Wall art, Columbia, South Carolina

Crossing

This map shows the 30 interstate highways featured in this book. All of them are contiguous except I-84, which has western and eastern segments. A gap in I-95 in the middle of New Jersey is filled by the N. J. Turnpike.

America

National Geographic's Guide To
THE INTERSTATES

Prepared by
The Book Division
National Geographic Society
Washington, D.C.

EASTERN

Credits

**Published by
The National
Geographic Society**

Gilbert M. Grosvenor
*President and
Chairman of the Board*
Michela A. English
Senior Vice President

**Prepared by
The Book Division**

William R. Gray, *Vice
President and Director*
Margery G. Dunn
Charles Kogod
Assistant Directors

Staff for this book

Elizabeth L. Newhouse
Editor

Cinda Rose
Art Director

Thomas B. Powell III
Illustrations Editor

Caroline Hickey
Dean A. Nadalin
Barbara A. Noe
Researchers

Carl Mehler
Map Editor and Designer

Carol B. Lutyk
Contributing Editor

Stewart Aitchison
Eddie Dean
Jay, Myra, and Suzanne
Gourley
Alison Kahn
Joyce B. Marshall
Dean A. Nadalin
Barbara A. Noe
John F. Ross
William G. Scheller

Downtown Atlanta, Georgia, at dusk

Thomas Schmidt
John A. Thompson
Robin S. H. Tunnicliff
Tony Wassell
Writers

Mary Ann Harrell
Consulting Editor

Joseph F. Ochlak
Larry Camp
Thomas L. Gray
Ann R. Perry
Map Researchers

Sandra F. Lotterman
Editorial Assistant

Karen Dufort Sligh
Artemis S. Lampathakis
Illustrations Assistants

Richard S. Wain
Production Project Manager
Lewis R. Bassford, Timothy
H. Ewing, H. Robert
Morrison, Lyle Rosbotham
Production

Karen F. Edwards, Elizabeth
G. Jevons, Peggy J. Oxford,
Teresita Cóquia Sison
Staff Assistants

Bryan K. Knedler
Susan G. Zenel, *Indexers*

Cover: Top row left to right: Arches National Park, Utah; Statue of Liberty, New York City; John F. Kennedy Space Center, Cape Canaveral, Florida. Bottom row: deer in forest; Delaware County Courthouse, New Castle, Delaware; Fremont Street, Las Vegas, Nevada; kayaker on Ocoee River, Tennessee. Background: Camelback Mountain, Arizona.

4

Contents

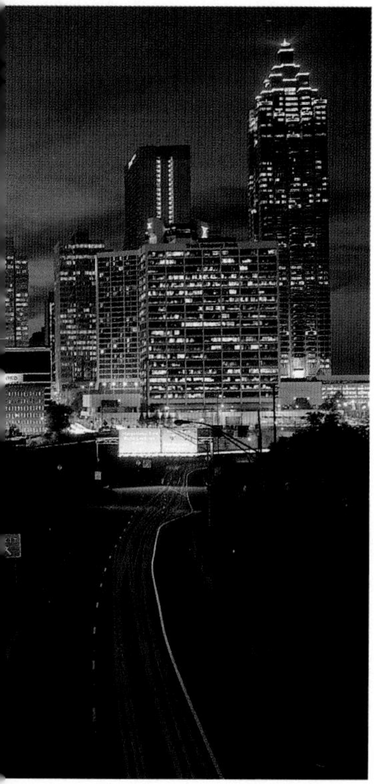

Manufacturing and Quality Management

George V. White, *Director*
John T. Dunn, *Associate Director*
Vincent P. Ryan, *Manager*
R. Gary Colbert

Map Production

Robert A. Ciepiela
Maryland Cartographics, Inc.

Edward Lanouette
Alexandra H. Lescaze
Miranda M. Lescaze
Rebecca F. Rooney
Susan Schafer
John R. Wagley, Jr.
Contributors

Library of Congress CIP data: page 352

Nothing speaks America like The Road—symbol of freedom and the pioneer spirit, celebration of democracy and individuality. Long before the automobile, Americans, obsessed with what lay beyond the horizon, blazed trails across the landscape, built railroad tracks through the western wilderness. When the motorcar rolled onto the scene, they embraced it as a pleasure machine that freed them to rediscover the country under their own steam.

But if the automobile revved the nation's restless frontier spirit, it caused a road crisis out of which came in mid-century the most ambitious and costly—129 billion dollars—public-works project in U. S. history: the Interstate Highway System (otherwise known as the Dwight D. Eisenhower System of Interstate and Defense Highways). Marked by uniform red-white-and-blue numbered shields, the 42,742-mile network makes up less than 2 percent of the country's roads, yet it carries more than 21 percent of the traffic. It's America's circulatory system, the modern Main Street.

Early in this century, the country boasted some 2 million miles of local thoroughfares, of which only about 140 miles were paved. Laid largely for the purpose of getting rural folks to town more eas-

> *"O public road...you express me better than I can express myself."*
>
> Walt Whitman
> "Song of the
> Open Road"

6

Interstate 15, Virgin River Gorge, Arizona

ily, roads often dead-ended at a state or county line, leaving on-going travelers to the vagaries of rustic byways.

The first national highway, begun in 1912, linked New York City and San Francisco—the route later traced by Interstate 80. No joy ride, the Lincoln Highway spurred federal highway advocates. Planning for the network began in the late 1930s, when public interest was piqued by the hype over Germany's fast, efficient Autobahns. On a more fantastic scale, General Motors' "Futurama" exhibit at the 1939 World's Fair wowed visitors with its vision of an America streamlined by superhighways. "Imagine the *possibilities*" was the seductive message. Behind it were the road industries, hoping to profit from the dream of a national expressway system.

President Eisenhower got things moving in the mid-fifties. He resolved the prickly problem of funding the system; the government would pick up 90 percent of the tab, paid for by a highway trust fund. The legislation also standardized highway design—at least four 12-foot-wide lanes and 10-foot-wide shoulders. Aesthetics, such as curves and plantings, evolved as the program expanded. In its wake, it reshaped the American landscape and culture. Eisenhower shared the view that superhighways would bring "greater convenience, greater happiness, and greater standards of living." And so they did. They transformed distance into time, making it possible to travel farther in the same time span. Faster commutes prompted an exodus to the suburbs, the American promised land.

Towns moved out to meet America at the edge of the new, fast roads. The strip became the traveler's mecca, where car culture rooted and flourished. Eye-catching diners, drive-ins, and fast-food franchises sprang up along the super-roads. Motor hotels, dubbed motels, replaced mom-and-pop establishments. Road signs flashed the logos of the new motel chains, safe harbors promising standardized lodging and no surprises. Roadside attractions—from drive-ins to miniature golf, alligator farms to dinosaur parks, campy architecture to living history—all were designed to lure the driving public off the highway.

Maligned by some as boring and alienating, the interstates tie us together. They provide a unique vantage point, the common landscape made cinematic, always in motion, always changing, of which we are the audience. At any moment we can stop the movement, exit, and enter the landscape. And engage. There lies the promise of the open road.

—ALISON KAHN

> "It is good to be out on the road, and going one knows not where."
>
> John Masefield
> "Tewkesbury Road"

Custer State Park, South Dakota

7

> "All the golden land's ahead of you and all kinds of unforseen events wait lurking to surprise you and make you glad you're alive to see."
>
> Jack Kerouac
> On the Road

This guide is designed to be concise, practical, and easy to use. It can serve both as a travel planner and a glove-compartment companion. When you're planning a trip, the book will help you decide which roads to follow and what sites to see (and how much time it takes to get to them). On the road, it can help relieve the tedium of a long drive by suggesting quick stops or longer excursions; there's something here for every family member.

Thirteen writers contributed to the guide. They drove the 30 major interstates we feature, more than 35,000 miles, as well as countless additional miles off the interstate exits. What they discovered not far beyond the strips of pavement was a wealth of sites—cities, towns, parks, recreation areas, historic buildings, battlefields, museums, monuments, and more—each of which they visited for possible inclusion in the book. Their assignment was to select a broad range of attractions, including some surprises, within easy reach of the interstates that would add pleasure and insight to your trip. To keep the thousands of sites to a number that would fit the book's space and be manageable for road travelers, they had to be highly selective. Regrettably, some places had to be left out. Herein are the writers' reports and recommendations.

> " 'Where we going, man?' "
> " 'I don't know but we gotta go.' "
>
> Jack Kerouac
> *On the Road*

The information about every site has been checked and, to the best of our knowledge, is accurate as of the press date. Much of it is perishable, however, so we suggest you telephone ahead whenever possible. In addition to the stated days of operation, many sites close on national holidays. All the mileages are approximate. The interstates are arranged numerically, from I-5 on the West Coast to I-95 on the East Coast. Although the coverage reads from west to east on the even-numbered routes and from north to south on the odd-numbered routes, it works in either direction. Just find the site nearest the place you wish to start and read either up or down the page. The sites are keyed to the map strips to help you quickly find a place, and the written directions correspond to the routes on the maps. Since many sites, especially cities, are served by more than one interstate, you will find frequent cross-references to descriptions and maps on other highways. When large sections of two interstates overlap, the sites are cross-referenced to one or the other interstate.

Starred and striped for Mardi Gras, New Orleans, La.

Locator maps begin every interstate chapter. Consult them for the page number(s) of the strip map that corresponds to the area you are traveling through. Also look at them for the route's overall orientation. Because of the strip maps' conical projection, the position of north varies; thus north arrows are not shown. On the maps, featured interstates are in red and nonfeatured interstates are in gray. Be sure to supplement the maps with a good road map.

Finally, enjoy your trip!

> "Whatever we may think, we move for no better reason than for the plain unvarnished hell of it."
>
> James Agee
> "The Great American Roadside"

8

MAP KEY and ABBREVIATIONS

National Battlefield	N.B.
National Conservation Area	N.C.A.
National Historical Park	N.H.P.
National Historic Site	N.H.S.
National Lakeshore	
National Memorial	N. Mem.
National Military Park	N.M.P.
National Monument	N.M.
National Park	N.P.
National Preserve	
National Recreation Area	N.R.A.
National Seashore	
National Scenic Area	N.S.A.
National Forest	N.F.
State Forest	S.F.
National Wildlife Refuge	N.W.R.
Natural Wildlife and Fish Refuge	
Wildlife Management Area	
State Historic Area	S.H.A.
State Historic(al) Park	S.H.P.
State Historic(al) Site	S.H.S.
State Memorial	
State Monument	S.M.
State Park	S.P.
State Recreation Area	S.R.A.
Indian Reservation	I.R.

■ Point of Interest

ROADS

80	Featured Interstate
15	Other Interstate
20	U.S. Federal Highway
1	Mexican Federal Highway
19	State and Provincial Road
212	County and Local Road
▼ 12 ▼	Mileage between ticks
★	State Capital

POPULATION

● Chicago	500,000 and over
● Madison	50,000 to under 500,000
● Quincy	Under 50,000

Cadillac Ranch, near Amarillo, Texas

"You road I enter upon and look around, I believe you are not all that is here,
I believe that much unseen is also here."

Walt Whitman
"Song of the Open Road"

Unless otherwise noted, directions are from interstate, and sites are free and generally open daily. Phone for further information.

(1) **Peace Arch State Park, WASHINGTON** *(On the Canadian border, near Blaine. 206-332-8221)* Surrounded by velvety lawns and flower-filled gardens, the Doric **International Peace Arch,** built in 1921, spans the U. S.-Canadian border and represents more than a hundred years of friendship between the two countries. The symbolic gates of the 67-foot-high structure can only be closed by mutual consent.

(2) **Lynden** Descendants of turn-of-the-century Dutch immigrants still carry on Calvinist traditions in this flower-bedecked village, including a Sunday business ban and a prohibition on dancing where alcoholic beverages are sold. Amid the European-style shops and restaurants stands the **Pioneer Museum** *(217 Front St. 206-354-3675),* known for its large buggy collection, antique tractors, and Native American artifacts. *Closed Sun.; donation requested.*

(3) **Ferndale** A dainty flower garden and white picket fence embellish the 1903 **Hovander Homestead** *(5299 Nielsen Rd. 206-384-3444. May-Sept.; adm. fee),* a restored frame house full of antiques that illustrate farm life at the turn of the century. Kids will enjoy the goats and geese outside the farm's red barn. Next door, at the **Tennant Lake Natural History Interpretive Center** *(206-384-3444. Feb.–mid-Oct.),* a boardwalk traces the lakeshore. An observation tower overlooking the 200-acre marsh is a great spot for watching ducks, trumpeter swans, bald eagles, and Canada geese.

(4) **Bellingham** *(Convention & Visitors Bureau, 904 Potter St. 206-671-3990 or 800-487-2032)* Settled in 1852 at the site of a sawmill, this small maritime city snuggles in the hills above Bellingham Bay. Its plank sidewalks and stately rose garden evoke the Victorian era in the Northwest. To absorb the town's quaint mood, stroll down by **Squalicum Harbor** *(1 mile NW on Roeder Ave. 206-676-2500),* where fishing boats float on mirrorlike water and, on a clear day, snowcapped Mount Baker looms behind the city. The ornate red-brick building dominating the skyline is the **Whatcom Museum of History and Art** *(121 Prospect St. 206-676-6981. Closed Mon.),* built in 1892 as the city hall. Inside you'll find paintings by Northwest artists and exhibits on logging and Native Americans. In the center of town, Western Washington University's **Sehome Hill** *(25th St., off Bill McDonald Pkwy., follow signs to university. 206-676-6985)* offers a 165-acre arboretum of native flora, as well as spectacular views of Puget Sound, the San Juan Islands, and Mount Baker.

(5) **Chuckanut Drive** Wash. 11 winds along dazzling Samish Bay, passing 2,765-acre **Larrabee State Park** *(7 miles S of Bellingham. 206-676-2093)* and tidal pools brimming with sea life.

Totem pole figure, Washington

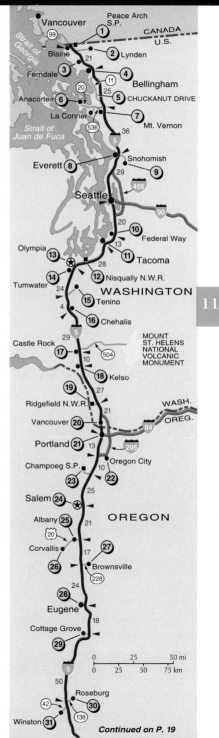

▶ **Anacortes** *(17 miles W on Wash. 20)* Ringed by snowy mountains, this serene seaport—a gateway to the San Juan Islands—lies at the northern tip of Fidalgo Island. The **Anacortes Museum** *(1305 8th St. 206-293-1915. Fri.-Sun.)* displays regional memorabilia. The **W. T. Preston** *(705 R Ave. 206-293-1916. Fri.-Sun.)*, a dry-docked stern-wheeler that broke up log jams on Puget Sound until 1981, has been turned into a maritime museum. Watch the sun set over the San Juans from **Washington Park** *(Wash. 20 spur to Sunset Ave.)*, a 200-acre forest preserve right on Rosario Strait.

▶ **Mount Vernon Region** Take time to explore the natural beauty just west of Mount Vernon. In springtime, fields of tulips, daffodils, and irises emblazon the **Skagit Valley,** one of the nation's largest bulb-growing regions. To find the blooms, pick up a map from the **Chamber of Commerce** *(Skagit Valley Sq., 200 E. College Way. 206-428-8547)*. Beyond, Puget Sound's indigo water reflects the Olympic Mountains. For a panoramic view, follow the steep, windy road up 934-foot **Little Mountain** *(Anderson Rd. exit, Cedardale Rd. to Blackburn Rd. to Little Mountain Rd. 206-336-6213)*. Across from the bulb fields lies **La Conner,** a late 1800s fishing village with a restored downtown of touristy shops and the **Skagit County Historical Museum** *(501 S. 4th St. 206-466-3365. Wed.-Sun.; adm. fee)*.

▶ **Everett** **Boeing Tour Center** *(3.5 miles W on Wash. 526 to Paine Field, follow signs.*

11

Boeing 767s under construction, Boeing plant, Everett, Washington

Continued on P. 19

206-342-4801) Jumbo 747s, 767s, and 777s in all stages of production fill the gigantic hangar of this 11-story assembly plant. Because the popular 90-minute tour is offered on a first-come, first-served basis, arrive two hours early. No children under ten admitted. *Tours Mon.-Fri. at 9 a.m. and 1 p.m.*

Elliot Point Lighthouse, Everett, Washington

⑨ **S n o h o m i s h**   On the banks of the Snohomish and Pilchuck Rivers sits the well-preserved Victorian town of Snohomish, surrounded by dairy farms and rolling hills. Born in 1859 as a trading center for settlers and Native Americans, Snohomish is a great place to stop for an ice-cream cone (the region tops the nation in pounds of milk produced per cow) and some antiquing. For a historical perspective, visit **Pioneer Village** *(Pine Ave. at 2nd St. 206-568-2526. June-Aug.; adm. fee)*, a collection of six restored houses and stores that represent early Snohomish, and the **Blackman House Museum** *(118 Ave. B. 206-568-2526. Daily June-Aug., Wed.-Sun. Sept.-May; adm. fee)*, an elegant 1878 mansion built by the town's first mayor, Hyrcanus Blackman.

S e a t t l e   See I-90, pp. 272-73.

⑩ **F e d e r a l   W a y**   **Rhododendron Species Botanical Garden** *(0.5 mile E on Wash. 18, 0.5 mile N on Weyerhaeuser Way. 206-661-9377. Sat.-Wed.; adm. fee)* Some 2,000 varieties of rhododendrons from around the world decorate this 24-acre garden. Next door, at the **Pacific Rim Bonsai Collection** *(206-924-5206. Sat.-Wed.)*, displays of 50-plus bonsai plants celebrate the importance of trade with Pacific Rim nations.

⑪ **T a c o m a**   *(Tacoma-Pierce County Visitor & Convention Bureau, 906 Broadway. 206-627-2836)* Gray and industrial, the deepwater port of Tacoma sprawls across

Tulips, Skagit Valley, Washington

12

rolling hilltops above Commencement Bay, with a front-row seat—on a clear day—of 14,410-foot Mount Rainier. Settled in 1852 as a mill town, the village was given an architectural makeover when the Northern Pacific Railroad arrived in 1873. Legacies include the 1891 Ferry Museum building, which now houses the marvelous **State Historical Society Museum** (*315 N. Stadium Way. 206-593-2830. Closed Mon.; adm. fee*), and **Wright Park** (*6th Ave. and S. G St.*), 30 grassy acres of exotic trees featuring the **Seymour Botanical Conservatory** (*206-591-5330*), an onion-domed Victorian greenhouse with striking seasonal displays. Don't miss **Point Defiance Park** (*N. 54th and Pearl Sts.*), 700 acres of old-growth forest and driftwood-strewn beaches; historical touches include the open-air **Camp 6 Logging Museum** (*206-752-0047. Jan.-Oct. Wed.-Sun.; adm. fee*) and **Fort Nisqually** (*206-591-5339. Daily June-Aug., Wed.-Sun. Sept.-May; adm. fee in summer*), a reconstruction of the Hudson's Bay Company's first outpost on Puget Sound.

Nisqually National Wildlife Refuge

(*Nisqually exit, 0.5 mile N on Brown Farm Rd., follow signs. 206-753-9467*) More than 300 species of wildlife, including red-tailed hawks, soft-shelled clams, red-legged frogs, and great blue herons, live in the refuge's marshes, tidal flats, wooded areas, and grasslands. Established in 1978 to protect the Nisqually River Delta on Puget Sound, the refuge serves as a stopover for more than 20,000 migratory birds in fall and winter. Eight miles of trails wander through the 2,817-acre preserve. Interpretive center. *Adm. fee.*

13

Olympia

Settled by pioneers in 1846, Washington's capital is a friendly city with parklike streets. The business of government takes place on the **Capitol Campus** (*Between 11th and 14th Aves., off Capitol Way*). This manicured, 30-acre setting forms a leafy backdrop to an impressive array of neoclassical structures dominated by the **Legislative Building** and its 287-foot-high dome. Begin your tour at the **Visitors Information Center** (*14th Ave. and Capitol Way. 206-586-3460*). A few blocks away, the **State Capital Museum** (*211 W. 21st Ave. 206-753-2580. Closed Mon.*),

Legislative Building overlooking Capitol Lake, Olympia, Washington

housed in a 1920s Spanish-style stucco mansion, portrays Washington's advancement to statehood with Native American art and pioneer artifacts. You can view ships in port at **Percival Landing** *(State Ave. and Water St.)*, where a mile-long boardwalk faces peaceful Budd Inlet. Kiosks describe how the tiny Olympia oyster, found only here, was harvested a century ago.

⑭ T u m w a t e r In 1845, pioneers moved into this region, originally occupied by Chinook Indians; they founded the first white settlement on Puget Sound and harnessed the Deschutes River to work their sawmills and gristmills. In **Tumwater Historical Park** *(Off Deschutes Way. 206-753-8583)*, probably the site of the original settlement, you can tour the town's oldest houses: the 1858 Crosby House and the 1905 Henderson House. An easy trail winds along the pleasant green river at nearby **Tumwater Falls Park** *(206-943-2550)*, where spawning Chinook salmon make their way up fish ladders in autumn. The six-story brick building at the river's edge is the 19th-century **Olympia Brewery**. You can't miss the company's modern facility *(206-754-5177)*; it's the bulky, salmon-colored building down the street, and it's open daily for tours and tastings.

⑮ T e n i n o **Wolf Haven International** *(3.5 miles E on 93rd Ave., 3.5 miles S on old US 99 to Offut Lake Rd. 206-264-4695)* More than 30 wolves prowl and play behind the fences of this 65-acre sanctuary, founded in 1982 to house abandoned and displaced wolves born in captivity. Tours outline their struggles in the wild, and summer howlins star residents. *Daily May-Sept., closed Tues. Oct.-April; adm. fee.*

14

Mount St. Helens, Washington

Chehalis **Lewis County Historical Museum** (*599 N.W. Front Way. 206-748-0831*) Housed in a 1912 railroad depot built for the Northern Pacific, this museum features extensive exhibits on early pioneers, Chehalis Indians, and the community's logging and farming activities. *Closed Mon.; adm. fee.*

Castle Rock When 9,677-foot Mount St. Helens exploded on May 18, 1980, blowing 1,300 feet off its top and spewing ash 80,000 feet into the air, the powdery gray substance covered this nearby timber town. Now Castle Rock is the jumping-off point for volcano-peering activities. Exhibits at the **Mount St. Helens National Volcanic Monument Visitor Center** (*5.5 miles E on Wash. 504. 206-274-2100*) put the mountain's actions in a global context. Worth the detour: The 43-mile **Spirit Lake Memorial Highway** (the new extension of Wash. 504) shoots through the blast zone, with breathtaking views of scorched trees and ravaged landscapes. At the road's end stands the impressive **Coldwater Ridge Visitor Center** (*206-274-2131*), where a 16-screen video show, touch-screen exhibits, and interpretive trails detail the region's re-birthing process. A further extension of Wash. 504 to Johnston Ridge should be completed in 1996.

Kelso **Cowlitz County Historical Museum** (*405 Allen St. 206-577-3119*) This cozy museum tells the history of Cowlitz County with Cowlitz Indian baskets, relics from the Oregon Trail, a re-created country store, and pioneer Ben Beighle's tiny split-log cabin, built in 1884. *Closed Mon. Apr.-Sept.*

Ridgefield National Wildlife Refuge (*3 miles W on Wash. 501 to Ridgefield, follow signs to refuge headquarters at 301 N. 3rd St. 206-887-4106*) Created on the floodplain of the Columbia River to protect the winter habitat of the Canada goose, this 5,149-acre sanctuary of woods, wetlands, and pastures also shelters otters, deer, ducks, red-tailed hawks, and bald eagles. A mile-long interpretive trail in the northern section winds past marshes and through oak groves.

Vancouver The gray timber stockade of **Fort Vancouver National Historic Site** (*Mill Plain Blvd. exit, 0.5 mile E on E. Evergreen Blvd., follow signs. 206-696-7655. Adm. fee*) once protected the headquarters of the Hudson's Bay Company, the huge fur-trading organization that secured the British claim in the Pacific Northwest and administered its fur brigades. Established in 1825, the fortified community bustled with activity until the Americans won the territorial claim in 1846. After the British pulled out in 1860, the fort was left to decay. The stockade and nine major structures have been reconstructed, including the trade shop, where Native Americans exchanged baskets for wool cloth, and the chief factor's house, with a graceful veranda.

Fort Vancouver NHS, Vancouver, Washington

The snowy *Cascades* punctuate the eastern horizons of Washington, Oregon, and northern California. Native Americans believed that three of the ethereal peaks resulted from a love triangle. The story goes that two brothers—sons of the Great Spirit Sehales—set forests afire and ravaged the countryside to win the love of a beautiful woman. Enraged at their behavior, Sehales turned his sons into Mount Hood and Mount Adams and the woman into the seductive and mercurial Mount St. Helens.

15

Green and progressive, the city sprawls across rolling hills above the salmon-filled Willamette River. Add a mild climate, clean air, magnificent mountain vistas, and a deepwater

Shucking oysters at a local restaurant

port, and you'll understand why Portlanders are determined to keep their city a secret. A good place to start uncovering its many facets is the *Portland Visitors Center* (26 S.W. Salmon St. 503-222-2223 or 800-962-3700).

Diving helmet, Oregon Maritime Center and Museum

Founded in 1844 in a wilderness clearing, Portland boomed with the 1848 California gold rush, the Indian wars of the 1850s, the discovery of gold in eastern Oregon, and the railroad's arrival in 1883. By the turn of the century, the pioneer town had become a sophisticated, flower-filled city.

Today Portlanders indulge their love of the outdoors in some 200 city parks (For information on all parks, call 503-823-2223), including *Forest Park* (Off US 30, NW of Fremont Bridge), 4,900 acres of primeval forest with some 50 miles of hiking trails; *Mount Tabor Park* (Off S.E. 60th Ave. via S.E. Harrison St. or Salmon St.), encompassing an extinct volcano; and *Tom McCall Waterfront Park* (Front St.), a grassy, 2-mile promenade along the Willamette popular with joggers and anglers. *Washington Park* (S.W. Park Place and Vista Ave.), the crown jewel of the park system, has 332 hilly acres of forests, sweeping vistas, and manicured gardens. Here you'll

find more than 400 varieties of roses at the *International Rose Test Garden;* the *Metro Washington Park Zoo* (503-226-1561. Adm. fee), noted for its Arctic animals and elephant breeding program; and the *World Forestry Center* (503-228-1368. Adm. fee), whose displays include a talking tree.

A tour of urban Portland—a pleasing blend of historic and state-of-the-art office buildings, cafés, and bookstores—begins at *Pioneer Courthouse Square* (Yamhill and Morrison Sts.), a block-long plaza where you can sip coffee by a fountain while listening to a political orator. Only a few blocks away are the *Portland Art Museum* (1219 S.W. Park Ave. 503-226-2811. Closed Mon.; adm. fee), displaying 35 centuries of art, and the *Oregon Historical Center* (1200 S.W. Park Ave. 503-222-1741. Closed Mon.; adm. fee). On the east side of the river stands the *Oregon Museum of Science and Industry* (1945 S.E. Water Ave. 503-797-4000. Adm. fee), with interactive exhibits on outer space, life sciences, and computers. Even landlubbers will take a fancy to the *Oregon Maritime Center and Museum* (113 S.W. Front Ave. 503-224-7724. Call for hours; adm. fee).

Japanese Garden, Washington Park

In town, be sure to stop by the **Clark County Historical Museum** *(1511 Main St. 206-695-4681. Closed Mon. year-round and Sun. Sept.-May).* Native American artifacts, pioneer quilts, and a reconstructed country store depict the westering of the county.

▶ **O r e g o n   C i t y**   This settlement marked the end of the Oregon Trail for the 300,000-plus pioneers who survived the treacherous 2,000-mile overland journey from Independence, Missouri, in the mid-19th century. Here, in the meadows along the Willamette River, they wintered before staking out homesteads in the fertile promised land of Oregon. **The Oregon Trail Interpretive Center** *(500 Washington St. 503-657-9336. Adm. fee)* fills you in on the trail's history. For a glimpse of 19th-century pioneer life, head to the **John McLoughlin House National Historic Site** *(713 Center St. 503-656-5146. Closed Mon. and Jan.; adm. fee),* the restored 1846 home of the Father of Oregon. The observation deck of the 90-foot **City Municipal Elevator** *(7th and Main Sts.),* one of only four municipal elevators in the world, commands an excellent view of 42-foot Willamette Falls and the surrounding hills.

17

▶ **C h a m p o e g   S t a t e   P a r k**   *(5 miles W of Aurora-Donald exit, follow signs. 503-678-1251)* Rolling farmland near the Willamette River was the site of Champoeg Village, where, in 1843, 102 settlers chafing under the rule of the British-owned Hudson's Bay Company voted to write a constitution. Oregon City subsequently became the seat of this provisional government, the first American governing body west of the Rockies. Champoeg Village thrived until a flood swept it away in 1861. At the Visitor Center paintings, photographs, and relics recount Champoeg's history. Hiking trails and picnic areas. *Adm. fee mid-May–Sept.*

▶ **S a l e m**   *(Convention & Visitors Association, 1313 Mill St. S.E. 503-581-4325)* Founded in 1840 by Methodist missionary Jason Lee, Salem retains provincial charm despite its status as the state capital. The multigabled **Deepwood Estate** *(1116 Mission St. S.E. 503-363-1825. Closed Sat. year-round and Tues. and Thurs. Oct.-April; adm. fee),* an 1894 Queen Anne mansion with golden oak woodwork and formal gardens, reflects the city's prosperity in the late 1800s. Well-preserved 19th-century buildings at **Mission Mill Village** *(1313 Mill St. S.E. 503-585-7012. Adm. fee)* include the prim **Jason Lee House,** the oldest wood-frame residence in the Pacific Northwest, and the **Thomas Kay Woolen Mill,** now a textile museum. Downtown, the angular, Greek-style **State Capitol** *(900 Court St. 503-378-4423. Tours hourly mid-June–Labor Day),* built of Vermont marble in 1938, features Depression-era murals of pioneers and a museum with geological and historical exhibits.

State Capitol, Salem, Oregon

▶ **A l b a n y**   Nearly 500 Victorian buildings—the largest collection in the state—line the streets of this quiet city on the east bank of the Willamette River. **Monteith House** *(518 2nd Ave. S.W.*

503-928-0911. June–mid-Sept. Wed.-Sun.), a restored frame residence, was built in 1849 by the two brothers who founded Albany. Nine covered bridges, dating from the 1930s, span the rivers outside town; you can pick up a map of the countryside from the **Albany Visitors Association** (300 S.W. 2nd St. 503-928-0911 or 800-526-2256).

26 **Corvallis** The Latin *corvallis* means "heart of the valley," an appropriate name for this university town cupped between two mountain ranges. Original furnishings embellish the 1881 Italianate **Benton County Courthouse** (120 N.W. 4th St. 503-757-6831).

By the turn of the century, more than 450 *covered bridges*—the largest collection west of the Mississippi—spanned Oregon's rivers. Roofs made of Douglas fir protected the plank decks and wooden tresses from drizzle, extending a bridge's life expectancy to 40 years. Roofs also protected sweethearts in search of privacy—hence the term "kissing bridges." Fifty-two restored bridges remain, mostly in the Willamette Valley. The one above crosses Mosby Creek, near Cottage Grove.

18

27 **Brownsville** Vintage storefronts line Brownsville's narrow streets, originally designed for wagons. Established in 1846, the town is one of Oregon's oldest settlements. The **Moyer House** (204 N. Main St. 503-466-3390. Weekends or by appt.), an ornate gingerbread mansion built in 1881, illustrates the success of one pioneer family with its 12-foot ceilings, Italian marble mantel, and grand piano transported by ship around Cape Horn. The **Linn County Historical Museum** (101 Park Ave. 503-466-3390), housed in an 1890 railroad depot and converted boxcars, depicts local history with a pioneer wagon, re-created early businesses, and other displays.

28 **Eugene** An outdoorsy university city on the Willamette River, Eugene was founded in 1846 by pioneer Eugene Skinner. You can see a reproduction of his home and other period buildings in **Skinner's Butte Park** (High to Pearl Sts., between 2nd and 5th Sts.). The **Lane County Historical Museum** (740 W. 13th Ave. 503-687-4239. Wed.-Sat.; adm. fee) contains important collections chronicling the emigration to Oregon. For a panoramic view of the city and the surrounding Cascades, hike the 9.6-mile South Hills Ridgeline Trail through coniferous forests to the 2,054-foot summit of Spencer Butte in **Spencer Butte Park** (3 miles S of town on Willamette St.).

29 **Cottage Grove** Named for an 1855 post office tucked in a grove of trees, this lumber town boomed after gold was discovered nearby in the late 19th century. Antique mining equipment and a working model of an 1870 stamp mill are among relics that recall those days at the octagonal-shaped **Cottage Grove Museum** (H St. and Birch Ave. 503-942-3963. Wed.-Sun. p.m. June-Aug. and Sat.-Sun. p.m. rest of year), built in 1897 as a church. Not far away, five graceful covered bridges cross Mosby Creek and Row River; ask for a map at the **Chamber of Commerce** (710 Row River Rd. 503-942-2411). South of town, 1,158-acre **Cottage Grove Lake** (Cottage Grove Lake exit, 4 miles S

Kayaking Oregon's Rogue River

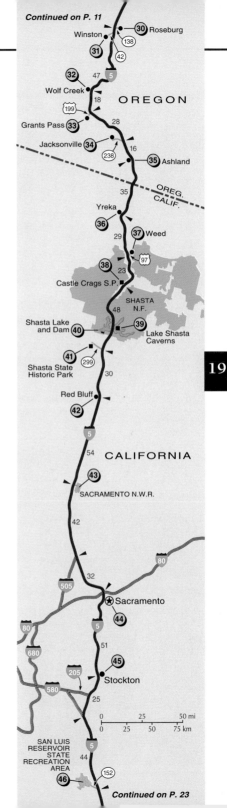

Continued on P. 11

on London Rd., follow signs. 503-942-5631) beckons boaters, swimmers, and anglers.

30 **Roseburg**   The center of a prosperous timber industry, this quiet little town overlooks the Umpqua River. The area's human and natural history are recounted in the marvelous **Douglas County Museum** (*Fairgrounds exit, just off I-5. 503-440-4507. Closed Mon.*). Displays include the million-year-old skeleton of a saber-toothed cat, tools used by Indians before the creation of nearby Crater Lake, and a reproduction of a settler's cabin.

Hidden in the misty Coastal Mountains 10 miles outside town, **HillCrest Vineyard** (*2 miles W on Garden Valley Blvd., left on Melrose Rd., right on Doerner Rd., follow signs. 503-673-3709*) is Oregon's oldest varietal winery. Renowned for its Rieslings and aged Cabernets, HillCrest lies at the end of a bucolic drive. Observation deck, tours, and tastings.

31 **Winston**   **Wildlife Safari** (*Winston-Coos Bay exit, follow signs for 2.5 miles. 503-679-6761*) Cheetahs, Bactrian camels, bison, and 113 other species of exotic animals prowl 600 acres of jungles and grasslands in Oregon's only drive-through zoological park. Paved roads wind through habitats found in North America, Asia, and Africa. *Adm. fee.*

32 **Wolf Creek**   **Wolf Creek Tavern** (*100 Front St. 503-866-2474*) Established in 1868, this classical revival inn served as a wayside stop for weary stagecoach travelers bouncing along the Oregon Territorial Road. Jack London stayed here in 1911 and wrote "The End of the Story." You can see his tiny second-floor room and the carved bed where he slept. The inn still serves meals and rents rooms.

33 **Grants Pass**   Just outside this lumber town, the **Rogue River** enters the remote Coastal Mountains through Hellgate Canyon, a stretch of turbulent water. You can arrange jet boat excursions and one- to five-day rafting trips with outfitters in Grants Pass, the region's white-water capital. Contact the **Grants Pass Chamber of Commerce** (*1501 N.E. 6th St. 503-476-7717*).

19

Continued on P. 23

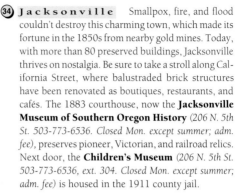

(34) Jacksonville Smallpox, fire, and flood couldn't destroy this charming town, which made its fortune in the 1850s from nearby gold mines. Today, with more than 80 preserved buildings, Jacksonville thrives on nostalgia. Be sure to take a stroll along California Street, where balustraded brick structures have been renovated as boutiques, restaurants, and cafés. The 1883 courthouse, now the **Jacksonville Museum of Southern Oregon History** (206 N. 5th St. 503-773-6536. Closed Mon. except summer; adm. fee), preserves pioneer, Victorian, and railroad relics. Next door, the **Children's Museum** (206 N. 5th St. 503-773-6536, ext. 304. Closed Mon. except summer; adm. fee) is housed in the 1911 county jail.

20

(35) Ashland This 19th-century frontier town supported itself for years on mining, logging, wood production, and agriculture. Since 1935, however, the main industry has been the elaborate **Oregon Shakespeare Festival** (Tickets 503-482-4331). From mid-February through October, actors perform the works of Shakespeare and his contemporaries on an open-air Elizabethan stage and in two indoor theaters. Near the main plaza, tranquillity suffuses **Lithia Park** (503-488-5340), 100 acres of trees, gardens, trails, and duck ponds.

(36) Yreka, CALIFORNIA Born as a gold-mining camp in 1851, Yreka sits in a lush valley near Mount Shasta. The town's rustic flavor lives on in preserved Victorian buildings along historic Miner Street, boomtown relics at the **Siskiyou County Museum** (910 S. Main St. 916-842-3836. Closed Sun.-Mon.; adm. fee), and dazzling gold nuggets from local mines at the **Siskiyou County Courthouse** (311 4th St. 916-842-8005. Closed Sun.).

(37) Weed This old lumber town, founded around the turn of the century by lumberman Abner Weed, sprawls across the western slope of Mount Shasta. The dusty **Lumber Town Museum** (303 Gilman Ave. 916-938-2352) chronicles Weed in its heyday, with logging tools and a diorama of a miner's cabin full of relics from the hills. May-Oct. and by appt.

(38) Castle Crags State Park (0.25 mile W of Castella exit. 916-235-2684. Adm. fee) Craggy granite spires formed more than 170 million years ago soar to 6,500 feet here. Originally named Devil's Castle by Spanish explorers, these glacier-polished peaks were the site of a bloody battle in 1855 between settlers and Modoc Indians. Today

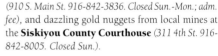

Lake Shasta Caverns, Shasta Lake, California

Mount Shasta, California

From miles away, 14,162-foot **Mount Shasta**—a dormant volcano with five active glaciers—looms above the landscape, often shrouded in clouds. Wintu Indians worshiped the peak, believing it the home of the Great Spirit. The first white settlers to arrive surmised that little people—bell makers—lived inside. Today stories still circulate of mysterious lights emanating from the mountain. New Age devotees consider it one of the world's power spots, along with the Great Pyramids and Stonehenge, and sometimes gather there to meditate.

they form the centerpiece of this forested, 4,250-acre park, where 18 miles of hiking paths twist through cool, quiet woods. If you're in a hurry, drive to the top of **Vista Point,** where an easy 50-yard trail yields a glorious view of the towering crags and Mount Shasta.

Lake Shasta Caverns (1.5 miles E of O'Brien exit on twisty Shasta Caverns Rd. 916-238-2341) Well-lit tunnels lead into fascinating limestone caves filled with 20-foot, crystal-studded stalactites and stalagmites. Take a sweater; it's always 58°F inside. The two-hour tour includes a boat ride across Shasta Lake. Adm. fee.

Shasta Lake and Dam Houseboats float quietly on Shasta Lake, poking into inlets of the largest man-made lake in California. Created in 1945 by the impoundment of Squaw Creek and the Sacramento, McCloud, and Pit Rivers with **Shasta Dam** (5 miles W of Central Valley exit on Shasta Dam Blvd. Visitor Center 916-275-4463), the 29,740-acre lake invites anglers and boaters. Shasta Dam is the nation's second largest concrete structure; its 602-foot-high spillway is three times higher than Niagara Falls.

Shasta State Historic Park (6 miles W of Redding on Calif. 299. 916-243-8194) Rough-and-tumble prospectors heading for the Mother Lode poured into Shasta in 1849, turning it into the Queen City of the North. The red-brick county courthouse contains a museum of California paintings, Victorian furnishings, and—out back—the gallows where murderers were hanged. Across the street, the 1855 Litsch General Store has plank

Bone-shaker bicycle, Shasta State Historic Park, near Redding, Calif.

floors, shelves stocked with dry goods and miner's supplies, and guides in period dress. *Closed Tues.-Wed.; adm. fee.*

(42) **Red Bluff**   Named for the area's reddish cliffs, this Victorian town on the Sacramento River was founded in 1850 as a supply center for the gold mines in Trinity County. A number of Italianate Victorian structures survived, including the 1880 **Kelly-Griggs House Museum** *(311 Washington St. 916-527-1129)*, an ornate white house with ten period rooms. The 4-acre **William B. Ide Adobe State Historic Park** *(E at Wilcox Rd. exit, follow signs. 916-529-8599. Parking fee)* features the reconstructed home of William Ide, president of the short-lived Republic of California, which was established in 1846 after a band of settlers revolted against Mexican authority. The revolt ended when the Mexican-American War broke out in the same year and U. S. troops occupied the area.

(44) Sacramento

22

In 1839, Swiss immigrant John Sutter built a colony around an adobe fort and prospered by raising wheat, milling flour, and distilling brandy. When gold was discovered near his sawmill in 1848, gold fever spread across the land. Relics of pioneer and gold rush days lend authenticity to reconstructed *Sutter's Fort* (27th and L Sts. 916-445-4422. Adm. fee).

The gold rush lured thousands of prospectors to the area, which became the bustling frontier town of Sacramento and, in 1854, the state capital. The *State Capitol* (10th St. and Capitol Mall. 916-324-0333), with marble mosaic floors and a 120-foot-high dome, resembles the U. S. Capitol. The wood sidewalks, cobblestoned streets, and false-front stores of *Old Sacramento* (Visitor Center, 1104 Front St.

Calif. State Railroad Museum

916-442-7644), the commercial district during the gold rush, have been lovingly restored. To learn more about the boom era, examine the memorabilia in the *Sacramento History Museum* (101 I St. 916-264-7057. Closed Mon.-Tues.; adm. fee).

The *California State Railroad Museum* (2nd and I Sts. 916-445-7387. Adm. fee) chronicles the city's role in launching the first transcontinental railroad. The largest museum of its kind, it showcases 21 shiny locomotives and railroad cars. The *B. F. Hastings Building* (2nd and J Sts. 916-445-7387) housed California's first supreme court and served as the western terminus of the Pony Express. The *California State Indian Museum* (2618 K St., next to Sutter's Fort. 916-324-0971. Adm. fee) exhibits baskets, beadwork, and other artifacts.

Old Sacramento National Historic Landmark

Sacramento Natl. Wildlife Refuge

(*Princeton exit, 2 miles N on Rte. 99W, follow signs. Visitor Center 916-934-2801*) For thousands of years the northern Sacramento Valley, an important wintering site on the Pacific flyway, has welcomed ducks, swans, and even geese from as far away as Siberia. This 10,783-acre refuge was created at the turn of the century, when farming threatened to destroy the natural habitat. Today its ponds, marshes, and grasslands safeguard more than 300 species of birds and mammals. November and December are peak birding months. Observation platform and 6-mile driving tour.

Stockton

The frontier town of Stockton boomed during the 1850s gold rush as prospectors came up the 86-mile deep-water channel that flows from its doorstep to San Francisco. Shipping and shipbuilding later made Stockton an international inland seaport. The **Haggin Museum** (*1201 N. Pershing Ave., in Victory Park. 209-462-4116*) eloquently tells Stockton's story with Native American baskets, farm equipment, and a re-created turn-of-the-century main street. The fine collection of American and French paintings is a surprise. *Closed Mon.; donation suggested.*

San Luis Reservoir S.R.A.

(*12 miles W of Los Banos exit on Calif. 152. 209-826-0718*) The shimmering waters of San Luis Reservoir, the largest off-stream reservoir in the United States, appear like a mirage at the base of Diablo Mountain's parched foothills. For a good view, stop at the **Romero Visitor Center** (*209-826-0718*) and then look at exhibits that explain how the water is transported from here to Central Valley fields via the California Aqueduct. Boating, swimming, and fishing.

Tule Elk State Reserve

(*3 miles W on Calif. 119 to Morris Rd., follow signs. 805-765-5004*) Before Europeans came to California, Tule elk—the smallest and rarest elk found in the United States—roamed the Central Valley's marshlands, sometimes in huge herds. By the 1850s, Spaniards and gold miners had killed off most of the species, and farmers threatened to do away with the rest.

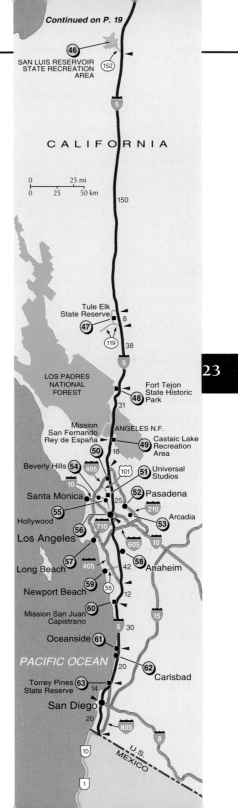

Continued on P. 19

23

The San Joaquin and Sacramento Valleys form California's great **Central Valley.** One of the nation's richest agricultural regions, it covers some 18,000 square miles between Bakersfield and Sacramento. From peaches and onions to rice and wheat, more than 200 different kinds of fruits, vegetables, and grains thrive in this agricultural patchwork. Naturally arid, the valley depends on an intricate network of canals and rivers for water—the source of ongoing, often acrid, political debate between northern and southern Californians.

In 1873, a remnant herd was given refuge on a private 950-acre preserve that became this sanctuary. You can see a small herd of the shaggy creatures from a viewing platform. *Phone ahead for tour; parking fee.*

(48) Fort Tejon State Historic Park *(W at Fort Tejon exit. 805-248-6692)* Restored adobe structures set against a backdrop of tawny mountains comprise Fort Tejon, the U. S. Army post established in 1854 to protect local miners and Native Americans, and later used to train officers during the Civil War. The fort also served as the western terminus of the U. S. Camel Corps, which hauled supplies to remote military posts in the Southwest. *Adm. fee.*

(49) Castaic Lake Recreation Area *(1 mile E of Castaic exit, follow signs. 805-257-4050)* A 2,235-acre mecca for swimmers, boaters, and anglers in the northern Santa Clarita Valley, Castaic Lake generates hydroelectric power for Los Angeles. The water originally fell as precipitation in the Sierra Nevada, then made its way via rivers and 388 miles of aqueducts to Castaic Lake. The lake is the centerpiece of an 8,000-acre recreation area. *Adm. fee.*

(50) Mission San Fernando Rey de España *(15151 San Fernando Mission Blvd. 818-361-0186)* Peacocks strut across the quiet grounds of this yellow adobe mission—California's 17th, founded in 1797. As ranchers moved into the area, the mission also acted as a cultural center. All but one of the original buildings were destroyed by earthquakes, but the excellent reconstruction includes the mission church and its arcaded convento. Don't miss the cemetery and flower-filled park across the street. *Adm. fee.*

Special effect: "Jaws" attack on Universal Studios tour, Universal City, California

(51) Universal Studios *(100 Universal City Plaza, off US 101 in Universal City. 818-508-9600)* In 1915, Bavarian immigrant Carl Laemmle converted a chicken farm into a production lot for his silent films. Today, 3.5 million visitors a year board brightly colored trams for an hour-long tour of his legacy: a 420-acre motion picture and television studio, the world's largest. Here you'll learn how filmmakers create such special effects as an earthquake, the parting of the Red Sea, and the collapse of a bridge. Other favorites include live shows, a tribute to Lucille Ball, and the sets for *Psycho, The Sting,* and other popular movies and TV programs. *Adm. fee.*

(52) Pasadena Thousands of people flock to this elegant L.A. suburb for its New Year's Day fete: the Tournament of Roses Parade, whose flower-bedecked floats first sashayed down Colorado Boulevard in 1890, and the accompanying football showdown at the Rose Bowl. Next to Old Town, the austere **Norton Simon Museum** (*411 W. Colorado Blvd. 818-449-6840. Thurs.-Sun.; adm. fee*) houses the world-class art collection of businessman Simon.

In neighboring San Marino, the august **Huntington Library** (*1151 Oxford Rd. 818-405-2100. Closed Mon.; donation requested*) was built by railroad tycoon Henry E. Huntington on his 207-acre estate. The museum showcases important 18th- and 19th-century French and British art, as well as such literary rarities as a Gutenberg Bible and a 1410 copy of *The Canterbury Tales.* Be sure to take a few minutes to enjoy the rare shrubs, dwarf maples, and 16th-century samurai's house in the 130-acre botanical garden.

Arcadia **Los Angeles State and County Arboretum** (*301 N. Baldwin Ave. 818-821-3222*) Peacocks roam the manicured gardens of exotic flora in this 127-acre oasis. Don't miss the prehistoric and meadowbrook gardens. In the late 19th century the estate belonged to E. J. "Lucky" Baldwin, who built the red-and-white Queen Anne Cottage later featured in the television series *Fantasy Island.* Hollywood producers have used the gardens for settings in films from *The African Queen* to *Roots. Adm. fee.*

Beverly Hills (*8 miles W on Hyperion Ave. and Santa Monica Blvd.*) The city's palm-lined streets encapsulate the carefree opulence of Hollywood's rich and famous, who live here in million-dollar Spanish haciendas and Tudor mansions. For a brief tour, pick up a walking map from the **Chamber of Commerce** (*239 S. Beverly Dr. 310-271-8174*). Head to **Roxbury Drive,** where you can stroll past the former residences of Lucille Ball (No. 1000), Jack Benny (No. 1002), and Jimmy Stewart (No. 918). You might see some current stars promenading along **Rodeo Drive,** an avenue of gilded boutiques. Up on Sunset Boulevard you'll find the pink

mission-revival-style **Beverly Hills Hotel** (*9641 Sunset Blvd. 310-276-2251*), the trysting place for such stars as Clark Gable, Marilyn Monroe, and Sophia Loren.

Hollywood (*5 miles W on Hyperion Ave. and Santa Monica Blvd.*) Excellent natural light and fine weather first enticed film producers here from the East Coast in 1911, when Hollywood was just a secluded orange grove. The 50-foot-high Hollywood sign still gleams from atop Mount Lee, but the golden era ended in the 1960s, when studios moved to the nearby San Fernando Valley.

Today's Hollywood is tawdry and junky, yet throngs of tourists walk **Hollywood Boulevard** each year in search of the legendary Tinseltown. The

Rock singer Angelyne, Hollywood, California

began as a Spanish pueblo in the late 1700s in an unlikely location: a basin threatened by floods, droughts, and battles. The fledgling town was saved by a series of booms brought on by the arrival of the railroad in 1885, oil strikes, and the movie business. Today

Look-alikes include Gerald Ford, Candace Bergen, Raquel Welch, and Jimmy Durante

Los Angeles is California's largest city, its 3.5 million residents crammed into 465 square miles.

L.A. juxtaposes multiculturalism with dazzle: Small neighborhoods, ranging from Latino barrios to the chic Westside, share space with a trendy city of steel-and-glass skyscrapers, Hollywood sets, and sophisticated tastes. A good place to start your tour is in the heart of downtown at the **L.A. Convention & Visitors**

Chinatown Gateway

Bureau *(685 Figueroa St. between 7th St. and Wilshire Blvd. 213-624-7300)*. Nearby, in the shadow of the ARCO building and the I. M. Pei-designed First Interstate

Bank headquarters, shines the **Museum of Contemporary Art** *(250 S. Grand Ave. 213-626-6222. Closed Mon.; adm. fee)*, an airy sandstone building devoted to works of art created since 1940. Nearby is the **Children's Museum** *(310 N. Main St. 213-687-8800. Weekends only; adm. fee)*, geared to youthful curiosities.

Just 5 blocks away, the open-air **Grand Central Public Market** *(317 S. Broadway. 213-624-2378)* is a great place to see L.A.'s ethnic mixture. Here in this bustling 1917 landmark, Westside chefs, Valley socialites, and Mexican housewives search shoulder-to-shoulder for the ripest tomatillos and the plumpest grapes. A few blocks east lies trim **Little Tokyo** *(1st and San Pedro Sts.)*, the center of one of the largest Japanese-American communities on the U. S. mainland. North on Broadway, more than 15,000 Chinese and Southeast Asians live in **Chinatown** *(900 block of N. Broadway)*, brimming with red-and-gold herbal shops, fish markets, and Buddhist temples.

The city traces its beginnings to a small adobe enclave near the art deco **City Hall** *(200 N. Spring St.; 360° views from observation deck on 27th floor. 213-485-4423)*. In 1781, when Spain ruled Mexico and Mexico included Alta California, a Spanish expedition established a pueblo on this site near the Los Angeles River. Shady **Olvera Street,** in the heart of the old pueblo—now a historic park—evokes those early years with an artsy marketplace where Hispanic locals sell tacos, piñatas, and blankets. The **Sepulveda House** *(622 N. Main St. 213-628-1274. Closed Sun.)*, built in 1887, now serves as a museum of Mexican-American culture. Nearby, you can tour L.A.'s oldest building: the restored 1818 **Avila Adobe** *(10 E. Olvera St. Closed Sun.-Mon.)*.

L.A. sprawls haphazardly from downtown, so that all other destinations lie in suburbs via one or another crowded freeway. Follow I-110 south

Street mimes

to **Exposition Park.** Here, at the vast **California Museum of Science and Industry** (213-744-7400), several exhibit buildings explore health, communications, space, and aviation. More than 16 million artifacts are on display right next door at the **L.A. County Museum of Natural History** (213-744-3414. Closed Mon.-Tues.; adm. fee). Highlights include pre-Columbian cultures, gemstones, and the skeleton of a rare megamouth shark.

Crawl through traffic west on I-10 to **Hancock Park** and the **La Brea Tar Pits,** a rich deposit of bubbling black morass that has yielded more than a hundred tons of Pleistocene fossils. Glimpse reconstructed skeletons of sloths, mammoths, and saber-toothed cats at the nearby **George C. Page Museum of La Brea Discoveries** (5801 Wilshire Blvd. 213-857-6311. Closed Mon.-Tues.; adm. fee). Also in Hancock Park is the impressive **Los Angeles County Museum of Art** (5905 Wilshire Blvd. 857-6111. Closed Mon.; adm. fee), with fine collections of Tibetan and Islamic art, among others.

I-5 runs north to **Griffith Park** (Los Feliz Blvd. exit), more than 4,000 acres of woods and oak-studded valleys tucked in the Hollywood Hills. Here you'll find the art deco, copper-domed **Griffith Observatory and Planetarium** (2800 E. Observatory Rd. 213-664-1191. Closed Mon. only Sept.-May; fee for planetarium), used as the film set for *Rebel Without a Cause,* and the **L.A. Zoo** (213-666-4090. Adm. fee), the 80-acre home of koalas,

Chiles Restaurant

tigers, orangutans, and more than 1,600 other animals.

Off Calif. 110, the mission revival-style **Southwest Museum** (234 Museum Dr. 213-221-2163. Closed Mon.; adm. fee) is L.A.'s oldest museum, founded in 1907. When L.A. traffic gets to be too much, head for 15-mile-long **Mulholland Drive** (Via Laurel Canyon Blvd., Hollywood Blvd., and other routes), a windy, ridge-top road across the Santa Monica Mountains, with fabulous views of the L.A. Basin, San Fernando Valley, and—most likely—those infamous smog banks.

27

Queen Mary, Long Beach, California

28

reminders are there. Visit the courtyard of the ornate **Mann's Chinese Theatre** (*6925 Hollywood Blvd. 213-464-8111*), where more than 160 celebrities have left footprints and handprints in cement. And stroll along the **Walk of Fame** (*Hollywood Blvd. between Gower St. and La Brea Ave.*), where the names of nearly 2,000 celebrities are engraved in metal stars. Look for Elvis's star in the 6700 block.

Santa Monica See I-10, p. 34.

㊏ Long Beach A regal presence, the elegant ***Queen Mary*** (*1126 Queens Hwy. 310-435-3511*) has been berthed at Long Beach Harbor since 1967. Launched in 1936, the 81,000-ton grande dame crisscrossed the Atlantic more than a thousand times, carrying celebrities, politicians, and royalty in her lavish salons and staterooms. You can stroll her polished decks and peek into a first-class stateroom. For a real treat, stay in one of the 365 staterooms and suites that have been turned into hotel rooms. *Adm. fee.*

㊄ Anaheim Walt Disney's idea of a "magical little park" exploded into the 80-acre (and ever growing) **Disneyland** (*1313 Harbor Blvd., follow signs. 714-999-4565*), which opened in 1955. Today the Magic Kingdom's eight theme parks create a child's paradise of rides, shows, and real-life storybook characters. Old favorites: the cutesy "It's a Small, Small World," Sleeping Beauty's Magical Castle, the scary Matterhorn ride, and the dazzling Electrical Parade that marches down Main Street every evening. The park is most crowded in July and August and around Christmas. *Adm. fee.*

㊣ Newport Beach In the early 1900s, affluent pleasure seekers from L.A. began swarming to Newport Beach, then a swath

In 1769, Spanish authorities sent Franciscan friar Junípero Serra to colonize the golden land of Alta California. Serra's legacy is the string of 21 adobe *missions* scattered a day apart by mule from San Diego to Sonoma along the 600-mile Camino Real. Rather than obliterate the Indians, the Franciscans "civilized" them with Christianity and enlisted their help in developing the missions into rich farms. After Mexico's independence from Spain in 1833, the missions were secularized; since then most have been restored to their original beauty.

Mission San Juan Capistrano, California

of sand at the edge of orange groves. Here they built seaside villas. Housing tracts have since replaced the groves, but the affluent still predominate. The 6-mile beach, though, is a good place for anyone to catch a few rays. The Newport dory fishermen, a fixture since 1892, still throw their lines from colorful wooden boats and sell their catch at **Newport Pier** *(Between 20th and 21st Sts.).*

Mission San Juan Capistrano *(Ortega Hwy. exit, follow signs. 714-248-2049)* Stolid bougainvillea-draped adobe walls surround one of the most romantic of the Franciscans' California missions, founded in 1776. Fountains and gardens grace the interior courtyard, and each year, around March 19 (St. Joseph's Day), the legendary swallows return to their mud nests from their winter homes in South America. A splendid stone church with seven domes, built between 1797 and 1806, was destroyed by an earthquake in 1812. Its ruins lie near the Serra Chapel; a simple adobe structure with an ornate gilded altar, this is the only remaining chapel actually used by Father Junípero Serra. A museum showcases Indian crafts, Spanish weapons, and early ecclesiastical artifacts. *Adm. fee.*

Mission San Juan Capistrano

Oceanside **Mission San Luis Rey de Francia** *(4 miles E on Calif. 76 through congestion, follow signs to 4050 Mission Ave. 619-757-3651)* The 18th and largest of California's 21 missions was named for King Louis IX of France. Founded in 1798 in the valley between the San Diego and San Juan Capistrano missions, its original 6 acres were once home to more than 2,000 Indians. Colorful paintings adorn the interior. The museum has a collection of antique vestments. *Adm. fee.*

Carlsbad In 1883, farmer John Frazier dug a well that tapped into water with the same mineral content as a famous spring in Karlsbad, Bohemia—hence the name of the village, whose downtown architecture reflects the Old World theme. For a refreshing dose of sunny California, don't miss 3-mile-long **Carlsbad State Beach** *(Tamarack Ave. W to Carlsbad Blvd.).*

Torrey Pines State Reserve *(1 mile W from Carmel Valley Rd. exit on Carmel Valley Rd., 0.5 mile S on Pacific Coast Hwy. Visitor Center 619-755-2063)* This 1,750-acre reserve protects the last mainland habitat of the rare Torrey pine. Believed to have once covered much of coastal southern California, these short, spindly trees were nearly killed off by development. Footpaths wind through the reserve, a beautiful headland overlooking the Pacific. *Vehicle fee.*

San Diego See I-8, pp. 30-31.

① San Diego

Mission San Diego de Alcalá, the first mission established in California, in 1769

In 1542, Portuguese sailor Juan Rodríguez Cabrillo landed near the tip of Point Loma and claimed the Pacific coast for Spain. Today the birthplace of California offers a relaxed lifestyle, balmy weather, and plenty of attractions (Visitor Information Center, 1st and F Sts. 619-236-1212).

Cabrillo National Monument *(End of Catalina Blvd. 619-557-5450. Adm. fee)* commemorates Cabrillo's discovery; this is also a favorite spot to view the gray whale migrations in spring and fall. To delve further into San Diego's rich history, stop by the **Mission San Diego de Alcalá** *(10818 San Diego Mission Rd. 619-281-8449. Adm. fee)*, built in 1769 under the direction of Father Junípero Serra, and the **Old Town San**

Orangutan, San Diego Zoo

Diego State Historic Park *(4002 Wallace St. 619-220-5422)*, which dates back to 1821, shortly after Mexico gained independence from Spain. The 16-block national historic district known as the **Gaslamp Quarter** *(Between 4th and 6th Aves. from Broadway to Harbor Dr.)*, with its many 1880s Victorian commercial buildings, was once the site of San Diego's notorious red-light district. In its heyday the Gaslamp Quarter counted more than 70 saloons and 120 bawdy houses, as well as opium dens, dance halls, and gambling houses. For information on walking tours, contact the **Gaslamp Quarter Association** *(410 Island Ave. 619-233-5227. Adm. fee)*.

In 1868, San Diego set aside 1,400 acres of cactus and chaparral as a public park. Today **Balboa Park** *(619-239-0512)*, the city's most elegant public space, provides a lush setting for serene gardens, striking architecture, picnic grounds, golf courses, and the world-class **San Diego Zoo** *(619-234-3153. Adm. fee)*, which showcases pygmy

Victor Ochoa mural, Balboa Park

30

Unless otherwise noted, directions are from interstate, and sites are free and generally open daily. Phone for further information.

Sailing a catamaran on Mission Bay

chimps, sun bears from Malaysia, and 22 new aviaries called the Wings of Australasia. Another star attraction, the **Reuben H. Fleet Space Theater and Science Center** *(619-238-1233. Adm. fee)* houses an Omnimax theater and hands-on exhibits. Also on the grounds are the **Museum of Photographic Arts** *(619-239-5262. Adm. fee),* the **Natural History Museum** *(619-232-3821. Adm. fee),* the **Model Railroad Museum** *(619-696-0199. Closed Mon.-Tues.; adm. fee),* and the **San Diego Museum of Art** *(619-232-7931. Closed Mon.; adm. fee).*

Down on the Embarcadero waterfront, sailors will delight in the three historic ships moored at the **Maritime Museum** *(1306 N. Harbor Dr. 619-234-9153. Adm. fee):* the 1863 tall ship *Star of India,* the 1898 San Francisco Bay ferry *Berkeley,* and the 1904

steam-powered yacht *Medea*. **Sea World** *(1720 S. Shores Rd. 619-226-3901. Adm. fee)* ranks as one of California's top attractions. The marine life park features six shows daily (its most famous star is Shamu the killer whale) and more than 30 educational exhibits, including the largest collection of penguins north of Antarctica, live sharks, a whale and dolphin petting zoo, and the new Rocky Point Preserve, a Pacific Northwest habitat where you look at sea otters and other marine creatures close-up.

Ready to soak up some sun? Take the San Diego-Coronado Bay Bridge *(toll)* or a pedestrian ferry *(San Diego Harbor Excursions leave from Broadway Pier. 619-234-4111. Fare charge)* to **Coronado Island** *(Visitor Center, 1111 Orange Ave., Suite A. 619-437-8788),* which is not really an island but a low, narrow peninsula that separates San Diego Bay from the Pacific Ocean. Be sure to visit the castlelike Victorian **Hotel del Coronado** *(1500 Orange Ave. 619-435-6611. Fee for cassette tour)* and take a stroll along the lovely beach.

31

Botanical Building and lily pond, Balboa Park

② **Cuyamaca Rancho State Park** *(9 miles N on Calif. 79. 619-765-0755)* Atypical of southern California, this 24,677-acre park has stands of pine and oak, mountain meadows, and spring-fed streams. A 3.5-mile walk leads from Paso Picacho Campground up Cuyamaca Peak, from which you can see the Anza-Borrego Desert and, on a clear day, the Pacific coast. The museum features exhibits on Indians, mining, and natural history. *Adm. fee.*

③ **San Diego Railroad Museum** *(14 miles SW on Calif. 94 in town of Campo. 619-697-7762)* Train buffs will revel in a 16-mile ride on a vintage 1920s train pulled by a diesel locomotive. *Weekends only; adm. fee.*

④ **Desert View Tower** *(1 mile N on In-Ko-Pah Park Rd. 619-766-4612)* This 600-foot observation tower offers a terrific view east across the Colorado Desert. A fun trail past huge granite boulders will appeal to kids. *Adm. fee.*

Anza-Borrego Desert State Park, California

⑤ **Anza-Borrego Desert State Park** *(Park boundary 8 miles N of Ocotillo on Rte. S2. Visitor Center, 200 Palm Canyon Dr., Borrego Springs. 619-767-5311)* The cooler months between November and April are the best time to explore this 600,000-plus-acre park, with its 12 wilderness areas, more than 500 miles of dirt roads, two dozen hiking trails, and myriad canyons. From Carrizo Badlands Overlook you can gaze across some 10 miles of tilted, twisted sedimentary rock formed five to six million years ago.

⑥ **Calexico** *(7 miles S on Calif. 111. Chamber of Commerce, 1100 Imperial Ave. 619-357-1166)* In this small border town you'll feel as though you've entered another country. Many signs are in Spanish, and only a simple fence separates the pleasant downtown from Mexicali, its south-of-the-border sister city. Besides the expected plethora of Mexican restaurants, Calexico bursts with Chinese eateries.

Imperial Sand Dunes, California

32

Imperial Sand Dunes BLM Recreation Area

(Access the dunes via Ogliby Rd. 619-353-1060) Also called the Algodones Dunes, these 300-foot-high dunes stretch more than 40 miles along the Imperial Valley's eastern edge. Scorching in summer, they attract droves of off-highway vehicle enthusiasts from Oct. to May.

Yuma, ARIZONA

(Convention and Visitor Center, 377 Main St., Suite 203. 602-783-0071) This city evolved from a series of forts and missions along the Colorado River. In 1852, Fort Yuma, one of the first military posts in the Arizona Territory, was built on a hilltop to protect those dashing off to California in search of gold. This early history comes alive at the **Fort Yuma-Quechan Museum** *(Picacho Rd. N to Indian Hill Rd. 619-572-0661. Closed Sun.; adm. fee)* and the **Yuma Crossing and Quartermaster Depot** *(N end of 2nd Ave. at Colorado River. 602-329-0404. Adm. fee).* The **Yuma Territorial Prison State Historic Park** *(Giss Pkwy. exit, follow signs. 602-783-4771. Adm. fee)* preserves the "hellhole of Arizona," where from 1876 to 1909 prisoners endured blistering heat and scorpions.

Painted Rocks Petroglyphs

(11 miles N on Painted Rocks Rd., follow signs. 602-780-8090) Prehistoric Hohokam petroglyphs cover a hill of boulders next to a campground. The rocks served as a landmark for travelers on the Gila Trail and the Butterfield Overland Stage, which linked St. Louis with San Francisco.

Gila Bend

Here, where the southbound Gila River makes a 90-degree turn west, Gila Bend took root in 1847 as a stop on the Gila Trail, but the town was moved 3 miles north when the tracks of the Southern Pacific Railroad were laid. The **Gila Bend Museum** *(644 W. Pima St. 602-683-2002)* displays prehistoric and historic exhibits, including baskets, tools, and pottery.

Casa Grande Ruins Natl. Mon. See I-10, p. 37.

The *route between Gila Bend and Yuma* may seem a tedious trip across the sun-blasted desert, but it's steeped in history. During the 18th century Spanish missionaries infiltrated this region via the Gila River. In the mid-1800s the Butterfield Overland Stage followed this route, and pioneers seeking fortune in California passed through. One family of nine was attacked by Indians, who killed all but three children. The Indians threw the boy over a cliff, leaving him for dead, and made off with the two girls. One was later rescued by her brother, traded for food and horses.

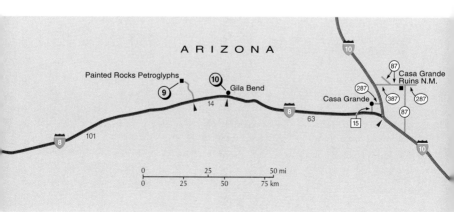

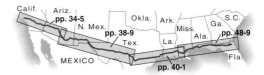

Unless otherwise noted, directions are from interstate, and sites are free and generally open daily. Phone for further information.

Venice Beach, California

1 **Santa Monica, CALIFORNIA** This bustling resort town shares the glitz and grit of nearby L.A., all bound up with sun and often cooling ocean breezes. A 3-mile bike path runs along the beach and crosses one of the West Coast's oldest pleasure piers, the 1908 **Santa Monica Pier** *(Foot of Colorado Ave.)*, home to restaurants, arcades, and an early carousel.

2 **Venice Beach** For a taste of California bohemianism, walk along the beach boardwalk here *(Foot of Wash. Blvd.)*. You'll smell incense, watch roller-bladers, pass tattoo parlors and body piercing shops, and get a look at a stream of unusual characters.

Los Angeles See I-5, pp. 26-27.

3 **Redlands** Some of the grand Victorian houses that grew up among the orange groves here in the 1880s are restored and visible today, though not open to the public. The **San Bernadino County Museum** *(2024 Orange Tree Lane, off Calif. St. exit. 909-798-8570. Closed Mon.; adm. fee)* contains history, anthropology, and natural history exhibits, including a collection of land and sea bird eggs.

4 **Palm Springs** This exclusive resort town in the shadow of 10,804-foot San Jacinto Peak attracts the well-to-do with miner-

34

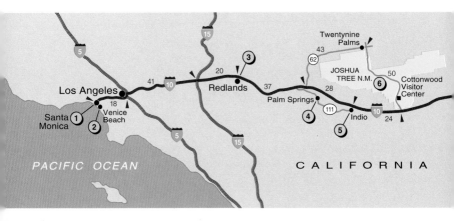

al springs, a generally balmy climate, golf courses, and chic shops. The **Palm Springs Desert Museum** (*101 Museum Dr. 619-325-0189. Closed Mon. and in summer; adm. fee*) is an excellent regional museum, with fine art and natural history, including Indian artifacts and live snakes. On the north edge of town, you can catch the **Palm Springs Aerial Tramway** (*Tramway Rd. off Calif. 111, 3.5 miles up the hill. 619-325-1391. Adm. fee*) for a 14-minute ride up to 8,516-foot Mountain Station for grand desert views.

I n d i o Some 3,000 acres of tall date palms shade the desert here in the nation's "date capital." **Shield's Date Gardens** (*80-225 Calif. 111. 619-347-0996*) offers date delights of all sorts.

J o s h u a   T r e e   N a t i o n a l   M o n u m e n t (*Adm. fee*) Some of the most spectacular desert scenery in California falls inside the boundaries of this 559,960-acre area of twisted rock, cactuses, and granite monoliths, slated to become a national park with expanded acreage. From the **Cottonwood Visitor Center** (*6 miles N of the Joshua Tree N.M. exit. No phone*), the park road climbs through the Colorado Desert and comes to the higher, wetter, and slightly cooler Mojave Desert, which bears the peculiar Joshua tree, the only tree that survives on the desert flatlands. The **Oasis Visitor Center** (*43 miles E on Calif. 62 to Twentynine Palms, follow signs. 619-367-7511*) features exhibits on regional wildlife and geology.

Joshua Tree National Monument, California

35

B l y t h e Just west of town, the Colorado River cuts through the desert like a long, thin oasis, its banks rich with vegetation. The **Cibola National Wildlife Refuge** (*20 miles S of town on Calif. 78, follow signs. 602-857-3253*) offers chances to study Canada geese, sandhill cranes, and other migratory birds amid sheltered wetlands.

Q u a r t z s i t e ,   A R I Z O N A Each January and February, this dusty desert town comes alive with gem and mineral shows.

Continued on P. 38

⑨ Phoenix

Hopi kachina doll and other Southwestern Indian artifacts, Heard Museum

The Hohokam people irrigated the Salt River Valley as early as A.D. 1300 Not until 1868, however, was a system of irrigation canals reestablished. A new city sprang up and was aptly named after the mythic Phoenix, the bird that arose from its ashes. Today, wide avenues lined with glass towers, museums, and restaurants dominate this sunny metropolis. A mix of Spanish, colonial, and adobe architecture adds to the Western flavor (Convention & Visitors Bureau 400 E. Van Buren St. 602-254-6500).

Head downtown to the small but outstanding *Heard Museum* (22 E. Monte Vista Rd. 602-252-8840. Adm. fee), showcasing Native American culture. The wall full of Hopi kachina dolls is especially impressive. Down the street is the more traditional *Phoenix Art Museum* (1625 N. Central Ave. 602-257-1222. Closed Mon.; adm. fee), with 16th-through 20th-century painting and sculpture. Across downtown, the copper-domed *State Capitol* (1700 W. Washington St. 602-542-4675. Closed weekends) has been restored to its original 1912 appearance. Two rooms of the *Phoenix Museum of History* (1002 W. Van Buren St. 602-253-2734. Closed Mon.-Tues.) are packed with early regional artifacts, including a bridle belonging to the Apache warrior Geronimo. For another taste of early history, tour the turn-of-the-century buildings of *Heritage Square* (Seventh and Monroe Sts. 602-262-5029. Closed Sun.-Mon.; adm. fee). Notable is the *Rosson House,* an example of the Victorian Eastlake style, with pressed-tin ceilings. Kids will enjoy the hands-on exhibits of thermal imaging, electricity, and much more at the *Arizona Museum of Science and Technology* (147 E. Adams St. 602-256-9388. Adm. fee). East of town at the Papago Park Military Reservation, the *Arizona Military Museum* (5636 E. McDowell Rd. 602-267-2676. Closed Mon., Wed., Fri.) features memorabilia from WW I to Desert Storm. Next door in Papago Park, hundreds of unusual lifeforms have adapted to desert conditions and flourish at the *Desert Botanical Garden* (1201 N. Galvin Parkway. 602-941-1225. Adm. fee), including three-crested saguaros and cardons, a Mexican cactus of massive stature. Nearby, the nocturnal house at the *Phoenix Zoo* (455 N. Galvin Pkwy. 602-273-1341. Adm. fee) shelters such night-active creatures as bats and scorpions. Opposite Papago Park is the *Hall of Flame Museum of Firefighting* (6101 E. Van Buren St. 602-275-3473. Closed Sun.; adm. fee) with all kinds of gear, from hand-held to computerized.

Zuni girl

State Capitol

Off the main street is the old graveyard with **Hi Jolly's Last Camp**, a small rock pyramid erected in honor of a Syrian camel driver who led an ill-fated attempt by the U. S. Army in the mid-1850s to enlist camels as pack animals. Southeast of town is the **Kofa National Wildlife Refuge** (*18 miles S on US 95, at Palm Canyon sign go E 9 miles on dirt road. 602-783-7861*), an area in the Kofa Mountains with 300 miles of rough roads, where you can see palm trees and perhaps glimpse bighorn sheep.

S c o t t s d a l e   The downtown here is dressed up like the Old West, with wooden sidewalks and old-fashioned storefronts. More modern sections of town are clogged with art galleries and shops that welcome browsers. You can ride the 5/12th-scale *Paradise and Pacific* over a mile of 15-inch track at the grassy **McCormick Railroad Park** (*7301 E. Indian Bend Rd. 602-994-2312. Fee for rides*). Full-size displays include a Baldwin steam engine and a Southern Pacific caboose. Northeast of town is the **Out of Africa Wildlife Park** (*NE on Beeline Rd., then N on Ft. McDowell Rd. 602-837-7779. Closed Mon.; adm. fee*), a cross between a zoo and a preserve.

M e s a   Affluent and growing, this city sits atop a plateau overlooking Phoenix. Mormons settled here in 1877, taking advantage of existing irrigation canals built by the ancient Hohokam people. You'll learn more about these vanished people at the **Mesa Southwest Museum** (*53 N. Macdonald St. 602-644-2230. Closed Mon.; adm. fee*). You can also pan for gold in the courtyard. Nearby, the **Champlin Fighter Museum** (*4636 Fighter Aces Dr. 602-830-4540. Adm. fee*) features 30 fighter planes from the Sopwith Camel to the F4 Phantom, as well as ace memorabilia and a machine gun collection.

C a s a   G r a n d e   R u i n s   N a t i o n a l   M o n u m e n t (*14 miles E via Ariz. 387 and Ariz. 87. 602-723-3172*) Worth a visit, this site contains the remains of the largest Hohokam structure known—35 feet tall—built in the 1300s of 3,000 tons of caliche (a concretelike hardpan) and timber. Exhibits in the Visitor Center tantalize you with clues about this little-known people. Beware of mid-summer temperatures; they can soar above 100°F. *Adm. fee.*

P i c a c h o   P e a k   S . P. (*Picacho Peak Rd. exit, then 0.5 mile S. 602-466-3183*) Picacho Peak served as a landmark to westwardbound stage passengers in the 19th century, and to Indians and Spaniards before that. The state's only Civil War battle is thought to have been fought nearby. Today, the 2-mile-long Hunter Trail winds up this 3,370-foot-tall eroded lava flow. The views are spectacular; gloves and hiking experience recommended. *Adm. fee.*

T u c s o n (*Convention & Visitors Bureau, 130 S. Scott Ave. 602-624-1817*) Sunny days almost always mark this energetic city, poised in a high desert valley and bounded by four mountain ranges. Some 12,000 years ago, Native Americans occupied this area, but were

Close-up of Curtiss P-40N Warhawk, Champlin Fighter Museum, Mesa, Arizona

37

Souvenir stands and museum shops across the Southwest are filled with imitations of the sacred Hopi religious figure, the *kachina doll*. Kachinas are spirits that serve as intermediaries, bearing prayers for rain and plentiful harvests from the Hopi to their deities. Traditionally, these dolls are carved from dried cottonwood root and given to Hopi children during religious ceremonies as a way of teaching about kachina spirits.

Mission San Xavier del Bac, 7 miles SW of Tucson off I-19

displaced gradually by Spanish missionaries, then Mexicans, and finally, Americans. Today, Tucson maintains ties to its past with low, adobe buildings, Mexican restaurants, and spoken Spanish. The best view of the city, especially at night, is atop **Sentinel Mountain** *(W on Congress St. and left at Sentinel Peak Rd.)*, locally referred to as "A" Mountain. The **University of Arizona** has two notable museums: the **Arizona State Museum** *(Park Ave. at University Blvd., inside main gate. 602-621-6302)*, with extensive exhibits on southwestern archaeology and ethnology and displays on 10,000 years of Native American culture; and the **Center for Creative Photography** *(Olive Rd. near Speedway Blvd. 602-621-7968. Closed Sat.)*, housing a collection of nearly 60,000 prints by more than 1,400 photographers. Outside the main university gate is the **Arizona Historical Society Museum** *(949 E. Second St. 602-628-5774)*, which has artifacts from colonial times to the present, including a full-scale mining tunnel. The small but well-arranged **Tucson Botanical Gardens** *(2150 N. Alvernon Way. 602-326-9686. Adm. fee)* illustrates the range of plants found in southern Arizona.

38

In the mountains west of downtown are three worthwhile stops. The dusty streets and weathered adobe storefronts of **Old Tucson Studios** *(201 S. Kinney Rd. 602-883-0100. Adm. fee)*, a theme park and production backdrop, have figured in more than 300 television and feature film projects, from *Gunsmoke* to *Three Amigos*. Up the road is the must-see **Ariz.-Sonora Desert Museum** *(2021 N. Kinney Rd. 602-883-2702.*

Biosphere 2, enclosed earth habitats, 35 miles NE of Tucson via Ariz. 77

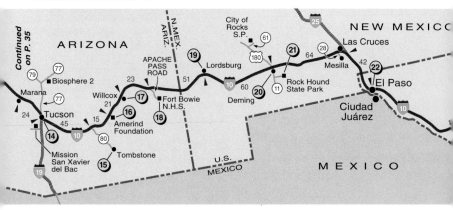

Continued on P. 35

Adm. fee), a superb outdoor showcase of desert life. You can walk through a hummingbird aviary, search for ocelots in a natural setting, and learn about the giant saguaro. Continue north on Kinney Road to **Saguaro National Monument West** *(602-883-6366)*, a park filled with saguaro cactus. A 6-mile dirt loop winds through saguaro forests, past rocks painted with Hohokam petroglyphs.

North of downtown is the **Tohono Chul Park** *(7366 North Paseo del Norte. 602-575-8468. Donations)*, a preserve of some 37 acres of desert containing 400 species of arid-climate plants that protects the desert tortoise and assorted lizards.

To the northeast, trails wind throughout **Sabino Canyon** *(5700 N. Sabino Canyon Rd. 602-749-3223)*, a deep cleft cut into the Santa Catalina Mountains by Sabino Creek. From the Visitor Center, shuttle buses run hikers to trailheads and picnic spots.

T o m b s t o n e *(26 miles S on Ariz. 80. Visitor Center, 4th and Allen Sts. 602-457-3929)* Despite its commercialism, this infamous town is loaded with Old West lore. Outlaws of all stripes came here in 1877, after a prospector discovered silver. Today, 19th-century vintage stores and saloons line dusty streets, where men in costume fire blanks. You can pay respects at the famous **Boothill Graveyard,** and stand on the actual spot of the **OK Corral** gunfight, amid dummy gunslingers. *Adm. fees for attractions.*

A m e r i n d   F o u n d a t i o n *(1 mile E of Dragoon Rd. exit, follow signs. 602-586-3666)* Spanish colonial-style buildings filled with archaeological and ethnological treasures compose this museum, art gallery, and research center. Highlights are the Apache spirit headdresses and the pottery, including pieces from the Hohokam site of Casas Grandes. *Closed Mon.-Tues. June-Aug.; adm. fee.*

W i l l c o x A cattle shipping center, this quaint town is best known for its apples—an experiment determined that Granny

Arizona-Sonora Desert Museum, Tucson

The tall and often ancient **saguaro cactus** solemnly presides over the arid Sonora Desert of central and southern Arizona, its arms raised skyward as if beseeching some larger presence. *Carnegiea gigantea* can grow as tall as 60 feet and weigh many tons. Arms only develop after 70 years; those individuals with several arms are more than 150 years old.

39

Continued on P. 40

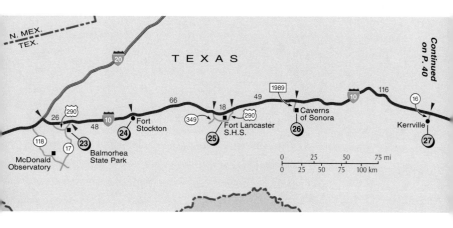

Smiths and other apples grow well here. Now there are more than a million trees in a 30-mile radius. The **Museum of the Southwest** (*1500 N. Circle I Rd. 602-384-2272*) is modest, but worth a peek if you combine it with a visit next door to **Stout's Cider Mill** (*1510 N. Circle I Rd. 602-384-3696*) for apple pie or fresh cider.

City of Rocks State Park, New Mexico, 28 miles NW of Deming via US 180 and N. Mex. 61

(18) **Fort Bowie Natl. Historic Site** (*12 miles S on Apache Pass Rd. 602-847-2500*) The outpost was built near Apache Springs in 1862 to protect travelers on the well-used route of the Butterfield Overland Stage from Apaches led by Cochise and Geronimo. The fort was abandoned 32 years later. From the ranger station, take a 1.5-mile path to the fort ruins.

(19) **Lordsburg, NEW MEXICO** The Southern Pacific Railroad gave rise to this small town, which soon overshadowed the older community of Shakespeare, 2.5 miles south on Main Street. Today, the latter is the well-preserved **Shakespeare Ghost Town** (*505-542-9034. Open 2nd and 4th weekends of month; adm. fee*), complete with buildings such as the Stratford Hotel, where Billy the Kid reputedly washed dishes. **Steins Railroad Ghost Town** (*16 miles SW on I-10 at Steins exit. 505-542-9791. Adm. fee for tour*) displays the remains of a pioneer town deserted overnight when the railroad was abandoned. Glimpses of the rough life can be had in nine buildings filled with artifacts.

WELCOME
THIS IS GOD'S COUNTRY
PLEASE DON'T
DRIVE THROUGH IT
LIKE HELL
HONDO, TEXAS

(20) **Deming** Surrounded by rugged mountains and cotton and grain fields, this busy town hosts the Great American Duck Race (ducks waddle competitively) in late August. The **Deming Luna Mimbres Museum** (*301 S. Silver St. 505-546-2382*) has a smattering of antique dolls, quilts, Mimbres Indian pottery, and more.

(21) **Rock Hound State Park** (*14 miles SE off N. Mex.*

40

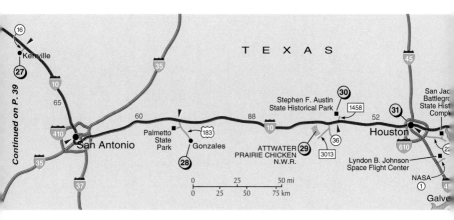

Continued on P. 39

11. 505-546-6182) This unusual park allows you to keep the rocks you find, including geodes, quartz, and agate. If you're unlucky, you can buy shiny agates just outside the park. *Adm. fee.*

Las Cruces and Mesilla See I-25, p. 85.

㉒ El Paso, Texas

It would be very difficult to tell where El Paso leaves off and Ciudad Juárez, Mexico, begins were it not for the bridges and the thin break in the buildings that is the Rio Grande (Visitor & Conv. Center, 1 Civic Center Plaza. 915-534-0696 or 800-351-6024).

The first recorded history in the area dates back to the **Spanish missions** (From Zaragoza exit, follow Mission Trail signs), built here in the mid-17th century. Three missions, including the rebuilt 1692 **Mission Ysleta** and the 1692 **Mission Socorro,** still stand along the Camino Real, a road first used by the conquistadores.

Near downtown, the **El Paso Museum of Art** (1211 Montana Ave. 915-541-4040. Closed Mon.) houses European and American works; and the **Chamizal Nation-**

Tigua Indian teenager

al Memorial (800 S. San Marcial. 915-534-6668) marks the peaceful settlement of a 99-year dispute between the U. S. and Mexico that began when the Rio Grande shifted, leaving formerly Mexican territory in the U. S. Less controversial history is celebrated in the **El Paso Museum of History** (15 miles SE of downtown at 12901 Gateway W. 915-858-1928. Closed Mon.), which tells of the area's early settlement with dioramas and artifacts.

Northeast of town, the **Fort Bliss Museum** (Pleasanton Rd., facing main parade grounds. 915-568-4518) shows how the now huge base looked in the mid-1800s. Farther north, the **Wilderness Park Museum** (4301 Transmountain Rd. 915-755-4332. Closed Mon.) depicts area Indian history to the 17th century.

41

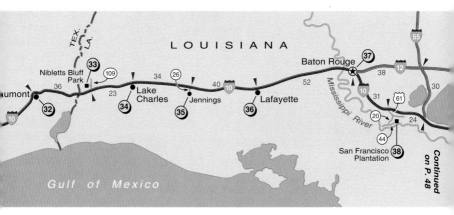

Continued on P. 48

㉓ Balmorhea S. P. *(4 miles SW of Balmorhea off US 290. 915-375-2370)* A spring-fed swimming pool is the main attraction of this park, shaded by Rio Grande cottonwoods. *Adm. fee.*

Attwater Prairie Chicken
NWR, Texas

㉔ Fort Stockton   In 1858, a cavalry post helped establish this small town atop a flat, 3,000-foot mesa. You can visit **Historic Fort Stockton** *(Rooney St., bet. 2nd and 5th Sts. 915-336-2400. Closed Sun.; adm. fee)* on the east side of town, with reconstructed barracks, a museum, and a Visitor Center. The **Annie Riggs Museum** *(301 S. Main St. 915-336-2167. Adm. fee)* preserves an adobe hotel built in 1900, with Victorian details, artifacts, and a memorable list of "house rules."

㉕ Fort Lancaster S. H. S. *(10 miles SE on US 290. 915-836-4391. Daily summer, closed Tues.-Wed. rest of year; adm. fee)* Built in 1855 to protect travelers along the San Antonio-El Paso Road, this outpost is now ruins. Visitor Center and museum.

㉖ Caverns of Sonora *(7 miles S on Rte. 1989. 915-387-3105)* Particularly delicate formations grow in this cavern, including fishtail helictites and chystalline "drapery." *Adm. fee.*

㉗ Kerrville   This resort town is on the Guadalupe River in the heart of beautiful Texas Hill Country. The **Cowboy Artists of America Museum** *(1550 Bandera Hwy. 210-896-2553. Closed Mon. in winter; adm. fee)* celebrates the cowboy with paintings and bronzes by well-known artists. Cypresses shade the riverbanks at **Kerrville-Schreiner S. P.** *(3 miles SE on Tex. Loop 534. 210-257-5392. Fee).*

San Antonio   See I-35, p. 105.

㉘ Gonzales   The first skirmish in the war for Texas independence erupted in this sleepy town in 1835. The **Gonzales Memorial Museum** *(414 Smith St. 210-672-6350. Closed Mon.)* remembers the 32 volunteers who marched the following year to the Alamo in San Antonio. The **Old Jail** *(414 St. Lawrence St. 210-672-6532),* used 1887-1975, now holds the Chamber of Commerce and a museum with restored cells, gallows, and dungeon. **Palmetto S. P.** *(10 miles N on US 183, follow signs. 210-672-3266. Adm. fee)* features rare palmetto palm bogs, thought to be 12,000-year-old relics.

McDonald Observatory, 35 miles south on
Tex. 118, in Davis Mountains

㉙ Attwater Prairie Chicken N. W. R. *(10 miles S on Tex. 36 and Rte. 3013, follow signs. 409-234-3021)* Known for its leaping and dancing during courtship, the once common prairie chicken is preserved here. Other residents include white-tailed hawks and whistling ducks.

㉚ Stephen F. Austin S. H. P. *(3 miles N on Rte. 1458. 409-885-3613)* In 1824, Stephen Austin brought the first 297

Classic American boomtown, Texas' largest city and the fourth largest in the nation exploded in the middle of the century with the growth of oil and petrochemicals. The legacy is reflected in several skylines of glass and metal skyscrapers, which give the city its spread-out, ultra-modern feel (Convention & Visitors Bureau, 801 Congress Ave. 713-227-3100 or 800-231-7799). The

Downtown skyline from Buffalo Bayou

Texas Commerce Tower (600 Travis St. 713-228-7261. Closed weekends), designed by I. M. Pei, offers splendid views from the Sky Lobby on the 60th floor. The tower is connected to the downtown area by some 6.5 miles of tunnels and skywalks, explaining why downtown often seems deserted during lunch. Several blocks away is fountain-studded *Tranquility Park* (E of Smith St., bet. Rusk and Walker), which celebrates the first words heard from the moon:

Space Center Houston

"Houston, Tranquility Base here. The Eagle has landed." A block away is *Sam Houston Park* (1100 Bagby. 713-655-1912. Adm. fee for tour), dedicated to the founder of the Texas republic and featuring seven 19th-century structures on pleasant grassy grounds.

Houston's cultural center, just southwest of midtown, includes the *Museum of Fine Arts* (1001 Bissonnet. 713-639-7300. Closed Mon.; adm. fee), a vast wealth of art highlighting Renaissance and 18th-century works, as well as Impressionism and post-Impressionism. Across the street is the *Contemporary Arts Museum* (5216 Montrose Blvd. 713-526-3129. Closed Mon.; adm. fee), an aluminum building of acute angles with changing modern

exhibits. The *Houston Museum of Natural Science* (1 Hermann Circle Dr. in Hermann Park. 713-639-4600. Adm. fee) boasts a marvelous collection of gems and minerals, as well as dioramas of Texas biota. In the same park are the *Houston Zoological Gardens* (1513 N. MacGregor. 713-523-5888. Adm. fee), where tropical paths lead you to snow leopards, white tigers, and more. Kids will appreciate the *Children's Museum of Houston* (1500 Binz. 713-522-1138. Closed Mon.; adm. fee), a treasure house with a fiberglass cow to milk and a bubbling bayou.

To the southeast, trams take you behind the scenes at the *Lyndon B. Johnson Space Flight Center* (25 miles S on I-45, then 3 miles E on NASA Rd. 713-244-2100), a large NASA facility. The Visitor Center—*Space Center Houston*—has interactive exhibits that show what it's like to land a shuttle. Near the center, on the western shore of Galveston Bay, is the 2,500-acre *Armand Bayou Nature Center* (8500 Bay Area Blvd. 713-474-2551. Closed Mon.-Tues.; adm. fee), the only remnant of this area's original ecosystems. Amid the oil towers east of Houston rises the 50-story obelisk at *San Jacinto Battleground S. H. Complex* (21 miles E on Tex. 225, 3 miles N on Tex. 134. 713-479-2421. Adm. fee), marking the spot where Texas won independence in 1836.

43

Astrodome, southwest of downtown on I-610 loop

families to colonize Texas here, under a contract with the Mexican government. The event is marked with modest but interesting presentations that include replicas of Austin's dog-run cabin and the J. J. Josey General Store Museum. *Adm. fee.*

(32) Beaumont On January 10, 1901, workers stood aghast as Texas' first giant oil gusher blew 100 feet into the air at the Lucas well. Within a month, this sleepy outpost was transformed into a city of 30,000. Today, Beaumont has one of the densest concentrations of petroleum refineries in the country. The **Spindletop/Gladys City Boomtown** (3 *miles S on US 69/96/287. 409-835-0823. Tues.-Sun. p.m.; adm. fee*) on the Lamar University campus re-creates the clapboard shanties that grew up around Beaumont's early wells. Just off the interstate is the **Babe Didrikson Zaharias Museum and Visitors Center** (*M.L. King exit, follow signs. 409-833-4622*), a tribute to this town's daughter, one of the century's finest athletes.

Cajun Music Festival, Lafayette, La.

44

Rollicking violins, swirling two-steps, French patois, and spicy gumbo are signs of the exuberant Cajun people, descendants of French-Canadian farmers exiled from Nova Scotia in the mid-1700s. Many of them found new homes along the bayous and rivers of Louisiana. Today *Cajun country* encompasses 22 parishes, or counties, west of New Orleans, where this unusual blend of Old and New World continues to thrive.

(33) Nibletts Bluff Park, LOUISIANA (3 *miles N on La. 109, then 2.5 miles W on Nibblets Bluff Rd. 318-589-7117*) The sandy bluffs overlooking the Sabine River here once served as a busy crossing point for westward travelers and, later, as the site of a Confederate fort. Today, people come to enjoy the shady banks, to fish, or to look at birds such as the red-headed woodpecker.

(34) Lake Charles The sawmills that fueled the growth of this attractive lakeside town are now gone, but evidence of the boom remains in the **Charpentier Historic District** (*Bounded by Kirby, Hodges, Broad, and Moss Sts. Tour info at the S.W. Louisiana Conv. & Visitors Bureau, 1211 N. Lakeshore Dr. 318-436-9588 or 800-456-SWLA*), a collection of houses built with an unusual mix of features recognized as Lake Charles-style architecture. A modest museum of local history, the **Imperial Calcasieu Museum** (*204 W. Sallier St. 318-439-3797. Closed Mon.*) re-creates an old pharmacy, kitchen, and barbershop and includes a small art gallery and a doll collection.

The **Creole Nature Trail** (*Maps available at Conv. & Visitors Bureau*) is a 105-mile-long auto trail that loops south to the Gulf of Mexico through bayou and alligator country, running by several wildlife refuges that are full of birdlife, especially in winter. There's good shelling for whelks, conch, and cockles.

(35) Jennings The Southern Pacific Railroad brought pioneers here in 1880. The contents of a country store that closed in 1949 are preserved at the **W. H. Tupper General Merchandise Museum** (*311 N. Main St. 318-821-5532. Closed Sun.; adm. fee*), with price tags hanging from items. Attached to the museum is the **Louisiana Telephone Pioneer Museum**, which traces the development of the telephone through full-scale dioramas. In a nearby residential neighborhood, the **Zigler Museum** (*411 Clara St. 318-824-0114. Closed Mon.; adm. fee*) houses a collection of European and American paintings, along with dioramas of southwest Louisiana wildlife.

Lafayette In the center of Cajun country is the **Acadian Village** (*5 miles, S on US 167, SW on Johnston St., then W on Ridge Rd. 318-981-2364. Adm. fee*), a folk-life museum that shows Acadian architecture, known for its outside stairways. A museum with a 400-year-old dugout canoe and paintings of early missionaries is here, too. On the banks of Vermillion Bayou is **Vermillionville** (*1600 Surrey St. 318-233-4077. Adm. fee*), a living-history park with re-creations of Acadian and Creole structures, as well as demonstrations of music, dance, food, and crafts. The handsome **Lafayette Museum** (*1122 Lafayette St. 318-234-2208. Closed Mon.; adm. fee*), housed in an 1800-era house, contains period furnishings, historical artifacts, and Mardi Gras costumes.

Baton Rouge (*Convention & Visitors Bureau, 730 North Blvd. 504-383-1825 or 800-527-6843*) Seven flags have flown over this capital city, named by a French explorer who described the red pole demarcating the boundary between two Native American tribes. The wide, languorous Mississippi River and the shady trees along the streets appear to set a slower pace for the city. But its location at the north end of a chemical corridor stretching to New Orleans and close to large sugar plantations makes it a major port. The 34-story, art deco **State Capitol** (*N. 3rd St. and State Capitol Dr. 504-342-7317*), the nation's tallest state capitol, rises above downtown. The controversial governor Huey Long is buried on the grounds. Sitting closer to the Mississippi is the Gothic Revival **Old State Capitol** (*North Blvd. at River Rd. 504-342-0500*), a lavish, castle-like structure completed in 1849.

Three miles south of town is **Louisiana State University** (*Off Highland Dr. 504-388-3202*), with 30,000 students and Indian mounds believed to be over 1,000 years old. The university operates the excellent **LSU Rural Life Museum** (*Just off I-10, Essen Lane exit. 504-765-2437. Closed weekends Nov.-Feb.; adm. fee*), a plantation with mostly original 19th-century buildings, including slave cabins and a church.

Rising from the dark shadows of swamps throughout the Southeast is the curiously shaped ***cypress tree,*** swollen at its base to protect it against the damp. Cousin of the redwood and giant sequoia, the cypress can grow to immense dimensions and live hundreds of years, though many of the finest specimens were logged for their rot-resistant wood. Surrounding each adult cypress are conical "knees," which are part of the root system and can grow as tall as 6 feet.

45

Bald cypress swamp, Louisiana

San Francisco Plantation (*Gramercy exit, then 8 miles S on US 61, right on La. 20 for 3.5 miles, then left on La. 44 for 5.5 miles. 504-535-2341. Adm. fee*) This richly decorated, 19th-century galleried house typifies the old Creole style, in which the dining and service rooms are on the ground floor and the living quarters are upstairs.

American alligator

An exotic jewel squeezed between the lazy Mississippi River and Lakes Pontchartrain and Borgne, the "Big Easy" casts a spell. In 1718, French Creoles settled the area now known as the Vieux Carré, or the French Quarter, with narrow streets and iron balconies. This historic heart of the city is now a lively 70 blocks filled with street musicians and artists. It is best seen on foot (Tourist and Convention Comm. Visitor Center, 1520 Sugar Bowl Dr. 504-566-5011). One of the country's oldest churches, the triple-spired 1794 *St. Louis Cathedral* (504-525-9585), on *Jackson Square,* lords over the Quarter. Flanking the cathedral are three of the four public museums of the *Louisiana State Museum* (504-568-6968. Closed Mon.; adm. fee). Artifacts at the *Cabildo,* the statehouse where the transfer papers for the Louisiana Purchase were signed in 1803, include

Mardi Gras celebrant

46

French Quarter

Preservation Hall, 726 St. Peter St. 504-522-2841

Napoleon's death mask and a slave collar and block. The *Presbytère,* built as the seat for the Bishop of Louisiana in 1797, now has displays on state culture and history and the Louisiana Portrait Gallery. And the *1850 House* (523 St. Ann St.) is the re-creation of a middle-class antebellum family residence.

A few blocks away, the state museum's popular *Old U. S. Mint* (400 Esplanade Ave.) contains mint artifacts, an entertaining exhibit on Mardi Gras, and a jazz display that includes Louis

Armstrong's first horn. Two small, quirky museums worth visiting are the *New Orleans Pharmacy Museum* (514 Rue Chartres. 504-565-8027. Closed Mon.; adm. fee), with mean-looking surgical instruments from the Civil War and an aquarium of live leeches; and the *New Orleans Historic Voodoo Museum* (724 Rue Dumaine. 504-522-5223. Adm. fee), which traces voodoo's roots to Africa.

On the river is the *Aquarium of the Americas* (One Canal St. 504-565-3006. Adm. fee), with albino alligators and black-footed penguins. The *World Trade Center* (2 Canal St. 504-581-4888. Adm. fee) offers an excellent view from its 31st floor, and the *La. Children's Museum* (428 Julia St. 504-523-1357. Closed Mon.; adm. fee) amuses the under-12 set.

Local favorite

In the 1,500-acre City Park, the handsome *New Orleans Museum of Art* (1 Collins Diboll Cir. 504-488-2631. Closed Mon.; adm. fee) has fine collections of Fabergé and pre-Columbian objects among its displays.

Gulfport, MISSISSIPPI Spread along the sandy Gulf coast, this resort town is also a busy port trading in seafood, lumber, and cotton. A Civil War fort, nature walks, and swimming in the bay attract visitors to West Ship Island, part of **Gulf Islands National Seashore.** Ferries leave from Yacht Harbor (*US 90 at US 49. 601-864-1014. March-Oct.; fare charge*).

For space buffs, a must-see is the **John C. Stennis Space Center** (*Stennis Space Center exit, follow signs. Visitor Center 601-688-2370*), where space shuttles' main engines are tested. Museum.

Biloxi A town in transition, Biloxi's Gulf waterfront now bears the gaudy neon and glitz of riverboat gambling, quite a contrast to the old Biloxi of quiet, tree-lined streets and clapboard houses. At the eastern end of 26-mile-long **Biloxi Beach** is the **Maritime Seafood and Industry Museum** (*115 1st St. 601-435-6320. Closed Sun.; adm. fee*), full of fish tales, including the one about the blessing of the shrimp fleet. There's also an interesting exhibit on hurricanes. Biloxi takes its history seriously, and **Beauvoir** (*2244 Beach Blvd. 601-388-1313. Adm. fee*), the last home of Confederate President Jefferson Davis, is treated like a shrine. The **Mississippi Sandhill Crane National Wildlife Refuge** (*N on Gautier Van Cleave Rd., then NE on Crane Rd to 7200 Crane Lane. 601-497-6322. Closed weekends. Tours Jan.-Feb. only, by appt.*) protects this bird's quickly vanishing habitat of savanna and bayou. It's not easy to spy a crane, but you may hear its raucous bugling.

Pascagoula Shipbuilding, lumber, and a large port sustain this industrial and resort town, noted for the singing sound that sometimes comes from the Pascagoula River, and is said to emanate from Indian spirits. The **Old Spanish Fort** (*4602 Fort Ave. 601-769-1505. Adm. fee*) was built by the French in 1718 and sealed with shells and mud. Its museum houses 18th-century artifacts.

Mobile, ALABAMA Perched on the western edge of Mobile Bay, Alabama's only port city was of critical importance to the Confederates, finally falling to Union forces in April 1865. In contrast to the busy port are sleepy, oak-lined avenues and a handful of pre-Civil War mansions. Visitors can climb high up on the bridge of the 35,000-ton, World War II U.S.S. *Alabama* at **Battleship Memorial Park** (*2703 Battleship Pkwy. 205-433-2703. Adm. fee*), which also has a submarine, a B-52 bomber, and World War II fighter planes. On the mainland opposite the 100-acre park is **Fort Conde** (*150 S. Royal St. Mobile Welcome Center 205-434-7304*), a partial reconstruction of a 1735 French fort, whose star-shaped foundation was rediscovered during the construction of I-10. Here, pick up a brochure for a walking or driving tour of the historic districts and houses, including the 20-room **Bragg-Mitchell Mansion** (*1906 Springhill Ave. 205-471-6364. Closed Sat.; adm. fee*). Its oak-lined driveway and white columns evoke antebellum opulence.

A pleasant 10-mile drive south on Ala. 59 leads to the **Bellingrath**

Mississippi Gulf coast

47

Roulette? Blackjack? Baccarat? No, this is not Las Vegas. It's a 35-mile stretch of Mississippi's coastline between Biloxi and Bay St. Louis—a **red-hot gambling strip** that's seen eight major casinos open in two years, and with plans for 20 more. "To say the least, we've hit a home run," says a Biloxi banker. "We're probably the hottest spot in the U. S. for growth. And when was the last time you heard Mississippi being first in anything?" Among other benefits, the bonanza has enabled Biloxi to stop charging for garbage collection.

Gardens and Home (*12401 Bellingrath Gardens Rd. 205-973-2217. Adm. fee*). A quarter-million azaleas, some reaching 16 feet in height, grow here, as do many other flowering plants.

State Capitol, Tallahassee, Florida

(44) Pensacola, FLORIDA Since the Spanish first established Fort San Carlos in 1698, this city has been a military town. Its restored 19th-century buildings in the Seville Square historic area are worth a quick visit, but the real action is southeast at the **U. S. Naval Air Station** (*From I-10, take I-110 S to downtown, follow signs*). The complex features the cavernous **Natl. Museum of Naval Aviation** (*904-452-3606*), a must-see for anyone interested in the subject. The flight deck of the U.S.S. *Cabot* is partly reconstructed to full scale, with Helldiver and Dauntless aircraft. Also on the grounds is the restored **Fort Barrancas** (*Part of Gulf Is. Natl. Seashore. 904-455-5167*), built by the Spanish in the 17th century, and the **Water Battery**, a 19th-century American fort.

48

(45) Ponce de León Springs S. R. A. (*0.5 mile N on Fla. 81, then E on US 90, follow signs. 904-836-4281*) The explorer might have ended his search for the fountain of youth right here if he'd found these two crystal-clear springs. Jump into the 68°F water on a hot day, and you're guaranteed to be refreshed. *Adm. fee.*

(46) Florida Caverns S. P. (*5 miles N on Fla. 71 and US 90 to Marianna, then 2.5 miles N on Fla. 166. 904-482-9598*) The pock-marked limestone that litters the woods here hints at the caves below ground. A high water table makes most of Florida's caves inaccessible, but here 23 are mapped. Only one is open to tour. *Fee.*

(47) Tallahassee (*Conv. and Visitors Bureau, 200 W. College Ave. 904-681-9200 or 800-628-2866*) Compromise as well as merit

Continued on P. 41

MISSISSIPPI ALA. MISS. ALABAMA

LOUISIANA

Mississippi Sandhill Crane N.W.R.

Mobile

Bellingrath Gardens

Biloxi

Pascagoula

Gulfport

New Orleans

San Francisco Plantation

GULF ISLANDS NATIONAL SEASHORE

Pensacola

Gulf of Mexico

0 25 50 mi
0 25 50 75 km

marked the selection of this pretty site, the halfway point between St. Augustine and Pensacola, as the capital of Florida in 1824. The city now boasts a number of attractive historic houses, beautiful gardens, and modern government buildings. Floridians have restored their original capitol, the **Old Capitol** (*Monroe St. and Apalachee Pkwy. 904-487-1902*), to its 1902 appearance. It sits adjacent to the new 22-story **State Capitol** (*N. Duval St. 904-488-6167*). Surrounding this complex are the **Historic Districts** of Park Ave. and Calhoun St., where you can enjoy a mix of colonial, Greek, and Renaissance Revival houses, including the newly restored **Knott House Museum** (*E. Park Ave. 904-922-2459. Adm. fee*). Pines and oaks tower over **Alfred B. Maclay State Gardens** (*1 mile N of I-10 on Fla. 319. 904-487-4556. Adm. fee*), originally the home of a New York financier who grew camellias and many other plants.

White Springs and Lake City   See I-75, p. 199.

Olustee Battlefield S. H. S. (*Sanderson/Olustee exit, 5 miles W on US 90. 904-758-0400*) In Florida's only notable Civil War battle, four hours of fighting here in February 1864 forced Union troops to retreat. *Closed Tues.-Wed.*

Jacksonville (*Conv. & Visitors Bureau, 3 Independent Dr. 904-798-9148 or 800-733-2668*) Straddling St. John's River, this seaport has preserved some of its waterfront in a 1.2-mile riverwalk. On the riverbank is the **Cummer Gallery of Art** (*829 Riverside Ave. 904-356-6857. Closed Mon.; adm. fee*), a beautiful spot to enjoy a 4,000-year span of fine and decorative arts. At the **Jacksonville Zoological Gardens** (*7 miles N on I-95 to Heckscher Dr., follow signs to 8605 Zoo Rd. 904-757-4462. Adm. fee*), you can see lions on the African veld and other fauna. On the south bank of the riverwalk is the **Museum of Science and History** (*1025 Museum Circle. 904-396-7062. Adm. fee*), full of hands-on exhibits.

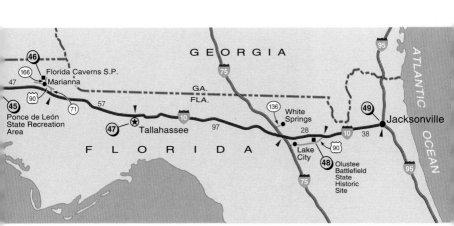

CANADA
Alta.

Mont.

P. 51 Idaho Wyo.

Nev.
P. 57 Utah

Calif.

Ariz.

MEX.

Unless otherwise noted, directions are from interstate, and sites are free and generally open daily. Phone for further information.

① **Shelby, MONTANA** This town's claim to fame is the famous Jack Dempsey-Tommy Gibbons world championship heavyweight fight, held here on July 4, 1923. You'll find memorabilia related to it at the **Marias Museum of History and Art** *(206 12th Ave. 406-434-2551)*, as well as exhibits on area homesteading and oil exploration and production.

② **Benton Lake N. W. R.** *(From Great Falls, N on 15th St./US 87 across the Missouri River to Bootlegger Trail, then go 10 miles N to office. 406-727-7400)* As many as 40,000 waterfowl have been raised here in good years. During migration, some 150,000 ducks, 6,000 tundra swans, 40,000 snow geese, and 2,500 Canada geese congregate on the marshes. The uplands teem with marbled godwits, sandpipers, gray partridges, and other species.

③ **Great Falls** *(Visitor Center, Broadwater Overlook Park. 406-761-4434)* Meriwether Lewis first saw the rapids on the upper Missouri River in 1805. While William Clark mapped the area, other members of the expedition portaged equipment. The **C. M. Russell Museum Complex** *(400 13th St. N. 406-727-8787. Closed Mon. Sept.-May; adm. fee)* preserves "America's Cowboy Artist" Charlie Russell's house and log cabin studio, as well as a comprehensive collection of his paintings and personal objects. The museum also displays the works of many other renowned Western artists and photographers. **Giant Springs Heritage State Park** *(4600 Giant Springs Rd., 3 miles E of town off River Dr. 406-454-3441. Adm. fee)* has one of the nation's largest freshwater springs—7.9 million gallons of water per hour at a constant 54°F. Across the road is the **Montana**

👉 ***Glacier National Park*** encompasses over a million acres of some of the world's finest alpine scenery. Dozens of glaciers, some 650 lakes, and scores of massive ice-carved mountains grace northwestern Montana. Originally the haunt of the Blackfeet and other Indians, the northern Rockies were penetrated by French and English trappers in the late 1700s. Within a century, the Great Northern Railroad was laying track and building huge hotels in anticipation of tourists. Today, most tourists arrive by car and, snow permitting, drive the dramatic Going-to-the-Sun Road. Its eastern entrance is about 85 miles W of Shelby via US 2 and US 89. 406-888-5441. Adm. fee.

50

Mounts Oberlin and Cannon, Glacier National Park, Montana

WATER FOWL CROSSING

Department of Fish, Wildlife and Parks (*406-454-3441*), with a small display on native animals. Picnicking and fishing are popular along this stretch of the Missouri.

Ulm Pishkun State Park (*Ulm exit, then 6 miles NW on county road, follow signs. 406-454-3441*) This prehistoric bison kill site consists of a mile-long, 30-foot pishkun, or buffalo jump, possibly the world's largest. Before the horse was introduced, early hunters often killed large game by scaring herds over cliffs. *Closed mid-Oct.–mid-April.*

Helena (*Chamber of Commerce, 201 E. Lyndale St. 406- 442-4120*) An 1864 gold strike touched off a boom era that transformed Helena into the "Queen City of the Rockies" and Montana's capital. By 1888 it was reputedly the richest city per capita in the U. S., boasting 50 millionaires. The **State Capitol** (*6th and Montana Aves. For tours, call the historical society 406-444-2694*) is worth a visit to see Charles Russell's famed mural, "Lewis and Clark Meeting the Flathead Indians at Ross' Hole," as well as other paintings. Close by is the original **Governor's Mansion** (*304 N. Ewing St. Tours 406-444-2694. April-Dec. Tues.-Sun. and by appt.*), a 22-room brick house built in 1888. The **Montana Historical Society Museum** (*225 N. Roberts St. 406-444-2694. Closed Sun. Labor Day-Mem. Day*) has over 60 works of art by Russell; the F. Jay Haynes photography collection, with early shots of Yellowstone National Park; and other Montana exhibits. To understand why prospectors roam the hills, go see the gold collection at **Norwest Bank** (*350 N. Last Chance Gulch. 406-447-2000. Mon.-Fri.*), which boasts nuggets, leaf and dust gold, and gold coins.

Canyon Ferry Recreation Area (*10 miles E on US 12/287, then 8 miles N on Mont. 284. 406-475-3310*) offers water sports, as well as history, geology, and beautiful scenery. In 1865, John Oakes started ferrying miners and prospectors across the Missouri River here, where now there's a man-made lake.

51

Continued on P. 57

Baled in Montana

6 **E l k h o r n** *(7 miles S of Boulder on Mont. 69, then 11 miles N on marked county road. 406-444-4720)* At their zenith during the 1880s, the Elkhorn mines produced $30,000 worth of silver ore a month. Now a ghost town, Elkhorn is notable for its two-story, wooden Fraternity Hall and for Gillian Hall, a bar and dance hall.

7 **B u t t e** *(Chamber of Commerce, 2950 Harrison Ave. 406-494-5595 or 800-735-6814)* The discovery of gold and silver lured the first miners to this spot, but it was 22 billion pounds of copper that led to Butte's epithet—"richest hill on earth." A walking tour covers a portion of the more than 4,500 buildings that make up the **Butte National Historic Landmark District**. The **Copper King Mansion** *(219 W. Granite St. 406-782-7580. Tours May-Oct.; adm. fee)* is the restored home of one of Montana's early senators, W. A. Clark. **Arts Chateau** *(321 W. Broadway St. 406-723-7600. Closed Mon.; adm. fee)*, originally the home of Clark's son, was built in 1898. A curved stairway leads from the first-floor gallery to the second-floor period museum to the fourth-floor ballroom. At the site of the former silver- and zinc-producing Orphan Girl Mine is now the **World Museum of Mining**, a vast collection of mining equipment; and **Hell Roarin' Gulch** *(End of W. Park St. 406-723-7211. Closed Mon. and Dec.-March)*, a faithful re-creation of an old Western town. Next door on the Montana Tech campus, the **Mineral Museum** *(406-496-4414. Closed Sat. Labor Day-Mem. Day)* displays over 1,300 specimens, including one of the largest gold nuggets found in the state. Be sure to take a gander at the **Berkeley Pit** *(Off Continental Dr. Closed Dec.-Feb.)*; 1,800 feet deep and a mile across, it was once the largest truck-operated open pit copper mine in the U. S.

Speed skater Dan Jansen, U. S. High Altitude Sports Center, Butte, Montana

8 **H u m b u g   S p i r e s   P r i m i t i v e   A r e a** *(Moose Creek exit, follow dirt road 3.5 miles E to main trailhead. 406-494-5059)* Here, nine 600-foot-high, 70-million-year-old steeple-like towers of white quartz monzonite jut into the sky above pine forest.

9 **D i l l o n** *(Chamber of Commerce, 125 S. Montana St. 406-683-5511)* This town began in 1880 as the northern terminus for the narrow-gauge Utah & Northern Railroad. At the chamber, pick up a **Historic Downtown** walking-tour brochure. Next door, the eclectic **Beaverhead County Museum** *(406-683-5027. Open daily June-Aug., closed Jan.-March and weekends rest of year)* includes an 1885 homesteader's cabin and Dillon's first flush toilet.

10 **B a n n a c k   S t a t e   P a r k** *(20 miles W on Mont. 278, then 4 miles S on gravel road. 406-834-3413)* Bannack became Montana's first territorial capital on the site of the region's first big gold strike in 1862. The well-preserved remnants of 60 buildings make it easy to imagine Bannack in its heyday, when 3,000 people lived (and many violently died) in "The Toughest Town in the West." *Adm fee.*

Camas Natl. Wildlife Refuge, IDAHO
(Hamer exit, follow signs 3 miles N, then 2 miles W to headquarters. 208-662-5423) Named after the blue lily whose bulb Indians once gathered as food, this refuge is an important link on the Pacific flyway. It is also a nesting place for trumpeter swans and peregrine falcons.

Montana gemstones

Idaho Falls *(Visitor Center, 505 Lindsay Blvd. 208-523-1010 or 800-634-3246)* The town was settled in 1864 as a ferry crossing on the Snake River. The **Bonneville County Museum** *(200 N. Eastern Ave. 208-522-1400. Closed Sun.; adm. fee)* features dioramas of local history, including the state's nuclear industry, and a walk-through facsimile of Eagle Rock, the early Idaho Falls. The actual **falls** *(0.5 mile E of I-15 on Broadway, then N on River Parkway)* are more like low cascades.

Blackfoot Idaho's World Potato Exposition *(Old train depot, 130 N.W. Main St., 1 mile E on Bus. 15. 208-785-2517)* shows a short film on the potato industry, displays the world's largest potato chip (25 x 14 inches), and sells such delicacies as potato ice cream and hand cream and potato fudge. *May-Oct., closed Sun.; adm. fee.*

Fort Hall Tours are available at the **Shoshone-Bannock Tribal Museum** *(Fort Hall exit, follow signs. 208-237- 9791. Fee for tour)* for viewing a buffalo herd and the original Fort Hall site, where you can see Oregon Trail ruts. Between 1841 and 1861, an estimated 300,000 people traveled through on the trail. The museum offers the Shoshone-Bannock perspective on Western history.

Idaho's World Potato Exposition, Blackfoot, Idaho

Pocatello *(Chamber of Commerce, 427 N. Main. 208-233-1525)* The city, whose historic downtown is being restored, was named after the 19th-century Bannock chief who granted the Utah & Northern Railroad a right-of-way for a Salt Lake City-to-Butte line. On the Idaho State University campus is the recently renovated **Idaho Museum of Natural History** *(S. 5th Ave. to E. Dillon St. 208-236-2262. Closed Sun.; adm. fee),* which has on permanent exhibit "The Nature of Idaho." **Ross Park,** on the southeast side of town, contains the **Bannock County Historical Museum** *(3000 Alvord Loop. 208-233-0434. Daily Mem. Day-Labor Day, rest of year Tues.-Sat.; adm. fee),* which houses a fine collection of 1895-1914 Shoshone-Bannock photos; the **Fort Hall Replica** *(208-234-1795. Daily June-Sept., Tues.-Sat. April-May; adm. fee);* and a small **Zoo** *(2700 S. 2nd Ave. 208-234-6196. Adm. fee)* of such native animals as bison, elk, pronghorns, wolves, bears, and mountain lions.

Lava Hot Springs South Bannock County Hist. Center *(110 Main St. 208-776-5254. Donations)* focuses on the history of southeast Idaho. **Lava Hot Springs** *(208-776-5221/5273 or 800-423-8597. Springs open all year, pools Mem. Day-Labor Day; adm. fee)* consist of outdoor mineral springs (110°F) on the town's east side and two huge hot-water swimming pools on the west side.

(17) Brigham City, UTAH The attractive Mormon town has many historic brick buildings along Main Street, over which an arch proclaims "Gateway—World's Greatest Bird Refuge." And, indeed, the **Bear River Migratory Bird Refuge** *(About 15 miles W on Forest St. 801-723-5887. May-Nov.)* is one of the last remaining marshlands where duck and goose concentrations resemble what early explorers described; waterfowl may number a half million.

(18) Ogden Don't miss **Historic 25th Street**; a free brochure is available from the museums listed below. The **Daughters of Utah Pioneers Museum** and the **Miles Goodyear Cabin** *(2148 Grant Ave. 801-393-4460. Mid-May–mid-Sept.)* display many fascinating artifacts from Ogden's pioneer past. The cabin, built in 1845, was the first permanent home in Utah of an Anglo-American. The 1924 **Union Railroad Station and Visitors Center** *(2501 Wall Ave. 801-629-8444. Closed Sun. Sept.-May. One adm. fee for museums)* includes the **State Railroad Museum**, the **Myra Powell Art Gallery**, the **Browning-Kimball Classic Car Museum**, the **Browning Firearms Museum**, and the **Natural History Museum**.

Included in the 3-mile long **Ogden River Parkway** *(Information 801-629-8284)*, along with playgrounds, picnic areas, golf courses, restaurants, and sports parks, is the fantastic **George S. Eccles Dinosaur Park** *(Exit at 12th St., follow signs about 5 miles E to 1544 E. Park Blvd. 801-393-DINO. April-Nov.; adm. fee)*. **Fort Buenaventura State Park** *(2450 A Ave. 801-621-4808. April-Nov.; adm. fee)* contains the 1846 fort, rebuilt using original construction techniques such as wooden pegs instead of nails and mortise-and-tenon joints. Guides relate the fort's exciting history.

(19) Hill Aerospace Museum *(Roy City exit, follow signs. 801- 777-6818. Closed Mon.)* displays several dozen vintage aircraft, as well as missiles, helicopters, and a restored WWII chapel and barracks.

George S. Eccles Dinosaur Park, Ogden, Utah

(20) Antelope Island State Park *(Syracuse exit, then 5 miles W on Antelope Dr. to causeway entrance. 801-451-3397 or 580-1043)* The largest island in the Great Salt Lake got its name from John C. Fremont, after he and Kit Carson hunted pronghorn antelope here in 1845. Twelve bison were introduced in 1893; now there's a herd of 600. In 1993, pronghorns were reintroduced. *Adm. fee.*

Salt Lake City See I-80, p. 222.

(21) Timpanogos Cave Natl. Monument *(10 miles E on Utah 92. Visitor Center 801-756-0351)* High on the rocky slopes of American Fork Canyon are three small limestone caves that contain stalactites, stalagmites, flowstone, and an unusually high concentration of helictites—fragile, intricate mineral deposits that resemble hand-blown glass. *Caves open mid-May–Sept.; adm. fee.*

Fossils, Earth Science Center, Brigham Young University, Provo, Utah

Bridal Veil Falls *(4 miles E on Utah 52, then 4 miles NE on US 189. 801-225-4461)* You can get a bird's-eye view of this double cataract plunging more than 600 feet by taking one of the world's steepest tramways. It rises 1,228 vertical feet above the canyon floor. *May-Oct.; adm. fee for tram.*

Provo *(Utah County Travel Council Visitor Center, 51 S. University Ave. 801-370-8393 or 800-222-UTAH)* Pick up the free guide, *Utah County Historic Sites.* Non-historical attractions in Utah's second largest city include **Brigham Young University** *(Information 801-378-4636),* with the following museums: the **Harris Fine Arts Center** *(801-378-2882);* the **Earth Science Center** *(801-378-5396. Adm. fee),* which has dinosaur exhibits and a planetarium; and the **Monte L. Bean Life Science Museum** *(801-378-5051. Closed Sun.).* Off campus, check out the **Museum of Peoples and Cultures** *(700 N. 100 E. 801-378-6112. Closed weekends)* and the **McCurdy Historical Doll Museum** *(246 N. 100 E. 801-377-9935. Closed Sun.-Mon.; adm. fee),* with a collection of more than 4,000 dolls.

Five miles west of Provo, **Utah Lake State Park** *(Center St. 801-375-0731 or 375-0733. Adm. fee),* a freshwater remnant of ancient Pleistocene Lake Bonneville, offers fishing and water sports.

Mount Nebo Scenic Loop Road *(Nephi Chamber of Commerce 801-623-2411, or Payson C. of C. 801-465-2634)* From Nephi, drive 5 miles east on Utah 132, then turn north to Payson. This gorgeous 38-mile drive around the eastern shoulder of Mount Nebo, one of the highest summits in the Wasatch Range at 11,877 feet, is especially stunning in autumn.

Yuba State Park *(Yuba State Park exit, then 5 miles S. 801-758-2611)* One of Utah's favorite boating sites, the park has warm summer water in Sevier Bridge Reservoir, with sandy beaches and excellent walleye fishing. *Adm. fee.*

Statue of Philo Farnsworth, Beaver, Utah

Fillmore In 1851, Brigham Young and a delegation of lawmakers chose this site for the capital of what they hoped would be the State of Deseret. The federal government denied them statehood, but the building preserved in the **Territorial Statehouse State Park** *(50 W. Capitol Ave. 801-743-5316)* served as the territorial capitol until 1858. *Adm. fee.*

Old Cove Fort *(2 miles E of Cove Fort exit, follow signs. 801-438-5547)* Built in 1867 as a way station between Fillmore and Beaver, the fort has been beautifully restored with authentic period furnishings and artifacts. *April-Sept.*

Beaver Settled in 1856, the town has more than 300 historic

Zion National Park, Utah

56

houses and other structures still standing today. The old **Beaver County Courthouse** (*90 E. Center St. 801-438-2975. Mem. Day-Labor Day Tues.-Sat.*), now a pioneer museum, is noted for its dungeonlike basement, which served as the jail. Outside is a statue of native son Philo Farnsworth, the "Father of Television."

㉙ C e d a r   C i t y   Today renowned for its annual Shakespeare Festival, the town got its start in 1851 with the discovery of iron deposits. This led to the construction, on Coal Creek, of the first iron foundry west of the Mississippi, which supplied iron to Mormon settlements. **Iron Mission State Park** (*585 N. Main St. 801-586-9290*) traces the history of the iron mission and preserves a collection of horse-drawn vehicles. *Adm. fee.*

㉚ Z i o n   N a t i o n a l   P a r k (*Kolob Canyons Visitor Center 801-586-9548*) At the entrance to the Kolob Canyons section of the park, one of its most accessible but least visited regions, a sinuous road leads 5.3 miles into 48,000 acres of spectacular canyon wilderness. If time and stamina permit, you can hike the 14-mile roundtrip to Kolob Arch, one of the world's largest freestanding natural arches, 310 feet long. See the sidebar on this page for more about the park. *Adm. fee.*

㉛ S n o w   C a n y o n   S t a t e   P a r k (*11 miles NW of St. George on Utah 18. 801-628-2255*) Towering red-and-white sandstone cliffs, volcanic cinder cones, and lava caves wait to be explored. Fee for facilities but not for the scenic Snow Canyon Highway.

㉜ S t .   G e o r g e (*Chamber of Commerce, 97 East St. George Blvd. 801-628-1658*) The success of cotton-raising experiments led to large-scale colonization of southwestern Utah in the 1860s. This rich historic area eventually became known as Little Dixie. **Brigham Young's Winter Home** (*200 North 100 West. 801-673-2517*) in this warm desert climate gave the head of the Mormon Church relief from his rheumatism. From here Young supervised the building of the St. George Temple, which preceded the Salt Lake Temple by two decades. **Jacob Hamblin's Home** (*5 miles W in Santa Clara via Bluff St./Utah 18 and Sunset Blvd. 801-673-2161*), a remnant of a more rugged pioneer life, stands in contrast to the genteel houses more typical of St.

The dramatic, towering sandstone walls of Zion Canyon, in **Zion National Park,** have inspired awe ever since the first Anazasi farmed along the Virgin River 1,000 years ago. Later the Paiutes feared the canyon as the dwelling place of deities. In 1858, Nephi Johnson, a young Mormon missionary, was probably the first white man to behold this wonderous place. Today, a paved road penetrates the main canyon, and from there numerous trails lead to secret canyon narrows and breathtaking vistas. The Zion Canyon Visitor Center (801-772-3256) is about 45 miles E of St. George on Utah 9. Adm. fee.

Valley of Fire State Park, Nevada

George. The **St. George Temple** is open only to Mormons in good standing, but a **Visitor Center** (*490 South 300 East. 801-673-5181*) tells the area's and church's histories. The **St. George Tabernacle** (*Main and Tabernacle Sts. 801-628-4072*), a remarkable structure of hand-quarried limestone, which took 13 years to build beginning in 1863, is open to all.

Overton, NEVADA The **Lost City Museum** (*1 mile S of town on Nev. 169. 702-397-2193*) has one of the most complete collections of the early Southwest Anasazi Indian culture, plus a partly restored ruin of Pueblo Grande de Nevada. At the pueblo's height, around A.D. 800, scores of villages filled the Moapa Valley. *Adm. fee.*

Valley of Fire State Park (*18 miles SE on Nev. 169. Visitor Center 702-397-2088*) Nevada's oldest state park gets its name from the extensive outcrops of red Mesozoic sandstone. The strange rock cliffs and hoodoos have served as backdrop for Western and science fiction movies. Anasazi prehistoric rock art can be found. *Adm. fee.*

Lake Mead N. R. A. (*Visitor Center, 28 miles SE on US 93. 702-293-8906*) The 726-foot-high Hoover Dam impounds the Colorado River to produce the country's largest artificial lake (110 miles long, 550 miles of shoreline). Boat rides, fishing, and swimming are available. *Fee for boat rides.*

Red Rock Canyon N. C. A. (*18 miles W on W. Charleston Blvd./Nev. 159. BLM Las Vegas District Office 702-363-1921*) A one-way, 13-mile scenic loop drive through this national conservation area in Joshua tree-studded high desert allows access to more than 20 miles of hiking trails. Towering sandstone and limestone cliffs serve as backdrop. Watch for desert burros and other desert wildlife.

Nearby is **Spring Mountain Ranch State Park** (*About 3 miles W on W. Charleston Blvd./Nev. 159. 702-875-4141. Adm. fee*), a ranch once owned by billionaire recluse Howard Hughes. It protects high desert flora and fauna and offers cultural events.

Continued on P. 51

57

③⑦ Las Vegas

Glittering Fremont Street

A trip here would not be complete without a cruise down the 3.5-mile, neon-lined *Strip* (Las Vegas Blvd.), with some of the world's largest and most luxurious resort hotels, each with a 24-hour casino. But Las Vegas has much more to offer (Chamber of Commerce, 711 Desert Inn Rd. 702-735-1616).

Once you have lost your stake and tired of the glitz, check out some of these museums and attractions. At the *Guinness World of Records Museum* (2780 Las Vegas Blvd. S. 702-792-3766. Adm. fee), you'll find out who was the tallest man ever, see life-size replicas of the strange and wonderful, and discover the lowest point in the Western Hemisphere. The *Liberace Museum* (1775 E. Tropicana Ave. 702-798-5595. Adm. fee), one of Nevada's most popular attractions, features a rare piano collection, customized automobiles, and the million-dollar wardrobe worn by the late entertainer. *The Las Vegas Natural History Museum* (900 Las Vegas Blvd. N. 702-384-3466. Adm. fee) is one of the country's finest paleontology museums, where you can enjoy animated dinosaur models, a marine-life exhibit, and a hands-on room for the kids. The *Nevada State Museum and Historical Society* (700 Twin Lakes Dr. 702-486-5205. Adm. fee) chronicles 10,000 years of Nevada's human and natural history. At the *Lied Discovery Children's Museum* (833 Las Vegas Blvd. N. 702-382-5437. Closed Mon.; adm. fee), more than 130 exhibits teach and entertain.

③⑧ **East Mojave National Scenic Area, CALIFORNIA** *(BLM Needles Office 619-326-3896)* Created in 1980 and slated to become a national park, this area of spectacular desert landscape preserves 1.5 million acres, with rich biological, cultural, and geologic resources, including huge sand dunes.

③⑨ **Calico Early Man Archaeological Site** *(Mineola Rd. exit, follow signs 2 miles. Info at California Desert Information Center, Barstow. 619-256-8313)* Unique among American archaeological sites, this presents some of the earliest dated evidence of human occupation in the Western Hemisphere. Louis Leakey began the excavations in 1964. A refurbished miner's shack displays replicas of artifacts; the originals are at the San Bernardino County Museum. An interpretive trail takes you around the main trenches, and guided tours are available Wed.-Sun. *Closed Mon.-Tues.*

④⓪ **Calico Ghost Town Regional Park** *(4 miles N of Yermo, Ghost Town Rd. exit. 619-254-2122)* Over $13 million in silver was mined from the mottled hills that gave the town its name. Restored in 1954 by Walter Knott of Knott's Berry Farm fame, the ghost town is no longer very ghostly. Its 1880s buildings are now shops and attractions, including a playhouse where you can still boo the villain. *Adm. fee.*

Barstow   The **California Desert Information Center** (*831 Barstow Rd. 619-256-8313*) provides a fine introduction to the southern California deserts. At the **Rainbow Basin Natl. Natural Landmark** (*8 miles N via Calif. 58 to Irwin Rd., then N to Fossil Bed Rd. Last 3 miles unpaved. 619-256-8313*), a 4-mile loop road gives a good overview of the colorful geology. Hiking and horseback riding.

Victorville   Housed in a Western-style fort, the **Roy Rogers/Dale Evans Museum** (*0.25 mile W at Roy Rogers Dr. 619-243-4547*) contains personal and professional memorabilia from their long career in movies, television, and music. *Adm. fee.*

Calico Ghost Town Regional Park, California

Riverside   The many fine museums include the **California Museum of Photography** (*3824 Main St. 909-784-3686. Closed Mon.-Tues.; adm. fee*), which houses historic cameras, an extensive permanent photo collection, and interactive exhibits; the **Riverside Art Museum** (*3425 7th St. 909-684-7111. Closed Sun.-Mon.; donations*); and the **Riverside Municipal Museum** (*3720 Orange St. 909-782-5273. Closed Mon.*), with Native American artifacts, early settlers' guns and tools, and interpretive displays about the local citrus industry. The **University of California-Riverside Botanical Gardens** (*909-787-4650*) occupy 39 acres of rugged terrain along the eastern boundary of the campus. Over 3,500 species, mostly from California, Australia, and southern Africa, have been planted since 1963. The **Mission Inn** (*3649 Seventh St. 909-784-0300. Tours except Mon.; fee for tour*) is Riverside's premier historical and architectural landmark. Christopher Columbus Miller started building the inn in 1876 as a two-story, 12-room adobe boardinghouse. Over the next half century, it became a grand hotel, with arcades and turrets, that occupied a city block and hosted Presidents and movie stars. Part of the inn, the Mission Inn Museum (*Closed Mon.*) exhibits more than 6,000 fine and decorative art pieces and artifacts.

Daguerreotype ca 1860, California Museum of Photography, Riverside

59

Lake Elsinore Recreation Area (*4 miles W on Calif. 74. 909-674-3178*) A cool respite from summer heat, the area has a shaded campground with grassy sites and showers, a boat ramp, fishing, bicycling, and picnicking sites. *Adm. fee.*

Temecula   The **Temecula Museum** (*41950 Main St. 909-676-0021. Wed.-Sun.*) displays the history of this quaint 1890s town through artifacts, antiques, and photos. The town also has 11 wineries (*Temecula Valley Vinters Assoc. 909-699-3626*).

Escondido   At **San Diego Wild Animal Park** (*E at Via Rancho Pkwy. exit, follow signs 6 miles. 619-747-8702*), a monorail and walkways allow you to view over 2,500 animals on 1,800 acres resembling Asian and African habitats. The Hidden Jungle features exotic insects, reptiles, and amphibians. *Adm. fee.*

Sampling wine, Temecula, California

San Diego   See I-8, pp. 30-31.

Unless otherwise noted, directions are from interstate, and sites are free and generally open daily. Phone for further information.

① Monahans Sandhills S.P. TEXAS *(N on Rte. 41. 915-943-2092)* At this 3,840-acre park and museum on desert geography, kids can play on sand dunes up to 70 feet high; other dunes that are bare of vegetation shift constantly in the wind. A less arid section of the park has a well-documented nature trail. *Vehicle fee.*

② Midland This accessible and friendly town of fewer than 100,000 people has some big-city attractions. The famous **Confederate Air Force** *(N on Rte. 1788 to Wright Dr. 915-563-1000. Adm. fee)* moved its headquarters and museum of World War II aircraft here in 1990. A flight simulator takes passengers on a wild ride in a World War II biplane trainer. Besides the CAF, Midland has two of the most professional museums in west Texas. The **Museum of the Southwest** *(1705 W. Missouri Ave. 915-683-2882. Closed Mon.)* is attempting to wrest from Santa Fe, New Mex-

ico, the right to define "Southwestern culture." The facility's new theme, "Under Starry Skies," presents art, artifacts, astronomy, flora, and fauna to explain what makes this part of America unique. It also has a children's section with hands-on art, archaeology, astronomy, and geology. The city's other professional museum is the **Petroleum Museum** *(1500 I-20 W. 915-683-4403)*, an institution with a message, that oil is strategic and foreign oil a snare. But its exhibits also give a serious explanation of how oilmen find and extract the fuel. *Adm. fee.*

③ Big Spring This small Texas community has a nice museum and a beautiful state park right in town. **Big Spring State Park** *(Rte. 700 at the S edge of town. 915-263-4931. Vehicle fee)* sits above the city on a high mesa. It has a well-documented nature trail, alive with desert critters, including some that rattle. The **Heritage Museum** *(6th and Scurry Sts. 915-267-8255)*, in a new building, preserves the history of the railroad and the community and has a large collection of Indian artifacts and old phonographs. *Closed Sun.-Mon.; adm. fee.*

④ Lake Colorado City S.P. *(6 miles S on Rte. 2836. 915-728-3931)* lies along half of the Lake Colorado City reservoir. The state has begun returning the park, overgrown with mesquite and cactus, to virgin grassland. Stop here to swim, picnic, hike, and see the prairie. *Adm. fee.*

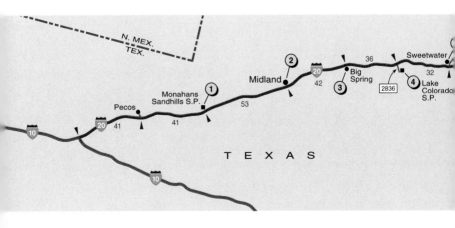

Sweetwater   The **City-County Pioneer Museum** (610 E. 3rd St. 915-235-8547) shows you what town life was like for the well-to-do in the Wild West. *Closed Sun.-Mon.; donations.*

Abilene   The area's principal city, Abilene became county seat when the Texas and Pacific Railway was routed through. The town's most touted attraction is the small but well-kept **Abilene Zoological Gardens** (*Tex. 36 and Loop 322. 915-676-6085. Adm. fee*). Abilene is also home to **Dyess Air Force Base** (*Signs W of downtown. 915-696-5609*), whose **Linear Air Park** exhibits 28 warplanes from World War II to Vietnam.

Cactus off I-20 in Texas

Buffalo Gap   **Buffalo Gap Historic Village** (*15 miles SW on Rte. 89 to town, right 2 blocks on Elm St. 915-572-3365*) is a fascinating collection of old buildings from the 1880s and 1890s that have been relocated to re-create an early settlement, with tools, furnishings, and other artifacts. Buildings include the area's first courthouse and jail, the home of Abilene's first marshal, and America's first Nazarene church. *Closed Mon.-Thurs. mid-Nov. to mid-March; admission fee.*

Fort Phantom Hill   (*9 miles N via Rte. 600*) The fort was established in 1851 to garrison five infantry companies that protected pioneers along the old Butterfield trail, which ran through here. Only a few buildings and several chimneys remain, but it's not hard to imagine what military life was like then.

Cisco   Not much happens between Fort Worth and Midland, but there was a bank robbery in Cisco around Christmas 1927. The ringleader wore a Santa Claus suit. Folks here published a book about it, but the short version is laid out in videotaped interviews with old-timers at the **Conrad N. Hilton Memorial Park Museum** (*4th St. and Conrad Hilton Ave. 817-442-2537*). The museum is

Few things as dangerous as *rodeos* are ☜ called sport. But almost everyone in every small town here regularly celebrates these blood-curdling, bone-crunching contests. Big-city commercial rodeos show better riding, but nothing gives outsiders such a candid look at local culture as the small-town "rodeo days," usually celebrated over a long weekend with fairs, parades, charity auctions, and cook-offs. Watch for the signs.

61

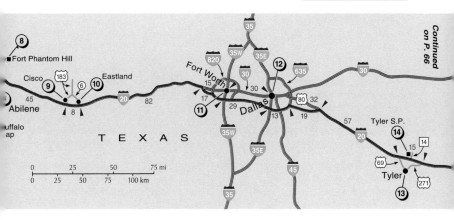

Continued on P. 66

Putting down roots near Dallas, Texas

also the first Hilton Hotel. Conrad came here in 1919 to buy a bank. When the deal fell through, he bought a hotel instead.

⑩ **Eastland** (*Chamber of Commerce 817-629-2332*) Old Rip has lain in state in his velvet coffin inside a glass display at the **Eastland County Courthouse** since 1929. His story is about the most exciting thing that ever happened in Eastland, population 5,000, annual rainfall 27.51 inches. To make it brief, Old Rip was a horned

⑪ Fort Worth

Nowhere is such a rich community struggling harder to preserve a Western cowtown image than is Fort Worth. The problem: There are no more cattle here. The sprawling *Fort Worth Stockyards* (About 2.5 miles N of downtown on Main St.) are filled with quaint Western boutiques that would send shivers down a real cowboy's spine (Convention and Visitors Bureau, 415 Throckmorton St. 800-433-5747). If you're here in January, be sure to see the *Southwestern Exposition and Livestock Show* (Will Rogers Mem. Center, 3301 W. Lancaster Ave. 817-877-2420. Adm. fee), a huge rodeo and county fair that recaptures the town's glory days. Start a walking tour of downtown, with its renovated turn-of-the-century buildings, at Sundance Square, where you'll find the *Sid Richardson Collection of Western Art* (309 Main St. 817-332-6554. Closed Mon.). The best place to learn the history of the ranching business is downtown at the *Cattleman's Museum* (1301 W. 7th St. 817-332-7064. Closed weekends).

A 2-mile strip along University Drive includes a half-dozen first-rate attractions. Among them are the well-funded *Fort Worth Zoo* (1989 Colonial Pkwy. 817-871-7050.

Painting by Charles M. Russell, Amon Carter Museum

Adm. fee) and its neighbor, the magnificent *Fort Worth Botanic Garden and Conservatory* (3220 Botanic Garden Blvd. 817-871-7689. Some adm. fees). Also here is the *Fort Worth Museum of Science and History* (1501 Montgomery St. 817-732-1631. Adm. fee). Nearby are three outstanding art museums: the *Amon Carter Museum* (3501 Camp Bowie Blvd. 817-738-1933. Closed Mon.), with 19th- and 20th-century American art; the exquisite *Kimbell Art Museum* (3333 Camp Bowie Blvd. 817-654-1034. Closed Mon.), with Old Masters and modern and ancient works; and the *Modern Art Museum* (1309 Montgomery St. 817-738-9215. Closed Mon.).

To the east, the new *American Airlines C.R. Smith Museum* (4601 Tex. 360 at FAA Rd. 817-967-1560. Closed Mon.-Tues.) tells the story of air carrier aviation and American Airlines.

Philip Johnson's Water Garden

⑫ Dallas

Planned as a trading post in 1841, Dallas still is a major collection and distribution center. It's also a major site for corporate and financial headquarters. Though popular for conventions, rush-hour traffic and construction delays can make it inhospitable to tourists driving through (Convention and Visitors Bureau, 1201 Elm St. 800-752-9222).

Skyline at dusk

Located in the downtown Arts District, the *Dallas Museum of Art* (1717 N. Harwood. 214-922-1200. Closed Mon.) is the city's finest cultural facility, an enormous complex with a wide-ranging collection that includes American and European paintings and a sculpture garden, as well as a new Museum of the Americas. Also there is the elegant *Morton H. Meyerson Symphony Center* (2301 Flora St. 214-670-3600. Free tours by appt.), designed by I. M. Pei. Nearby, the most visited attraction in town is a grim reminder from the city's past. The *Sixth Floor* (411 Elm St. 214-653-6666. Adm. fee), in the former Texas School Book Depository, is the place from which Lee Harvey Oswald shot President John F. Kennedy on Nov. 22, 1963. It is now a museum examining JFK's legacy, with films, photographs, and documents. A block away is *Dealey Plaza* (Houston, Elm, and Main Sts.), the assassination site. To the south, *Old City Park* (1717 Gano St. 214-421-5141. Tours available except Mon.; adm. fee) has relocated and restored 37 1840–1910 buildings, including log cabins, elegant houses, and a school to create a turn-of-the-century town.

Southeast of downtown, the city's largest concentration of cultural attractions is at *Fair Park* (Off I-30 on Parry Ave. 214-890-2911), where the famous Texas State Fair takes place annually. Besides the fair, it has

a number of museums, many in art deco style. Among them are the *Dallas Museum of Natural History* (214-670-8457); the *Dallas Aquarium* (214-670-8443. Adm. fee); the *Dallas Civic Garden Center* (214-428-7476. Indoor garden closed Mon.); the *Dallas Historical Society* in the Hall of State (214-421-4500. Closed Mon.); and the *Age of Steam Railroad Museum* (214-428-0101. Closed Mon.-Wed.; adm. fee). The best is *Science Place* (214-428-5555. Adm. fee), an outstanding hands-on museum with its own planetarium. The *African American Museum* (214-565-9026. Closed Monday) opened in late 1993. Northeast of the area is the *Dallas Arboretum and Botanical Garden* (8525 Garland Rd. 214-327-8263. Adm. fee), a lovely 66-acre park on the shore of White Rock Lake, with themed gardens and self-guided tours.

Lee Harvey Oswald's view from the Sixth Floor

Also worth seeing: the 25-acre "Wilds of Africa" exhibit at the *Dallas Zoo* (621 E. Clarendon Dr. 214-946-5154. Adm. fee), across Trinity River from downtown. Africa's six major habitats have been re-created, and animals roam freely. Visitors view them on a 1-mile monorail ride.

South Fork Ranch, home of J. R. Ewing of *Dallas* fame

toad, and in 1897 the justice of the peace thought it would be amusing to put him in the cornerstone of the new courthouse along with other memorabilia. Thirty-one years later when they tore down the courthouse, Old Rip was still alive and kicking, or so the story goes. He died a year later of pneumonia, but Eastlanders honor their heroes, and Old Rip is now the town emblem.

Rose garden, Tyler, Texas

(13) Tyler *(10 miles SE via US 69 or 11 miles SW via US 271)* The **Caldwell Zoo** *(2203 Martin Luther King Blvd. 903-593-0121)* is a 50-acre private park open to the public. Hidden barricades keep the most interesting animals unobstructed within a few feet of visitors, giving an impression of predators roaming among potential prey.

(14) Tyler State Park *(2 miles N on Rte. 14. 903-597-5338)* This beautiful 985-acre park has campsites and picnic tables around a reservoir that invites swimming. Nature trail. *Vehicle fee.*

(15) Kilgore *(5 miles S on US 259)* This was a sleepy agricultural community until 1930, when Dad Joiner brought in the Daisy Bradford well. Two successor wells quickly confirmed that Kilgore sat atop the largest pool of black gold ever discovered—the East Texas Field. The town went crazy. World crude oil prices plummeted. Troops were sent in. The state set up the first OPEC-style commission to control production. And this part of the world has never been the same. The **East Texas Oil Museum** *(US 259 at Ross St. 903-983-8295)* is dedicated to that moment when Kilgore was on top. It is an indoor amusement park with puppets and special effects that will delight children and enlighten everyone. *Closed Mon.; adm. fee.*

(16) Oil City, LOUISIANA **Caddo-Pine Island Oil Historical Society Museum** *(18 miles N on La. 1, right on Savage to Land Ave. 318-995-6845)* preserves artifacts from the 1900 oil boom at Oil City. It's a good museum, but it lacks the youth appeal of its counterpart in Kilgore, Texas. *Mon.-Fri., weekends by appt.; adm. fee.*

(17) Shreveport It's hard to imagine a place less open to casino gambling than this Bible-belt town of 300,000. Until 1993, its boldest bid for attention was to combine a botanical garden with an art museum. Now Shreveport aspires to be the glitziest spot on I-20. Nightclub and casino developers have poured millions into the city, and some $15 million in public money has been spent to gussy up the business district—$500,000 of it to decorate a rusty steel bridge with red, pink, and orange neon and spotlights. You won't miss it. On top is a laser that paints the night streets with flickering designs. The real cultural attraction remains the breathtaking collection of Western art at the **R. W. Norton Art Gallery** *(4747 Creswell Ave. 318-865-4201. Closed Mon.)*, including paintings by Charles Russell and Frederic Remington. The gallery also has tapestries, Wedgwood china,

Civil War Fort Turnbull a.k.a. Fort Humbug, Clyde Fant Parkway, Shreveport, La.

antique dolls, firearms, and Steuben glass. The **Meadows Museum of Art** (*2911 Centenary Blvd. 318-869-5169. Closed Mon.*), part of Centenary College, displays a fascinating collection of art as journalism. Jean Despujols was commissioned by the French Society of Colonial Painters to record Indochina on canvas from 1936 to 1938. The **Barnwell Garden and Art Center** (*601 Clyde Fant Pkwy. 318-673-7703*), the scandalous mix of plants and paintings, also has a fragrance garden for the blind.

G e r m a n t o w n   C o l o n y (*3 miles N of Minden via La. 159, La. 534, and Rte. 114. 318-377-1875*) A band of Germans immigrated here for religious reasons in 1835 and stayed for more than three decades. What they didn't bring, they grew or made. Their tools, books, and houses compose a valuable collection that may not last unless better protected. *Closed Mon.-Tues.; adm. fee.*

H o m e r (*21 miles N on US 79*) At the center of this quaint town is a stately 1860 antebellum courthouse with large white columns and a statue honoring Confederate dead. The old hotel is now the **Ford Museum** (*519 S. Main St. 318-927-9190*), where volunteers artfully exhibit the town's attic matter. *Adm. fee.*

65

L a k e   C l a i b o r n e   S t a t e   P a r k (*8 miles N on La. 9, 8 miles E on La. 518, right on La. 146 to entrance on left. 318-927-2976*) Here is a pleasant place to picnic and swim. Campsites available. *Vehicle fee.*

M o u n t   L e b a n o n (*6 miles S on La. 154*) Seven structures at this crossroads have been recognized as historically significant. The 1850s **Mount Lebanon Baptist Church** is still in use, its pews divided so that the sexes need not mix. About 5 miles south of town beside La. 154, a monument marks the spot where lawmen in 1934 ambushed Bonnie Parker and Clyde Barrow. Old-timers recollect all the hubbub that followed.

Germantown Colony, Louisiana

R u s t o n This small college town, home to Louisiana Tech University, includes a little-known but fascinating stop: the **LTU Equine Center** (*Exit at the univ. and continue through on Tech Dr. to California Ave./US 80, right 2 blocks to Tech Farm Rd., left 1 block to Ag Dr. and follow to end. 318-257-4502. Closed weekends*). Students and an enthusiastic staff are eager to introduce visitors to the world of horses. Top racing stock such as Raise a Bid is here; reportedly, his offspring have won more than $15 million. Visitors can see grooming and training daily and farriers less frequently. In season, you can watch—and even help with—the natural breeding and foaling of the thoroughbreds. On Saturday night the place to be is the **Dixie Theater** (*206 N. Vienna St. 318-255-0048*), where the town showcases local country music talent.

Bayou Bodcau, Louisiana, 10 miles north on La. 157

(23) Autrey House (*12 miles N on US 167 to Dubach, then 1 mile W on La. 151, on right. 318-251-0018*) A log cabin built in 1848, the house is a beautifully restored example of the "dogtrot" plan, in which every room opens onto a central breezeway. The cabin is locked except for weekends in summer, but the grounds are always open, and visitors can appreciate the architecture without going inside.

(24) Monroe After he made his fortune developing a method for bottling Coca-Cola, Joseph A. Biedenharn came here from Vicksburg, Mississippi, in 1913. Among his investments was stock in a small, local crop-dusting service, known today as Delta Airlines. The giant company, now headquartered in Atlanta, still holds its annual board meetings here, where its largest block of stock is held.

The **Emy-Lou Biedenharn Mansion** (*2006 Riverside Dr. 318-387-5281. Closed Mon.*) has the Biedenharn Bible collection and is surrounded by the ELsong Garden and Conservatory. Only some of the 1,500 Bibles are on display at a time, but the elegant grounds with fountains and statuary are open to visitors. Different gardens provide background music appropriate to the motif when visitors trip hidden laser switches. Tours available.

The town's most sumptuous institution of learning is the Junior League's **Cotton Country Cooking School** (*2811 Cameron St. 800-*

Continued on P. 61

*256-4888), producer of the best-selling *Cotton Country Collection* cookbook. By prior arrangement, the faculty will enroll visitors passing through. At **Northeast Louisiana State University,** the **Museum of Natural History** *(Room 316, Hanna Hall, University Dr. 318-342-1878. Closed weekends)* has a large collection of artifacts from Poverty Point, the archaeological park east of here. There's also the **Herbarium** *(Room 232, Stubbs Hall, Bayou Dr. 318-342-1812)* and the **Museum of Zoology** *(Room 231, Garrett Hall, Northeast Dr. and Univ. Ave. 318-342-1799. Closed weekends).* The **Louisiana Purchase Gardens and Zoo** *(Bernstein Park Dr. 318-329-2400. Adm. fee)* holds more than 750 animals; a lagoon ride allows visitors to see many of them.*

Poverty Point La. State Comm. Area

(18 miles NE via La. 17, La. 134, and La. 577. 504-342-8111) At this archaeological park, scientists study a pre-pottery Indian culture centered here from 1700 to 700 B.C. The earthworks are not nearly as impressive as those at Moundville, Alabama, but the culture is much older. It probably flourished as a center for trade in the lower Mississippi Valley. Visit in late spring or in summer when excavations are under way. *Adm. fee.*

Vicksburg, MISSISSIPPI

The nation's products moved down the Mississippi at the sufferance of Vicksburg, high above a narrow bend in the river. After the state seceded, the river closed. Reopening it became key to winning the Civil War, said Lincoln. The campaign ended after a 6-week siege and merciless bombardment in the summer of 1863—an ordeal that made Vicksburg a permanent symbol of Southern resolve, as strong in civilians as in soldiers. The city's architecture has been well preserved, and the **Visitor Center** *(Clay St. and Miss. 27. 601-636-9421)* publishes a map for a rewarding driving tour. The most important attraction is the 16-mile driving-walking tour of **Vicksburg Natl.**

The wide, covered *porches* that surround most older southern houses are an adaptation to sultry climate and an architectural expression of the famous southern hospitality. The porch substitutes for living and dining rooms of northern latitudes. Before air conditioning, folks sat here to read their papers, snap their beans, and wave to neighbors. The empty chairs are a friendly sign that no invitation is needed to step up, say howdy, and sit a spell.

67

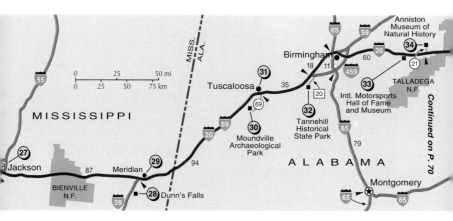

Steamboat on the Missis-
sippi River

68

Military Park (*3201 Clay St. 601-636-0583. Vehicle fee*). Its placid hills still stir a feeling of anger that men should have suffered so long and so bitterly here—in Lincoln's words, to "the last full measure of devotion." Gen. U. S. Grant relied on siege, shellfire, and starvation; for both sides it was a ghastly test of human resolve.

Vicksburg's place in history has insured a steady supply of tourists, and today almost every building with a room full of heirlooms calls itself a museum and charges admission. It's a tourist town, and its carnivalization is likely to continue as casino gambling on the river gains popularity. One museum worth a visit is the **Old Court House Museum** (*1008 Cherry St. 601-636-0741. Adm. fee*). Among its quirky exhibits is an explanation of how the Ku Klux Klan was established "to restore some semblance of decency to the government." Another exhibit, heavily anecdotal, shows thousands of aging veterans from both North and South at the 1917 reunion called the "Peace Jubilee." By nightfall, some of the old soldiers raised their walking sticks and once again set upon one another. Across the street is the **Toys and Soldiers Museum** (*1100 Cherry St. 601-638-1986. Adm. fee*), which includes an enormous private collection of toy soldiers. And a few blocks away is the **Museum of Coca-Cola** (*1107 Washington St. 601-638-6514. Adm. fee*), a restored turn-of-the-century candy store, where in 1894 Joseph A. Biedenharn first bottled what was until then just a soda fountain beverage.

The **Waterways Experiment Station** (*2 miles S of town at 3909 Halls Ferry Rd. 601-634-2502*) conducts guided tours weekdays at 10 a.m. and 2 p.m. One especially interesting demonstration is on liquefaction; visitors see how solid ground acts as a liquid during an earthquake.

Cemetery at Vicksburg National Military Park, Mississippi

Jackson   At the top of the attractions list of this state capital and university town is the **Jim Buck Ross Mississippi Agriculture and Forestry/National Agricultural Aviation Museum** *(1150 Lakeland Dr. 601-354-6113. Adm. fee).* It depicts a 1920s crossroads farming community and its daily commerce. Visitors can watch a cane press in action and then buy the syrup at the general store. It's a fascinating look at the rural economies that gave rise to today's complex marketplace. The museum is heavily into agricultural aviation (crop dusting), which helps keep kids interested.

Toys and Soldiers Museum,
Vicksburg, Mississippi

The **Mississippi Museum of Art** *(201 E. Pascagoula St. 601-960-1515. Closed Mon.; adm. fee)* has works by Renoir, Picasso, and O'Keeffe, among other artists, as well as the acclaimed Impressions Gallery, where the younger set use computers and conventional art supplies to learn about color, perspective, shape, and more. Next door, the **Russell C. Davis Planetarium** *(601-960-1550. Adm. fee)* serves both as a vehicle for astronomical education and for rock-and-roll entertainment, mostly on weekend evenings. The **Old Capitol** *(100 S. State St. 601-359-6920),* a Greek Revival building completed in 1839 that served as capitol until 1903, is now the state historical museum with an excellent presentation. It has been named a national historic landmark.

Jackson has an assortment of historically important, mostly Greek Revival, restored houses, but the **Manship House** *(420 E. Fortification St. 601-961-4724. Closed Sun-Mon.),* a Gothic Revival, is especially interesting. Its original owner, the town's mayor during the Civil War, was also a craftsman who painted pine and cypress to look like marble, mahogany, and oak. His home became a showcase for his trade. It is also notable for the painstaking detail of its restoration.

Dunn's Falls   *(Follow signs from Savoy exit off I-59 10 miles S of I-20. 601-655-8550)* This is a clean, well-kept old mill pond on the high east bank of the scenic Chunky River, a delightful and uncrowded place for a picnic and a swim. The gristmill, with its huge waterwheel, still operates. Visitors can see and touch every part of it. *Closed Mon.-Tues.; adm. fee.*

State Capitol, completed in 1903,
Jackson, Miss.

Meridian   At the turn of the century, Meridian was Mississippi's largest and most prosperous city. But today much of it is dilapidated. The city's most popular attraction is the small **Jimmie Rodgers Memorial Museum** *(8th St. N.W. from downtown to 39th Ave., turn N to Highland Park. 601-485-1808. Adm. fee).* Rodgers was an important figure in early country music. Exhibits include his guitar, concert clothing, and sheet music. The museum is in a public park that also has a carousel, built in 1892 by the famous German master Gustav Dentzel. It still operates to the delight of children. The **Grand Opera House of Mississippi** *(2208 5th St. 601-693-5239. Closed Mon.; adm. fee),* built in 1890, can be toured in its unrenovated condition.

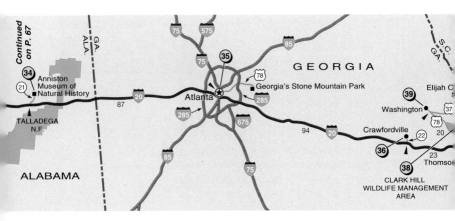

ALABAMA
CLICK-1

The Old South had moonlight and magnolias; the New South has *kudzu*—and more kudzu. The weedy vine throws its curtain of green over anything in its path: trees, telephone lines, buildings, abandoned cars. A post-Civil War invader, it has changed the landscape more than Sherman's March to the Sea. In the 1930s, the U. S. government imported the Oriental plant to control erosion. At first, it was championed by farmers; kudzu festivals were even held. But the fast-growing plant spread, endangering forests. Now decried as a weed and a plague, kudzu covers 2 million acres.

70

30 Moundville Archaeological Park, ALABAMA (*20 miles S on Ala. 69. Museum 205-371-2572*) On the high east bank of the Black Warrior River, the 317-acre archaeological park may have been the capital of a nation of Mississippian Indians that thrived from A.D. 900 to 1500. Two days a week in autumn, visitors can watch the excavations of University of Alabama archaeology students. There are a museum and some outdoor exhibits, but most interesting are the huge mounds. *Adm. fee.*

31 Tuscaloosa The grounds where the capitol building of Alabama's fourth capital (1826-1847) once stood are now a public park (*28th Ave. and University Blvd.*). The **Old Tavern Museum** (*205-758-8163. Fri.-Sat.; adm. fee*), a two-story brick stagecoach inn, houses memorabilia from days when pols tipped a glass here, as well as exhibits on local archaeology. Modern Tuscaloosa is home of the **University of Alabama** (*Information 205-348-6010*), which opened its doors in 1831. Yankees torched most of its buildings in 1865, but four survived, including the beautiful Greek Revival **President's Mansion** (*Closed to the public*). Football mania has made the **Paul W. Bryant Museum** (*300 Paul W. Bryant Dr. 205-348-4668. Adm. fee*), honoring the late head coach, a popular and worthwhile stop. Park in the rear and ignore the posted restrictions meant for students. The **Children's Hands-On Museum** (*2213 University Blvd. 205-349-4235. Closed Sun.-Mon.; adm. fee*) is an indoor playground where children will be amused by interactive historical and science exhibits. Older children can be left alone here.

32 Tannehill Historical State Park (*12 miles south of Bessemer via I-459 and Route 20. 205-477-5711*) It's hard to imagine not enjoying a few hours at this park, dedicated to the industrial and economic history of the Confederacy, which relied on foundries here for some of its war matériel. The old Confederate ironworks stands next to a spring-fed stream deep in a forest where campers are welcome. Several Civil War-era buildings and much of the ironworks have been restored. *Adm. fee.*

The **Bessemer Pioneer Homes** *(205-425-3253),* spread along Eastern Valley Rd./Route 20 north of the park, are beautifully restored Civil War-era houses with interesting furniture; the upstairs rooms of one were divided by sex. Tours available.

Birmingham See I-65, p. 155.

President's Mansion, University of Alabama, Tuscaloosa

Intl. Motorsports Hall of Fame and Museum

(Next to I-20 at its own exit. 205-362-5002) Adjacent to the Talladega Superspeedway, this hall of fame has more than 100 automotive exhibits, including a rocket car that propelled a driver to Mach 1.1 only 18 inches above the Bonneville Salt Flats in Utah. The biggest draw is a race car simulator—a vibrating car body in front of a big screen. It will give anyone a rush who's never blasted down the road at 200 mph, but if you think this is fun, don't miss the exhibits of what's left when a heavily reinforced NASCAR racer hits the wall at that speed. *Admission fee.*

Anniston Museum of Natural History

(6 miles N on Ala. 21. 205-237-6766) A valuable collection of mounted birds and mammals is imaginatively exhibited here in the heart of Christian fundamentalism. It deftly makes two points—that natural selection is plausible and that man's ability to alter his environment exceeds his understanding of it. Displays tell how predators and prey discipline one another, how environment influences evolution, and how evolution shapes environment. It's no wonder 100,000 people visit every year. *Closed Mon.; adm. fee.*

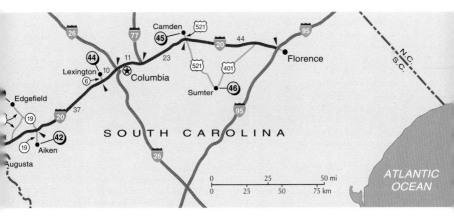

Already a commercial center before the Civil War—and a crucial railroad link during it—Atlanta was reduced to ruins by General Sherman's army in 1864. It soon re-built and has been growing ever since.

Swan House, built in 1928, part of Atlanta History Center, 130 W. Paces Ferry Rd. 404-814-4000

Today it is not only Georgia's capital but also the commercial, industrial, and financial capital of the Southeast, with a modern, burgeoning skyline and crowded expressways. A convention town, Atlanta draws 16.5 million visitors annually, who when added to the 2.9 million residents create congestion that detracts from its Southern charm. A stop at one of the *Atlanta Visitor Centers* (404-222-6688) will lessen the pain.

Atlanta's most popular attraction is outside the city. The 3,200-acre *Georgia's Stone Mountain Park* (16 miles E of Atlanta on US 78. 404-498-5600. Adm. fee) encompasses Stone Mountain, a massive granite dome into which three huge equestrian figures have been sculptured as a Confederate memorial. The park also has a wide range of other historical and recreational facilities, including an antebellum plantation, riverboat cruises, and a lakefront beach.

Georgia's Stone Mountain Park

In town, two popular attractions are corporate exhibits created to promote their sponsors. The *World of Coca-Cola* (55 M.L. King, Jr. Dr. 404-676-5151. Adm. fee) is a museum with all the razzle-dazzle appeal of a Coke commercial. A monument to American marketing, it offers a taste, literally, of Coke's worldwide diversity. The *CNN Studio Tour* (Marietta St. at Techwood Dr. 404-827-2300. Adm. fee) allows you to see how TV news comes together. A favorite of foreigners, it is offered every 15 minutes; 24-hour notice is required.

After Stone Mountain, Atlanta's most visited area is the *Martin Luther King, Jr., Natl. Historic Site* (Info Center, 522 Auburn Ave. 404-331-5190). The civil rights leader is entombed in a fountain between the *Ebenezer Baptist Church* (407 Auburn Ave. 404-688-7263), where he preached, and the *King Center* (449 Auburn Ave. 404-524-1956), which exhibits photos. Nearby at 501 Auburn Ave. is his restored birthplace. A few blocks away, the *APEX* (African–American Panoramic Experience) *Museum* (135 Auburn Ave. 404-521-2739. Closed Sun.-Mon.; adm. fee) tells about the Sweet Auburn District, the center of the black community for much of this century.

Zoo Atlanta (800 Cherokee Ave. S.E. 404-624-5600. Adm. fee) has 20 gorillas living in natural family groups and a huge reptile collection, as well as a petting zoo. Children will also like *Scitrek* (395 Piedmont Ave. N.E. 404-522-5500. Closed Mon. Labor Day-Memorial Day; adm. fee), a hands-on science and technology museum.

Crawfordville   Incorporated in 1826, this town is younger than many of its neighbors and still looks as it did in the mid-1900s. Its main attraction is the **A. H. Stephens State Historic Park** (*Just N of town center. 706-456-2602. Closed Mon.*), which memorializes a fascinating Civil War figure. Stephens was a U. S. congressman and outspoken opponent of secession, who in a show of unity became vice president of the Confederacy. Even so, he opposed the war and especially its mandatory draft. Imprisoned at war's end, he later served as state governor. *Adm. fee.*

Thomson   Near this crossroads stands Georgia's oldest documented dwelling, the **Rock House** (*3 miles S on US 78/Ga. 17 to town, then 5 miles W on Ga. 223/Lumpkin St. and left 1 mile on Rock House Rd.*), a beautifully restored 1780s pioneer house in a peaceful pine forest. There's little to see inside, but visitors can arrange to enter by contacting the **Thomson-McDuffie Tourism Bureau** (*111 Railroad St. 706-595-5584. Closed weekends*).

Clark Hill Wildlife Management Area (*N on US 78 10 miles, follow sign right onto dirt road, Smith Mill Rd., 2.5 miles to check station. 706-595-4222*) The state welcomes sightseers, hikers, and campers (except during hunting season) to this beautiful 12,700-acre, forested hunting preserve with a nature trail along J. Strom Thurmond Lake.

Washington   (*20 miles N on US 78*) Fort Heard was established here in 1773. It became a hotbed of patriotic resistance to the British during the Revolution and, at the end of the Civil War, the site of the Confederate government's last official meeting. The community has preserved a number of historic buildings, including the **Washington Historical Museum** (*308 E. Robert Toombs Ave. 706-678-2105. Closed Mon.; adm. fee*), which exhibits Confederate relics and papers. A historical walking-tour map is available at the museum and at the **Washington-Wilkes Chamber of Commerce** (*104 E. Liberty. 706-678-2013*).

Elijah Clark State Park   (*28.5 miles NE via US 78, Ga. 43, and US 378. 706-359-3458*) is a 447-acre park memorializing a Revolutionary War hero, whose reconstructed log home is now a museum of local colonial life. The park offers picnicking, camping, and swimming. *Cabin open April-Nov. weekends; adm. fee.*

Augusta   (*6 miles S on Ga. 28*) Founded in 1735 as a fur-trading post on the Savannah River, Augusta was the site of the Confederacy's largest gunpowder factory. By the mid-1800s, Augusta was one of the region's largest cotton markets. Cotton trading still goes on, as does textile manufacturing. Golfers gather annually for the famous Masters Tournament. Many well-preserved buildings recall Augusta's historic past. The **Welcome Center** (*At the Cotton Exchange. 706-724-4067*) publishes a map, and **Historic Augusta**

73

Uncle Remus Museum, Eatonton, Georgia, 21 miles south of I-20 on US 441/129

(111 10th St. 706-724-0436) sponsors a weekly trolley tour *(Infoline 706-722-2034)* that drives by such high points as the old **Cotton Exchange Building** *(8th and Reynolds Sts.),* circa 1886, the center of Augusta's cotton trade; the 1797 **Ezekiel Harris House** *(1822 Broad St.);* the **Woodrow Wilson Boyhood Home** *(419 7th St. Not open for tours);* the **First Presbyterian Church** *(642 Telfair St. 706-823-2450. Weekdays),* of 1812, designed by Robert Mills; and the **Augusta-Richmond County Museum** *(540 Telfair St. 706-722-8454. Closed Mon.; adm. fee),* in an edifice built about 1802 and full of interesting history exhibits. **Riverwalk Augusta** *(15 8th St. 706-821-1754)* is a jogging, walking, and picnicking park along the river, with many markers describing what it once was like.

㊷ **A i k e n ,   S O U T H   C A R O L I N A** *(8 miles S on S.C. 19. Chamber of Commerce, 400 Laurens St. N.W. 803-641-1111)* The town was settled in the 1830s as a railroad stop on the Charleston-to-Hamburg line. In the 1870s it became a winter haven for rich New Yorkers, who introduced their equine sports. Today these define the town. Equestrian activities—races, hunts, steeplechases, horse trials and shows, and polo—go on from November through April. The **Thoroughbred Racing Hall of Fame** *(In Hopeland Gardens, Whiskey Rd. and Dupree Pl. 803-649-7700. Oct.-May p.m., closed Mon.)* depicts the town's role in the training of thoroughbreds. The countless horse facilities include a 2,000-acre preserve called **Hitchcock Woods** *(Off S. Boundary Ave.),* woven with sandy bridle paths. Pedestrians are welcome.

㊸ **E d g e f i e l d** *(15 miles N on US 25)* One of the state's earliest up-country towns, it is named for the **Old Edgefield District,** which supplied the region with stoneware from the early 1800s to the 1930s. In its heyday, millions of gallons of pottery poured out of kilns in Edgefield and nearby towns. The industry's history is preserved at the **Old Edgefield Pottery** museum *(230 Simkins St. 803-637-2060. Closed Sun.-Mon.),* which plans to be in a new facility by 1995. The United Daughters of the Confederacy maintain **Oakley Park Museum** *(300 Columbia Rd. 803-637-4010 or 637-4027. Thurs.-Sat.; adm. fee),* the former home of Confederate officer Martin Witherspoon Gary who, in 1876, led 1,500 "Red Shirts," torches ablaze, to rally white Democrats against the Reconstruction government. For another century, white supremacy reigned supreme.

㊹ **L e x i n g t o n** Swiss and German immigrants settled here in the early 1700s to scratch a living from the relatively unproductive land. In 1785, the county was renamed Lexington in honor of the first battle of the Revolution. Citizens have relocated several historical buildings on a plot adjacent to the **Lexington County Museum** *(US 378 3 miles to town center, left on Fox St. 803-359-8369).* No carriages or fine crys-

☞ The old *shanties* of the segregated South are disappearing. Rusty tin and unpainted timber are giving way to trailers and cinder blocks. Historical societies don't work to preserve this heritage beyond the pavement. No longer called "quarters districts" or "nigger-towns," they are witnesses to changing standards and economic conditions. For now, in many small towns you can still see shanties, often supplying eggs and chickens from illegal coops.

74

Old Edgefield Pottery, Edgefield, South Carolina

Magnolia Dale House, Edgefield, South Carolina

tal here. This is a lesson in the hardiness and ingenuity of 19th-century life. *Closed Mon.; adm. fee.*

Columbia See I-77, p. 211.

Camden Laid out in 1733, this lovely town—the oldest inland settlement in South Carolina—was the site of a disastrous Revolutionary War battle. Soon after the town was captured by the British in 1780, American troops attempted to retake it. Most were raw militia, however, and they bolted at the first enemy charge. Their commander, Gen. Horatio Gates—the "hero of Saratoga"—fled with them, never to live it down. Near a partially reconstructed British wall, the town has established a 98-acre park called **Historic Camden** *(From I-20, N on US 521 for 1.4 miles. 803-432-9841. Guided tours except Mon.; adm. fee. Free self-guided tours daily)*, where visitors can tour five historic buildings, some relating to the occupation. You can also take a driving or walking tour of the **Camden Historic District,** with more than 60 houses and public buildings, most dating before 1860. Pick up a booklet at the **Camden Archives and Museum** *(1314 Broad St. 803-425-6050. Weekdays)* for a small charge. The museum has exhibits on county history.

Sumter *(24 miles S on US 521)* boasts a thriving local arts tradition. The **Sumter Gallery of Arts** *(421 N. Main St. 803-775-0543. Closed Mon.)* is in the Elizabeth White House, built in 1850. Among well-presented history exhibits at the **Sumter County Museum** *(122 N. Wash. St. 803-775-0908. Closed Mon.)* is Rembrandt Peale's portrait of Revolutionary War Gen. Thomas Sumter.

Kershaw-Cornwallis House, Historic Camden, South Carolina

Florence See I-95, p. 340.

Unless otherwise noted, directions are from interstate, and sites are free and generally open daily. Phone for further information.

1 Buffalo, WYOMING *(Chamber of Commerce, 55 N. Main St. 307-684-5544)* Founded by ranchers in 1879, Buffalo lies among the rumpled grassland hills at the base of Wyoming's Bighorn Mountains. It thrived early on and played a major role in the 1890s range wars, but today its historic downtown looks a bit saddlesore. Nonetheless, three buildings are listed on the National Register of Historic Places: The **Occidental Hotel** *(10 N. Main St. Summer only)*, where Owen Wister's hero, the Virginian, got his man and which today is open for tours, not guests; the neoclassic **Johnson County Courthouse** *(104 Fort St. 307-684-7281)*, circa 1884; and a red sandstone Carnegie Library, circa 1909. The Carnegie now forms part of the **Jim Gatchell Memorial Museum of the West** *(100 Fort St. 307-684-9331. Daily in summer, weekdays only May and Sept.-Oct.; adm. fee)*, a fine collection of Old West relics.

2 Teapot Dome *(19 miles S of Midwest on Wyo. 259)* Now known as U. S. Naval Petroleum Reserve No. 3, this large oil field lay at the heart of a famous 1920s political scandal. Interior Secretary Albert B. Fall took a $100,000 "loan" for secretly allowing an oil company to tap into the Navy's reserve. The rock formation that gave the dome its name juts from a hillside, but no longer looks like a teapot now that its "spout" and "handle" have broken off.

Frontier Days, Cheyenne, Wyoming

3 Casper Here at the base of the Laramie Mountains, the town's refineries, office buildings, and shady neighborhoods stretch along the banks of the North Platte River. Though most recently a center for oil and gas production, the area traces its history to the mid-19th century, when waves of emigrants passed by on their way west via the Oregon Trail. Here, too, the U. S. Army briefly established an outpost and fought Indians during the 1860s. The Army post was reconstructed in 1936 as the **Fort Caspar Museum** *(Poplar St. exit, follow signs to 4001 Fort Caspar Rd. 307-235-8462. Closed Sat. in winter).* Its log buildings, furnished in period style, depict military life on the High Plains.

4 Fort Fetterman *(On Wyo. 93, 10 miles NW of Douglas. 307-358-2864)* This site lies on a windy, sunbaked plateau overlooking the North Platte River and the seemingly endless plains of northeastern

Ayres Natural Bridge, 5 miles west of
Douglas, Wyoming, on Wyo. 91

Wyoming. Established in 1867 to supply
troops fighting along the Bozeman Trail, the
fort was named for Capt. William Fetterman,
killed the previous winter with 80 others in a
Lakota ambush. The Army abandoned the fort
after the 1870s war for the Black Hills. Two
buildings survive as a museum. *Summer only.*

Douglas   This small town sprang to
life in 1886 and enjoyed a colorful history as
a place where ranch hands celebrated payday
by getting drunk, gambling, and fighting—
usually in that order. Today Douglas is a pleasant, laid-back town set among the sinuous
oasis of cottonwoods and poplars that is the
North Platte River Valley. It has an excellent
museum of Native American and pioneer
memorabilia—the **Wyoming Pioneer Memorial Museum** (*W. Center St., just inside the
State Fairgrounds. 307-358-9288. Closed Sun. in
summer and weekends in winter*).

Guernsey Area (*15 miles E on US
26. Follow signs for the Oregon Trail Ruts and
Register Cliff*) Some of the most impressive
physical evidence of Wyoming's covered-
wagon era survives in the cliffs and hills near
Guernsey. About a mile south of town, travelers on the Oregon Trail crossed a grassy ridge
of soft sandstone. Their wagons left ruts as
deep as 5 feet. Many of the emigrants who
helped cut those ruts spent the previous night
a few miles downriver at **Register Cliff,** where
they carved their names into the tannish sandstone. Some signatures date back to the 1840s,
but part of the surface is marred by names
added during the past 25 years.

Fort Laramie Natl. Hist. Site
(*28 miles E on US 26, follow signs. 307-837-*

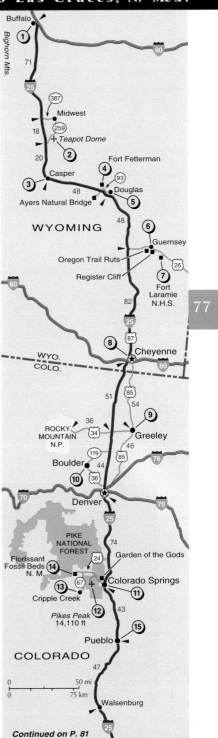

Continued on P. 81

State Capitol, Cheyenne

☞ Three important ***19th-century trails*** crossed the rolling prairies of eastern Wyoming. The Oregon Trail followed the great bend of the North Platte River before striking out across central Wyoming. John Bozeman blazed his famous trail through Wyoming's Powder River country to reach the goldfields of central Montana. And Black Hills gold spawned the Cheyenne to Deadwood stage line, which ran from Cheyenne to Fort Laramie and then skirted the Wyoming border.

78

2221) Built in 1834 near the confluence of the Laramie and North Platte Rivers, Fort Laramie casts a long shadow over Wyoming's early history. Considered the first permanent white settlement on the northern plains, it began as a fur-trading post and became a large military garrison. Emigrants and Pony Express riders traveling the Oregon Trail stopped here. So did passengers taking the stagecoach between Cheyenne and Deadwood. Fort Laramie was also the site of two important treaties with the Plains tribes—and a staging area for Army campaigns when those treaties failed. Today it is one of the finest living history museums in the West, with a dozen structures restored to their original appearance. *Adm. fee.*

⑧ **Cheyenne** *(Convention & Visitors Bureau, 309 W. Lincolnway St. 307-778-3133 or 800-426-5009)* Born in 1867 as a rough-and-tumble construction camp on the Union Pacific line, Cheyenne has since developed into a sedate capital city where manicured lawns, flower gardens, and shade trees are the rule and cowboys the exception. The city has not, however, forgotten about boots and spurs. Each July it still throws the state's biggest rodeo bash, which is enshrined at the **Cheyenne Frontier Days Old West Museum** *(4501 N. Carey Ave. 307-778-7290. Adm. fee)* in Frontier Park.

During the cattle boom and gold rush years of the 1870s and '80s, wealthy citizens built fabulous mansions, now mostly demolished, as well as beautiful churches and commercial buildings, many of which survive downtown on Capitol Avenue between the magnificent **Union Pacific Depot** *(121 W. 15th St.)* and the **State Capitol** *(307-777-7777)*. One fine old residence still opens its doors to visitors: the **Historic Governors' Mansion** *(300 E. 21st St. 307-777-7878. Closed Sun.-Mon.),* a gracious Georgian-style house decorated with eclectic furnishings.

⑨ **Greeley**, COLORADO *(19 miles E on US 34)* In 1870, Nathan Meeker, agricultural editor of the *New York Tribune,* founded this prosperous city as a utopian community. Based on the principles of family, temperance, religion, and education, Greeley flourished as a lavishly irrigated agricultural district. At **Centennial Village** *(1475 A St. 303-*

Fiske Planetarium, University of Colorado, Boulder

350-9224. Closed Sun.-Mon.; adm. fee), lovingly preserved buildings depict the range of homes, businesses, and lifestyles common to the region between 1860 and 1920. The **Meeker Home** *(1324 9th Ave. 303-350-9221. Closed Sun.-Mon.; adm. fee)*, the founder's two-story adobe house, adapted Victorian style to the building materials at hand—mud and grass. It is filled with Meeker family belongings.

Boulder *(26 miles W on US 36. Convention & Visitors Bureau, 2440 Pearl St. 303-442-2911 or 800-444-0447)* Located just a half hour's drive northwest of Denver, this attractive university town spills out of the rugged foothills of Colorado's Front Range. Gold, silver, and oil fueled the city's early growth, but today Boulder is a major technical and scientific center. Nature trails, open spaces, and

Purple sky pilot,
Rocky Mountains

greenbelts abound, making the simple act of walking one of the city's greatest pleasures. Three major trail systems loop through **Boulder Mountain Park** at the edge of town, climbing high into the Flatirons for boffo vistas of the city and plains. Boulder also boasts three distinct historic districts, including **Chautauqua Park,** the only intact Chautauqua site surviving in the West. The city concentrates 30 art galleries into its downtown area and hosts summer-long festivals of Shakespeare and classical music. Star talks and laser shows are offered at the **Fiske Planetarium** *(303-492-5002. Call for show times; adm. fee)* on the University of Colorado campus. A

Rocky Mountain National Park, Colo., 75 mins. west of I-25 on US 34

short drive up Table Mesa leads to the **National Center for Atmospheric Research** *(1850 Table Mesa Dr. 303-497-1174)*, where scientists study severe storms and other interesting phenomena. The building alone, designed by I. M. Pei, is worth the stop.

Denver See I-70, p. 164.

Colorado Springs *(Visitor Bureau, 104 S. Cascade Ave. 719-635-7506)* Founded as a resort town in 1871 by railroad tycoon William J. Palmer, Colorado Springs now sprawls across the plains east of Pikes Peak. Huge crowds flock to it all summer to visit museums, shops, and intensely developed scenic areas. First stop on most agendas is the **U. S. Air Force Academy** *(719-472-2555)*, just north of town, with its ultra-modern Cadet Chapel and exhibits on Air Force history. Just across I-25 from the academy's north gate stands the **Western Museum of Mining and Industry** *(125 Gleneagle Dr. 719-488-0880. Daily March-Nov., by appt. Dec.-Feb.; adm. fee)*, where a colossal steam engine spins a 14-foot

Cadets at U. S. Air Force Academy,
Colorado Springs, Colorado

Garden of the Gods, Colorado Springs

From Buffalo, Wyoming, to Albuquerque, New Mexico, I-25 parallels the leading edge of the *Rocky Mountains.* For nearly 1,000 miles, the peaks rise abruptly from the plains. Major ranges include the Bighorns, the Laramies, the Front Range, and the Sangre de Cristos. Each has its own creation story, but all originated with a colossal collision of tectonic plates that began some 150 million years ago off the West Coast. Like a fender bender in slow motion, the Pacific oceanic plate ran in and slipped under the North American plate—crumbling and uplifting the continent's margin.

flywheel in the lobby. Perhaps the city's best stop is the **U. S. Olympic Complex** (*1750 E. Boulder St. 719-578-4618*), where hundreds of Olympic contenders train. You might see gymnasts, boxers, weight lifters, and other athletes working out.

On the edge of Colorado Springs rises the **Garden of the Gods** (*3500 Ridge Rd. 719-578-6939*), a tranquil pocket reminiscent of the slickrock country of southern Utah. In this park, broad rock flakes and slender stone pinnacles the color of salmon flesh serrate a landscape of gentle hills and small basins. Laced with roads and gravel footpaths, the Garden of the Gods is at its best in early morning, when the red rock seems incandescent and cool air sifts through the trees. On the east side of the park, you'll find the **White House Ranch** (*3202 Chambers Way. 719-578-6777. Wed.-Sun.; adm. fee*), an excellent living-history museum that depicts life in the Pikes Peak region from 1860 to 1910.

⑫ **Pikes Peak** (*19 miles W on US 24*) Despite the hype, Pikes Peak does not present a dramatic profile. It is simply a broad peak that rises far above the timberline and tops out in a squat, dome-shaped summit. Still, at 14,110 feet, Pikes Peak is impressive, and its summit views are spectacular. You can hike, bike, or drive 19 miles along a toll road to reach the top. But the most comfortable (and expensive) conveyance is the **Cog Railway,** which leaves from 515 Ruxton Ave. in Manitou Springs (*6 miles W on US 24. 719-685-5401*) eight times daily in summer, less often the rest of the year.

If Time Permits...

⑬ **Cripple Creek** (*45 miles W on US 24 and Colo. 67*) This former gold-mining town burned to the ground twice before its present attractive redbrick buildings were erected in the 1890s. Today the big draw is casino gambling, but you can still ride the **Cripple Creek & Victor Narrow Gauge Railroad** (*On Colo. 67. 719-689-2640. Memorial Day-early Oct.; fare charge*), pulled by miniature steam locomotives. While waiting for the next train, wander through the **Cripple Creek District Museum** (*511 E. Bennett. 719-689-2634. Memorial Day-early Oct.*), a three-story, brick-and-stone train depot given over to pioneer and mining memorabilia.

⑭ **Florissant Fossil Beds National Monument** (*35 miles W on US 24. 719-748-3253*) Roughly 500,000 years of intermittent volcanic activity buried the Florissant area with mud,

Cog Railway, Pikes Peak, Colorado

pumice, and ash, preserving excellent specimens of insects and plants that lived here more than 35 million years ago. At the Visitor Center and along nature trails, you'll see the shadowlike carbon imprints of leaves, beetles, and dragonflies, as well as the petrified stumps of ancient sequoias. Also on the grounds: cross-country ski trails and an 1870s homestead. *Adm. fee (except in winter).*

Pueblo *(Visitor Center, 302 N. Santa Fe Ave. 719-542-1704)* A natural crossroads for hundreds of years, Pueblo grew from a prosperous agricultural community in the 1870s into a major industrial center around the turn of the century. Vestiges of this era abound in the Victorian buildings of the **Union Avenue Historic District,** which include an immense and stately train depot. The best Victorian structure, by far, stands on a hill overlooking downtown: the **Rosemount Museum** *(419 W. 14th St. 719-545-5290. Closed Mon.; adm. fee),* a stunning, 37-room stone mansion built in 1893. Exceptionally well preserved, with original furnishings, Rosemount depicts the gracious life of the late 1800s. Reaching deeper into the past, exhibits at the **El Pueblo Museum** *(324 W. 1st St. 719-583-0453. Adm. fee)* span the region's history from prehistoric times to 1900. At the airport you'll find an excellent collection of more than two dozen vintage military aircraft parked at the **Fred E. Weisbrod/International B-24 Memorial Museum** *(31001 Magnuson Ave. 719-948-9219),* including jet fighters, a B-29 bomber, and a Boeing Stratojet.

Raton Pass *(Colorado-New Mexico border)* From Trinidad, I-25 more or less follows the original route of the **Santa Fe Trail.** Opened in 1821, the trail was an important trade route linking Missouri with the fur- and silver-rich region of Santa Fe. First blazed over Raton Pass, the Mountain Branch proved longer for wagons, so most traffic turned south at Dodge City and crossed the Cimarron Desert to Santa Fe.

Continued on P. 77

81

Walsenburg
25
37
Trinidad
Raton Pass (16)
59
COLO.
N. MEX.
Springer
(17)
70
Fort Union
N.M.
161
25
SANTA FE
N.F.
84
(18)
BANDELIER
N.M. 502 84
285
(19) 50
63
Las
Vegas
(21) 4
Santa Fe
42 15 9
Coronado (23) (22) (20) Pecos N.H.P.
S.M. 38
44 El Rancho
de las Golondrinas
556 Sandia Mts.
+ Sandia Peak 40
(24) 16
40 13 Albuquerque
(25) Isleta
ISLETA Pueblo
I.R. CIBOLA
NATIONAL
FOREST
76 NEW
MEXICO
25
San Antonio
15 (1) BOSQUE DEL APACHE
N. W. R.
(26)
50
195 (27)
(28) Elephant Butte Lake S.P.
Truth or Consequences
51
68 (29)
25
Las Cruces Dripping
(30) Springs
(28) Mesilla N. MEX.
TEXAS
10
10
U.S.
MEXICO
0 25 mi
0 50 km

(17) **Fort Union National Monument, NEW MEXICO** *(8 miles N on N. Mex. 161. Visitor Center 505-425-8025)* Built in 1851 to protect travelers on the Santa Fe Trail, Fort Union later served as a base for Federal troops who beat back a Confederate invasion of the Southwest during the Civil War. It was the largest military installation on the southwestern frontier, supplying a network of outposts through the 1870s. The fort was abandoned in 1891; foundations and parts of walls remain. *Adm. fee.*

(18) **Las Vegas** Mexicans founded Las Vegas in 1835 along the lush bottomland of the Gallinas River. The town thrived because of its strategic location on both the Santa Fe Trail and, later, the railroad. Las Vegas boasts more than 900 buildings on the National Register of Historic Places, and interesting history crops up all over. From the central plaza, Gen. S. W. Kearny claimed New Mexico for the

(19) Santa Fe

82

This famous center of southwestern art and architecture rests against the wooded foothills of the Sangre de Cristo Mountains. Founded in 1610, Santa Fe enjoys a rich multicultural heritage. People come to visit its galleries, sample southwestern cuisine, and admire the gentle play of light and shadow on the smooth lines of its adobe buildings (Convention & Visitors Bureau, 201 W. Marcy St. 505-984-6760 or 800-777-CITY).

Inn at Loretto, next to historic Loretto Chapel

In 1609-10, Spanish settlers erected the *Palace of the Governors* (505-827-6483. Adm. fee for museum) on the central plaza. Considered the oldest capitol building in the United States, it served as the capital of this part of New Spain for two centuries. Today it houses an excellent museum, and its porticos serve as a thriving bazaar for Native Americans

Pueblo pottery and chile *ristras*

selling pottery and jewelry.

Legend has it that the bell in 17th-century *San Miguel Chapel* (401 Old Santa Fe Trail. 505-983-3974) was cast in 1356 from 780 pounds of copper, silver, and gold. Just down the street is the *Loretto Chapel* (211 Old Santa Fe Trail. 505-984-7971. Adm. fee), one of the first Gothic churches built west of the Mississippi. Its spiral staircase was constructed without nails or visible support.

A cluster of museums overlooks the city 2 miles southeast of the plaza. These include the *Museum of International Folk Art* (706 Camino Lejo. 505-827-6463. Adm. fee), one of the world's largest collections of Hispanic folk art, and the *Museum of Indian Arts and Culture* (710 Camino Lejo. 505-827-8941. Admission fee), with displays of magnificent Pueblo pottery.

Bandelier Natl. Monument, N. Mex.

United States in 1846. Doc Holliday gunned down a fellow on Center Street in 1880. While visiting Las Vegas in 1900, Teddy Roosevelt announced his candidacy for President of the U. S. The **Rough Riders Memorial and City Museum** *(925 Grand Ave. 505-425-8726. Closed Sun.)* preserves memorabilia from Roosevelt's liberation of Cuba, as well as local historical items.

Pecos National Historical Park *(5 miles N on N. Mex. 63. 505-757-6032)* Pre-Hispanic Pecos was a farming community and trading center with a past that reached back to the 12th century. By 1450 the pueblo had grown into a five-story fortress housing 2,000 people. After the Spanish arrived, the inhabitants helped build two missions. The first was destroyed in the Pueblo Revolt of 1680. The second, completed in 1717, survives only in the crumbled walls you see today. *Adm. fee.*

If Time Permits...

Bandelier National Monument *(24 miles N on US 285, 10 miles W on N. Mex. 502, 12 miles S on N. Mex. 4. 505-672-3861)* Nearly 50 square miles of spectacular canyon country embrace the ruins of many pre-Hispanic cliff and pueblo dwellings open to visitors. In a few hours you can tarry at the ruins of a two- to three-story circular pueblo, peer into a reconstructed cliff dwelling, and climb a series of ladders to a ceremonial cave—all inhabited between the 13th and 16th centuries. *Adm. fee.*

El Rancho de las Golondrinas *(Cienega exit, follow signs. 505-471-2261)* This outstanding living-history museum re-creates Spanish colonial life on the grounds of an early 18th-century ranch. The estate was a stopover along the Camino Real, the trail from Santa Fe to Mexico City. Today you can stroll through the original residence. During festivals, costumed interpreters cook, weave, and chop wood. *April-Oct. Wed.-Sun.; adm. fee.*

Coronado State Monument *(1 mile W on N. Mex. 44. Visitor Center 505-867-5351)* Out on the desert floor near the banks of the Rio Grande, this monument preserves the ruins of the 14th-century Kuaua Pueblo, which was probably visited by the Spanish conquistador Francisco Vásquez de Coronado in 1541. Archaeologists unearthed a kiva here with 17 layers of beautiful murals; you can climb into the restored underground ceremonial chamber and see some of them. *Adm. fee.*

Albuquerque *(Convention & Visitors Bureau, 121 Tijeras Ave. N.E. 505-243-3696 or 800-284-2282)* Founded in 1706 by a Spanish noble and a small group of colonists, Albuquerque sprawls along both banks of the Rio Grande at the foot of the Sandia

Perhaps nowhere else in the United States is **Native American culture** celebrated, studied, and commercialized with such vigor as in the Southwest. In the midst of all the adobe walls, jewelry, sand paintings, and pottery, you may find the history of these artistic people a bit confusing. The past is dominated by the Anasazi, who came to the upper Rio Grande about A.D. 600 and who, 600 years later, developed the adobe architectural style that now characterizes the Southwest. Their descendants are the Pueblo Indians, some of whom live in 19 villages in northern New Mexico.

83

Storyteller figurine, Santa Fe, N. Mex.

Balloon festival, Albuquerque, New Mexico

84

Mountains. Although sometimes overlooked in favor of Santa Fe, Albuquerque has much to offer. Start with a visit to **Old Town,** Albuquerque's historic core, which surrounds a shady central plaza graced by the smooth adobe walls of **San Felipe de Neri Church,** erected in 1706. Most of the shops, galleries, and restaurants in Old Town are also adobe structures; some date back to 1750. Native Americans from surrounding villages sell their marvelous jewelry and pottery from blankets spread on the sidewalks.

If museums appeal, you'll find several that cater to specific interests. The **National Atomic Museum** *(Kirtland Air Force Base East, E. Gibson Blvd. 505-845-6670)* displays nuclear bomb casings, missiles, cannon, and a B-52 bomber. At the **Maxwell Museum of Anthropology** *(University Dr., UNM campus. 505-277-4404),* you can tour one of the region's best exhibits of Native American rugs and pottery. The **Meteorites Museum** *(Northrop Hall, UNM campus. 505-277-4204. Closed Sat.-Sun.; adm. fee)* showcases meteorites from around the world. The **Indian Pueblo Cultural Center** *(2401 12th St. N.W. 505-843-7270. Adm. fee to museum)* chronicles the history of the 19 pueblos in northern New Mexico.

Other museums take a broader view. Folk art, sculptures, and photographs highlight the **Albuquerque Museum** *(2000 Mountain Rd. N.W. 505-243-7255. Closed Mon.).* Don't miss the **New Mexico Museum of Natural History** *(1801 Mountain Rd. N.W. 505-841-8837. Adm. fee),* with its top-drawer treatment of the history of the planet from the Big Bang through the evolution of species to the present day. Albuquerque also offers two excellent outdoor experiences: The **Rio Grande Nature Center State Park** *(2901 Candelaria Rd. N.W. 505-344-7240. Adm. fee)* explains the river's unique ecology; **Petroglyphs National Monument** *(3 miles W on I-40. 505-839-4429. Adm. fee)* preserves prehistoric designs chipped into volcanic cliffs.

☞ The *Sandia Mountains,* a spectacular arch of Precambrian granite capped by late Paleozoic limestone and shale, burst 5,000 feet from the desert floor and loom above Albuquerque. The peaks formed during the last 30 million years as areas of the valley west of them dropped an astonishing 26,000 feet and then filled with alluvial debris. You can drive to the top on the Sandia Crest Highway (via I-40, N. Mex. 14, and N. Mex. 536) or take the Sandia Peak Tramway (Tramway Rd. 505-856-7325. Fare charge), which links northwest Albuquerque with Sandia Peak.

㉕ Isleta Pueblo *(Isleta exit, 15 miles S of Albuquerque. 505-869-3111)* Once the largest of the Rio Grande pueblos, this village of dirt streets and low-slung adobe houses lies along the river. The pueblo dates from the early 1200s and includes a beautiful old church, **St. Augustine Mission,** built in 1613 and reconstructed in 1680. Several shops sell Isleta pottery, jewelry, and baked goods.

㉖ Bosque del Apache National Wildlife Refuge *(8 miles S of San Antonio on N. Mex. 1. 505-835-1828)* Every autumn, thousands of greater sandhill cranes leave their nesting grounds in eastern Idaho and fly south to this refuge among the wetlands of the Rio Grande. Snow geese, many types of ducks, and whooping cranes with their sandhill crane foster parents join them every winter. In summer look for snowy egrets, pheasants, quail, and sandpipers. A 15-mile loop road and three trails traverse the refuge. *Adm. fee.*

㉗ Elephant Butte Lake State Park *(7 miles N of Truth or Consequences on N. Mex. 195. 505-744-5421)* Created by a dam built across the Rio Grande in 1916, Elephant Butte Lake extends 40 miles along the base of the heavily eroded Fra Cristobal Mountains. The lake was named for an elephant-shaped volcanic neck that protrudes from the water just above the dam. *Adm. fee.*

Truth or Consequences This sun-soaked town beside the Rio Grande voted in 1950 to change its name from Hot Springs in order to meet a challenge made by the *Truth or Consequences* radio program. The radio show petered out, but natural hot springs still flow through several bathhouses here.

Organ Mountains Named for the craggy pinnacles of granite that to some eyes resemble organ pipes, this small but dramatic mountain range cuts across the skyline east of Las Cruces. For an intimate encounter with the Organs, visit the **Dripping Springs Natural Area** (*E of Las Cruces via University Ave. and 10 miles of gravel road*). One trail leads to the ruins of a resort built around Dripping Springs, a seasonal waterfall at the base of 2,700-foot-high pinnacles. Another path runs to a cave shelter occupied off and on for 7,000 years. *Adm. fee.*

Fiberglass Allosaurus in sculptor's pickup, near Albuquerque

85

Las Cruces and Mesilla Although most of the big names in Spanish colonial history passed through this valley at one time or another—de Vaca, Coronado, Oñate—these towns were not established until the mid-19th century, late for New Mexico. Until 1881, Las Cruces existed as a sleepy farming community, in the shadow of nearby Mesilla. Then the railroad arrived, and Las Cruces boomed while Mesilla faded. Although Las Cruces may have won the railroad—as well as the county seat, university, and symphony—Mesilla still garners the lion's share of interest, history, and tourists. You can get a good feel for the past in **Old Mesilla Plaza,** whose historic buildings include the courthouse where Billy the Kid was sentenced to hang, the station where coaches of the Butterfield Overland Stage clattered to a stop, and a lovely 1850s church. Most of the old buildings are now shops, galleries, and restaurants.

Greater sandhill cranes, Bosque del Apache National Wildlife Refuge, New Mexico

Unless otherwise noted, directions are from interstate, and sites are free and generally open daily. Phone for further information.

(1) Pembina State Historic Site, NORTH DAKOTA *(1 mile E on Stutsman St. 701-825-6209)* This shady spot at the confluence of the Pembina and Red Rivers marks the site of North Dakota's earliest white settlement, Fort Panbian, established in 1797 by the North West Company. Here you can picnic, camp, or inspect an 1860s log house. *Memorial Day-Labor Day.*

(2) Grafton *(10 miles W on N. Dak. 17. Chamber of Commerce, 432 Hill Ave. 701-352-0781)* Maple and oak woodwork and a carved staircase add elegant touches to **Elmwood** *(2nd St. and Stephen Ave. Sun. only Memorial Day-Labor Day, or phone C. of C. for appt.)*, an 1895 Victorian mansion. For another look back at bygone days, tour the farmhouse, church, depot and caboose, working carousel, and taxidermy shop at the **Walsh County Heritage Village** *(N. Dak. 17. Sun. only Memorial Day-Labor Day, or phone C. of C. for appt.).*

(3) Grand Forks First a French fur-trading post, then a frontier river town, this leafy city lies at the fork of the Red Lake River and the Red River of the North. The **Myra Museum** *(2405 Belmont Rd., on the S edge of Lincoln Park. 701-775-2216. May-Sept.; adm. fee)* chronicles the history of Grand Forks and the surrounding area. The **North Dakota Museum of Art** *(Univ. of North Dakota/Grand Forks campus. 701-777-4195)* showcases contemporary art from around the world.

(4) Fargo *(Convention and Visitors Bureau, 2001 44th St. S.W. 701-282-3653)* William George Fargo founded both the famed Wells Fargo Express Company and, in 1872, this city. Now North Dakota's largest, it's the leading commercial center in the Red River Valley. At **Bonanzaville, USA** *(4.5 miles W on Main Ave., in West Fargo. 701-282-2822. May-Oct.; adm. fee)*, more than 40 reconstructed buildings re-create 19th-century prairie life, from a railroad museum with an 1883 locomotive and caboose to Fargo's first house and an antique car museum. Across town, at the **Children's Museum at Yunker Farm** *(1201 28th Ave. N. 701-232-6102. Closed Mon. during school year; adm. fee)*, youngsters can build a toy house, play in Legoland, or watch a puppet show.

Crop duster spraying sunflowers, Red River Valley, North Dakota

Moorhead (Minn.) See I-94, p. 311.

86

Fort Abercrombie S.H.S.
(4 miles E on Rte. 4, 3 miles S on Rte. 81, follow signs. 701-553-8513) Established in 1858, the fort was besieged by a band of Dakota (Sioux) for nearly six weeks in 1862 before reinforcements arrived. Abandoned in 1877, Fort Abercrombie now survives as a peaceful field surrounded by a tall palisade and reconstructed blockhouses. The museum brings pioneer days to life. *Fort open year-round, museum May-Sept.; adm. fee for museum.*

Wahpeton *(10 miles E on N. Dak. 13)* Thick woods gave this delightful town its Native American name—"village of the leaves." Set where the Ottertail and Bois de Sioux Rivers meet to form the Red River of the North, Wahpeton is the home of woodsy **Chahinkapa Park and Zoo** *(1004 R. J. Hughes Dr. 701-642-8709).* Here you can camp, picnic, ride the fully restored antique Prairie Rose Carousel, and visit the small but appealing zoo. *Zoo open year-round, carousel Memorial Day-Labor Day; charge for rides.*

Mooreton   Bagg Bonanza Farm Historic Site *(3 miles W on N. Dak. 13, follow signs. 701-274-8989)* The first bonanza farms in the United States date back to the 1860s, when the bankrupt Northern Pacific Railroad offered huge tracts of land for sale. J. F. Downing bought more than 9,000 acres and started a farm managed by his nephew, F. A. Bagg. When Downing died in 1913, Bagg established his own bonanza farm a mile away—the one you can tour today. *Memorial Day-Labor Day Tues.-Sun.; adm. fee.*

Canada geese

⑧ **Sisseton, SOUTH DAKOTA** *(3 miles W on S. Dak. 10)* Located in the middle of the triangular Sisseton-Wahpeton Indian Reservation, this small town takes pride in its **Tekakwitha Fine Arts Center** *(410 S.*

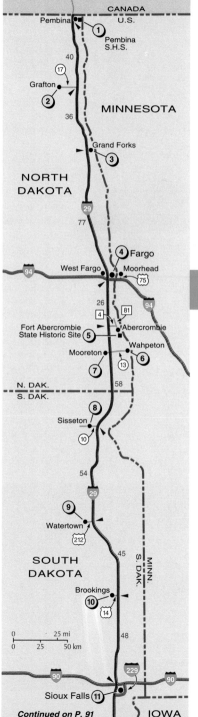

Continued on P. 91

Joseph N. Nicollet Tower,
Sisseton, South Dakota

(410 S. 8th Ave. W. 605-698-7058. Closed Mon. Labor Day-Memorial Day), a delightful museum featuring brightly colored paintings by local Native American artists. On a small hill outside town stands the **Joseph N. Nicollet Tower** *(3.5 miles W on S. Dak. 10. 605-698-7672. Tower open year-round; interpretive center May-Sept. Tues.-Sun., by appt. rest of year)*, a 75-foot-high observation deck with spectacular views of North Dakota, South Dakota, and Minnesota. The interpretive center recounts the story of Joseph Nicollet, the French mapmaker who explored this region in the late 1830s.

⑨ W a t e r t o w n *(3 miles W on US 212)* The **World Wildlife Museum** *(US 212 at Clock Tower Sq. 605-882-4724. Sept.-May weekends only; adm. fee)* displays mounted animals in realistic dioramas. To see the real thing, check out the hundred-plus species at **Bramble Park Zoo** *(S. Dak. 20, follow signs. 605-882-3464. Adm. fee)*. The restored **Mellette House** *(421 5th Ave. N.W. 605-886-4730. May-Oct. Tues.-Sun.)* takes visitors back to 1883, when it was built by Arthur C. Mellette, the first governor of South Dakota.

⑩ B r o o k i n g s Named after W. W. Brookings, an influential politician and judge, this picturesque town is now dominated by South Dakota State University. At its **McCrory Gardens** *(6th St. and 22nd Ave. 605-688-5136)*, rose, iris, and other gardens sprawl across more than 60 acres. On campus you can also visit two excellent museums: The **South Dakota Art Museum** *(Medary Ave. at Harvey Dunn St. 605-688-5423)* safeguards the state's art treasures, and the **State Agricultural Heritage Museum** *(Medary Ave. at 11th St. 605-688-6226)* highlights the development of farming and ranching with an original homesteader's shack, old steam and gas tractors, horse-drawn implements, and more.

⑪ S i o u x   F a l l s *(Convention and Visitors Bureau, 200 N. Phillips Ave. 605-336-1620 or 800-333-2072)* Like a moat around a castle, the Sioux River encircles this city, the region's meat-packing center. Its top attraction is the **Great Plains Zoo and Delbridge Museum of Natural History** *(805 S. Kiwanis Ave. 605-339-7059. Daily Apr.-Oct., weekends only in winter; adm. fee)*. The zoo shelters more than 300 reptiles, birds, and mammals, while the museum displays one of the world's largest collections of mounted animals. Down the street looms the **U.S.S. South Dakota Battleship Memorial** *(12th St. and Kiwanis Ave. 605-339-7060. Memorial Day-Labor Day)*, a full-size concrete outline of the battleship rising out of a field. In its center you can tour a museum packed with World War II mementos.

Falls Park, Sioux Falls, South Dakota

Downtown you'll find two other museums. South Dakota's first U. S. senator once owned the **Pettigrew Home and Museum** (*131 N. Duluth Ave. 605-339-7097. Closed Mon.*), a restored 1889 Queen Anne house crammed with souvenirs from his travels. At the 1890 Romanesque **Old Courthouse Museum** (*200 W. 6th St. 605-335-4210. Closed Mon.*), exhibits tell the story of the early settlers and the Plains Indians; on the second floor you can examine a restored circuit courtroom and law library. One of the town's oldest parks, **McKennan Park** (*26th St. and 2nd Ave.*) has fabulous gardens and pillars made of rocks from all 50 states. Well worth a stop are the waterfalls that gave the city its name; paved walkways at **Falls Park** (*Falls Park Dr.*) lead to the base of the crashing cascades.

Vermillion (*8 miles W on S. Dak. 50*) After an 1881 flood drowned the original town, Vermillion was relocated on top of the bluffs, away from the Missouri River. The community revolves around the University of South Dakota. Its **Shrine to Music Museum** (*414 E. Clark St. 605-677-5306*), one of the great institutions of its kind, features a fascinating collection of 5,000 musical instruments, including wooden music boxes, Elizabethan ivory lutes, a South Pacific trumpet mask, and two Stradivarii. On the other side of campus stands the **W. H. Over State Museum** (*1110 Ratingen St. 605-677-5228*), with displays of South Dakota's natural history and cultural heritage. Of special interest are the fine Dakota (Sioux) artifacts and Stanley J. Morrow's photographs documenting the Little Bighorn Battlefield and the changing West in the late 19th century.

Sioux City, IOWA (*Tourist Bureau, 801 4th St. 712-279-4800 or 800-593-2228*) One of the country's leading grain and livestock centers, Sioux City lies at the confluence of the Big Sioux and Missouri Rivers. An excellent collection of Native American artifacts and displays recounting local history make the **Sioux City Public Museum** (*2901 Jackson St. 712-279-6174*) well worth visiting. The **Sioux City Art Center** (*513 Nebraska St. 712-279-6272. Closed Mon.*) houses a small but impressive collection of contemporary midwestern art. From woodsy **Stone State Park** (*Memorial Dr., follow signs. 712-255-4698*), in the northwest part of the city, you'll have a spectacular view of Iowa, South Dakota, and Minnesota from Dakota Point Lookout atop the local Loess Hills.

DeSoto National Wildlife Refuge, Iowa

Lewis and Clark State Park (*2 miles W on Iowa 175, follow signs. 712-423-2829*) Besides camping, picnicking, hiking, and water sports on Blue Lake, you'll find a full-size reproduction of the 55-foot keelboat that Lewis and Clark's party sailed, pulled, and poled through this area in August 1804. *Adm. fee.*

DeSoto National Wildlife Refuge (*4 miles W on US 30. 712-642-4121*) Thousands of migrating

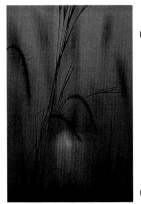

Wild grasses, Nebraska

90

mallards, as well as snow, Canada, and white-fronted geese, descend on this 7,823-acre refuge in autumn. *Adm. fee.*

(16) Council Bluffs President Abraham Lincoln's selection of Council Bluffs as the eastern terminus of the soon-to-be-built Union Pacific Railroad solidified the city as a major rail hub. The beautifully restored **Historic General Dodge House** (605 3rd St. 712-322-2406. Closed Mon. and Jan.; adm. fee) was built in 1869 by Grenville Mellen Dodge, a Civil War officer, U. S. congressman, and top railroad official. The 1885 **Historic Pottawattamie County Jail** (226 Pearl St. 712-323-2509. May-Aug. Mon.-Sat., spring and fall Tues.-Sat., closed Nov.-Feb.; adm. fee) is one of the few remaining "lazy Susan" or "squirrel cage" prisons, in which a rotary cage let wardens keep tabs on inmates from one vantage point.

(17) Omaha, NEBRASKA (Information Center, 13th St. exit from I-80, follow signs. 402-595-3990) A major outfitting center for early pioneers and today a major telecommunications center, Omaha prizes its acclaimed **Henry Doorly Zoo** (3701 S. 10th St. 402-733-8401. Adm. fee), home of North America's largest cat complex and the fabulous Lied Jungle, an indoor rain forest. A magnificent art deco building holds the **Joslyn Art Museum** (2200 Dodge St. 402-342-3300. Closed Mon.; adm. fee) and its collection of art from antiquity to the present. A few blocks away, the **Union Pacific Historical Museum** (1416 Dodge St. 402-271-3530. Closed Sun.) depicts the development of the railroad and preserves a large collection of Lincoln memorabilia. In old Union Station, the **Western Heritage Museum** (801 S. 10th St. 402-444-5071. Closed Mon. Sept.-May; adm. fee) features exhibits on Omaha's history. The **Great Plains Black Museum** (2213 Lake St. 402-345-2212. Closed weekends; donation requested) contains one of the largest African-American historical and cultural collections west of the Mississippi. Kids will enjoy the hands-on **Omaha Children's Museum** (500 S. 20th St. 402-342-6164. Closed Mon.; adm. fee).

(18) Waubonsie State Park, IOWA (5 miles E on Iowa 2, right on Iowa 239 for 1 mile. 712-382-2786) A windy ridge offers fine views of Nebraska, Iowa, Missouri, and Kansas. *Camping fee.*

(19) Squaw Creek National Wildlife Refuge, MISSOURI (2 miles W on US 159. 816-442-3187) Migrating birds begin congregating at this 7,178-acre refuge in September. Pelicans are among the first arrivals, followed by cormorants, snow and Canada geese, and mallards. As many as 300 bald eagles move in by December. *Daily during fall migration, weekdays rest of year.*

(20) St. Joseph (Tourist Information Center, Frederick Blvd. 816-232-1839) Once the outfitter of gold seekers headed for California, this historic city also served as the eastern terminus of the short-lived Pony Express. Today it bursts with museums. The **Glore Psychi-**

An unusual landform juts from the prairie along the Missouri River's eastern floodplain. **Loess Hills,** found only here and in China, were formed during the last ice age, when the Missouri was a major runoff channel filled with silt. As the silt dried, huge amounts of fine sediment settled on the floodplain. Strong winds deposited the sediment on the edge of the valley, and erosion and flowing water shaped the hills into what you see today.

atric Museum, on the grounds of the St. Joseph State Hospital (*3400 Frederick Ave. 816-387-2300*), tells how psychiatry developed over the last 400 years. Down the street, in a 1935 Georgian mansion, the **Albrecht-Kemper Museum of Art** (*2818 Frederick Ave. 816-233-7003. Closed Mon.*) spotlights 18th- to 20th-century American art. The **St. Joseph Museum** (*1100 Charles St. 816-232-8471. Adm. fee*), in an 1879 Gothic sandstone house, delves into local natural history, St. Joseph's past, and Native American art. Four other museums are clustered in the same area. The largest, the **Patee House Museum** (*12th and Penn Sts. 816-232-8206. Daily May-Oct., weekends only Nov.-April; adm. fee*), in the old Pony Express headquarters, focuses on transportation, with an 1860 train, horse-drawn buggies, and a 1920s service station. Directly behind it stands the **Jesse James Home** (*816-232-8206. Adm. fee*), where gang member Bob Ford shot and killed Jesse James in 1882 for a $10,000 reward. You can still see the bullet hole in the wall. On the other side of the intersection you'll find some 700 antique dolls, toys, and miniatures in the **Society of Memories Doll Museum** (*1115 S. 12th St. 816-233-1420. May-Sept. Tues.-Sun., Oct.-Apr. Mon.-Wed.; adm. fee*). Down the street, the **Pony Express National Memorial** (*914 Penn St. 816-279-5059. Adm. fee*) illustrates the operation of the Pony Express in the stables where the brave riders set out from April 1860 until October 1861.

Weston (*3 miles W on Mo. 273, 1 mile NW on Mo. JJ*) Sometimes called Sin City, this charming town is home to the **McCormick Distilling Company** (*1 mile SE on Mo. JJ, follow signs. 816-386-2276. Tours March-Nov.*). Established in 1856 by stagecoach king Ben Holladay, it's the nation's oldest continuously operated distillery. **Pirtle's Weston Vineyard Winery** (*502 Spring St. 816-386-5728/ 5588*), located in a historic church, offers fine local wines—and free samples. Not far away you can also try tasty local wines at the **Mission Creek Winery** (*1099 Welt St. 816-386-5770. Tours and tastings on weekends*).

Kansas City See I-70, p. 168.

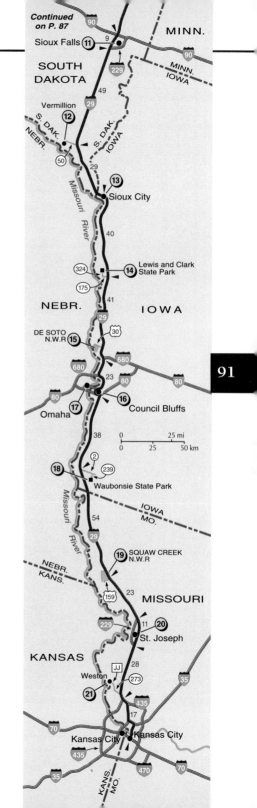

Continued on P. 87

91

CANADA
Ont.
N.Dak. Minn.
P. 93
S.Dak. Wis.
Nebr. Iowa
P. 97
Ill.
Kans. Mo.
Okla. Ark.
P. 103
Tex. La.
MEX.

Unless otherwise noted, directions are from interstate, and sites are free and generally open daily. Phone for further information.

① Duluth, MINNESOTA *(Convention and Visitors Bureau, 100 Lake Place Dr. 218-722-4011 or 800-438-5884)* Named for the French explorer Daniel de Greysolon, Sieur du Luth, who landed here in 1679, Duluth—with its 49 miles of docks—is a thriving inland port on the western tip of Lake Superior.

The Army Corps of Engineers' **Canal Park Marine Museum** *(At the end of Canal Park Dr. 218-727-2497. Closed Mon.-Thurs. in winter)* uses ship models, films, and other exhibits to tell the fascinating story of commercial shipping on the Great Lakes. Visitors can walk along the canal outside the museum and get a close-up view of giant lake carriers and foreign ships as they pass under the **Aerial Lift Bridge**, which rises 138 feet in less than a minute to let them through. A few blocks away in a renovated 1892 railroad station is the St. Louis County Heritage and Arts Center, an eclectic mix of museums that is best known as **The Depot** *(506 W. Michigan St. 218-727-8025. One admission fee for all)*. The four-level structure includes **Depot Square**, a reproduced 1910 Duluth street scene complete with storefronts, summertime trolley rides, and an ice-cream parlor; the **Lake Superior Museum of Transportation's** excellent collection of historic railroad cars and memorabilia; the **Duluth Children's Museum**; the **St. Louis County Historical Society,** which tells the story of northern Minnesota's European and Native American history; and the **Duluth Art Institute,** with its wide variety of fine art. On the shore of Lake Superior, **Glensheen** *(3300 London Rd. 218-724-8864. Reservations recommended; admission fee)* is a stately 39-room Jacobean-style mansion, completed in 1908, with formal gardens and a carriage house.

Polar bears, penguins, and other Arctic and Antarctic animals can be found at the **Lake Superior Zoo** *(Grand Ave. at 72nd Ave. W. 218-624-1502. Adm. fee)*. The Children's Zoo has a petting area. And not to be missed is the **Skyline Parkway** *(Spirit Mountain exit)*, a 16-mile drive that offers spectacular views from 600-foot bluffs. Also on the parkway is the five-story octagonal **Enger Tower**, which is set in a lovely wooded park.

Jay Cooke State Park, Minnesota, 5 miles east on Minn. 210

② Moose Lake State Park *(0.25 mile E on Rte. 137. 218-485-4059)* offers a beautiful respite to any road-weary traveler. Echo Lake is stocked with fish and is great for swimming, and the surrounding forests are laced with hiking trails that bring visitors close to the wide variety of wildlife found here. Camping and picnic sites are also available. *Adm. fee.*

Banning State Park *(0.5 mile E on Minn. 23 to Visitor Center. 612-245-2668)* Within its forested boundaries are the rapid-filled Kettle River, a state wild and scenic river popular with canoeists and kayakers. Hiking trails above the 40-foot cliffs offer fine views of the river below and also lead to the ruins of a 19th-century sandstone quarry that once employed 500 stonecutters. *Admission fee.*

North West Company Fur Post *(2 miles W of Pine City on Rte. 7. 612-629-6356)* Located on the original site, this entirely reconstructed 1804 trading post comes complete with period furnishings and costumed tour guides who demonstrate frontier survival techniques and describe the harsh living conditions endured by the traders at their winter post. *May-Labor Day Tues.-Sun.*

Taylors Falls *(27 miles E on US 8)* Once an important lumbering center, this quaint town is situated on the edge of a rugged gorge overlooking the St. Croix River. Today, it is home to 293-acre **Interstate State Park** *(Directly across US 8 from downtown. 612-465-0516)*, established in 1895 and one of the oldest state parks in the country, with more than 200 glacial potholes of various sizes. Exhibits at the Visitor Center explain the geology of the area and the history of the local lumber industry. *Visitor Center open Memorial Day-Labor Day; adm. fee.*

In town, the **W.H.C. Folsom House** *(120 Government St. 612-465-3125)* combines both federal and Greek Revival styles popular with many of the New Englanders who settled here. The 1855 house, originally owned by businessman and state senator W.H.C. Folsom, is now open for tours. *Memorial Day–mid-Oct.; admission fee.*

Minnesota bull moose

Continued on P. 97

93

❻ Minneapolis

Spoonbridge and Cherry, Minneapolis Sculpture Garden

After the War of 1812, the U.S. established a chain of forts to protect its interests on the Northwest frontier. In 1819, the military arrived at the junction of the Mississippi and Minnesota Rivers and started construction of Fort Snelling. Soldiers built a sawmill and gristmill at nearby St. Anthony Falls, and the settlement expanded from there. Today, Minneapolis has grown into the major processing and distribution center for America's farms and dairies, as well as the cultural capital of the upper Midwest (Information Center in the City Center Mall. 612-348-2453).

Historic Fort Snelling (Fort Rd. at Minn. 5 and 55. 612-725-2413. May-Oct.; adm. fee) has been restored to its original 1820s appearance; guides dressed in costumes demonstrate various aspects of life on the frontier in the early 19th century. Also on the grounds is the Fort Snelling History Center (May-Oct. and weekdays in winter), with more information about the fort's history. Just north of the fort is *Minnehaha Park* (Minnehaha Pkwy. and Minnehaha Ave. 612-348-8942. Closed Oct.-March), site of the beautiful Minnehaha Falls, immortalized in

Minnehaha Falls

Longfellow's epic poem, *Song of Hiawatha*. Northwest of the quiet park are the bustling streets of downtown, an area of many cultural landmarks. The *Hennepin History Museum* (2303 Third Ave. S. 612-870-1329. Closed Mon.; adm. fee) uses assorted historical material to tell the history of Hennepin County and the city of Minneapolis. Nearby, the *Minneapolis Institute of Arts* (2400 Third Ave. S. 612-

Historic Fort Snelling

870-3131. Closed Mon.) has more than 80,000 art objects ranging from Roman sculpture and European painting to textiles and photography. A few blocks away, *The American Swedish Institute* (2600 Park Ave. 612-871-4907. Closed Mon.; adm. fee), in a medieval-style mansion, houses social and cultural artifacts that recount the Swedish experience in America. The *Upper St. Anthony Falls Lock and Dam* (Foot of Portland Ave. 612-332-3660. April-Nov.) has a small Visitor Center and an observation deck with good views of the falls and the upper lock of the Mississippi River.

St. Paul

Como Park Conservatory Sunken Garden

Like its neighbor Minneapolis, Minnesota's capital city has much to offer visitors (Conv. and Visitors Bureau, 55 E. Fifth St. 612-297-6985 or 800-627-6101). Two large domed buildings, one devoted to government and the other to religion, dominate the skyline. More than 20 varieties of marble went into building the **State Capitol** (Cedar and Aurora Sts. 612-297-3521. Tours), and it features one of the largest self-supported domes in the world. The **Cathedral of St. Paul** (239 Selby Ave. 612-228-1766), styled after St. Peter's Basilica in Vatican City, has beautiful stained-glass windows and a 175-foot-high dome. A half block west is the stately **James J. Hill House** (240 Summit Ave. 612-297-2555. Closed Sun.-Tues.; adm. fee), a red sandstone edifice that was completed in 1891 for the founder

Science Museum of Minnesota

of the Great Northern Railway. Two excellent museums can be found downtown. The **Minnesota History Center** (345 Kellogg Boulevard W. 612-296-6126. Closed Mon.) innovatively explores the history of the state. A few blocks away is the **Science Museum of Minnesota** (30 E. 10th St. 612-221-9488. Adm. fee), where anthropology, biology, geography, paleontology, and technology are intriguingly presented; it also has an Omnitheater. Northwest of downtown is **Como Park** (612-266-6400), oasis and home of **Como Zoo** (Midway Pkwy. and Kaufman Dr. 612-488-5571), a small zoo with a large selection of animals, including bison, polar bears, Siberian tigers, penguins, and gorillas. Next to the zoo is the **Como Conservatory** (612-489-1740. Admission fee), with plants from many parts of the world.

95

Northfield (7 miles E on Minn. 19) Founded in 1855 on the banks of the Cannon River, the town's streets were bustling with shoppers and businessmen on the afternoon of September 7, 1876, when Jesse James and his gang rode in to rob the First National Bank. Shots rang out and Joseph Lee Heywood, the acting cashier, was killed when he refused to open the safe. With the raid thwarted, the gang rode out of town on what is now called the Outlaw Trail. The Northfield Historical Society's **Bank Museum** (408 Division St. 507-645-9268) is in the original bank and is furnished as it was during the attempted robbery. Exhibits offer more information about the event. Closed Mon.; adm. fee.

Faribault The **Alexander Faribault House** (12 N.E. 1st Ave. 507-334-7913. May-Oct.; adm. fee) was built in 1853 by the local fur trader and town founder and has now been restored and decorated with period furniture. The **Rice County Historical Museum** (1814 N.W. 2nd Ave. 507-332-2121. Closed weekends Nov.-

Iowa pig farmer

The triangle of land between the Mississippi and Missouri Rivers was still a cartographic unknown in 1836, when Frenchman *Joseph Nicollet,* astronomer and mathematician, set out to map it. He crisscrossed the vast prairies, making more than 90,000 mathematical calculations including longitudes, latitudes, and elevations. The detailed map he completed in 1840, the only source of Indian names of landscape features in the region, became the basis for further western exploration.

96

Memorial to Buddy Holly, Clear Lake, Iowa

May) introduces visitors to local history with slide and video presentations and exhibits of Indian and turn-of-the-century artifacts. On the outskirts of town is the 646-acre **River Bend Nature Center** (*E on Division St., follow signs. 507-332-7151*). With the purpose of "impacting lives with nature," this area is woven with hiking trails through forest, prairie, wetland, and riverbank.

⑩ **O w a t o n n a** boasts **The Village of Yesteryear** (*1448 Austin Rd. 507-451-1420. May-Sept.; adm. fee*), an assemblage of 19th- and early 20th-century buildings including two log cabins, a church, a railroad station, a firehouse, and an 1869 mansion. Most buildings are filled with period artifacts. **Rice Lake State Park** (*7 miles E of town on Rte. 19. 507-451-7406. Adm. fee*) contains remnants of the vast oak savanna that once covered this part of the state and has mostly disappeared due to farming and development. The park's 5 miles of hiking trails take you through a variety of habitats.

⑪ **A l b e r t   L e a** In 1855, a dam was constructed here to power a mill, creating Fountain Lake; the city developed around it. The **Freeborn County Museum and Historical Village** (*1031 Bridge Ave. 507-373-8003. April–mid-Dec. Tues-Sun.; adm. fee*) retains the past via a collection of fourteen 19th-century buildings and numerous artifacts. The museum features a period kitchen and living room, musical instruments, and a doll collection. Drivers on I-35 zoom right over Albert Lea Lake, site of **Myre-Big Island State Park** (*1 mile SE on Rtes. 46 and 38, follow signs. 507-373-5084. Adm. fee*). Evidence of early man in this area dates back 9,000 years, and the interpretive center on Big Island displays one of the state's largest prehistoric artifact collections. Camping, hiking, and fishing.

⑫ **C l e a r   L a k e ,   I O W A** This is the home of the **Surf Ballroom** (*460 N. Shore Dr. 515-357-6151. Closed Tues., Sun.*), the site in 1959 of the last performance by Buddy Holly, the Big Bopper, and Ritchie Valens. The plane carrying the performers crashed the next morning—now known as "The Day the Music Died." The ballroom is filled with rock-and-roll pictures and memorabilia.

⑬ **M a s o n   C i t y** (*8 miles E on US 18*) The **Stockman House** (*530 1st St. N.E. 515-423-1923. Mem. Day-Labor Day Thurs.-Sun., and Sept.-Oct. weekends; adm. fee*), designed by Frank Lloyd Wright in 1908, is Iowa's only prairie school-style house. Built to reflect the natural beauty of the prairie, it features an open floor plan, a central fireplace, and overhanging eaves. One of the country's largest collections of restored old-time trucks can be admired at **Van Horn's Antique Truck Museum** (*3 miles N of town on US 65. 515-423-0550. June-Sept.; adm. fee*). It includes a 1920 GMC circus truck, a 1918 Pierce Arrow whiskey truck, and a 1908 carpet cleaning truck. The **Kinney Pioneer Museum** (*1 mile E of I-35 on US 18. 515-423-1258. May-Sept.; closed Mon.-Tues., Sat.; adm. fee*) has an original horse-drawn dairy wagon, an early dentist's office, a 1912 blacksmith shop, and a broom factory.

Beeds Lake State Park (*11 miles E on Iowa 3. 515-456-2047*) is a wonderful place to stop. The water cascading over the 40-foot-high spillway creates a restful atmosphere. Picnicking, swimming, fishing, boating, and camping are all offered. *Camping fee.*

Ames One of the oldest land-grant institutions in the country, **Iowa State University** was founded here in 1858. The **Farm House Museum** (*Knoll Rd. 515-294-3342. April-Dec. Tues., Thurs., Sun. p.m.*), the first building constructed on campus, has been restored and furnished to reflect the 1860-1910 period. The beautifully landscaped campus is also known for its Christian Petersen sculptures and Grant Wood murals. Walking tour brochures are available at **University Museums** (*290 Scheman Bldg. 515-294-3342*).

Des Moines See I-80, p. 229.

Indianola (*13 miles E on Iowa 92*) The **National Balloon Museum** (*1601 N. Jefferson. 515-961-3714*) is filled with artifacts and memorabilia relating to both hot air and gas ballooning. Fascinating exhibits chronicle more than 200 years of ballooning history.

Winterset (*13 miles W on Iowa 92*) has at least two claims to fame. It is the town where Marion Morrison, a.k.a. John Wayne, was born. Two rooms at the **Birthplace of John Wayne** (*224 S. 2nd St. 515-462-1044. Adm. fee*) have been restored to look as they did in 1907, the actor's birth year. Other rooms display photos and movie memorabilia, including the eye patch Wayne wore in *True Grit.* Also of interest are the famous (thanks to Robert Waller's novel) and scenic **Covered Bridges** of Madison County. Contact the

John Wayne birthplace, Winterset, Iowa

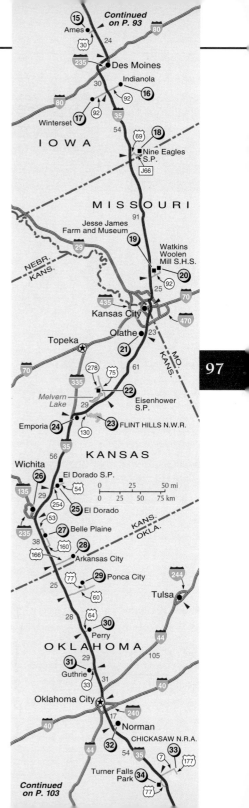

Continued on P. 93

97

Continued on P. 103

Bridge in Madison County, Iowa

Madison County Chamber of Commerce *(515-462-1185)* for more information about the bridges.

⑱ Nine Eagles State Park *(4 miles E on US 69, 5.5 miles S on Rte. J66. 515-442-2855)* Among rugged wooded hills and valleys, this park is packed with oak trees, some as old as 300 years. White-tailed deer and wild turkeys can be seen morning and evening. A 60-acre lake offers fishing, boating, and swimming. Camping available for a fee.

☞ Born in western Missouri in 1847, *Jesse James* became one of the most notorious outlaws of the Wild West. He started his career during the Civil War when, at age 15, he joined a group of pro-Confederate guerrillas. After the war, Jesse and his brother Frank assembled several men who successfully robbed numerous banks and trains. The gang finally broke up in 1876 after a failed bank robbery in Northfield, Minnesota. Six years later, Jesse James was killed by a fellow gang member—out to collect a reward.

98

⑲ Jesse James Farm and Museum, MISSOURI *(2 miles E on Mo. 92, then 2 miles N on Jesse James Farm Rd. 816-635-6065)* Visitors can tour the authentically restored birthplace and family home of the notorious Jesse James. The museum, which has the largest collection of James family artifacts in the country, tells the story of both Jesse and his brother Frank. *Adm. fee.*

⑳ Watkins Woolen Mill State Historic Site *(6 miles E on Mo. 92, follow signs. 816-296-3357)* This fully equipped 19th-century textile mill, the only one left in the country, was the centerpiece of Waltus Watkins's Bethany Plantation. Visitors can tour the mill, as well as Watkins's 1850 home, a smokehouse, and other historic buildings. **Watkins Mill State Park** adjoins the site and offers fishing, swimming, bicycling, and camping. *Adm. fee to historic site.*

Kansas City See I-70 p. 168.

㉑ Olathe, KANSAS At the **Prairie Center** *(26325 W. 135th St. 913-856-8832)*, a preserved tallgrass prairie of 300 acres lush with wildflowers and native grasses, trails wind through primitive campsites by fishing ponds and a 5-acre lake. *Camping fee.*

㉒ Eisenhower State Park *(10 miles NW via US 75 and Kans. 278. 913-528-4102 for park or 913-549-3318 for lake)* The 1,800-acre park on Melvern Lake abuts 23,000 acres of federal land managed by the Army Corps of Engineers. The whole comprises a vast and beautiful place to camp, hike, swim, or picnic. An abundant bird population includes large flocks of prairie chickens. *Day-use and camping fees.*

㉓ Flint Hills National Wildlife Refuge *(8 miles S on Kans. 130. 316-392-5553)* This 18,500-acre waterfowl refuge around John Redmond Reservoir has well-kept facilities for boating, fishing, and picnicking. Located in the middle of the vast central flyway, the refuge attracts as many as 100,000 migratory ducks and 70,000 geese, including snow and blue geese, accompanied by dozens of predaceous bald eagles. White pelicans also stop by. Nature trails.

Emporia Founded in 1857, Emporia gained fame in the 1920s as the home of William Allen White ("the sage of Emporia"), colorful and distinguished editor and publisher of the *Emporia Gazette,* one of the country's most notable small newspapers. The **Emporia Gazette** *(517 Merchant St. 316-342-4800),* still published six days a week, preserves the original newspaper building and exhibits White memorabilia.

Flint Hills National Wildlife Refuge, Kansas

El Dorado On the edge of the Flint Hills, El Dorado is an 1860 oil boom town whose heritage is preserved in the **Kansas Oil Museum** *(383 E. Central. 316-321-9333. Daily p.m. only).* Its full-size outdoor exhibits include a 100-foot steel derrick and cable-tool drilling rig and a Kansas Oil Hall of Fame, with exhibits on oil-men W. G. Skelly, Alf Landon, and Fred Koch, among others.

El Dorado State Park *(3 miles E on US 54 to Bluestem Rd., then left 1.5 mile to Visitor Center. 316-321-7180)* has almost 8,000 acres of park and refuge land, mostly open prairie grassland, surrounding 8,000-acre El Dorado Lake. Opened in 1983, the well-tended park offers excellent camping (more than 1,000 campsites), swimming, picnicking, and nature trails. *Day-use and camping fees.*

㉖ Wichita

Old Cowtown Museum

The largest city in Kansas, with a population of 300,000, Wichita was established in the late 19th century as a cattle center, and it has since prospered with the growth of its wheat and aviation industries. Boeing, Cessna, and Lear all operate facilities here (Conv. & Visitors Bureau, 100 S. Main St. Suite 100. 316-265-2800).

In the pleasant downtown, the Little Arkansas River runs into the Arkansas River, forming a peninsula for "Museums on the River," a network of four museums linked by a continuous trolley on summer Saturdays. The *Wichita Art Museum* (619 Stackman Dr. 316-268-4921. Closed Mon.) has an extensive collection of American masterpieces. The *Indian Center Museum* (650 N. Seneca. 316-262-5221. Adm. fee) displays only Native American artists in its arrowhead-shaped building. Its permanent collection includes the 44-foot-tall "Keeper of the Plains" by sculptor Blackbear Bosin. The Gallery of Indian Nations is a 500-seat atrium auditorium, displaying the flags of 250 Indian nations. A beautiful and tranquil garden, *Botanica* (701 Amidon. 316-264-0448. Closed weekends Jan.-Mar.; no adm. fee in winter) has both exotic plants and native prairie wildflowers and tallgrasses. The *Old Cowtown Museum* (1871 Sim Park Dr. 316-264-0671. Closed weekdays Nov.-Feb.; adm. fee) re-creates frontier Wichita, with historic buildings, 1870s cooking demonstrations, and reenactments of such special events as the Fourth of July.

The *Sedgwick County Zoo* (5555 Zoo Blvd. 316-942-2212. Adm. fee) claims to be Kansas' biggest visitor attraction. Some 1,300 members of 300 species live in near-native habitats on 212 acres. The zoo includes an impressive North American prairie exhibit with bison, prairie dogs, American elk, and soft-shell turtles that feed in the zoo's river.

Pioneer Woman Statue, Ponca City, Oklahoma

100

Traveling through north Texas, Oklahoma, and Kansas, especially in spring and early summer, you might chance to see an awesome natural phenomenon that meteorologists call a "supercell." These giant rotating thunderstorms can be 20 miles in diameter and extend more than 10 miles into the atmosphere. They sometimes reach the ground with deadly tornadoes that can destroy cars and buildings like paper toys. Common down a band along I-35 known as *Tornado Alley*, you can sometimes see them from 100 miles away.

(27) **Belle Plaine**   The **Bartlett Arboretum** (*301 N. Line St. 316-488-3451*) is a beautiful, 20-acre garden woven with interesting trails and footbridges over a lake. Some 30,000 tulips bring the park to blazing beauty in April, and a late October mums show attracts hundreds of visitors. *Closed mid-Nov.–March; adm. fee.*

(28) **Arkansas City**   (*17 miles E on US 166*) This is the place where 30,000 land seekers registered to run for a piece of Oklahoma land in the Cherokee Strip Land Rush of 1893. The 6.5 million acres were awarded to the swiftest in "the largest race in world history." The **Cherokee Strip Land Rush Museum** (*US 77 1 mile S of town. 316-442-6750*) commemorates the event in more than 21,000 artifacts, pictures, documents, and manuscripts. *Closed Mon.; adm. fee.*

(29) **Ponca City, OKLAHOMA**   (*16 miles E on US 60, then N on US 77*) A Conoco Oil Co. refinery dominates the economy here. The town's historical interest is tied to the colorful oilman and reform governor E. W. Marland (1894-1941). Marland lost his wealth, but its memory lives on in the opulent **Marland Mansion and Estate** (*901 Monument Rd. 405-767-0420 or 800-532-7559. Adm. fee*). Built between 1925 and 1928 and known as the "Palace on the Prairie," the $5.5-million, 43,000-square-foot house has a leather-lined elevator and 12 bathrooms. The **Pioneer Woman Statue and Museum** (*701 Monument Rd. at US 77. 405-765-6108. Closed Mon.; donation requested*) was Marland's tribute to the women who helped settle the West. The **Ponca City Cultural Center and Museums** (*1000 E. Grand Ave. 405-767-0427. Closed Tues.; adm. fee*) is another legacy of Marland, who lived in this restored 22-room house before building the bigger mansion. Its Indian Museum exhibits a scalp and Geronimo's moccasins. The colorful history of the 101 Ranch road show, which starred the likes of Will Rogers and Bill Pickett, is depicted in the former game room.

(30) **Perry**   Founded in 1893, this farming community is home to the **Cherokee Strip Museum** (*2617 W. Fir St. 405-336-2405*), which depicts the history of the land rush. Cherokees, who owned the land in the area, later sold it to the federal government, triggering the land rush. The museum—more extensive than the museum at Arkansas City—displays area Indian and pioneer artifacts. On the grounds are an 1895 schoolhouse and an excellent display of pioneer farm implements. *Closed Mon.*

(31) **Guthrie**   Founded in 1889, Guthrie was the capital of Oklahoma from 1907 until one night in 1910 when champions of Oklahoma City reportedly absconded with the state seal, thus moving the capital. Guthrie declined rapidly, but in the 1980s citizens restored the downtown. Continuous **trolley tours** (*223 S. First. 405-282-6000. Adm. fee*) explain "Historic Guthrie," a quaint and enjoyable experience. The **Oklahoma Territorial Museum** (*406 E. Oklahoma Ave. 405-282-1889. Closed Mon.*) exhibits the area's colorful history, such as an early Guthrie saloon targeted by temperance crusader Carry Nation. The **State Capital Publishing Museum** (*301 W. Harrison. 405-282-4123. Closed Mon. and last two weeks of Jan.*) claims to be the nation's largest and most complete newspaper museum. It is in the office of the old *Oklahoma Capital,* which folded after the state capital was stolen away.

Oklahoma City   See I-40, p. 111.

Norman   Home of the University of Oklahoma, this town is fast becoming a suburb of Oklahoma City. The university operates the **Oklahoma Museum of Natural History** (*1335 Asp Ave. 405-325-4711*), with sophisticated exhibits on vertebrate paleontology and prehistoric Indian cultures. *Closed Mon.*

Thunderstorm along Tornado Alley in Oklahoma

Chickasaw National Recreation Area (*14 miles E on Okla. 7, US 177 into park. 405-622-3165*) The Chickasaw tribe that lived in the area in the 1800s believed the mineral springs here to be medicinal. To prevent commercial development, the tribe deeded the land to what is now the National Park Service. It's a naturalist's paradise, with roadrunners, prickly pear cactus, and wild turkeys. Rangers lecture and guide nature walks. Campsites are available, and lakes and streams offer places to wade and swim. *Camping fee.*

101

Turner Falls Park (*1 mile from S. Davis exit on US 77, follow signs. 405-369-2917. Adm. fee*) Operated by the city of Davis, this is a commercial swimming hole beneath a beautiful mountain waterfall.

Lake Murray State Park (*Just E on US 70. 405-223-6600*) Surrounding Lake Murray with mixed meadows and scrub oak forest, the park offers all manner of recreation, from solitary hiking trails and secluded swimming to highly organized activities such as night horseback rides. Campsites and cabins available.

Gainesville, TEXAS   Established as a way point on the California Trail during the gold rush, Gainesville is still a transportation hub. The **Morton Museum of Cooke County** (*210 S. Dixon. 817-668-8900. Closed Sun.-Mon.*) has more to offer than most small community museums, but it's still primarily a one-room display of artifacts donated by townsfolk. Two local historical organizations published an interesting walking tour of the town, which is available from the **Chamber of Commerce** (*101 S. Culberson St. 817-665-2831*).

Fort Worth   See I-20, p. 62.

Dallas   See I-20, p. 63.

Turner Falls Park, Oklahoma

37 Lake Whitney State Park *(17 miles W on Tex. 22 to Rte. 933 in Whitney, then 3 miles SW on Rte. 1244. 817-694-3793)* Meadows and scattered groves of post oak and live oak ring the shores of the state's fourth largest lake. The park offers camping and water sports; it can be crowded in summer. *Day-use and camping fees.*

38 Waco   Established as a Texas Ranger outpost in 1837, Waco came to be known as "Six-Shooter Junction," as ranchers and cattlemen began driving cattle north through the area on the Chisholm Trail after the Civil War. The town grew in importance in 1870 when a majestic suspension bridge was built across the Brazos River. At the turn of the century, cotton barons from the South moved in, tempering the town's rough ways. This strange mix of Old South–Old West still is present today. Waco is striving to become an important way point on I-35's heavily traveled tourist trail to San Antonio. Most touted of its attractions is the **Texas Ranger Museum** *(Follow signs from University Parks Dr. exit. 817-750-5986. Adm. fee),* whose memorabilia includes badges, chaps, and Colt 45s—the pistols the rangers made famous. A repository of Texas history is the **Strecker Museum** *(4th and Speight, in the basement of the Sid Richardson Bldg. 817-755-1110. Closed Mon.)* at Baylor University. It has an extensive collection of archaeological artifacts from central Texas and many exhibits on local prehistoric culture. The museum also runs the **Gov. Bill and Vara Daniel Historic Village** *(University Parks Dr. 2 blocks E of I-35. 817-755-1160. Closed Mon.; adm. fee),* an 1890s Texas river town, created with relocated buildings and offering tours and lectures. Besides driving and walking tours, Waco has a 45-minute **mule-drawn wagon tour** *(817-836-4845. Closed Sun.; adm. fee)* of historic downtown, beginning at the Ranger Museum.

39 Temple   Founded in 1881 around the railroad, Temple has a **Railroad and Pioneer Museum** *(31st and Ave. H. 817-778-6873. Closed Sun.-Mon.; adm. fee)* featuring a few locomotives and cars and a lot of memorabilia. To the west of town is **Belton Lake,** with facilities for picnicking and boating. Downstream from the dam is the **Miller Springs Natural Area** *(10 miles SW of town via Rtes. 2305 and 2271. 817-939-1829),* 266 acres of rock cliffs, running springs, canyons, and delta wetlands woven with hiking trails and historic ruins along the Leon River.

40 Salado   Scarcely a wide spot on Old US 81, adjacent to I-35, this artist community—with galleries along Main Street—has a beautiful swimming hole and picnic area called **W. A. Pace Memorial Park,** where a natural spring feeds into Salado Creek.

41 Austin *(Convention and Visitors Bureau, 201 E. 2nd St. 512-474-5171 or 800-926-2282)* The state capital and an attractive university town, Austin was settled in 1835 on bluffs overlooking the Colorado River. The river has been dammed into a string of lakes, and **Town Lake,** which threads the city, is rimmed with parkland. Near

The development of San Antonio as a major tourist destination has turned the ☞ **strip of I-35** between there and Austin into a huckster's paradise. The incessant billboard offerings range from Ralph the Swimming Pig—thought to be the strip's biggest draw—to miniature goat farms and marching chicken bands. The ads often include such words as "Fantastic" and "Enchanting." But "Weird" covers them all. Local historians say the phenomenon is rooted in the 19th century, when Harry Landa ran excursion trains to his park in New Braunfels, and began promoting the town as the "beauty spot" of Texas.

102

Texas cowboy boot

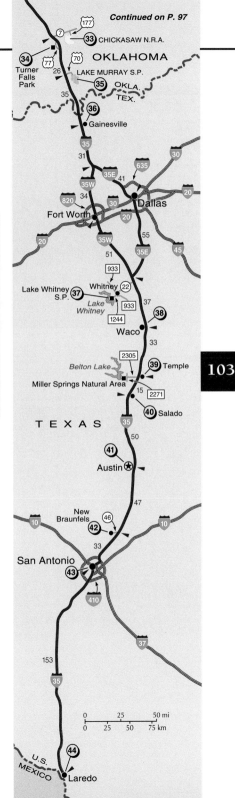

Continued on P. 97

the city center in 46 acres of landscaped grounds stands the **State Capitol** (*11th and Congress Ave. 512-463-0063. Guided tours*). Made of Texas pink granite, it is filled with state history. The main campus of the **University of Texas** (*Info 512-471-3434*) lies nearby. The university's principal museum is

...in High School prom

the **Texas Memorial Museum** (*2400 Trinity St. 512-471-1604*), with expansive exhibits on geology, paleontology, Texas history, natural history, and anthropology. Also on campus are the **Huntington Art Galleries** (*Locations at 21st and Guadalupe Sts. and 23rd and San Jacinto Sts. 512-471-7324*), with more than 9,000 works ranging from ancient to contemporary; and the **Lyndon Baines Johnson Library and Museum** (*2313 Red River St. 512-482-5279*). Exhibits detail the political and cultural agonies of the 1960s. The **Elisabet Ney Museum** (*304 E. 44th St. 512-458-2255. Closed Mon.-Tues.*) honors the work of a German sculptor who immigrated to Texas in 1872. Her statues of Sam Houston and Stephen F. Austin stand in the State Capitol and the U. S. Capitol; other works are in European palaces. Exhibits on African American history can be seen at the **George Washington Carver Museum** (*1165 Angelina St. 512-472-4809. Closed Sun.-Mon.*). For a bit of local culture, head to the **Sixth Street Historic District** (*Bet. I-35 and Congress Ave.*), a lively

103

Football game, University of Texas, Austin

downtown mix of shops, galleries, restaurants, and music clubs, many in restored 19th-century buildings. Live music—especially country, rock, and blues—echoes here and throughout the city.

㊷ New Braunfels Prince Carl of Braunfels, Germany, brought several hundred immigrants here in the 1840s, making this city the fourth largest in Texas by 1850. It's far down the list now, but volunteer efforts keep its German heritage alive. Many 19th-century buildings survive and can best be seen on a downtown walking tour, accompanied by a brochure from the **Chamber of Commerce** (*390 S. Seguin St. 210-625-2385*). The **Sophienburg Museum and Archives** (*401 W. Coll St. 210-629-1572. Adm. fee*) has an extensive collection of artifacts from the early days. The **Museum of Texas Handmade Furniture** (*N on Tex. 46, follow signs 1 mile to 1370 Church Hill Dr. 210-629-6504. Mem. Day-Labor Day closed Mon.; rest of year open weekends, p.m. only; adm. fee*) is an 1858 farmhouse with 70 pieces of 19th-century Biedermeier furniture. Adjacent is **Conservation Plaza** (*1300 Church Hill Dr. 210-629-2943. Closed Mon.; adm. fee*), a small village of 19th-century buildings—including a store, barn, and music studio—relocated from downtown. The new **Hummel Museum** (*199 Main Plaza. 210-625-5636. Adm. fee*) exhibits drawings by Sister M. I. Hummel, whose designs for figurines of cherubic German children became familiar during World War II. **Landa Park** (*Lake McQueeney exit. 210-608-2160*) is a 196-acre city park and a lovely place to swim, tube, and boat in spring water, as well as to picnic and hike. *Water activities Easter-Labor Day; fees for swimming, boat rentals.*

Ballet Austin, Texas

㊹ Laredo The streets of Laredo are safer now than they were for the cowboy memorialized in ballad, but they still offer unsavory entertainment, mostly at night and mostly south of the Rio Grande in the bustling border city of Nuevo Laredo. There, the most popular daylight attraction is **El Mercado** (*Guerrero Ave. at Calle Belden*), a traditional Mexican market district a short walk across International Bridge I. It's worth seeing even if you're not looking for the bargains it offers. Stateside, the **Laredo Children's Museum** (*Far W end of Washington St. 210-721-5321.Closed Mon.-Wed.; adm. fee*) is a safe and illuminating place for youngsters 3 to 12 years old to play and learn. An adult companion is required.

San Antonio

This festive city dates from 1718, when Spain established a mission here (later called the Alamo) to Christianize the Indians. The site remained a Spanish, then a Mexican, stronghold until the Texas revolution (Visitor Information Center, 317 Alamo Pl. 210-270-8748). Today, San Antonio is one of the state's most visited cities and home to several of its most popular attractions. An inexpensive bus line called *VIA Vistas* (210-227-2020) takes in most of the cultural high spots in two big loops that intersect at the *Alamo* (300 Alamo Plaza. 210-225-1391). Known as the "Cradle of Texas Liberty," the Alamo was the site of a 13-day siege by thousands of Mexican troops in 1836; 189 Texan volunteers died defending it. A block away is the number two attraction, *River Walk,* a modern park trail 20 feet below street level that follows the San Antonio River several miles through town. Along with trees and tropical foliage are hotels, restaurants, shops, and cafés. Riverboat taxis and cruises are available.

To the north, the *San Antonio Museum of Art* (200 W. Jones Ave. 210-978-8100. Adm. fee) specializes in the art of the Americas. The *Zoological Gardens*

The Alamo

and Aquarium (3903 N. St. Mary's St. 210-734-7183. Adm. fee) is so breathtaking in its collection of animals that it has become a bit cramped in its old limestone quarry. The lovely *Japanese Tea Gardens* (3835 N. St. Mary's St. 210-299-8480) are next door. The *San Antonio Botanical Gardens* (555 Funston Pl. 210-821-5115. Closed Mon.; adm. fee), a few bus stops away, also has wonderful gardens and a stunning conservatory. The *Witte Museum* (3801 Broadway. 210-820-2111. Adm. fee) exhibits prehistoric Texas artifacts and the state's ecology. Next door, *Pioneer Hall* (3805 Broadway. 210-822-9011. Closed Mon., also Tues. Sept.-April; adm. fee) displays Wild West memorabilia. The glitzier *Cowboy Museum* (210-229-1257. Adm. fee), back on Alamo Plaza, focuses on the same period but includes a re-created Western town. The Alamo was only one of several Spanish missions on the San Antonio River. Four others are now part of the *San Antonio Missions National Historical Park* (210-229-5701) along the Mission Trail. The VIA Vistas bus line connects them.

Mariachi player

River Walk

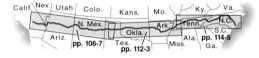

Unless otherwise noted, directions are from interstate, and sites are free and generally open daily. Phone for further information.

Barstow, CALIF. See I-15, p. 59.

(1) Providence Mountains S. R. A.
(16 miles N on Essex-Black Canyon Rd., follow signs to the Mitchell Caverns Natural Preserve. 805-942-0662) The Bonanza King, a turn-of-the-century silver mine, was located near this rugged park, part of the East Mojave National Scenic Area (see I-15, p. 58). The Visitor Center and nature trails have dramatic views of 7,170-foot Edgar Peak and the desert. *Cavern tours except mid-June–mid-Sept.; adm. fee.*

(2) Needles The road descends down the eastern slopes of the Dead Mountains into town, named for the jagged peaks to the southeast. Here, the Colorado River forms the Calif.-Ariz. border, creating an oasis of cottonwood, palm, and tamarisk trees. **Moabi Regional Park** *(Off Park Moabi Rd. 619-326-3831. Adm. fee)* offers camping and water sports.

(3) Havasu N. W. R., ARIZONA

(First exit after crossing the Colorado River, follow signs. 619-326-3853) This refuge, which extends south along the river to Lake Havasu, includes Topock Marsh, an area of bullrushes and cattails inhabited by waterfowl in winter. The best way to see 18-mile-long Topock Gorge is by a day-long canoe trip.

(4) Kingman The town's location—in a high mountain basin surrounded by three mountain ranges—has made it a crossroads for Mojave Indians, westward-headed pioneers, the railroad, and modern-day motorists. The **Mohave Museum of History and Arts** *(400 W. Beale St., next to info center. 602-753-3195. Adm. fee)* tells the story through dioramas and a mural that includes art created out of Kingman turquoise. First-hand history is found just north of town at the **wagon tracks** *(N on Grandview Ave. to Lead St., then 0.5 mile to a footbridge on right in small canyon)*, deep ruts carved by pioneer wagon wheels between 1870 and 1912 and preserved in the area's soft volcanic rock. Also outside town are several ghost towns, the legacy of mining booms in silver, gold, and minerals.

(5) Hualapai Mountain Park
(14 miles SE from Stockton Hill Rd. exit. 602-757-0915) Dominated by bizarre granite formations amid ponderosa pines and gambel oaks, the park offers views from rocky crags ranging from 6,315 to 8,240 feet high.

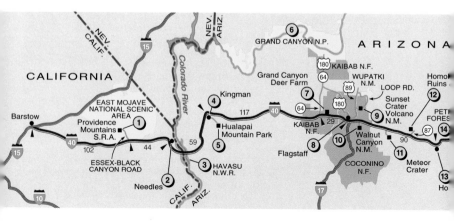

If Time Permits...

Grand Canyon National Park *(56 miles N via Ariz. 64/US 180. Visitor Center 6 miles N of south entrance. 602-638-7888)* No photograph or description will prepare you for the thrill of standing on the canyon's rim and feeling its sheer immensity. The mile-deep cleft is a geologic tour de force, a kaleidoscope of earth tones that changes with the sunlight. At the South Rim, there's a Visitor Center and Grand Canyon Village, with lodges and many chances to peer over the edge. The Bright Angel Trail descends to the canyon floor; you can hike it or ride down on a mule. *Adm. fee.*

Grand Canyon Deer Farm *(Just off I-40 at 100 Deer Farm Rd. 602-635-4073)* On this 8-acre farm you can feed the spotted, white, and black deer that run free. Behind fences are four-horned Jacob sheep, pygmy goats, a llama, a bison, and many other animals. *Adm. fee.*

Grand Canyon, as seen from Hopi Point, Arizona

107

Flagstaff   The rugged, often snowcapped San Francisco Peaks lend drama to this thriving town, enlivened by Northern Arizona University and downtown craft shops. Legend has it that a stripped ponderosa pine, used as a flagpole for the 1876 Centennial, gave the town its name. Built largely by the lumber industry, Flagstaff was dominated by the Riordan family, whose American craftsman-style mansion is open at **Riordan State Historic Park** *(1300 Riordan Ranch St. 602-779-4395. Adm. fee for tour)*. West of town is the **Lowell Observatory** *(1400 W. Mars Hill Rd. 602-774-2096. Adm. fee)*, from which the ninth planet, Pluto, was discovered in 1930. The **Museum of Northern Arizona** *(3 miles NW on US 180. 602-774-5211. Adm. fee)* has displays on Indian cultures.

Astronaut training in lunar rover, near Flagstaff, Arizona

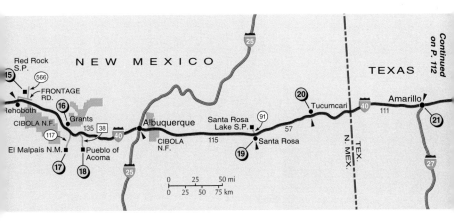

Continued on P. 112

⑨ Sunset Crater Volcano & Wupatki Natl. Mons. *(12 miles N on US 89. 602-556-7040)* Otherworldly lava fields and flanks of black ash characterize this 1,000-foot-high volcano, thought to be one of the youngest cinder-cone volcanoes in the continental U. S. Take the loop road 20 miles farther for views of Anasazi and Sinagua dwellings, dating from the 13th century. *One adm. fee for both.*

Meteor Crater, Arizona

⑩ Walnut Canyon Natl. Mon. *(3 miles S from Walnut Canyon exit. 602-556-7040)* Sinagua structures are set in the cliff face, and a 0.75-mile footpath leads to 25 of the cliff-dwelling rooms. *Adm. fee.*

⑪ Meteor Crater *(6 miles S on Meteor Crater Rd. 602-774-8350)* A multimillion-ton meteorite violently struck the surrounding plain some 50,000 years ago, creating the enormous chasm. It measures 3 miles around and is deep enough to swallow a 60-story building. NASA astronauts have used it as a training ground. *Adm. fee.*

108

☞ The **petrified forests** scattered about the deserts of northeastern Arizona look as though whole forests had been magically transformed to brilliantly colored stone. Here, about 200 million years ago—when winged pterosaurs glided over rivers filled with armored fish, and herds of dinosaurs ran nearby—forests of pinelike trees grew in a wetlands environment similar to the Everglades. Gradually, fallen trees buried under the wet sediments began petrifying, a geologic process in which the cells of organic material are replaced by quartz.

⑫ Homolovi Ruins State Park *(2 miles N, off Ariz. 87. 602-289-4106)* The Anasazi, predecessors of the Hopi, built the large pueblo buildings here between A.D. 1150 and 1400. Archaeological excavation continues, especially in June and July. *Adm. fee.*

⑬ Holbrook A motel strip, this small town lies near Navajo and Hopi Indian reservations. The **Navajo County Historical Museum** *(100 E. Arizona St. 602-524-6558),* inside the turn-of-the-century courthouse, highlights prehistoric Indian life and the rough times of pioneers. *Closed weekends; donation requested.*

⑭ Petrified Forest National Park *(Visitor Center 602-524-6228)* Here in a corner of the Painted Desert, extraordinary examples of petrified pinelike trees lie scattered among barren hills, colored gentle shades of red, gray, and orange. Scientists have identified more than 100 species of fossil animals and plants. I-40 bisects the park's two main sections. In the south are the major concentrations of petrified wood and the Rainbow Forest Museum; in the north are colorful badlands of the Painted Desert. The park also has Anasazi ruins and petroglyphs. *Adm. fee.*

⑮ Red Rock State Park, NEW MEXICO *(About 3 miles E on Frontage Rd. north of Rehoboth, then 1 mile N on N. Mex. 566. 505-863-1337)* Crowded against cliffs of weathered sandstone, this park has special summer events including rodeos and the Inter-tribal Indian Ceremonial *(Second week in August).* *Closed Sun.; donation requested.*

⑯ Grants In the 1950s, a local Navajo rancher discovered a piece of yellowish rock that turned out to be uranium

Petrified Forest National Park, Arizona

ore; scientists believe that half of America's uranium is located here. Though demand for the material has waned, the town celebrates the discovery at the **New Mexico Mining Museum** (*100 N. Iron St. 505-287-4802. Adm. fee*). Visitors can descend into a simulated uranium ore mine.

El Malpais Natl. Monument (*25 miles S on N. Mex. 117. 505-285-4641*) An immense black lava bed speaks of violent

Pueblo of Acoma, New Mexico

Apache Indians in New Mexico

volcanic activity over the past three million years. The highlights include a spectacular natural arch, large lava tubes, and a 7.5-mile nature trail along an old Pueblo Indian trade route.

Pueblo of Acoma (*14 miles S on Rte. 38. 505-252-1139*) This village atop a sheer mesa has been occupied since A.D. 1150. Buses carry visitors to the top, where the buildings are positioned and terraced to receive the winter sun. *Adm. fee*.

Albuquerque See I-25, p. 83.

Santa Rosa As early as 1540, Spaniards explored this area. Despite its semidesert location, this small town is situated near bodies of water that attract anglers and scuba divers. **Blue Hole City Park** (*E of town on Blue Hole Rd. 505-472-3404*) contains an artesian well; it's filled with crystal-blue spring water that's only 60 feet wide but more than 80 feet deep. Scuba divers are certified here. At the **Rock Lake Rearing Station** (*2 miles S of town, off River Rd. 505-472-3690*), you can feed rainbow trout year-round and walleye in March and April. **Santa Rosa Lake State Park** (*7 miles N on N. Mex. 91. 505-472-3115. Day-use and camping fees*), built on the Pecos River for flood control and irrigation, offers nature trails and fishing for bass, walleye, and catfish.

Tucumcari Now a center for trucking, this former frontier town earned the name "Six-Shooter Siding" for the numerous shootings here. Then the Canadian River was dammed for irrigation, and the place calmed down. The dusty **Tucumcari Historical Museum** (*416 S. Adams St. 505-461-4201. Closed Mon. in winter; adm. fee*) offers a look at pioneer life, with a moonshine still.

21 **Amarillo, TEXAS** (*Chamber of Commerce, 1000 S. Polk. 806-374-1497*) Once a railhead for cattle drives and later an oil and gas boomtown, this lively Western city now enjoys a tourist boom. Bidding commences every Tuesday at the **Amarillo Livestock Auction** (*100 S. Manhattan. 806-373-7464*), where some 200,000 head are sold annually. A tribute to the modern Amarillo, the **Don Harrington Discovery Center** (*Harrington Regional Medical Center, 1200 Streit Dr. 806-355-9547. Closed Mon.; adm. fee in summer only*) is a hands-on museum with planetarium. Outside is the silver, 60-foot-tall **Helium Monument**, marking Amarillo's status as the world's top helium supplier. One of Amarillo's famous landmarks is **Cadillac Ranch** (*0.5 mile W of town, S of Hope Rd. exit*), not a ranch but a piece of landscape art created in 1974 and featuring ten Cadillacs (vintage 1948 to 1964) upended grille-first into the ground.

Cadillac Ranch, Amarillo, Texas

22 **Palo Duro Canyon State Park** (*27 miles SE via I-27 and Texas 217. 806-488-2227*) You can drive down into the 1,200-foot-deep canyon, where the popular romantic musical *Texas* (*806-655-2181. Adm. fee*) plays every summer evening except Sunday. *Admission fee.*

23 **Elk City, OKLAHOMA** The Great Western Trail came within a few miles of here. Some of this history is retold at the **Elk City Old Town Museum Complex** (*US 66 and Pioneer Rd. 405-225-2207. Closed Mon.; adm. fee*), a turn-of-the-century Victorian house. One exhibit tells about the Beutler brothers, well-known producers of rodeo stock.

24 **Red Rock Canyon State Park** (*5 miles S, off US 281. 405-542-6344*) Sugar maples provide pleasant shade in the red Permian sandstone canyons, once enjoyed by Cheyenne Indians, pioneers, and forty-niners. Picnicking, hiking, camping.

25 **El Reno** When the Rock Island line was built in the late 1800s on the North Canadian River's south bank, many residents of Reno City, on the north bank, moved their town—buildings and all—across the shallow river. The **Canadian County Historical Museum** (*300 S. Grand. 405-262-5121. Closed Mon.-Tues.*) is located in the turn-of-the-century Rock Island Depot. Here you'll also find the late 1800s Darlington Indian Agency Jail and Gen. Phil Sheridan's cabin, used during the Indian Wars. If possible, visit the **Darlington Game Bird Hatchery** (*3 miles N of town on US 81, then 3 miles W on Darlington Rd. 405-262-2372. Closed Tues. March-May; no tours on weekends*) between March and June, when thousands of quail and pheasant chicks are hatched. On the grounds are mountain lions, bobcats, pheasants, foxes, coyotes, and white prairie dogs.

㉖ Oklahoma City

This city began with the firing of a cannon at sunrise on April 22, 1889, when thousands of settlers rushed across the Kansas boundary in the Great Land Run. By afternoon, a small town had replaced empty, treeless prairie. The capital city has since grown wealthy from oil and an aviation industry (Convention & Visitors Bureau, 4 Santa Fe Plaza. 405-297-8912).

In the heart of downtown, the **Oklahoma State Capitol** (Lincoln Blvd. and N.E. 23rd St. 405-521-3356. Closed weekends) sits on an active oil field. A block away is the **State Museum of History** (2100 N. Lincoln Blvd. 405-521-2491. Closed Sun.), with a rare, painted bison-hide tepee, a land-run wagon, and other artifacts. Nearby, the **Harn Homestead Museum** (313 N.E. 16th St. 405-235-4058. Closed Sun. and Mon.; adm. fee) demonstrates early pioneer life with period buildings filled with relics. Symbolic of the new Oklahoma City is **Crystal Bridge** at **Myriad Botanical Gardens** (Reno and Robinson Sts. 405-297-3995. Adm. fee). The large tube, spanning a spring-fed pond, houses 600 species of trees and other plants.

To the northeast, the giant **Kirkpatrick Center Muse-** **um Complex** (2100 N.E. 52nd St. 405-427-5461. One fee for all) houses a space museum, a hands-on science center, a planetarium, the Red Earth Indian Cen-

Myriad Botanical Gardens

ter, and more. Not far are the **National Softball Hall of Fame** (2801 N.E. 50th St. 405-424-5266. Closed weekends in winter; adm. fee) and the **Oklahoma Firefighters Museum** (2716 N.E. 50th St. 405-424-3440. Adm. fee), full of fire engines and equipment. Don't miss the **National Cowboy Hall of Fame** (1700 N.E. 63rd St. 405-478-2250. Adm. fee), with oil paintings, Remington bronzes, and John Wayne's kachina dolls and Bowie knives.

Natl. Cowboy Hall of Fame

㉗ **Shawnee** Founded during a late 19th-century land rush, the town was enriched by the discovery of oil in the 1920s. Jim Thorpe, the famed Indian athlete, was born near here in 1888. On the grounds of St. Gregory's College is the **Mabee-Gerrer Museum** (1900 W. MacArthur Dr. 405-878-5300. Closed Mon.), a fine collection from many civilizations, including Egyptian mummies.

㉘ **Wewoka** (21 miles S on Okla. 56) Located at the end of the brutal Trail of Tears— the route to Indian Territory, later Oklahoma, that southeastern Indians were forced to travel by the government in the 1830s—Wewoka was established as the capital of the Seminole Indian nation. The **Seminole Nation Museum** (524 S. Wewoka. 405-257-5580. Tues.-Sun. p.m.) commemorates Seminole heritage with displays that include a full-size chickee, a stilt house thatched with palmetto leaves.

㉙ O k m u l g e e *(14 miles N on US 62/US 75)* This was the end of the Trail of Tears for Creek Indians, who established their capital here. The impressive **Creek Council House Museum** *(Grand and 6th Sts. 918-756-2324. Closed Sun.-Mon.),* built of native stone in 1878 as the center of tribal affairs, now has exhibits on Muscogee Creek tribal history.

㉚ F o u n t a i n h e a d S t a t e P a r k *(6 miles S on Okla. 150. 918-689-5311)* The recreational park on the shores of Eufaula Lake features camping, fishing for bass and catfish, and nature trails.

㉛ S e q u o y a h N a t i o n a l W i l d l i f e R e f u g e *(3 miles S of Vian exit. 918-773-5251)* A 6-mile dirt road meanders near the confluence of the Arkansas and Canadian Rivers, past wetlands and cottonwoods. In winter, bald eagles flock, and thousands of geese and ducks inhabit the fields and wetlands. In spring and summer you might see a scissor-tailed flycatcher, the state bird.

㉜ S e q u o y a h ' s H o m e S i t e *(3 miles N of Sallisaw on US 59, then 7 miles E on Okla. 101. 918-775-2413. Closed Mon.)* Sequoyah, the Cherokee diplomat, artist, and linguist, spent the last 15 years of his life here. Rangers show the written Cherokee alphabet he devised, enabling thousands of his people to read and write.

112

Judge Parker's gavel and ink-stand, Fort Smith NHS, Fort Smith, Arkansas

㉝ F o r t S m i t h , A R K A N S A S   Perched on the Arkansas River, this border town feels more western than southern. **Miss Laura's** *(2 N. B St. 501-783-8888),* a famous turn-of-the-century bordello—the only one on the National Register of Historic Places—now houses a Visitor Center. At the **Fort Smith National Historic Site** *(3rd St. and Rogers Ave. 501-783-2861. Adm. fee),* the restored courtroom, gallows, and jail of "Hanging" Judge Parker, who strung up 79 desperadoes in the late 1800s, recall the town's frontier legacy. The excavated ruins of the original Fort Smith, built in

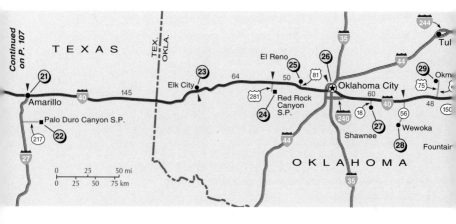

1817, are also here. Nearby, the **Old Fort Museum** (*320 Rogers Ave. 501-783-7841. Adm. fee*) has a working soda fountain, memorabilia about war hero Brig. Gen. William Darby, and early town artifacts.

Storefronts, Van Buren, Arkansas

Van Buren Replicas of gaslights line the streets of this pretty river town, restored to its 19th-century appearance, when it was a lively steamboat port and stage stop. A stroll down Main Street—filled with antique and knickknack shops—brings you to the old-est active courthouse west of the Mississippi. Board a vintage passenger car for a 3-hour tour through the rugged Boston Mountains on the **Ozark Scenic Railway** (*Departs from Old Frisco Depot, 813 Main St. 800-452-9582. Adm. fee*). Or you can cruise the Arkansas River on the riverboat ***Frontier Belle*** (*501-471-5441. April-Nov. Reserve; adm. fee*), docked at Riverfront Park.

Mountainburg (*12 miles N on US 71*) With a population of 600, Mountainburg is the largest of several mountain towns in this region of the Ozarks. Just north is **Lake Fort Smith State Park**. (*501-369-2469. Day-use fee*), in a wooded valley surrounded by thousands of acres of national forest.

Arkansas River Visitor Center (*11 miles S on Ark. 7. 501-968-5008. Closed weekends Nov.-March*) Displays here explain the development of the Arkansas River Valley, including the creation of a system of locks and dams that enables ocean-going vessels to travel upstream. Outside you can watch a ship navigate the lock, or stroll along the sandy banks of the Arkansas River at the adjacent **Old Post Road Park.**

Woodcarving, Mountainburg, Ark.

Pottsville This quiet hamlet bustled with activity in the 1800s, when streams of travelers passed through on the Butterfield

Continued on P. 114

Overland Mail route between Memphis and Fort Smith. The ante-bellum **Potts Tavern** (*Ask at the general store. 501-968-8369 or 968-6703*), once a stagecoach station and frontier home, now houses period furniture and stagecoach exhibits. *Adm. fee.*

Petit Jean State Park, Arkansas

(38) **Petit Jean Mountain** (*9 miles S on Ark. 9, then 12 miles W on Ark. 154*) This flat-topped mountain was named for a French girl who, the story goes, disguised herself as a boy so that she could accompany her sailor sweetheart to America. Here you'll find **Petit Jean State Park** (*501-727-5441. Adm. fee*), with 24 miles of trails through forests and past springs, caves, and 95-foot Cedar Falls. North of the park is **Winrock Farms** (*501-727-5421. Open for self-guided tours*), where Gov. Winthrop Rockefeller bred cattle beginning in the 1950s. Part of the property is now the non-profit **Winrock Intl. Institute for Agricultural Development** (*Visitor Center 501-727-5435*).

114

(39) **Conway**   This tree-shaded community, near the winding Arkansas River and Lake Conway, is a central gateway to the Ozarks. Downtown in Courthouse Square is the **Greathouse Home and Museum** (*501-329-6446. By appt. only*), an 1830s dogtrot house that served as an inn on the Butterfield Overland Mail route. In the 1770s, the French established a trading outpost along the Arkansas at what is now **Cadron Settlement Park** (*W on Ark. 319 to river. 501-329-2986*), with several bluff overlooks and trails. Farther south on the river is **Toad Suck Ferry Park** (*W on US 60. 501-759-2005*), with boating and fishing at the site of an early ferry crossing.

(40) **Little Rock**   (*Convention & Visitors Bureau, Markham and Main Sts. 800-844-4781*)   The state's capital and largest city, Little

Continued on P. 113

Rock still retains a small-town air. The first settlement arose on the bluffs overlooking the Arkansas River near a "little rock." Later, the town became a point along the busy Southwest Trail. A 9-mile-square area encompassing Little Rock's early boundaries has been preserved as the **Quapaw Quarter** and divided into three historic districts. Here you'll find **Riverfront Park** (*La Harpe Blvd. bet. Arch and Commerce Sts.*), containing the remains of the little rock, as well as strolling paths, plazas, and benches. The nearby **Old State House** (*300 W. Markham St. 501-324-9685*), with its stately Doric columns, served as a center of state government in the 19th century and is now a museum with historical exhibits, including one on President Clinton's campaign. The neoclassic **State Capitol** (*W. Capitol Ave. and Woodlane St. 501-682-5080*) has brass doors and Tiffany chandeliers, as well as a portrait of a youthful Bill Clinton, the state's youngest governor at 32. The **Arkansas Territorial Restoration** (*E. Third and Scott Sts. 501-324-9351. Adm. fee for tours*) features four restored buildings, including the city's oldest standing structure, the 1820s **Hinderliter Grog Shop**. Jefferson Davis once rented the **Villa Marre** (*1321 S. Scott St. 501-374-9979. Closed Sat.; adm. fee*), an elaborate Victorian southeast of downtown. Don't miss the nearby **Arkansas Museum of Science and History** (*MacArthur Park. 501-324-9231. Adm. fee*) and the Arkansas Arts Center's **Decorative Arts Museum** (*E. Seventh and Rock Sts. 501-372-4000. Donations*), an 1840s Greek Revival structure. **Central High School** (*1500 S. Park St.*), southwest of downtown, remains a symbol of the civil rights era. In 1957, President Eisenhower sent federal troops to enable nine black students to enter the all-white school.

Old State House, Little Rock, Arkansas

▶ **Scott Environs** (*6 miles SE on I-440 and US 165*) Near the small agricultural community of Scott, **Marlsgate Plantation** (*Off US 165. 501-961-1307. Tours by appt. only. Closed Sun.; adm. fee*),

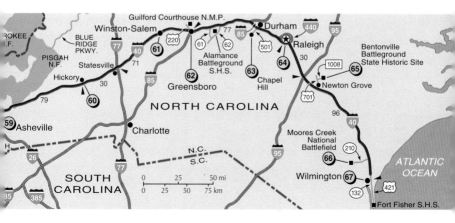

Appalachian quilting bee

116

features an antebellum mansion amid cotton fields and a quiet, cypress-edged lake. Steam tractors and other machines of Arkansas' once-thriving cotton industry are on display at the **Plantation Agriculture Museum** *(US 165 at Ark. 161. 501-961-1409. Closed Mon.; adm. fee)*. Fascinating **Toltec Mounds Archeological State Park** *(About 5 miles S of Scott, off US 165. 501-961-9442. Closed Mon.; adm. fee for tour)* contains the remains of ancient Indian earthworks, the religious and social centers of an Arkansas Indian culture known as Plum Bayou, which inhabited this site from A.D. 600 to 950.

42 **L o n o k e** This small town devoted to cotton and rice farming lies on east-central Arkansas' Grand Prairie. At the **Joe Hogan State Fish Hatchery** *(1 mile S on US 70. Visitor Center 501-676-6963)*, one of the nation's largest state-owned, warm-water fish hatcheries, you can feed catfish and see a 200-pound mounted alligator gar.

43 **L o u i s i a n a P u r c h a s e H i s t o r i c S t a t e P a r k** *(21 miles S on US 49, then 2 miles E on Ark. 362. 501-238-2188)* A 950-foot-long boardwalk stretches across a headwater swamp filled with bald cypress and tupelo trees. A granite monument marks the point from which land surveys of the Arkansas area began in 1815.

44 **V i l l a g e C r e e k S t a t e P a r k** *(13 miles N on Ark. 284. 501-238-9406)* Cherokees once lived on this ridge, a geologic formation running some 300 feet above sea level, near Village Creek. The 7,000-acre park offers hiking, fishing, and camping. *Adm. fee.*

M e m p h i s , TENNESSEE See I-55, p. 132.

45 **H a t c h i e N . W . R .** *(0.25 mile S on Tenn. 76. 901-772-0501)* A 12-mile gravel road passes through the seasonally flooded bottomlands of the refuge, which holds some of the Mississippi's last virgin swamp forest. *Bird area closed mid-Nov.–mid-March.*

46 **J a c k s o n** This town served as a busy railroad center during the Civil War. The **Casey Jones Home and Railroad Museum** *(I-40 at US 45 Bypass. 901-668-1222. Adm. fee)* honors the engineer who died in a 1900 train wreck and was immortalized in song. Artifacts fill the house, and you can climb aboard a replica of his engine. For a quiet time, visit **Cypress Grove Nature Park** *(2 miles W on US 70. 901-425-8364)*, a preserve on the Forked Deer River.

47 **P i n s o n M o u n d s S t a t e A r c h a e o l o g i c a l A r e a** *(17 miles SE of Jackson via US 45 and Tenn. 197. 901-988-5614)* Silent and mysterious, the 12 ceremonial Indian mounds here are accessible by boardwalk and trail. Museum. *Closed weekends Dec.-Feb.*

48 **N a t c h e z T r a c e S t a t e R e s o r t P a r k** *(3 miles S on Tenn. 114. 901-968-3742)* A western spur of the famous Natchez Trace once wended through the quiet forests. Today, the park con-

☞ One of the nation's most famous pioneer roads, the *Natchez Trace* describes a southwesterly path from Nashville, Tenn., 500 miles through Mississippi to the city of Natchez. In the early 1800s, rugged pioneers followed the old Indian trace, or trail, to settle the lower Mississippi Valley. Settlers moving to the Gulf area often traveled this way. Traders and preachers, bandits and cutthroats, gamblers, soldiers, and slaves added to the rich folklore of the route, now mostly preserved as the Natchez Trace Parkway.

tains old graves, miles of trails, and a huge pecan tree.

Montgomery Bell State Resort Park
(10 miles NW on Tenn. 46 to US 70, then E for 4 miles. 615-797-9052)
The wooded hills in this preserve contain the birthplace of the Cumberland Presbyterian Church and the remains of an early iron-mining operation.

㊿ Nashville

Country music and fundamentalist Christianity pervade not only the airwaves but also the soul of this capital city. Steady steamboat and railroad traffic helped make it a commercial mecca during the mid-1800s. The Union occupation early in the Civil War prevented much destruction. Today it supports a large music industry, as well as insurance, banking, and printing businesses (Conv. & Visitors Bureau, 161 Fourth Ave. N. 615-259-4700). Relatively small and easy to navigate, downtown spreads along the west bank of the Cumberland River. On the highest hill is the 1859 Greek Revival **State Capitol** (Charlotte Ave. bet. 6th and 7th. 615-741-2692). President James Polk is buried on the grounds. Nearby, the **Tennessee State Museum** (Fifth Ave. bet. Union and Deaderick Sts. 615-741-2692. Closed Mon.) is filled with reproductions and artifacts from early area history, including Davy Crockett's rifle.

At Riverfront Park is **Fort Nashborough** (170 First Ave. N. 615-862-8400. Closed Sun.-Mon.), a reconstruction of the 1780s palisaded settlement that preceded Nashville. The **Museum of Tobacco Art & History** (800 Harrison St. 615-271-2349. Closed Sun.) traces the economic and social impact of the weed through art and antiques. More recent history is housed at the **Ryman Auditorium** (116 Fifth Ave. N. 615-254-1445. Adm. fee), home of the Grand Ole Opry from 1943 to 1974 and now

Nashville star Dolly Parton

a museum. Live shows begin in June 1994.

Southwest of downtown lies **Music Row,** with many recording studios and talent agencies. The **Country Music Hall of Fame** (4 Music Square E. 615-255-5333. Adm. fee) displays Elvis's solid gold Cadillac among its memorabilia. Centerpiece of Nashville's fame is the radio show that has run since 1925, launching the careers of country music's greats. If you want to watch them sing in person, the place to go on Friday or Saturday night is the **Grand Ole Opry** (2804 Opryland Dr. 615-889-6611. Adm. fee), 10 miles northeast of downtown.

South of town, magnolias line the drive of the 1799 **Travellers Rest** (636 Farrell Pkwy. 615-832-2962. Closed Mon.; adm. fee), filled with locally crafted furniture. Not far is the Georgian **Governor's Residence** (882 S. Curtiswood Lane. 615-383-5401. Tues. and Thurs. p.m.; closed Jan.-May).

Ryman Auditorium

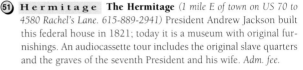

(51) Hermitage **The Hermitage** (*1 mile E of town on US 70 to 4580 Rachel's Lane. 615-889-2941*) President Andrew Jackson built this federal house in 1821; today it is a museum with original furnishings. An audiocassette tour includes the original slave quarters and the graves of the seventh President and his wife. *Adm. fee.*

The Hermitage, Hermitage, Tenn.

(52) Cedars of Lebanon State Park (*6 miles S on US 231. 615-443-2769*) The pencil industry logged the area of all its cedar during the Depression, but the WPA replanted. The result is this park, with the nation's largest remaining red cedar forest. Hiking trails.

(53) Joe L. Evins Appalachian Center for Crafts (*6 miles S on Tenn. 56. 615-597-6801. Tours June-July Mon. and Fri.*) A steep road through forest brings you to this professional crafts center. You can buy pieces at the gallery or walk around the grounds.

(54) Cumberland Mountain State Park (*6 miles S through Crossville, off US 127. 615-484-6138*) features a 50-acre lake and a stone dam and bridge that is the largest masonry structure built by the CCC. Picnicking, camping, and water sports in season.

118

(55) Oak Ridge Cloaked in secrecy, the entire town was built during World War II as part of the Manhattan Project, which led to the building of the first atom bomb and the dawn of the nuclear age. Today, high-tech companies make this a thriving city. The U. S. Department of Energy's **American Museum of Science and Energy** (*300 S. Tulane Ave. 615-576-3200*) has exhibits beginning with a top-secret uranium processing plant. See more history at the **Graphite Reactor**, the world's oldest nuclear reactor and part of the **Oak Ridge Natl. Laboratory** (*S of town on Bethel Valley Rd., 10 miles W of Tenn. 62. 615-574-4160. Phone ahead for tours. Closed Sun.*).

(56) Knoxville (*Convention and Visitors Bureau, 810 Clinch Ave. 615-523-7263*) From the observation deck of the golden **Sunsphere**, the signature structure of the 1982 World's Fair, you can see this pleasant city spreading out along the banks of the Holston and French Broad Rivers, as they join to form the Tennessee. **James White Fort** (*205 E. Hill Ave. 615-525-6514. Closed Sun. March-Dec.; Mon., Wed., Fri. only Jan.-Feb.; adm. fee*) reconstructs the area's first white settlement, built on land given to General White after his service in the Revolution. Nearby is the 1792 **Blount Mansion** (*200 West Hill Ave. 615-525-2375. Closed Mon.; adm. fee*), the residence of William Blount, governor of the Southwest Territory. Later, the state constitution was drafted here. Minutes away, the **Beck Cultural Exchange Center** (*1927 Dandridge Ave. 615-524-8461. Closed Sun. and Mon.*) celebrates the historical and cultural contributions of African Americans. Over the bridge is the **Candy Factory** (*408 10th St.*), home to craft galleries, and the **Knoxville Museum of Art** (*410 10th St. 615-525-6101. Closed Mon.*), featuring contemporary exhibits. South of downtown, the **University of Tennessee** has the **Frank**

H. McClung Museum of natural history and archaeology (*1327 Circle Park Dr. 615-974-2144*), with 315-million-year-old amphibian footprints. South across the river is **Marble Springs** (*1220 W. Gov. John Sevier Hwy. 615-573-5508. Closed Mon.; adm. fee*), home of John Sevier, who became the state's first governor in 1796. You can tour his relic-filled original cabin.

Forbidden Caverns (*18 miles SE on Tenn. 66 and US 411 through Sevierville. 615-453-5972*) A wall of onyx, underground streams, and natural chimneys characterize this cavern, inhabited 2,000 years ago by Indians and used much later for moonshine production. *April-Nov.; adm. fee.*

Great Smoky Mountains National Park, N.C.

Great Smoky Mountains National Park, TENN./NORTH CAROLINA (*From W, 22 miles S on Tenn. 66 and US 441 to Gatlinburg entrance. From E, 31 miles W on US 19 and US 441 to southern entrance near Cherokee, N.C. 615-436-1200*) Few superlatives adequately describe this preserve, one of the last true wildernesses in the East. Doused by rain, the area supports a staggering diversity of plants and animals over a wide range of elevations. Only one highway (*US 441*) crosses its half-million-acre expanse, but hundreds of miles of trails go through forests and by rock domes, streams, and waterfalls. *Adm. fee.*

Asheville A good part of the cultural life of this pretty mountain resort town is concentrated at Pack Place, which includes three small museums: the **Asheville Art Museum** (*704-253-3227. Closed Mon.; adm. fee*), featuring 20th-century art; **The Health Adventure** (*704-254-6373. Closed Mon.; adm. fee*); and the **Colburn Gem & Mineral Museum** (*704-254-7162. Closed Sun.-Mon.; adm. fee*), boasting a 376-pound hunk of aquamarine. Fans of Thomas Wolfe's work should visit his boyhood home, the **Thomas Wolfe Memorial** (*48 Spruce St. 704-253-8304. Closed Mon. Nov.-March; adm. fee*), featured in much of his writing. Asheville's other famous abode is the **Biltmore Estate** (*3 blocks N of I-40 on US 25. 704-255-1700 or 800-543-2961. Adm. fee*), George Vanderbilt's 255-room

The ***Smoky Mountains*** are among the oldest on earth. Ice Age glaciers stopped their journey south just short of these mountains, which became a junction of southern and northern flora. Here live the world's best examples of deciduous forest, more than 1,500 species of flowering plants, and a matchless variety of animals. The tangle of brush and trees forms a close-packed array of leaves that exude water and hydrocarbons, producing the filmy "smoke" that gives the mountains their name.

119

Biltmore Estate, Asheville, N.C.

mansion, completed in 1895. It's packed with fine art and treasures.

60 **Hickory**   Numerous showrooms flaunt the region's thriving furniture industry. Kids will enjoy the **Catawba Science Center** *(Arts and Science Center, 243 Third Ave. N.E. 704-322-8169. Closed Mon.),* with dioramas of local wildlife and an aquarium.

Statesville   See I-77, p. 209.

North Carolina state flag

61 **Winston-Salem**   *(Visitor Center, 601 N. Cherry St. 910-777-3796 or 800-331-7018)* Salem was settled in 1766 by German-speaking Moravians from Pennsylvania; nearby Winston was founded in 1849. With strong tobacco, textile, and furniture industries, Winston thrived, and the two towns were joined in 1913. The Moravian settlement is faithfully restored at **Old Salem** *(910-721-7300. Adm. fee),* comprising some 80 structures. Also here is the **Museum of Early Southern Decorative Arts** *(924 S. Main St. 910-721-7360. Adm. fee),* with 19 period rooms and 6 galleries. **Historic Bethabara Park** *(2147 Bethabara Rd. 910-924-8191. Exhibits closed Dec.-March)* features the 130-acre archaeological site of the Moravian settlement, including a restored 1788 church.

62 **Greensboro**   *(Visitor Info Center, 317 S. Greene St. 910-274-2282 or 800-344-2282)* Ravaged by fire in 1872, the city was rebuilt in the 1890s thanks largely to the booming textile industry. A different fire roared here in the 1960s, when African Americans started a famous sit-in at Woolworth's lunch counter. The **Greensboro Historical Museum** *(130 Summit Ave. 910-373-2043. Closed Mon.)* displays four of the counter stools. You can also walk through a reconstruction of the old town as native writer O. Henry saw it.

Northwest of town is the **Guilford Courthouse Natl. Military Park** *(6 miles NW on US 220. 910-288-1776),* where in 1781 the colonists lost a Revolutionary War battle, but inflicted so many casualties that the British withdrew. A 2.5-mile road winds through it.

Alamance Battleground S.H.S.   See I-85, p. 257.

Durham   See I-85, p. 256.

University of North Carolina, Chapel Hill

63 **Chapel Hill**   *(Welcome Center, 113 W. Franklin St. 919-929-9700)* This bustling college town, home of the **University of North Carolina**—the nation's oldest state university, chartered in 1789—has shady streets and old buildings *(Campus info 919-962-1630).* On campus is the **Morehead Planetarium** *(Chapel Hill/Durham exit, turn left and follow signs to E. Franklin St. 919-962-1236. Adm. fee for shows),* with constellation shows and science exhibits.

64 **Raleigh**   *(Conv. and Visitors Bureau, 225 Hillsborough St., Suite 400. 919-834-5900)* In 1792, commissioners selected this spot as the state capital. Today, along with Chapel Hill and Durham, Raleigh

Bell tower, N. C. State University, Raleigh

is one point of the "Research Triangle," a large center for industrial and governmental research.

The modest **State Capitol** (*Wilmington and Morgan Sts. at Union Sq. 919-733-4994*) looks as it did in the 1840s. Nearby at Bicentennial Plaza is the **North Carolina State Museum of Natural Sciences** (*919-733-7450*), with locally mined gems and a poisonous snake display. **Mordecai Historic Park** (*1 Mimosa St. 919-834-4844. Adm. fee*), to the north, contains a 1785 plantation house where five generations of a family lived. On the grounds is the tiny birthplace of 17th President Andrew Johnson. Outside the Beltline, the **North Carolina Museum of Art** (*2110 Blue Ridge Rd., off Wade Ave. exit. 919-839-6262. Closed Mon.*) has a collection that spans 5,000 years.

Bentonville Battleground S. H. S. (*2.5 miles N of Newton Grove, right on Rte. 1008 for 2.5 miles. 910-594-0789*) Here in 1865, Sherman's Union troops defeated Johnston's Confederates in the state's bloodiest land battle. A trail takes you to see breastworks and a house that was once a hospital. *Closed Mon. in winter.*

Moores Creek Natl. Battlefield (*15 miles W on N.C. 210. 910-283-5591*) In the swampy forests and thickets along this coastal creek, independence-minded colonists fought Tory sympathizers, winning a victory against the British early in the Revolutionary War. Two interpretive trails wind through the park.

Wilmington (*Conv. and Visitors Bureau, 24 N. Third St. 910-341-4030 or 800-222-4757*) A deepwater port on the Cape Fear River, Wilmington was incorporated in 1739. The center of Stamp Act resistance before the Revolutionary War, it was a coastal bastion of the Confederacy. Now the waterfront has been renovated and the large **Historic District** spruced up. The **Burgwin-Wright House** (*224 Market St. 910-762-0570. Closed Sun.-Mon.; adm. fee*) served as British headquarters during the occupation. Just across Cape Fear Memorial Bridge is the **U.S.S. *North Carolina* Battleship Memorial** (*Off US 421. 910-251-5797. Adm. fee*). The ship earned 15 World War II battle stars and now houses a museum. Not far to the south at the **Brunswick Town State Historic Site** (*N.C. 133 and Plantation Rd. 910-371-6613. Closed Mon. in winter*), you can see the remains of a thriving port town abandoned during the Revolution. Farther south are beach resorts and **Fort Fisher State Historic Site** (*20 miles S of town on US 421. 910-458-5538. Closed Mon. in winter*), a much-besieged Civil War fort.

U.S.S. *North Carolina*, Wilmington, N.C.

Unless otherwise noted, directions are from interstate, and sites are free and generally open daily. Phone for further information.

(1) Wichita Falls, TEXAS   Allegedly won in a New Orleans poker game, the town was settled in the 1870s and has been a distribution center for this farming region ever since. The best attraction is the **Kell House Museum** (*900 Bluff St. 817-723-0623. Closed Mon. and Sat.; adm. fee*), the elegant 1909 residence of a city father. You can pick up a driving-tour map of other historic buildings here. The **Museum and Art Center** (*2 Eureka Cir. 817-692-0923. Closed Mon.; adm. fee*) offers a modest children's science museum and a state-of-the-art planetarium. A new **Railroad Museum** (*8th St. and the tracks. 817-723-2331. Call for hours.*) has 13 cars and is growing.

(2) Lawton, OKLAHOMA   The fourth largest city in the state, Lawton is a dusty military town, newer than the Army post it serves. **Fort Sill** (*Exit into main gate. 405-351-5123*) was founded in 1869 during a campaign against the South Plains Indians. Today, Army artillery are trained on the 94,000-acre range. The fort's museum, a 21-building complex, includes the guardhouse where the Apache renegade Geronimo was jailed. He's buried in a cemetery nearby. The most impressive exhibit is **Cannon Walk,** an outdoor display of artillery pieces, including the 280-mm "Atomic Annie" that fired the first nuclear shell in 1953. Also available for visitor inspection is the **Old Post Headquarters,** built in 1870.

(3) Wichita Mountains Wildlife Refuge (*6 miles W on Okla. 49. 405-429-3222*) The sprawling 59,020-acre refuge has bison, longhorn cattle, elk, and deer roaming the rolling prairie. In certain areas, visitors in cars can get close to the animals.

122

Wichita Mountains Wildlife Refuge, Oklahoma

Anadarko (*From N, 19 miles W on US 62; from S, 32 miles N on US 62*) Founded in 1901, Anadarko justifiably calls itself the "Indian Capital of America." **Indian City USA** (*2 miles S of town on Okla. 8. 405-247-5661. Adm. fee*) is an 80-acre collection of historical and cultural exhibits. A serious effort to preserve Indian culture, it's also fun. Several re-created villages and encampments invite you to contrast lifestyles among the Navajo, Apache, Wichita, Caddo, and Pawnee tribes. A 45-minute tour includes ritual dances. The **National Hall of Fame for Famous American Indians** (*US 62 E of town. 405-247-5555*) is a museum and park. Among the exhibits are 37 statues of figures such as Geronimo, Pontiac, and Jim Thorpe.

Indian City USA, Anadarko, Oklahoma

Oklahoma City   See I-40, p. 111.

Chandler   The **Lincoln County Historical Society Museum of Pioneer History** (*717-719 Manvel Ave. 405-258-2425*) works to preserve the history of western pioneer life and of "America's Main Street," the famous Route 66. *Closed Sun.*

Tulsa (*Visitor Center, 616 Boston Ave. 918-585-1201*) Oklahoma's second largest city, Tulsa is one of the few oil boom towns that continued to prosper after the rush in 1901. It now calls itself the "Oil Capital of the World." Among the country's finest museums of the American West, the **Gilcrease Museum** (*1400 Gilcrease Museum Rd. 918-596-2700. Donations*) has more than 10,000 paintings, including works by Frederic Remington, Charles M. Russell, and George Catlin, and over 50,000 Indian artifacts. The gallery of battlefield pictures fascinates young people. The **Philbrook Museum of Art** (*2727 S. Rockford Rd. 918-749-7941 or 800-324-7941. Closed Mon.; adm. fee*) is housed in the 90,000-square-foot home of the late oilman Waite Phillips on beautifully landscaped grounds.

Oral Roberts University, Tulsa, Okla.

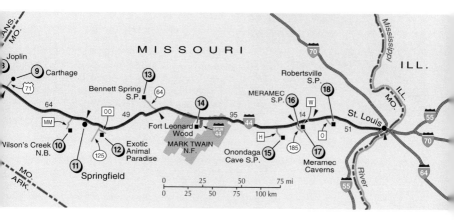

It includes Italian Renaissance and 19th- and 20th-century European and American paintings, and a large collection of Indian works. The 70-acre **Tulsa Zoological Park and Living Museum** (*5701 E. 36th St. N. 918-669-6200. Adm. fee*) has more than 1,200 animals and an Elephant Encounter. Striking modern buildings make up **Oral Roberts University** (*7777 S. Lewis Ave. 918-495-6807*); its dazzling "Prayer Tower" offers a good view of the city.

☞ Outsiders who stay glued to I-44 may miss the breathtaking landscape of the **Ozarks**. The only extensive relief between the Appalachians and the Rocky Mountains, it rivals them in scenic beauty. Old hardwood forests and sparkling lakes cover the 50,000-square-mile semiwild region, comprising most of southern Missouri and northern Arkansas and spilling over into Oklahoma, Kansas, and Illinois. State parks and caves abound. Isolation has bred a colorful rural culture of self-reliant farmers whose pleasures still include storytelling, fiddling, and square dancing.

(7) **Claremore** Established in 1874, this town and Oologah to the north are Will Rogers country. The **Will Rogers Memorial** (*1720 W. Will Rogers Blvd. 918-341-0719*) is a seven-gallery museum founded in 1938. It includes the larger-than-life Joe Davidson statue of the famous humorist, identical to the one in the U. S. Capitol. Rogers' movies, such as *State Fair* and *Connecticut Yankee,* and recordings of his radio shows are continually run. A display depicts the tragic crash that killed him and aviator Wiley Post in Point Barrow, Alaska, in 1935. **Will Rogers' Birthplace** (*12 miles N in Oologah on Okla. 88. 918-275-4201*) is a 400-acre spread with 60 longhorn cattle, nothing like the 10,000 head on 60,000 acres the family once owned. The Rogers' home, built in 1875, is open to visitors.

Also in Claremore is the **J. M. Davis Gun Museum** (*333 N. Lynn Riggs Blvd., Okla. 66. 918-341-5707*), with more than 20,000 historic firearms and related items and a firearms library. Its outlaw gallery includes weapons used by Pancho Villa and the Jesse James gang.

(8) **Joplin, MISSOURI** Here, in the mineral-rich hills of southwest Missouri, the **Tri-State Mineral Museum** (*Mo. 43 S exit, but go N on Schifferdecker Ave. about 3 miles, left into Schifferdecker Park. 417-623-2341. Closed Mon., also Tues. Oct.-March*) exhibits an impressive zinc-lead collection, as well as mining tools and models of machinery. At the **Thomas Hart Benton Exhibit** in the Municipal Building (*303 E. 3rd St. 417-625-4789. Closed weekends*), the artist's work and memorabilia are on display. He got his start as a newspaper cartoonist here in 1906.

Canoeing in the Ozarks

(9) **Carthage** Victorian houses and a marble courthouse bedeck the town's historic square. Nearly a million visitors a year reportedly visit the **Precious Moments Chapel and Museum** (*480 Chapel Rd. 417-358-7599. Tours*), where artist Samuel J. Butcher designs porcelain figurines of wide-eyed children, sold worldwide. His stained-glass windows and murals adorn the chapel. **Red Oak II** (*3 miles E on Mo. 96, then 1 mile N on Rte. 12, on left. 417-358-1943*) is a complex of 17 historic buildings relocated to create a small 1930s town

(10) **Wilson's Creek National Battlefield** (*8 miles S on Mo. MM across US 60 to Mo. M to Mo. ZZ, follow signs. Visitor Center 417-732-2662*) After terrible fighting here in 1861, Missourians sympathetic to the South won Bloody Hill in a Pyrrhic victory over

Union forces. Missouri remained in Union hands, albeit barely. The park shows a film and offers a self-guided 5-mile auto tour. *Adm. fee.*

Springfield *(Conv. & Visitors Bureau, 3315 E. Battlefield Rd. 417-881-5300 or 800-678-8766)* This is the gateway to the Ozark Mountains vacation region; nearby lakes offer fishing, boating, picnicking, and hiking trails. Aficionados of the outdoors will like **Bass Pro Shops Outdoor World** *(1935 S. Campbell Ave. 417-887-1915)*, a "sportsman's mall" with exhibits. The **Springfield Nature Center** *(4600 S. Chrisman. 417-882-4237. Closed Mon.)* is an 80-acre park offering nature trails, guided walks, and exhibits on Ozark flora and fauna. First explored by 12 women in 1867, the limestone cave at **Fantastic Caverns** *(1.5 miles N on Mo. 13, follow signs. 417-833-2010. Adm. fee)* was a speakeasy in the 1920s and a country music hall in the 1960s. A 45-minute tram tour takes you through it.

Wilson's Creek National Battlefield, Missouri

Exotic Animal Paradise *(S side of I-44 bet. N. View and Stafford exits. 417-859-2159)* The 3,000 animals here are mostly free and the visitors caged as they drive the 9.5 miles of road. *Adm. fee.*

125

Bennett Spring State Park *(10 miles W on Mo. 64, follow signs. 417-532-4338)* In this popular 3,099-acre park, nearly 100 million gallons of springwater a day feed the Niangua River. Trails, campsites, cabins available. *Closed Nov.-Feb.; fee for camping and cabins.*

Fort Leonard Wood *(St. Roberts exit, then 4.5 miles S on Missouri Ave./I-44 Spur. 314-596-0169)* The Army's **Fort Leonard Wood Engineer Museum** features weapons and a bridge exhibit. Reconstructed World War II barracks are located nearby. *Closed Sun.*

Onondaga Cave State Park *(Leasburg exit, 7 miles S on Mo. Secondary H. 314-245-6576)* Among the state's many caves and caverns open to the public, Onondaga Cave is one of the largest and least developed. The 1,317-acre park offers swimming, fishing, and canoeing on the Meramec River. *Cave tours March-Oct.; adm. fee.*

Meramec State Park *(4 miles S on Mo. 185. 314-468-6072)* At this beautiful 6,878-acre area of rolling forests and pleasant trails along the bucolic Meramec River, outfitters rent rafts and canoes.

Meramec Caverns *(Stanton exit, 2.5 miles S on Mo. Secondary W. 314-468-3166)* These commercially developed caves, with 1.5 miles of paved paths, are some of Missouri's best known. *Adm. fee.*

Robertsville State Park *(US 50 exit, 6 miles E on Mo. Secondary O, follow signs. 314-257-3788)* Wetland habitat, with several oxbow sloughs, attracts many kinds of waterfowl to this 1,110-acre park along the Meramec River. Hiking trails and camping.

St. Louis See I-55, p. 130.

Unless otherwise noted, directions are from interstate, and sites are free and generally open daily. Phone for further information.

① Chicago

Along the shore of Lake Michigan, Chicago's towers of stone and steel explode from ground to sky in a dizzying spectacle. Chicago's rise, however, has not been a steady accumulation of buildings since fur trader Jean Baptiste Point du Sable built his lonely cabin here in 1779. The city, with its stockyards, steel mills, canals, and railroads, was growing at a healthy clip in the late 19th century when, in a flash, the Great Fire of 1871 destroyed nearly all of it. But a new Chicago soon began to rise. Architect Daniel Burnham's 1909 plan envisioned a monumental city of wide avenues and magnificent public parks and buildings. As a result, today's Chicago is a collection of 20th-century architectural landmarks. The **Chicago Architecture Foundation Shop and Tour Center** *(224 S. Michigan Ave. 312-922-3432)* suggests a variety of tours via bus, bicycle, and elevated train. Or simply get a map and start walking; the grid pattern of the city's streets makes getting lost nearly impossible.

For a good city overview, see the multimedia show at the 1869 **Water Tower Pumping Station** *(N. Michigan Ave. and Pearson St. Visitor Info Center in lobby. 312-467-7114 or 800-428-8557. Adm. fee),* tucked among the trendy stores along North Michigan Avenue's Magnificent Mile. The Gothic-style **castle** across the street, built to hide a water pipe, survived the Great Fire. For a bird's-eye view, try the 103rd floor of the 110-story

Overlooking downtown

126

Chicago River and Wacker Drive

Sears Tower (233 S. Wacker Dr. 312-875-9696. Adm. fee), the world's tallest building.

Two blocks away, traders buy and sell bushels of midwestern grain by the thousand—not out in the street, as in former days, but on the floor of the **Chicago Board of Trade** (114 W. Jackson Blvd. 312-435-3590. Closed weekends). From the fifth floor viewing gallery, you can watch the digital display boards and the frenzy below as traders shout and

John Hancock Center

gesticulate and litter the floor with slips of paper. A film helps explain it all. For more of the action that makes Chicago the country's second leading financial center, step over to the **Mercantile Exchange** (30 S. Wacker Dr. 312-930-8249. Closed weekends), where

d," by John Olitski, at Institute of Chicago

the futures of pork bellies and currencies are decided.

Of Chicago's 30-plus museums, the most popular cluster is on the lakefront round Grant Park: The **Adler Planetarium** (1300 S. Lake Shore Dr. 312-922-STAR. Adm. fee) features sky shows and collection of early scientific instruments; the **John G. Shedd Aquarium** (1200 S. Lake Shore Dr. 312-939-438. Adm. fee) exhibits ea creatures; the **Field Museum** (S. Lake Shore Dr. and Roosevelt Rd. 312-922-9410. Adm. fee) encompasses 20 acres f anthropology, geology, zoology, and botany isplays; the **Art Insti-**

tute of Chicago** (Adams St. and S. Michigan Ave. 312-443-3500. Adm. fee) is considered one of the world's top art museums. Another nearby museum, the **Museum of Broadcast Communications** (Chicago Cultural Center, 78 E. Washington St. 312-629-6000), traces popular culture and contemporary history through TV and radio.

Just beyond the Loop (downtown), the **University of Chicago** (5801 S. Ellis Ave. 312-702-8370) takes pride in various museums and in a Frank Lloyd Wright masterpiece—the **Robie House** (5757 Woodlawn Ave. 312-702-8374. Tours at noon only; adm. fee)—as well as in buildings by other great 20th-century architects. Nearby, the interactive exhibits at the **Museum of Science and Industry** (57th St. and S. Lake Shore Dr. 312-684-1414) demonstrate the principles of those fields and of technology. On the Chicago campus of the University of Illinois stands **Jane Addams' Hull-House Museum** (800 S. Halsted St. 312-996-2793. Closed Sat.), home of the famed social worker and Nobel Prize winner.

Lincoln Park (N of downtown on N. Lake Shore Dr.), Chicago's largest and most popular park, wins high

Field Museum

marks for its conservatory, zoo, and statuary, including "Lincoln" by Augustus Saint-Gaudens. West of downtown, 5,000 species of plants, flowers, and trees adorn mammoth **Garfield Park Conservatory** (300 N. Central Park Blvd. 312-533-1281).

Chicago Bears at Soldier Field

127

Oak Park See I-90, p. 286.

(2) **Naperville** *(16 miles W on I-355 and I-88)* In this well-to-do Chicago suburb, the attractive **Riverwalk,** adorned with fountains, sculptures, and covered bridges, traces the West Branch of the Du Page River and runs past the **Naper Settlement Museum Village** *(201 W. Porter Ave. 708-420-6010. Wed.-Sun. in summer, weekends in spring and fall, second Sun. of month in winter; adm. fee).* Here, 25 buildings re-create 19th-century rural life.

(3) **Aurora** *(22 miles W on I-355 and I-88)* Though home to nearly 100,000 people, Aurora feels like a small town. An agreeable walkway connects sites along the Fox River, including the **Grand Army of the Republic Memorial** *(23 E. Downer St. 708-897-7221),* an ornate structure housing a small military museum, and **SciTech** *(18 W. Benton St. 708-859-3434. Closed Mon.-Tues.; adm. fee),* a hands-on science center. Not far away, the **Schingoethe Center for Native American Cultures** *(Aurora University, 347 S. Gladstone Ave. 708-844-5402. Closed Wed., Sat., and Aug.)* showcases tribal artifacts.

Joliet See I-80, p. 232.

(4) **Bloomington** Tallgrass prairie ablaze with wildflowers inspired the town's original name—Blooming Grove. The **McLean County Historical Society Museum** *(200 N. Main St. 309-827-0428. Closed Sun.; adm. fee),* lodged in a magnificent 1903 courthouse, focuses on county history, including an exhibit on Abraham Lincoln, who delivered his Lost Speech here about preserving the Union (no one bothered to record it). One of Lincoln's Supreme Court appointees later built an elegant Italianate house here, now known as the **David Davis Mansion State Historic Site** *(1000 E. Monroe St. 309-828-1084. Closed Tues.-Wed.).*

(5) **Lincoln** As a lawyer, Abraham Lincoln helped plan this town, which was named for him even before he became famous. He christened it with watermelon juice, saying that "nothing named Lincoln ever amounted to much"; a historical marker near the train station commemorates the site. The **Lincoln College Museum** *(300 Keokuk St. 217-735-5050. Closed mid-Dec.–Jan.)* houses Lincoln memorabilia.

(6) **Springfield** *(Visitors Bureau, 109 N. 7th St. 217-789-2360 or 800-545-7300)* Abraham Lincoln moved here to practice law in 1837, the same year Springfield became the state capital. During his 24-year residence, he rode the circuit, made a name for himself in politics, married, buried a child, and won the Presidency. Still the state capital, this friendly town proudly promotes its Lincoln lore. The **Lincoln Home National Historic**

Before the interstates, interstate travel meant narrow highways, tacky motels, and goofy billboards. No road conjures more memories of the romance of long-distance car travel than old *Route 66.* It started in Chicago, ran parallel to much of today's I-55 in Illinois, then raced clear to California. Every stop, every tourist court and gas station had a gimmick to lure travelers: SEE AUTHENTIC INDIAN DANCES! REPTILE GARDENS! BUFFALO! The road that inspired songs, a TV series, and a subculture of kitsch survives mostly in pictures and in the Route 66 Hall of Fame at the Dixie Truckers Home in McLean, Illinois.

128

Mary Todd Lincoln's room, Lincoln Home National Historic Site, Springfield, Illinois

Site (*413 S. 7th St.*), which the Lincolns owned for 17 years, has been a tourist attraction since 1887; pick up a free ticket and walking-tour map at the **Visitor Center** (*426 S. 7th St. 217-492-4150*). Two blocks away, at the **Lincoln Depot** (*9th and Monroe Sts. 217-544-8695. Closed Sept.-March*), the President-elect bid farewell to Springfield before heading east in 1861. Other Lincoln sites worth a look: the **Lincoln-Herndon Law Offices** (*6th and Adams Sts. 217-785-7289*) and the **Lincoln Tomb** (*Oak Ridge Cemetery. 217-782-2717*), a towering granite obelisk where Lincoln and his family are buried.

Downtown, the **Old State Capitol** (*1 S. Old State Capitol Plaza. 217-785-7961*) is rich in historical associations, and the new **State Capitol** (*2nd St. and Capitol Ave. 217-782-2099*) boasts an eye-popping rotunda with intricately detailed murals and bas-reliefs. Not far from the new capitol stands the **Executive Mansion** (*5th and Jackson Sts. 217-782-6450. Tours Tues., Thurs., Sat.*), dating from 1855.

Edwardsville This small town preserves much of its pre- and post-Civil War past in stylish federal and Greek Revival houses, particularly along St. Louis Street. The **Leclaire Historic District** was founded as an industrial age experiment in creating a harmonious working and living environment; you can pick up tour maps at the **Madison County Historical Museum** (*715 N. Main St. 618-656-7562. Closed Mon.-Tues., Sat., and Jan.*), an 1836 house with period rooms, Native American artifacts, and pioneer relics.

Cahokia Mounds S.H.S. (*Ill. 111 exit, follow signs for 1.5 miles. 618-346-5160*) The largest prehistoric settlement north of Mesoamerica, this site marks the center of the Mississippian culture, which flourished from A.D. 900 to 1200. At least 10,000 people lived here, farming, hunting, and building large platform mounds; many are visible, including 100-foot-high Monks Mound. A first-rate interpretive center has evocative full-scale dioramas. *Closed Mon.-Tues. Dec.-Feb.*

Cahokia See I-64, p. 134.

Continued on P. 133

A bluff-top setting just below the confluence of the Mississippi and Missouri Rivers attracted French fur traders to this wildlife-rich area in the 1760s. In 1803, Lewis and Clark came here to outfit their expedition to the Northwest. A few decades later, the railroad brought German and Irish immigrants. When St. Louis began to experience 20th-century decay and congestion, citizens rallied. The downtown area, once an eyesore, is now the city's showpiece (Convention & Visitors Commission, 10 S. Broadway. 314-421-1023 or 800-325-7962).

Eero Saarinen's Gateway Arch

At the 82-acre Jefferson National Expansion Memorial, the gleaming *Gateway Arch* (314-425-4465. Adm. fee; during busy periods, buy tram tickets for later in the day) offers unsurpassed views of the city and river from its 630-foot-high observation room, reachable by tram. In the Visitor Center below the arch, the *Museum of Westward Expansion* honors Thomas Jefferson and western pioneers. Nearby stand the *Old Cathedral* (209 Walnut St. 314-231-3250), built in the 1830s, and the *Old Courthouse* (11 N. 4th St. 314-425-4468), where the Dred Scott slavery trial began in 1847. The *Mercantile Money Museum* (Mercantile Tower, 7th and Washington Sts. 314-421-1819) exhibits counterfeiting and printing errors.

Old Courthouse

Baseball fans can take in a Cardinals game at ultramodern *Busch Stadium* (Bounded by Walnut, Broadway, Spruce, and 7th Sts. 314-241-3900 or 800-421-3263. Tours available). Next door, the *National Bowling Hall of Fame and Museum* (111 Stadium Plaza. 314-231-6340. Adm. fee) traces the history of the sport.

The city's premier museums lie to the west, in leafy Forest Park. The *Saint Louis Art Museum* (1 Fine Arts Dr. 314-721-0072. Closed Monday) dazzles with more than 30,000 international masterpieces. At the top-flight *Science Center* (5500 Oakland Ave. 314-289-4400. Adm. fees to planetarium and theater), you can check the speed of traffic on I-64 with a radar gun or explore a mock-up of a cool cavern, the kind that made St. Louis a brewing capital. Sample local brews—and see the famous Budweiser Clydesdales—at the *Anheuser-Busch Brewery* (13th and Lynch Sts. 314-577-2626).

Missouri Botanical Garden

Don't miss the *Missouri Botanical Garden* (4344 Shaw Blvd. 314-577-5100. Adm. fee), whose 79 manicured acres include a tropical greenhouse and a tranquil Japanese garden. A bit farther out, the 115-acre *Laumeier Sculpture Park* (12580 Rott Rd. W. 314-821-1209) spotlights contemporary works by renowned artists.

Ste. Genevieve *(Tourist Information Office, 66 S. Main St. 314-883-7097)* The town's original French inhabitants put up with flooding for 50 years before moving to higher ground in 1785. Fortunately, most of this attractive town—the state's oldest permanent settlement—was left dry during the 1993 flood. Several houses welcome visitors, including the 1785 French colonial **Bolduc House** *(125 S. Main St. 314-883-3105. Closed Nov.-March; adm. fee)* and the 1818 federal-style **Felix Valle House State Historic Site** *(Merchant and 2nd Sts. 314-883-7102. Adm. fee).*

Trail of Tears State Park *(11 miles E on Mo. 177. 314-334-1711. Visitor Center closed Mon.-Tues.)* During the winter of 1838, hundreds of Cherokee tramped through these 3,306 woodsy acres on their forced march to Oklahoma.

Cape Girardeau Soon after the United States acquired this town in 1803 as part of the Louisiana Purchase, it was enjoying a flourishing riverboat trade. Its historical buildings and lovely parks are protected by a sturdy wall, which in 1993 spared the main town from the swollen Mississippi. The 1883 **Glenn House** *(325 S. Spanish St. 314-334-1177. Closed Mon.-Wed.; adm. fee)* contains Victorian furnishings, 12-foot-high stenciled ceilings, and displays about the steamboat era. Slaves were auctioned at the 1854 **Common Pleas Courthouse** *(Spanish and Themis Sts. 314-335-1631 or 800-777-0068. Closed weekends),* whose dungeon held Southern sympathizers during the Civil War.

New Madrid Hugging a loop in the Mississippi, this town was established in 1789 as a Spanish outpost but became a U. S. holding with the Louisiana Purchase. The area was still largely unsettled in 1811, when several earthquakes whiplashed the land and altered the river's course. The **New Madrid Historical Museum** *(1 Main St. 314-748-5944. Adm. fee)* details the disaster, and a seismograph charts the current movement of the ground along the fault zone. An exhibit indicates that another major quake may hit here by 2040. At the north end of town you'll find the 1850s **Hunter-Dawson State Historic Site** *(312 Dawson Rd. 314-748-5340. Adm. fee),* a 15-room Greek Revival house with original furnishings.

Wilson, ARKANSAS A local amateur archaeologist spent 30 years unearthing the remains of an agrarian culture that thrived from A.D. 1400 to 1650 in what is now **Hampson Museum State Park** *(0.25 mile N on US 61. 501-655-8622. Closed Mon.; adm. fee).* The museum displays beautifully made pottery and tools.

Wapanocca National Wildlife Refuge *(2 miles E on Ark. 42. 501-343-2595)* Though fishing and hunting are permitted, these 5,500 acres of woods, swamps, and farmland exist mainly as a habitat for a variety of animals, including wood ducks, mallards, herons, egrets, mink, muskrats, and bobcats.

Bolduc House, Ste. Genevieve, Missouri

131

You still see a few docked at St. Louis, New Orleans, and Louisville—queens of the river, the grand old *steamboats,* now reduced to floating restaurants, casinos, or museums. For a brief 40 years in the mid-1800s, paddle wheelers proudly churned the Mississippi and the Ohio, ferrying freight and passengers. They made the rivers a showplace, their brass bands playing, whistles and bells sounding, stacks belching. Inside, ladies and gentlemen twirled under crystal chandeliers in salons fit for palaces. But the new railroads soon ran where rivers couldn't, and the days of luxurious river travel were gone forever.

⑯ Memphis, Tennessee

Its central location on the Mississippi made Memphis a major port by the 1860s. During the Civil War the city fell on hard times, followed by a yellow fever epidemic in the 1870s. A brisk cotton trade revived turn-of-the-century Memphis. Today the city is known for its music (Visitor Info Center, 340 Beale St. 901-543-5333). Underscoring its fame is *Graceland* (3765 Elvis Presley Blvd. 901-332-3322 or 800-238-2000. Closed Tues. Nov.-Feb.; adm. and parking fees), Elvis Presley's 15,000-square-foot mansion. Downtown on *Beale Street,* W.C. Handy and other musicians developed and performed the blues early in this century. Stretching east from the Mississippi, this 4-block entertainment area produces some of the finest sounds around. *Confederate Park* (N. Front St. and Jefferson Ave.) affords good views of the Wolf

Elvis's Cadillac

River. On Front Street, you can take the monorail or walkway to *Mud Island* (125 N. Front St. 901-576-7241. Daily in summer, closed Mon. mid-Sept.–Nov. and Apr.-May, closed Dec.-March; adm. fee), a 50-acre park on the Mississippi. A three-quarter-mile-long model of the lower Miss. lets you follow the river, at one mile per step, all the way to the delta. The *River Museum* chronicles the area's natural and cultural history.

Other fine museums include the bustling *Children's Museum* (2525 Central Ave. 901-458-2678. Closed Mon.; adm. fee), the *Memphis Brooks Museum of Art* (Overton Park. 901-722-3525. Closed Mon.; adm. fee except Fri.), and the *National Civil Rights Museum* (450 Mulberry St. 901-521-9699. Closed Tues.; adm. fee), built around the motel where Martin Luther King, Jr., was killed in 1968.

132

☞ **The blues** took root in the Mississippi Delta, nourished by gospel music and minstrel shows, field hollers and work songs. The music eased upriver, first on steamboats, then with African Americans migrating north during the Depression. Memphis, St. Louis, Chicago—each has its own sound and its own stars, but the heart and soul of the blues belong to Memphis.

⑰ Oxford, MISSISSIPPI *(23 miles E on Miss. 6. Chamber of Commerce, 299 W. Jackson Ave. 601-234-4651)* In 1836, Oxford's founders bought land from a Chickasaw woman and named their town with scholarly intentions. The **University of Mississippi,** which opened 12 years later, made the headlines in 1962 when James Meredith became the first African American to enroll. An earlier student, Nobel Prize winner William Faulkner, lived at **Rowan Oak** *(Old Taylor Rd. 601-234-3284. Closed Mon.),* a pre-Civil War house behind the university. His boots sit by his bed, and his plot for a novel remains outlined on the office wall. A short trail behind the property leads to the **University Museums** *(University Ave. and 5th St. 601-232-7073. Closed Mon.),* which house classical antiquities, southern folk art, and 18th-century scientific instruments.

⑱ Grenada Lake *(Off Miss. 8, 5 miles NE of Grenada. Visitor Center 601-226-1679)* This 35,000-acre lake offers all kinds of water sports. On the lakeshore, **Hugh White State Park** *(5 miles E of Grenada on Miss. 8. 601-226-4934. Adm. fee)* has some of the same, plus boat and bike rentals, camping, and cabins.

⑲ Vaughan   Engineer Casey Jones, trying to make up lost time, rammed his steam locomotive into a freight train here in 1900—and died. He was reborn in a song written and sung by a fellow crewman and later immortalized by two vaudevillians. At the dusty **Casey Jones Railroad Museum State Park** *(10901 Vaughan Rd. 601-673-*

9864. *Closed Sun.; adm. fee*), you can hear a recording of the ballad and learn about Jones and early railroading.

Jackson   See I-20, p. 69.

Tangipahoa, LOUISIANA
Founded in the early 1800s, this village is remembered as the site of **Camp Moore** (*US 51, just N of town. 504-229-2438*), a Confederate boot camp where recruits were inducted by the thousand—and died by the hundred. A one-room museum displays Confederate uniforms and artifacts. *Closed Sun.-Mon.; adm. fee.*

Hammond   Settled by a Swede in the 1820s, Hammond prospered when the railroad came to town in 1854. Near the old depot, the **Chamber of Commerce** (*Thomas and Railroad Sts. 504-345-4457*) dispenses information on the area, including a walking-tour map of the attractive downtown. For a different kind of outing, visit the **Global Wildlife Center** (*6 miles E on I-12, 10.5 miles N on La. 445, follow signs. 504-624-WILD. Fare charge for wagon tours*), a Jurassic Park-like preserve where endangered animals roam free.

Ponchatoula   Laid out along the railroad in the 1850s, this town thrived on strawberries and lumber. Take a peek at the one-room **Collinswood School Museum** (*165 E. Pine St. 504-386-2741. Closed Mon.-Wed.*). A must-see is the **Joyce Wildlife Management Area** (*2 miles S on I-55, Frontage Rd. exit. 504-542-7520*), whose 1,000-foot boardwalk leads into a cypress swamp festooned with Spanish moss, known as *ponchatoula* in Choctaw.

Faulkner reading, Rowan Oak, Oxford, Mississippi

Continued on P. 129

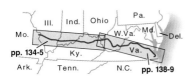

Unless otherwise noted, directions are from interstate, and sites are free and generally open daily. Phone for further information.

St. Louis, MISSOURI See I-55, p. 130.

① Cahokia, ILLINOIS *(7.5 miles S on I-255, 2 miles W on Ill. 157)* This small St. Louis suburb dates back to the days when the French occupied the area and built structures using logs set vertically instead of in the usual horizontal style. The circa-1740 **Cahokia Courthouse State Historical Site** *(107 Elm St. 618-332-1782. Thurs.-Sat. p.m.)* exemplifies this building method, called *poteau sur solle* (post on sill), as does the nearby **Church of the Holy Family** *(116 Church St. 618-337-4548. Summer and by appt.)*, in use since 1799.

② Belleville Emma Kunz Home Museum *(6 miles S on Ill. 159 to 602 Fulton St. 618-234-0600)* Built in 1830, this one-story brick cottage is an early example of Greek Revival architecture in Illinois. *Sun. and by appt.*

③ Mount Vernon Motorcyclist think they've gone to heaven at **Wheel Through Time** *(2 miles N on Ill. 37, left on Waltonville Rd., right at motorcycle dealership 618-244-4116. Closed Wed., Sun.)*, a small warehouse crammed with vintage bikes and memorabilia. The **Illinois Appellate Court, Fiftl District** *(14th and Main Sts. 618-242-3120 Closed weekends)* convenes in the courtroor where Abraham Lincoln presented an oral argument on behalf of the Illinois Central Railroad in an 1859 tax case. Clara Barton once used the building as a temporary hospital

Cahokia Courthouse State Historical Site, Cahokia, Illi

④ New Harmony, INDIAN *(7 miles S on Ind. 68, follow signs)* The peacefu atmosphere and early 19th-century woode houses reflect New Harmony's original pur pose as a haven for Lutheran separatists awai ing the Second Coming. In 1825, Welsh ir dustrialist Robert Owen bought the town i

134

hope of turning it into a utopia of universal education and social equality. Though that didn't happen, New Harmony remained a haven for naturalists and educators. Orientation tours begin at the ultramodern **Atheneum** *(Arthur and North Sts. 812-682-4482. April-Oct., call for winter hours; fee for tours)*, a light-filled structure offering views of the countryside. On the same street stands another modern creation: Philip Johnson's **Roofless Church** *(North and Main Sts. 812-682-4431)*. Heading south on Main Street, you'll come to the **Labyrinth,** a boxwood maze symbolizing man's troubled road to perfection. Relic of Owens's vision, the **Workingmen's Institute** *(W. Tavern St. 812-682-4806. Closed Mon. all year and Sun. in winter)* once served as a model school; now it's a museum and library. The best time to visit **Harmonie State Park** *(4 miles S on Ind. 69, 1 mile W on Ind. 269. 812-682-4821. Adm. fee)* is late afternoon, when deer feed along the banks of the Wabash River.

Fall Kunstfest, New Harmony, Indiana

Evansville *(13 miles S on I-164. Visitor Center, 623 Walnut St. 812-425-5402)* Founded in 1819, Evansville owes its prosperity to the Ohio River and the transcontinental railroad. A century ago, the commercial fortunes made here were used to create fancy Victorian buildings. In the city's ritzy Riverside Historic District stands the **John Augustus Reitz Home** *(224 S.E. 1st St. 812-426-1871. Closed Mon.-Tues.; adm. fee)*, an opulent example of 1890s interior decorating. The entrance hall is Moorish, the parlor Italianate, and the gilded drawing room French, capped by a painted canvas ceiling. The townsfolks' taste for the elaborate carried over to public buildings, such as the **Old Vanderburgh County Courthouse** and **Jail** *(4th and Vine Sts. 812-423-3361. Courthouse Mon.-Fri., jail by appt.)*. The 1890 courthouse is a French beaux arts landmark; the jail, completed the same year, was modeled after a German castle. To give visitors a feel for Victorian life, the **Evansville Museum of Arts and Science** *(411 S.E. Riverside Dr. 812-425-2406. Closed Mon.)* has re-created a Gay Nineties village called Rivertown

135

SMILE: YOU MAY BE ON RADAR

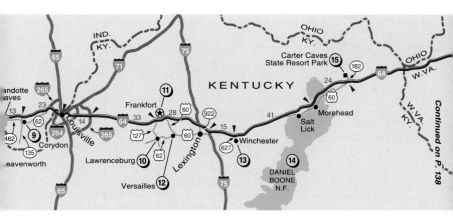

Continued on P. 138

U.S.A. People have lived in the area for a very long time; **Angel Mounds State Historic Site** *(Visitor Center, 8215 Pollack Ave. 812-853-3956. Mid-March–Dec. Tues.-Sun.)* preserves the locale where some 3,000 prehistoric mound builders resided until their village was mysteriously abandoned around A.D. 1450. Eleven mounds—building platforms—remain. Animal lovers can watch captive wildlife in open-terrain settings at the **Mesker Park Zoo** *(Bement and St. Joseph Aves. 812-428-0715. Adm. fee).* Centuries-old trees and a wide variety of birds find a home at the **Wesselman Woods Nature Preserve** *(551 N. Boeke Rd. 812-479-0771. Closed Mon.).*

(6) **L i n c o l n   C i t y**   In 1816, seven-year-old Abe Lincoln helped his father clear some of the land now known as the **Lincoln Boyhood National Memorial** *(6 miles S on US 231, 2 miles E on Ind. 162. 812-937-4541. Adm. fee).* A cozy log cabin stands on what is thought to be the original site, and "pioneers" run the farm as the Lincolns would have done. Across the road, Lincoln's sister, Sarah, is buried in **Lincoln State Park** *(812-937-4710. Fri.-Sun.; adm. fee).*

(7) **S a n t a   C l a u s**   **Betsy Ross Doll House** and **Toyland Museum** *(7 miles S on Ind. 162, follow Holiday World signs. 812-937-4401 or 800-GO-SANTA)* Tucked away in a theme park where Christmas and American history clash with water slides are two unique collections of antique toys. The dolls reside in the town's original 1856 post office; the toy museum displays trains, dolls, and doll furniture that would have appeared under Victorian Christmas trees. On the way out, mail yourself a letter; the postmark is famous. *Daily in summer, weekends mid-May–mid-Oct.; adm. fee.*

(8) **L e a v e n w o r t h**   **Wyandotte Caves** *(3.5 miles S on Ind. 66, 5 miles E on Old Ind. 62. 812-738-2782)* More than 1,800 years ago, Indians used the huge hall in the largest cave as a meeting place and shelter. *Closed Mon. in winter; adm. fee.*

(9) **C o r y d o n**   *(2 miles S on Ind. 135, 0.5 miles E on Ind. 62)* Indiana's history began in this sleepy village. The **Old State Capitol** *(N. Capitol Ave. 812-238-4890. Closed Mon.),* made of native limestone, served as the state's political center from 1816 until Indianapolis became the capital in 1825. The **Constitution Elm Monument** *(High St.)* marks the site where, on a hot June day in 1816, delegates drafted the state constitution. The **Battle of Corydon Memorial Park** *(1 mile S of town on Ind. 135 Bus.)* was the site of Indiana's only Civil War fighting. Led by Brig. Gen. John H. Morgan, the Rebel cavalry shelled the town on July 9, 1863, then confiscated its food.

South of Corydon, **Squire Boone Caverns** *(10 miles S on Ind. 135, left on Squire Boone Caverns Rd. for 3 miles. 812-732-4381. Closed Jan.-Feb.; adm. fee)* glows with colored lights. The caverns were discovered by Daniel Boone and his brother, Squire, in 1790. Several years later, Squire hid there from Indians and chose it as his burial place. His wooden coffin adds an eerie note to the tour.

Lincoln Boyhood National Memorial, Lincoln City, Ind.

136

Ten miles east of Corydon lies **Needmore Buffalo Farm** (*Lanesville exit, follow buffalo signs to 4100 Buffalo Rd. S.E. 812-968-3473. Closed Tues.*). The shaggy brown herd, led by a 2,500-pound bull named Arthur, is one of 20 herds in Indiana.

Louisville, KENTUCKY See I-65, p. 148.

Lawrenceburg **Kentucky Boulevard Distillery and Imports Inc.** (*10 miles S on US 127, 3 miles E on US 62, follow signs to 1525 Tyrone Rd. 502-839-4544*) The home of Wild Turkey bourbon is a century-old bottling plant where a label overseer still checks each bottle to make sure the bird goes on straight. *Weekday tours.*

Gainsborough Farm, Versailles, Kentucky

(11) Frankfort For history and variety, Kentucky's capital is one of the best surprises on I-64. Its quaint residential side streets and charming downtown are easily explored on foot. The **Tourist and Convention Commission** (*100 Capital Ave. 502-875-8687*) provides excellent maps and is conveniently located across the street from **Rebecca-Ruth Candies** (*112 E. 2nd St. 502-223-7475 or 800-444-3766. Tours except Aug., Nov., and Dec.*), which makes delicious sweets using the same recipes—with smatterings of Kentucky bourbon—and equipment the founders did in 1919.

Across the Kentucky River you'll find the **Old State Capitol** and the **Kentucky History Museum** (*Broadway at St. Clair Mall. 502-564-3016*). Built in 1830, the capitol has a stone staircase that spirals beneath the dome without any visible support. The 1798 Georgian **Lt. Governor's Mansion** (*420 High St. 502-564-3449. Tues. and Thurs.*), 3 blocks east of the old capitol , once served as the governor's residence. It became known as the Palace after hosting several U. S. Presidents and the Marquis de Lafayette. The marquis also visited **Liberty Hall** (*218 Wilkinson St. 502-227-2560. Closed Mon.; adm. fee*), a Georgian mansion with original furniture. U. S. Senator John Brown built it in the 1790s for his elder son, then constructed a smaller but fancier house next door for his other son. The 1910 **Zeigler House** (*509 Shelby St. 502-227-7164. By appt.; adm. fee*), designed by Frank Lloyd Wright, is a flowing example of his prairie style. Nearby, the **Governor's Mansion** (*704 Capital Ave. 502-564-3000. Tues. and Thurs. a.m.*) mimics Marie Antoinette's Petit Trianon. Across the lawn, the **Capitol** (*Capital Ave. 502-564-3000*) presides over the Kentucky River. Inside are statues of famous Kentuckians and colorful frescoes of state history. The

The smooth-tasting whiskey called *bourbon* was born in Kentucky, and natives insist that anything else just isn't bourbon. A Baptist minister invented the amber liquid in 1789 in the county named for the French royal family. Corn, rye, and barley—combined with water from the limestone-bedded Kentucky River—give bourbon its distinctive taste. It gets its potency from aging up to eight years in white oak barrels.

137

Governor's Mansion, Frankfort, Ky.

Kentucky Vietnam Veterans Memorial *(Coffee Tree Rd.)* honors the more than 1,000 Kentuckians killed; a sundial points to the name of each on the day he died. Daniel Boone is buried in the **Old Frankfort Cemetery** *(215 E. Main St.).* At the **Ancient Age Distillery** *(1000 Wilkinson Blvd. 502-223-7641),* in operation since 1869, some 10,000 bottles of bourbon are capped during peak periods.

(12) **Versailles** *(10 miles E on US 60)* Train buffs should allow time to hop aboard the **Bluegrass Scenic Railroad** *(1.5 miles W on US 62 to Woodford County Park. 606-873-2476 or 800-755-2476. Weekends May-Oct.; fare charge),* which makes a 90-minute trip through Bluegrass country to a historic bridge over the Kentucky River. Trains on a smaller scale line the walls and cases of **Nostalgia Station** *(279 Depot St. 606-873-2497. Closed Mon.-Tues.; adm. fee).*

Natural Arch, Daniel Boone
National Forest, Kentucky

Lexington See I-75, p. 192.

(13) **Winchester** Built in the 1790s, the **Old Stone Church** *(Bypass to Ky. 627, right on Boonesborough Ave. for 3 miles, right on Old Stone Church Rd. 606-744-6420)* has enough historic appeal to make the bumpy jaunt down a dirt road tolerable. Again, the long arm of Daniel Boone reaches out: His family worshiped here.

(14) **Daniel Boone National Forest** *(Salt Lick exit, 10 miles E on US 60, right on Ky. 801 for 2 miles. Visitor Center 606-784-6428)* Woods, lakes, and streams cover more than 672,000 acres of the area Daniel Boone settled in 1769. Boaters and beachgoers enjoy Cave Run Lake. *Daily in summer, Mon.-Fri. in winter.*

(15) **Carter Caves State Resort Park** *(5 miles N on Ky. 182. 606-286-4411)* If you don't mind bats, the cave tours are fascinating. The X Cave is a good choice for those on a tight schedule. If you have more time, visit Cascade Cave, known for its wa-

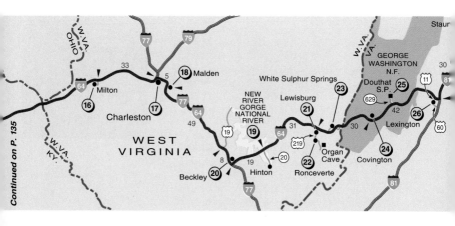

Continued on P. 135

terfall. If bats are a problem, the Natural Bridge Trail offers a beautiful 0.5-mile hike along a pebbly stream. *Fee for tours.*

Milton, WEST VIRGINIA Glass has been blown at the **Blenko Glass Company** (*0.5 mile W on US 60, left at first stoplight, factory 0.5 mile on right. 304-743-9081. Weekday tours*) since 1893. To see it done in all types and colors—using 19th-century methods—arrive before 3 p.m. If you miss the glassblowing, visit the plant's Japanese garden, decorated with stained glass, or head for the **Mud River Covered Bridge** (*Right out of factory*), built in 1876.

Blenko stained glass, West Virginia

Charleston (*Visitor Center, 299 Civic Center Dr. 304-344-5075 or 800-733-5469*) Sprawled along the Kanawha River, West Virginia's capital is dominated by its gold-domed **Capitol** (*Kanawha Blvd. E. 304-558-3809*), finished in 1932. On the north side of the

Capitol, Charleston, West Virginia

capitol's shady, manicured grounds stands a bronze bust of Booker T. Washington; his stint in nearby Malden made him an honorary native son. To the west, in the **West Virginia Cultural Center** (*Capitol Complex. 304-558-0220*), a museum chronicles the state's history. Several yards away is the **West Virginia Executive's Mansion** (*304-558-3809 or 800-225-5982. Thurs.-Fri. a.m.*), a gracious brick house completed in 1925. Two of Charleston's more impressive houses constitute the **Sunrise Museum Complex** (*746 Myrtle Rd. 304-344-8035. Closed Mon.-Tues.; adm. fee*). Crowning 16 hilly acres above the Kanawha, the stone mansions

139

Stern-wheeler, Charleston

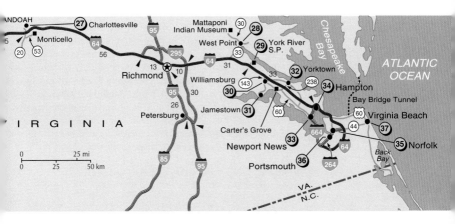

New River Gorge Bridge, W. Va.

140

hold rotating art and science exhibits. In South Charleston 13 prehistoric skeletons were unearthed at the **Adena Burial Mound** (*MacCorkle Ave. and D St. 304-768-5552 or 800-238-9488*).

(18) Malden (*1 mile E on US 60, right on Malden Dr., bear left*) Salt created this tiny town in 1755 when two white women, Mary Ingles and Betty Draper, churned out the white stuff for their Indian captors. A hundred years later, the Buffalo Salt Licks had become a big business. Young Booker T. Washington worked there and attended the white-frame **African Zion Baptist Church** (*4100 Malden Dr. 304-768-2635. By appt.*), built by slaves in 1852.

(19) New River Gorge National River (*10 miles S from Sandstone exit on W. Va. 20, through Hinton, to Visitor Center on W. Va. 20 Bypass. 304-466-0417. See map for locations of other approaches*) The drive along this 53-mile wild river is breathtaking. At least 65 million years old—one of the continent's most ancient rivers—the New River existed even before the surrounding Allegheny Mountains were formed. White-water rafters consider it a real treasure. *Visitor Center open daily in summer, weekends year-round.*

(20) Beckley **Beckley Exhibition Coal Mine** (*1.5 miles E on W. Va. 3, left on Ewart Ave., follow signs to New River Park. 304-256-1747. April-Nov.; adm. fee*) Small trains carry passengers through 1,200 feet of restored mines for a look at life in this dark, chilly workplace. In the adjacent **Youth Museum of Southern West Virginia** (*304-252-3730. Daily in summer, closed Sun.-Mon. in winter*), colorful railroad cars have been transformed into exhibit galleries. Kids may also enjoy a romp in the surrounding park.

(21) Lewisburg (*Visitor Center, 105 Church St. 304-645-1000 or 800-833-2068. Closed Sun.*) Settled in the 1770s as a fort on the Virginia frontier, the town has many old buildings still in fine shape, and much of the downtown has been preserved as a national historic district. Two churches, both still in use, are located within walking distance of each other: the **Old Stone Presbyterian Church** (*200 Church St.*) and the **John Wesley Methodist Church** (*209 E. Foster St.*). The former, built in 1796 of native limestone, survived a Civil War battle. The brick Methodist church did not fare as well. During an engagement in 1862, a Confederate cannonball struck the building's southwest wall, where it remains.

(22) Ronceverte **Organ Cave** (*About 8 miles S on US 219, follow signs. 304-647-5551 or 800-258-CAVE*) Bring a sweater because the cave registers 55°F year-round. Guides give an amusing spiel as

Some 350 million years ago, much of the land between western Virginia and Missouri lay under a vast sea. As marine creatures died, their remains sank to the ocean floor and decayed, turning into limestone. When the carbonic acid in groundwater hit the porous limestone, it ate away holes that eventually became *caverns.* The region near I-64 is honey-combed with caverns in various stages of development.

Organ Cave, Ronceverte, West Virginia

you pass huge formations and abandoned saltpeter hoppers once used to store material needed for gunpowder. *Adm. fee.*

Greenbrier River, West Virginia

White Sulphur Springs
Presidents' Cottage Museum *(2 miles W from White Sulphur Springs exit on US 60, right at Greenbrier Resort. 304-563-1110, ext. 7314)* The healing powers of the springs and mountain air have made this a resort area for almost 200 years. In the 1830s Martin Van Buren was the first of 22 U. S. Presidents to visit; the cottage perched on a hillside became the first summer White House. The museum is decorated with pictures taken over the years of the resort's chic clientele. *Daily Apr.-Oct., Sat. only rest of year; adm. fee.*

Covington, VIRGINIA Humpback Bridge
(1 mile E on US 60) This covered bridge—made without nails—may be unique. Built in 1835 as part of the James River–Kanawha Turnpike, the bridge rises 8 feet in the center without support.

141

Douthat State Park *(5.6 miles N on Va. 629. 703-862-7200)* Fishermen flock to Douthat Lake and rocky Wilson Creek during trout season. In warm weather you can rent a paddleboat or stretch out on the beach. *Parking fee.*

Lexington Named for the 1775 Battle of Lexington and Concord, this gracious college town has been associated with four American generals. History pervades the well-preserved business district and 19th-century houses, best seen on walking tours suggested by the excellent **Visitor Center** *(106 E. Washington St. 703-463-3777)*. High on the list for Civil War buffs is the brick, three-story **Stonewall Jackson House** *(8 E. Washington St. 703-463-2552. Adm. fee)*. On the **Washington and Lee University** campus, the revered general Robert E. Lee is buried in the **Lee Chapel** *(703-463-8768)*. A reproduction of his office and a family museum are located downstairs. The **Virginia Military Institute** was founded next to the university in 1839. The **George C. Marshall Museum and Library** *(703-463-7103)* honors the World War II general and Nobel Peace Prize winner, who was VMI's most famous graduate.

Staunton See I-81, p. 243.

Shenandoah National Park *(Southern entrance at Afton)* See I-81, p. 241.

Greenbrier Resort, White Sulphur Springs, West Virginia

Charlottesville At the foot of the Blue Ridge Mountains, Thomas Jefferson designed his "academical village" in 1819, and it became the **University of Virginia** *(Univ. of Virginia exit, follow signs. 804-924-1019)*. Tours of the grounds begin at the Rotunda, which Jefferson modeled after the Roman Pantheon. His home at **Monticello** (*0.5 mile S on Va. 20, left on Va. 53 for 2 miles, follow signs. 804-984-9822. Adm. fee*) reflects his love of classical buildings. While waiting to get in, you can wander the gardens. Jefferson's friend James Monroe owned a farm just 2.5 miles away. Today called **Ash Lawn-Highland** (*S on Va. 53, right on Rte. 795. 804-293-9539. Adm. fee*), it was one of two houses owned by the fifth President. Money trouble forced its sale in 1826. The original portion is furnished with pieces in the French style beloved by Elizabeth Monroe.

R i c h m o n d   See I-95, p. 338.

Humpback Bridge, Covington, Va.

(28) **W E S T   P O I N T**   The artifacts at the **Mattaponi Indian Museum** (*21 miles N on Va. 30, right on Va. 625, follow signs in reservation. 804-276-7696*) mostly pertain to the Mattaponi tribe, ruled by Powhatan in the 1600s. Look for the club the chief almost used on Capt. John Smith. *Daily summer, by appt. rest of year; adm. fee.*

(29) **Y O R K   R I V E R   S T A T E   P A R K**   (*1 mile N on Croaker Rd., right on Riverview Rd. for 1.5 miles. Visitor Center*

142

(30) # Williamsburg

Colonial Williamsburg (Visitor Center 804-229-1000 or 800-447-8679. Adm. fee) is too big to tour in an hour or two, so set aside time and money; massive restorations do not come cheap, even for John D. Rockefeller, Jr. In 1926, he began his affair with the second capital of 18th-century Virginia, then a rundown southern village.

Today about 85 percent of Colonial Williamsburg is restored, and visitors

Governor's Palace

from around the globe converge to see where Patrick Henry thundered his defiance of the crown. While strolling down *Duke of Gloucester Street* past shops run by costumed staffers, it's easy to return to a time when the Colonies were chafing under British rule. Sights include the reconstructed *Capitol,* where Virginia's burgesses de-

clared independence in 1776, and the *Wren Building* on the manicured campus of the *College of William and Mary.* Completed by 1700, this building is thought to have been designed by the great British architect Sir Christopher Wren.

Farther afield, *Carter's Grove* (4 miles E on US 60, right on Va. 194 for 1.5 miles. 804-229-1000. Adm. fee) recalls colonial living at its height. Set on gracious grounds, the 1750 brick home of Carter Burwell is furnished with antiques from several periods. Nearby, the underground museum of *Wolstenholme Town* (Adm. fee) offers an excellent way to experience an archaeological dig. Established in 1619, the settlement was wiped out only three years later by Indians.

804-566-3036) This 2,505-acre park is far enough off the beaten path to be truly peaceful. Hikers can take several trails, and a volleyball net is set up for spikers (equipment available). *Parking fee.*

Jamestown *(7 miles W on Colonial Pkwy. Visitor Center 804-229-1733)* Capt. John Smith arrived here in 1607 and founded the first permanent British settlement in North America. The **Old Church Tower** is the only standing structure left on what is now Jamestown Island. Other buildings must be imagined from foundations; work continues on excavations. To see the land as the first settlers saw it, follow the **Wilderness Loop Drive** past woods and marshes little changed in four centuries. Some of the settlement has been reconstructed: At the **Glass House** craftsmen shape molten glass near the ruins of the original 1608 building. *Adm. fee.*

Copies of 17th-century settlers' ships, Jamestown, Virginia

Yorktown The 12-mile drive along the Colonial Parkway linking Yorktown with Williamsburg and Jamestown is a scenic pleasure. So is Yorktown itself, a sleepy village that never regained its pre-Revolutionary bustle. But at this spot, Great Britain lost the last major campaign of the Revolution, and American independence was finally won. The model in the Visitor Center at **Yorktown Battlefield** *(Follow signs. 804-898-3400)* explains the events leading to October 19, 1781, the day British troops surrendered to George Washington's army. When the news reached Congress, members voted to construct a **Victory Monument,** which towers over a bluff between the town and the battlefield. In town you'll find the **Nelson House** *(Main St. Summer only),* the Georgian estate of Maj. Gen. Thomas Nelson, Jr., who signed the Declaration of Independence and commanded the Virginia militia at the siege of Yorktown. Legend says that Nelson ordered his troops to fire at the house, thinking it the headquarters of British Gen. Lord Charles Cornwallis. Cornwallis's emissaries met with American and French representatives to draft surrender terms at the **Augustine Moore House** *(1.3 miles E of battlefield on Va. 238. Daily summer, weekends rest of year).*

Costumed as a British soldier, Jamestown

Newport News *(Visitor Center, 8 San Jose Dr. 804-873-0092)* Like the other cities that make up southeastern Virginia's coastal megalopolis, Newport News bears the influence of its maritime and military past. The **Mariners Museum** *(100 Museum Dr. 804-595-0368. Adm. fee)* covers maritime history so well that even the staunchest landlubber will be enthralled. Guarding the galleries is Alexander Calder's statue of Leif Eriksson, the first European to set foot in North America. Other must-sees are the collections of miniature ships and small crafts. The **War Memorial Museum of Virginia** *(9285 Warwick Blvd. 804-247-8523. Adm. fee)*

Launching the submarine U. S. S. *Chicago,* Newport News, Virginia

includes part of a Nazi concentration camp. U. S. Gen. Jacob L. Devers donated it and other grim artifacts after his troops freed Dachau at the end of World War II. The **U. S. Army Transportation Museum** (*Follow signs for Fort Eustis. 804-878-1183*) presents a lighter side of the military. In the exhibit on experimental craft, be sure to look for the 1955 Delackner Aerocycle, an unusual contraption that lifted soldiers into the air with a four-cylinder engine mounted on two propellers. If you're overdosing on war, take a break at the **Virginia Living Museum** (*524 J. Clyde Morris Blvd. 804-595-1900. Adm. fee*). A 0.6-mile trail twists through natural habitat that bobcats, river otters, and bald eagles call home. There's also a planetarium and two aviaries.

Virginia hams aging

(34) Hampton   Settled in 1610, Hampton claims to be the oldest English-speaking city in continuous existence in the United States. It lends itself to walking tours. Start at the **Visitor Center** (*710 Settlers Landing Rd. 804-727-1102 or 800-800-2202*), steps away from the 1920 **Hampton Carousel** (*610 Settlers Landing Rd. Adm. fee*), still operating by the James River. Nearby, at the **Virginia Air and Space Center/Hampton Roads History Center** (*600 Settlers Landing Rd. 804-727-0900 or 800-296-0800. Adm. fee*), visitors can launch rockets, become an astronaut for a minute, and gaze at aircraft suspended from a ceiling. Two blocks from the river and two centuries back in time is **St. John's Church** (*100 W. Queen's Way. 804-722-2567*). Home to the country's oldest English-speaking parish, the church dates back to 1728. In the graveyard look for a marker for Virginia Laydon, one of the first surviving children born to English parents in the New World. At **Fort Monroe,** a busy Army post, don't miss the **Casemate Museum** (*Follow signs for fort. 804-727-3391*) inside an old fort. Confederate President Jefferson Davis was imprisoned in the fort for, among other charges, plotting Lincoln's assassination. A Union stronghold during the Civil War, the fort became a haven for runaway slaves. Later a Union general opened a school for freedmen that became **Hampton University** (*Hampton Univ. exit. 804-727-5000. Tours weekdays*).

Convention center, Norfolk, Virginia

(35) Norfolk (*Visitor Center, 236 E. Plume St., 804-441-5266*) Nucleus of the Hampton Roads area, Norfolk is home to one of the world's largest naval installations. Be sure to drive through the **Norfolk Naval Base,** where you can gawk at the hulking gray ships lined up along the piers. To understand the base and its components, take the bus tour (*9079 Hampton Blvd. 804-444-7955. Adm. fee*). On weekends, certain ships lay down the gangplank for visitors. The naval base and much of the city's success as a port is due to the 45-foot-deep harbor. With the trade came merchants. Back in 1792, one of them built the magnificent brick **Moses Myers House** (*Bank and Freemason Sts. 804-622-1211. Closed Mon.; adm. fee*), which remained in the family until 1930. About 70 percent of the furnishings are original. Two blocks away stands one of Norfolk's oldest structures, **St. Paul's Church** (*201 St. Paul's Blvd. 804-627-4353*). Built in 1739, it survived the Revolutionary War practically intact, except for a cannonball lodged high in one wall. In the graveyard you'll find interesting and legible headstones, some from the 17th century. Gen. Douglas MacArthur, America's most decorated soldier, is buried under a slab of black marble in the **MacArthur Memorial** (*Bank St. and City Hall Ave. 804-441-2965*). Norfolk has two museums that shouldn't be missed. The **Chrysler Museum** (*245 W. Olney Rd. 804-622-1211. Closed Mon.; donation requested*) is noted for its Tiffany glass and impressive collection of ancient Egyptian and Roman art. The **Hermitage Foundation Museum** (*7637 N. Shore Rd. 804-423-2052. Adm. fee*), a Tudor mansion built in 1908 as a summer home for William and Florence Sloane, showcases their art collection.

Cape Henry Lighthouse, Virginia Beach

Portsmouth   The best way to see Portsmouth is on a five-minute ride aboard the **Elizabeth River Ferry** (*Norfolk's Waterside. Fare charge*). Once docked, pick up a walking guide at the **Visitor Center** (*6 Crawford Pkwy. 804-393-5111 or 800-PORTSVA*). To get a feel for this small city, laid out more than 300 years ago to resemble its British namesake, walk along the water, then turn up High Street. On the right is the **Portsmouth Naval Shipyard Museum** (*420 High St. 804-393-8983. Closed Mon.; adm. fee*), with relics of the city's maritime legacy. Four blocks up, at the **Children's Museum** (*Court and High Sts. 804-393-8718. Adm. fee*), kids can try on uniforms and hard hats or encase themselves in giant bubbles.

Virginia Beach (*10 miles E on Va. 44. Visitor Center, 2100 Parks Ave. 804-437-4888*) The Atlantic meets Chesapeake Bay at Virginia Beach, a popular resort with a 3-mile boardwalk. Before it evolved into a sun-worshipers' paradise in the early 1900s, the beach was desolate and the ocean a ships' graveyard. In 1607, three vessels navigated the waters, and the English colonists who would settle Jamestown stepped ashore. They placed an oak cross on the point, which they named Cape Henry for King James I's son; the **Cape Henry Memorial** (*At Fort Story*) marks this landing. Across the road stands the **Cape Henry Lighthouse** (*At Fort Story. 804-422-9421. Mid-March–Oct.; adm. fee*). Built in 1791, it guided ships until 1881. A steep roof and diamond pane windows give the cozy **Adam Thoroughgood House** (*1636 Parish Rd. 804-460-0007. Closed Mon.; adm. fee*) a medieval look. Completed about 1680, it is one of the country's oldest brick houses. At the south end of Virginia Beach lie the **Back Bay Natl. Wildlife Refuge** (*Visitor Center, 4005 Sandpiper Rd. 804-721-2412. Adm. fee*) and **False Cape State Park** (*4001 Sandpiper Rd. 804-426-7128. No cars; camping fee*). Their well-trailed dunes and forests offer chances to see a variety of wildlife.

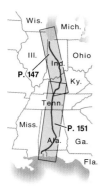

Unless otherwise noted, directions are from interstate, and sites are free and generally open daily. Phone for further information.

① Wood's Historic Grist Mill, INDIANA *(4 miles E on US 30, left on Randolph St. for 0.5 mile, right 1 mile to 9410 Old Lincoln Hwy. 219-947-1958)* Dating from 1838, this restored flour mill in Deep River County Park will appeal to those with a yen for times past. A garden gazebo and willows arching over a pond make for a picturesque setting. *Closed Nov.-Apr.; adm. fee to mill.*

② Lowell *(6 miles W on Ind. 2)* A farming community since the 1830s, the area didn't become favorable to intensive settlement until the 1870s, when sections of swamp around the Kankakee River were drained for the railroad. The **Buckley Homestead** *(2 miles SE of town, off Ind. 2, follow signs. 219-696-0769)* invites visitors to step into the past. An early 1900s farm and schoolhouse and an 1850s pioneer farm show how people made a living from the land. *Grounds open year-round, buildings open weekends only May-Oct.; adm. fee.*

③ Lafayette *(Visitor Center, 301 Frontage Rd. 317-447-9999 or 800-872-6648)* Founded in 1825 along the Wabash River, this trading center has kept pace with changing times. The river, the Erie Canal, and then the railroad brought early prosperity; in this century, manufacturing and the rise to prominence of nearby Purdue University have maintained the town's fortunes. In 1717, the French built Indiana's first fortified white settlement here. At **Fort Ouiatenon** *(5 miles W on S. River Rd. 317-743-3921. Memorial Day-Labor Day Tues.-Sun., weekends only fall and spring)*, a copy of the blockhouse recalls frontier days. Lafayette is perhaps best known for the 1811 Battle of Tippecanoe, when territorial governor William Henry Harrison led a thousand men against an Indian federation organized by Tecumseh. Harrison's victory drove out the Indians and helped launch his successful bid for the Presidency. The interpretive center at the **Tippecanoe Battlefield** *(Ind. 43 exit, follow signs N. 317-567-2147. Adm. fee)* presents a collection of battle artifacts.

For an in-depth look at local history, visit the **Moses Fowler House** *(909 South St. 317-742-8411. Tues.-Sun. p.m., closed Jan.)*, a grand old English Gothic mansion whose exhibits document local lore from Indians to pioneers to railroads. Just up the street, the small **Greater Lafayette Museum of Art** *(101 S. 9th St. 317-742-1128. Tues.-Sun. p.m.)* displays regional art. For an unusual excursion, drive out to **Wolf Park** *(N to Battle Ground, follow signs. 317-567-2265. Park open May-Nov., howl nights year-round on Fri.; adm. fee)*, a research center where you can see and learn about wild wolves. On Friday evenings you can howl with the wolves and on Sundays watch them interact with bison.

④ Zionsville *(4 miles E on Ind. 334. Chamber of Commerce, 135 S. Elm St. 317-873-3836)* Hard by Indianapolis but decades away in temperament, this gentrified Victorian village harbors quiet parks,

Bartholomew County Courthouse, Third
and Wash. Sts., Columbus, Indiana

including one where Lincoln spoke, and a brick
Main Street chockablock with shops and restaurants. Founded as a railroad town in the
1850s, Zionsville became something of a cultural center with regular appearances by such
leading lights as William Jennings Bryan.

Indianapolis   See I-70, p. 172.

Columbus *(Visitor Center, 506 5th St.
812-372-1954)* Beauty seems to be a point of
pride in this small town, starting with the drive
in from the interstate along cornfields lined
with graceful willows. Columbus holds more
modern architectural landmarks than all but
a few big cities. After World War II, a private
foundation offered to pay the design fees for
new buildings by prominent architects. Perhaps the best way to take in the architectural
wonders is by joining a guided bus tour *(Fee)*
sponsored by the Visitor Center. Across the
street from it rises the 166-foot bell tower of
the **First Christian Church,** designed in
1942 by Eliel Saarinen. A block down Fifth
sits an **I. M. Pei library** (1969), graced out
front by a giant Henry Moore bronze. Treat
yourself afterward at **Zaharako's** *(329 Washington St. 812-379-9329. Closed Sun.),* an old-
fashioned ice-cream parlor, circa 1900, with
a marble counter, working player pipe organ,
and homemade ice cream.

Clarksville Along the north shore
of the Ohio River, 1,404-acre **Falls of the Ohio
State Park** *(Jeffersonville exit, 0.75 mile to*

147

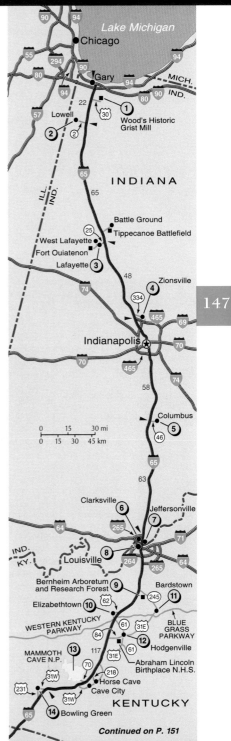

Continued on P. 151

Riverside Dr. 812-280-9970) was created to protect the unusual exposed fossil beds laid down by an inland sea 400 million years ago, when land creatures were evolving from marine life. For best viewing, come between August and October, when the river is low. The falls and dam are also worth a look. *Adm. fee to interpretive center.*

⑦ **Jeffersonville**   Once a major boat-building center, this town showcases its grand past in the **Howard Steamboat Museum** *(1101 E. Market St. 812-283-3728. Closed Mon.; adm. fee),* a late Victorian mansion that once belonged to an important boat-building family. The house and its treasures, including riverboat artifacts and models, have survived flood and fire, and feel a bit moldy and creaky—more like a dusty old attic than a pristine museum. Also in town, the **Hillerich & Bradsby Co.** *(1525 Charlestown-New Albany Rd. 502-585-5226. Museum and plant tours Mon.-Fri.)* has been turning out Louisville Slugger baseball bats since 1884. A museum displays the bats used by famous players.

148

⑧ Louisville, Ky.

Kentucky Derby, Churchill Downs

Horses and bourbon have fueled Kentucky's economy for generations. These two powers unite each spring in the state capital for a ten-day party called the Kentucky Derby. For those who visit at other times, the *Kentucky Derby Museum* (704 Central Ave. 502-637-7097. Adm. fee includes a tour of adjacent Churchill Downs, where the races are run) offers the next best thing. Exhibits on betting, breeding, and training are winners, but the trophy goes to the multimedia show on a wraparound screen, a heart-pounding presentation of Derby Day and the Run for the Roses.

Louisville's downtown has undergone renovation, though much remains to be done (Louisville-Jefferson County Visitor Bureau, 400 S. 1st St. 502-582-3732). An excellent state-of-the art museum, the *Museum of History and Science* (727 W. Main St. 502-561-6100.

Making Louisville Slugger baseball bats

Adm. fee) has three floors of hands-on exhibits and an IMAX theater. In the neo-classic *J. B. Speed Art Museum* (2035 S. 3rd St. 502-636-2893. Closed Mon.) hang 5,000 works from antiquity to modern times.

Southeast of town, the *Colonel Harland Sanders Museum* (1441 Gardiner Ln. 502-456-8353. Closed weekends) traces the growth of Kentucky Fried Chicken from a small restaurant to a megachain. The nearby *Louisville Zoo* (1100 Trevilian Way. 502-459-2181. Adm. fee) safeguards more than 1,600 animals. The *John Conti Coffee Museum* (4023 Bardstown Rd. 502-499-8602 or 800-528-JAVA. Closed weekends) tells the story from beans to brew, with antique grinders and roasters.

Bernheim Arboretum and Research Forest

(2 miles E on Ky. 245. 502-543-2451) Owned by a private foundation, this preserve encompasses 14,000 acres of lovely meadows and woodlands. There's also a nature center, hiking trails, and picnic areas. *Closed mid-Nov.–mid-March; vehicle fee on weekends.*

Elizabethtown

(Tourism and Convention Bureau, 24 Public Sq. 502-765-2175 or 800-437-0092) Founded in 1797, Elizabethtown owes its fame to a relative latecomer—Coca-Cola. Collectors' mania overtook the owners of the local bottling plant, and over the last 20 years they've amassed an impressive array of memorabilia, all displayed in the **Schmidt Coca-Cola Museum** *(Coca-Cola Bottling Co., 2 miles N on US 31W. 502-737-4000. Closed weekends; adm. fee)*. For historical offerings, try the **Lincoln Heritage House** *(Freeman Lake Park, just S of the Coca-Cola museum. 502-769-3916. June-Sept. Tues.-Sun.; donations)*, a log cabin partly built by Abraham Lincoln's father. Also at Freeman Lake Park: the **Sarah Bush Johnston Lincoln Memorial** *(502-737-8727. June-Sept. p.m.; adm. fee)*, a copy of the cabin where Lincoln's stepmother lived.

Bardstown

(20 miles E on Blue Grass Pkwy., 2 miles N on US 31E. Visitor Center, 107 E. Stephen Foster Ave., just off Court Sq. 502-348-4877 or 800-638-4877) This quaint town is soaked in history. Start with the **St. Joseph's Cathedral** *(Junction of US 31E and US 62. 502-348-3126. Tours Apr.-Oct.; donation requested)*, the first Roman Catholic cathedral west of the Alleghenies. Paintings and gifts from Pope Leo XII adorn its walls. For a change of pace, wander behind the cathedral to the **Oscar Getz Museum of Whiskey History** *(114 N. 5th St. 502-348-2999. Closed Mon. Nov.-Apr.; donation requested)* for a first-rate introduction to the state's liquid gold. Here you'll see confiscated copper stills, a saloon room, and displays on Prohibition and Kentucky native Carry Nation. (The museum shares a building with the Bardstown Historical Museum.) To learn more about whiskey, visit one of the four local distilleries; you can pick up a map at the Visitor Center.

The 19th-century **Old County Jails** *(111 W. Stephen Foster Ave. 502-348-5551. March-Dec.; adm. fee)* now open their doors to the curious. The door is also open (and meals are served) at the **Old Talbott Tavern** *(107 W. Stephen Foster Ave. 502-348-3494)*, once patronized by George Rogers Clark, Andrew Jackson, Jesse James, and other notables. The house now known as **My Old Kentucky Home** *(1 mile E of Court Sq. on US 150, follow signs. 502-348-3502 or 800-323-7803. Adm. fee)*, the centerpiece of a state park, inspired Stephen Foster to write what would become the state song. Tours are conducted by ladies in hoop skirts. *The Stephen Foster Story*, a popular musical drama, plays in the park amphitheater *(June-Labor Day Tues.-Sun. 502-348-5971 or 800-626-1563)*. Three governors—two from Kentucky and one from Louisiana—lived at various times in the Georgian **Wickland** mansion *(1 mile E of Court Sq. on US 62. 502-348-5428. Daily spring-fall, weekends only in winter; adm. fee)*.

Homegrown butter beans

☞ Traces of the *Civil War in western Tennessee* tell of the Confederacy's last-ditch efforts to stop the inevitable. In late 1864, while the war's final act played out in Virginia, desperate battles at Franklin and Nashville took nearly 3,000 lives, wrecking the Rebel army in Tennessee. The state had been badly split by the war—the mountaineers in the east siding with the Union, the landowners in the flatlands with the South. Only Virginia saw more battles. To survive, Tennesseans could only fight on as the great conflict exhausted itself.

⑫ **Hodgenville** *(11 miles E on Ky. 84 and US 31E)* Memorials to Abraham Lincoln are scattered among the rolling hills near here. In town, the **Lincoln Museum** *(66 Lincoln Sq. 502-358-3163. Adm. fee)* showcases Lincoln memorabilia and Civil War relics. Tucked in a grove of cedars, oaks, and maples, the marble-and-granite memorial at the **Abraham Lincoln Birthplace National Historic Site** *(3 miles S of town at the junction of Ky. 61 and US 31E. 502-358-3874)* belies Lincoln's humble origins, but the log cabin inside attests to the hardscrabble life led by the future President's parents. At **Abraham Lincoln's Boyhood Home** *(7 miles NE of town on US 31E. 502-549-3741. Closed Nov.-March; adm. fee)*, you can see a cabin reconstructed on the site where young Abe lived from 1811 to 1816.

⑬ **Mammoth Cave National Park** *(9 miles W on Ky. 70 and Ky. 255. 502-758-2251 or -2328. Adm. fee. Advance reservations, which are recommended in summer and on holidays and spring and fall weekends, can be obtained up to eight weeks ahead by calling 800-967-2283.)* For millions of years, water flowed through a land of limestone, creating the world's longest known cave system. Mammoth Cave's underground passages snake away into the black, punctuated by rooms decorated with gypsum crystals and other fantastic formations. The known passageways traverse more than 330 miles; no one knows the full extent of the cave. Guided tours range from an easy 75-minute walk to a strenuous 6-hour, 5-mile wild cave adventure, so pick ones that match your time and stamina.

While in the area, you may want to sample other caves. In the town of Horse Cave, you'll learn more about caves and groundwater by visiting the crowd-free **American Cave Museum and Hidden River Cave** *(Main St. 502-786-1466. Adm. fee)*. Children will like **Kentucky Down Under** *(Horse Cave exit, 0.5 mile NE on Ky. 218 and Ky. 335. 502-786-2634 or 800-762-2869. Animal displays open Apr.-Oct.; adm. fee)*, a 75-acre park featuring animals from the Australian outback, a petting zoo, and Mammoth Onyx Cave. **Crystal Onyx Cave** *(From Cave City, 2 miles S on Ky. 90, follow signs. 502-773-2359. Adm. fee)* is noted for its rare onyx formations.

⑭ **Bowling Green** *(Bowling Green-Warren County Tourist and Convention Commission, 352 Three Springs Rd. 502-782-0800)* Founded in 1798 in a bowl of hills that are still much in evidence (the green less so), the town is webbed by highways and one-way streets. Visitors will want to take a walking tour of the historic district *(Maps available at Tourist and Convention Commission)* and visit the **Kentucky Museum** *(Kentucky Bldg., Western Kentucky Univ. 502-745-2592. Closed Mon.; adm. fee)*, whose artifacts range from prehistoric

Mammoth Cave National Park, Kentucky

to present-day. Car enthusiasts will enjoy the tour of the **General Motors Corvette Assembly Plant** (*Follow signs to Corvette Dr. 502-745-8419. Tours at 9 a.m. and 1 p.m. Mon.-Fri.*) and the display of vintage Corvettes at the **National Corvette Museum** (*Just S of assembly plant. 502-781-7973. Closed Sun.*).

Cross Plains, TENNESSEE

(*3 miles W on Tenn. 25*) This 19th-century pioneer settlement is worth a visit if you fancy old-fashioned drugstores with working soda fountains. **Thomas Drugs** (*7802 Tenn. 25. 615-654-3877*), one of the town's oldest businesses, makes delicious milk shakes. *Closed Sun.*

Gallatin

(*15 miles SE on Tenn. 25*) Named for Albert Gallatin, the treasury secretary under John Adams and Thomas Jefferson, the town serves as the center of agriculture and industry for Sumner County. Several historic houses remain from the early 19th century. **Trousdale Place** (*183 W. Main St. 615-452-5648. Closed Mon.; adm. fee*), a two-story brick mansion, contains 19th-century furniture and a military history library.

A pleasant drive past tobacco farms and hardwood forests brings you to **Cragfont** (*5 miles E of town on Tenn. 25. 615-452-7070. Mid-Apr.–Oct. Tues.-Sun.; adm. fee*). Built about 1800 by Revolutionary War hero James Winchester, Cragfont is an outstanding example of a period patrician home. Famous visitors to the upstairs ballroom include Andrew Jackson, Sam Houston, and the Marquis de Lafayette. A little farther east you'll come to **Wynnewood** (*7 miles E of town, off Tenn. 25. 615-452-5463. Closed Sun. Nov.-March; adm. fee*), a former stagecoach inn and mineral springs resort. The rooms and furnishings reveal the habits of early wayfarers. Don't miss the doctor's cabin with its chilling displays.

Goodlettsville

Though clogged with generic strip growth, this town is worth a stop to see two historic buildings in a lovely park setting. In its first incarnation, **Mansker's Station** (*Moss-Wright Park. 615-859-FORT. Closed Sun.-Mon. and Jan.-Feb.; adm. fee includes Bowen-Campbell House*), a

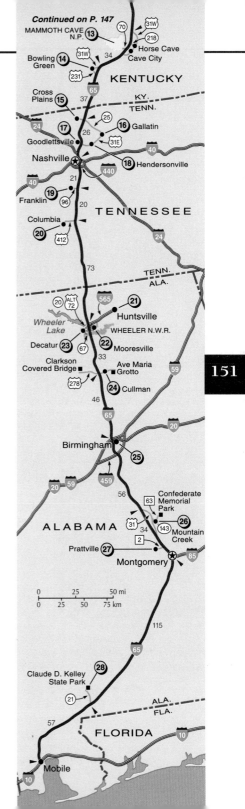

Continued on P. 147

151

reconstructed log fort, was attacked and burned by Indians. Volunteers built the present fort in 1986, a testament as much to the town's community spirit as to its pioneer heritage. The federal-style **Bowen-Campbell House**, also in Moss-Wright Park, was first occupied in the 1780s. It's on the National Register of Historic Places.

Just north of Goodlettsville you'll find an unusual collection: the **Museum of Beverage Containers & Advertising** (*Millersville exit, follow signs 1.5 miles W to 1055 Ridgecrest Dr. 615-859-5236. Adm. fee*), sporting more than 30,000 different soda and beer cans.

(18) **Hendersonville** (*Goodlettsville exit, 4 miles E on US 31E*) Part of Nashville's urban sprawl, Hendersonville boasts its own country music shrines. The **House of Cash** (*3 miles E of town on US 31E. 615-824-5110. Apr.-Oct. Mon.-Sat.; adm. fee*) displays the singer's awards, photos, antiques, guns, guitars, and other belongings. If your taste runs to Conway Twitty, head over to **Twitty City** (*1 Music Village Blvd., across the street from the House of Cash. 615-822-6650. Call for special Dec. hours; adm. fee*), a compound featuring the homes of the country music star and his four children.

At the end of a quiet residential lane, **Historic Rock Castle** (*2 miles S on Indian Lake Rd. to Rock Castle Lane. 615-824-0502. Closed Mon.-Tues. and Jan.; adm. fee*) stands as a reminder of the early days in Tennessee. Though hardly a castle, the limestone structure dates from the late 1700s, when surveyor and statesman Daniel Smith brought his family to this frontier settlement.

Nashville See I-40, p. 117.

Carnton Mansion, Carnton Plantation, Franklin, Tennessee

(19) **Franklin** This peaceful farming community erupted into a bloody battleground late on November 30, 1864, when Confederates charged entrenched Federals. Nearly 2,000 Rebels died, and most of them are buried at McGavock Confederate Cemetery, on the grounds of the **Carnton Plantation** (*2.5 miles S of town, off Lewisburg Pike, at 1345 Carnton Ln. 615-794-0903. Adm. fee*). The Carnton Mansion, a spacious neoclassical house, served as a hospital. Thick bloodstains on the floorboards remain as testimony to the suffering endured here. Closer to town, the **Carter House** (*1140 Columbia Ave. 615-791-1861. Adm. fee*) stood in the middle of the fighting. This national historic landmark features battle-scarred outbuildings, a farmhouse, and a small museum with a descriptive film.

(20) **Columbia** (*9 miles W on US 412*) Set on the limestone bluffs of the Duck River, Columbia is a center for limestone quarrying and phosphate mining. The surrounding fertile farmlands, wooded hills, and meadows attracted settlers in the early 19th century, including the parents of James K. Polk. The 11th President lived here in his early 20s, and the painstakingly restored **James K. Polk Ancestral**

Home *(301 W. 7th St. 615-388-2354)* displays family heirlooms and furnishings from his White House years. *Adm. fee.*

H u n t s v i l l e ,   A L A B A M A   *(20 miles E on I-565. Huntsville-Madison County Convention and Visitors Bureau, 700 Monroe St. 205-533-5723 or 800-SPACE4U)* This city was the birthplace of both Alabama in 1819 and the U. S. space program in the 1950s. Alabama's first constitution was drafted in **Constitution Hall** *(Franklin St. and Gates Ave. 205-535-6565 or 800-678-1819. Closed Sun. and Jan.-Feb.; adm. fee),* now a low-key living-history village with costumed guides, gardens, a print shop, and other buildings. The near-by **Historic Huntsville Depot Transportation Museum**

Historic Huntsville Depot Transportation Museum, Huntsville, Alabama

(320 Church St. 205-539-1860. Closed Sun.-Mon. and Jan.-Feb.; adm. fee), a polished, three-floor display of local history, includes talking robots, Civil War-era graffiti, and extensive railroad memorabilia. The museum also offers a half-hour trolley tour of downtown and the historic districts. The **Huntsville Museum of Art** *(Von Braun Civic Center, 700 Monroe St. S.W. 205-535-4350. Closed Mon.)* features regional and American art.

U. S. Space & Rocket Center, Huntsville

Huntsville is best known as the place where Wernher von Braun and his team of German scientists developed the Saturn V moon rocket. The Marshall Space Flight Center has headed all phases of the space program, from satellites to shuttles. The colossal rockets, visible from I-565, form part of the **U. S. Space & Rocket Center** *(Tranquility Base, 1 mile W of town. 205-837-3400. Adm. fee),* a huge museum and outdoor complex where visitors can experience the closest thing to space exploration. Simulators used by astronauts, hands-on exhibits, IMAX movies, and tours bring the earthbound into contact with cutting-edge technology.

Those in search of quieter pleasures should try the **Burritt Museum and Park** *(7 miles E of town on US 431, left at Monte Sano Blvd. to Burritt Dr. 205-536-2882. Closed Mon. and mid-Dec.–Feb.; donation requested),* a woodland preserve atop a knoll with fine views, nature trails, and reconstructed 19th-century log buildings.

M o o r e s v i l l e   Exiting off high-speed I-565, you might feel that you've entered a time tunnel as you drive into this unobtrusive village bypassed by the 20th century. The state's first incorporated town (1818), Mooresville embraces a small, all-but-forgotten clutch of antebellum structures, most still in use. The nearly dilapidated wooden **Stagecoach Inn,** circa 1825, is undergoing slow restoration. Around the corner, an 1840 post office still uses the original wooden call boxes. And the brick church has a balcony where slaves sat.

Close-up of Alabama flag

(23) **Decatur**   Founded in 1820 and named for naval hero Stephen Decatur, this town sits beside Wheeler Lake, one of the TVA reservoirs on the Tennessee River. Though badly damaged during the Civil War, Decatur rose again to become an important railroad and industrial center. One survivor, the **Old State Bank** (*925 Bank St. 205-350-5060*), built in the 1830s, has served as a bank, Union supply depot and hospital, residence, and now a museum where you can obtain maps for walking tours of the adjacent Old Decatur and Albany Historic Districts. Wildlife enthusiasts will be fascinated by the rocks, shells, and mounted animal specimens in **Cook's Natural Science Museum** (*412 13th St. S.E. 205-350-9347*). To see the real thing, head for the **Wheeler National Wildlife Refuge** (*Just W of I-65 on Ala. 67. 205-350-6639. Visitor Center closed Mon.-Tues. March-Oct.*), a peaceful preserve that bursts into life every winter with the arrival of thousands of migrating ducks and Canada geese.

☞ The history of towns like Birmingham, Alabama, and Lafayette, Indiana, is tied to the *railroad,* which could move people and cargo much faster than canals, rivers, or horses. By the 1870s, train tracks from the Deep South to the northern prairie meant prosperity to the connected towns, doom to those bypassed. Small towns sprang up around depots; many now preserve their heritage in train museums.

154

(24) **Cullman**   When Johann Cullman arrived with five families from Germany in 1873, he intended to establish a wine-making community here. Finding the soil unsuitable for grapes, the industrious immigrants turned to strawberries, sweet potatoes, and corn, and over the next several years the thriving town attracted 20,000 German settlers. The **Cullman County Museum** (*211 2nd Ave. N.E. 205-739-1258. Closed Sat.; adm. fee*), a copy of Cullman's German Victorian house, features exhibits on Native American culture and the area's rural and German heritage. The town has become famous for the work of another, later, German immigrant. Brother Joseph came to study at the local Benedictine abbey and began assembling a collection of miniature buildings made of stone, glass, and odds and ends. The **Ave Maria Grotto** (*4 miles E of I-65 on US 278. 205-734-4110. Adm. fee*) contains 125 models of buildings in Rome, the Holy Land, and other places. In the vicinity you can visit several well-preserved covered bridges, including the picturesque **Clarkson Covered Bridge** (*9 miles W of town, off US 278*), built in 1904.

Model of St. Peter's Basilica and Square, Ave Maria Grotto, Cullman, Alabama

(26) **Mountain Creek**   (*9 miles SE on US 31 and Ala. 143*) In 1902, this small summer resort community became the site of Alabama's only Confederate veterans' home. Now a hundred acres of secluded woods, **Confederate Memorial Park** (*1 mile N on Rte. 63, follow signs. 205-755-1990*) remembers the boys in gray with a memorabilia-packed museum and a walking or driving tour.

(27) **Prattville**   (*3 miles W on Rte. 2*) In 1835 Daniel Pratt, one of Alabama's first industrialists, built cotton gins and mills here on the swampy lands by Autauga Creek. Prattville's present vitality

Not until the railroad arrived in the 1870s did Birmingham really take off. But with the essentials for steel production—iron ore, limestone, and coal—readily available in the hills nearby, the town quickly became a thriving industrial city. The iron and steel industries lapsed after the Depression, and the Birmingham of the 1960s became a focal point for violent racial upheaval. Now traces of the Old South have all but vanished, and Alabama's largest city is making its mark in the medical and engineering fields (Chamber of Commerce, 2027 1st Ave. N. 205-323-5461).

To explore the city's recent history, tour the new Civil Rights District. *Kelly Ingram Park* (6th Ave. N. and 16th St.), once the forum for demonstrations, is now a quiet greensward with stunning sculptures honoring the struggle for equality. Catercorner is the *Sixteenth Street Baptist Church,* the site of the infamous 1963 bombing that killed four black girls. Across the street, the attractive *Birmingham Civil Rights Institute* (520 16th St. N. 205-328-9696. Closed Mon.) chronicles the civil rights era. While

Arlington Antebellum House, 331 Cotton Ave. S.W.

downtown, visit the *Alabama Sports Hall of Fame* (2150 Civic Center Blvd. 205-323-6665. Adm. fee) and see how seriously Alabamians take their sports. Three floors of exhibits memorialize Jesse Owens, Paul B. "Bear" Bryant, and others.

For a terrific overview of the city and surroundings, head up to *Vulcan Park* (20th St. S. and Valley Ave. 205-328-2863. Adm. fee), where the world's tallest (55 feet) cast-iron statue honors Birmingham's industrial past. Nearby you'll find two top attractions: the *Birmingham Zoo* (2630 Cahaba Rd. 205-879-0408. Adm. fee) and the *Birmingham Botanical Gardens* (2612 Lane Park Rd. 205-879-1227). *Red Mountain Roadcut,* not far away, offers a fascinating walk through the area's geological history.

155

Downtown skyline in morning

attests to its founder's success. Textile mills, a paper mill, and a cotton-ginning factory are key businesses. Visitors can tour the renovated historic district and **Buena Vista** (*3 miles S on Ala. 14, left on Rte. 4 for 2.5 miles. 205-361-0961. Tues. and by appt.; adm. fee*), an early 1800s plantation house. **Wilderness Park** (*Upper Kingston Rd. 205-361-3623*), a small, jungly tract, is luxuriant with towering bamboo, laurel oaks, and scuppernong vines.

Montgomery   See I-85, p. 261.

Claude D. Kelley State Park   (*9 miles N on Ala. 21. 205-862-2511*) Located off a Deep South back road that winds past farms, piney hills, and kudzu-choked ravines, this 960-acre park beckons travelers with a picturesque lake for boating, swimming, and fishing. Camping, picnic areas. *Adm. fee.*

Mobile   See I-10, p. 47.

Unless otherwise noted, directions are from interstate, and sites are free and generally open daily. Phone for further information.

① **Port Huron, MICHIGAN**   One of the state's oldest settlements, this delightful port city on the choppy St. Clair River took root in 1686 as a French fort. It now welcomes foreign incursion—the **Blue Water International Bridge** links it to Canada. The **Museum of Arts and History** (*0.5 mile N of Mich. 25 at 1115 6th St. 313-982-0891. Wed.-Sun.*) features Indian and maritime items, as well as Thomas Edison memorabilia (he grew up here).

② **Dryden**   At the **Seven Ponds Nature Center** (*Lapeer Rd. exit, S on Mich. 53, follow signs 12 miles to 3854 Crawford Rd. 313-796-3200*), almost 5 miles of hiking trails cross 250 tranquil acres of fields, marshes, gardens, woods, and glacial lakes. *Closed Mon.; adm. fee.*

Flint   See I-75, p. 187.

③ **Durand**   Settled in the 1870s as a railroad stop, Durand grew into one of Michigan's major train centers. Picturesque **Union Station** features château revival architecture.

④ **East Lansing**   With nearly 40,000 students, 5,200-acre **Michigan State University** (*517-353-8700*) has one of the largest enrollments in the country. Visitor attractions include the **W. J. Beal Botanical Garden** (*W. Circle Dr. 517-355-9582*), the dinosaur skeletons in the **MSU Museum** (*Opposite the library. 517-355-2370*), the **Abrams Planetarium** (*Shaw La. and Science Rd. 517-355-4672. Open weekends; adm. fee for programs*), and the **Kresge Art Museum** (*Auditorium Rd. 517-355-7631. Closed Aug.*).

156

Barge near Port Huron, Michigan

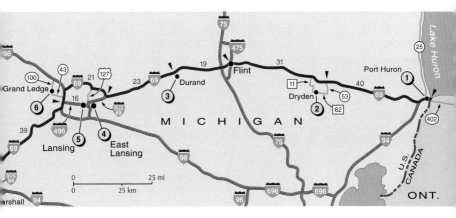

Lansing   In 1847, the state legislature settled on Lansing as the capital, provoking laughter since there was little here but a log cabin and a sawmill. Now a clean, orderly city, the capital welcomes visitors (*Follow Capitol Loop signs to the downtown area*). To delve deeper into state history, stop at the **Michigan Library and Historical Center** (*717 W. Allegan St. 517-373-3559*). The ornate **State Capitol** (*Capitol and Michigan Aves. 517-373-2353. Tours daily*) is the city's focal point. Continue a few blocks east on Michigan Avenue to a cluster of museums: The **Impression 5 Science Museum** (*200 Museum Dr. 517-485-8116. Adm. fee*) offers visitors a top-notch hands-on experience; the **Michigan Museum of Surveying** (*220 S. Museum Dr. 517-484-6605. Closed Mon.; adm. fee*) houses historical surveying artifacts; and the **R. E. Olds Transportation Museum** (*240 Museum Dr. 517-372-0422. Adm. fee*), named for Oldsmobile's founder, showcases antique cars and memorabilia.

Grand Ledge (*5 miles W on Mich. 43*) Sandstone ledges 300 million years old rise 60 feet above the Grand River. Climbers like to tackle the craggy wall in **Oak Park** (*Off Front St. 517-627-2149*), while fishermen and canoeists head for adjacent **Fitzgerald Park** (*133 Fitzgerald Park Dr. 517-627-7351. April–mid-Oct.; free on Wed.*).

Coldwater   This town on the turnpike between Detroit and Chicago boasts the **Tibbits Opera House** (*14 S. Hanchett St. 517-278-6029*), an 1882 Victorian theater that was a favorite of traveling troupes. It now puts on concerts, art exhibits, and summer theater performances for adults and children. *Tours on request.*

Angola, INDIANA (*2 miles E on US 20*) This small town sits on the former hunting lands of the Potawatomi and Miami Indians. Mid-19th-century settlers traded with Indians in the public square, where the 1868 **Courthouse,** a copy of Boston's Faneuil Hall, still stands. The area's many lakes attract vacationers.

Hood ornament, Auburn-Cord-Duesenberg Museum, Auburn, Ind.

⑨ Auburn The world-famous **Auburn-Cord-Duesenberg Museum** (*E on Ind. 8, follow signs to 1600 S. Wayne St. 219-925-1444*) pays tribute to top-of-the-line automobiles from horseless carriages to modern sports cars. *Adm. fee.*

⑩ Fort Wayne (*5 miles E on Ind. 14. Visitor Info Center, 1021 S. Calhoun St. 219-424-3700 or 800-767-7752*) Now Indiana's second largest city, Fort Wayne started off as a French trading post. In 1794, U. S. Maj. Gen. "Mad" Anthony Wayne built a fort here and gave the city its name. The past is recounted at **Historic Fort Wayne** (*211 S. Barr St. 219-424-3476. Adm. fee*), a living history museum with a blacksmith shop, smokehouse, and baker's house. For a more in-depth look at local history and geography, stop by the **Allen County–Fort Wayne Historical Museum** (*302 E. Berry St. 219-426-2882. Closed Mon.*), housed in the old city hall. Nearby is the turn-of-the-century, classical-style **Allen County Courthouse** (*715 S. Calhoun St. 219-428-7555*). You can visit the grave of John Chapman, better known as Johnny Appleseed, in **Johnny Appleseed Park** (*Parnell Ave. S of War Memorial Coliseum*). Kids of all ages will enjoy the 22-acre "African veldt" at the **Fort Wayne Children's Zoo** (*3411 Sherman St. 219-482-4610. May-Sept.; adm. fee*) and the colorful blooms at **Lakeside Gardens** (*1401 Lake Ave. 219-483-0057*), one of the nation's largest rose gardens. You can view tropical and desert plants at the **Foellinger-Freimann Botanical Conservatory** (*1100 S. Calhoun St. 219-427-1267. Adm. fee*) and a large collection of Lincoln family photographs, paintings, and letters at the **Lincoln Museum** (*1300 S. Clinton St. 219-455-3864*).

⑪ Bluffton (*12 miles E on Ind. 116*) Downtown Bluffton prides itself on its many turn-of-the-century buildings. Bikers, joggers, and walkers take to the **Rivergreenway Trail** (*Ind. 316*), which meanders east from downtown along the Wabash River. Just beyond the trail lies **Ouabache State Park** (*4 miles E of town on Ind. 216. 219-824-0926. Daily Apr.-Oct., weekdays rest of year; adm. fee on weekends Apr.-Oct.*). The 1,116-acre site, once the nation's largest producer of pheasant and quail chicks, offers trails, boating, and camping.

⑫ Marion (*7 miles W on Ind. 18*) On the **Mississinewa Battlefield** (*7 miles N of town on Ind. 15. 317-662-0096. Adm. fee*), 600 Federal troops fought Miami and Delaware Indians during the War of 1812. In town, the Greek Revival **Hostess House** (*723 W. 4th St. 317-664-3755. Mon.-Fri.; tours and lunch available*) was built in 1912 by black architect Samuel Plato.

⑬ Fairmont (*5 miles W on Ind. 26*) Between the **James Dean Gallery** (*425 N. Main St. 317-948-3326. Adm. fee*), run by a James Dean look-alike, and the **Fairmont Historical Museum** (*203 E. Washington St. 317-948-4555. March-Nov.; donation requested*), you'll see enough Dean memorabilia to last a lifetime. The idolized Fairmont native is buried in **Park Cemetery** (*0.5 mile N on Main St.*).

How did Michigan take the driver's seat in *auto manufacturing*? Capitalizing on the state's wagon- and buggy-making heritage and its raw materials, R. E. Olds opened a car company in Lansing in the 1890s. Other companies followed, and competition grew fierce. But in 1908 a new car left the others in the dust—the Model T Ford, a cheap version made on an assembly line. Detroit, Flint, and Lansing became auto capitals. Michigan's economy boomed so much it didn't bother to diversify, an error that took a toll in the 1980s.

Muncie *(10 miles E on Ind. 32. Visitor Center, 425 N. High St. 317-284-2700)* Built on the homeland of the Munsee clan of the Delaware Indians, this small city, now surrounded by cornfields, became industrialized in the late 19th century with the discovery of natural gas and the arrival of the railroad. The Ball family moved their glass manufacturing plant here from New York in 1888; today the **Ball Corporation Museum** *(345 S. High St. 317-747-6100. Mon.-Fri.)* displays glass containers from those early years. The Balls also helped establish a university here in 1918. The collection at the **Ball State University Museum of Art** *(Fine Arts Bldg. 317-285-5242. Closed Mon.)* spans 5,000 years. The **Emily Kimbrough House** *(715 E. Washington St. 317-282-1550)* was home to the author who wrote of her Muncie childhood in *How Dear to My Heart*. The **Minnetrista Cultural Center** *(1200 Minnetrista Pkwy. 317-282-4848. Closed Mon.; adm. fee for special shows)* presents exhibits on local history, as well as outdoor concerts in summer.

Anderson *(6 miles W on Ind. 32)* More than 2,000 years ago, Adena and Hopewell mound builders occupied this area; you can still see their huge earthworks in **Mounds State Park** *(From I-69, 4 miles W on Ind. 32 to 4306 Mounds Rd. 317-642-6627. Summer adm. fee)*. In town, visit the **Gruenwald House** *(626 Main St. 317-646-5771. April-Dec. Tues.-Fri.; adm. fee)*, dating from 1860; the **Anderson Fine Arts Center** *(226 W. 8th St. 317-649-1248. Closed Mon.)*, with works by local and national artists; the **Historical Military Armor Museum** *(2330 Crystal St. 317-649-TANK. Tues. and Thurs. by appt.)*; and the 1929 **Paramount Theatre** *(1124 Meridian St. 317-642-1234)*, a movie palace showing classic films.

Noblesville *(11 miles N on Ind. 37)* Originally an Indian trading post, Noblesville grew with the railroad. For a taste of pioneer life, visit **Conner Prairie** *(4 miles S on Allisonville Rd., follow signs. 317-776-6000. Closed Mon. and Dec.-April; adm. fee)*, a re-created village with costumed interpreters.

Indianapolis   See I-70, p. 172.

159

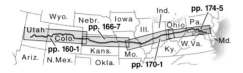

Unless otherwise noted, directions are from interstate, and sites are free and generally open daily. Phone for further information.

(1) **Fremont Indian State Park, UTAH** *(Fremont Indian State Park exit. 801-527-4631 or 800-662-8898)* Fremont Indians flourished in southern Utah a thousand years ago, vanishing before the first Spaniards arrived. The site of one of their largest known villages was destroyed during the construction of I-70, but archaeologists excavated tons of pottery, arrowheads, grinding stones, and other relics, as well as the remains of 80 pit houses. A museum displays the best finds. Hiking trails, campsites. *Adm. fee for museum.*

(2) **Palisade State Park** *(25 miles N on US 89. 801-835-7275)* Set in a semiarid farming valley, the park centers on a 70-acre reservoir created as a resort in the 1870s. Swimming, boating, camping. *Adm. fee.*

(3) **San Rafael Swell** I-70 bisects this 2,400-square-mile sandstone wonderland

of buttes, pinnacles, deep canyons, and mesas that is sometimes called Utah's Little Grand Canyon. A series of uplifts created these formations 50 million years ago; wind and water have been sculpturing the rock ever since. Especially dramatic is **San Rafael Reef** on the eastern face. Utah 24 has numerous access points; you can pick up a map at I-70 rest areas.

(4) **Green River** Surrounded by melon farms, this tiny highway stopover is a popular launching point for river expeditions. **Green River State Park** *(Green River Blvd. 801-564-3633 or 800-322-3770. Adm. fee)* attracts boaters, anglers, and campers. Park rangers will give directions to **Crystal Geyser** *(10 miles S on unpaved roads)*, whose unpredictable seven-minute bursts usually occur twice daily. The **John Wesley Powell River History Museum** *(88. E. Main St. 801-564-3427)* outlines the natural and human history of the Green and Colorado Rivers. Exhibits chronicle the exploits of Powell, the one-armed explorer who first mapped the Grand Canyon, and other river runners.

(5) **Sauropod Track Site** *(8.5 miles S on US 191, left before passing microwave tower, cross train tracks, follow unpaved road 2 miles. Do not attempt after rain.)* Some 150 million years ago, when this area was a damp river channel, at least four dinosaurs left their footprints. Among them were a brontosaurus with 2-foot-wide prints and a large carnivore with a limp

Arches National Park *(Crescent Junction exit, 27 miles S on US 191. Visitor Center 801-259-8161)* Enfolding the world's highest concentration of naturally formed stone arches, this 77,379-acre park boasts a wealth of spectacular sights. You can drive to many of the major arches and other formations, which wind and water carved from red sandstone over the last 150 million years. Many hiking trails. *Adm. fee.*

Delicate Arch, Arches National Park, Utah

You won't see any THEROPOD CROSSING signs, but the arid badlands along the Utah-Colorado border were a ***dinosaur stomping ground*** some 150 million years ago. Back then, the area was a broad, river-laced plain, though scientists debate whether it was tropically lush or merely seasonally humid. Muddy riverbanks and occasional dustings of volcanic ash preserved both the bones and the footprints of diplodocus, allosaurus, and other prehistoric creatures. From such dinosaur highways, scientists can deduce a lot about Jurassic social life.

161

Sego Canyon Petroglyphs *(Thompson exit, 1 mile N to train tracks, follow signs 3 miles on unpaved road)* Hundreds of petroglyphs etch the steep sandstone walls of Sego Canyon. Three groups of Native Americans carved these humanoid forms, animals, and mysterious abstract symbols over a 2,000-year period. You'll find information at the Silver Grill Café in Thompson.

Grand Junction, COLORADO Dwarfed by sprawling mesas, this city thrives on ranching, orchards, and recreation. In its small downtown, you'll encounter more than two dozen sculptures and the **Museum of Western Colorado.** Its **Main**

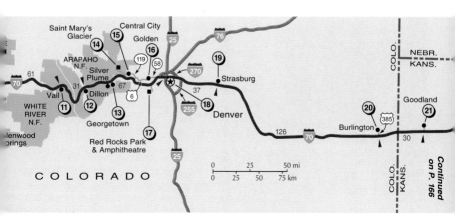

Continued on P. 166

East of Glenwood Springs, I-70 enters 12-mile-long **Glenwood Canyon**, a steep, narrow chasm cut by the Colorado River. The canyon is a marvel not only for its beautiful vistas and sheer cliffs but also for the interstate itself, whose four lanes squeeze through the gorge with little detriment to the environment or the view. Completed in 1993 after 11 years of work at a cost of 490 million dollars, this stretch of I-70 includes tunnels, bridges, and sections where the roadbed is cantilevered over the rock face.

Museum (*4th and Ute Sts. 303-242-0971. Closed Sun. year-round and Mon. Labor Day-Memorial Day*) is devoted to the region's post-1880 history. At the **Dinosaur Valley** branch (*4th and Main Sts. 303-243-3466 or 241-9210. Closed Sun.-Mon. Labor Day-Memorial Day; adm. fee*), lifelike automated dinosaurs re-create the area's rich paleontological past, while guides at the museum's **Cross Orchards Historic Site** (*3073 F/Patterson Rd. 303-434-9814. May-Oct. Tues.-Sat.; adm. fee*) reenact life at a turn-of-the-century orchard, once the valley's most modern. On the high plateaus surrounding the city, you can fish, hike, camp, and enjoy the view. Another place to savor fine vistas is 23-mile Rim Rock Drive in **Colorado National Monument** (*10 miles W of town on Colo. 340. 303-858-3617. Adm. fee in summer*), a breathtaking preserve of canyons and sandstone formations.

⑨ **Rifle**   This small, recreation-oriented town on the Colorado River is so named because an early surveyor lost his firearm nearby and wrote the word "rifle" on his map to help an assistant retrieve it. **Rifle Gap State Park** (*9 miles N on Colo. 13 and Colo. 325. 303-625-1607. Adm. fee*), set on a 359-acre reservoir, offers boating, swimming, fishing, and camping. Four miles up the canyon at **Rifle Falls State Park** (*N on Colo. 325. 303-625-1607. Adm. fee*), East Rifle Creek plunges over a steep, cave-punctured limestone cliff.

⑩ **Glenwood Springs**   Ensconced in the crimson foothills just west of where the Rockies begin to steepen, unpretentious Glenwood Springs attracts skiers and hikers to its mineral springs, used by Ute Indians and then developed by wealthy Easterners in the 1880s. **Hot Springs Pool and Lodge** (*401 N. River Rd. 303-945-6571 or 800-537-7946. Adm. fee*) claims the world's largest outdoor mineral hot springs pool. At **Yampah Spa Vapor Cave** (*709 E. Elm St. 303-945-0667. Adm. fee*), located inside a natural vapor cave, you can indulge in a steam bath and massage.

⑪ **Vail**   In the 1960s a trio of developers transformed this remote sheep-ranching valley into one of the country's leading ski resorts. Although central Vail, with its Tyrolean-facaded buildings, is restricted to pedestrians, a free bus system links the village with outlying areas. The **Colorado Ski Museum–Hall of Fame** (*231 S. Frontage Rd. E., in Vail Village Transportation Center. 303-476-1876. Closed Mon.; adm. fee*) recounts the history of the sport, introduced here by Norwegian miners who had skied to work. The **Lionshead Gondola** and the **Vista Bahn Express Lift** (*183 Gore Creek Dr. 303-479-4290 in summer. Adm. fee*) carry skiers in winter, mountain bikers in summer.

⑫ **Dillon**   Longtime residents, mainly ranchers, may not have been thrilled about relocating their town to make way for Denver's main water supply in 1961, but the resulting **Dillon Reservoir** (*Dillon Marina. 303-468-5100*) is a boon for those who like to boat, sail, swim, and fish in its high-elevation waters

Vail, Colorado

Georgetown and Silver Plume   The high valleys just east of the Continental Divide shelter two of Colorado's best preserved mining towns. The prospectors who poured in after gold was struck in 1859 soon realized these hills were rich in silver. The mine owners lived in large Victorian houses in Georgetown. Miners, mainly Italian and British immigrants, occupied Silver Plume, whose dirt streets and weathered wooden buildings look much as they did in the late 1880s, when the town was rebuilt after a fire. The **Georgetown Loop Railroad** (*Information and tickets at Old Georgetown Station or Silver Plume Depot. 303-569-2403. Memorial Day-Oct.; fare charge*), completed in 1884 and rebuilt in 1984, snakes between the two towns and includes an optional tour of the defunct **Lebanon Silver Mine.** An engineering wonder in its day, the railroad carried as many sightseers as silver loads. You can see the tracks from an I-70 overlook between Georgetown and Silver Plume.

St. Mary's Glacier   (*9 miles N on Fall River Rd.*) Tucked beneath blustery 13,294-foot James Peak, this glacier entices skiers, snowmobilers, and hikers year-round. The hairpin road up the mountain twists past old mining camps to a parking lot, where a half-mile trail leads to St. Mary's Lake and the 2,000-foot-long glacier. It can get bitter cold up here!

Central City   (*2 miles E on US 6, 8 miles N on Colo. 119*)   Dubbed "the richest square mile on earth" following the gold strike of 1859, raucous Central City grew from the largest of several mining camps. In 1991, the state authorized casino gambling here and in neighboring Black Hawk, turning the historic towns into mini-Las Vegases. Narrow

Victorian house in Georgetown, Colorado (upper); mining students at an old Colorado silver mine (lower)

roads are clogged, parking is scarce, and construction mars vistas. At the 1872 **Teller House** (*120 Eureka St. 303-279-3200*), visitors can still make out the woman's face painted on the floorboards. The well-appointed 1878 **Opera House** (*200 Eureka St. 303-292-6700. Tours from Teller House; adm. fee*) hosts summer performances.

Golden   (*13 miles E on US 6*)   The **Adolph Coors Company** (*13th and Ford Sts. 303-277-BEER. Closed Sun.*) runs tours of its mammoth plant, which produces 1.5 million gallons of beer a day. Two miles outside town, the **Colorado Railroad Museum** (*17155 W. 44th Ave. 303-279-4591 or 800-365-6263. Adm. fee*) displays more than 50 old railroad cars and a model train.

Adolph Coors Company, Golden, Colo.

Red Rocks Park & Amphitheatre   (*1.5 miles S on Colo. 26. 303-697-8935*)   Jewel of Denver's regional mountain park system, Red Rocks—a 9,050-seat theater framed by 400-foot-high sandstone slabs and noted for its acoustics—has hosted open-air performances each summer since the 1940s. The dramatic geology and hiking trails alone are worth a visit.

⑱ Denver

Skyline at sunset

Brightened by as many sunny days a year as Miami, with the jagged peaks of the Rockies for a backdrop, Denver is a mecca for outdoor enthusiasts and home to an unusually young populace. The city boomed in 1859 with wildly exaggerated tales of gold found in Cherry Creek, then kept growing when sizable veins were struck in the mountains soon afterward. Mineral wealth from oil and coal continues to fuel Denver's economy. The inexpensive *Cultural Connection Trolley* (303-299-6000. May-Oct.) runs daily between many of the city's most popular attractions (Convention & Visitors Bureau, 225 W. Colfax Ave. 303-892-1112).

Maya plaque, Denver Art Museum

164

The gold-domed *Colorado State Capitol* (200 E. Colfax Ave. 303-866-2604. Closed weekends), completed in 1908, is a good first stop in the Mile High City: The top of its west steps is exactly 5,280 feet above sea level. Within a few blocks are the *U. S. Mint* (320 W. Colfax Ave. 303-844-3582. Closed weekends), where 32 million coins are stamped a day; the *Colorado History Museum* (Broadway and 13th Ave. 303-866-3682. Adm. fee), with fine exhibits on the region's Indians and mining boom; the *Denver Art Museum* (100 W. 14th Ave. 303-640-2793. Closed Mon.; adm. fee), whose varied collection highlights Native American art; the *Denver Firefighters Museum* (1326 Tremont Pl. 303-892-1436. Closed weekends; adm. fee), which houses early fire equipment; and the *Museum of Western Art* (1727 Tremont Pl. 303-296-1880. Closed Sun.-Mon.; adm. fee),

Museum of Western Art

with more than 125 works by Frederic Remington, Charles Russell, and others.

Across the South Platte River, near Mile High Stadium, youngsters will enjoy the interactive exhibits and plastic-tile practice ski slope at the *Children's Museum of Denver* (2121 Children's Mu-

Lunchtime at the Buckhorn Exchange Restaurant

seum Dr. 303-433-7444. Closed Mon. except summer; adm. fee). In City Park, east of downtown, you'll find the *Denver Zoo* (Colorado Blvd. and 23rd Ave. 303-331-4110. Adm. fee), featuring tropical animals, and the *Denver Museum of Natural History* (2001 S. Colorado Blvd. 303-322-7009. Adm. fee), with first-rate displays on prehistoric animals and Colorado geology, among others. The serene *Denver Botanic Gardens* (1005 York St. 303-331-4000. Adm. fee) showcases 22 acres of flowers, trees, and shrubs. The *Black American West Museum and Heritage Center* (3091 California St. 303-292-2566. Wed.-Sun.; adm. fee) tells the story of African Americans on the frontier.

Strasburg   The last tracks of the Kansas Pacific Railroad were laid on the flat plains of Strasburg in August 1870, making uninterrupted, coast-to-coast rail travel possible for the first time. The **Comanche Crossing Museum** *(On Colo. 36 at W end of town. 303-622-4668. June-Aug. p.m.)* contains exhibits on the railroad and frontier life, as well as several restored buildings.

Burlington   This small High Plains city is home to the **Kit Carson County Carousel** *(Fairgrounds, Colorado Ave. and 15th St. Memorial Day-Labor Day; adm. fee)*, built in 1905 and moved here from Denver in 1928. The **Old Town Museum** *(420 S. 14th St. 719-346-7382 or 800-288-1334. Adm. fee)*, a living-history museum with 20 restored buildings, depicts turn-of-the-century life on the plains.

Prairie Museum of Art and History, Colby, Kansas

Goodland, KANSAS   After a dispute with nearby Eustis over which would become the county seat, a band of armed Goodland men stormed Eustis in the late 1880s and seized the county record books. Eustis no longer exists; Goodland remains the county seat. Its **High Plains Museum** *(1717 Cherry St. 913-899-4595)* boasts a full-scale copy of the country's first patented helicopter, built in 1910 by two locals. The original self-destructed on its maiden flight.

Colby   *(2 miles N on Kans. 25)*   The **Prairie Museum of Art and History** *(1905 S. Franklin St. 913-462-4590)* spotlights decorative art objects acquired by a Colby couple over 40 years, including finely cut glass, 18th-century porcelain figures, antique furniture, clothing, and dolls. *Closed Mon. except June-Aug.; adm. fee.*

Cedar Bluff State Park   *(13 miles S on Kans. 147. 913-726-3212)* Named for high, wooded limestone bluffs that fracture the Kansas plains, this park encompasses an 1,100-acre reservoir. You can see deer, turkeys, pheasants, and other wildlife in the surrounding public lands, and pioneer carvings in a canyon to the west. *Drinking water is limited mid-Oct.–mid-Apr.; adm. fee.*

Hays   Built to protect post-Civil War settlers and railroad workers from Indian attacks, Fort Hays hosted such notables as Buffalo Bill Cody and Lt. Col. George Armstrong Custer. Its blockhouse, officers' quarters, and other original buildings are preserved at **Frontier Historical Park** *(4 miles S on US 183 Bypass. 913-625-6812)*. Fort Hays State University *(US 183 Bypass)* is home to the **Sternberg Memorial Museum** *(1st floor of McCartney Hall. 913-628-4286)*, which features the fossils of plants and animals from an inland sea that covered western Kansas a hundred million years ago.

Victoria   Founded by British settlers, the town saw an influx of Germans fleeing Russian persecution in the late 1870s. With

165

Wood was scarce on the treeless plains of central Kansas, but the Europeans who settled there in the 1870s and needed to pen livestock had ingenuity to spare. Just beneath the topsoil lay a foot-thick bed of limestone some 60 million years old, the rocky remnant of an ancient inland sea. The stone could easily be cut and notched to make durable posts for barbed wire fences. As recently as 1950, Kansas had more than 40,000 miles of these **stone-post fences.** Today, limestone posts, not to mention limestone sundials and birdbaths, are more likely to be found in backyards than on the range.

Cathedral of the Plains, Victoria, Kansas

its 140-foot twin towers, the Romanesque St. Fidelis Church, completed in 1911 and often called the **Cathedral of the Plains** (*900 Cathedral St. 913-735-2777*), stands as a monument to their faith.

㉖ **S a l i n a**   A business center for hard wheat and alfalfa crops, Salina started off as a trading post. The town came into its own during the 1860s, first as a supply outlet for Colorado-bound gold prospectors and later as a stop on the Union Pacific Railroad. For a look at exhibits on Native Americans and pioneers, visit the **Smokey Hill Museum** (*8th and Iron Sts. 913-826-7460. Closed Mon.*).

㉗ **A b i l e n e**   This small plains city became the country's first cow town in 1867, when a young entrepreneur built large pens at the Kansas Pacific Railroad's terminus. Over the next five years, three million cattle and hordes of rowdy drovers moseyed up the Chisholm Trail from Texas, while the likes of Marshal Wild Bill Hickok tried to keep the peace. Review Abilene's colorful past at the **Dickinson County Historical Museum** (*412 S. Campbell St. 913-263-2681. Closed weekends Nov.-March*), where you'll also find a large collection of early telephone equipment at the **Museum of Independent Telephony** (*Closed weekends Nov.-March; adm. fee*). Abilene takes pride in its **Eisenhower Center** (*2 miles S on Kans. 15. 913-263-4751. Adm. fee for museum*), which encompasses the childhood home of Dwight D. Eisenhower, the graves of the 34th President and his wife, a museum, and a library.

㉘ **J u n c t i o n   C i t y**   This town owes its existence to **Fort Riley,** built in the 1850s to help open the frontier. The still active post, home of the Army's First Infantry Division, includes the **Custer House** (*Fort Riley exit, follow signs to Bldg. 24. 913-239-2737. By appt. on weekends*), believed to have been occupied by the ill-fated Lt. Col. George A. Custer

Museum of Independent Telephony, Abilene, Kansas

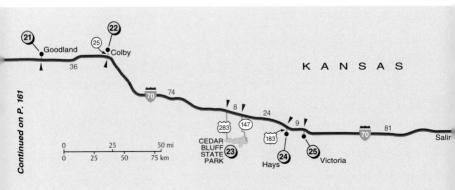

Continued on P. 161

Goodland

Colby

K A N S A S

36

74

CEDAR BLUFF STATE PARK

Hays

Victoria

Salir

0   25   50 mi
0   25   50   75 km

in 1866, and the **U. S. Cavalry Museum** *(913-239-2737),* housed in an early post hospital. Also on the base stands Kansas' **First Territorial Capitol** *(913-784-5535. Phone ahead for hours),* a warehouse used for four days in 1855 by a bogus legislature elected with the help of proslavery Missourians who had voted illegally in Kansas.

Topeka Lying on the south bank of the Kaw River in the Flint Hills, the state capital boomed in the 1850s and '60s as a rail junction; the Santa Fe Railroad remains a major presence. A John Steuart Curry mural of abolitionist John Brown adorns the copper-domed **State Capitol** *(10th and Harrison Sts. 913-296-3966. Tours Mon.-Sat.),* built of native limestone. North of downtown, **Historic Ward-Meade Park** *(124 N.W. Fillmore Ave. 913-295-3888. Closed Mon. year-round and weekends Nov.-March; adm. fee)* preserves an 1870s Victorian mansion, with tours twice daily. On Topeka's west side, 160-acre **Gage Park** *(Gage Blvd. between W. 6th and W. 10th Sts.)* embraces the **Topeka Zoo** *(913-272-5821. Adm. fee);* don't miss the gorilla exhibit and tropical rain forest. Eight miles west of downtown, the excellent **Kansas Museum of History** *(6425 S.W. 6th St. 913-272-8681)* traces the state's past.

State Capitol, Topeka, Kansas

Lawrence *(2 miles S on US 59)* Settled in 1854 by New England abolitionists, Lawrence was burned by proslavery raiders in 1863. Today it's home to the University of Kansas, whose **Natural History Museum** *(Dyche Hall, 14th St. and Jayhawk Blvd. 913-864-4540. Donation requested)* displays fossils, wildlife dioramas, and a mounted horse that survived Little Big Horn. A 7,000-acre reservoir at **Clinton State Park** *(7 miles SW of town via US 40 and Rte. 13. 913-842-8562. Adm. fee)* is popular with anglers and boaters.

Bonner Springs In this western suburb of Kansas City, exhibits at the **National Agricultural Center and Hall of Fame** *(630 N. 126th St. 913-721-1075. Closed Dec.–mid-March; adm.*

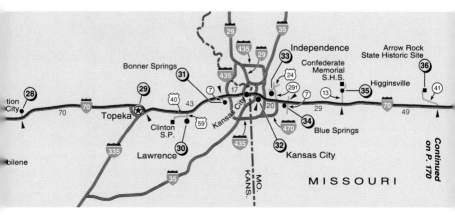

fee) depict the history and development of agriculture. Nearby, the newly expanded **Wyandotte County Historical Society and Museum** (*631 N. 126th St. 913-721-1078. Closed Mon.*) features fossils, Native American artifacts, and pioneer heirlooms.

㉜ Kansas City, Missouri

A sprawling metropolis of 1.5 million people straddling the Missouri River, a state line, and seven counties, Kansas City began as a lowly steamboat landing for Westport, a trading post 4 miles south that thrived in the mid-1800s. Today's skyscraping downtown, with its tangle of railroad tracks, is far from lowly. Yet Kansas City's heart is still to the south, in Westport's stately houses and in posh Country Club Plaza, a midwestern version of L.A.'s Rodeo Drive. A *trolley* (816-221-3399. March-Dec. Fare charge) links major tourist sights (Convention & Visitors Bureau, 1100 Main St. 816-221-5242. Closed weekends).

Topping the list of museums is the *Nelson-Atkins Museum of Art* (4525 Oak St. 816-751-1278. Closed Mon.; adm. fee except Sat.), with its outstanding Oriental collection and 12 monumental bronzes by Henry Moore. The nearby *Toy and Miniature Museum of Kansas City* (5235 Oak St. 816-333-2055. Closed Mon.-Tues.; adm. fee) is one of the best of its kind. The *Wornall House Museum* (146 W. 61st Terr. 816-444-1858. Closed Mon.; adm. fee), a restored 1858 Greek Revival mansion, spotlights life on a plantation.

For a panoramic view of downtown, ride the elevator to the top of the 217-foot *Liberty Memorial* (Memorial Dr., near Penn Valley Park. 816-221-1918. Closed Mon.-Tues.; adm. fee). Down on the waterfront, the *Arabia Steamboat Museum* (400 Grand Ave. 816-471-4030. Adm. fee) displays goods salvaged from a side-wheeler that sank in the Missouri River in 1856. The *Kansas City Museum* (3218 Gladstone Blvd. 816-221-3466. Closed Mon.; donation requested), in the 1910 mansion of a lumber magnate, chronicles the region's frontier past.

Dawn in the heartland

㉝ **Independence** (*2 miles N on Mo. 291*) For thousands of westbound migrants in the 1840s and '50s, this was civilization's edge; here wagons were stocked and beasts fattened before journeying into the unknown. At the **National Frontier Trails Center** (*318 W. Pacific Ave. 816-325-7575. Adm. fee*), exhibits and a film recount the town's role as trail outfitter. In 1890, six-year-old Harry S. Truman moved to town, grew up to be the 32nd President, and died here in 1972. The best of numerous local shrines are the comprehensive **Truman Library and Museum** (*US 24 and N. Delaware*

Truman Home, Independence, Missouri

St. 816-833-1225. Adm. fee) and the **Truman Home** *(219 N. Delaware St. Closed Mon. Labor Day-Mem. Day)*, where Harry and Bess lived for five decades. Tickets for the latter must be purchased at the **Truman Home Ticket and Information Center** *(Truman Rd. and Main St. 816-254-7199)*. The 1881 **Vaile Mansion** *(1500 N. Liberty St. 816-325-7430. Apr.-Oct. and special holiday tours; adm. fee)* exemplifies Second Empire Victorian architecture.

Blue Springs At **Burr Oak Woods** *(1 mile N on Mo. 7, follow signs. 816-228-3766)*, shady trails wind past streams, boulders, and the remains of a prairie homestead; the nature center *(Closed Mon.)* holds a 3,000-gallon aquarium. At **Fleming Park** *(5 miles S on Mo. 7 and 3 miles W on Cowherd Rd.)*, you can fish in two lakes, view elk, bison, and white-tailed deer in a fenced preserve, or tour **Missouri Town 1855** *(816-795-8200. Wed.-Sun. mid-Apr.–mid-Nov., weekends only rest of year; adm. fee)*, an outdoor museum where costumed interpreters re-create life in a pre-Civil War farm community.

Higginsville Although their state didn't secede, 40,000 Missourians fought under the Stars and Bars. Some of the 600-plus Rebels laid to rest at the **Confederate Memorial State Historic Site** *(9 miles N on Mo. 13. 816-584-2853)* took part in the 1861 Battle of the Hemp Bales, fought about 10 miles northwest, near Lexington. Using the bales for cover, they took 3,000 Union prisoners.

Arrow Rock State Historic Site *(13 miles N on Mo. 41. 816-837-3330)* Named for the flint bluffs where Indians sharpened their arrows, this rejuvenated town bustled in the 1830s because of its location at the junction of the Santa Fe Trail and the Missouri River, then dwindled with the decline of river traffic. Today's population numbers 70, many of whom run quaint shops and inns. Guided walking tours visit a dozen old buildings.

Columbia This small city is home of the main campus of the **University of Missouri** *(Visitor and Guest Relations, Conley Hall. 314-882-6333)*, the oldest (1839) state university west of the Mississippi. On Francis Quadrangle six Ionic columns mark the site of the Academic Hall, which burned in 1892. The nearby **Museum of Art and Archaeology** *(University Ave. and 9th St. 314-882-3591. Closed Mon.)* displays a small, eclectic collection of paintings, sculpture, and artifacts. For a close-up look at the region's karst topography, drive to **Rock Bridge Memorial State Park** *(4 miles S on Mo. 163, follow signs. 314-449-7402)*. Wooded trails lead to a natural bridge, formed when part of an ancient limestone seafloor collapsed, and the Devil's Icebox, a chilly cave.

Site of the original Academic Hall at the University of Missouri, Columbia

Fulton *(7 miles S on US 54)* Here at Westminster College, Winston Churchill coined the term "Iron Curtain" in a 1946 speech; 46 years later in 1992, Mikhail Gorbachev delivered a speech on the end of the Cold War. The **Winston Churchill Memorial and Library** (*7th St. and Westminster Ave. 314-642-6648. Adm. fee*) commemorates the first event. The 17th-century **Church of St. Mary the Virgin, Aldermanbury,** which was moved to the campus from London, now holds a museum on Churchill's life and times.

ILLINOIS

(39) **Graham Cave State Park** (*2 miles W on Rte. TT. 314-564-3476*) Archaeological and radiocarbon evidence shows that Indians lived here at least 10,000 years ago. The cave is closed pending excavation, but visitors may view interpretive signs at its entrance and in the park office. Camping, hiking, and access to the Loutre River.

(40) **Defiance** **Daniel Boone Home** (*13 miles S via US 40, Mo. 94, and Rte. F. 314-987-2221*) Spain controlled the hilly, wooded farmland near Defiance when Kentucky woodsman Daniel Boone, aging and in debt, settled here about 1800. In return for his services as a territorial judge, Boone was granted 845 acres from Spain. The stone-walled Georgian edifice, his home until his death in 1820, preserves period furnishings and family artifacts. *Daily Apr.–mid-Dec., weekends only mid-Dec.–March; adm. fee.*

170

(41) **St. Charles** Settled by French Canadians, this bustling Missouri River port was the state capital from 1821 to 1826. You can visit the four second-story rooms, perched above a general store, that served as the **First Missouri State Capitol** (*200-216 S. Main St. 314-946-9282. Adm. fee*). The **Lewis and Clark Center** (*701 Riverside Dr. 314-947-3199. Adm. fee*) pays homage to the exploring duo, whose party camped in the area before striking west in 1804.

St. Louis See I-55, p. 130.

(42) **Lewis and Clark S.H.S. and Park, ILLINOIS** (*From I-270, 3 miles N on Ill. 3*) A concrete mon-

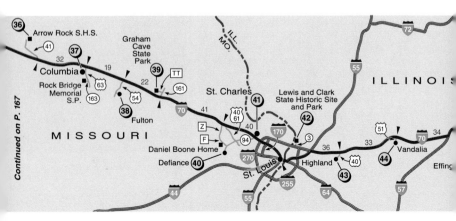

Continued on P. 167

36 Arrow Rock S.H.S.
41
32 **37**
Columbia 19
Rock Bridge Memorial S.P. **63**
163
Graham Cave State Park
22
39 TT
161
54
38 Fulton
MISSOURI
Z
F
Daniel Boone Home
Defiance **40**
270
94
40 61
40
41
St. Charles
41
170
Lewis and Clark State Historic Site and Park
42
3
36
St. Louis
Highland
43
72
55
ILLINOIS
55
51
33
Vandalia
40
44
70 34
Effing
255
44
55
64
57

ument at the confluence of the Missouri and Mississippi Rivers commemorates the 1804 departure of Meriwether Lewis and William Clark on their historic search for a water passage to the Pacific Ocean. *In spring 1994 the park was being restored after flood damage.*

Highland *(5 miles W on US 40)* Named by a homesick Scottish surveyor, this town was settled by Swiss immigrants in the 1830s. Half a century later, native son Louis Latzer developed the process of condensing milk; the family business became the Pet Milk Company. The 1901 **Latzer Homestead** *(2 miles S of town on Old Trenton Rd. 618-654-7957. By appt. only; adm. fee)* features running water, telephones, and other amenities considered modern at the turn of the century.

Vandalia Hastily carved out of the wilderness, this town served as Illinois's state capital from 1820 until 1839, when Springfield took that honor. Abraham Lincoln made an antislavery speech in the restored federal-style **Vandalia Statehouse** *(315 W. Gallatin St. 618-283-1161. Closed Mon.-Tues. Dec.-Jan.; donation requested)*, which dates from 1836.

Small-town Illinois

171

Effingham Named after a British lord who refused to fight the rebelling colonists, Effingham features an ornate 1871 **County Courthouse** *(3rd and Jefferson Sts. 217-342-4065)*.

Lincoln Trail State Recreation Area *(5 miles S on Ill. 1, follow signs. 217-826-2222)* A wooded lake is the star attraction of this park, so named because Lincoln's family passed through after leaving Indiana in 1830. Camping, hiking.

Terre Haute, INDIANA *(Visitor Center, 643 Wabash Ave. 812-234-5555)* French for "high ground," Terre Haute

Continued on P. 174

was settled in 1816 on a bluff above the Wabash River. The National Road, the railroad, and nearby coal deposits spurred industry. Today much of the city's vitality comes from Indiana State University and four other colleges. The fine **Sheldon Swope Art Museum** (*25 S. 7th St. 812-238-1676. Closed Mon.*) displays 19th- and 20th-century American paintings. The **Eugene V. Debs Home** (*451 N. 8th St. 812-232-2163. Wed.-Sun. p.m.*), a Victorian house occupied by the union leader and American Socialist Party founder from 1890 to 1926, contains period furnishings and labor movement exhibits. For a look at an early Terre Haute suburb, tour the tree-lined **Farrington's Grove Historical District** (*Bounded by 4th, 7th, Poplar, and Hulman Sts. Maps at Visitor Center*). The district includes 800 houses and the **Historical Museum of the Wabash Valley** (*1411 S. 6th St. 812-235-9717. Tues.-Sun.*), with artifacts and Victorian rooms.

(48) G r e e n c a s t l e (*8 miles N on US 231*) You'll find the 1880 **Dunbar Bridge,** one of the area's oldest covered bridges, just north

(49) Indianapolis

This site was little more than a swamp on an unnavigable river when it became Indiana's capital in 1821. Since then, Indianapolis has grown into a major crossroads with a monument-studded downtown. Hundreds of thousands flock here each Memorial Day for the nation's most famous car race. Indianapolis is also home to pharmaceutical giant Eli Lilly and many high-tech firms (*Visitor Center, City Center, 201 S. Capitol Ave. 317-237-5206*).

Indianapolis's streets radiate from the *Soldiers' and Sailors' Monument* (Monument Circle). Within walking distance are the *State Capitol* (*317-233-5293. Closed weekends*), a

Renaissance Revival structure of Indiana limestone; the *Hoosier Dome* (100 S. Capitol Ave.), home of the Indianapolis Colts football team; and *Union Station* (*39 W. Jackson Pl. 317-267-0701*), renovated with restaurants and shops.

The Children's Museum of Indianapolis (*3000 N. Meridian St. 317-924-5431. Closed Mon. except summer; adm. fee*) ranks as one of the world's largest. If your taste runs to Native American and Western art, stop by the *Eiteljorg Museum* (*500 W. Washington St. 317-636-WEST. Closed Mon.; adm. fee*). The *Indianapolis Motor Speedway Hall of Fame Museum* (*4790 W. 16th St. 317-241-2500. Adm. fee*) shows off dozens of racing vehicles and offers bus tours of the Indy 500 racetrack when it's not in use. The 1872 *Riley House* (*528 Lockerbie St. 317-631-5885. Closed Mon.; adm. fee*) displays Victorian furnishings and poet James Whitcomb Riley's personal effects. The *President Benjamin Harrison Home* (*1230 N. Delaware St. 317-631-1898. Adm. fee*), a three-story Italianate house on the north side of town, showcases original furnishings and exhibits on the life of the 23rd President.

Indianapolis 500 race, Indianapolis Motor Speedway

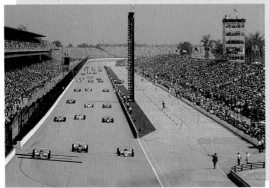

of town; pick up a map at the **Visitor Center** (*25 Jackson St. 317-653-8687*). Across the street, in front of the courthouse, a World War II German buzz bomb serves as a county war memorial.

Greenfield (*3 miles S on Ind. 9*) Founded in 1828 on the busy National Road, Greenfield struck it rich in the 1880s with the discovery of natural gas nearby. You can see vestiges of this prosperity in the elaborate **Hancock County Courthouse** (*W. Main and South Sts. 317-462-1109*) and the surrounding Romanesque and Italianate buildings of the **Courthouse Square Historic District**, where poet James Whitcomb Riley was born and raised. The **Riley Birthplace** (*250 W. Main St. 317-462-8539. Closed Jan.-March*) is an original log cabin around which a two-story structure was added in the 1850s. The **Old Log Jail** (*Main and N. Apple Sts. 317-462-7780*), in use from 1853 to 1871, is now a county museum.

Cambridge City (*3 miles S on Ind. 1, W on US 40*) A sprawl of buildings strung out along US 40, Cambridge City has the long, thin layout of many towns that sprang up overnight on the National Road. The first floor of the well-preserved 1840 **Huddleston Farmhouse Inn Museum** (*3 miles S on Ind. 1, left on US 40. 317-478-3172. Closed Jan., Mon. year-round, and Sun. Sept.-Apr.; donation requested*) was once a kitchen for travelers, who could sleep in their wagons in the yard. Four sisters created the bright ceramics displayed in the **Overbeck Museum** (*33 W. Main St., in the basement of the city library. 317-478-3335. Closed Sun.*). Dating from 1911, the pieces include art deco vases and humorous figurines.

Hagerstown (*4 miles N on Ind. 1*) Settled by several Maryland families who operated mills along nearby creeks in the 1830s, Hagerstown retains a shady, old-fashioned ambience. During business hours you can tour **Abbott's Candy Shop** (*48 E. Walnut St. 317-489-4442*), in operation since before 1890.

Richmond (*3 miles S on US 27*) Still a thriving industrial center, Richmond hit its stride around the turn of the century, when its factories turned out pianos, automobiles, and lawn mowers. Some of the country's first 78 rpm recordings, including many by Louis Armstrong and Hoagy Carmichael, were made here. Both of the Wright brothers graduated from Richmond High School. An 1864 Quaker meetinghouse holds the excellent **Wayne County Historical Museum** (*1150 N. A St. 317-962-5756. Closed Mon.; adm. fee*), which details the city's past with displays of Native American pottery, vintage cars, and exquisite furniture. Also worth a visit are two historic residences: the 1858 **Scott House** (*126 N. 10th St. 317-962-5756. Sun. p.m. and by appt.; adm. fee*) and the **Gaar Mansion** (*2593 Pleasant View Rd. 317-966-7184. First and third Sun. p.m.; adm. fee*), the elegant 1876 home of a local industrialist. Richmond takes pride

Few states are as proud of their monikers as Indiana, the Hoosier state. But what, exactly, is a *Hoosier*? No one knows for sure. In pioneer days, to be called a "hoozer" or "hoodger" meant you were a) big and burly, b) an unrefined, backwoods type, or c) both. Some say Indiana settlers greeted visitors with a brusque "Who's here?," which came out as "Hoos yer?" Others contend that Sam Hoosier, a Kentucky canal contractor, hired Indiana laborers who became known as Hoosier's men. Whatever the derivation, Hoosier today connotes a) an Indiana native or b) a member of Indiana University's renowned basketball team.

173

O. H. Little Livery, Wayne County Historical Museum, Richmond, Indiana

in the three rose gardens in **Glen Miller Park** (*2500 National Rd. E.*); the blooms reach their peak in June and September.

54 Fountain City (*6 miles N on US 27*) Like several other towns in the region, Fountain City (originally known as Newport) was settled by North Carolina Quakers who relocated here because of their opposition to slavery. The **Levi Coffin House** (*113 N. Main St. 317-847-2432. June-early Sept. p.m. except Mon., weekends only mid-Sept.–Oct.; adm. fee*), the restored 1840s home of one such couple, served as an important hiding place on the Underground Railroad. Between 1826 and 1847, the Coffins sheltered some 2,000 runaway slaves fleeing north to freedom.

Dayton, OHIO See I-75, p. 190.

55 Yellow Springs (*6.5 miles S on US 68*) The spring that gave this secluded village its name and attracted cure seekers in the 19th century is located in **Glen Helen** (*405 Corry St. Visitor Center closed Mon. 513-767-7375*), a wooded, 1,000-acre nature preserve owned by Antioch College. Twenty miles of trails lead to quiet glades and cascading streams. Glen Helen also operates a raptor center, where you can see injured birds of prey being nursed back to health for release into the wild. Take time out to enjoy a picnic at the adjacent **John Bryan State Park** (*3790 Ohio 370. 513-767-1274*).

56 Clifton (*7 miles S on Ohio 72*) This hamlet of wood-frame and stone buildings dates from the early 1800s, when at least five mills on the Little Miami River produced paper, distilling grain, and cloth. Only **Clifton Mill** (*75 Water St. 513-767-5501. Adm. fee*), built in 1802, remains; it still grinds wheat and corn. From a parking area just outside town, trails lead to **Clifton Gorge** (*W on Ohio 343*), a 130-foot-deep canyon with dolomite rock faces and lush vegetation that's part of John Bryan State Park (see Yellow Springs entry above).

Clifton Gorge, near Clifton, Ohio

174

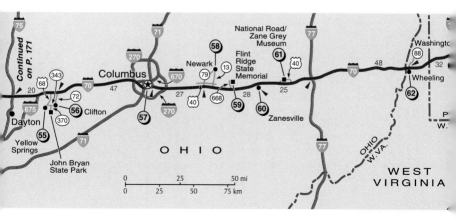

⑤⑦ Columbus

Skyscrapers overlooking the Scioto River

A clean, compact metropolis on the Scioto River, Columbus has a demographic profile so like the rest of the country that new products are often tested here. Although the area was once a swamp, its central location led to its selection as the state capital in 1812. The establishment of Ohio State University in 1873 helped Columbus develop into a leading high-tech center (Visitor Center, 10 W. Broad St. 614-221-6623 or 800-345-4-FUN).

The city radiates from the **State Capitol** (High and E. Broad Sts. 614-466-2125), a domeless, Greek Revival structure built in 1861. A few blocks west along the river, you can board a reproduction of the **Santa Maria** (Broad and High Sts. 614-645-8760), Christopher Columbus's flagship.

Museum goers will delight in **Ohio's Center of Science and Industry** (280 E. Broad St. 614-228-COSI. Adm. fee), an interactive technology extravaganza. The nearby **Columbus Museum of Art** (480 E. Broad St. 614-221-6801. Closed Mon.) spotlights Impressionist and 20th-century masterworks. The **Ohio Historical Center** (17th Ave. and I-71. 614-297-2300. Adm. fee) showcases an extensive collection of prehistoric arti-

facts and a re-created Civil War town.

The restored houses in **German Village** (Tours leave from Meeting Haus, 588 S. 3rd St. 614-221-8888. Adm. fee), one of Columbus's largest historic neighborhoods, date from the 1840s. In the 1920s humorist James Thurber, a Columbus native, lived at the **Thurber House** (77 Jefferson Ave. 614-464-1032. Sun.-Fri. p.m., phone for Sat. hours), where you can see manuscripts, drawings, and other memorabilia. Exotic vegetation luxuriates in the **Franklin Park Conservatory** (1777 E. Broad St. 614-645-8733. Closed Mon.; adm. fee for special exhibits), a huge, ornate greenhouse styled after London's Crystal Palace.

58 **Newark** *(9 miles N on Ohio 79)* Damaged by centuries of erosion and encroachment, the Newark Earthworks, built by the prehistoric Hopewell, preserve remnants of the largest known set of geometric earthworks. **Mound Builders State Memorial** *(S on Ohio 79, follow signs. 614-344-1920. Museum open Wed.-Sun. in summer and some fall weekends; adm. fee)* encompasses a circular earthwork 1,200 feet in diameter, while **Octagon State Memorial** *(W of town, off 33rd and N. Main Sts.)* features a 20-acre circular enclosure connected to a 50-acre octagonal enclosure. On a more modern note, the **National Heisey Glass Museum** *(6th and W. Church Sts. 614-345-2932. Closed Mon.; adm. fee)* displays handmade crystal once considered both elegant and affordable. At the **Dawes Arboretum** *(7770 Jacksontown Rd. S.E. 614-323-2355 or 800-44-DAWES)*, you can admire 1,150 acres of splendid gardens, hedges, and trees.

A novel way to get to Newark on summer weekends is aboard the **Buckeye Central Scenic Railroad** *(National Road Station on US 40, 3 miles E of Hebron. 614-366-2029. Memorial Day–mid-Oct.; fare charge)*, which runs along an 1854 spur of the Baltimore & Ohio Railroad.

59 **Flint Ridge State Memorial** *(2 miles N on Ohio 668. 614-787-2476)* The flint outcroppings along the wooded trails of this 5-square-mile park supplied spearpoints and knives to the Paleo-Indians who occupied the region as early as 10,000 years ago. The Hopewell, who vanished a thousand years before Columbus, traded the flint they quarried here for items from far away. A museum outlines flint-working techniques and local geology. *Museum open Wed-Sun. in summer and some fall weekends; adm. fee.*

60 **Zanesville** This city was settled by pioneering road builder Ebenezer Zane, whose grandson, adventure writer Zane Grey, was born here in 1872. Zanesville was the state capital for two years before Columbus was chosen in 1812. The 1809 **Stone Academy** *(456 Putnam Ave. 614-452-0742)* didn't become Ohio's permanent capitol, as residents had hoped; abolitionists later used it as a meetinghouse.

61 **National Road/Zane Grey Museum** *(0.7 mile E on US 40/22. 614-872-3143)* This informative museum focuses on Zane Grey's life, regional pottery, and the National Road, the first federally funded interstate highway. *Daily May-Sept., Wed.-Sun. March-Apr. and Oct.-Nov., closed Dec.-Feb.; adm. fee.*

62 **Wheeling, WEST VIRGINIA** Served by riverboats, the Baltimore & Ohio Railroad, and the National Road, this mountain city on the Ohio River rivaled Pittsburgh as an inland port in the mid-19th century. Wheeling's coal mines and iron foundries attracted a large, multiethnic workforce in the early 1900s, and the downtown, perched above the river, has changed little

From Vandalia, Illinois, to Cumberland, Maryland, US 40—which for long stretches parallels I-70—follows the route of America's first interstate highway. Just 30 feet wide and paved with broken stone, the *National Road* was authorized by Congress in 1806 after the Louisiana Purchase gave the country a vast frontier to settle. The only alternative to river transport into the interior, the 600-mile-long road took three decades and some seven million dollars to complete. Many stone mileposts, some dating from the 1830s, can still be seen along US 40, reminders of a time when the fastest coaches traveled 5 miles an hour.

176

Oglebay Park Zoo, Wheeling, West Virginia

since then. During the early years of the Civil War, Union sympathizers seceded from Virginia and presided over their new state from the **West Virginia Independence Hall** (*1528 Market St. 304-238-1300*), in the old Custom House, where you can examine period rooms and historical exhibits. The **Wheeling Suspension Bridge** (*10th and Main Sts.*) held the title of world's longest single-span bridge when it was built in 1849. The largest concentration of the city's Victorian houses lines the 2300 block of Chapline Street; for information on tours, contact the **Victorian Wheeling Landmark Foundation** (*810 Main St. 304-232-6400. Adm. fee*). The 1,500 acres of **Oglebay Park** (*5 miles N on W.Va. 88, follow signs. 304-243-4000 or 800-624-6988. Adm. fee for mansion, museum, and zoo*), a city-owned mountain resort, provide a lovely setting for formal gardens, greenhouses, a historic mansion, glass museum, and zoo.

Washington, PENNSYLVANIA Yesteryear comes alive at the **Pennsylvania Trolley Museum** (*1 Museum Rd. 412-228-9256. Weekends in May, daily in summer*), where you can ride on a restored trolley or visit a streetcar named *Desire*. History also plays a role at the **LeMoyne House** (*49 E. Maiden St. 412-225-6740. Closed Mon., Sat., and Jan.; adm. fee*), the home of a fervent abolitionist who built the nation's first crematory in 1876.

Manns Choice Stalactites and stalagmites embellish **Coral Caverns** (*Bedford exit, 7 miles W on Pa. 31. 814-623-6882. Memorial Day-Labor Day, weekends Sept.-Halloween; adm. fee*), part of a 400-million-year-old coral reef.

Bedford At **Old Bedford Village** (*1 mile S on US 220 Bus. 814-623-1156 or 800-622-8005. May-Oct. and special holiday hours; adm. fee*), costumed interpreters re-create the crafts and activities of a 1790s frontier village.

Fort Frederick State Park, MARYLAND (*1 mile S on Md. 56. 301-842-2155*) Built in 1756 to protect settlers from Indian raids, Fort Frederick was later used by rebellious colonists to imprison British and Hessian troops. Its stone construction and design were unusual for the time. Imposing 17-foot walls enclose two restored barracks, which now house a museum. From April through October you can camp in the park's wooded hills, which are bisected by the Potomac River and the Chesapeake & Ohio Canal.

Old Bedford Village, Bedford, Pennsylvania

Hagerstown (*3 miles N on I-81, exit E onto US 40*) The seat of fertile Washington County, this manufacturing city was settled in 1739 by German immigrant Jonathan Hager. His impregnable **Hager House** (*19 Key St. 301-739-8393. Apr.-Dec. Tues.-Sun.; adm. fee*), built above two springs to protect the water supply, served as home, fort, and warehouse. The surrounding **City Park**, a shady green space, beckons visitors to its lake and pleasant picnic spots.

68 **Antietam National Battlefield** (*10 miles S on Md. 65. Visitor Center 301-432-5124*) It's hard to imagine this peaceful farmland as the scene of the Civil War's bloodiest day of battle. On September 17, 1862, from positions on opposite sides of Antietam Creek, the armies of Confederate Gen. Robert E. Lee and Union Maj. Gen. George B. McClellan clashed repeatedly. By sunset, more than 22,000 soldiers were missing, wounded, or dead. A film and spirited talks by rangers help bring the battle alive. *Adm. fee.*

Antietam National Battlefield, Maryland

69 **Boonsboro** (*5 miles S on Md. 66*) The founders of this small, rustic town are said to have been kin to Daniel Boone. The **Museum of History** (*113 N. Main St. 301-432-5151. May-Sept. Sun. p.m. and by appt.; adm. fee*) features Indian artifacts and Civil War relics. Not far from town, you can walk along illuminated paths and gaze at the limestone formations of the **Crystal Grottoes Caverns** (*1.5 miles W on Md. 34. 301-432-6336. Apr.-Oct., weekends rest of year; adm. fee*). For an excellent view of Washington County, climb to the top of the 34-foot granite turret dedicated to the first President in **Washington Monument State Park** (*3 miles E of town on Md. 40 Alt., left on Wash. Mon. Rd. 301-432-8065. Museum closed weekends Dec.-March*); here you can picnic and hike.

70 **Frederick** The legend you'll hear most often in this valley community deals with Barbara Fritchie, the 95-year-old heroine of John Greenleaf Whittier's poem. In 1862, as Confederate general Stonewall Jackson led his troops through town, she defiantly flew the U. S. flag. The **Barbara Fritchie House** (*154 W. Patrick St. 301-698-0630. Mon., Thurs., and Sat.-Sun. Apr.-Sept., weekends only Oct.-Nov.; adm. fee*) was reconstructed from material salvaged from the original residence. You can see Mrs. Fritchie's grave, as well as the Francis Scott Key Monument, in **Mount Olivet Cemetery** (*515 Market St.*). Ask at the **Visitor Center** (*19 E. Church St. 301-663-8687 or 800-999-3613*) for a walking-tour map of the **Historic District** with its impressive federal houses. North of town, kids can try their hand at carding wool and operating a cream separator at the **Rose Hill Manor Children's Museum and Historic Park** (*1611 N. Market St. 301-694-1648 or 694-1646. Daily Apr.-Oct., weekends in Nov.; adm. fee*), the 1790s Georgian mansion of Maryland's first governor.

71 **Ellicott City** (*3 miles S on US 29*) Built into a rocky hillside, Ellicott City's downtown—a jumble of tourist shops, restaurants, and law offices—manages a not-quite-restored, workaday character. Founded in 1772, the settlement had become an important industrial center by the 1850s. At the **B&O Railroad Station Museum** (*2711 Maryland Ave. 410-461-1944. Memorial Day-Labor Day Wed.-Mon., rest of year Fri.-Mon.; adm. fee*), a restored 1830s train station, you can examine old railcars and a partly excavated turntable.

Inner Harbor

Founded in 1729, Baltimore and its deepwater harbor played a vital role in early America as an outlet for tobacco, grain, and other products. Baltimore repelled British soldiers during the War of 1812, but its Confederate sympathies led to skirmishes with Federal troops during the Civil War (Visitor Center, 300 W. Pratt St. 410-837-4636 or 800-282-6632).

.S. Constellation

Most visitors start at Baltimore's revamped *Inner Harbor* (Pratt and Light Sts.), a fine example of urban renewal; glass-enclosed shopping pavilions and outdoor cafés are linked by elevated walkways and water taxis. The first-rate *National Aquarium* (Pier 3. 410-576-3810. Adm. fee) simulates a variety of aquatic ecosystems. The *U.S.S. Constellation* (Constellation Dock, Pier 1. 410-539-1797. Adm. fee), built in 1797 as the Navy's first commissioned ship, is a floating museum. You'll find another landmark of Baltimore's military past at the *Fort McHenry National Monument and Historic Shrine* (Foot of E. Fort Ave. 410-962-4290. Adm. fee), which withstood British shells in 1814. Mary Pickersgill, who sewed the flag that inspired Francis Scott Key, resided at the *Star-Spangled Banner Flag House* (844 E. Pratt St. 410-837-1793. Closed Mon.; adm. fee).

The renowned *Walters Art Gallery* (600 N. Charles St. 410-547-9000. Closed Mon.; admission fee) showcases more than 25,000 works. Just a hard-hit pop foul away from *Camden Yards* (33 Camden St. 410-685-9800), the beautiful new home of the Baltimore Orioles, lies the *Babe Ruth Birthplace and Baseball Center* (216 Emory St. 410-727-1539. Adm. fee), with vintage broadcasts and memorabilia. Scores of food kiosks crowd *Lexington Market* (400 W. Lexington St. 410-685-6169. Closed Sun.), one of the nation's oldest (1782) markets.

West of downtown, you can visit the *Mencken House* (1524 Hollins St. 410-396-7997. Weekends or by appt.), the home of journalist H. L. Mencken (1880-1956), as well as the *Poe House* (203 N. Amity St. 410-396-7932. Wed.-Sat.; adm. fee), where Edgar Allen Poe lived from 1832 to 1835.

North of downtown, the note-

Fort McHenry National Monument

worthy collections of the *Baltimore Museum of Art* (N. Charles and 31st Sts. 410-396-7100. Wed.-Sun.; adm. fee) range from French post-Impressionism to African tribal art. At the *Cab Calloway Jazz Institute* (2500 W. North Ave. 410-383-5926. By appt.), photographs and show posters commemorate one of the city's own jazz greats.

Camden Yards, home of the Orioles

Unless otherwise noted, directions are from interstate, and sites are free and generally open daily. Phone for further information.

Davenport/Bettendorf, IOWA See I-80, p. 230-31.

① Moline and Rock Island, ILLINOIS
This is an area with a violent past. Both the Revolutionary War and the War of 1812 found their way to the western outpost. Then, in 1832, the Sauk brave Black Hawk returned to the region to try to win back tribal lands; the hostilities became known as the Black Hawk War. During the Civil War, **Rock Island,** an island in the Mississippi not to be confused with the mainland city of Rock Island, was the site of a military prison where nearly 2,000 Confederate soldiers died. Their cemetery remains on the island. Other sites worth a look include the **Mississippi River Project Visitor Center** (*W end of island. 309-794-5338*), where you can watch barges lock through Lock & Dam No. 15; and the **Colonel Davenport House** (*W end of island. 309-786-7336. May–mid-Oct. Fri.-Sun.; adm. fee*), home of the area's first white settler. Housed in one of the many drab stone buildings of arsenal row, the **Rock Island Arsenal Museum** (*Bldg. 60. 309-782-5021*) tells the story of this arms-making complex. At the glass-and-steel headquarters of **Deere & Company** (*John Deere Rd., Moline. 309-765-4793*), designed by Eero Saarinen, visitors can check out expensive farm machinery.

② Andover This tidy prairie town was founded by a Presbyterian minister in the mid-1830s. Swedish immigrants settled here between 1848 and 1900, and many descendants still live here. The **Jenny Lind Chapel** (*6th St. May-Sept., or get key from post office or bank*), a beautifully restored church with a museum in the basement, was built in the 1850s with help from the Swedish singer. A cholera epidemic in 1852 diverted to coffins boards intended for the steeple.

Imagine the astonishment of settlers arriving from the East after the Revolutionary War. Beyond Lake Michigan spread *prairie*—a seemingly limitless expanse of high, golden grass stippled with wildflowers of every hue. No forbidding forest here. And rich soil—perfect for corn and fruit. As I-74 crosses Illinois' central plains (the "garden spot of the nation"), here and there along the edges of the great grain farms you can still see tallgrass and vivid flowers, remnants of the once vast Illinois prairie.

Galesburg   Built around Knox College (est. 1837), this small town was a stop on the Underground Railroad and the site of an 1858 Lincoln-Douglas debate on slavery. Several notable old churches and buildings dignify the townscape. The ornate **Orpheum Theatre** (*57 S. Kellogg St. 309-342-2299*) began as a vaudeville stage and hosted such stars as Harry Houdini and the Marx Brothers. Concerts, plays, and operas are now presented. A few blocks away, the **Galesburg Railroad Museum** (*423 Mulberry St. 309-342-9400. Mem. Day-Labor Day Tues.-Sun. p.m., plus some weekends in Sept.-Oct.; donations*) recounts train history in a restored Pullman parlor car. The poet and Pulitzer Prize-winning Lincoln biographer, Carl Sandburg (1878-1967), grew up in Galesburg; his birthplace is now the **Carl Sandburg State Historic Site** (*313 E. Third St. 309-342-2361. Closed Mon.-Tues. Jan.-March; donations*).

Jubilee College State Park (*Kickapoo-Edwards exit, 0.5 mile W, off US 150. 309-446-3758*) commemorates the remarkable but unsuccessful effort of Episcopal Bishop Philander Chase to establish an educational community here in the 1830s. The restored stone chapel and dormitory stand in a cool, green park.

Peoria   (*Convention and Visitors Bureau, 403 N.E. Jefferson St. 309-676-0303*) One of the oldest European settlements in the state, Peoria commands a position on a bulge in the Illinois River. White occupation began in 1673 with explorer Jacques Marquette. By the mid-1800s, the city had become a manufacturing center and the leader in whiskey production. For a good look at the lay of the land, ride the glass-enclosed elevator to the top of the tower in **Tower Park** (*Glen Ave. and Prospect Rd. Adm. fee*). From here, take a turn down Grandview Drive for beautiful views of the lake. The **Peoria Historical Society** (*309-674-1921*) operates two fine historical houses: The **John C. Flanagan House** (*942 N.E. Glen Oak Ave. Closed weekends; adm. fee*) has striking ironwork and a river view;

Mississippi River Project Visitor Center, Rock Island, Illinois

Fort Armstrong Blockhouse, Rock Island Arsenal, Rock Island, Illinois

181

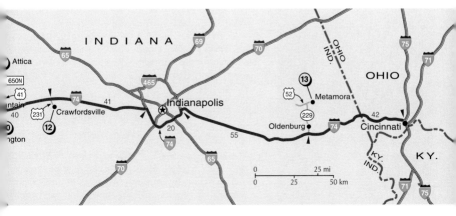

and the **Pettengill-Morron House** (*1212 W. Moss Ave. Closed Sun.-Mon.; adm. fee*) contains family heirlooms from three centuries. Another first-class museum, **Wheels O' Time** (*11923 N. Knoxville/Rte. 88. 309-243-9020. May-Oct. Wed.-Sun. p.m.; adm. fee*), marks the passage of history with vintage autos, steam engines, and tractors. If gambling or riverboats appeal, try the **Par-a-Dice Riverboat Casino** (*E. Peoria riverfront. 800-DEAL ME IN. Adm. fee*).

A bit farther afield, the **Wildlife Prairie Park** (*10 miles W of downtown, Kickapoo-Edwards exit, follow signs to 3826 N. Taylor Rd. 309-676-0998*) offers a primo encounter with such Illinois wildlife as bison and cougars. *Closed mid-Dec.–mid-March; adm. fee.*

Carl Sandburg State Historic Site, Galesburg, Illinois

⑥ Pekin (*6 miles S on Ill. 29*) This Peoria suburb boasts the **Everett McKinley Dirksen Congressional Leadership Research Center** (*Pekin Public Library, Broadway and 4th. 309-347-7113*), a fascinating, if overly reverent, exhibition on politics and the U. S. Congress, with emphasis on the life and career of Illinois Senator Dirksen (1896-1969), Republican leader and orator. *Mon.-Fri. and by appt.*

Bloomington See I-55, p. 128.

⑦ Mahomet The **Lake of the Woods Park,** with its manicured lawns wrapping a central lake, is the setting for the **Botanical Gardens** and the **Early American Museum** (*1 mile N on Ill. 47. 217-586-2612. Daily Mem. Day-Labor Day, weekends May, Sept.-Oct.; adm. fee*), with items relating to 19th-century life in the area.

⑧ Champaign-Urbana On a windswept prairie in the mid-1800s, these towns grew up around the railroad. Champaign has more people and most of the commerce, and Urbana the county seat and the **University of Illinois.** Among the university's offerings are: the **Krannert Art Museum & Kinkead Pavilion** (*500 E. Peabody Dr. 217-333-1860. Closed Mon.*), whose spacious displays include drawings by Picasso and Matisse; and the **World Heritage Museum** (*Lincoln Hall, 702 S. Wright St. 217-333-2360. Closed Sat. and June-Aug. In 1995, the museum is moving and being renamed the Spurlock Museum.*), a wonderful grab bag of culture with such diverse items as a mummified adolescent from Egypt, medieval chain mail, and Chinese imperial robes. Champaign has the **Champaign County Historical Museum** (*709 W. University Ave. 217-356-1010. Tours Wed.-Fri. and Sun. p.m.; adm. fee*), with more than 10,000 items including costumes, decorative art, and furniture; and the **William M. Staerkel Planetarium** (*2400 W. Bradley Ave. 217-351-2446. Adm. fee*).

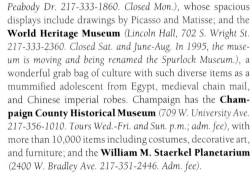

⑨ Kickapoo State Park (*Just off I-74, 6 miles W of Danville. 217-442-4915*) spreads along the Middle Fork of the Vermilion River near the site of a former Kickapoo village. Salt springs attracted early settlers, and by the 1840s

Caterpillar Tractor Co., Peoria, Illinois

salt production reigned here. Then the area was strip-mined for coal. Nature has returned the riverbanks to forest. Hiking and fishing.

Covington, INDIANA The **Fountain County Courthouse** (*301 4th St. 317-793-2243*) is graced with murals depicting area history. Also on exhibit are historical artifacts. *Weekdays.*

Attica (*12 miles N on US 41*) When the Wabash and Erie Canal opened in 1847, this town became a lively mix of packing houses, docks, and factories for saddles and whips. The railroad came along in 1856 and displaced the canal. Then, as nearby Lafayette grew, Attica waned. But the town's leaders have preserved the history and Victorian charm. The **Old Church** and the **William Brown House** (*300 Main St. 317-762-2511. Open by appt.; adm. fee*) are restored to their elegant 1850s appearance. South of town lies the **Portland Arch Nature Preserve** (*From US 41, 5 miles W on 650 N. Rd. to Fountain, follow signs. 317-232-4052*), with a 1-mile loop trail past sandstone cliffs.

Crawfordsville Renaissance man Lew Wallace lived and worked here in the late 1800s. His résumé includes Civil War general, governor of New Mexico Territory, musician, painter, and author of historical novels, the most famous being *Ben Hur*. Learn about Wallace and his work at the **Ben Hur Museum** (*E. Pike St. and Wallace Ave. 317-362-5769 or 800-866-3973. April-Oct. Tues.-Sun.; adm. fee*). The **Henry S. Lane Place** (*Pike and Water Sts. 317-362-3416. April-Oct. Tues.-Sun. p.m. and by appt.; adm. fee*) houses the historical society in the 1845 home of the former governor and U. S. senator. The **Visitor Center** (*412 E. Main St. 317-362-5200 or 800-866-3973*) has information about many other old houses. Also worth a visit: the **Old Jail Museum** (*225 N. Wash. St. 317-362-5222. Closed Mon. and Nov.-March*), featuring a rotary jail and exhibits on local and natural history.

Indianapolis See I-70, p. 172.

Whitewater Canal State Historic Site, Metamora, Indiana

183

Metamora (*12 miles N on Ind. 229 to US 52*) The Whitewater Canal and then the railway made this town a robust business center, but things went downhill by the 1930s. Local citizens restored the canal, and by the 1970s tourists were coming. Now Metamora has more than 100 businesses, including craft and antique shops and museums. The **Whitewater Canal State Historic Site** (*Just S of town. 317-647-6512. Mid-March–Nov. Wed.-Sun., boat ride May-Oct. Wed.-Sun.; adm. fee for boat*) features rides on a horse-drawn canal boat. On the way back to I-74, stop at **Oldenburg,** a "village of spires" plotted in 1837 by German speculators and still Germanic. **Koch's Brau Haus** (*812-934-4840*) offers literature.

Cincinnati, OHIO See I-75, p. 191.

CANADA

Wis. Ont.
Mich.
P. 185
Ohio
P. 189
Ind.
W.Va.
Ky. Va.
Tenn. N.C.
P. 195 S.C.
Ala. Ga.

P. 199 Fla.

184

Unless otherwise noted, directions are from interstate, and sites are free and generally open daily. Phone for further information.

① **Sault Ste. Marie, MICHIGAN** This town perches at the edge of St. Mary's Rapids, a barrier between Lakes Superior and Huron that once forced Ojibwa Indians and early pioneers to portage their canoes. Then, in 1855, the passage was opened to large boats with the completion of the first Soo Lock. Now a series of four parallel chambers, the **Soo Locks** give passage to 12,000 vessels a year. The U. S. Army Corps of Engineers runs a fine **Visitor Center** *(W. Portage Ave. 906-632-0888)*,

Soo Locks, Sault Ste. Marie, Michigan

with a film, models, and observation decks. The **Tower of History** *(326 E. Portage Ave. 906-632-3658)* offers a panorama of the city's historic sites and many-gabled houses and, on the horizon, Canada's Laurentian Hills. Across the street, the **Museum Ship *Valley Camp*** *(501 E. Water St. 906-632-3658)* is a floating cornucopia of Great Lakes maritime history. *Both open mid-May–mid-Oct.; adm. fees.*

② **St. Ignace** In November 1957, the Mackinac Bridge, one of the world's longest suspension bridges, opened across the Straits of Mackinac. St. Ignace crouches on the northern side and owes its existence to the amazing Father Jacques Marquette. The young Jesuit priest established a mission here in 1671 and then set out on a 3,000-mile exploration of Lake Michigan and the Mississippi River Valley. His presumed burial site is at the **Marquette Mission Park and Museum of Ojibwa Culture** *(500 N. State St. 906-643-9161. Closed early Oct.-late May and Sun.-Mon. in Sept.; adm. fee).* The **Father Marquette National Memorial and Museum** *(Just NW of the bridge off US 2. 906-643-8620. April-Sept.; adm. fee)* does an excellent job depicting Marquette's life and the clash of European and Indian cultures he represented.

Colonial Michilimackinac,
Mackinaw City, Michigan

③ **Mackinaw City and Mackinac Island** The site of a French fort built in 1715, Mackinaw City stands at the gateway to Michigan's Upper Peninsula and is now a lure for vacationers en route to Mackinac Island and the north. Fort Michilimackinac passed from the French to the British to the Indians and back to the British. A reconstructed fort staffed by costumed reenactors, **Colonial Michilimackinac** *(616-436-5563)* is at the foot of Louvigny St. near Mackinac Bridge. Another good living-history complex, **Mill Creek State Historic Park** *(3 miles SE on US 23. 616-436-7301)* has a water-powered sawmill, nature trails, and a museum. *Both mid-May–mid-Oct.; adm. fees.* The Straits of Mackinac dividing Lakes Huron and Michigan are 5 miles wide at the narrowest point. The ferry ride to Mackinac (pronounced "mackinaw") Island gives you a sense of why the British moved **Fort Mackinac** *(906-847-3328. Mid-May–mid-Oct.; adm. fee)* from the mainland to the more strategic island bluffs. From 1780 to 1875, British and then American troops were garrisoned at the fort. Visitors to the island, now a popular resort, may tour original buildings and watch cannon and musketry demonstrations.

Cheboygan *(9 miles E on Rte. 66)* The name comes from an Indian term meaning "through passage" and refers to the Inland Waterway. A series of lakes and rivers connecting Lake Huron with Crooked Lake and, by portage, Lake Michigan, the route has been used by Indians, explorers, loggers, and fishermen. Among indoor attractions, the plush **Opera House** *(403 N. Huron St. 616-627-5841. Tours in summer. Donations)* is noteworthy, but the real draw here is the outdoors. **Cheboygan State Park** *(3.5 miles E on Mich. 23. 616-627-2811. Adm. fee)* is a secluded haven of trails, beaches, and wildflowers.

Petoskey and Harbor Springs *(23 miles W on Mich. 68, follow signs)* Unlike other places in the area whose early success depended on lumber, these two towns, situated on either side of Little Traverse Bay, started as summer resort communities in the late 19th century. In Petoskey, the **Little Traverse Historical Society** *(100 Depot Ct. 616-347-2620. May-Oct., closed Mon.; admission fee)* offers a good introduction to the area, including an exhibit on Ernest Hemingway, who spent some of his early life on the lakes and in the woods near here. Tonier and more sedate, the Harbor Springs side boasts stately yachts and tasteful galleries and storefronts. For history buffs, there are two museums: the **Ephraim Shay House** *(396 E. Main St.)*, built in 1891 by a locomotive pioneer; and the **Andrew J. Blackbird Museum** *(368 E. Main St. 616-526-7731. Memorial Day-Labor Day;*

185

Continued on P. 189

donation requested), which maintains a collection of Ottawa artifacts.

⑥ Hartwick Pines State Park *(2 miles E on Mich. 93. 517-348-7068)* Of the many gorgeous parks in central Michigan, this one stands out for its tract of virgin pines, untouched by the 19th-century logging boom. A museum introduces the 9,672-acre park's human and natural history; exhibits depict the rough lot of lumberjacks. *Some exhibits closed Nov.–mid-March; adm. fee.*

⑦ Roscommon This small resort town outfits boaters and fishermen. **Houghton Lake,** largest inland lake in the state, is south of **Higgins Lake,** known for its clear, deep water and gentle beach. Two state parks are on Higgins Lake, offering hiking and camping. The south park *(106 State Park Dr. 517-821-6374. Closed Dec.-May; adm. fee)* is popular with families; the north park *(11511 W. Higgins Lake Dr. 517-821-6125. Closed Dec.-May; adm. fee)* runs the **Civilian Conservation Corps Museum.**

⑧ Saginaw, Bay City, and Midland Once the pine forests were played out, the Saginaw Valley switched from lumber to beans and beets. Iron and automobiles now bolster the economy of this Tri-City Area. All three cities have recently put money into tourism, and the results are evident in the many fine parks and cultural attractions. Highlights in Saginaw include the **Art Museum** *(1126 N. Michigan Ave. 517-754-2491. Closed Mon.),* housed in a turn-of-the-century Georgian Revival building; the **Japanese Cultural Center and Tea House** *(Ezra Rust Dr. and Wash. Ave. 517-759-1648. Closed Mon.; adm. fee),* with a lovely pond, gardens, and teahouse; the **Children's Zoo** *(Across Wash. Ave. from the Japanese Center. 517-759-1657. May-Sept.; adm. fee);* and the **Castle Museum of Saginaw County History** *(500 Federal Ave. 517-752-2861. Closed Mon.; adm. fee).*

A Bay City landmark, **City Hall** *(301 Wash. Ave.)* is a striking late 19th-century edifice. Next door, the **Historical Museum of Bay County** *(321 Wash. Ave. 517-893-5733. Closed Sat.)* tells about the town's decline. Yet out **Center Avenue,** Victorian mansions have kept their vitality.

In Midland, the place to visit is the **Midland Center for the Arts** *(2 miles S of US 10, Eastman Rd. exit, at 1801 W. St. Andrews Rd. 517-631-5930. Adm. fee),* which houses a concert hall, theater, and the Hall of Ideas, an outstanding arts and sciences display.

Grand Hotel, opened in 1887, Mackinac Island, Michigan

Adjacent **Dow Gardens** *(517-631-2677. Adm. fee)* make for delightful wandering. The **Herbert H. Dow Historical Museum** *(3100 Cook Rd. 517-832-5319. Closed Mon.-Tues.; adm. fee)* portrays the life of the founder of Dow Chemical Co., which originated here.

Frankenmuth *(1 mile S on Dixie Hwy., left on Junction Rd. 4 miles)* In 1845, the Bavarian Lutherans sent missionaries here to teach the Chippewa. Today the town's outreach is more toward the pocketbook, but it retains a German air. Tour the **Frankenmuth Brewery** *(425 S. Main St. 517-652-2088. Adm. fee)*; peek into the **Frankenmuth Historical Museum** *(613 S. Main St. 517-652-9701. Closed mid-week Jan.-March; donation requested)*, which recounts the lives of German immigrants; or sit at one of the sidewalk cafés, listen to the glockenspiel, and enjoy the passing show.

Flint Once a key Indian river crossing on the Pontiac Trail, Flint has been making vehicles ever since the mid-1800s logging boom brought a need for carts and wagons. Birthplace of General Motors, Flint has suffered with the recession in the automotive industry, yet it is recharging its batteries. Drop by the **Flint Cultural Center** *(E. Kearsley St. Adm. fees)*, which includes the **Sloan Museum** *(810-760-1169. Closed Mon. except July-Aug.)*, a showcase of local history from mastodons to motor cars; the **DeWaters Art Center** *(810-234-1695. Closed Mon.)*, with the Flint Institute of Arts and an art museum; and the **Longway Planetarium** *(810-760-1181)*.

North of town, **Crossroads Village and Huckleberry Railroad** *(Saginaw St. exit, N to Stanley Rd., then E to Bray Rd. and follow signs S. 810-736-7100 or 800-648-7275)* re-create pioneer life of the mid-1800s with costumed interpreters. *Adm. fee.*

Rochester Nearly 30 miles from central Detroit, the widow of auto baron John Dodge built a palatial residence. She deeded **Meadow Brook Hall** *(University Dr. exit to Oakland Univ., follow signs. 810-370-3140)* and the 1,400-acre estate to found Oakland University. Visitors may tour the 100-room Tudor mansion. Note the ballroom, the tapestries, and the playhouse furnished with antiques. *Adm. fee.*

Bloomfield Hills In rolling country, Detroit newspaper publisher George Booth and architect Eliel Saarinen designed **Cranbrook Educational Community** *(Main entrance to all sites: 1221 N. Woodward Ave. Admission fees)*, now a world-renowned center for the arts and sciences. The **Cranbrook House and Gardens** *(810-645-3149. May-Oct.)* includes formal landscaping, fountains, and woods; **Cranbrook Academy of Art Museum** *(810-645-3312)* showcases paintings and sculpture by faculty and graduates, ranging from

Flour mill, Frankenmuth, Michigan

⑬ Detroit

Renaissance Center

On a crook in the river connecting Lake St. Clair to Lake Erie, the skyscrapers of Detroit rise in a concentrated mass. Here, in 1701, the French founded a trading post that became the automobile capital of the world. Dubbed Motor City, Detroit prospered until the riots of the late 1960s. Although many areas still look rundown, the city is intent on shedding its blighted image. Start your downtown tour aboard the *People Mover* (At any of 13 stations. 313-962-7245), an elevated train that links several buildings and provides choice angles on architecture, street life, and the bright Detroit River. While downtown, wander over to *Hart Plaza* (Jefferson and Wood) and check out the scene. A *Visitor Information kiosk* (313-567-1170) dispenses friendly advice. Opposite the plaza hangs a 24-foot bronze fist, honoring Detroit boxing legend Joe Louis. Just north of the plaza loom the black towers of the 1977 *Renaissance Center* (313-568-5600). Detroit's tallest landmark includes offices and stores.

The city's major museums are about

People Mover

a mile and a half farther north on Woodward Ave. The *Detroit Institute of Arts* (Woodward and Kirby Aves. 313-833-7900. Closed Mon. and Tues.; donations) is a trove of fine art from classical to Impressionist. For some local history, visit the *Detroit Historical Museum* (5401 Woodward Ave. 313-833-1805. Closed Mon.-Tues.; donation requested), which features a full-scale model of an old Detroit cobblestone street with shops. The *Museum of African American History* (301 Frederick Douglass Ave. 313-833-9800. Closed Mon.-Tues.; donations) includes

Motown Museum

an exhibit on the Underground Railroad, of which Detroit was a northern terminus. The small *Children's Museum* (67 E. Kirby. 313-494-1210. Closed Sun.) focuses on animal exhibits, planetarium programs, and workshops. Northwest of museum central sits another Detroit landmark: the *Motown Museum* (2648 W. Grand Blvd. 313-875-2264. Adm. fee), where the world's largest independent record company began in 1959 with a $700 loan. To catch the city's flavor and rhythm, visit the 100-year-old *Eastern Market* (2934 Russell St. 313-833-1560).

sublime to wacky; and the **Cranbrook Institute of Science** *(810-645-3200)* offers informative natural history and hands-on exhibits, a planetarium, and laser shows.

Monroe By the 1780s, the French were moving their families down from Detroit, where they felt unwelcome after the Revolutionary War. Still surviving from that era, the **Navarre-Anderson Trading Post** *(N. Custer and Raisinville Rds. 313-243-7137. Weekends Mem. Day-Labor Day)* is said to be Michigan's oldest wooden structure. A conflict between Indians and whites during the War of 1812 is outlined at the **River Raisin Battlefield Visitor Center** *(1403 East Elm Ave. 313-243-7137. Mem. Day-Labor Day Wed.-Sun.; weekends only rest of year)*. An equestrian statue at North Monroe St. and West Elm Ave. honors native son George Armstrong Custer, whose story is told at the **Monroe County Hist. Museum** *(126 S. Monroe St. 313-243-7137. Closed Mon.-Tues. Labor Day-Mem. Day)*.

Toledo, OHIO In 1835, Ohio gained a Great Lakes port that grew into a booming industrial center with considerable culture and recreation. About 6 miles out Central Avenue, the **Toledo Botanical Garden** *(5403 Elmer Dr., off N. Reynolds Rd., just S of Central Ave. 419-536-8365)* invites visitors to a 57-acre sanctuary of meadows and gardens. A bit closer in, the fine **Toledo Museum of Art** *(2445 Monroe St. at Scottswood Ave. 419-255-8000. Closed Mon.)* displays artists from Rembrandt to Picasso. While in the area, cruise up to the **Old West End** *(Along Collingwood Blvd. from Bancroft St. to Central Ave.)*, a neighborhood of (mostly) restored Victorians. The old houses feature turrets and gables, columns and wide porches. Self-guided tour maps are available at the **Toledo Visitors Bureau** *(401 Jefferson Ave. 419-321-6404 or 800-243-4667)*. Back downtown, near the modern business district, people stroll the riverfront, a promenade with sculptures and fountains. Across the Maumee River, the **Willis B. Boyer** *(419-698-8252. April-Sept. Wed.-Sun.; adm. fee)* is berthed; a tour shows how the Great Lakes freighter plied its trade in 1911. The **Toledo**

Continued on P. 185

189

Continued on P. 195

Ohio state flag

Back when Americans were carving the country into states, it was a serious matter where the lines were drawn. So serious, in fact, that Michigan nearly started a war with Ohio in 1835 over a 520-square-mile tract of land where the up-and-coming village of Toledo stood. Governors on both sides sent troops to the boundary. Thanks to President Jackson's diplomacy, no one was killed in the *"Toledo War."* Instead, both states won— Toledo went to Ohio and Michigan took a piece of the Wisconsin Territory, now known as the Upper Peninsula.

Zoo (*US 25. 419-385-5721*) houses 2,500 animals in simulated habitats, including a hippoquarium. *Adm. fee.*

(16) **L i m a** ("lie-ma") made headlines in 1933, when John Dillinger's gang murdered the sheriff. The **Allen County Museum** (*620 W. Market St. 419-222-9426. Closed Mon.*) displays steam engines made locally. **Lincoln Park** (*E. Elm St.*) has a restored 1895 railroad station and the last locomotive built here.

(17) **W a p a k o n e t a** The hometown of the first man on the moon boasts the **Neil Armstrong Air and Space Museum** (*Just W on Bellefontaine St. 419-738-8811*). Through model airplanes, films, spacesuits, and spacecraft, it tracks the history of flight, with special emphasis on Armstrong's career. *March-Nov.; adm. fee.*

(18) **S i d n e y** The **Titanic Memorial Museum** (*Ohio 47 W to Vandemark Rd., 1 mile N to Russell Rd., then 3 miles W. 513-492-7762*) houses more than 3,300 items relating to the great sea disaster, including clothes worn by the survivors. *Sat.-Wed.; adm. fee.*

(19) **P i q u a** Maj. Gen. Anthony Wayne built Fort Piqua in 1794 during the campaign against the northern Ohio Indians. The fort is gone, but John Johnston's nearby farm remains to tell the story of Ohio pioneer life. The **Piqua Historical Area** (*4 miles NW off Ohio 66. 513-773-2522*) depicts the life of this federal Indian agent, once a soldier in Wayne's army. Johnston's farm of fields and woods includes his restored house, an Indian earthwork, a museum of local Indian culture, and a mule-drawn boat ride along a canal. Here you get a sense of the changes history works on the land. *Mem. Day-Labor Day Wed.-Sun., weekends Sept.-Oct, closed rest of year; adm. fee.*

(20) **D a y t o n** Settled in 1796 at the confluence of four streams, Dayton today swirls around two interstates and their associated spurs and bypasses. Consequently, you need a map. Visitor attractions are generally either in the downtown area or scattered around the interstates. Head first to the **Dayton Convention Center** (*E. Fifth and Main Sts. 513-226-8248 or 800-221-8235*) to pick up information. This puts you at the hub of the attractive business district. Concerts and other events often take place across the street in Dave Hall Plaza Park. In the **Oregon Historic District** (*SE of Patterson Blvd. and E. Fifth St.*), 12 blocks of formerly blighted houses have been resettled by urban pioneers. Exhibits on the Wright brothers (local heroes) and on area history are found in the **Old Courthouse Museum** (*E. Third and Main Sts. 513-228-6271. Closed Sun.-Mon.*). The **Dayton Art Institute** (*456 Belmonte Park N. 513-223-5277. Closed Mon.; adm. fee*) contains a small but good collection of fine art in an Italianate building. Farther afield are the popular **U. S. Air Force Museum** (*Springfield Pike at Wright Field, 6 miles E of Needmore*

U. S. Air Force Museum, Dayton, Ohio

Rd. exit. 513-255-3284), which depicts the history of aviation with more than 200 aircraft; **Carillon Historical Park** *(2001 S. Patterson Blvd. 513-293-2841. May-Oct., closed Mon.; adm. fee),* featuring a Wright flyer and a full-scale replica of an early 20th-century village; and **SunWatch Prehistoric Indian Village** *(S of city, 1 mile W on Edwin C. Moses Blvd., then 1 mile S on W. River Rd. 513-268-8199. Adm. fee),* an archaeological site where you can learn about ancient Indians.

㉑ Cincinnati

191

Cityscape with 1867 suspension bridge by John Roebling and Riverfront Stadium

Situated on the Ohio River and surrounded by green hills, Cincinnati's beauty has long been praised. By 1811 steamboats from New Orleans reached the city, opening it up to commerce. Today, the culture and esthetic appeal of the Queen City keep pace with its diversified business enterprises. Start at *Fountain Square* (5th and Vine Sts.), the city's thriving core, where the 1871 Tyler Davidson Fountain plays a refreshing counterpoint to the lively beat of downtown. A kiosk here dispenses visitor information; or stop by the *Convention and Visitors Bureau* (300 W. 6th St. 513-621-2142 or 800-344-3445). A second-level skywalk connects the offices and hotels surrounding the square, allowing movement free of traffic and weather. Ascend the 49 floors of *Carew Tower* (5th and Vine Sts. 513-579-9735. Closed Mon. Sept.-May; adm. fee), the city's tallest building, for a great view. *Mount Adams* rises in the northeast part of the city. This former German-Irish working-class neighborhood is now lined with boutiques and restaurants. Driving up steep streets, you arrive at *Eden Park,* known for its views of the city, river, and Kentucky hills. Here you'll find the *Cincinnati Art Museum* (513-721-5204. Closed Mon.; adm. fee), with the work of most major civilizations over the past 5,000 years. The *Krohn Conservatory* (513-352-4090. Donations) has desert, tropical, and seasonal flora.

Museum Center has two top museums. The *Cincinnati Historical Society Museum* and the *Museum of Natural History* (1301 Western Ave. 513-287-7000 or 800-733-2077. Adm. fees) are housed in the splendidly restored *Union Terminal,* worth a visit in itself. The *William Howard Taft Natl. Historic Site* (2038 Auburn Ave. 513-684-3262) preserves the memory of the 27th President. The *Taft Museum* (316 Pike St. 513-241-0343. Adm. fee) contains a small but excellent collection of fine art. Children enjoy the *Zoo* (N of the city off Mitchell Ave. exit. 513-281-4700. Adm. fee), with its many exotic animals.

22 Covington, KENTUCKY Part northern big city, part southern small town, Covington finds itself historically and geographically between two worlds. As if this weren't confusing enough, the town's main architectural influence is Old World. A restored 5-block, 19th-century German neighborhood, **MainStrasse Village** consists of shops, restaurants, and **Goebel Park**, boasting a carillon that accompanies a mechanical Pied Piper. Two lovely cathedrals are open to the public: the **Cathedral Basilica of the Assumption** (*1130 Madison Ave. 606-431-2060*), modeled after Notre Dame, and the **Mother of God Church** (*119 W. 6th St. 606-291-2288*), an 1870s structure with wonderful interior space.

Just east of the 1867 suspension bridge, designed by John Roebling, lies the **Riverside Historic District**, with Civil War-era houses. To the west, **Riverboat Row** offers floating restaurants, waterside nightclubs, and a great view of the Cincinnati skyline.

23 Big Bone Lick State Park (*6 miles W on Ky. 338. 606-384-3522*) Mammoths and mastodons roamed this area after the last Ice Age, grazing and licking the salty earth around the springs. Many became stuck in the morass and died. Thomas Jefferson sent William Clark to excavate the site in 1807. Now plaques and a small museum interpret the area's geology and history.

24 Lexington This is Kentucky's second largest city and the heart of horse country. More than 400 horse farms carpet the countryside, a soft, rolling dream of green. To immerse yourself in the lore and tradition of the favorite animal, stop at **Kentucky Horse Park** (*10 miles N of city, Iron Works Rd. exit. 606-233-4303. Adm. fees*). A haven of white fences and groomed fields, this working farm fea-

Some say it's the lime in the *bluegrass* pasturage that gives horses strong, light bones; others maintain that the ground has the perfect resistance for a foal's muscles and tendons. Whatever the reason, Kentucky has been a leading nursery of thoroughbred champions for more than 150 years. Originally brought from Virginia, Lexington's racehorses were run in the streets until the 1780s, when pioneers laid out a racing path. Since then, horses have become a multibillion-dollar industry for Kentucky, and the Derby—held in May—is the country's premier racing event.

192

Bluegrass country, near Lexington, Kentucky

tures horse shows, self-guided walking tours, and the definitive **International Museum of the Horse**. Also on the grounds is the **American Saddle Horse Museum**. Visit **Keeneland** (*5 miles W of downtown on US 60. 606-254-3412. Major races in April and Oct.; adm. fees for races*) for a free equine encounter from dawn to 10 a.m. Historic buildings open to the public include the **Mary Todd Lincoln House** (*578 W. Main St. 606-233-9999. April to mid-Dec.; closed Sun.-Mon.; adm. fee*), the elegant girlhood home of Lincoln's wife. **Lexington Cemetery** (*833 W. Main St. 606-255-5522*) is where members of the Todd family are buried.

Calumet horse farm, producer of Kentucky Derby winners, Lexington, Ky.

Richmond This town has seen the march of history from pioneer days to the Civil War. Daniel Boone and his followers passed through, and **Fort Boonesborough State Park** (*5 miles NE on Ky. 627. 606-527-3131. April-Oct.; closed Mon.-Tues. after Labor Day; adm. fee*) includes a reconstruction of the fort they built in 1775. A Civil War battle, fought south of town in 1862, ended in a Confederate victory. Not everyone was sympathetic to the South. Cassius M. Clay, fiery emancipationist and Lincoln's minister to Russia, lived in **White Hall,** now a state historic site (*7 miles NW of Richmond to White Hall Shrine Rd. exit. 606-623-9178. April-Oct.; closed Mon.-Tues. after Labor Day; adm. fee*). The 44-room house gives a glimpse into the life of this complex man, who once fired a cannon at tax collectors.

Berea Where Kentucky's rolling hills step up to the Cumberland Mountains, **Berea College** was founded in 1855 upon lofty ideals—"anti-slavery, anti-caste, anti-rum and anti-sin, giving an education to all colors, classes, cheap and thorough." The college admits talented, financially needy students from southern Appalachia; tuition is free. Both school and town promote the region's rich tradition in arts and crafts. The **Berea College Appalachian Museum** (*103 Jackson St. 606-986-9341. Adm. fee*) is a repository of folk arts. At many shops visitors can watch artisans work at such specialties as weaving and glassblowing. Pick up information at the **Berea Welcome Center** (*N. Broadway and Adams Sts. 606-986-2540 or 800-598-5263*).

Boone Tavern Hotel, built in 1909, Berea, Kentucky

Levi Jackson Wilderness Road S.P. (*2 miles E on Ky. 192, then 2 miles S on US 25, follow signs. 606-878-8000*) This 815-acre park underscores the area's history and beauty. The **Mountain Life Museum** offers insights into the lives of the mountain settlers. *Museum April-Oct.; adm. fee.*

Cumberland Falls State Resort Park (*15 miles W on Ky. 90. 606-528-4121*) is famous for its waterfall, which drops 68 feet into the Cumberland River gorge.

Knoxville, **TENNESSEE**   See I-40, page 118.

194

Fog over the Appalachian Mountains

㉙ V o n o r e   The center-piece of **Fort Loudoun State Historic Area** (*18 miles E on Tenn. 72, N on US 411, follow signs. 615-884-6217*) is a replica of the 18th-century British palisaded fort that staved off French efforts to penetrate the Appalachian frontier. Cherokees later captured the fort and killed all but one officer. Besides nature trails, the site—now surrounded by water—has a fishing pier and a breathtaking view of the Smokies. On tribal grounds sits the **Sequoyah Birthplace Museum** (*Citico Rd. 615-884-6246. Adm. fee*), a memorial to the Cherokee statesman who in the early 1800s invented a writing system for his people. It took 12 years to perfect but only hours to learn.

㉚ S w e e t w a t e r   **Lost Sea** (*7 miles S on Tenn. 68, follow signs. 615-337-6616*) Discovered in 1905, this 4.5-acre underground lake takes 15 minutes to cross by boat. Fish leap about eerily in the clear water as dim lights flicker on the cave walls. Carved by water inside a Tennessee mountain, the caverns were once used by Cherokees for council meetings, by Confederates mining saltpeter from bat droppings (for gunpowder), and more recently during Prohibition, by locals who opened a tavern with a dance floor. The 90-minute guided tour includes a glass-bottomed boat ride. *Adm. fee.*

㉛ C l e v e l a n d   "No Kissing, No Shorts or Mini-skirts" warn signs at the meeting hall of the **Primitive Settlement** (*7 miles E on US 64, follow signs. 615-476-5096. April-Oct.; adm. fee*), where Saturday dances are still ruled by old ways. This group of century-old log cabins salvaged from hollows shows how pioneers improvised.

㉜ R e d   C l a y   S t a t e   H i s t o r i c a l   A r e a (*15 miles E on Tenn. 317, follow signs. 615-478-0339. Visitor Center closed Dec.-Feb.*) After being banished from Georgia in 1832, Cherokee leaders moved to this area, before signing the treaty that forced them on the Trail of Tears to Oklahoma. Exhibits re-create the Eastern Cherokee Nation's last days and illuminate this dark period in history.

㉝ C h a t t a n o o g a (*Visitor Center, 2 Broad St. 615-266-7070 or 800-322-3344*) In the shadow of Lookout Mountain on the Ten-

☞ *Cumberland Gap National Historical Park* preserves more than 20,000 acres of rugged Appalachian terrain, including a natural passage that was crucial in opening the American West. By the 1750s explorers started pushing through the gap, followed hard by settlers. Daniel Boone blazed a trail in 1775. Until canals linked east with west in the 1820s, the gap remained the major route to the frontier. Today, you can drive through the gap or up to Pinnacle Overlook for a magnificent view. Or hike some of the park's 50 miles of trails. About 45 miles E on US 25E. Visitor Center 606-248-2817.

nessee River, this city was the site of some of the toughest fighting in the Civil War. Before touring the area military parks, see the fascinating show at **Confederama** (*3742 Tennessee Ave. 615-821-2812. Adm. fee*), where an electric 3-D map puts the military maneuvers in perspective. Down the street, catch a ride up the **Incline Railway** (*827 E. Brow Rd. 615-821-4224. Adm. fee*), the world's steepest passenger rail, to the top of Lookout Mountain, where on clear days you can see several states. Three blocks from the upper station lies **Point Park** (*Visitor Center 615-821-7786*), a precarious rock formation where Confederate cannons perched during the "Battle Above the Clouds." The park is one parcel of the vast **Chickamauga and Chattanooga National Military Park,** which spreads around the city and across the state line into Georgia.

Chattanooga's refurbished waterfront shows off the town's incarnation as a modern commercial center. As tall as a skyscraper, the **Tennessee Aquarium** (*1 Broad St. 800-262-0695. Adm. fee*) has the world's largest freshwater exhibit tank. The **Hunter Museum of Art** (*10 Bluff View. 615-267-0968. Closed Mon.*) houses an extensive collection of American art. Computerized displays at the **TVA Energy Center** (*1101 Market St. 615-751-2631. Closed weekends*) explain water-powered electricity and the New Deal project that harnessed the Tennessee Valley river systems. A young Bessie Smith used to sing for pennies on street corners along old 9th Avenue (now Martin Luther King Blvd.). An exhibit about her extraordinary life and career as one of the world's most famous blueswomen can be found in the **Chattanooga African-American Museum** (*730 E. Martin Luther King Blvd. 615-267-1076*).

On the city's outskirts are two peaceful retreats. **Audubon Acres** (*900 N. Sanctuary Rd. 615-892-1499. Adm. fee*) offers nature trails, and the **Nature Center and Reflection Riding** (*400 Garden Rd. 615-821-160. Adm. fee*) is a lush area on the slope of Lookout Mountain.

Chickamauga Battlefield, GEORGIA (*8 miles, W on Ga. 2, S on US 27. Visitor Center 706-866-9241*) A 7-mile, self-guided driving tour is the best way to see

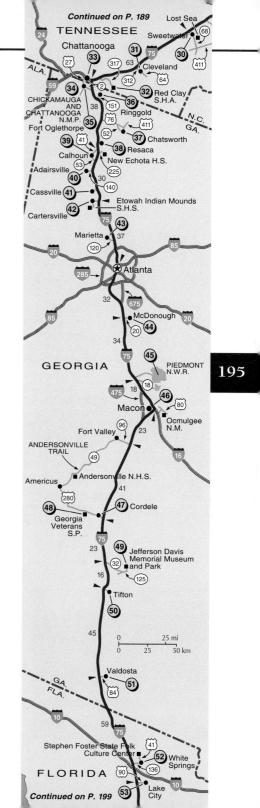

Continued on P. 189

195

Continued on P. 199

this battlefield, where in September 1863, Union and Confederate armies fought savagely for Chattanooga. This last major Southern victory cost some 34,000 casualties. On display are the guns that wrought the carnage. Later that fall, the Federals took Chattanooga and prepared to invade Atlanta.

(35) Fort Oglethorpe Near the entrance to Chickamauga Battlefield off US 27, the **Sixth Calvary Museum** (*Barnhardt Circle. 706-861-2860*) traces the saga of the renowned fighting unit that has seen service in every American conflict from the Civil War to the Persian Gulf War. *Closed Sun. and Nov.-April.*

(36) Ringgold This quiet mountain town witnessed the horror of war up close, as casualties from nearby battles were carted in by the hundred. Blood still stains the floor of the **Old Stone Presbyterian Church** (*At US 41 and Ga. 2*), a humble 1850 sandstone sanctuary that became a hospital. A driving tour brochure can be had at the **Catoosa County Chamber of Commerce** (*306 E. Nashville St. 706-965-5201*); it includes the 1863 **Whitman-Anderson House** (*Tennessee St. Closed to public*), which U. S. Grant visited that year.

(37) Chatsworth **Chief Vann House Historic Site** (*14 miles E via US 76 and Ga. 52, follow signs. 706-695-2598*) The master of this elegant 1804 mansion was James Vann, a wealthy Cherokee planter who owned more than 100 slaves. A hard-drinking polygamist, he was killed at a tavern for shooting a brother-in-law. The family's rise and fall is told in a house tour. *Closed Mon.; adm. fee.*

(38) Resaca The sun sets through the solemn gateway of **Resaca Confederate Cemetery** (*3.5 miles N on US 41, follow signs*), the oldest Georgia graveyard memorial. Marble tablets mark the final resting places of 300 mostly unknown Confederates killed at the Battle of Resaca, the first major clash of the Atlanta Campaign.

(39) Calhoun Before this town existed, the Cherokee Nation had established a busy capital at **New Echota Historic Site** (*1 mile E on Ga. 225. Visitor Center 706-629-8151*), with a courthouse and newspaper office. Now these and other structures have been rebuilt. In 1838, the state stripped the Cherokees of their sovereignty, forcing them into exile in Tennessee. From there they were sent on the Trail of Tears to Oklahoma. *Closed Mon.; adm. fee.*

Etowah Indian Mounds State Historic Site, Cartersville, Georgia

(40) Adairsville As a gift to his wife British-born cotton planter Godfrey Barnsley lovingly re-created a formal English garden at their antebellum estate. After a century of neglect **Barnsley Gardens** (*9.5 miles, W on Ga. 140, fol-*

low signs. 404-773-7480) have been restored. The boxwood parterre and rose gardens are highlights, along with the profusions of daffodils, azaleas, and rhododendrons. The ruins of Barnsley's 24-room Italianate manor serve as an apt symbol of his broken dream. Ravaged by the Civil War and his wife's death, he died penniless in 1873. *Closed Mon. and mid-Dec.–Jan.; adm. fee.*

C a s s v i l l e The hillside **Cassville Confederate Cemetery** *(2.5 miles W on Cassville-White Rd.)* serves as a haunting memorial not only to fallen Southern soldiers, but also to a town that was wiped off the map—the largest city in northwest Georgia before Union troops burned it to the ground in October 1864. A few miles west, post-Civil War African-American heritage is remembered at the **Noble Hill-Wheeler Memorial Center** *(US 41. 404-382-3392. Closed Sun.-Mon.).* Housed in a beautifully restored 1923 school for blacks, exhibits and photos offer a glimpse of a rural community in the late 1800s and early 1900s, the era after Emancipation but long before equal rights.

C a r t e r s v i l l e This sleepy mountain town is the seat of Bartow County, devastated in General Sherman's Georgia campaign. Begin a walking tour of the historic downtown at the **Visitor Center** *(16 W. Main St. 404-387-1357 or 800-733-2280).* Nearby is the first outdoor Coca-Cola ad, hand-painted on the side of a brick pharmacy by a Coke syrup salesman in 1894. On the town's outskirts, the **Etowah Indian Mounds State Historic Site** *(813 Indian Mounds Rd. 404-387-3747. Closed Mon.; adm. fee)* stands above cornfields. The mounds, one 63 feet high, served as ceremonial centers for a large Indian settlement from A.D. 700 to 1650. A museum displays a pair of marble mortuary statues and other finds.

M a r i e t t a Suburbs share the hallowed ground where Civil War soldiers died at the 2,884-acre **Kennesaw Mountain Natl. Battlefield Park** *(4 miles W on Barrett Pkwy., follow signs. 404-427-4686).* Digging in on high ground, the Rebels gave Sherman's men a bloody rebuff on June 27, 1864. Car and foot trails to the peak reveal Confederate trenches and a view of Atlanta's skyline.

A t l a n t a See I-20, p. 72.

M c D o n o u g h *(3 miles E on Ga. 20)* Daily life at the seat of Henry County still revolves around the 1897 Romanesque **Courthouse** *(1 Courthouse Sq.),* which fronts on a busy public square with a Confederate monument. Now a county annex, the **Old Post Office** *(34 Covington St.)* was one of the last of President Franklin D. Roosevelt's public works projects. The lobby has a dramatic mural by French artist Jean Charlot. Antique shops, cafés, and a hardware store add to the ambience of this slice of small-town Dixie. Pick up a brochure for a walking tour at the **Henry County Chamber of Commerce** *(0.25 mile W on Ga. 20. 404-957-5786).*

Like guardians of the past, they stand alone and tall in nearly every small southern town that has a courthouse. Perched high on stone shafts, *statues of Confederate soldiers* pay silent homage to the Lost Cause. Memorial groups like the United Daughters of the Confederacy erected them in the era after Reconstruction, when the South's elite regained power. Often, the pedestal bases list every local man who fell. Unlike many of Dixie's battlefield and big-city monuments—the gargantuan, sword-carrying, horseback-riding heroes—these are anonymous, life-size Rebel soldiers who stand at ease and face defeat with an even gaze.

197

Let's Keep Georgia Peachy Clean

☞ A scenic 80-mile loop through a countryside of peach and pecan orchards, the **Anderson-ville Trail** has as its highlight and midpoint the Andersonville National Historic Site (Ga. 49. 912-924-0343), where nearly 13,000 Union soldiers perished at the notorious Confederate prison camp. Its commandant, Henry Wirz, who was later executed, is memorialized in the town, and a Welcome Center & Museum (114 Church St. 912-924-2558) present the Southern side of the conflict. South on Ga. 49 is historic Americus, whose streets are lined with Victorian houses.

45 **Piedmont National Wildlife Refuge** *(18 miles E on Juliette Rd. 912-986-5441)* A tract of eroded farmland makes up most of this 35,000-acre refuge, established in 1939. It offers sanctuary to more than 200 species of birds, especially the endangered red-cockaded woodpecker, which only nests in old-growth pines. Self-guided driving tour and nature trails.

46 **Macon** Founded in 1823 on the Ocmulgee River, Macon soon became known as the "Queen Inland City of the South," for its bustling trade, wide streets, and cherry blossom parks. The downtown business district is still a pedestrian's paradise of shops and Southern charm. Pick up a pamphlet at the **Welcome Center** *(200 Cherry St. 912-743-3401. Closed Sun.),* in a restored 1916 railroad depot. The antebellum **Johnston-Felton-Hay House** *(934 Georgia Ave. 912-742-8155. Adm. fee)* is a rare example of Italian Renaissance Revival architecture in the South. A guided tour takes visitors through the lavish, cupola-crowned mansion, completed in 1859. Down the street, a 12-pound Union cannonball sits where it landed in 1864, in the front hall of the 1853 Greek Revival **Old Cannonball House** *(856 Mulberry St. 912-745-5982. Adm. fee).* The servants' quarters now house a **Confederate Museum.** Another quintessentially Southern mansion, the white-columned **Woodruff House** *(988 Bond St. 912-752-2715. Weekdays by appt.; adm. fee)* offers a magnificent view of Macon. In the heart of downtown, one of the world's largest copper domes shines atop the **City Auditorium** *(Cherry and First Sts. 912-751-9152).* Inside, a 60-foot-long painting tells the area's history. Another mural graces the foyer at the **Harriet Tubman Museum of African-American Art and Culture** *(340 Walnut St. 912-743-8544. Closed Sun.).* Painted by a local artist, it salutes black Americans from the 1700s to Oprah Winfrey. The museum has a fine collection of West African artifacts and modern works. The nearby **Otis Redding Memorial Bridge,** spanning the Ocmulgee River, pays tribute to the legendary soul singer and composer. For a self-guided Black Heritage tour, pick up a brochure at the Welcome Center. Also worth seeing: the **Ocmulgee National Monument** *(1207 Emery Hwy. 912-752-8257),* a 700-acre archaeological preserve; and the **Museum of Arts and Sciences** *(4182 Forsyth Rd. 912-477-3232. Adm. fee),* with a 40-million-year-old whale fossil found near Macon.

47 **Cordele** *(Just W on US 280)* In the so-called "Watermelon Capital of the World," locals sell the fruit from trucks and stands

Woodruff House, built in 1836, Macon, Georgia

in season. For a walking tour of historic down-town, pick up a brochure at the **Chamber of Commerce** (*302 E. 16th Ave. 912-273-1668*).

Georgia Veterans S. P. (*10 miles W on US 280, follow signs. 912-276-2371. Adm. fee*) Tanks, planes, and other military exhibits are gathered at this 1,322-acre site on Lake Blackshear's shore. It's also a haven for model-airplane enthusiasts.

Jeff. Davis Mem. Museum & Park (*17 miles E on Ga. 32, follow signs. 912-831-2335*) An obelisk in a pine grove marks the spot where the Confederate president was cap-tured in May 1865. The museum displays Civil War artifacts. *Closed Mon.; adm. fee.*

Tifton As interstate traffic whizzes by, horses slowly pull plows in the fields at **Georgia Agrirama** (*0.25 mile W on 8th St., follow signs. 912-386-3344*), a 95-acre living-history museum that re-creates a 19th-century rural community. *Closed Mon.; adm. fee.*

Valdosta A manufacturing center with a name like a Southern belle, turn-of-the-century Valdosta was one of the richest towns per capita in the U. S. Its historic district bears testament. Pick up a driving-tour pamphlet at the **Ola Barber Pittman House** (*416 N. Ashley St. 912-247-8100. Closed weekends*). Now hosting the Chamber of Commerce, the neo-classical 1915 building was the former resi-dence of a Coca-Cola bottling tycoon.

White Springs, FLORIDA Stephen Foster State Folk Culture Center (*3 miles E on Fla. 136, follow signs. 904-397-2733*) The 19th-century northern composer never saw the Suwannee River he immortal-ized in "Old Folks At Home." But this beau-tiful hilltop site epitomizes the romance of the Old South enshrined in his songs. In the mu-seum, dioramas illustrate the songs. *Adm. fee.*

Lake City A shrine to the sports-crazy South, the **Florida Sports Hall of Fame** (*0.25 mile W on US 90. 904-758-1310*) displays memorabilia of more than 100

Continued on P. 195

199

Florida athletes and others who have retired here. Videos show career highlights. *Adm. fee.*

⑤④ Gainesville **Devil's Millhopper State Geological Site** *(3 miles E on Fla. 232, follow signs. 904-336-2008. Adm. fee)* Winding stairs descend to the bottom of this 500-foot-wide, 120-foot-deep sinkhole formed when an underground cavern collapsed. Below, visitors can watch streams trickle down the steep sides and vanish into crevices. The cool temperatures nurture plants and animals more common in the Appalachians. A display explains this geological wonder. The late archer Fred Bear bagged big-game animals all over the globe. Many are displayed at the **Fred Bear Museum** *(0.25 mile W on Archer Rd., follow signs. 904-376-2411 or 800-874-4603. Closed Mon.-Tues.; adm. fee)*, including an elephant, a lion, and a Bengal tiger. A recorded commentary describes the mounted animals.

⑤⑤ Paynes Prairie State Preserve *(1 mile E on Rte. 234, then 2 miles N on US 441. 904-466-4100)* Herds of Spanish horses gallop across the plain that dominates the 20,000-acre preserve; sandhill cranes nest here in winter. Trails. *Adm. fee.*

⑤⑥ Cross Creek **Marjorie Kinnan Rawlings State Historic Site** *(13 miles, E on Rte. 234, follow signs to Rte. 325. 904-466-3672)* At this one-story farmhouse, where she lived from 1928 until her death in 1953, Rawlings wrote *The Yearling* and other famous works about the Florida backwoods. Cross Creek inspired the transplanted Northerner's love of cracker culture and what she called the "encroaching jungle." *Closed Tues.-Wed.; tours; adm. fee.*

⑤⑦ Ocala **Don Garlits' Museum of Drag Racing** *(0.5 mile E on Rte. 484. 904-245-8661)* A car-crammed tribute to the auto sport that roared out of the '50s, the museum displays more than 75 racing machines, from early fuelers to today's funny-car champions. Films and exhibits relate the saga of drag racing. *Adm. fee.*

Florida Museum of Natural History,
Museum Rd. and Newell Dr.
University of Florida, Gainesville

⑤⑧ Bushnell **Dade Battlefield State Historic Site** *(2 miles E on Fla. 48, follow signs. Visitor Center 904-793-4781)* Not really a battlefield, this path through pines and palmettos is where U. S troops were ambushed and killed by Seminole Indians and runaway slaves one rainy morning in 1835. Only 3 of Maj. Francis Dade's 108 soldiers survived the massacre, which began the bloody Second Seminole War. Museum and self-guided tour. *Adm. fee.*

⑤⑨ Tampa *(Convention and Visitors Assoc., 111 Madison St. 813-223-1111 or 800-826-8358)* Now a cosmopolitan metropolis, Tampa was a frontier railroad stop when Cuban exile Don Vicente Martinez Ybor built a company town in 1886 that became the "Cigar Capital of the World." More than 10,000 immigrants worked in the factories here until the 1930s, when the boom ended. **Ybor City State Museum** *(1818 Ninth Ave. 813-247-6323. Closed Sun.-Mon.; adm. fee)*, in a his-

Gondola touring, Tampa, Florida

toric brick bakery, tells of the rise and fall of the Ybor dynasty. A block away, visitors can watch modern workers hand-roll cigars at the restored factory at **Ybor Square** (*8th Ave. and 13th St. 813-247-4497*), a quaint marketplace of shops and restaurants. Piped-in jazz provides the perfect ambience for perusing the collection at the downtown **Museum of African-American Art** (*1308 N. Marion St. 813-272-2466. Closed Mon.; adm. fee*), featuring works by more than 80 black artists.

There isn't a cage in sight at the lush, natural setting of **Lowry Park Zoo** (*7530 N. Blvd. 813-932-0245*). Next door, children follow a rainbow bridge into **Fun Forest** (*813-935-5503*), a delightful theme park filled with fairy-tale characters. *Adm. fees at both.* At the **Museum of Science and Industry** (*4801 E. Fowler Ave. 813-987-6300. Adm. fee*), you can experience the 75-mph gusts of a simulated hurricane. Hands-on exhibits keep children busy for hours.

St. Petersburg The Gulf shore of this popular peninsular resort boasts sparkling white-sand beaches; its Tampa Bay side has one of the nation's longest public waterfronts. The historic **Pier** (*800 2nd Ave. N.E.*), a concrete walkway ending in an inverted pyramid of shops, cafés, and an observation deck, has attracted crowds since the early 1900s. On the pier, a life-size replica of the Benoist airboat hangs in the foyer of the **St. Petersburg Historical and Flight One Museum** (*335 2nd Ave. N.E. 813-894-1052. Adm. fee*). The small plane's 1914 flight across the bay to Tampa launched the commercial airline industry. Next door, the **Museum of Fine Arts** (*255 Beach Dr. N.E. 813-896-2667. Closed Mon.; adm. fee*) spreads its treasures throughout a Mediterranean-style villa. The late Spanish surrealist hovers ominously in a white-light hologram at the **Salvador Dali Museum** (*1000 3rd St. S. 813-823-3767. Adm. fee*), as if keeping watch over his works. An ancient sinkhole provides the dramatic setting at **Sunken Gardens** (*1825 4th St. N. 813-896-3186. Adm. fee*), a botanical wonderland of 1930s Americana, with a Biblical wax museum.

Manatee cow and calf, Florida

Bradenton The **Manatee Village Historical Park** (*604 15th St. E. 813-749-7165. Closed Sat.*) displays a group of late 19th-century buildings. After watching Snooty, a 45-year-old manatee at the downtown **South Florida Museum & Bishop Planetarium** (*201 10th St. W. 813-746-4131. Closed Mon.; adm. fee*), you wonder how sailors could have mistaken these sea cows for mermaids.

Sanibel Island, Florida

Conquistador Hernando de Soto and his men began their cross-country search for gold after landing at the Manatee River in 1539. Exhibits at the **De Soto National Memorial** (*7 miles from Bradenton, W on Fla. 64, N on 75th St. N.W. 813-792-0458*) tell the story of his doomed quest. The trail through a mangrove swamp shows what the explorers had to contend with.

202

(62) **Sarasota** High- and lowbrow culture meet in magnificent surroundings at the **John and Mable Ringling Museum of Art** complex (*5401 Bay Shore Rd. 813-359-5700. Adm. fee*), the circus tycoon's gift to the people of Florida. His renowned collection of Baroque paintings hangs in the **Art Galleries** with other treasures, near the gaudy memorabilia of the **Circus Galleries.** Reflected in Sarasota Bay, **Ca'd'Zan** (Venetian for "John's House"), the Ringling's 32-room winter residence, was inspired by the Doge's Palace in Venice and built in 1926. Across the highway, **Bellm's Cars & Music of Yesterday** (*5500 N. Tamiami Trail. 813-355-6228. Adm. fee*) is home to more than 2,000 mechanical music machines. Player pianos, cylinder phonographs, and crank-up hurdy-gurdies from the Gilded Age make a quaint racket. Thousands of orchids bloom at the **Marie Selby Botanical Gardens** (*811 S. Palm Ave. 813-366-5730. Adm. fee*), spilling fragrance on Sarasota's waterfront.

Circus Galleries, Ringling Museum of Art, Sarasota, Florida

(63) **Osprey** **Historic Spanish Point** (*9.5 miles, W on Fla. 72, S on US 41. 813-966-5214*) Centuries of human settlement—from prehistoric Indians to northern homesteaders—converge at this 30-acre site, featuring restored buildings and trails; a footbridge lets you view ospreys and other wildlife. *Tours; adm. fee.*

(64) **Fort Myers** Founded as a military post, Fort Myers became an important port and cowtown for Florida's 19th-century cattle industry. Thomas Edison's **Winter Home** (*2350 McGregor Blvd 813-334-7419. Tour; adm. fee*), built in 1886, has spacious porches and a sprawling botanical garden. A museum showcases his most important inventions. Next door, vintage Model T's gleam in the garage of the **Henry Ford Winter Home** (*813-334-3614*), also on the tour. The men were friends and vacationed here for decades.

(65) **J. N. "Ding" Darling Natl. Wildlife Refuge** (*18 miles W on Sanibel Island Wildlife Dr. 813-472-1100*) A 5-mile self-guided car ride through a mangrove swamp is one way to ex

plore this 5,393-acre refuge, named for the late Pulitzer Prize-winning cartoonist and conservationist. Walking and canoe trails allow for a better look at the numerous bird and other wildlife species. There is also a bird-watching tower. To get here, you pass the posh resorts that crowd the rest of the island, famous for its seashell-strewn Gulf beaches. *Bridge toll and adm. fee.*

Bonita Springs **Everglades Wonder Gardens** (*3 miles, W on Fla. 865, N on Old US 41. 813-992-2591*) The first creature to greet visitors at this wildlife menagerie is "Old Joe," a snaggle-tooth crocodile and the zoo's star attraction since 1936. The garden setting makes for easy access and pleasant shade. *Adm. fee.*

Corkscrew Swamp Sanctuary (*17 miles E on Fla. 846, follow signs. 813-657-3771*) To protect the endangered wood storks that nest here, the Audubon Society in 1954 took over the 11,000-acre property and saved the country's oldest stand of virgin bald cypresses. A 2-mile boardwalk loops through the majestic trees. Winter offers the best chance to see wildlife, such as alligators, bobcats, and more than 200 bird species. *Adm. fee.*

Great egret, J. N. "Ding" Darling NWR, Florida

203

Naples Named for the Italian city, the former fishing village boomed briefly in the early 1900s as a railroad town. Now it's an upscale resort community known for its golf courses and 10 miles of public beaches. A historic port district of tin-roofed warehouses has been converted into trendy shops and restaurants at **Old Marine Marketplace** (*1200 Fifth Ave. S.*); fishing boats still dock here with their daily catch from the Gulf of Mexico.

Miami See I-95, p. 345.

With more than 2,400 square miles, *Big Cypress National Preserve* is no mere subtropical swamp, but rather a complex landscape of wet and dry prairies, pine islands and hardwood hammocks, marshes and mangrove forests. Not long ago, the area was filled with loggers, oil rigs, and cattle ranches; plans to drain it for real estate in the 1960s spurred establishment of the preserve. Now you can see nature taking back the land. The Visitor Center (813-695-4111) is about 40 miles from I-75 via Fla. 29 and US 41.

Big Cypress National Preserve, Florida

Unless otherwise noted, directions are from interstate, and sites are free and generally open daily. Phone for further information.

❶ Cleveland

Cleveland
Museum of Art

Monstrous iron bridges span the Cuyahoga River, where steel mills belch fire and smoke, and ships laden with coal and iron still leave port for Lake Erie. Above all, Cleveland is an industrial city whose growth in the 19th century was fueled by the industrial revolution and its immigrant labor force.

Public Square (Euclid and Ontario Aves.) was the spot that surveyor Moses Cleaveland chose in 1796 to plot the town commons. Today the square is Cleveland's commercial heart, dwarfed by gleaming skyscrapers. The observation deck of the 52-story *Terminal Tower* (Tower City Center. 216-621-7981. Open weekends; adm. fee) offers a magnificent view of the city. Here, too, is the *Greater Cleveland Convention & Visitors Bureau* (216-612-4110 or 800-321-1001).

Five miles east of the square, the art galleries, cafés, and studios of *Little Italy* (Marfield Rd., off Euclid Ave.) still evoke an Old World atmosphere. Nearby *University Circle,* a tree-shaded hub of world-class museums, embraces the cultural legacy of the 19th-century industrial barons. Don't miss the *Cleveland Museum of Art* (11150 East Blvd. 216-421-7340. Closed Mon.), a sumptuous beaux arts building with masterpieces from the Americas, Europe, Asia, and Africa. Nearby, giant insects, dinosaur fossils, and a cast of three-million-year-old "Lucy"—one of the world's oldest hominid skeletons—can be seen at the *Museum of Natural History* (1

Wade Oval Dr. 216-231-4600. Adm. fee)

The *Western Reserve Historical Society Museum* (10825 East Blvd. 216-721-5722. Closed Mon.; adm. fee) illustrates American and Ohio history with displays that include Shaker crafts and Early American costumes. Hands-on exhibits predominate at the *Children's Museum* (10730 Euclid Ave. 216-791-KIDS. Adm. fee) and the *Health Education Museum* (8911 Euclid Ave. 216-231-5010. Adm. fee), with a walk-through tooth and transparent talking woman.

Also worth visiting are 19th-century *Dunham Tavern* (6709 Euclid Ave. 216-431-1060. Wed. and Sun.; adm. fee), the *African-American Museum* (1765 Crawford Rd. 216-791-1700. Closed Wed. adm. fee), and, near Hopkins Airport, the *NASA Lewis Visitors Research Center* (21000 Brookpark Rd. 216-433-2001) with its supersonic wind tunnel.

Aerial view of downtown and waterfront area

❷ Akron

(*Akron and Summit County Visitors Bureau, Cascade Plaza sublevel. 216-376-4254 or 800-245-4254*) Benjamin Franklin Goodrich arrived in the small town of Akron in 1870 to open the first rubber company west of the Alleghenies. With the invention of the automobile, the rubber industry exploded between 1910 and 1920, and Akron became the world's rubber capital. The **Goodyear World of Rubber** (*1144 E. Market St. 216-796-7117. Mon.-Fri.*) tells

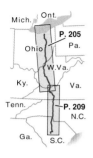

about rubber-tire making, including how Charles Goodyear came up with the formula for rubber over his cookstove. Admire the riches reaped during the rubber era at **Stan Hywet Hall** (*714 N. Portage Path. 216-836-5533. Closed Mon.; adm. fee*), a 65-room Tudor manor that was once the home of Frank Seiberling, co-founder of the Goodyear Tire and Rubber Company. From here, drive south along **Portage Path**—the western boundary of the U. S. for almost 20 years—to the **Simon Perkins Mansion** (*550 Copley Rd. 216-535-1120. Closed Mon.; adm. fee*), the 1835 stone home of Akron's founder, now restored with pre-Civil War and Victorian furnishings. Across the street stands the white-frame **John Brown Home** (*514 Diagonal Rd. 216-535-1120. Closed Mon.; adm. fee*), where the fiery abolitionist raised sheep in the 1840s. **Quaker Square** (*120 E. Mill St. 216-253-5970*) is an upscale shopping center housed in an old Quaker Oats factory and grain silos. Nearby, the **Akron Art Museum** (*70 E. Market St. 216-376-9185. Closed Mon.*) showcases foreign and American masterworks.

Canton (*Canton–Stark County Visitor Center, 2141 George Halas Dr. N.W. 216-452-0243*) An important steel center, Canton is famous for its **Pro Football Hall of Fame** (*2121 George Halas Dr. N.W. 216-456-8207. Adm. fee*), where the big heroes and the big moments of football are relived. The Taj Mahal-like **McKinley National Memorial** (*800 McKinley Monument Dr. N.W. 216-455-7043*) honors native son William McKinley, 25th President of the U. S., who is buried here with his wife and daughters. Another native son is lionized at the **Hoover Historical Center** (*2225 Easton St. N.W., near Walsh Univ. 216-499-0287. Closed Mon.*). The restored Victorian boyhood home of vacuum-cleaner mogul William Hoover displays antique and modern sweepers.

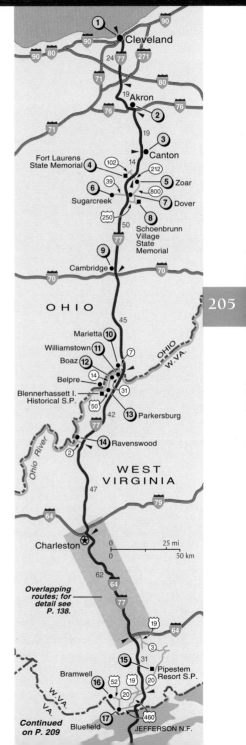

Overlapping routes; for detail see P. 138.

Continued on P. 209

④ Fort Laurens State Memorial *(0.5 mile N on Ohio 212, 0.5 mile S on Rte. 102. 216-874-2059)* Ohio's first fort once stood on the site of this tranquil 80-acre park and served as a western outpost during the Revolutionary War. A museum contains uniforms, weapons, and a crypt with the remains of 21 soldiers who fought in that war. *Wed.-Sun. in summer, weekends in fall; adm. fee.*

Pro Football Hall of Fame, Canton, Ohio

⑤ Zoar *(3 miles E on Ohio 212, follow signs. 216-874-3011)* An experiment in communal living, the town was founded in 1817 by German separatists fleeing religious persecution. The self-sustaining group of farmers, bakers, and weavers flourished for 81 years, disbanding in 1898. **Zoar Village** encompasses a 12-block historic district, with restored communal dwellings, a garden, and a tavern. On walking tours, costumed guides tell tales of old Zoar. *Wed.-Sun. in summer, weekends in May and Oct.; adm. fee to museums.*

206

⑥ Sugarcreek *(8 miles W on Ohio 39. 216-852-4113)* With restaurants and craft shops lining its commercialized but cheery streets, this hamlet is the gateway to Ohio's Amish country. The **Alpine Hills Historical Museum** *(106 Main St. 216-852-4113. April-Nov. Mon.-Sat.)* depicts Swiss and Amish life and includes a re-created 1890s kitchen, woodworking shop, and cheese factory.

☞ About 35,000 **Amish**—the world's largest community—reside in the frame farmhouses of Holmes County, Ohio, and four neighboring counties. Following a doctrine of simplicity, the Old Amish, whose forefathers fled religious persecution in Germany and Switzerland in the 1700s, drive horse-drawn buggies, use kerosene lamps, wear plain clothes, and support themselves through farming and cottage industries. Simple living, they believe, fosters family togetherness and preserves their heritage in a complex world.

⑦ Dover Warther Museum *(331 Karl Ave. 216-343-7513)* This popular museum commemorates Ernest Warther (1885-1973), a part-time craftsman who carved 63 intricate models of steam locomotives and events in American history from walnut, ebony, and ivory. Displays include a model of Lincoln's funeral train. *Adm. fee.*

⑧ Schoenbrunn Village State Memorial *(4 miles E on US 250, follow signs. 216-339-3636)* In 1772, David Zeisberger led a group of Delaware Indians and Moravian missionaries here from Pennsylvania to serve the local Indians. Refusing to join in frontier raids, the pacifists destroyed their little settlement—Ohio's first—in 1777 and moved away. Today, in the re-created, tree-shaded village, you can see 17 log buildings, the original cemetery, and period demonstrations. Picnic area. *May-Oct.; adm. fee.*

⑨ Cambridge Ever since the Cambridge Glass Company created its first pressed-glass pitcher in the early 1900s, the region's reputation for high-quality glass has blossomed. The **Cambridge Glass Museum** *(1.5 miles N on Ohio 209 to 812 Jefferson Ave. 614-432-3045. June-Oct. Mon.-Sat.; adm. fee)* displays 5,000 pieces of art glass made before 1954. Peek at glassmaking in the works at **Boyd's Crystal Art Glass** *(1203 Morton Ave., off Ohio 40. 614-439-2077. Closed Sun.)*, a tiny factory with friendly artisans.

Marietta and Environs (*Marietta Area Tourist Bureau, 316 Third St. 614-373-5178 or 800-288-2577*) The first organized settlement in the Northwest Territory, Marietta became an important stopover in the 1800s for stern-wheelers chugging down the Ohio River to the Mississippi. Several museums preserve this heritage, including the **Campus Martius Museum** (*601 2nd St. 614-373-3750. Daily May-Sept., Wed.-Sun. March-April and Oct.-Nov.; adm. fee*), which contains historical artifacts from Ohio and the Northwest Territory, and the **Ohio River Museum** (*601 Front St. 614-373-3750*), which traces the river's great steamboat era. Nearby is moored the **W. P. Snyder Jr.**—the nation's only surviving steam-powered stern-wheeler towboat. The well-preserved toys, dolls, and dollhouses of the wealthy Bosley children, who grew up in the Marietta area at the turn of the century, are arrayed inside a restored B&O railroad car at the **Children's Toy and Doll Museum** (*100 Maple St. 614-373-5900. Tues.-Sun. in summer, Sat.-Sun. in fall; adm. fee*). Nearby, **Butch's Cola Museum** (*118 Maple St. 614-376-COKE. Tues.-Sun. spring–fall, Fri.-Sat. in winter*) salutes America's Coke-drinking habit with antique vending machines and other memorabilia. Children will enjoy watching artisans create realistic baby dolls from porcelain and vinyl at the **Lee Middleton Original Doll Factory** (*1301 Washington Blvd. in Belpre, across the bridge from Parkersburg, W. Va. 614-423-1305. Call ahead for hours*), a dollhouse-like building with life-size toy soldiers standing guard.

Pinnacle Rock State Park, near Bluefield, W. Va., 12 miles west of I-77 on US 52

Williamstown   Fenton Art Glass Factory (*Williamstown exit, follow signs. 304-375-7772*) Craftsmen hand-blow glass into jewel-colored vases, lamps, bowls, and more. An interesting museum features more than 1,500 pieces of Ohio Valley glass made between 1880 and 1980. *Tours Mon.-Fri.*

Boaz, WEST VIRGINIA Henderson Hall (*Williamstown exit, 2 miles S on W. Va. 14 to Old River Rd. 304-375-2129*) Hostesses give tours of this Italianate mansion, one of the state's best preserved antebellum homes. *Sun. only May-Oct.; adm. fee.*

Parkersburg (*Greater Parkersburg Area Chamber of Commerce, 720 Juliana St. 304-422-3588. Mon.-Fri.*) The oak-shaded streets of the **Parkersburg Historical District** depict a refined, progressive city at the confluence of the Ohio and Little Kanawha Rivers that prospered from shipping in the 19th century. That era is epitomized by the **Cook House** (*1301 Murdoch Ave. 304-422-6961. By appt.; adm. fee*), an early federal-style house with period furnishings. The centerpiece of picturesque **Blennerhassett I. Historical State Park** (*Accessible via stern-wheeler from Point Park. 304-428-2436 or 614-423-7268; park information 304-428-3000. May-Oct. Tues.-Sun.; adm. fee*) is the reconstructed **Harman Blennerhassett Mansion**, home of a wealthy Irishman arrested in 1806 for plotting with Aaron Burr to establish a southwest empire. The charges were later dismissed. The **Blennerhassett Museum** (*2nd and*

Juliana Sts. May-Dec. Tues.-Sun., Jan.-April Sat.-Sun.; adm. fee) highlights area history and Blennerhassett family possessions.

 A number of subsistence farmers, loggers, and coal miners dwell in rough-hewn log cabins deep in the Appalachian Mountains. The *mountain people* of West Virginia and eastern Virginia have managed to retain their handicrafts—quilting, toy making, wood carving—and their hymns and folk songs, accompanied by dulcimers and fiddles. This rich heritage can be traced back to their Scottish, Irish, and German roots.

208

⑭ **R a v e n s w o o d** Col. William Crawford surveyed the land along the Ohio River for George Washington, who camped nearby in 1770. At **Washington's Lands Museum and Park** *(W. Va. 68 in South Ravenswood),* a converted lock building and restored log cabin hold a sizable collection of relics from the pioneer and riverboat eras. Picnic tables. *Museum Sun. p.m. May-Sept.*

C h a r l e s t o n See I-64, p. 139.

I - 6 4 / 7 7 Overlapping routes; see sites pp. 139-40.

⑮ **P i p e s t e m   R e s o r t   S t a t e   P a r k** *(20 miles NW on W. Va. 20, follow signs. 304-466-1800)* Perched atop a woodland plateau at the edge of a 1,000-foot gorge, this 4,024-acre park is an upscale operation with two lodges, one accessible only by aerial tram. For the rugged, cabins and campsites are available, as are hiking trails. Stables, championship golf courses, and scenic overlooks.

⑯ **B r a m w e l l** *(6 miles W of Bluefield on US 52)* Narrow, shaded streets meander past Bramwell's fanciful Victorian and Tudor homes, which cling to hillsides above the Bluestone River. During the Gilded Age 14 coal barons resided in this town, once considered America's richest. Information at **Town Hall** *(Main St. 304-248-7114).*

⑰ **B l u e f i e l d** *(4 miles W on US 52)* Named for the chicory flowers growing wild on the surrounding mountainsides, Bluefield thrives on coal from the nearby Pocahontas bituminous coalfield, mined since 1892. At the **Eastern Regional Coal Archives** *(Craft Memorial Library, 600 Commerce St. 304-325-3943. Mon.-Fri.),* historical photographs, rare books, diaries, and films shed light on this important regional industry. **Old City Hall,** a classical revival edifice built in 1924, now holds the bustling **Bluefield Area Arts and Crafts Center** *(500 Bland St. 304-325-8000),* with an art gallery, craft shop, restaurant, transportation museum, and performing arts center.

Jefferson National Forest, Virginia

⑱ **Shot Tower Historical State Park, V I R G I N I A** *(1.5 miles N on US 52. 703-699-6778)* A dizzying staircase leads up the narrow interior of this fortress-like stone tower, built by a miner about 1807 to make ammunition for settlers' firearms. The crude process included

NASCAR racing, Charlotte Motor Speedway,
North Carolina

carrying lead from the
nearby mines to the
top of the 75-foot
tower, melting it, then
dropping it to the bot-
tom of the shaft into a
large kettle of water. A
park ranger stands by to answer questions.
*Daily in summer, park only weekends rest of
year; adm. fee.*

**Stone Mountain State Park,
NORTH CAROLINA** (*14 miles
NW on US 21, 1.5 miles W on N.C. 1002, 4 miles
on John P. Frank Pkwy. 910-957-8185*) The
600-foot-high granite dome resembling a
moonscape isn't immediately visible from beneath the 13,000-acre park's cool canopy of
pines and oaks. Drive to the Visitor Center to
see the magnificent view from the deck, or hike
one of the many trails. Camping, picnic areas.

Pilot Mountain State Park
(*14 miles S of Mount Airy on US 52. 910-325-
2355*) Rising 1,400 feet above the rolling
countryside, this solitary quartzite monad-
nock was used as a landmark by both Indians and pioneers. You can drive to the summit of nearby **Little Pinnacle,** where short
trails lead to scenic overviews of Pilot Mountain and, in the distance, the hazy Blue Ridge
Mountains. Camping, picnic areas.

Statesville (*Chamber of Commerce,
115 E. Front St. 704-873-2892. Mon.-Fri.*) A
pretty city with wide streets, Statesville has
neighborhoods dating from the 19th century.

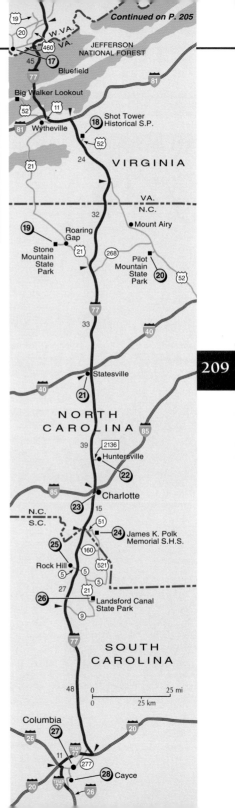

Continued on P. 205

Carolina Raptor Center,
Huntersville, North Carolina

The largest district, encircling **Mitchell College** (*W of downtown*), contains two of Statesville's oldest houses, both privately owned: the **George Anderson House** (*313 S. Mulberry St.*), built in 1860, and the **William Franklin Hall House** (*203 N. Race St.*), constructed of handmade brick in 1870. Also of interest is the **Fourth Creek Burying Grounds** (*202 W. End Ave.*), where Revolutionary War soldiers lie beneath crumbling tombstones.

(22) Huntersville In a picturesque setting by the Catawba River, a white clapboard house and working farm tell the story of 19th-century plantation life at **Latta Place** (*5225 Sample Rd., in Latta Plantation Park. 704-875-2312. Feb.-Dec. Tues.-Sun.; adm. fee*). At the **Carolina Raptor Center** (*Latta Plantation Park. 704-875-6521. Tues.-Sun.; adm. fee*), a woodsy trail winds past captive American kestrels, hawks, and owls.

210

(23) Charlotte Towering above the tree-clad Carolina foothills, Charlotte's glass-and-metal skyscrapers proclaim the city's status as a major financial and convention center. Strolling down the main street, though, you get a picture of a laid-back town, with flower beds and benches where locals have time to sit and chat. For kids, the action is at **Discovery Place** (*301 N. Tryon St. 704-372-6261 or 800-935-0553. Adm. fee*). Here, mynahs fly free in a rain forest, and the Science Circus says "Touch!" The **Mint Museum of Art** (*2730 Randolph Rd. 704-337-2000. Tues.-Sun.; adm. fee*), dating from a nearby gold rush in 1836, displays more than 5,000 pieces of European art, pre-Columbian artifacts, period costumes, and regional crafts.

Tobacco plants, South Carolina

(24) James K. Polk Memorial S.H.S. (*3 miles E on N.C. 51, 0.5 mile S on US 521. 704-889-7145*) Reconstructed log buildings with period relics depict the 1795 birthplace of the 11th President of the U. S. The Visitor Center has interesting artifacts from Polk's time. *Closed Mon. in winter.*

Glencairn Garden, Rock Hill, South Carolina

(25) Rock Hill, SOUTH CAROLINA While the town of Rock Hill, founded in 1852 as a station on the Charlotte-Columbia Railroad, appears gray and industrial, its downtown neighborhoods reflect a colorful Victorian heritage. In the **Oakland-College-Ebenezer Avenue** area (*Maps at City Hall, Hampton and Black Sts. 803-329-7000. Mon.-Fri.*), mansions line the streets, including the 1907 neoclassical **Stokes-Mayfield House** (*353 Oakland Ave.*) and the 1898 **Anderson-Gill House** (*227 Oakland Ave.*). Nearby, 6-acre **Glencairn Garden** (*Charlotte Ave. and Crest St.*) offers a quiet retreat with manicured trails weaving past dogwoods, primroses, azaleas, and Japanese maples. Children will want to have their picture taken next to the "Casey at the Bat" statue in **Cherry Park** (*1466 Cherry Rd.*). Outside town, the **Museum of York County** (*4621 Mount Gallant Rd., follow signs. 803-329-2121. Tues.-Sun.; adm. fee*) houses a display of 500 mounted animals, including a majestic elephant at a water hole. Other exhibits include the artwork of Vernon Grant (creator of Kelloggs' "Snap, Crackle, and Pop") and regional Catawba pottery. Nature trail.

Wall mural, Columbia, South Carolina

Landsford Canal State Park *(10 miles S of Rock Hill on US 21. 803-789-5800)* A tiny museum on the banks of the slow-moving Catawba River shows how the adjacent early 19th-century canal was supposed to work—but didn't. Relax in the shade of maple and pine trees and admire the endangered rock shoal spider lilies. Playground, picnic area. *Thurs.-Mon.; museum by appt.*

㉗ Columbia

Columbians haven't forgotten February 16, 1865, the day their genteel southern capital went up in flames while occupied by General Sherman's army. The Italian Renaissance **State House** (Main and Gervais Sts. 803-734-2430. Tours Mon.-Fri.) wears six brass stars where Union cannonballs hit. Not far away, the classical revival **First Baptist Church** (1306 Hampton St. 803-256-4251. Mon.-Fri.)—with original furniture—was the site of the first Secession Convention, which led to the Civil War.

Columbia's tree-shaded streets harbor many elegant old houses; for tours, contact **Historic Homes** (803-252-1770. Tues.-Sat.; adm. fee). Some examples of antebellum living include the **Hampton-Preston Mansion** (1615 Blanding St.), built in 1818, and the **Robert Mills House** (1616 Blanding St.), designed in 1823 by Robert Mills, the first federal architect of the United States. The tiny,

white-frame **Mann-Simons Cottage** (1403 Richland St.) was the home of Celia Mann, a former slave who purchased her freedom. The Italian villa-style **Woodrow Wilson Boyhood Home** (1705 Hampton St.) contains period furnishings and family keepsakes of the 28th President of the United States.

Don't miss the **South Carolina State Museum** (301 Gervais St. 803-737-4595. Adm. fee), whose exhibits explore state history, industry, transportation, and natural history. The **Columbia Museum of Art** (Senate and Bull Sts. 803-799-2810. Tues.-Sun.) displays a modest but impressive art collection in the soft-hued, classical rooms of a restored 1908 house.

Kids of all ages will love the **Riverbanks Zoo** (Greystone Riverbanks exit, off I-26. 803-779-8717. Adm. fee), where more than 2,000 animals—including bald eagles and Siberian tigers —live in simulated natural habitats.

State House

Cayce *(Adjacent to Columbia to the SW)* Built as a trading post in 1765, **Cayce Historic Museum** *(1800 12th St. 803-796-9020, ext. 3030)* is a hewn-pine house that changed hands several times during the Revolutionary War. Its history includes the imprisonment of Emily Geiger, captured while delivering a message behind enemy lines. The Visitor Center displays old farm tools. *Closed Mon.*

CANADA
Ont.
Mich.
N.Y.
Ohio   Pa.
Md.
Ky. W.Va.
Va.

Unless otherwise noted, directions are from interstate, and sites are free and generally open daily. Phone for further information.

① Presque Isle State Park, PENNSYL-VANIA *(2 miles N of Erie on Pa. 832. 814-871-4251)* On this 7-mile-long peninsula wrapping a protective arm around Erie's waterfront, visitors can enjoy the beaches, the sheltered bays, and the rustle of cottonwoods along easy hiking trails. A road loops past duck ponds, a historical monument, and a lighthouse; turnouts offer excellent views of Erie's skyline. Boating, swimming, picnicking, and environmental programs easily fill the day, and leave enough time to watch the spectacular sunsets.

② Erie *(Tourist and Convention Bureau, 1006 State St. 814-454-7191)* Snugged against a sliver of shoreline, Erie gained fame as a shipyard during the War of 1812. Industry fueled the city's growth in the late 1800s, and today its uncongested downtown bustles against the backdrop of Lake Erie. For a look at the city's past, drive along its wide, shady streets to a magnificent brownstone mansion that is now the **Erie Historical Museum & Planetarium** *(356 W. 6th St. 814-453-5811. Closed Mon.; adm. fee).* Built by an industrial magnate in 1889, the house alone—with its ornate woodwork, mosaics, friezes,

and stained-glass windows—is worth a visit. Self-guided tours lead past period settings to exhibits on regional and maritime history and to a children's playroom with an 1872 dollhouse, computer games about Victorian life, and a trunk with try-on clothes. The carriage house has been turned into a planetarium. Down on the bay front, the square-rigged, two-masted **Niagara** *(Foot of Holland St. 814-871-4596. April-Oct.; adm. fee)* is a faithful reproduction of the warship used by Comdr. Oliver Hazard Perry to capture the British fleet during the 1813 Battle of Lake Erie. Visitors can walk the wood decks and admire the rigging and cannon on this floating piece of history, now the state's official flagship. Picnic tables.

③ Guys Mills A haven for waterfowl, the **Erie National Wildlife Refuge** *(17 miles E on Pa. 198. 814-789-3585)* attracts 236 species of birds to its wetlands and grasslands. Three trails loop through the refuge, and an observation blind provides photo opportunities of pond life. Easy to spot from March through November are wood ducks and hooded mergansers. In summer sandpipers and other shorebirds feed on the mud flats. The activity peaks during spring and fall migrations, when up to 2,500 ducks and 4,500 Canada geese fill the sky.

④ Greenville **Railroad Museum** *(13 miles W on Pa. 358. 412-588-4009. Daily Memorial Day-Labor Day,*

Clayton, Henry Clay Frick's estate in Pittsburgh, Pa. (upper); breakfast room (lower)

weekends Sept.-Oct.) The largest switch engine ever built, requiring a unique wheel arrangement, is the gleaming focal point of this small park and museum; a coal tender, hopper car, and walk-through caboose complete the line-up. Railroad memorabilia are displayed in the reconstructed stationmaster's quarters and dispatcher's office. In the nearby **Canal Museum** (*Lock 22, Alan Ave. 412-588-7540. Memorial Day-Labor Day Tues.-Sun.; adm. fee*), a quieter mode of transportation is recalled by the 40-foot copy of a freighter that once plied the 200-mile extension of the Erie Canal. Artifacts and a diorama of a canal boat passing through a lock complement the canal-era exhibits in this new museum.

South of town, the **Brucker Great Blue Heron Sanctuary** (*3 miles S on Pa. 18. 814-432-3187*) safeguards Pennsylvania's largest colony of the 4-foot-tall birds. The best months for watching them nest are March through May, although fledglings and adults can be seen through July.

Old Stone House Museum
(*9 miles E on Pa. 108 through Slippery Rock, then S on Pa. 173 to its junction with Pa. 8. 412-794-4296*) Built in 1822, the Old Stone House thrived at this crossroads for some 50 years as a stagecoach stop and lodging. Now reconstructed, the two-story tavern features a museum of pioneer artifacts and four rooms furnished in 18th- and 19th-century styles. *May-Oct. Fri.-Sun.; donation requested.*

McConnell's Mill State Park
(*2 miles W on US 422. 412-368-8091/8811*) Hidden by rolling landscape, a spectacular 400-foot-deep gorge cuts through the park. Ice Age glaciers carved the gorge, leaving behind house-size boulders. The gristmill, built in 1868, was powered by Slippery Rock Creek until 1928. Sports enthusiasts come to challenge the white-water rapids or climb and rappel the gorge. Picnic tables and playing fields.

Harmony (*1.5 miles W on Pa. 68, right on Main St., right on Mercer St., follow signs*) Founded in 1804, Harmony was the first home of pious German immigrants in search

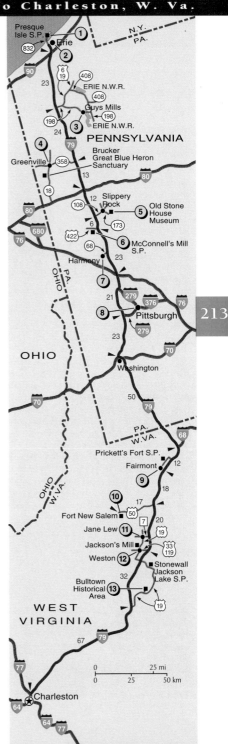

213

of a utopian society based on communal living and brotherhood. The town prospered before the Harmonists moved on in 1814, leaving behind the buildings you see today on the main square. The **Harmony Museum** *(412-452-7341)* houses one of the oldest clocks in western Pennsylvania. *Daily June-Sept., Oct.-May closed Tues., Thurs., Sat.; admission fee.*

⑧ Pittsburgh

This wedge of skyscrapers, parks, and neighborhoods sits where the Allegheny and Monongahela Rivers join and form the Ohio River. The discovery of gas, coal, and oil had made Pittsburgh the steel capital of the world by the late 1800s. Today no steel is produced within the city limits, and Pittsburgh has emerged from its smoky past as a center of technology, culture, and education (Convention and Visitors Bureau, 4 Gateway Center. 412-281-7711 or 800-359-0758). *Point State Park* (101 Commonwealth Pl.) occupies the site where, in 1754, British and French troops clashed over the strategic "golden triangle" between the rivers. *Fort Pitt Museum* (412-281-9284. Closed Mon.; adm. fee), near the British blockhouse, tells the history.

Pittsburgh boasts more than 20 museums, perhaps none better known than *The Carnegie* (4400 Forbes Ave. 412-622-3131. Closed Mon.; adm. fee). This cultural center includes an art museum featuring Impressionist and contemporary works, as well as a natural history museum with a huge collection of dinosaur skeletons. Across the street, on the University of Pittsburgh campus, stands the *Cathedral of Learning* (412-624-6000. Adm. fee for tours). The 42-story Gothic tower pays tribute to Pittsburgh's

Headquarters of PPG Industries

ethnic heritage. Twenty-three Nationality Classrooms are decorated in Byzantine, classical, folk, and other styles. The nearby *Phipps Conservatory* (Schenley Park. 412-622-6914. Closed Mon.; adm. fee) is an oasis of orchids and cactuses in Victorian glasshouses surrounded by gardens.

More art and flowers can be seen at *Clayton* (7227 Reynolds St. 412-371-0606. Closed Mon.; adm. fee for tours), the estate of industrialist Henry Clay Frick. It includes a magnificent Gilded Age mansion, greenhouse, and carriage museum. Also on the grounds, the *Frick Art Museum* (412-371-0600. Closed Mon.) showcases European art from the Renaissance to the 18th century, as well as bronzes, tapestries, and porcelains.

Across the river, the outstanding *Carnegie Science Center* (One Allegheny Ave. 412-237-3400. Adm. fee) uses hands-on interactive exhibits to explore industry, energy and matter, lasers, nutrition, and much more. The smaller *Pittsburgh Children's Museum* (Allegheny Center, follow signs. 412-322-5058. Closed Mon. Sept.-May; adm. fee) welcomes kids to three stories of fun-filled displays, including a creative workshop, vertical maze, puppet gallery, and silk screen studio.

Fireworks above the downtown skyline

:kett's Fort State Park, Fairmont, West Virginia

Washington See I-70, p. 177.

⑨ Fairmont, WEST VIRGINIA Prickett's Fort State Park *(2.5 miles W on Montana Rd., follow signs. 304-363-3030)* When Indians threatened frontier families in colonial western Virginia, the settlers sought refuge in Prickett's Fort. The 1774 log fort has been reconstructed as part of a scenic state park along the Monongahela River. Interpreters demonstrate late 18th-century crafts, and each July the park hosts the popular show *An American Frontier Musical.* Near the fort, the **Job Prickett House,** circa 1859, is filled with family antiques. *Mid-April–Oct.; adm. fee for historical attractions and show.*

⑩ Fort New Salem *(17 miles W on US 50, follow signs. 304-782-5245)* This re-created frontier settlement celebrates the Appalachian culture of 1790 to 1900 as old-time skills are brought to life by modern-day weavers, printers, tinsmiths, and apothecaries. Summer programs feature concerts and a dulcimer festival. *Memorial Day-Oct. Wed.-Sun., April-May weekdays only; adm. fee.*

⑪ Jane Lew Glass Swan *(1 mile W at junction of Rte. 7 and US 19. 304-884-8014. Closed Sun.)* This small outlet carries a wide variety of handmade crystal and glassware. Demonstrations are given weekdays at the glassblower's studio, just a few doors away.

⑫ Weston Jackson's Mill *(6 miles S from Jane Lew exit on US 19, follow signs. 304-269-5100)* Admirers of Stonewall Jackson will enjoy walking the wooded land the Civil War hero knew as a boy. More than just his childhood home, Jackson's Mill was a flourishing business. The mill where young Jackson worked now holds a collection of machinery and artifacts from the mid-1800s. *Memorial Day-Labor Day Tues.-Sun.; adm. fee.*

⑬ Bulltown Historical Area *(From Flatwoods exit, 12 miles N on US 19, left on Millstone Rd. 304-452-8170)* An original farmstead, circa 1815, and log structures relocated here offer visitors a unique look at 19th-century Appalachian building styles. From an interpretive center, a trail leads past trenches dug by Union soldiers in a skirmish with Confederates. *May-Sept.*

Charleston See I-64, p. 139.

If you've ever shot glass marbles or admired the stained glass in Washington National Cathedral, you've seen the work of **West Virginia glassmakers.** Abundant deposits of silica-rich sandstone, along with coal and gas to fuel furnaces, have made the state a leading producer of American glassware—from delicate stemware and Christmas tree ornaments to Jack Daniels bottles and the Country Music Award. Centuries-old techniques and tools are used to form hand-blown glass, with skills often passed down from father to son.

215

Stonewall Jackson Lake State Park, West Virginia
2.5 miles south on US 19

San Francisco ①

A precarious jumble of skyscrapers and pastel houses clinging to a hilly peninsula in a sparkling bay, the "City" is the urban jewel of California's rugged coast. Half-heartedly settled by Spain in

A camera's angle on Telegraph Hill

the 1770s, San Francisco had a rude awakening in 1848, when gold was struck near Sacramento. In a few short months, the population burst from 800 to 25,000. Expansion continued over the following decades, as San Francisco banks financed new mineral strikes, the Union Pacific Railroad began building eastward, and shipping bloomed. Despite a catastrophic fire and leveling earthquakes, the city on the bay has been growing ever since. Today little damage is visible from the tremblor of 1989.

New and old buildings in the Financial District

One of America's most demographically diverse cities, San Francisco is tolerant to the point that nonconformity seems the norm. While finance and shipping remain important, tourism also plays a major role in the city's economy (Visitors Bureau, 900 Market St., on lower level of Hallidie Plaza. 415-391-2000).

In this city of spectacular vistas, practically any high spot affords a good view. A popular vantage is the 27th-floor observation area of the 853-foot **Transamerica Corporation pyramid** *(600 Montgomery St. 415-983-4000. Closed weekends)*, the downtown skyline's tallest structure. The top of **Coit Memorial Tower** *(Summit of Telegraph Hill. 415-362-0808. Adm. fee for elevator)* isn't as tall—180 feet, plus the height of the hill—but you can feel the bay wind on your face. Built in 1933 as a monument to volunteer firefighters, its lobby has Depression-era murals. View seekers can also walk out along the city's most famous landmark, the **Golden Gate Bridge** *(US 101)*. Completed in 1937, after 4 years of work and at a cost of 11 lives, the 2-mile span was an engineering feat that many said couldn't be done. From the deck beneath the 48-story towers, you can see across the bay to the downtown skyline or out to the Pacific Ocean.

The large, columned rotunda nearby, built as a mock-Roman ruin for the city's 1915 Panama-Pacific International Exposition, is part of the **Palace of Fine Arts**. Behind the gaudy structure stands the **Exploratorium** *(3601 Lyon St. 415-563-7337. Closed Mon. Labor Day-Mem. Day; adm. fee)*, a huge collection of hands-on science experiments for children. Formerly a fort, **Alcatraz Island** *(415-705-1045)*, or the "Rock," was a maximum-security

Golden Gate Bridge from Fort Baker

216

pp. 218-9 | Idaho | Wyo. | S. Dak. | Iowa | Wis. | Mich. | Ont. | N.Y.
pp. 228-9
Calif. | Nev. | Utah | pp. 224-5 | Nebr. | Ohio | Pa. | N.J.
Colo. | Kans. | Mo. | Ill. | Ind. | W.Va. | pp. 234-5

Lion Dancer, New Year's Parade, Chinatown

Palace of Fine Arts

federal prison from 1934 to 1963 that housed such characters as Al Capone and "Machine Gun" Kelly. Visitors can now enter its cell blocks. Catch a ferry at Pier 41 *(415-546-2628 or 800-229-2784. Fare charge)*; tickets are limited and reservations recommended.

Chinatown *(Bounded by Broadway, Bush, Kearny, and Stockton Sts.)*, a collection of restaurants, temples, residences, and shops, is home to the largest concentration of Chinese outside of China. **Chinatown Gate** *(Grant and Bush)* is the ornate entrance to the district. **Grant Street** is its main thoroughfare, but the back streets are also worth the time to explore.

The city's famous **cable cars,** designed to cope with the steep hills, date from the late 1800s. Among three remaining lines are Powell-Mason, run-

Japanese Tea Garden, Golden Gate Park

ning from Hallidie Plaza *(Powell and Market)* to Bay Street at Fisherman's Wharf, and Powell-Hyde, from Hallidie Plaza to Ghirardelli Square, also on the waterfront. A fee is charged, and lines at the terminals are often long.

On the city's west side is **Golden Gate Park** *(Bounded by Fulton, Stanyan, Lincoln Way, and the Pacific Ocean)*, a marvelously landscaped sanctuary of lakes, meadows, and glades created on a sandy waste in the late 1800s. Larger than New York's Central Park, Golden Gate includes a variety of exotic gardens and several fine museums. The **M. H. de Young Memorial Museum** *(Teagarden Dr. 415-750-3600. Closed Mon.-Tues.; adm. fee)* highlights art from the Americas and Africa. In the same building, the **Asian Art Museum of San Francisco** *(415-668-8921. Closed Mon.-Tues.; adm. fee)* features a stunning collection of paintings, ceramics, lacquerware, and sculpture from China, Japan, Korea, India, and Southeast Asia. Across the way, the **California Academy of Sciences** *(415-750-7145. Adm. fee)* houses an aquarium, a planetarium, and a natural history museum, with mounted animals and a room that simulates earthquakes.

Just east of Golden Gate Park lies **Haight-Ashbury.** The district has been gentrified since the late 1960s, when thousands of young people flocked there to drop out, but it retains a tie-dyed, gritty aura, with myriad New Age shops and natural-food cafés.

San Francisco's oldest standing building is **Mission Dolores** *(16th and Dolores Sts. 415-621-8203. Adm. fee)*, founded in 1776 and completed in 1791. The ceiling replicates the native designs of the Ohlone Indians, who

Steaming crabs, Fisherman's Wharf, end of Taylor Street

helped erect the adobe structure. The modest mission withstood the 1906 earthquake, while the large basilica next door required rebuilding.

217

Unless otherwise noted, directions are from interstate, and sites are free and generally open daily. Phone for further information.

Oakland Athletics baseball game, Oakland, California

218

(2) **Oakland** Although blessed with a winning baseball team, a bustling port, and sunnier weather than its glitzy neighbor across the bay, Oakland may always be known as San Francisco's bedroom. Settled in 1820, Oakland's downtown is centered on **Lake Merritt**, a tidal saltwater lake and waterfowl sanctuary ringed by a 3.5-mile walking trail. **Lakeside Park**, on the northern shore, features gardens and fountains. The huge **Oakland Museum** (*1000 Oak St. 510-834-2413. Closed Mon. and Tues.; donations*) is devoted to art, ecology, and history. **Dunsmuir House & Gardens** (*2960 Peralta Oaks Ct. 510-562-0328. April-Sept. and Christmastime, phone for schedule; adm. fee*) preserves a 37-room colonial revival mansion built in 1899. The **Northern California Center for Afro American History and Life** (*Golden Gate Library, 56th St. and San Pablo Ave. 510-658-3158. Tues.-Sat. p.m.*) exhibits materials that tell the story of black Californians.

DNA model on the plaza at Lawrence Hall of Science, Berkeley, Calif.

(3) **Berkeley** Known primarily for the University of California's main campus, Berkeley is also a pharmaceutical and chemical manufacturing center and site of some of the Bay Area's prettiest houses. Founded in 1866, the city grew after the disastrous 1906 earthquake, when thousands of refugees resettled here. **U.C. Berkeley** (*Visitor Center, Univ. and Oxford. 510-642-5215*), which climbs up steep hills on the east side of town, boasts the excellent **University Art Museum** (*2625 Durant Ave. 510-642-1207. Closed Mon.-Tues.; adm. fee*), with a large collection of Asian and modern works and a

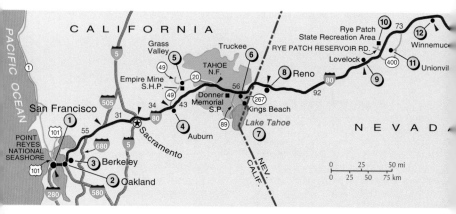

repository of avant-garde movies. Above campus is the **Lawrence Hall of Science** (*Centennial Dr. near Grizzly Peak Blvd. 510-642-5132. Adm. fee*), an interactive science museum.

Sacramento   See I-5, p. 22.

Auburn   In 1848, a French miner heading for Sutter's Mill, now Coloma, stuck his pan into a stream here and pulled out three gold nuggets. His statue in **Old Town Auburn** honors the event. The 1851 **Bernhard Museum** (*291 Auburn-Folsom Rd. 916-889-4156. Closed Mon.; adm. fee*) has been a stagecoach stop and boarding house. Recreation abounds in these Sierra foothills. **Auburn State Recreation Area** (*S on Calif. 49. 916-885-4527*) is a 30,000-acre park with gorges of two forks of the American River.

Grass Valley (*23 miles NE on Calif. 49*) The gold rush started at Sutter's Mill, but Grass Valley is where they found the mother lode. Between 1850 and 1956 an estimated 5.8 million ounces of gold were removed from the Empire Mine south of town. Visitors to **Empire Mine State Historic Park** (*10791 E. Empire St. 916-273-8522. Call for tour info; adm. fee*) can walk a short distance into the main shaft. The park includes the mansion of Empire owner William Bourn, Jr. Nearer town, the **North Star Power Station Museum** (*S. Mill St. to Allison Ranch Rd. 916-273-4255. Closed mid-Oct.–April; donations*) is a place to learn about hard-rock mining.

Truckee   This former railroad town on the main pass over the Sierras still has an Old West look, but most visitors today come for the alpine beauty. A museum at **Donner Memorial State Park** (*0.5 mile W of Truckee exit. 916-582-7892. Adm. fee*) tells the tragic story of the pioneer families who were trapped by a blizzard during their 1846 journey west and resorted to cannibalism to survive. The park borders **Donner Lake**, with boating, fishing, and hiking.

The infamous *San Andreas Fault,* a 650-mile tectonic rift responsible for the Bay Area earthquakes of 1906 and 1989, actually skirts the San Francisco peninsula, heading to sea south of the city and hitting land again north in Marin County. In one massive shift during the 1906 quake, Point Reyes lurched 18 feet north in relation to the mainland. The fault line, marked by Bolinas and Tomales Bays, is roughly followed by Calif. 1. The Earthquake Trail at Point Reyes National Seashore (32 miles N of San Francisco on US 101 and Calif. 1. 415-663-9029) includes a fenceline broken clean by the fault in 1906.

219

Lake Tahoe, California

Nevada Club Reno,
Reno, Nevada

(7) **Lake Tahoe** (*15 miles S on Calif. 89*) Straddling the California-Nevada border at 6,225 feet, Lake Tahoe offers water sports, hiking, and skiing, and on the Nevada side, casino gambling. The north shore of the 22-mile-long, crystal-clear lake blends woods, beaches, and cafés; high-rise casinos dominate its south shore. To appreciate the lake's personalities, drive its 72-mile circumference. The closest beach to I-80 is **Kings Beach** (*13 miles S on Calif. 267*). Especially worth seeing is **Emerald Bay** (*25 miles S of Tahoe City on Calif. 89*), with the 38-room castle **Vikingsholm** (*916-525-7277. Closed mid-Sept.–mid-June. Tours; adm. fee*) beside it.

(8) **Reno, NEVADA** (*Visitor Center, 275 N. Virginia St. 702-827-RENO or 800-FOR-RENO*) Walking into any of the casinos along the neon-lit 6 blocks of **Virginia Street** in downtown Reno is like entering the guts of a pinball machine, with flashing lights, beeps, and the crash of coins. Yet Reno isn't all glitz and show. The downtown is also home to the **Nevada Museum of Art and E. L. Wiegand Gallery** (*160 W. Liberty St. 702-329-3333. Closed Mon.; adm. fee*), exhibiting 19th- and 20th-century regional works. The **Natl. Automobile Museum** (*10 Lake St. S. 702-333-9300. Adm. fee*) shows 200 vehicles, including antiques and cars of the stars. North of downtown on the Reno campus of the University of Nevada, the **Nevada Historical Society Museum** (*1650 N. Virginia St. 702-688-1190. Closed Sun.; donation requested*) offers an overview of state history, covering Indians, mining, railroads, and gambling.

(9) **Lovelock** In the valley just east of where the Humboldt River ends in a marshy sink, thousands of 19th-century pioneers grazed and watered their animals before continuing west through 40 miles of desert. Lovelock is home to the **Pershing County Courthouse** (*Main and Central*), one of two round courthouses in the U. S.

(10) **Rye Patch State Recreation Area** (*2 miles W on Rye Patch Reservoir Rd. 702-538-7321*) Hidden in the desert hills is this 11,000-acre reservoir, with boating, fishing, and camping. *Day-use fee.*

(11) **Unionville** (*17 miles S on Nev. 400 to gravel road on right, continue for 3 miles*) Rustic and remote don't begin to describe this dusty canyon oasis where Mark Twain once staked a silver claim. Initially called Dixie, Unionville took its name in the early 1860s after its loyalties shifted to the Northern cause. For several years the town supported 50 businesses, but the mining went bust. It's now a ghost town. Great hiking begins where the road peters out.

(12) **Winnemucca** Named for a Paiute chief, the town began as a covered-wagon stop near where the Little Humboldt meets the main river. The First National Bank here was robbed by Butch Cas-

Wild mustangs on the Nevada flatlands

sidy's gang in 1900; the group later posed for a picture and sent it to the bank with a thank-you note. The **Humboldt Museum** (*N on US 95 to Jungo Rd. and Maple Ave. 702-623-2912. Closed Sun.; donations*) exhibits Indian relics, antique autos, and memorabilia.

Elko Gold mining, cattle, and tourism support Elko, which began as a drop-off point for miners after the railroad came through in 1868. Many early settlers were Basque sheep ranchers from the Pyrenees. The **Northeastern Nevada Museum** (*1515 Idaho St. 702-738-3418*) focuses on the region's natural history and settlement. An exhibit on Halleck Bar (1869-1915) tells how some patrons met their deaths. Still working, the **Barrick Goldstrike Mine** (*702-738-8381*) offers summer tours by appointment.

Wells This spring-fed ranch and farm community began with the Central Pacific Railroad and survives as an interstate pit stop. Winter weekends are enlivened by races of chariots made from 50-gallon oil drums and pulled by horses. To the south, the towering Humboldts shelter alpine Angel Creek and Angel Lake in **Humboldt Natl. Forest** (*Follow signs 7.5 miles S from W. Wells exit to the Angel Creek turnoff, then 3.5 miles farther to the lake. 702-752-3357. Parking fee for developed areas*), both offering fishing, swimming, camping, and hiking. The steep drive features spectacular views.

Bonneville Salt Flats, UTAH This snow-white, hard-packed crust of salt is the remnant of Lake Bonneville, an ancient body of water that covered a third of Utah some 20,000 years ago. Although the flats fan out to the north of I-80 for about 40 miles, they are at their whitest near a rest area about 15 miles east of the Nevada border. In summer and fall, speed trials are held on the flats, which have been used since 1914 to achieve record-breaking land speeds. The Bureau of Land Management (*801-977-4300*) has brochures and racing schedules.

Nevada's arid sagebrush range, marginal for cattle, was ideal for sheep, and many early settlers in the mid-1800s were **Basque shepherds** from the Pyrenees region of France and Spain. Some Basques were lured here by gold but most turned to the more stable, if lonesome, life of herding. Others came via the pampas of South America seeking better wages. Some descendants speak Euskara, the Basque tongue, believed to predate French and Spanish. Elko holds a Basque festival, with traditional dances and strength contests, on the weekend nearest July 4th. The hearty soups and meats of Basque cuisine spice the menus of many Nevada restaurants.

Speed trial, Bonneville Salt Flats, Utah

American white pelicans, Great Salt Lake, Utah

⑯ Great Salt Lake Its distant islands cloaked in a brackish haze, the landlocked Great Salt Lake stretches like a primitive landscape forgotten by time. Mistaken by early trappers for an inlet of the Pacific Ocean, the lake is actually as much as 7.5 times saltier than the sea. Only brine shrimp and certain types of algae can survive in its waters. Although the lake rises and falls seasonally, depending on precipitation, it is in a long process of drying out. **Great Salt Lake State Park** (*Saltair exit. 801-250-1822*), with a beach and showers, is at the mercy of its fluctuations.

⑰ Salt Lake City

222

Spilling from the Wasatch foothills onto the desert flats, Salt Lake City offers a rare mix of natural wonder, monumental architecture, and unfamiliar tradition. The first Mormon pioneers, spurred by years of forced westward migration, arrived here in 1847. Within hours they were planting crops and laying out a city. Today, about half of Salt Lake's population belongs to the Church of Jesus Christ of Latter-day Saints. Many modern-day migrants are attracted by the outdoor life and a growing high-tech and retail-based economy (Visitor Center, 180 S. West Temple. 801-521-2868).

The heart of the city is *Temple Square* (Bounded by Main St. and N., S., and W. Temple Sts.), a 10-acre landscaped complex of buildings and monuments around which the downtown street grid emanates. Although the multispired *Salt Lake Temple* is open only to Mormons, visitors can enter most of the other buildings, and tours of the

Mormon Temple

square are offered every few minutes. The domed roof of the *Mormon Tabernacle,* completed in 1867, affords excellent acoustics, and the public can attend the renowned choir's Sunday a.m. broadcasts and Thursday p.m. rehearsals. The *Beehive House* (67 E. South Temple. 801-240-2671), home of Brigham Young from 1854 to 1877, is named for the Mormon symbol of industriousness. The copperdomed *State Capitol* (801-538-3000), perched at the north end of State Street, offers a commanding view of the city. One block west, the three-story *Pioneer Memorial Museum* (300 N. Main St. 801-538-1050. Closed Sun. Sept.-May; donation requested) displays hundreds of everyday items used by early settlers. *Pioneer Trail State Park* (2601 Sunnyside Ave. 801-584-8391. Closed Mon. Labor Day-Mem. Day; adm. fee) marks where Brigham Young, coming down Emigration Canyon from the east, purportedly said, "This is the place."

Antelope Island State Park See I-15, p. 54.

⑱ Park City (*5 miles S via Utah 224*) Set amid the slopes of the Wasatch Range, Park City boomed after soldiers discovered silver in the winter of 1868, marked the spot, and returned in the spring to get rich. The Hearst fortune sprang partly from this mining town.

Today crowds of vacationers are drawn by skiing, hiking, mountain biking, restaurants, and shops. The **Park City Museum** *(528 Main St. 801-649-6104. Donations)* offers a historical overview; in its basement is the dungeon-like Territorial Jail, used until 1964.

Rockport State Park *(5.5 miles S via Utah 32, follow signs. 801-336-2241 or 800-322-3770)* Tucked into a craggy valley of the Wasatch Range, 3-mile-long Rockport Reservoir offers water sports. Deer and jackrabbits live amid the sagebrush and junipers around the lake, and elk, moose, and bald eagles can be spotted. The land along Weber River, which supplies the reservoir, was settled in 1860. Colonists built a rock fort for protection—hence the park's name. *Day-use fee.*

Wyoming state flag

Piedmont, WYOMING *(From Leroy exit, 7 miles S on Rte. 173, a gravel road along a stream. Go straight at all crossroads.)* A starkly beautiful drive through desolate ranch country leads to this ghost town that once supplied charcoal for Union Pacific engines. Four dome-shaped stone kilns, three restored, were built in 1869. The wooden ruins down the road are unsafe to enter.

223

Fort Bridger The ramshackle trading post founded here in 1843 by ex-trapper Jim Bridger outfitted thousands of westbound pioneers. Among them were Brigham Young's Mormons, whose acquisition of the post sparked confrontation with the federal government. In 1858, the U. S. Army established a fort to protect pioneers and, later, rail workers. **Fort Bridger State Historic Site** *(2 miles E of Fort Bridger exit, off I-80 Bus. 307-782-3842. Closed Dec.-Feb. and weekdays in spring and fall; adm. fee in summer)* preserves the officers' quarters and other buildings, displays a re-created picket-walled trading post, and has an informative museum.

Costumed "officer," Fort Bridger SHS, Wyoming

Green River An oasis amid rocky canyons, Green River was the starting point for John Wesley Powell's landmark 1869 voyage down the Green and Colorado Rivers and through the Grand Canyon. A series of plaques at **Expedition Island** *(S on Wyo. 530, right on 2nd S., left on 2nd E.)*, where Powell embarked, recount the history of river running on the Green, from before Powell into the 20th century. The **Sweetwater County Historical Museum** *(80 W. Flaming Gorge Way, ground floor of courthouse. 307-872-6435. Closed Sun. year-round and Sat. Sept.-June)* displays Shoshone art, the cast of a dinosaur footprint, and exhibits on the mining of soda ash, used to make glass and detergents; it's important to the area economy. Green River is a good base for exploring **Flaming Gorge Reservoir** *(801-784-3445)*, a recreation area that begins about 10 miles south of town and stretches into northern Utah.

Rawlins When Wyoming became a state in 1890, lawmakers chose Rawlins as the prison site. True to Wyoming's violent frontier legacy, the prison's history was marked by inmate uprisings and mass escapes; cells didn't have hot water until 1978. Now a museum, the **Wyoming Frontier Prison** (*5th and Walnut. 307-324-4422. Adm. fee*) can be toured March-Oct. and by appt.

㉔ Saratoga (*20 miles S on Wyo. 130*) A small resort in the North Platte River Valley, Saratoga's main attraction is its hot spring, which bubbles from the ground at 117°F. **Hobo Pool** (*E on Walnut Street*) is an enclosure around the spring. For a less scalding dip, bathe along the banks of the Platte, where chilly river water mixes with the hot. **Saratoga Museum** (*104 Constitution Ave. 307-326-5511. Mem. Day-Labor Day p.m.*), in the original 1915 railroad depot, exhibits a general store, a Union Pacific caboose, and railroad equipment.

㉕ Arlington (*Exit at Arlington, drive a short way S past "No Services Ahead" sign to marker on left. 307-378-2333 in summer, 379-2721 in winter*) Aspen-shaded Arlington, a former stagecoach stop and toll bridge over Rock Creek, would be a ghost town if not for Chet and Goldie Pitcher, the couple who own its log structures, one of which is their home. An official stone marker tells the basics. If you can catch Mrs. Pitcher at home, however, ask her to open the cabin built in 1862 by squatter Joe Bush. A larger cabin, whose hanging pots and boarded-up smells freeze it in time, served as a saloon, post office, and store before being converted to an informal museum. Mrs. Pitcher is full of stories about the families who lived here.

㉖ Laramie Named for a French trapper, Laramie became a notoriously lawless frontier outpost once the Union Pacific arrived in 1868. **Wyoming Territorial Park** (*975 Snowy Range Road. 307-745-6161 or 800-845-2287. Closed winter, Sat. in May, weekends Mem. Day–mid-June, and Mon. in Sept.; adm. fee*), centered around the territory's original prison, does an excellent job of interpreting those times. Mugs of inmates and their real-life stories line the restored cell blocks. The park also features a living-history frontier town dur-

---

Among the world's fastest animals, capable of running 50 miles an hour, *American pronghorns* often browse in herds on the sagebrush and grasses of the high, arid plains along I-80 in southern Wyoming. Named for the curved, forked horns males use to fight off rivals, pronghorns have keen eyesight and flash the white patches of hair on their rumps to warn of danger. Although their numbers had fallen to 15,000 by 1910, pronghorns are carefully managed today. In Wyoming alone, the population ranges from 350,000 to 500,000, depending on the severity of winter and the number harvested during the fall hunt.

224

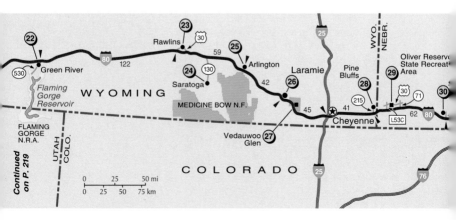

ing the summer and the National U. S. Marshals Museum. Early Laramie had a civilized side, as shown by the **Laramie Plains Museum** (*603 Ivinson Ave. 307-742-4448. Closed Sun. Sept.-May; adm. fee*), an 1892 Victorian mansion. Period furnishings include a piano shipped west in 1868 via riverboat, train, and wagon.

Vedauwoo Glen (*1 mile N on Vedauwoo Glen Rd./Rte. 700. Medicine Bow Natl. Forest 307-745-8971*) This picnic and camping area is a wonderland of huge, weirdly formed chunks of pink granite that tower above the treeless plain to the east. Pine trees and other vegetation somehow take root in fissures and terraces of the volcanic stone. *Camping fee and services Mem. Day-Labor Day.*

Cheyenne See I-25, p. 78.

Pine Bluffs Sioux Indians often camped on the ridges overlooking this small rail and ranch town, which became a large shipping point for cattle in the 1870s. The **Texas Trail Museum** (*3rd and Market. 307-245-3713. May-Sept.; donation requested*) commemorates frontier crossroads in the region, including those forged by buffalo, Indians, cowboys, emigrants, trains, and autos. Indian artifacts, some 10,000 years old, unearthed at nearby digs can be seen at the **University of Wyo. Archaeological Education Center** (*2nd and Elm. 307-245-3695 or 800-426-5009. June to mid-Aug.*).

Oliver Reservoir State Rec. Area, NEBRASKA (*6 miles NE on Nebr. L53C and US 30. 308-235-4040*) This pretty reservoir in west Nebraska's lonely ranching country offers fishing, boating, picnicking, and a playground. *Vehicle fee.*

Sidney As Union Pacific rail construction reached western Nebraska, raids by angry Cheyenne, Sioux, and Arapaho bands became more frequent. In 1867, the Army dispatched soldiers to

Vedauwoo Glen, Medicine Bow National Forest, Wyoming

225

Stag pronghorn

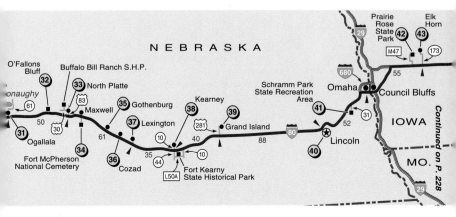

what would later become Fort Sidney. The settlement boomed in the late 1870s, when thousands came through en route to the gold-rich Black Hills. The **Officers' Quarters** (*6th Ave. and Jackson St. 308-254-2150. Shorter winter hours*) serve as a history museum. The **Post Commander's Home** (*1108 6th Ave.*) offers summer tours.

Front Street Cowboy Museum, US 30, Ogallala, Nebraska

226

31 Ogallala In the 1870s and '80s, cattle drivers on the Texas Trail spent their money in this town, known as Gomorrah of the Plains. Gunfights were common, and many who met their deaths are buried on **Boot Hill** (*W. 10th and Parkhill Drive*), where boards still mark graves. A kiosk quotes newspaper accounts of some who died. Up the street is the **Mansion on the Hill** (*W. 10th and N. Spruce Sts. 800-658-4390. Mem. Day-Labor Day; donation requested*), built in 1887 and luxuriously furnished for the frontier. **Lake McConaughy** (*308-284-3542. Vehicle fee*), set like an inland sea among the dry hills, is formed by a hydroelectric dam 8 miles north of town. The lake offers water recreation, and the shore has more than 100 miles of beach.

👉 ***William "Buffalo Bill" Cody,*** born in Iowa in 1846, was an early version of today's media star. By age 26, he'd been a cowboy, Pony Express rider, Army scout, and buffalo hunter, killing 4,280 in 8 months to feed Kansas railroad workers. Then, amazingly, he turned to showbiz, playing himself in a series of badly acted but popular dramas and eventually starting a world-touring Wild West show, with rodeos, sharpshooting contests, and mock Indian battles. The Old West of Cody's youth was gone, but its image lived. In 1917, he died in debt, but 25,000 fans attended his funeral.

32 O'Fallons Bluff On this stretch of the Oregon Trail, settlers had to take a narrow path between sandy hills and the Platte. A depression where wagons passed is faintly visible at the east end of the rest area on eastbound I-80 between Sutherland and Hershey (*Mile marker 158*). A sculpture and plaques mark the spot.

33 North Platte Positioned at the fork of the North and South Platte Rivers, this town was the longtime home of William "Buffalo Bill" Cody, who bought his 4,000-acre ranch in 1878. In 1886, during the heyday of his Wild West show, he built an 18-room Victorian mansion, preserved along with the barn and memorabilia at **Buffalo Bill Ranch State Historical Park** (*US 83 to town, left on US 30, right on Buffalo Bill Ave. 308-535-8035. Closed Nov.-March and weekends April-May, Sept.-Oct.; vehicle fee*).

34 Fort McPherson National Cemetery (*2 miles S of Maxwell exit on county road*) The former site of a fort that protected the Oregon Trail now serves as Nebraska's only national cemetery. Soldiers from the 1860s Indian wars lie beside those killed in Vietnam.

35 Gothenburg This processing center for the region's alfalfa preserves a slice of the past with a **Pony Express station** (*Ehmen Park. May-Sept.*). The 1854 log cabin, moved to its present spot from its Oregon Trail site, was a trading post before serving as one of 157 Pony Express relay stations in 1860-61. Riders would cover up to 100 miles in a shift. Later, the post became a stagecoach stop.

ebraska meadowlark

36 **C o z a d**   Traveling west by train in 1872, Cincinnati gambler and entrepreneur John J. Cozad was so intrigued with the Platte River Valley at the 100th meridian sign that he decided to start a town. Ten years later, after shooting a man in an argument, Cozad fled his settlement. Son Robert Henri (he dropped the surname after the shooting) became a successful artist. The family's stucco hotel is now the **Robert Henri Museum** (*218 E. 8th St. 308-784-4154. May–Sept.; adm. fee*), with period rooms, copies of Henri works, and one early original.

L e x i n g t o n   Plum Creek, the trading post that preceded Lexington, made headlines in 1864 when Indians attacked a wagon train, killing 11 men and taking a woman and young boy captive. The **Dawson County Museum** (*805 N. Taft St. 308-324-5340. Adm. fee*) provides a driving-tour map to the massacre site and other points around Lexington, now a beef-packing town. The museum also exhibits an elliptical-winged biplane built in the county in 1919.

K e a r n e y   Established on the Platte River's south bank in 1848 to protect Oregon Trail traffic, Fort Kearny was a way station and supply depot for westbound pioneers. Wooden fortifications, constructed during the Indian wars of 1864-65, have been re-erected at **Fort Kearny State Historical Park** (*2 miles S on Nebr. 44 and 4 miles E on Nebr. L50A. 308-234-9513. Visitor Center closed Labor Day–Mem. Day; vehicle fee*). A mile east of the park at **Fort Kearny State Recreation Area** (*308-234-9513. Vehicle fee*), hikers can get great views of the Platte from a trail over an old railroad bridge. Fishing and camping offered. Today Kearney is home to the expanded **Museum of Nebraska Art** (*2401 Central Ave. 308-234-8559. Closed Mon.*), with the state's collection of works by 19th- and 20th-century area artists.

Covered wagon and blacksmith shop, Fort Kearny SHP, Nebraska

G r a n d   I s l a n d   Initially settled in the 1850s near an island on the Platte River, the town moved north the following decade to be nearer the Union Pacific tracks. The hardships European immigrants faced are presented at the **Stuhr Museum of the Prairie Pioneer** (*4.5 miles E on US 34. 308-385-5316. Railroad town closed mid-Oct.–April; adm. fee*). The grounds include a re-created railroad town with 60 buildings. One cottage is the birthplace of actor Henry Fonda (born 1905), relocated from town. In spring, thousands of migrating sandhill cranes rest along the nearby Platte. You can also see them at the **Heritage Zoo** (*2103 W. Stolley Park Rd. 308-385-5416. Mid-March–mid-Oct.; adm. fee*), which focuses on Nebraska species and endangered animals from abroad.

L i n c o l n   Although far smaller than its rival Omaha, Lincoln was chosen capital in 1867 because of its location south of the Plat-

University of Nebraska State
Museum, Lincoln

te River. Rivalries in today's Lincoln center mainly around the University of Nebraska's football team. The campus is also home to the **University of Nebraska State Museum** (*Morrill Hall, 14th and U Sts. 402-472-2642. Donation requested*), whose collection of fossils includes one of the country's largest mammoth skeletons. Near campus, the **Museum of Nebraska History** (*15th and P Sts. 402-471-4754*) has outstanding exhibits on Plains Indians and Nebraska's settlement. Nebraska's **State Capitol** (*1445 K St. 402-471-0448*), a 400-foot domed tower completed in 1932, is one of the country's most unusual. Tours of its ornate interior include a 14th-floor city view. The **Natl. Museum of Roller Skating** (*4730 South St. 402-483-7551. Closed weekends*) boasts a large skate collection. **Folsom Children's Zoo and Botanical Gardens** (*1222 S. 27th St. 402-475-6741. Late April-Sept.; adm. fee*) features exotic animals, pony rides, and a miniature train.

228

41 **Schramm Park State Rec. Area** (*6 miles S on Nebr. 31. 402-332-3887. Vehicle fee*) Situated on the sandy north bank of the Platte River, this 340-acre park offers picnicking, hiking, and views of the river. It has a 12-tank **aquarium** (*402-332-3901. Closed Tues. Labor Day-Mem. Day and Mon. Dec.-March; adm. fee*).

Omaha See I-29, p. 90.

Council Bluffs, IOWA See I-29, p. 90.

42 **Prairie Rose State Park** (*7.5 miles N on Rte. M47, follow signs. 712-773-2701*) The 422-acre park's 218-acre artificial lake has campsites, a beach, boat ramps, and fishing for bass and catfish. *Camping fee.*

"The Sower," bronze statue atop
the State Capitol, Lincoln, Nebr.

43 **Elk Horn** In this town settled largely by Danes, the main

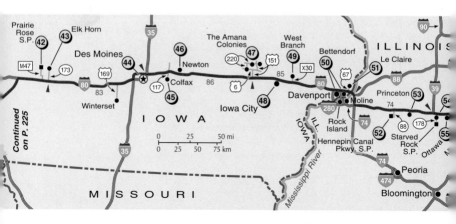

attraction is an 1848 **windmill** *(6.5 miles N on Iowa 173. 712-764-7472)* from Norre Snede, Denmark. The 60-foot structure, with a pointed dome, was reassembled here in 1976 as a Bicentennial project. Visitors can climb to the third floor to see the gears. *Adm. fee.*

W i n t e r s e t *(14 miles S on US 169)* See I-35, p. 97.

D e s   M o i n e s *(Convention & Visitors Bureau, 2 Ruan Center, 601 Locust, Suite 222. 515-286-4960 or 800-451-2625)* Originally a fort at the confluence of the Raccoon and Des Moines Rivers, Des Moines replaced Iowa City as state capital in 1857. Besides being an important grain center, this heartland city is home to numerous insurance companies and factories.

Iowa's ornate **State Capitol** *(Grand Avenue bet. E. 9th and E. 12th. 515-281-5591. Tours Mon.-Sat.)*, dedicated in 1884 and topped with a 23-karat gold-leaf dome, is a beauty. Two blocks west, the **State Historical Building** *(600 E. Locust St. 515-281-5111. Closed Mon.)* features fine exhibits on Iowa's past. The **Des Moines Botanical Center** *(909 E. River Dr. 515-242-2934. Adm. fee)*, a tropical hothouse beneath an 80-foot Plexiglas dome, displays 15,000 plants including Japanese bonsai and a Colombian papaya tree, as well as exotic birds. Thanks largely to architects Eliel Saarinen, I. M. Pei, and Richard Meier, the **Des Moines Art Center** *(4700 Grand Ave. 515-277-4405. Closed Monday; adm. fee)* is regarded as one of the country's finest examples of museum design; inside are 20th-century paintings and sculptures. Nearby in Greenwood Park is the **Science Center of Iowa** *(4500 Grand Ave. 515-274-4138. Adm. fee)*, with a planetarium and exhibits.

West of town, **Living History Farms** *(I-80 and US 6. 515-278-5286. May–mid-Oct.; adm. fee)* is an exemplary museum of its type. Tours of the 600-acre park start at a re-created pre-railroad town, Walnut Hill. Tractors take visitors to the farming area, where agricultural methods of Ioway Indians and pioneers are demonstrated.

Cornfields near Des Moines, Iowa

229

Des Moines Art Center, Iowa

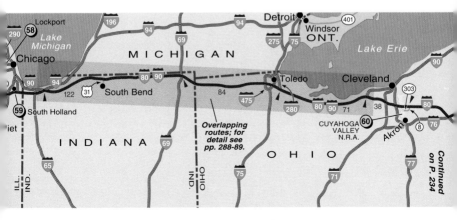

Overlapping routes; for detail see pp. 288-89.

Continued on P. 234

Staircase in the Old Capitol,
University of Iowa, Iowa City

230

Figure of President Herbert
Hoover, Hoover NHS, Iowa

45 **Colfax** **Trainland USA** *(2.5 miles N of I-80 on Iowa 117. 515-674-3813)* Model train enthusiasts will like this collection of trains running all at once on 4,000 feet of track, begun in 1964 by a farmer. Backdrops include a Kentucky coal mine, San Francisco's cable car lines, and an operating roundhouse. *Closed Labor Day-Mem. Day and weekdays in Sept.; adm. fee.*

46 **Newton** This farming community boomed after F. L. Maytag began manufacturing hand-powered washing machines in 1907. The small but informative **Jasper County Historical Museum** *(1700 S. 15th Ave. W. 515-792-9118. May-Sept. p.m.; adm. fee)* exhibits dozens of Maytag washers from the earliest wooden tubs to today's computer-paneled models. Also featured are a diorama of county history and local pioneer and Native American artifacts.

47 **The Amana Colonies** *(About 10 miles N on US 151 to Iowa 220)* A sect of ex-Lutheran Germans called Inspirationists began settling this rolling farm country in 1855. Their seven villages, scattered along Iowa 220, preserve many late 19th-century buildings. Residents still speak a German dialect, although communal life was abandoned in 1932. A good place to start a tour is at the **Museum of Amana History** *(In "main" Amana. 319-622-3567. April-Nov.; adm. fee)*, which explains the group's beliefs and how they settled the area. Museums in Middle Amana and South Amana focus on communal cooking and agricultural methods respectively. Unlike the Amish, who shun modern inventions, Inspirationists embraced new technology. A 1930s refrigerator shop grew into the Amana Refrigeration Company, whose plant sits across the street from quaint Middle Amana.

48 **Iowa City** *(Convention and Visitors Bureau, 325 E. Washington, Suite 200. 319-337-6592 or 800-283-6592. Closed weekends)* Straddling the Iowa River, this small but sophisticated college city served as Iowa's original capital from 1846 to 1857. The gold-domed, Greek Revival **Old Capitol** *(Clinton St. at Iowa Ave. 319-335-0548)* features a 650-pound crystal chandelier in the senate chamber. When the seat of government shifted to Des Moines in 1857, the building was given to the University of Iowa, whose campus sprang up around it. Another vestige of the city's early prominence is **Plum Grove** *(1030 Carroll St., off Kirkwood Ave. 319-337-6846 or 351-5738. April-Oct. Phone for schedule; donations)*, the 1844 brick home of Iowa Territory's first governor, Robert Lucas.

49 **West Branch** The **Herbert Hoover Natl. Historic Site** *(Visitor Center, Parkside and Main. 319-643-2541)* re-creates the 1870s Quaker farming village of the 31st President's childhood, complete with wood-plank sidewalks, a schoolhouse, the two-room birthplace cottage, and a blacksmith shop. The site includes the graves of Hoover and his wife and a presidential library-museum. *Adm. fee.*

Davenport/Bettendorf Iowa's half of the Quad Cities metro area was where the treaty ending the Black Hawk War was signed in 1832. Davenport's **Putnam Museum of History and Natural Science** (*1717 W. 12th St. 319-324-1933. Closed Mon.; adm. fee*) features an excellent exhibit on the region's history from the end of the Ice Age to the present. Next door, the **Davenport Museum of Art** (*1737 W. 12th St. 319-326-7804. Closed Mon.; donation requested*) specializes in 19th- and 20th-century American works and has a large collection of Mexican colonial paintings. In an old school building, the **Children's Museum of Bettendorf** (*533 16th St. 319-344-4106. Closed Mon.; adm. fee*) offers hands-on activities for youngsters 12 and under.

Loading corn, Davenport, Iowa

Le Claire This tiny Mississippi River town was the 1846 birthplace of "Buffalo Bill" Cody. The actual birth site is now a cornfield, and the family moved to Kansas when Bill was 7, but the **Buffalo Bill Cody Museum** (*1.5 miles N on US 67, right on Jones St. to levee. 319-289-5580*) preserves a small hodgepodge of Cody photographs and artifacts, as well as Indian arrowheads and pioneer relics. A section is devoted to another native son, James Ryan II, inventor of the seat belt and the in-flight recorder. *Closed weekdays mid-Oct.–mid-May; adm. fee.*

Moline and Rock Island, ILLINOIS See I-74, p. 180.

Hennepin Canal Parkway State Park (*2.5 miles S on Ill. 88, follow signs. 815-454-2328*) The waterfowl observation trail through beautiful fields is a bird-watcher's paradise. The park accesses the towpath trail along the 104-mile Hennepin Canal, which linked the Illinois and Mississippi Rivers. Completed in 1907, the Hennepin was soon rendered obsolete by the railroad.

Princeton Now a modest assortment of weathered houses, Princeton was a hotbed of 19th-century abolitionism. The **Owen Lovejoy Homestead** (*E of town on US 6. 815-879-9151. May-Sept. Sun. and Thurs. p.m.; adm. fee*), the home of a preacher and U. S. congressman, was an important way station on the Underground Railroad. About a mile north of I-80 (*Via Ill. 26*) is the **Red Covered Bridge**, one of a handful left in Illinois. A sign warns against driving more than 12 horses, mules, or cattle across at a time.

Fall maples, La Salle County, Ill.

Utica Dating from 1836, tiny Utica is one of the oldest towns on the western stretch of the Illinois & Michigan Canal. The small **La Salle County Historical Society Museum** (*E. Canal and Mill Sts. 815-667-4861. Closed Mon.-Tues.; adm. fee*), in an 1840s warehouse, has exhibits on the canal and a Visitor Center. The area south

Starved Rock State Park on Illinois River, near Utica, Illinois

of Utica has a rich Indian heritage. Thousands of Illinois Indians were living in a riverside village when explorers Marquette and Jolliet came through in 1673. **Starved Rock State Park** *(1.5 miles S of town on Ill. 178, first left past the river. 815-667-4726)* is named for a 125-foot bluff where, according to legend, a band of Illinois starved in 1769 rather than surrender to foes below. Trails, picnicking, and water activities.

(55) Ottawa Settled at the confluence of the Illinois and Fox Rivers, Ottawa was the site in 1858 of the first Lincoln-Douglas debate. A rock in **Washington Park** *(Bordered by Lafayette, Jackson, Columbus, and La Salle Sts.)* marks the event. Across the street is the 1856 Italianate **Reddick Mansion** *(100 W. Lafayette St. 815-433-5121 or 433-0084. Closed weekends; adm. fee for tours)*, with period furnishings.

(56) Morris With its low-rise downtown, annual Corn Festival, and diner displaying high-school emblems, Morris is the picture of a small midwestern town. **Goose Lake Prairie State Natural Area** *(6 miles SE of town via Ill. 47 and Pine Bluff Rd. 815-942-2899)* preserves 2,500 acres of tallgrass prairie, the largest remnant in a state that was once 60 percent prairie.

(57) Joliet Founded in 1833 as construction on the Illinois & Michigan Canal was gearing up, Joliet grew into a shipping and industrial center. Local limestone is evident in many of the city's buildings. The city is home to one of the last vaudeville-era venues, the 1926 **Rialto Square Theatre** *(102 N. Chicago St. 815-726-6600. Tours Tues.; adm. fee for tours)*, still used for shows. Inside are a two-and-a-half-ton crystal chandelier and a large pipe organ.

(58) Lockport *(About 5 miles N on Ill. 171)* In the restored 1837 home of the canal commissioner, the **Illinois & Michigan Canal Museum** *(803 S. State St. 815-838-5080. Open p.m.only)* has period furnishings, documents, and canal photos.

(59) South Holland Some 800 wood carvings, most produced locally and including a 7-foot-tall wooden Indian, are on display at the **Midwest Carvers Museum** *(16236 Vincennes Ave. 708-331-6011. Closed Sun.; donations)*, run by the South Suburban Chiselers, the largest of five area wood-carving clubs.

Chicago See I-55, pp. 126-27.

I-80/I-90 Overlapping routes, see sites pp. 286-88.

Cleveland, OHIO See I-77, p. 204.

(60) Cuyahoga Valley National Recreation Area *(2 miles SW on Ohio 8 and Ohio 303 to Happy Days Visitor Center. 800-*

The trappers and missionaries have been gone for centuries, but place names like La Salle, Marseilles, and Des Plaines recall an era when Illinois was the frontier of **New France,** with Quebec its capital. The Illinois River Valley was a vital link between Lake Michigan and the Mississippi River, which, as French explorers Louis Jolliet and Jesuit Father Jacques Marquette discovered in the 1670s, flowed clear to the Gulf of Mexico. Although it established several forts, France didn't actively colonize the interior and eventually lost its North American holdings to Britain and the U. S.

257-9477) This history-rich preserve of woods and rolling pastures along a 22-mile stretch of the Cuyahoga River is popular with Cleveland and Akron urbanites for a quick nature fix. The river is paralleled by the **Ohio & Erie Canal**, whose old towpath is now a gravel bike and walking trail. The **Canal Visitor Center** *(800-445-9667)*, at the north end of the park, is housed in a period building that's seen use as hotel, tavern, and dance hall. The **Cuyahoga Valley Scenic Railroad** *(800-468-4070. Mem. Day–foliage season Wed.-Sun., phone for additional hours; fare charge)* runs the park's length on tracks dating from 1880. It offers several route packages, some combining stops in the park and downtown Akron. **Hale Farm & Village** *(2686 Oak Hill Rd. 216-666-3711. June-Oct. Wed.-Sun., call for add'l hours; adm. fee)*, a living-history museum at the park's south end, depicts life in rural Ohio from 1825 to 1850. Buildings have been moved here to re-create a typical village.

Akron See I-77, p. 204.

Niles *(4 miles N on Ohio 46)* Exhibits at the **Natl. McKinley Birthplace Mem.** *(40 N. Main St. 216-652-1704. Closed Sun. June-Aug.)* recount William McKinley's life as soldier and 25th President.

233

Youngstown *(I-680)* Surrounded by the Mahoning River Valley's rich deposits of iron ore and block coal, Youngstown had the world's largest concentration of steel mills by the early 1900s. Today, the empty shells of former steel plants attest to the industry's collapse by the 1980s. The high-tech **Youngstown Historical Center of Industry and Labor** *(151 W. Wood St. 216-743-5934. Closed Mon.-Tues.; adm. fee)* articulates the story with photos, videos, and artifacts. The fine collection at the **Butler Institute of American Art** *(524 Wick Ave. 216-743-1107. Closed Mon.)* ranges from colonial to contemporary. Up the street, the **Arms Family Museum of Local History** *(648 Wick Ave. 216-743-2589. Closed Mon.; adm. fee)* displays the furnished 1905 Arts-and-Crafts-style mansion of a wealthy family. The huge indoor waterwheel of **Lanterman's Mill** *(Off Canfield Road in Mill Creek Park. 216-740-7115. May-Oct. Tues.-Sun.; adm. fee)*, a restored 1845 gristmill, is housed in a rock foundation. For a taste of a sweeter industry, tour the factory of **Gorant Candies** *(8301 Market St., about 5 miles S of town. 800-572-4139. Closed weekends. Phone for tour)*, founded in 1945.

Franklin, PENNSYLVANIA *(18 miles NE on Pa. 8 and US 62)* In the days before jukeboxes and phonographs, ready-made music came from nickelodeons; for a five-cent investment, you could hear the merry strains of several instruments being played from inside a box. A spirit-lifting demonstration of more than 50 rare old music boxes, band organs, and calliopes awaits visitors to the **DeBence Antique Music World** *(1261-63 Liberty. 814-432-5823. Closed Mon.; adm. fee)*. Guides play each piece and explain its history. The museum is crammed with curiosities.

234

On August 27, 1859, a century before OPEC and a time when most people lit their homes with candles (or, if wealthy, whale oil), one of modern times' significant events occurred near the tiny lumber town of Titusville, Pennsylvania. After weeks of drilling, ex-railroad conductor Edwin L. Drake, working for a small petroleum company, struck oil at 69.5 feet. With the creation of the *world's first commercial oil well,* Titusville land prices soared and the petroleum age began. The Drake Well Museum (814-827-2797. Adm. fee) in Titusville (38 miles N on Pa. 8) tells the story.

64 Emlenton Spread out along the foot of the Allegheny River's steep east bank, Emlenton can trace a long industrial past. In the 1820s, wagons brought crude iron from nearby furnaces, where it was held until barged to Pittsburgh. The town boomed with the region when oil drilling took off in the late 1860s. Many of the town's historic buildings date from then. Walking-tour maps are available at the **Emlenton Borough Building** (*Left after the bridge, 501 Main St. 412-867-2472. Closed weekends*). The 1875 **Emlenton Mill** (*201 Main St.*) now houses shops, a café, and a hardware store.

65 Cook Forest State Park (*16 miles N on Pa. 36. 814-744-8407*) The park preserves 1,500 acres of virgin white pine and hemlock, the state's largest stand of uncut trees, some more than 300 years old. Hike a half mile up the Longfellow Trail to reach Forest Cathedral, the densest stand of big trees. The pristine Clarion River is popular for canoeing and fishing. You may also climb a 70-foot fire tower for spectacular views. Maps are available at the office.

66 Brookville Tucked into the steep hills along the river, Brookville was settled in 1830 and thrived on timber, gristmills, and its location on the Susquehanna & Waterford Turnpike. By the early 1900s, a factory was producing four-wheel-drive cars. Many of the town's 19th-century buildings were designed from pattern books and reflect function, not flourish. Pick up a walking-tour map at the **Chamber of Commerce** (*233 Main St. 814-849-8448. Closed weekends*). The **Jefferson County Historical Museum** (*232 Jefferson St. 814-849-8415. Tues.-Sun. p.m.*) displays furnishings and artifacts.

67 Punxsutawney (*About 25 miles S on Pa. 36*) This is the home of Phil, the prognosticating groundhog whose shadow is the focus of national attention on February 2. According to a tradition attributed to German settlers who believed in the perspicacity of groundhogs, Phil's casting a shadow means another six weeks of win-

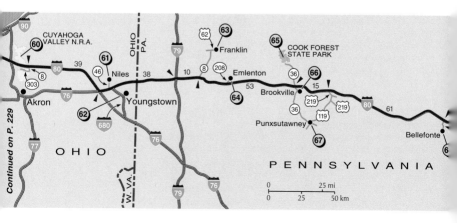

Continued on P. 229

ter; no shadow means an early spring. The **Groundhog Zoo** *(301 W. Mahoning St. 814-938-5020)* is little more than a den at the library housing Phil and a few cousins. Besides the annual ritual, dating from 1887, the town holds a Groundhog Festival in June.

Bellefonte *(4 miles S on Pa. 150)* Named for a spring that still provides this town's drinking water, Bellefonte gained prosperity as an iron center in the early 19th century. It has been home to seven governors, including Andrew G. Curtin, who helped persuade state Republicans to back Lincoln's 1860 presidential nomination. Among its fine historic structures are the **Centre County Courthouse** *(Alleghany and High Sts.)*, whose porch dates from 1835, and the antebellum **Hastings Mansion** *(Alleghany and Lamb Sts.)*, with a hodgepodge of styles added later. Walking-tour maps are available at the **Chamber of Commerce** *(Railroad station at bottom of High St. 814-355-2917)*. **Curtin Village** *(2 miles N on Pa. 150. 814-355-1982. Daily Mem. Day-Labor Day, Wed.-Sun. Labor Day to mid-Oct.; adm. fee)* preserves Curtin's iron furnace and mansion.

Football weather in small-town Pennsylvania

Williamsport *(21 miles N on US 15. Visitor Center, 848 W. 4th St. 717-326-1971 or 800-358-9900)* Vast tracts of trees and the Susquehanna River made Williamsport a wealthy city in the mid-19th century. But the industry reeled in 1889, when a disastrous flood washed away lumber mills. Vestiges of the heyday remain along **Millionaires' Row** *(W. Fourth St.)*. The town is also the home of Little League baseball, which started here as a three-team league in 1939. The **Peter J. McGovern Little League Baseball Museum** *(Just S of town, off US 15. 717-326-3607. Adm. fee)* outlines the development of the sport. Visitors of all ages can try to pitch or hit a ball, then watch an instant replay video for style pointers.

Hickory Run State Park *(5 miles SE on Pa. 534. 717-443-9991)* When glaciers receded from the Pocono foothills 20,000

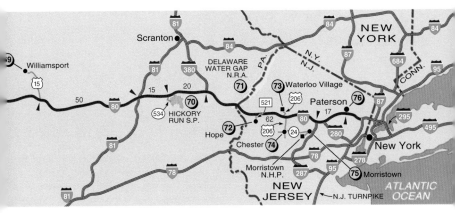

years ago, they left a huge scar of broken rock. What remains is a field of pink sandstone and quartz, surrounded by forest. The graffiti on the rocks decreases the farther you get into the 1,800-foot field. The park also offers lakes, streams, and wooded trails.

(71) Delaware Water Gap Natl. Recreation Area, NEW JERSEY Formed by millions of years of erosion and geologic upheaval, the Delaware Water Gap is a dramatic S-shaped bend in the Delaware River between 1,500-foot shale peaks, one in New Jersey and one in Pennsylvania. Although I-80 takes you through the gorge on the Jersey side, you need to get out and hike, swim, or boat to experience its beauty. The area encompasses unspoiled shoreline along 40 miles of the river and offers a wide variety of recreation. **Kittatinny Point Visitor Center** (*Off I-80 just E of the bridge. 908-496-4458. May–mid-autumn, weekends in winter*) gives information. Trails to Mount Tammany in New Jersey and Mount Minsi in Pennsylvania afford great views. (See I-84, p. 252, for information about the area's northern section.) On the Pa. side, the **Water Gap Trolley** (*Depot on Pa. 611. 717-476-0010. April-Oct.; fare charge*) can be boarded in the town of Delaware Water Gap.

(72) Hope Members of a German Protestant sect, Moravians settled Hope in 1769 and sold it in 1808 to help pay a church debt. The limestone-and-brick houses they left make this an appealing town.

Of note are the **Gemeinhaus** (*Rte. 521 and High St.*), built in 1781 as a church and social center and now a bank; the 1769 **Moravian Grist Mill** (*High St. and Millbrook Rd.*), now an inn; and the **Moravian Cemetery** (*High St. W of town*), which appeared in the movie *Friday the 13th.* Walking-tour maps are available in town.

(73) Waterloo Village (*Exit at Stanhope, follow signs N about 3 miles. 201-347-0900*) This restored hamlet along the Musconetcong River prospered with the Morris Canal in the 1830s but faded in the early 20th century. Costumed guides and original buildings highlight Waterloo's

Canoeists at the Delaware Water Gap National Recreation Area, N.J.

ups and downs. The park includes a simulated 400-year-old Lenape Indian village. *Mid-April–Dec. Tues.-Sun.; adm. fee.*

(74) Chester (*8 miles S on US 206*) A profusion of gristmills made this a strategic region during the Revolutionary War. **Cooper Mill** (*From US 206, 1 mile W on N.J. 24. 908-879-5463. July-Aug. Fri.-Tues., weekends only May-June and Sept.-Oct.; donations*), one of the few left that still grinds, is on the Black River. Its grindstones, together weighing 3,000 pounds, can mill up to 400 pounds of meal per hour. Farther south is **Willowwood Arboretum** (*6 miles SW of town*

ristown National Historical Park, N.J.

via US 206 and Pottersville Rd./Rte. 512, follow signs. 201-326-7600), with 3,500 plant species, including wildflowers and over 100 willows.

⑦ **Morristown** (*5 miles S via I-287*) In 1779, Gen. George Washington and 10,000 troops converged on the small, reluctant farming community to tough out what would be the century's worst winter. **Washington's Headquarters**, the main section of **Morristown National Historical Park** (*Morris Ave. exit off I-287, follow signs. 201-539-2085. Adm. fee for headquarters*), were in the mansion of a leading citizen; the museum has a first-rate display of period weapons. Other sections of the park include **Fort Nonsense**, the site of a 1777 earthen fortification, and **Jockey Hollow**, a wooded area south of town with reconstructed soldier huts. Several of Morristown's fine early houses can be toured. The **Schuyler-Hamilton House** (*5 Olyphant Pl. 201-267-4039. Sun. and Tues. p.m. and by appt.; adm. fee*), circa 1760, is where Alexander Hamilton courted his future wife, Betsy Schuyler. **Macculloch Hall Historical Museum and Gardens** (*45 Macculloch Ave. 201-538-2404. Sun. and Thurs. p.m.; adm. fee*), built in 1810, displays drawings by cartoonist Thomas Nast. **Historic Speedwell** (*333 Speedwell Ave. 201-540-0211. May-Oct. Thurs.-Sun.; adm. fee*), north of town center, preserves the estate of Stephen Vail, whose iron foundry produced some of the earliest steam engines. It's also where the telegraph was first perfected and publicly demonstrated in 1838. Morristown is home to **Seeing Eye** (*Washington Valley Rd. 201-539-4425. Tours by appt.*), which trains guide dogs for the blind.

▶ **Paterson** This crumbling factory city, the country's first planned industrial community, owes its existance to Alexander Hamilton's vision and the power of the Passaic River's awesome **Great Falls**. By the mid-1800s, flumes channeled water to more than 300 textile mills. By the 1960s, native Beat poet Allen Ginsberg was smoking pot here, trying to envision the falls as the Indians might have. **Overlook Park** (*Spruce and McBride Aves.*) offers distant views; a nearby footbridge takes you over the gorge. Several dozen mills, in varying states of repair, highlight Paterson's **Historic District**. Pick up a map at the **Great Falls Visitor Center** (*65 McBride Ave. 201-279-9587*). The **Paterson Museum** (*2 Market St. 201-881-3874. Closed Mon.; donation requested*) features an industrial-strength spinning wheel. To see how some of the wealth was spent, visit 1892 **Lambert Castle** (*Valley Rd. 201-881-2761. Wed.-Sun. p.m.; adm. fee*), built by a silk magnate to house his art.

New York, NEW YORK See I-95, pp. 328-29.

The 102-mile **Morris Canal,** one of dozens built in the wake of New York's successful Erie Canal, was New Jersey's first trans-state canal, linking the Hudson and Delaware Rivers. Finished in 1836, it relied on 24 lift locks and 23 inclined planes to haul boats a total of 1,674 feet up and down the state's hilly interior. Little is left of the canal today, although I-80 crosses its course near Paterson and at Lake Hopatcong, which was its main water source. The western New Jersey towns of Port Colden and Port Murray, today landlocked, carry names recalling their origins.

On the road in New Jersey

CANADA

Ont.

N.Y.

P. 239

Ohio   Pa.

W.Va.   Md.

Ky.   **P. 243**

Va.

Tenn.   **P. 245**

N.C.

Ga.   S.C.

Unless otherwise noted, directions are from interstate, and sites are free and generally open daily. Phone for further information.

① **Clayton, NEW YORK** *(7 miles W on N.Y. 12)* Jutting into the St. Lawrence River, the seaside resort of Clayton affords a sweeping view of the **Thousand Islands.** The village thrived early on as a river port, but turned to tourism when the area became a playground for the rich in the late 19th century. Overlooking the river, the **Antique Boat Museum** *(750 Mary St. 315-686-4104. Mid-May–mid-Oct.; adm. fee)* boasts the nation's largest collection of antique freshwater boats and engines. One of the best ways to see the Thousand Islands region is via **Uncle Sam Boat Tours** *(604 Riverside Dr. 315-482-2611 or 800-253-9229)*, which depart from Clayton and nearby Alexandria Bay. Summer houses dot the islands; grandest is **Boldt Castle** *(May-Oct.; adm. fee)*, the turreted extravagance begun in 1900 by George Boldt, owner of the Waldorf-Astoria.

238

② **Watertown** **Jefferson County Historical Society Museum** *(2 miles E on N.Y. 3 to 228 Washington St. 315-782-3491)* Built in 1878 and known as the Paddock Mansion, this unusual Victorian house is trimmed like a Swiss chalet. It features a "please touch" kitchen, as well as original furnishings, tools, and looms. The garden is a favorite lunchtime retreat for locals. *Tues.-Sat.; donation requested.*

③ **Sackets Harbor** **Sackets Harbor Battlefield S. H. S.** *(9 miles W on N.Y. 3. 315-646-3634)* Here, Americans repulsed an attempt by British and Canadian forces to capture the Navy shipyard during the War of 1812. The village is located on the **Seaway Trail,** a 454-mile scenic byway and national recreational trail edging the

Alexandria Bay, Thousand Islands section of the St. Lawrence River between New York and Ontario, Canada

shorelines of Lakes Erie and Ontario and the St. Lawrence River in northwestern New York.

Selkirk Shores State Park
(5.5 miles W on N.Y. 13 through Pulaski, 1.5 miles S on N.Y. 3. 315-298-5737) This peaceful bit of land sits on a forested bluff above Lake Ontario. Boating, swimming, and fishing for salmon and trout are the big draws. *Camping fee.*

Salmon River Fish Hatchery
(8 miles E on N.Y. 13 to Altmar, left on Rte. 22. 315-298-5051) This high-tech hatchery produces a whopping five million trout and salmon each year for stocking Lakes Ontario and Erie. On a self-guided tour you can view the 56 start tanks, fish ladder, and outdoor raceways, and also observe egg-taking and fish-tagging. Best time to visit is during spawning season—October for salmon, late March or early April for steelhead. *Mid-March–Nov.*

Syracuse
(Chamber of Commerce, 572 S. Salina St. 315-470-1800) Syracuse grew up around Onondaga Lake when settlers, like the Indians before them, came to boil the water's brine for salt. Founded in 1805, Salt City quickly became the nation's leading supplier. With the arrival of the Erie Canal soon after, the lakeside settlement was on its way to becoming the prosperous city you see today. The **Erie Canal Museum** *(318 Erie Blvd. E. 315-471-0593. Donation suggested)* celebrates the waterway that runs 363 miles from Albany to Buffalo. Completed in 1825, the canal was a vital link between eastern cities and the western frontier. A reconstructed canal boat and exhibits on canal life are housed in the Weighlock Building, built in 1850 to weigh the 100-foot-long boats. A few blocks away, the **Museum of Science and Technology** *(Franklin St. at W. Jefferson St. 315-425-0747. Closed Mon.; adm. fee)* is filled with hands-on exhibits that make it fun to learn about things like light, sound, and gravity. Just outside the city in Liverpool, **Sainte Marie among the Iroquois** *(0.5 mile W on N.Y. 370. 315-453-6767. Closed Mon.; adm. fee)* is a living-history museum where costumed interpreters re-create daily life, 1657-style, in a French Jesuit mission.

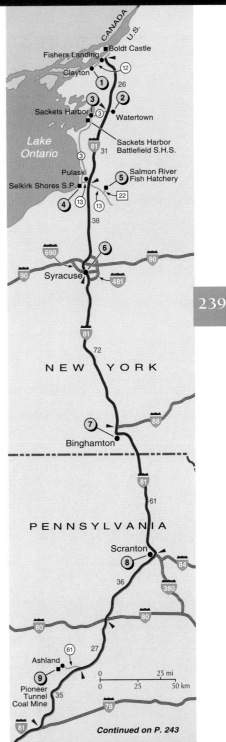

239

Continued on P. 243

(7) Binghamton   Roberson Museum and Science Center (30 Front St. 607-772-0660) Attached to the 1907 Roberson Mansion, the museum features regional exhibits, as well as a planetarium and hands-on science education area. *Closed Mon.; adm. fee.*

Steamtown National Historic
Site, Scranton, Pennsylvania

(8) Scranton, PENNSYLVANIA   It could be said that Scranton's foundations are made of iron, so completely did the city's growth and prosperity fuse with the coal and iron ore beneath it. The **Scranton Iron Furnaces** (159 Cedar Ave. 717-963-3208) stood at the heart of the immense Lackawanna Iron and Steel Company complex, which in its heyday produced 500,000 tons of railroad track per year. Only four massive stone stacks remain. One block west, **Steamtown National Historic Site** (150 S. Washington St. 717-961-2033. Memorial Day-Oct.; fee for longer excursions) offers a short ride through the rail yards to see a large collection of steam locomotives. The **Lackawanna Coal Mine** (McDade Park off Keyser Ave. 717-963-6463. May-Nov.; adm. fee) gives a hard-core look at anthracite 300 feet below ground.

(9) Pioneer Tunnel Coal Mine   (In Ashland, 8 miles W on Pa. 61, follow signs. 717-875-3850) Above the trim wood houses and steepled churches of Ashland, open-air cars carry visitors 1,800 horizontal feet into Mahanoy Mountain for the inside scoop on coal mining. A steam locomotive takes passengers around the mountain to view strip mining. *Memorial Day-Labor Day; adm. fee.*

(10) Harrisburg   The riverside approach past fine old mansions and historic bridges is a pleasant introduction to this capital city. Visitors can enjoy views of the Susquehanna from the many plazas, benches, and gardens in 5-mile-long **Riverfront Park;** a footbridge leads to **City Island,** a 63-acre recreational area where you can jog, swim, bike, or simply watch sailboats skim by.

Designated the capital in 1812, Harrisburg has preserved many of its 19th- and early 20th-century buildings. Begin with a tour of the elegant **Capitol Building** (N. 3rd and State Sts. 717-787-6810), whose green-tiled dome, reminiscent of St. Peter's Basilica in Rome, dominates the skyline. Flanking the capitol are two excellent museums: the **State Museum of Pennsylvania** (N. 3rd and North Sts. 717-787-4978. Closed Mon.), which features exhibits on history, natural science, technology, and state art; and the **Museum of Scientific Discovery** (N. 3rd and Walnut Sts. 717-233-7969. Adm. fee), where touching is encouraged. The latter is part of Strawberry Square, which offers specialty shops, restaurants, and galleries. Across the interstate, stately **Fort Hunter Mansion** (5300 N. Front St. 717-599-5751. May-Dec. Tues.-Sun.; adm. fee), built in 1787 and enlarged in 1814, presides over a delightful riverfront park. A walking tour leads past a tavern, barn, springhouse, and other outbuildings.

Pride of the Susquehanna, Harrisburg, Pennsylvania

Martinsburg, WEST VIRGINIA Commercial center of the state's eastern panhandle, the town has seven historic districts spanning 220 years. Its founder built his home, the **General Adam Stephen House** (*309 E. John St. 304-267-4434. Weekends May-Oct.*), above a creek where mills and foundries were later established. This imposing rectangular structure of native limestone was completed in 1789. Another building with a past, now headquarters of the county historical society, is the renovated **Belle Boyd House** (*126 E. Race St. 304-267-4713. March-Labor Day Fri.-Sun., Labor Day-Dec. Fri.-Sat.*). The ten-year-old girl who defiantly rode her horse into the ballroom of this 1853 Greek Revival mansion went on to become the Confederacy's most colorful spy.

Museum of Scientific Discovery, Harrisburg, Pa.

Morgan Cabin (*2 miles S from Inwood exit on US 11, 1 mile W on W. Va. 26. 304-229-8946. Weekends May-Aug.*) In 1731, West Virginia's first settler, Morgan Morgan, built a one-room cabin here. The reconstruction uses many of the original logs, including one in the north wall with an opening for shooting at Indians. Just down the road stands **Morgan Chapel,** a two-story Episcopal church. Original pews, an antique organ, and graffiti written by Civil War soldiers mark this 1851 brick Greek Revival. The interior is not open, but visitors may look through the windows.

241

Winchester, VIRGINIA Its strategic location at the hub of pioneer routes gained Winchester early prominence as a provision stop. The same position made it a prize for both Union and Confederate forces; as a result, the town changed hands more than 70 times during the Civil War. Today Winchester enjoys a gentler fame as host of the Shenandoah Apple Blossom Festival each spring. The **Visitor Center** (*1360 S. Pleasant Valley Rd. 703-662-4135 or 800-662-1360*) occupies an old gristmill next to **Abram's Delight Museum** (*703-662-6519. Apr.-Oct.; adm. fee*), a loving restoration of the town's oldest house. From there, proceed downtown to the historic district, where you'll find buildings of renown on almost every corner. The two not to be missed are **Stonewall Jackson's Headquarters** (*415 N. Braddock St. 703-667-3242. Apr.-Oct.; adm. fee*), home of the popular Confederate general during the winter of 1861, and **George Washington's Office Museum** (*Braddock and Cork Sts. 703-662-4412. Apr.-Oct.; adm. fee*), the crude cabin used by the young colonel in 1755, when he was in charge of protecting the Virginia frontier.

Shenandoah National Park (*10 miles E on I-66 and US 340 to northern entrance at Front Royal. Visitor Center 703-999-2266*) For generations, people lived in the jumble of forests and mountains that now comprise this long, narrow 194,630-acre park. In the decade before it opened in 1935, some 2,000 mountain people were resettled outside it. Today the marks of lumbering and

Quilter in Virginia's Blue Ridge

View of Piedmont Plateau from Blue Ridge Parkway in Virginia

farming are disappearing as forests make a steady comeback. About two million people visit the park each year, nearly a quarter of them in October to see the foliage. To avoid fall traffic jams, arrive early, park at an overlook, and walk a trail. There are nearly 500 miles of them. *Admission fee.*

15 Woodstock Tower *(Va. 42 exit to Woodstock, 1 mile N on US 11, right on Mill Rd. for 0.5 mile, left on Va. 758 for 3.5 miles. 703-984-4101)* The last stretch of road, steep and gravelly, twists up through a scenic slice of the George Washington National Forest. Park at the top and watch for a path on the right. The view from the tower, which stands at 2,000 feet on Massanutten Mountain, is superb on a clear day. Look for the seven bends of the Shenandoah River.

16 New Market In May 1864, this rural town saw outnumbered Rebels rout Federal troops to give the Confederacy its last victory in the Shenandoah Valley. I-81 bisects the 8-mile-long Civil War battlefield. The first-rate **New Market Battlefield Military Museum** *(0.5 mile N of US 211 on Va. 305. 703-740-8065. Mid-March–Nov.; adm. fee)* houses artifacts from the Revolutionary War to Desert Storm. Outside the museum, markers show battlefield positions. The **New Market Battlefield Historical Park** *(1 mile N of US 211 on Va. 305. 703-740-3101. Adm. fee)* uses murals and dioramas to interpret the Civil War in its **Hall of Valor Museum.** A 2-mile trail loops around a farmstead where some of the worst fighting took place.

☞ The core of the *Blue Ridge Mountains* was formed a billion years ago, when molten magma solidified beneath the earth's surface. Uplift exposed the granite core, evident in Shenandoah National Park's 3,268-foot Old Rag Mountain. Subsequent volcanic forces spewed layers of lava, up to 1,800 feet thick at the park's treeless Big Meadows. Today wind, water, and frost continue to sculpture the ancient landscape.

Civil War reenactment, New Market, Va.

17 Luray Reptile Center and Dinosaur Park *(16 miles E on US 211. 703-743-4113)* The dinosaurs are stiff, but the snakes are thrilling. So, too, is the assortment of alligators and other reptiles. If you're dying to touch, there's an outdoor petting zoo with burros, llamas, goats, and deer. *Mid-April–Nov.; adm. fee.*

18 Luray Caverns *(12 miles E on US 211, follow signs. 703-743-6551)* Despite overkill advertising, this spectacular hole in the ground doesn't disappoint. An hour-long tour leads through a fantasyland of chambers where crystalline columns, translucent draperies, and other bizarre formations crowd around dangling stalactites. Highlights include ethereal Dream Lake and the Stalacpipe

Saracen's Tent, Luray Caverns, Virginia

Organ. *Adm. fee (also covers entrance to a vintage car museum).*

Natural Chimneys *(12 miles W on Va. 646 and Va. 747, follow signs. 703-350-2510)* When part of an ancient inland seabed was thrust up and then scoured by erosion, it left seven chunky limestone pillars brooding over the valley floor. Ranging in height from 65 to 120 feet, they are the focal point of a well-run regional park offering camping, swimming, hiking, and biking. *Adm. fee.*

Grand Caverns *(6 miles E on Va. 256, follow signs. 703-249-5705. April-Oct.; adm. fee)* Caverns honeycomb the limestone beneath the Shenandoah Valley; most have spectacular formations and an average temperature of 55°F. Grand Caverns was the first stumbled upon in 1804, early enough to intrigue Thomas Jefferson. In the 19th century, candlelight dances enlivened the cave's 5,000-square-foot Grand Ballroom; today the softly illuminated passageways kindle a childlike feeling of exploration. The caverns form part of a regional park, with a swimming pool, tennis courts, miniature golf, and picnic tables.

Staunton Near the junction of I-81 and I-64, Staunton keeps a proud hold on a past that dates back to 1732. Historical and architectural gems abound. Pick up information about five walking tours at the **Visitor Center** *(1303 Richmond Ave. 703-332-3972).* One beauty is the **Woodrow Wilson Birthplace & Museum** *(18-24 N. Coalter St. 703-885-0897. Adm. fee).* This magnificent Greek Revival house has a lovely formal garden, but the 28th President's shiny Pierce-Arrow quietly steals the show. Two miles away, at the **Museum of American Frontier Culture** *(Off*

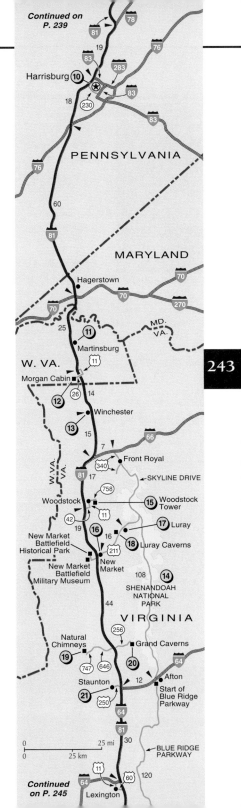

Continued on P. 239

PENNSYLVANIA

MARYLAND

Harrisburg 10

Hagerstown

MD. VA.

W. VA.

Martinsburg

Morgan Cabin 11

12 Winchester

13

Front Royal

SKYLINE DRIVE

Woodstock 15 Woodstock Tower

17 Luray

16 18 Luray Caverns

New Market Battlefield Historical Park

New Market Battlefield Military Museum

New Market

14

SHENANDOAH NATIONAL PARK

VIRGINIA

Natural Chimneys 19

Grand Caverns

20

Staunton 21

Afton

Start of Blue Ridge Parkway

BLUE RIDGE PARKWAY

0 25 mi
0 25 km

Continued on P. 245

Lexington

243

Autoharpist, Staunton, Virginia

US 250, follow signs. 703-332-7850. Adm. fee), costumed interpreters work 17th- to 19th-century farmsteads.

Shenandoah National Park (*Southern entrance 12 miles E on I-64, at Afton*) See p. 241.

Lexington See I-64, p. 141.

(22) **Natural Bridge** (*2.5 miles E on US 11, follow signs*) This beautiful, 23-story-high natural limestone phenomenon has been somewhat overwhelmed by rampant commercialism. *Adm. fee.*

(23) **Roanoke** (*Visitor Center, 114 Market St. 703-345-8622*) Roanoke started life as little more than a salt-lick crossing and grew, with the coming of the railroad, into the largest city in the Blue Ridge Mountains. Today this center of commerce still hums to the tune of its steel rails. The **Virginia Museum of Transportation** (*303 Norfolk Ave. 703-342-5670. Adm. fee*) pays homage to the iron horse. The country's largest collection of diesel engines makes this primarily a railroad museum, although everything from autos to airplanes is on display. A few blocks away, **Market Square**, lined with Roanoke Valley produce, embraces the state's oldest farmers market. The sleek building overlooking the square is a restored 1914 warehouse that houses the **Science Museum of Western Virginia** (*703-342-5710*), as well as art and history museums and a theater. *Adm. fees.*

If Time Permits...

(24) **Booker T. Washington National Monument** (*27 miles SE, through Roanoke, on Va. 116 and Va. 122. 703-721-2094*) In 1856, one of America's great educators began his journey from slave to college president on this small plantation in the rolling piedmont. It's now a reconstructed working farm with a lingering smell of tobacco in the old barn. *Adm. fee.*

Running parallel to I-81, the *Blue Ridge Parkway* threads 469 miles along the crest of the southern Appalachians. White dogwoods emerge in May, followed by flame azaleas and mountain laurels. By June showy catawba rhododendrons attract crowds. In summer look for orange day lilies and butterfly weed. Wildflowers linger until fall, when dogwood and black gum turn deep red. Hickories answer in yellow, sassafrases in orange, and red maples blaze. With oaks' soft russet the season gently closes, leaving evergreens— and a few hardy travelers—to face winter.

Natural Bridge, near Lexington, Virginia

Shot Tower Historical State Park
(8 miles S on I-77) See I-77, p. 208.

Wytheville Dating from 1792, when it was first known as Evansham, this town served as a supply stop for settlers heading west on Daniel Boone's Wilderness Trail. The historic district includes the stately antebellum houses of Civil War officers and Virginia politicians. Most are privately owned, but the **Rock House** *(Monroe and Tazewell Sts. 703-228-3111)*, once a Confederate hospital, is open Sunday afternoons. *Adm. fee.*

Big Walker Lookout *(12 miles N on US 52. 703-228-4401)* A 100-foot tower offers an expansive view of five states: Virginia, West Virginia, Kentucky, Tennessee, and North Carolina. *April-Oct.; adm. fee.*

Hungry Mother State Park *(4 miles N of Marion on Va. 16. 703-783-3422)* Words purportedly uttered by a child rescued from Indians gave this popular woodland park its name. Today hearty meals are served in the rustic lodge, and laughter drifts across the tranquil mountain lake. Children's activities and spontaneous old-time music jams augment the usual recreational offerings of swimming, hiking, boating, and horseback riding. *Day-use and camping fees.*

Abingdon Famed for theater, Abingdon saw plenty of drama when three major fires swept through town in the 19th century. The attractive frame and brick houses lining the historic district today are the survivors, some more than 200 years old. Most historic is the **Barter Theatre** *(133 W. Main St. 703-628-3991 or 800-368-3240. April-Nov.; adm. fee)*, so named when Depression-era patrons traded "ham for Hamlet." Lively productions run from April through December; children's plays are performed in summer. Another summer highlight is the **Virginia Highlands Festival** *(First two weeks of Aug.)*, with arts and crafts, antiques, and music. A few blocks from the theater, you'll find the trailhead for the **Virginia Creeper Trail**, a hiking-biking path that rolls 34 miles through the southwest highlands to

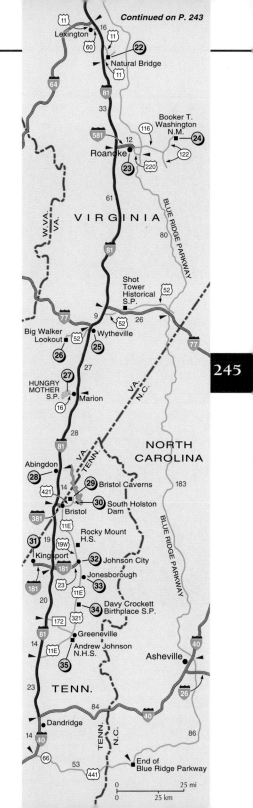

Continued on P. 243

245

Catawba rhododendrons, Cherokee National Forest, Tennessee, east of Johnson City on I-181

246

Black bear, Blue Ridge Mountains

the North Carolina border. Or try the 3-mile self-guided nature walk. Just outside town, **White's Mill** (*3.5 miles N on Va. 692. 703-676-0285. Daily Oct.-Memorial Day, closed Mon. rest of year; adm. fee*) is a picturesque, much photographed working flour mill dating from 1790.

㉙ **B r i s t o l C a v e r n s**, **T E N N E S S E E** (*4 miles SE of Bristol, just off US 421, follow signs. 615-878-2011*) An underground river carved these caverns about 200 million years ago, then served as a hidden pathway for Indians to launch raids on frontier families. Today the quiet water reflects the colorful rock turrets and columns that must have awed the Cherokee warriors. *Adm. fee.*

㉚ **S o u t h H o l s t o n D a m** (*6 miles E of Bristol on US 421, follow signs*) Impressive is the word that comes to mind as you gaze 285 feet up the terraced embankment of this huge earthen dam, completed in 1950 by the Tennessee Valley Authority. The paved summit leads to an observation deck with a splendid view of the 24-mile-long lake and the hazy ridge of Holston Mountain. The lake's gin-clear water is a magnet for scuba divers. Just below the dam, a labyrinth weir boosts the fish population, luring anglers to the **Osceola Island Recreation Area.** Hiking trails, picnic tables.

㉛ **K i n g s p o r t**   **Bays Mountain Park** (*8 miles N on I-181, follow signs. 615-229-9447*) Opened in 1971 to acquaint schoolchildren and the public with the natural world, this forested preserve provides 3,000 acres' worth of environmental education. Wildlife exhibits, nature programs, an aquarium, and a planetarium encourage a healthy interest in the outdoors; but if recess is more your thing, you can hike, bike, ramble, or fish in this marvelous mountain retreat. *Fee for parking and some programs.*

㉜ **J o h n s o n C i t y**   (*19 miles S on I-181*) Tucked around the urban sprawl of Johnson City, once known as Blue Plum, are little pockets of Tennessee's early history. On the **Tipton-Haynes Historic Site** (*I-181 to S. Roan St., follow signs. 615-926-3631. Closed week-*

ends Nov.-March; adm. fee), a battle for the state of Franklin (the original name of northeast Tennessee, after Benjamin) was fought and lost on the handsome farmstead you see today. **Rocky Mount Historic Site** (US 11E at Piney Flats. 615-538-7396. Closed weekends Jan.-Feb.; adm. fee), a two-story log cabin built in 1770-72, served as a territorial capitol before Tennessee became a state. On the East Tennessee State University campus, the **Carrol Reece Museum** (615-929-4392) displays antique musical instruments and frontier artifacts. Not historical but educational, the **Hands On! Regional Museum** (315 E. Main St. 615-434-4263. Closed Mon.; adm. fee) has an aquarium, an ark, and more to engage youngsters in entertaining scientific activities.

Jonesborough (7 miles S of Johnson City on US 11E) Founded in 1779, Jonesborough first belonged to North Carolina and the short-lived state of Franklin. Today Tennessee's oldest town is distinguished by brick sidewalks, eclectic architectural styles, antique shops, and cafés along its lively Main Street. The **Visitor Center** (117 Boone St. 615-753-5961) arranges tours of the following four houses. The **Chester Inn** (116 W. Main St.), where President Andrew Jackson was threatened with a tar and feathering, is thought to be the oldest frame structure, and **Sister's Row** (205-209 W. Main St.) the oldest brick building. The **Gammon-Sterling House** (204 W. Main St.) features one of the best examples of a stepped gable. The **Mansion House** (200 W. Main St.), a simple federal building garnished with elaborate woodwork, is an outstanding example of the blend of styles characteristic of this historic town.

Davy Crockett Birthplace State Park

(Midway between Jonesborough and Greeneville, 3.5 miles off US 11E, follow signs. 615-257-2167) Davy Crockett wasn't born on a mountaintop, as the ballad would have it, but you can still see the site next to the reconstructed log cabin on the Nolichucky River. For more information about the frontiersman, head over to the Visitor Center and museum, then strike out on a delightful self-guided tour of the bluff-top trail through Crockett's woods. Swimming pool. Museum closed weekends Labor Day-Memorial Day; camping fee.

Andrew Johnson National Historic Site

(13.5 miles to Greeneville on US 11E or Rte. 172, follow signs. 615-638-3551) Andrew Johnson snipped silk and polished rhetoric in his tailor shop, the local center of political debates, before becoming 17th President of the United States after Lincoln's assassination. The site comprises the shop and an adjoining Visitor Center, as well as the statesman's two homes and final resting place, each several blocks apart. Adm. fee to Johnson Homestead.

Not all states make it to statehood. Take *Franklin*. In 1784, frontiersmen primed a remote swath of the western Appalachians for self-government. They named it after Benjamin Franklin, penned a constitution, signed treaties with Indians, even set up a monetary system. The problem: Congress and North Carolina—to whom the land belonged—refused to recognize the fledgling state, forcing its dissolution in 1788. Today it is part of Tennessee.

Kayaking Tennessee's
Ocoee River

CANADA

Wash.

Mont.

Oreg.

Idaho

Wyo.

Calif.

Nev.

Utah

For the eastern segment of I-84 see pages 252-55.

Unless otherwise noted, directions are from interstate, and sites are free and generally open daily. Phone for further information.

Portland, OREGON   See I-5, p. 16.

(1) **Historic Columbia River Highway** *(US 30 bet. Troutdale and Bonneville Dam, follow signs)* As this asphalt band curls through the forest corridors of the Columbia River Gorge, it passes beautiful waterfalls, spans fern-laden glens, and climbs to stunning vistas—all in about 20 miles. **Multnomah Falls**, best known of the cascades, is a 620-foot double falls that slips over mossy cliffs and drops into a pool. **Vista House** *(10 miles W of the falls)*, a small but elaborate stone rotunda, offers terrific views.

(2) **Bonneville Lock and Dam** *(Follow signs from own exit. Visitor Center 503-374-8820. Tours)* Bonneville was the first of eight federal lock and dam projects built on the Columbia and Snake Rivers during the 1930s. The dams supply hydroelectric power and irrigation, but they also are blamed for the virtual extinction of the Snake River sockeye salmon. A viewing room allows you to watch fish migrate upstream.

248

(3) **Cascade Locks**   Before the first locks were built in 1896, steamboats docked here, and rails portaged their cargo around powerful rapids. The rapids are submerged now, but you can see the original locks at **Cascade Locks Marine Park** *(Cascade Locks exit)*, and pick up river lore at the **Cascade Locks Historical Museum** *(503-374-8535. May-Sept.; donations)*. A modern stern-wheeler, *Columbia Gorge (503-223-3928. Mid-June–Sept.; fare charge)*, offers excursions through the gorge.

Bonneville Dam, on the Columbia River, Oregon

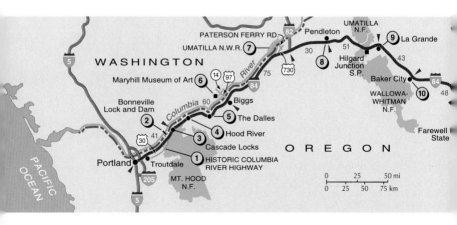

UMATILLA N.F.

PATERSON FERRY RD.   Pendleton

UMATILLA N.W.R. **(7)**

(9) La Grande

WASHINGTON

30   51

(8) Hilgard Junction S.P.

43

Maryhill Museum of Art **(6)**   **(14)** 97

75

730

Baker City

(10)   48

60

Biggs

WALLOWA-WHITMAN N.F.

Bonneville Lock and Dam

Columbia   River

(2)   30   41

(5) The Dalles

(3)   **(4)** Hood River

Farewell State

Cascade Locks

O R E G O N

Portland   Troutdale

(1) HISTORIC COLUMBIA RIVER HIGHWAY

PACIFIC OCEAN

MT. HOOD N.F.

0   25   50 mi

0   25   50   75 km

5

205

Hood River *(Chamber of Commerce, Port Marina Park. 503-386-2000 or 800-366-3530)* Founded in 1854, when traffic along the Oregon Trail was heaviest, this beautiful town lies among the lush foothills of Mount Hood. **Panorama Point** *(0.5 mile S on Oreg. 35 to Eastside Rd.)* offers a fine view of Mount Hood and the Edenic landscape emigrants trudged 2,000 miles to find. Follow signs from the Mount Hood/White Salmon exit for the **Hood River County Tour Route,** or ride the **Mount Hood Railroad** *(110 Railroad Ave. 503-386-3556. Phone for schedule; fee).* You'll find good displays of area history at the **Hood River County Hist. Museum** *(Port Marina Park. 503-386-6772. Closed Mon.-Tues. and Nov.-March).*

The Dalles *(Chamber of Commerce, 404 W. 2nd St. 503-296-2231)* Built among the steep, forested walls of the Columbia River Gorge, the town was settled in 1838. Many emigrants ended their overland journey at The Dalles; from here they could float to the Willamette Valley. The **Fort Dalles Museum** *(15th and Garrison. 503-296-4547. Daily March-Oct., closed Mon.-Tues. Nov.-Feb. and Jan. 1-15; adm. fee)* houses pioneer relics in a surviving building of the old fort. From **Sorosis Park,** a fine view opens up of the town, gorge, and mountains. Visitors are welcome at **The Dalles Lock and Dam** *(E edge of town. 503-296-1181. Closed weekends).*

Maryhill Museum of Art *(In Wash., 5 miles NW of Biggs, via US 97 and Wash. 14. 509-773-3733. Closed mid-Nov.–mid-March; adm. fee)* On the rim of the Columbia River Gorge, Maryhill includes a large collection of Rodin sculpture and drawings, as well as furniture, jewelry, and icons given by a Romanian queen. The mansion was built by an entrepreneur who added a replica of **Stonehenge** *(3 miles E of museum)* in memory of World War I dead.

Umatilla National Wildlife Refuge *(NE on US 730, left on Paterson Ferry Rd. 503-922-3232)* Stretching

As mighty as the ***Columbia River*** seems today, it carries a trickle compared to the floodwaters that blasted through the Columbia River Gorge during the last ice age. Beginning about 18,000 years ago, a glacier repeatedly blocked the Clark Fork River near Coeur d'Alene. Each time, the ice dam created a huge lake up to 2,000 feet deep; then the dam burst, releasing a wall of water that rushed across eastern Washington and filled the gorge to depths of 1,000 feet.

249

Stonehenge, Maryhill Museum of Art, Washington

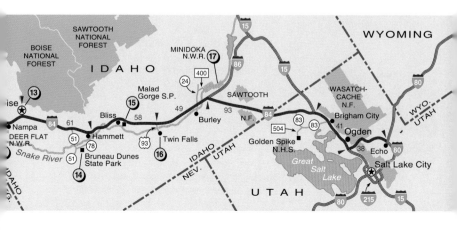

for 20 miles along the Columbia River, the refuge protects a ribbon of high desert. Sloughs, islands, and woodlands draw waterfowl, as well as bald eagles, long-billed curlews, and rare burrowing owls.

(8) Pendleton *(Chamber of Commerce, 25 S.E. Dorion. 800-547-8911)* Founded in 1868 beside the Umatilla River, Pendleton prospered as a commercial center for ranchers and as a party town (32 saloons, 18 bordellos) for cowboys. In September, frontier days return in the form of the Pendleton Round-up. One fascinating aspect of Pendleton is its Underground—16 square blocks of foundations connected by tunnels. Built by Chinese laborers as service tunnels, the Underground became a honky-tonk at the turn of the century. Contact **Pendleton Underground Tours** *(37 S.W. Emigrant. 503-276-0730. Closed Sun. in winter; adm. fee).* For more history, visit the **Umatilla County Hist. Society Museum** *(108 S.W. Frazer. 503-276-0012. Closed Sun.-Mon.; donation requested).*

(9) La Grande *(Chamber of Commerce, 2111 Adams Ave. 800-848-9969)* The route of the Oregon Trail runs through the Grande Ronde Valley and La Grande. A brochure guides visitors to important landmarks; emigrants probably camped near what is now **Hilgard Junction State Park** *(8 miles W of town, off Oreg. 244. 503-983-2277)* before crossing the Blue Mountains. At the **Oregon Trail Interpretive Park at Blue Mountain Crossing** *(13 miles W of town, off Oreg. 30, follow signs. 503-963-7186),* a fine stretch of wagon ruts threads through forest and meadow. *Late May–mid-Oct.*

(10) Baker City Lying in a fertile valley at the foot of the Blue Mountains, the town sprang up with the 1860s Rockies gold rush. It boasts more than 100 historical buildings, but its main draw is the **National Historic Oregon Trail Interpretive Center** *(5 miles E on Oreg. 86. 503-523-1843. Donation requested).* With its living-history programs and miles of trails, the center ranks as the preeminent memorial to the Oregon Trail. The **Oregon Trail Regional Museum** *(Campbell and Grove Sts. 503-523-9308. Closed Nov.–mid-April; donations)* houses memorabilia from Baker City's early days.

(11) Farewell Bend State Park *(1.25 miles N of Farewell Bend exit. 503-869-2365)* Here, Oregon Trail emigrants spent a final night on the Snake River before heading northwest. *Fee May-Sept.*

(12) Deer Flat N. W. R., IDAHO *(4.5 miles W on Idaho 55, left on Lake Rd. for 3 miles, follow signs. 208-467-9278)* The refuge takes in a large impoundment of the Boise River via a 20-mile canal and 107 islands that stretch along the Snake. Mild winters attract Canada geese and mallards. *Visitor Center closed weekends.*

(13) Boise *(Convention & Visitors Bureau, 168 N. 9th St. 208-344-7777)* Built among shady groves on the Boise River, the city took root during the 1860s gold rush as a mining center and military post

Peregrine falcon, Idaho

Morrison-Knudson Nature Center, Boise, Idaho

Today it's the state capital and home of Boise State University. The **Boise River Greenbelt** stretches through the heart of the city, linking eight major parks with walkways. At **Julia Davis Park** (*Bet. Myrtle St. and the river*), you'll find a small amusement park for kids, boat rentals, and three other attractions: **Zoo Boise** (*208-384-4260. Adm. fee*); the **Idaho Historical Museum** (*208- 334-2120. Donations*); and the **Boise Art Museum** (*208-345-8330. Closed Mon.; adm. fee*). Nearby, kids routinely mob the **Discovery Center of Idaho** (*131 Myrtle St. 208-343-9895. Closed Mon.; adm. fee*), with hands-on science. Also downtown, the **Basque Museum and Cultural Center** (*611 Grove St. 208-343-2671. Closed Sun.-Mon.; donations*) celebrates the Basque heritage. Haunting self-guided tours of the 1870 **Old Idaho Penitentiary** (*2.5 miles E via Warm Springs Ave. 208-334-2844. Adm. fee*) lead through cell blocks in use to the 1970s. If aquatic biology interests you, don't miss the **Morrison-Knudson Nature Center** (*600 S. Walnut Ave. Visitor Center 208-368-6060. Donations*) with its cross-sectional views of a living stream. Another good stop is the **World Center for Birds of Prey** (*6 miles S on S. Cole Rd. 208-362-8687. Closed Mon.; adm. fee*).

Shoshone Falls, Twin Falls, Idaho

Bruneau Dunes State Park (*20 miles SE via Idaho 51 and Idaho 78, or 15 miles W on Idaho 78. Visitor Center 208-366-7919*) Two huge dunes connected by a sand ridge loom over olive trees and crystalline lakes. Nature trails. *Vehicle fee.*

Malad Gorge S. P. (*7 miles E of Bliss, follow signs from Tuttle exit. 208-837-4505*) The gorge is a narrow side canyon that joins the Snake River Canyon. At **Devil's Washbowl**, a footbridge spans the gorge. Upstream, Malad River cascades through a cleft; downstream, a waterfall stairsteps over the rim. Hiking trails.

Twin Falls This city lies at the rim of **Snake River Canyon**, a spectacular gorge 500 feet deep and 2,000 feet wide. Far below, the river wanders among grassy islands. **Shoshone Falls** (*3 miles E on Falls Ave., follow signs. 208-736-2265. Adm. fee mid-May–Sept.*), the "Niagara of the West," is little more than a damp cliff much of the year. Exhibits at the **Herrett Museum** (*College of Southern Idaho. 208-733-9554, ext. 355. Closed Sun.-Mon.*) interpret early human life on the Snake River plain. The **Twin Falls Historical Society Museum** (*3 miles W on US 30. 208-734-5547. Mid-May–Aug. Tues.-Sat. p.m.; donations*) celebrates pioneer days.

Minidoka National Wildlife Refuge (*16 miles NE of Burley via Idaho 24, follow signs. 208-436-3589*) Extending 25 miles along the Snake River, the refuge includes areas of open water, bays and inlets, islands, and marshes. It attracts geese and tundra swans and harbors white pelicans. Roads are rough.

Brigham City and Ogden, U T A H See I-15, p. 54.

On May 10, 1869, an exuberant throng gathered at Promontory Point, Utah, to drive the last spike in America's first transcontinental railroad. The celebration culminated seven years of surveying, grading, and track laying between Omaha and Sacramento—1,776 miles. Today, at *Golden Spike National Historic Site* (32 miles NW of Brigham City via Utah 83. Visitor Center open all year. 801-471-2209), replicas of the steam locomotives that met ply 1.7 miles of rails across the prairie in a reenactment of the original ceremony (May-Oct.; fee).

For the western segment of I-84 see pages 248-51.

Unless otherwise noted, directions are from interstate, and sites are free and generally open daily. Phone for further information.

Scranton, PENNSYLVANIA See I-81, p. 240.

(1) **Lake Wallenpaupack** *(Visitor Center, 14 miles NE on Pa. 507 and US 6. 717-226-2141)* This huge summer recreation area is built around a 13-mile-long, man-made lake. *Adm. fee for some activities.*

(2) **Milford** **Grey Towers** *(2 miles E of I-84 on US 6. 717-296-6401)*, the 1885 châteaulike summer home of governor and conservationist Gifford Pinchot, was designed by Richard Morris Hunt. It's nestled amid 102 acres of formal gardens, meadows, and expansive lawns. *Memorial Day-Labor Day and by appt.; donations.*

(3) **Delaware Water Gap National Recreation Area** Some 70,000 acres of land are preserved for public use along a 40-mile stretch of the Delaware River. The gap, a mile-wide notch cut through the Kittatinny Ridge by the Delaware River, is at the south end of the park *(About 35 miles S through Milford on US 209. See I-80, p. 236)*. Closer to I-84, the **Dingmans Falls Visitor Center** *(10 miles S, off US 209, follow signs. 717-828-7802. May-Oct.)* is the starting point for a half-mile nature trail to two waterfalls. The **Pocono Environmental Education Center** *(About 5 miles S of Dingmans Ferry, off US 209. 717-828-2319)* maintains 12 miles of trails on its grounds, with access to 200,000 acres of adjacent public lands.

(4) **Cuddebackville, NEW YORK** In Delaware & Hudson Canal Park, the **Neversink Valley Area Museum** *(8 miles N on US 6 and US 209 to town, left on Hoag Rd. 914-754-8870)* tells the story of the 108-mile canal, dug in 1825-28 to carry coal from Honesdale, Pa., to the Hudson River. *March-Dec. Thurs.-Sun.; fee.*

252

Goshen (*3 miles S on N.Y. 17*) The **Trotting Horse Museum** (*240 Main St. 914-294-6330. Adm. fee*) celebrates America's standard-bred trotting horses, raised here for over 150 years. Nearby **Goshen Historic Track** (*914-294-5333*), still a year-round training facility, is America's first sporting site designated a national historic landmark. The best time to visit is in the morning.

Vails Gate **New Windsor Cantonment State Historic Site** (*3 miles S of I-84 on N.Y. 300. 914-561-1765. Mid-April–Oct. Wed.-Sun.*) A year after the 1781 Battle of Yorktown, General Washington brought his victorious troops to this 1,600-acre site for their final winter encampment. Today, Continental Army "soldiers" demonstrate their drills. Nearby, **The Last Encampment of the Continental Army** (*914-562-6397. Mid-April–Oct. Tues.-Sun.*) preserves part of the campground.

Erie Depot Museum, in an 1892 railroad station, Jersey Ave., Port Jervis, New York

Fishkill Part of the **Van Wyck Homestead Museum** (*I-84 and US 9. 914-896-9560*), reputed to be the setting for James Fenimore Cooper's novel *The Spy*, was built in 1732. An American officers' headquarters during the Revolution, it is maintained as a museum. *Mem. Day-Columbus Day Sun p.m. and by appt.; adm. fee.*

253

Ridgefield, CONNECTICUT (*3 miles S on US 7 to Conn. 35 for 4 mi.*), retains much of the charm of an 18th-century village. In **Keeler Tavern** (*132 Main St. 203-438-5485. Wed., Sat.-Sun. p.m. Closed Jan.; adm. fee*), it's easy to imagine patriots plotting over ale. A sculpture garden is a focus of the **Aldrich Museum of Contemporary Art** (*258 Main St. 203-438-4519. Tues.-Sun.; adm. fee*), one of the first U. S. museums devoted to contemporary art.

Danbury America's former hat-making capital is also the birthplace of composer Charles Ives. On summer weekends the town honors him with concerts at the **Charles Ives Center for the Arts** (*W.*

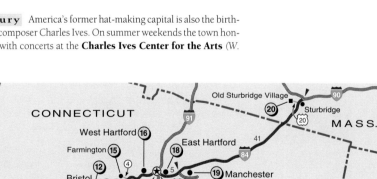

When Mark Twain scribed his story about a 19th-century technological wizard in King Arthur's court, it wasn't by accident he made the protagonist a ***Connecticut Yankee.*** The U. S. industrial revolution came of age in Connecticut, largely along the path of I-84. Samuel Colt shipped revolvers west from Hartford; Seth Thomas kept America on time with clocks and watches from his Plymouth Hollow factory; New Britain made hardware; and Danbury made hats. The Connecticut Yankees were ever an industrious lot.

Conn. State Univ./Westside campus, Mill Plain Rd. 203-837-8200). The **Scott-Fanton Museum** (43 Main St. 203-743-5200. Wed.-Sun. p.m.) includes the 1790 John Rider House; the John Dodd Hat Shop next door, chronicling the local industry; and the Charles Ives Birthplace (5 Mountainville Ave. 203-778-3540).

(10) Kettletown State Park (5 miles S of Southbury off Conn. 484, follow signs. 203-264-5169) Take a dip in the lake, hike along the Appalachian Trail, or just picnic. Adm. fee weekends.

(11) Waterbury The **Mattatuck Museum** (144 W. Main St. 203-753-0381) brings to life the history of western Connecticut and displays the work of state artists. Closed Mon. year-round and Sun. in July-Aug.

(12) Bristol The ornate wooden ponies of your childhood are at the **New England Carousel Museum** (95 Riverside Ave. 203-585-5411. Closed Mon. Nov.-March; adm. fee), one of America's largest collections of antique carousel pieces. The animated miniature circus took one man 50 years to build. More than 3,000 timepieces are on display in the **American Clock & Watch Museum** (100 Maple St. 203-583-6070. Closed Dec.-Feb.; adm. fee), in an 1801 mansion.

(13) New Britain The **New Britain Museum of American Art** (56 Lexington St. 203-229-0257. Tues.-Sun. p.m.) holds more than 5,000 American works from 1740 to the present. Kids can explore the history and cultures of the state and world in the **New Britain Youth Museum** (30 High St. 203-225-3020. Closed Sun.-Mon.).

(14) Hungerford Outdoor Education Center (6 mi. E on Conn. 72 and Conn. 372. 203-827-9064) Here's fun for the family—farm and exotic animals, hiking trails, gardens. Tues.-Sat.; adm. fee.

(15) Farmington This is the quintessential New England town—quaint and manicured. McKim, Mead & White designed turn-of-the-century **Hill-stead** (35 Mountain Rd. 203-677-9064. Closed Mon.; adm. fee) to showcase a private French Impressionist collection. The colonial revival house is now a museum. The **Stanley-Whitman House** (37 High St. 203-677-9222. May-Oct. Wed.-Sun. p.m.; adm. fee), of 1720, is an example of early New England frame architecture.

Bushnell Park, Hartford, Conn.

(16) West Hartford Costumed guides give tours of the late 18th-century **Noah Webster's House** (227 S. Main St. 203-521-5362. Closed Wed.; adm. fee), birthplace of America's first lexicographer. The **Science Center of Connecticut** (950 Trout Brook Dr. 203-231-2824. Closed Mon. except July-Aug.; adm. fee) features a mini-zoo, discovery room, and planetarium. The **Museum of American Political Life** (Univ. of Hartford, 200 Bloomfield Ave. 203-768-4090. Closed Mon.) exhibits artifacts of Presidents and campaigns.

(17) Hartford Connecticut's capital has gone through many metamorphoses since the Dutch established a trading post here in 1633. Today its multicultural vitality belies its staid image as "the insurance capital of the nation." The acclaimed **Wadsworth Atheneum** (*600 Main St. 203-278-2670. Closed Mon.; adm. fee*), America's oldest continuously operating public art museum, has more than 45,000 objects. Cap a stroll through lovely **Bushnell Park** (*Adj. to the State Capitol*) with a look at the **Soldiers and Sailors Memorial Arch** (*Trinity St.*), dedicated to Hartford's Civil War dead. The gold-domed 1879 **State Capitol** (*210 Capitol Ave. 203-240-0222. Tours Mon.-Fri.; also Sat. April-Oct.*) is a trove of state history. A Revo-

Mark Twain House, Hartford, Connecticut

lutionary War replica cannon is fired thrice daily (except Sun.) by a corps in Continental uniform at the **Old State House** (*800 Main St. 203-522-6766. Under restoration through April 1995*), designed by Charles Bulfinch; its museum has changing exhibits. Don't miss the neighboring **Mark Twain House** (*351 Farmington Ave. 203-493-6411. Closed Tues. Columbus Day-May; adm. fee*) and **Harriet Beecher Stowe House** (*73 Forest St. 203-525-9317. Closed Mon. Columbus Day-May; adm. fee*). Twain's 19-room "steamboat Gothic" was decorated by Louis C. Tiffany in 1881. Stowe's "cottage" holds many of her possessions. In summer, more than 900 varieties of roses are on display in **Elizabeth Park** (*Prospect and Asylum Aves. 203-722-6543. Greenhouses open weekdays*). The **Historical Museum of Medicine and Dentistry** (*Hartford Medical Soc. Bldg., 230 Scarborough St. 203-236-5613. Weekdays*) exhibits 200 years of artifacts.

East Hartford   The **Edward King Museum** (*840 Main St. 203-289-6429. Closed Sun. May-Sept.*) chronicles the local histories of tobacco and aviation. At Martin Park, visit the **Huguenot House** (*307 Burnside Ave. 203-568-6178*), the restored home of a colonial saddlemaker; the one-room **Goodwin Schoolhouse** (1820); and the **Burnham Blacksmith Shop** (1850). *Mem. Day-Sept. Thurs., Sun. p.m.; donation requested.*

Manchester   The small but compact **Lutz Children's Museum** (*247 S. Main St. 203-643-0949. Closed Mon.; adm. fee*) features absorbing hands-on exhibits and a big playground. The **Fire Museum** (*230 Pine St. 203-649-9436. Mid-April–mid-Nov. Fri.-Sun. and by appt.; donation requested*), a former fire station, houses equipment from nearly every era of American fire fighting.

Old Sturbridge Village, MASSACHUSETTS (*1 mile W, off US 20. 508-347-3362*) Plan on *at least* a half day to visit this full-scale reconstruction of an 1830s New England rural community. More than 40 buildings were moved here and staffed with farmers and craftspeople. *Closed Mon. Nov.-Mar.; adm. fee.*

Old Sturbridge Village, Mass.

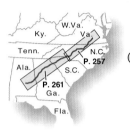

Unless otherwise noted, directions are from interstate, and sites are free and generally open daily. Phone for further information.

① Petersburg, VIRGINIA This city on the Appomattox River quickly grew from a 17th-century frontier trading post into a busy commercial center. Much of the **Old Towne** has been restored. Pick up walking-tour maps at the **Visitor Center** (*Cockade Alley. 804-733-2400 or 800-368-3595*). Sites include the **Appomattox Iron Works** (*20-28 Old St. 804-733-7300. Adm. fee*), a collection of industrial age factories with much of their original equipment; the **Trapezium House** (*Market St. April-Oct.; adm. fee*), built in 1817 by a superstitious Irishman who believed ghosts lived in right-angled corners; and the 1823 brick **Centre Hill Mansion** (*Between Adams and Jefferson Sts. 804-733-2401. Adm. fee*). The **Siege Museum** (*15 W. Bank St. 804-733-2404. Adm. fee*) gives visitors a feel for what Petersburg was like during the Civil War, when Union troops held it under a ten-month siege, the war's longest. The 1735 **Blandford Church** (*321 S. Crater Rd. 804-733-2396. Adm. fee*) is Petersburg's oldest building, with stained-glass windows by Louis Tiffany.

Outside town, at the **Petersburg National Battlefield** (*3 miles E on Va. 36. Visitor Center 804-732-3531. Adm. fee*) and beyond, Union forces besieged the city, threatening Confederate supply lines from June 1864 to April 1865. What once resembled a lunar landscape, ravaged by trenches and shellbursts, is now a shady park.

② Blackstone **Doll House Museum** (*21 miles W on Va. 40 into Blackstone, left on US 460 through town, right on Church St. 804-292-3487*) Fans of things Lilliputian won't mind the long drive through farmland to this museum, crammed with some 4,000 dolls, along with dollhouses and stuffed animals. *Closed Mon.; adm. fee.*

③ John H. Kerr Dam and Reservoir (*16 miles W on US 58 through South Hill, left on Va. 4 past dam to main entrance on left. 804-738-6143*) Travelers wishing to stretch their legs or take home a suntan (in season) should consider any of the numerous parks along this 50,000-acre reservoir, also called Buggs Island Lake. Picnicking, swimming, boating, fishing, and camping. *Fees in summer.*

Trapezium House, Petersburg, Va.

④ Durham, NORTH CAROLINA The **Duke Homestead** (*2828 Duke Homestead Rd. 919-477-5498. Closed Mon. in winter*), built in 1852, provides a glimpse of the modest origins of a wealthy tobacco family. The Duke family endowed Trinity College, which became **Duke University** in 1924. Pick up university maps and brochures at the **Information Office** (*615 Chapel Dr. 919-684-3973/2823*). On the east side of the Gothic campus are the magnificent, 55-acre **Sarah P. Duke Gardens** (*Anderson St.*). Farther in town, at the **North Carolina Museum of Life and Science** (*433 Murray Ave. 919-220-5429. Adm. fee*), kids can simulate earthquakes, look inside a lunar pod, and hear a rabbit's heartbeat.

North of Durham lies **Stagville Center** *(3 miles N on US 501 Bus., right on N.C. 1004 for 7 miles. 919-620-0120. Mon.-Fri.)*, a rustic plantation with four slave houses. An exposed wall inside the plantation house shows how birdlime was mixed with animal hair to fill in the chinks.

Petersburg National Battlefield, Petersburg

West of Durham, **Bennett Place State Historic Site** *(From the south, 1 mile E on US 70, follow signs; from the north, 1 mile W on US 70, follow signs. 919-383-4345. Daily April-Oct., closed Mon. Nov.-March)* marks the spot where Gen. Joseph Johnston surrendered his command to Maj. Gen. William T. Sherman days after Robert E. Lee's surrender at Appomattox in April 1865.

Chapel Hill See I-40, p. 120.

Burlington **Burlington City Park Carousel** *(1 mile N on Alamance Rd., right on Church St. for 0.5 mile. 910-570-1444 or 800-637-3804)* The animals and carriages on this working carousel were hand-carved almost a century ago. *Easter-Halloween Tues.-Sun.; adm. fee.*

Alamance Battleground S.H.S. *(6 miles S on N.C. 62. 910-227-4785)* Here, almost a hundred years before the Civil War, a group of backcountry farmers, known as "Regulators," protested what they considered a corrupt colonial government. They were crushed by militia on May 16, 1771. *Daily April-Oct., closed Mon. Nov.-March.*

Sedalia **Charlotte Hawkins Brown Memorial State Historic Site** *(Rock Creek exit, left on US 70 for 1 mile. 910-449-4846)* Established in 1902 as a pioneer prep school for blacks, the former Palmer Institute is now a monument to an educator's vision. Visitors can see the home of founder Brown, whose labor of love closed in 1971 after graduating more than a thousand students.

Greensboro See I-40, p. 120.

257

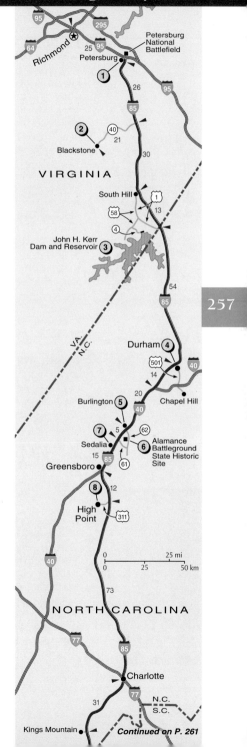

Continued on P. 261

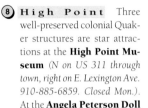 **High Point** Three well-preserved colonial Quaker structures are star attractions at the **High Point Museum** (*N on US 311 through town, right on E. Lexington Ave. 910-885-6859. Closed Mon.*).

Angela Peterson Doll and Miniature Museum, High Point, North Carolina

At the **Angela Peterson Doll and Miniature Museum** (*N on US 311, left on W. Green Dr., left into Visitors Bureau parking lot. 910-885-3655. Closed Mon.; adm. fee*), collectors will love the Nursery, devoted to baby dolls. The Shadow Box Room displays tiny worlds, including a Mexican bullfight.

Charlotte See I-77, p. 210.

Supporters of the *American Revolution* took heart at the news of clear victories in the Carolina backcountry. In the fall of 1780, "over-mountain men" with long rifles crushed a Loyalist force encamped on Kings Mountain. Three months later, Brig. Gen. Dan Morgan won a brilliant success over Col. "Bloody Ban" Tarleton and his mixed force of British Regulars and American Tories. These successes inspired patriots to resist British General Lord Cornwallis's invasion of the South.

258

 **Kings Mountain Natl. Military Park, N.C./S.C.** (*Road to park begins on N.C. 216, which turns into S.C. 216; follow signs. Visitor Center 803-936-7921*) Sprawling across almost 4,000 acres, this park offers a gorgeous 1.5-mile hike through the woods. Fighting among the trees, patriot "over-mountain men" defeated Loyalist militia here in 1780. The living-history farm at neighboring **Kings Mountain State Park** (*803-222-3209*) captures frontier life of the 1850s.

 **Cowpens National Battlefield, SOUTH CAROLINA** (*From the south, 8 miles NW on S.C. 110, right on S.C. 11; from the north, 10 miles NW on S.C. 11. Visitor Center 803-461-2828*) On January 17, 1781, crusty Brig. Gen. Daniel Morgan deployed raw militia and Continental veterans to defeat the enemy in what has been called the "best planned battle of the Revolution."

 **Paris Mountain State Park** (*N on US 25, right on S.C. 253, follow signs. 803-244-5565*) Renting a paddleboat on Lake Placid is an ideal way to see this piney park, established in 1890. Its 4 miles of mountainous roads take time to drive. *Adm. fee.*

 **Greenville** Begin your tour of this attractive city at the **Visitors Bureau** (*500 E. North St. 803-233-0461 or 800-476-8687*). The **Greenville County Museum of Art** (*420 College St. 803-271-7570. Closed Mon.*) sports an impressive collection of contemporary art by Georgia O'Keeffe, Jasper Johns, and others. Stroll down tree-lined Main Street to **Reedy River Falls Park** for a picnic near the falls. The **Greenville Cultural Exchange Center** (*Arlington Ave. and Sumner St. 803-232-9162. Closed Mon.*) has dedicated a room to the memorabilia of native son Jesse Jackson.

"Peachoid" water tower, Gaffney, South Carolina

 **Pendleton** **Historic Pendleton** (*7 miles W on US 76, 1 mile N on S.C. 28. 803-646-3782*) Everything on and around Pendleton's early 19th-century square speaks of history. Many of the houses are privately owned, but two are open as museums. *April-Oct. Sun. only.*

Clemson **Fort Hill** (*11 miles W on US 76, 1 mile S on S.C. 93, follow signs to Clemson University, left on Calhoun Dr., left into Trustees House parking lot. 803-656-2475*) The antebellum home of John C. Calhoun sits in a gardenia-scented garden on Clemson's shady campus. Be sure to take a stroll through the rows of boxwood and magnolia trees. Furnishings are typical of the 1825 to 1850 period, when the statesman and U. S. Vice President lived here.

Carnesville, GEORGIA **Cromer's Mill Covered Bridge** (*9 miles S on Ga. 106 through Carnesville, cross Nail's Creek, take immediate left onto gravel road. On left around bend*) Built about 1907, this wooden bridge saw lots of horse-and-buggy traffic. Now it is safe only for pedestrians.

Winder **Fort Yargo State Park** (*10 miles S on Ga. 211 into Winder, right after courthouse, 1 mile S on Ga. 81. 404-867-3489*) Fort Yargo, a log blockhouse built by settlers in 1792 as protection against Indians, still stands in this woodsy, 1,850-acre park. *Adm. fee.*

Atlanta See I-20, page 72.

Fayetteville **Fayette County/Margaret Mitchell Public Library** (*12 miles S on Ga. 85, left on Johnson Ave., right into Fayette County Annex, follow signs. 404-461-8841*) In this unassuming building, Margaret Mitchell fans find heaven. Hardback first editions of her Pulitzer Prize-winning novel, *Gone With the Wind*, share space with commemorative dolls and plates. A scrapbook of clippings chronicles the Atlanta native's life and work. *Closed Sun.*

Newnan **Shenandoah Environment and Education Center** (*Newnan/Shenandoah exit, right toward Newnan, right at first stoplight onto Amlajack Blvd. into Shenandoah Industrial Park, left on Solar Circle. 404-253-0218 or 800-342-6547 in Ga.*) Kids get hands-on experience with all forms of energy in this joint project of the Georgia Power Company and the Georgia Department of Education. With the touch of a button, they can see how acid rain is tested or a Geiger counter works. A 15-minute walk along the nature trail will stretch your legs. *Closed weekends.*

If Time Permits...

Warm Springs **Little White House** (*31 miles S on US 27 Alt. into Warm Springs, right at stoplight, follow signs. 706-655-3511*) This site will interest students of the Presidency and admirers of FDR. Crippled by polio in 1921, Franklin Delano Roosevelt discovered the soothing powers of the springs near Pine Mountain a few years later. The waters and the mountain air prompted him to build a rustic lodge. Here, in April 1945, FDR died while sitting for a portrait, which stands unfinished in the study. His dog Fala's leash still hangs in the closet. *Adm. fee.*

Little White House, Warm Springs, Georgia

⑳ La Grange **Chattahoochee Valley Art Museum** (*3 miles W on Ga. 109 into La Grange, cross bridge, left on Hines St. 706-882-3267*) This small museum of modern regional art is a delightful surprise. You can see the tiny sculpture garden and exhibitions in less than an hour. *Closed Sun.*

㉑ Pine Mountain **Callaway Gardens** (*7 miles S on I-185, left on US 27 for 11 miles. 706-663-2281 or 800-282-8181*) Plan to spend several hours touring these splendid gardens, where some 700 types of native azaleas bloom from late March through summer. A butterfly center shelters 50 different species. The shores of Mountain Creek Lake are ideal for strolling or sunning. Golf course. *Adm. fee.*

Callaway Gardens, Pine Mountain, Georgia (upper); azaleas at Callaway Gardens (lower)

㉒ Tuskegee National Forest, ALABAMA (*2 miles E on Ala. 186. 205-727-2652*) Parts of this 11,000-acre forest look as they did two centuries ago when William Bartram, King George III's naturalist, hiked through. Today you can view some of the 200 plant species Bartram identified. In the Taska Recreation Area stands a copy of the log cabin where Booker T. Washington was born in Franklin County, Virginia.

260

㉓ Tuskegee **Tuskegee Institute National Historic Site** (*5 miles S on Ala. 81, right on Old Montgomery Rd., right at second stoplight, follow signs. 205-727-3200*) Giving blacks the knowledge and skills to support themselves after slavery was Booker T. Washington's goal when he opened this school in 1881, with 30 students in one room. Today it has more than 161 buildings and an enrollment of 3,500. Begin your tour in the **George Washington Carver Museum** with a look at biographical films and artifacts, then stroll across the campus to see Washington's home, **The Oaks.** If you're interested in the famous Tuskegee Airmen of World War II, the **Chappie James Center** has information and memorabilia.

㉔ Wetumpka **Fort Toulouse–Jackson Park** (*12 miles N on US 231, follow signs. 205-567-3002*) Indians and French soldiers erected a fort here in 1717 to keep a check on nearby British forces. During the War of 1812 American troops built another fort on the site. Today visitors can see the rebuilt French fort, but only the moat of the American fort remains. *Adm. fee.*

㉕ Jasmine Hill Gardens and Outdoor Museum (*14 miles N on US 231, right on Jasmine Hill Rd. for 2 miles. 205-567-6463*) Classical sculpture buffs should budget several hours for this site. The gardens' founders gathered reproductions of famous Greek and Roman sculptures as a hobby; flower gardens atop a high hill serve as backdrop for the vast collection. *Closed Mon.; adm. fee.*

Montgomery *(Visitor Center, 401 Madison Ave. 205-262-0013)* From the Civil War to civil rights, two opposing principles held sway over this hilly city, and the spirit of both is alive and well. The **First White House of the Confederacy** *(644 Washington Ave. 205-242-1861)* claimed that title for only a few months until the capital moved to Richmond in May 1861. President Jefferson Davis's bedroom still holds his belongings. Across the street in the domed **Alabama State Capitol** *(205-242-3184. Closed Sun.)*, Davis was elected president of a new nation in February 1861. Just to the west stands the **Alabama Department of Archives and History** *(624 Washington Ave. 205-242-4363. Closed Sun.)*, home of the state history museum. Two blocks away, the names of 40 civil rights martyrs are inscribed on the **Civil Rights Memorial.** A block north, Dr. Martin Luther King, Jr., served as pastor of the **Dexter Avenue King Memorial Baptist Church** *(454 Dexter Ave. 205-263-3970. Tours weekdays)* from 1954 to 1960. In 1955, Dr. King and his parishioners launched the civil rights movement with a boycott of Montgomery's segregated bus system.

On the city's south side, the **Governor's Mansion** *(1142 S. Perry St. 205-834-3022. By appt. Tues.-Thurs.)* is worth seeing, as is the **F. Scott and Zelda Fitzgerald Museum** *(919 Felder Ave. 205-264-4222. Wed.-Sun.)*. The couple lived here in 1931-32 while the novelist wrote *Tender Is the Night*. On the east side of town, the **Montgomery Museum of Fine Arts** *(One Museum Dr. 205-244-5700. Closed Mon.)* showcases American art and fascinating interactive exhibits for children.

UNTIL JUSTICE ROLLS DOWN LIKE WATERS
ND RIGHTEOUSNESS LIKE A MIGHTY STREAM

MARTIN LUTHER KING JR.

l Rights Memorial, Montgomery, Alabama

Continued on P. 257

Unless otherwise noted, directions are from interstate, and sites are free and generally open daily. Phone for further information.

(1) Adirondack Park, NEW YORK Sprawling between Lake Champlain and the St. Lawrence River is one of the nation's largest areas of near-wilderness—6,000,000 magnificent acres of state-protected mountains, uplands, meadows, plains, lakes, and rivers. The **Newcomb Interpretive Center** (*Frontier Town exit, right on Blue Ridge Rd., then 20 miles to railroad tracks, right onto 28N, follow signs. 518-582-2000*) offers information, programs, and trails.

262

Heart Lake and Algonquin Peak, Adirondack Park, New York

Adirondack Park in autumn

(2) Ausable Chasm (*Ausable Forks or Keeseville exit, follow signs on N.Y. 9N. 518-834-7454*) The chasm was formed more than 500 million years ago, when an arm of the sea partly bordered the Adirondack Mountains. Hike sandstone cliffs, cross the gorge on bridges, or shoot rapids by boat. *Mem. Day-Columbus Day; adm. fee.*

(3) Lake George (*3 miles N on N.Y. 9N to Lake George Village*) The 32-mile-long lake dotted with more than 200 islands offers something for everyone—from the village with its T-shirt shops, arcades, and lovely public beaches to expensive lakeside resort hotels. Cruise the lake on **Lake George Steamboat Company** boats (*Steel Pier, Beach Rd. 518-668-5777. Mid-May–Labor Day; adm. fee*), carrying passengers since 1817. Kids will enjoy the *Minne-Ha-Ha*, which leaves port with its steam calliope merrily playing. At **Fort William Henry** (*Beach Rd. 518-668-5471. May–mid-Oct.; adm. fee*), across from Steel Pier, military drills and cannon firings are reenacted at the restored 18th-century fort.

Steamboat on Lake George, New York

Glens Falls **The Hyde Collection** *(161 Warren St. 518-792-1761)* exhibits Botticelli, El Greco, Whistler, and other artists in a 1912 Florentine Renaissance villa-museum complex. *Closed Mon.; adm. fee.*

Wilton **Grant Cottage State Historic Site** *(Follow signs for 3 miles toward US 9 and Mt. McGregor Correct. Facility. 518-587-8277)* Ulysses S. Grant finished his memoirs here, days before he died in 1885. The cottage is preserved as he left it. *Mem. Day-Labor Day Wed.-Sun., weekends in Sept.; adm. fee.*

Saratoga Springs *(W on N.Y. 50, follow signs. Chamber of Commerce, 494 Broadway. 518-584-3255)* The downtown jewel of this longtime mecca for the health and horse conscious is **Congress Park**, where fashionable travelers of 100 years ago strolled the promenades and took the waters. In the park, **Canfield Casino**, an 1870s Italianate former gambling casino, now houses the historical society museums, including the **Walworth Memorial Museum** *(518-584-6920. Adm. fee)*, which portrays the life of a prominent Saratoga Springs family. The 2,000-acre, mineral-spring-studded **Saratoga Spa State Park** *(1 mile S on US 9. 518-514-2000)* offers year-round recreation. On its grounds, the **National Museum of Dance** *(S. Broadway. 518-584-2225. Mem. Day-Labor Day Tues.-Sun.; adm. fee)* is the nation's only museum devoted exclusively to American professional dance. **Saratoga Performing Arts Center** *(518-587-3330. Adm. fee)*, also in the park, hosts summer performances by the New York City Ballet, the Philadelphia Orchestra, and the New York City Opera. The **Roosevelt Mineral Baths** *(518-584-2011. July-Aug. Tues.-Sun., Wed.-Sun. rest of year; adm. fee)* offers relaxing baths and massages. The **Saratoga Harness Hall of Fame** *(352 Jefferson St. 518-587-4210. Tues.-Sat. in summer, Thurs.-Sat. in spring and fall; closed Dec.-April)* at the raceway exhibits harness-racing memorabilia; and the **National Museum of Racing and Hall of Fame** *(Union Ave. 518-584-0400. Adm. fee)* traces over 300 years of thoroughbred history.

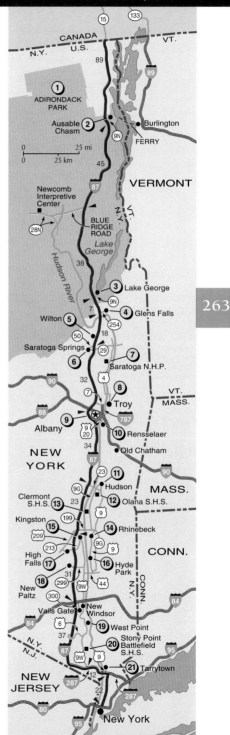

(7) Saratoga National Historical Park *(11 miles E on N.Y. 29, 13 miles S on US 4. Visitor Center 518-664-9821)* Here in 1777, American troops proved they could beat the British, thus convincing the French to enter the Revolutionary War on their side. Among the highlights at this 2,800-acre park are the **Saratoga Monument,** a 155-foot memorial marking British Maj. Gen. Burgoyne's surrender; and the **Schuyler House** *(Mem. Day-Labor Day Wed.-Sun.; adm. fee),* restored summer home of American Maj. Gen. Philip Schuyler, with period furnishings.

(8) Troy *(4 miles E on N.Y. 7)* Exhibits at the **Junior Museum** *(3 miles N on US 4 to 282 5th Ave. 518-235-2120)* include a discovery room, an 1855 log cabin, and a planetarium. *Wed.-Sun.; adm. fee.*

(9) Albany The nation's oldest city (1686) still operating under its original charter was settled by the Dutch. Albany's present-day bustle reminds us that this is the capital of the Empire State. At the excellent **Visitor Center** *(25 Quackenbush Sq. 518-434-6311),* pick up a copy of *Capital Capital! A cityWalk Tour,* which traces the city's development through its buildings and street patterns. The tour passes the 1798 **First Church of Albany** *(N. Pearl St. at Clinton Sq. 518-463-4449),* with America's oldest pulpit and weathervane (1656); and the 1881 Romanesque **City Hall** *(Eagle St. 518-434-5132. Closed weekends),* designed by H. H. Richardson. Nearby, the **State Capitol** *(518-474-2418. Tours)* is noted for its elaborate carvings and "Million Dollar Staircase." In the Plaza, the **New York State Museum** *(518-474-5877),* one of the nation's oldest and largest state museums, recounts New York history through full-scale dioramas, sound, and video. One block away is the **Schuyler Mansion** *(32 Catherine St. 518-434-0834. Mid-April–Oct. Wed.-Sun.; by appt. in winter),* the elegantly furnished Georgian home of Maj. Gen. Philip Schuyler. On the other side of the capitol, the **Albany Institute of History and Art** *(125 Wash. Ave. 518-463-4478. Closed Mon.)* celebrates the culture of Albany and the Upper Hudson Valley region.

State Capitol, Albany, New York

(10) Rensselaer **Crailo State Historic Site** *(Across the river from Albany on US 9, 9 1/2 Riverside Ave. 518-463-8738)* Exhibits in this early 18th-century Dutch house tell the story of the region's Dutch heritage. *Mid-April–mid-Oct. Wed.-Sun.*

Old Chatham *(15 miles E on I-90)* See I-90, p. 291.

Hudson *(6 miles E on N.Y. 23)* The **American Museum of Firefighting** *(Harry Howard Ave. 518-828-7695)* holds one of the U. S.'s best collections of firefighting equipment and memorabilia.

Olana State Historic Site *(Exit at Rip Van Winkle Bridge, cross bridge, bear right for 1 mile on N.Y. 9G. 518-828-0135)* The Persian Gothic castle and gardens of Hudson River school artist Frederic Edwin Church, who designed the mansion, command a fabulous river view. *Mid-April–Oct. Wed.-Sun., gardens year-round; adm. fee. Reservations suggested for house tour.*

Warren Street in historic Hudson, New York

Clermont State Historic Site *(Past Olana on N.Y. 9G for 10 miles, follow signs. 518-537-4240)* Oldest of the mid-Hudson's great riverfront estates, Clermont was the home of Robert R. Livingston, negotiator of the Louisiana Purchase and benefactor of steamboat inventor Robert Fulton (hence Fulton's boat *Clermont*). *Mid-April–last Sun. in Oct. Wed.-Sun., grounds open all year.*

Rhinebeck **Old Rhinebeck Aerodrome** *(4 miles E on N.Y. 199, 1 mile N on US 9, then right on Stone Church Rd. 914-758-8610)* Take to the air in a 1929 open cockpit biplane, watch a live dogfight *(Sun. only)*, or just wander through three buildings filled with vintage aircraft, automobiles, and other vehicles. *Air shows on weekends June–mid-Oct. Aerodrome open mid-May–Oct.; adm. fee.*

Kingston Settled in 1652, Kingston was New York's first state capital. Its attractions are concentrated in two sections. The **Rondout Area** is a revitalized 19th-century waterfront community. Exhibits in the **Hudson River Maritime Museum** *(1 Rondout Landing. 914-338-0071. May-Oct.; adm. fee)* recall the golden age of river commerce. Excursion boats go to the 20th-century Rondout II Lighthouse. Many other points of interest lie within the **Uptown Area**, which includes the **Stockade**, rich in prerevolutionary sites. Tours and self-guided walking maps are offered at the **Kingston Urban Cultural Park Center** *(308 Clinton Sq. 914-331-9506. Jan.-April Wed.-Mon., Thurs.-Sun. rest of year)*, devoted to preserving the city's history. The **Senate House State Historic Site** *(296 Fair St. 914-338-2786. Mid-April–Oct. Wed.-Sun., off-season by appt.)* commemorates the first meeting of New York's senate in Sept. 1777. Today the museum exhibits paintings and artifacts. The 1852 ceiling in the **Old Dutch Church** *(Main and Wall Sts. 914-338-6759. Closed weekends)* is reminiscent of English architect Christopher Wren.

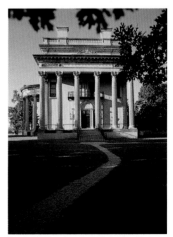

Hyde Park McKim, Mead & White executed one of their most extravagant commissions at the **Vanderbilt Mansion National Historic Site** *(S of Rhinebeck on US 9.*

Vanderbilt Mansion, Hyde Park, New York

Homecoming Parade, U. S. Military Academy, West Point, New York

266

Henry Hudson claimed the territory you see along I-87 for the Netherlands in 1609, and a *Dutch flavor* lingers in the names of local towns and natural features. Berg means "mountain"; Dunderberg is "Thunder Mountain." A kil is a "stream," as in Kaaterskill or Beaver Kill. The Tappan Zee, a broad basin of the Hudson between Tarrytown and Nyack, is the "cold spring sea," a hybrid of a local Indian word and the Dutch "zee."

Visitor Center 914-229-9115. Closed Tues.-Wed. Nov.-March; adm. fee), a 54-room beaux arts mansion with 212-acre grounds. The sprawling colonial revival birthplace and home of FDR at **Franklin Delano Roosevelt National Historic Site** (*US 9. 914-229-9115. Closed Tues.-Wed. Nov.-March; adm. fee*) is decorated as it was at the time of his death in 1945. The President and his wife are buried here, and the **FDR Library/Museum** (*914-229-8114. Adm. fee*) is on the grounds. While the President was alive, **Val-Kill—the Eleanor Roosevelt National Historic Site** (*2 miles E of the FDR Site to N.Y. 9G. 914-229-9115. April-Oct. and winter weekends*) was a recreational retreat; after he died, Eleanor lived here until her death in 1962.

⑰ **High Falls** **Delaware & Hudson Canal Museum** (*Kingston exit, S on US 209, left on N.Y. 213 to High Falls, and right onto Mohonk Rd. 914-687-9311*) Located near original canal locks, this hands-on museum tells the story of life along the canal. *Mem. Day-Labor Day Thurs.-Mon., weekends in May, Sept.-Oct.; adm. fee.*

⑱ **New Paltz** **Huguenot Street** (*Info at Deyo Assembly Hall, 6 Broadhead. 914-255-1889*) is the oldest street in America with original houses. Six of the stone houses, built between 1692 and 1712, are authentically furnished and open for tours. *Weekends June-Sept.*

Vails Gate See I-84 E, p. 253.

⑲ **West Point** (*Harriman exit, 12 miles, E on US 6, N on US 9W, follow signs*) Strategically situated above the Hudson, the Point has been a military stronghold since 1778. Thomas Jefferson authorized the **U. S. Military Academy** (*914-938-2638; parade info 914-938-3614*) in 1802. The **West Point Museum** (*914-938-2517*) contains one of the hemisphere's largest military collections.

⑳ **Stony Point Battlefield S. H. S.** (*6 miles E on US 6, 7 miles S on US 9W. 914-786-2521*) The storming of Stony Point by Americans under Brig. Gen. Anthony Wayne was one of the Rev-

olution's brilliant actions. Museum. *Mid-April–Oct. Wed.-Sun.*

㉑ Tarrytown Lyndhurst
(From Tappan Zee Bridge, 0.5 mile S on US 9 to 635 S. Broadway. 914-631-0046. May-Oct. Tues.-Sun., weekends rest of year; adm. fee), the 1838 Gothic Revival home of railroad robber baron Jay Gould, overlooks the Hudson from the east. A mile south on US 9, Washington Irving renovated a two-room Dutch tenant farmer's cottage in 1835 into **Sunnyside**

Philipsburg Manor, N. Tarrytown, N. Y.

(W. Sunnyside La. 914-591-8763. March-Dec. Wed.-Mon., weekends Jan.-Feb.; adm. fee), which he described as "all made up of gable ends, and as full of angles…as an old cocked hat." Irving's gardens are still maintained. The Dutch manor house at **Philipsburg Manor Upper Mills** *(N on US 9 for 2 miles to N. Tarrytown. 914-631-3992),* on a 52,000-acre estate, has costumed guides; a walking bridge over a dam leads to a working gristmill. The farm features colonial-era animal breeds. *March-Dec. Wed.-Mon.; adm. fee.*

267

New York City   See I-95, pp. 328-29.

Lyndhurst, Jay Gould's country retreat, Tarrytown, New York

Interior of Lyndhurst

Unless otherwise noted, directions are from interstate, and sites are free and generally open daily. Phone for further information.

(1) Missisquoi National Wildlife Refuge, VERMONT *(5 miles W of Swanton on Vt. 78. 802-868-4781)* Canoeing and birding are favorite activities at this 5,839-acre wetlands at the head of the Missisquoi River. Waterfowl, marsh hawks, great blue herons, and some 200 other species of birds live here.

(2) Lake Champlain Islands *(N on US 2)* Sparsely populated and agricultural, Grand Isle County encompasses an elongated archipelago and the southern end of a peninsula stretching south from Canada between two bays of Lake Champlain. Four miles from the exit, en route to the islands, lies **Sand Bar State Park** *(802-893-2825. Memorial Day-Labor Day; adm. fee)*, one of Lake Champlain's finest beaches. Continue 14 miles north on US 2 to the **Hyde Log Cabin** *(802-828-3226. July 4-Labor Day Thurs.-Mon.; adm. fee)* in Grand Isle. Built in 1783 by frontiersman Jedediah Hyde, Jr., it is reputedly one of the oldest log cabins in the country. In North Hero, another 5 miles north, you can admire the **Royal Lipizzan Stallions of Austria** *(802-372-5683. July-Labor Day Thurs.-Sat. at 6 p.m. and Sat.-Sun. at 2:30 p.m.; adm. fee)* as they step to music with intricate promenades, graceful pirouettes, and soaring leaps.

Colchester Reef Lighthouse, Shelburne Museum, Vermont

(3) Burlington *(Lake Champlain Regional Chamber of Commerce, 60 Main St. 802-863-3489)* Before heading downtown, visit the **Ethan Allen Homestead** *(W on US 2 to Vt. 127, N to first exit for North Ave. Beaches, first right at green sign. 802-865-4556. Daily mid-June–Labor Day, Tues.-Sun. p.m. mid-May–mid-June, p.m. only Labor Day-Oct.; adm. fee)*. The Revolutionary War hero spent the last two years of his life in this 1780s farmhouse.

Compact Burlington sits on a hillside overlooking Lake Champlain. Most of its sites are located downtown, within a few blocks of each other. Begin with a stroll down **Church Street,** a lively outdoor mall filled with shops, cafés, and pushcart vendors. At the head of Church Street stands the 1816 Georgian **First Unitarian Church** *(152 Pearl St. 802-862-5630. Closed Mon.)*. Its bell is a copy of one cast by Paul Revere. Then head downhill to the shores of Lake Champlain and **Waterfront Park,** a new pedestrian walkway and bike path with a great view of the Adirondacks. For an inexpensive cruise on Lake Champlain, take a ride on the **Port Kent Ferry** *(802-864-9804. Mid-May–mid-Oct.; fare charge)*, which leaves from the pier at nearby King Street. Excursion boats also depart from nearby **Burlington Boathouse** *(802-862-9685. May-Oct.; fare charge)*. Walk up Lake Street to **Battery Park,** site of an artillery battery that repelled the British during the War of 1812. Burlington's hill is topped with the spires of the **University of Vermont,** founded by Ethan Allen's brother, Ira. Its **Robert Hull Fleming Museum** *(61 Colchester Ave. 802-656-0750. Closed Mon. and university holidays; donation*

Sign at Ben & Jerry's, Waterbury, Vermont

requested) houses both Western and non-Western art and ethnographic material.

Shelburne Farms (*5 miles S of Burlington on US 7 to Bay Rd. 802-985-8686*) Frederick Law Olmsted designed the grounds of this thousand-acre estate on Lake Champlain, now a working farm you can tour on a 90-minute wagon ride. *Tours mid-May–mid-Oct., Visitor Center open year-round; adm. fee.*

Shelburne Museum (*7 miles S of Burlington on US 7. 802-985-3344*) It's been called "New England's Smithsonian." And deservedly so. The state's largest attraction offers a 45-acre, 37-building assemblage of 18th- and 19th-century folk art, artifacts, and architecture that includes everything from the 220-foot side-wheeler *Ticonderoga* to an impressive group of wildfowl decoys. *Late May–late Oct. self-guided tours, rest of year guided tours at 1 p.m. (reservations suggested); adm. fee.*

Richmond **Old Round Church** (*Richmond exit, 2 miles S on US 2 to Richmond, 0.5 mile SW on Bridge St. 802-434-2556*) This 16-sided church, which appears round, was built in 1813 by five different denominations. *Daily July 4–Labor Day, weekends only Memorial Day–early Oct.; donation requested.*

Waterbury **Ben & Jerry's** (*1 mile N on Vt. 100. 802-244-TOUR. No ice cream production on Sun.; adm. fee*) Cherry Garcia, Wavy Gravy, Chunky Monkey—it's all made here in the ice cream capital of Vermont. Watch the process while sampling the flavor of the day. For a more traditional treat, continue 2 miles north on Vt. 100 to **Cold Hollow Cider Mill** (*Waterbury Center. 802-244-8771*), Vermont's largest producer of fresh apple cider. Watch the press in action and sip a free cup of cider.

Montpelier A drive through downtown Montpelier will confirm that it is, indeed, the nation's smallest state capital. But what it lacks in size, it makes up for in charm. Parking is easy, people are friendly, and the shops and cafés give it a cosmopolitan flair. The Greek Revival **State House** (*State St. 802-*

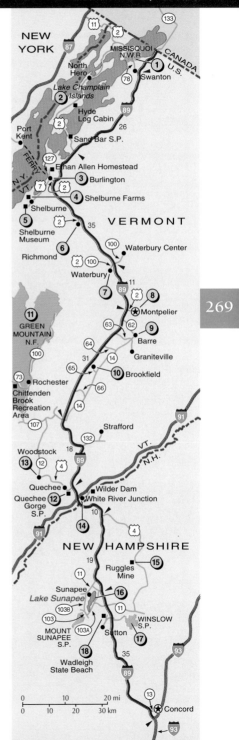

828-2228. *Tours weekdays and Sat. July-Oct.)* was built between 1857 and 1859 of granite from nearby Barre. That's Ceres, the Roman goddess of agriculture, atop the gold-leaf dome; patriot-statesman Ethan Allen guards the massive front doors. Next door you'll find the **Vermont Historical Society Museum** *(Pavilion Bldg., 109 State St. 802-828-2291. Closed Mon.; adm. fee),* which explores the state's past through costumes, furnishings, tools, and other memorabilia. To visit the **T. W. Wood Gallery and Arts Center** *(College St. 802-828-8743. Closed Mon. and Christmas-Jan.; adm. fee),* walk 6 blocks down State Street to College Hall. Founded in 1895, the gallery houses an excellent collection of Vermont fine art.

No trip through Vermont would be complete without a tour of a working sugarhouse. The Morse family has been making maple syrup at **Morse Farm** *(2.5 miles N on Main St. and County Rd. 802-223-2740)* for seven generations and welcomes visitors.

⑨ B a r r e *(4 miles E on Vt. 62)* Built on a vein of granite 4 by 6 miles in area and at least 10 miles deep, this city is known as the Granite Capital of the World. **Rock of Ages quarry** *(8 miles E of I-89 on Vt. 63, follow signs through Graniteville. 802-476-3119. Visitor Center daily May-Oct., tours June–mid-Oct. Mon.-Fri.; fee for tours)* offers tours of a working quarry. You can guide yourself around the **Rock of Ages Manufacturing Division** *(1 mile W of quarry on Vt. 63. Closed weekends),* where monuments are cut and carved. **Hope Cemetery** *(1 mile N on Vt. 14)* is filled with fine examples of local craftsmanship.

⑩ B r o o k f i e l d **Floating Bridge** *(11 miles SE on Vt. 64, Vt. 14, and Vt. 65)* Because Sunset Lake is too deep for pilings, this 1820s wood bridge once floated on logs. It now rests on plastic pontoons.

⑪ G r e e n   M o u n t a i n   N a t i o n a l   F o r e s t With more than 350,000 acres stretching nearly two-thirds the length of Vermont, this forest embraces half of the state's public lands. The ranger station in **Rochester** *(14 miles W on Vt. 107, 9 miles N on Vt. 100. 802-767-4261)* provides information on activities and car tours. You can camp at the **Chittenden Brook Recreation Area** *(8 miles SW of Rochester on Vt. 100 and Vt. 73. Camping fee in summer),* a trailhead for several hiking and cross-country ski trails.

⑫ Q u e c h e e   G o r g e *(4 miles W on US 4. 802-*

Camels Hump, Green Mountains, Vermont

When the sap begins to rise in the sugar maples, it's time for ***sugar on snow.*** To make this Vermont rite of spring, simply boil maple syrup down and cool it on packed snow. The result: a cloyingly delicious, taffylike candy. (Don't eat the snow!) Revive your palate the Vermont way, with a dill pickle and raised doughnut. No one knows who first combined these unlikely foods. Perhaps the housewife who sent her husband off to the sugarhouse with a lunch box filled with her kitchen's bounty.

270

295-7900) This deep chasm, the centerpiece of a state park, is called the Grand Canyon of Vermont. Near the bridge spanning the gorge are an overlook and a trail down to the bottom.

Church on the Green, Strafford Village, Vt., 8 miles north on Vt. 132 and Justin Smith Morrill Hwy.

Woodstock *(10 miles W on US 4 through Quechee to junction with Vt. 12)* Its green surrounded by tidy federal houses, Woodstock more than lives up to your fantasy of the perfect New England town. The **Billings Farm & Museum** *(0.5 mile N on Vt. 12. 802-457-2355)* portrays 1890s farm life. *Daily May-Oct., weekends only Nov.-Dec.; adm. fee.*

White River Junction *(N on I-91 to first exit)* A century-old steam locomotive known as **Old 494** *(Railroad Row, intersection of N. and S. Main Sts.)* proclaims the town's former prominence as a train depot. (Amtrak's *Montrealer* still stops here.) It's now better known as the home of a leading regional microbrewery, **Catamount Brewing Company** *(58 S. Main St. 802-296-2248. Tours daily July-Oct., Sat. only Nov.-June).*

Wilder Dam See I-91, p. 294.

Ruggles Mine, NEW HAMPSHIRE *(22 miles E on US 4, follow signs. 603-523-4275)* Worth the detour, this 190-year-old mine atop Isinglass Mountain has yielded more than 150 types of minerals. Visitors can prospect and keep their finds. *Daily mid-June–mid-Oct., weekends only mid-May–mid-June; adm. fee.*

Lake Sunapee *(4 miles S on N.H. 11 to N.H. 103)* Ten-mile-long Lake Sunapee is set like a jewel amid the surrounding hills. Picturesque **Sunapee**, just off N.H. 11, bustles with shops, restaurants, and excursion boats. Artifacts in the **Historical Society Museum** *(603-783-2449. Mid-June–Labor Day, no set schedule)* date from the turn of the century, when Lake Sunapee was a grand resort. **Mount Sunapee State Park** *(5 miles S of Sunapee on N.H. 103B. 603-763-2356 or 800-258-3530)* offers downhill skiing in winter and a scenic chairlift ride in summer. Across the road you can rent canoes and sailboards at a lovely public beach. *Beach open all year, but lifeguard only on duty daily mid-June–Labor Day and weekends Mem. Day–mid-June; adm. fee Mem. Day-Labor Day only.*

Winslow State Park *(N from Sutton exit, right on North Rd. for 0.5 mile, left on Kearsarge Valley Rd. for 3.5 miles, right on Mountain Rd. for 2 miles. 603-526-6168)* Mount Kearsarge affords magnificent 360° views, especially at sunset. Hiking trails. *Adm. fee.*

Wadleigh State Beach *(Sutton exit, right on N.H. 114. 603-927-4724)* For a few relaxing hours at an uncrowded beach, make a stop at Kezar Lake. *Memorial Day-Labor Day; adm. fee.*

Concord See I-93, p. 302.

Marina on Puget Sound

When asked her opinion of Seattle, humorist Fran Liebowitz replied, "It's cute. Why are they tearing it down?" She was referring to the city's propensity for remodeling: During the past century, Seattle refashioned itself in brick after the Great Fire of 1889, raised its streets, regraded its steep waterfront, buried its tidelands, sacrificed a river, binged on skyscrapers—and it's still changing.

In the 1980s word got out that damp,

272

remote, lovely Seattle was a sleeper, a last best place ruled by mountains and water. The media hyped it, and the rush was on. Now even Seattle has to contend with big-city problems. Still, it's a city at the edge whose spirit is young and brash, a conglomerate of distinct neighborhoods (Visitor Center, 8th and Pike

Aluminum sculptures in the Fremont district

Sts. 206-461-5840).

Plunge in downtown and join the throng at **Pike Place Market** (*Pike St. and 1st Ave.*). Founded in 1907, this 7-acre, 16-building market is a colorful, kinetic circus where you'll find everything from pottery to fresh fish. Choose your picnic fixings, then feast on views of the bay, the islands, and Mount Rainier. More visual pleasures are at hand in the dramatic new **Seattle Art Museum** (*100 University St. 206-654-3100. Closed Mon.; adm. fee*), noted for its Asian and African collections.

Pike Place Hillclimb is the scenic route down to the waterfront and the incomparable **Seattle Aquarium** (*Pier 59, Waterfront Park. 206-386-4320. Adm. fee*), where innovative exhibits reveal the world beneath Puget Sound. Next door, the **Omnidome** (*206-622-1869. Adm. fee*) screens a changing repertoire of films projected on a 180° dome. If the weather is fine, take a **harbor tour** (*Piers 55 and 57. 206-623-4252. Schedules vary; fare charge*) or hop a **ferry** (*Pier 50, for passengers only, or Pier 52, for autos and passengers. 206-464-6400. Fare charge*) to Seattle's commuter islands.

Walk east on 1st Avenue, and you'll run into historic **Pioneer Square,** where settlers put down the city's roots. Now it's rife with galleries, restaurants, Euro-style cafés, nightclubs, shops, and gold rush-era architecture. After the 1889 fire, a new city went up on top of the ruins.

Space Needle and downtown skyline

The **Underground Tour** *(Doc Maynard's Public House, 610 1st Ave. 206-682-1511 or, for reservations, 682-4646. Adm. fee)* offers a fascinating walk through subterranean Seattle. The **Klondike Gold Rush National Historical Park** *(117 S. Main St. 206-553-7220)* presents this lively chapter in the city's story.

A mania for coffee

Nearby Chinatown testifies to Seattle's Asian heritage, honored at the modest **Wing Luke Asian Museum** *(407 7th Ave. S. 206-623-5124. Closed Mon.; adm. fee, except Thurs.).* Across town, the inimitable 605-foot **Space Needle** *(Adm. fee to observation deck)* marks the 74-acre **Seattle Center** *(Visitor Center, 305 Harrison St. 206-684-8582),* legacy of the 1962 World's Fair. Highlights include the six-building **Pacific Science Center** *(200 2nd Ave. N. 206-443-2001. Adm. fee)* and the **Children's Museum** *(Center House. 206-298-2521. Closed Mon., except holidays; adm. fee),* featuring a pint-size play neighborhood.

Among Seattle's outstanding parks are **Discovery Park** *(3801 W. Government Way. 206-386-4236),* a 534-acre urban wilderness with 7 miles of hiking trails; the **Washington Park Arboretum**

(2300 Arboretum Dr. E. 206-543-8800); the serenely beautiful **Japanese Garden** *(Lake Washington Blvd. E. 206-684-4725. March-Nov.; adm. fee);* and **Volunteer Park** *(E. Prospect St. and 14th Ave. N. 206-625-8901)* in the funky Capitol Hill area. **Woodland Park Zoological Gardens** *(5500 Phinney Ave. N. 206-684-4800. Adm. fee),* rated one of the country's top ten zoos, has replaced bars and cement with innovative natural habitats.

Along the Lake Washington Ship Canal in Ballard, you can watch boats pass through historic **Hiram M. Chittenden Locks** *(3015 N.W. 54th St. 206-783-7059).* Added bonuses: a botanical garden and a fish ladder with windows for observing migrating trout and salmon.

Pike Place Market

Seattle boasts a number of good **microbreweries** that welcome callers. Pick up a list at the Visitor Center.

Fishing for steelhead, Snoqualmie Falls, Washington

274

Unless otherwise noted, directions are from interstate, and sites are free and generally open daily. Phone for more information.

② **North Bend-Snoqualmie Area** (*Upper Snoqualmie Valley Chamber of Commerce, 1422 N. Bend Blvd. 206-888-4440*) Fame came to these valley towns thanks to David Lynch's dark television series *Twin Peaks.* Die-hard fans will recognize North Bend's **Mount Si,** the show's commercial signature—and one of Washington's most popular hikes. For train buffs, the Puget Sound & Snoqualmie Valley Railroad maintains a **Railroad Museum** (*109 King St. in Snoqualmie. 206-746-4025 or 888-0373. Sun. only April-Memorial Day, Thurs.-Sun. Memorial Day-Labor Day*) in the historic 1890 Snoqualmie Depot. From here, you can hop on a vintage steam or diesel train (*Weekends only Apr.-Oct. and two weekends in Dec.; fare charge*) for a 10-mile round-trip to North Bend, where you can also get aboard. Tucked between Snoqualmie and Fall City in the foothills of the Cascades, **Snoqualmie Falls Park** (*3 miles N on Wash. 202*) overlooks the Snoqualmie River's spectacular 268-foot cascade—100 feet higher than Niagara Falls. Not far away is the **Snoqualmie Winery** (*Snoqualmie Falls exit to 1000 Winery Rd. 206-888-4000. Tours and tastings*), worth a visit for the mountain views alone.

③ **Ellensburg** The county seat and hub of central Washington's cattle trade, Ellensburg considers itself a cowboy town. The biggest event of the year is the Labor Day rodeo, ranked among the top ten in the United States. Another highlight: the **Clymer Museum & Gallery** (*416 N. Pearl St. 509-962-6416. Adm. fee*), which honors renowned Western artist and native son John Clymer and also spotlights other American painters. Historic **Olmstead Place State Park** (*Canyon Rd. exit, 4.5 miles E on Kittitas Hwy. 509-925-1943.*

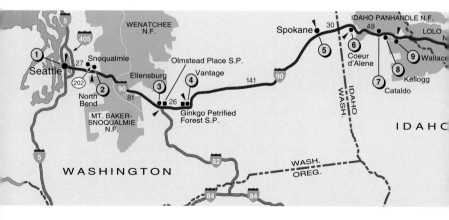

Tours Mem. Day-Labor Day Sat.-Sun. and by appt.) brings to life one of the valley's earliest homesteads, including original furnishings.

Vantage   **Ginkgo Petrified Forest State Park** *(Old Vantage Hwy., follow signs. 509-856-2700. Park open year-round, interpretive center mid-May–mid-Sept.)* A fossil forest set in the scruffy sagebrush desert of central Washington, the park harbors a greater diversity of petrified wood than anywhere else in the world. Rarest of all are specimens of the ancient ginkgo tree. Interpretive trail.

Along I-90 just east of Vantage, look to the east and you'll see silhouetted horses dancing across a barren hilltop; it's a monumental sculpture, **"Grandfather Cuts Loose the Ponies,"** carved by David Govedare. Eastbound travelers can exit for a closer look *(Follow signs to Wild Horses Sculpture).*

Spokane   *(Convention & Visitors Bureau, 926 W. Sprague Ave. 509-747-3230 or 800-248-3230)* Spokan-ee Indians called their fishing grounds Spokan. Despite the "e," added later, it's still pronounced "spo-CAN." Regional history dominates the **Cheney Cowles Museum** *(W. 2316 1st Ave. 509-456-3931)*, which also houses an art gallery. Next door stands the historic **Campbell House** *(Closed Mon.; adm. fee)*, a turn-of-the-century mansion.

The city devotes acres to green space. **Riverfront Park** *(Adm. fees to attractions)*, site of Expo '74, harbors a 1909 carousel, park train, gondola ride over Spokane Falls, and an IMAX theater. Other beauty spots include **Manito Park and Botanical Gardens** *(4 W. 21st Ave. 509-625-6622. Park open year-round, Japanese Garden Apr.-Oct.)* and the **John A. Finch Arboretum** *(3404 Woodland Blvd. 509-625-6655)*. The 60-mile **Spokane River Centennial Trail,** which wends from downtown well into Idaho, attracts bicyclists and walkers. At the east edge of town you'll find **Arbor Crest** *(N. 4705 Fruithill Rd. 509-927-9894)*. More than just a winery—of which Spokane boasts four—it occupies an enchanting bluff-top estate.

The Pacific Northwest loves its ***coffee***. Not just any coffee, mind you. The beans of choice are high quality (about 25 percent are specialty blends) and roasted by one of a dozen or so area companies. Coffee bars abound. Best explained as an antidote to the damp weather, the coffee mania began in the 1970s, when Starbucks opened Seattle's first roasting company. Today caffeine is a hard-core habit; junkies even speak in code when ordering their hits: "a double tall *latte* with two percent," "a Yankee Dog with a White Hat on a Leash," or "a Thunder Thighs." Go figure.

275

Continued on P. 278

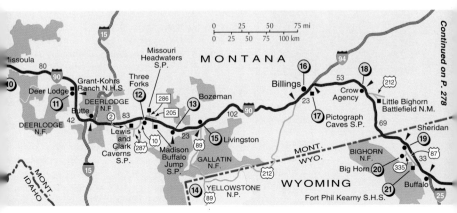

Lake Coeur d'Alene sunset, Idaho

⑥ Coeur d'Alene, IDAHO True blue and pine bound, splendid **Lake Coeur d'Alene** is the star attraction of this upscale playground. A delightful vantage point is the 3,300-foot-long floating boardwalk at **Coeur d'Alene Resort** (*On the waterfront*), which may inspire you to take a **cruise** (*Lake Coeur d'Alene Cruises. 208-765-4000. May-Oct.; fare charge*). More challenging are the scenic trails at **Tubbs Hill** (*Loop trailhead at parking lot between McEuen Park and the resort; park office, 221 S. 5th St. 208-769-2252*). For a lesson in Kootenai County history, stop by the **Museum of North Idaho** (*115 Northwest Blvd. 208-664-3448. Tues.-Sat. Apr.-Oct., Sun. only July-Aug.; adm. fee*).

⑦ Cataldo The **Old Mission State Park** (*208-682-3814. Adm. fee*) shelters the Old Sacred Heart Mission (1850-53), the oldest standing structure in Idaho.

⑧ Kellogg This small town takes its name from the discoverer of the Bunker Hill silver bonanza. The current boom is skiing on **Silver Mountain** (*610 Bunker Ave. 208-783-1111. Adm. fee*). The resort sports seven lifts, including one of the world's longest single-stage gondolas, stretching 3.1 miles and rising 3,400 vertical feet. Summer offerings include gondola rides, mountain biking, horseback riding, and concerts in the amphitheater at the top of the gondola ride.

Old Sacred Heart Mission, Cataldo, Idaho

⑨ Wallace This old mining camp lies in Silver Valley, a leading silver producer. (Wallace also produced Lana Turner.) You can see an underground operation on the **Sierra Silver Mine Tour** (*420 5th St. 208-752-5151. May–mid-Oct.; adm. fee*). Train history and memorabilia dominate the **Northern Pacific Depot Railroad Museum** (*219 6th St. 208-752-0111. Adm. fee*) in the restored 1901 station.

⑩ Missoula, MONTANA (*Chamber of Commerce, 825 E. Front St. 406-543-6623*) Geographical hub of five forested valleys, this mill town and university seat is also a cultural center, notoriously liberal despite its blue-collar core. Art enthusiasts will want to check out the **Missoula Museum of the Arts** (*335 N. Pattee St. 406-728-0447. Closed Sun.; adm. fee*), the **Monte Dolack Gallery** (*139 W. Front St. 406-549-3248. Closed Sun.*), and the **Sutton West Gallery** (*121 W. Broadway. 406-721-5460. Closed Sun.*). There's also the **Historical Museum at Fort Missoula** (*Off South

Ave., follow signs. 406-728-3476. Closed Mon.) and the **Rocky Mountain Elk Foundation's Wildlife Visitor Center** *(2291 W. Broadway. 406-523-4545).* For a behind-the-scenes look at a training center for U. S. Forest Service firefighters, stop at the **Smokejumper and Aerial Fire Depot Visitor Center** *(7 miles W on Broadway. 406-329-4900. Memorial Day-Labor Day; call about off-season tours).*

Smoke jumpers, Missoula, Montana

Deer Lodge Since the 1850s, livestock has been the trade of Montana's second oldest city, named for a popular salt lick. Memorializing the frontier cattle era, **Grant-Kohrs Ranch National Historic Site** *(Main St. 406-846-2070. Adm. fee in summer only),* one of the state's oldest and biggest ranches, is also the best preserved in the country, with 90 structures on 1,500 acres. Downtown, you can examine the grim grounds of the **Old Montana Prison** *(1106 Main St. 406-846-3111. Feb.-Nov.; adm. fee),* the antique Ford cars in the adjoining **Towe Ford Museum** *(Feb.-Nov.; adm. fee),* and the doll and toy collection at nearby **Yesterday's Playthings** *(1017 Main St. 406-846-1480. Mid-May–Sept.; adm. fee).*

Butte See I-15, page 52.

Three Forks In 1805, Lewis and Clark discovered the triple-streamed headwaters of the Missouri just north of here. Today, the dusty little town of Three Forks is home to the **Headwaters Heritage Museum** *(Main and Cedar Sts. 406-285-3495. Memorial Day-Labor Day),* jam-packed with vintage collectibles, and **Three Forks Saddlery** *(221 S. Main St. 406-285-3459. Closed Sun.),* "the working cowboy's store," where you can watch their famous chaps and saddles being made. Historic state parks nearby include **Lewis and Clark Caverns** *(Mont. 2 exit. 406-287-3541. Daily May-Sept., weekends only in Apr. and Oct.; adm. fee),* with colorful rock formations; **Missouri Headwaters** *(Three Forks exit, E on Rte. 205, 3 miles N on Rte. 286. 406-994-4042. Adm. fee);* and **Madison Buffalo Jump** *(Logan exit, 7 miles S on mostly unpaved Buffalo Jump Rd. 406-994-4042. May-Sept.; adm. fee),* featuring self-guided trails to the cliff where Plains Indians stampeded buffalo.

Bozeman *(Chamber of Commerce, 1205 E. Main St. 406-586-5421 or 800-228-4224)* In 1862, John Bozeman led the first wagon train to the Gallatin Valley, blazing a trail that became a frontier thoroughfare across Indian hunting grounds. Now Bozeman is a lively college town (home of Montana State University), its Main Street an affable mix of Western and sophisticate. Don't miss the **Museum of the Rockies** *(600 W. Kagy Blvd. 406-994-2251),* whose planetarium, dinosaur hall, and Native American exhibits whisk you through four billion years of earth's history. *Adm. fee.*

Old Faithful, Yellowstone National Park, Wyoming

278

IF TIME PERMITS . . .

(14) **Yellowstone National Park** (*53 miles S on US 89 to the North Entrance, the only one open to cars in winter. 307-344-7381*) For beauty, the drive to Yellowstone is one of the best in the West. Founded in 1872, the world's first national park is also the largest in the lower 48 states, with 2.2 million acres of backcountry, 150 waterfalls, and more than 10,000 springs, geysers, and other hydrothermal features. If your time is limited, the 142-mile **Grand Loop Road** passes the main attractions: Old Faithful, Mammoth Hot Springs, Yellowstone Lake, and the Grand Canyon of the Yellowstone. Better still, take a hike; some 1,200 miles of trails beckon. *Limited access Nov.-Apr.; adm. fee.*

(15) **Livingston** This is a frontier town with a bohemian streak. The railroad put it on the map; today the 1902 **Depot Center** (*200 W. Park St. 406-222-2300. Mid-May–mid-Oct.; adm. fee*) exhibits art, culture, and history. Among resident writers and artists is Russell Chatham, whose **Chatham Fine Art** (*120 N. Main St. 406-222-1566. Closed Sun.*) is one of many galleries here.

(16) **Billings** (*Visitor Center, 815 S. 27th St. 406-252-4016 or 800-735-2635. Daily in summer, weekdays only rest of year*) Originally a stagecoach stop between Bozeman and Miles City, Montana's largest city got a jump start in 1882 with the arrival of the Northern Pacific Railroad. Sparkling galleries of regional, national, and international art fill the refurbished old county jail, now the **Yellowstone Art Center** (*401 N. 27th St. 406-256-6804. Closed Mon. and Jan.*). The **Western Heritage Center** (*2822 Montana Ave. 406-256-6809. Closed Mon.*), in the magnificent 1909 Romanesque library building, presents multimedia exhibits on cultural life, while the **Peter Yegen Jr. Yellowstone County Museum** (*27th St. to Logan Airport, follow signs. 406-256-6811. Closed Sat.*) displays a bit of everything in an

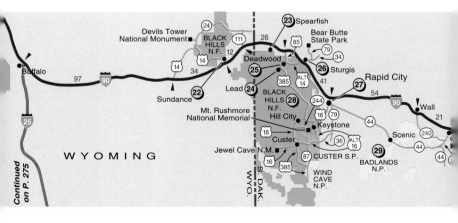

Continued on P. 275

1890s log cabin. **Moss Mansion** (*914 Division St. 406-256-5100. Adm. fee*), the former home of entrepreneur P. B. Moss, contains 28 opulent rooms virtually unchanged since 1903. You'll find a world-class collection of antique farm machinery, plus 5,000 other wonders, at **Oscar's Dreamland** (*1 mile S, off Shiloh Rd. 406-656-0966. May-Oct.; adm. fee*). An obligatory drive is spectacular **Black Otter Trail** (*E on Main St., follow signs*), which traces the 400-foot-high rimrocks and passes Boothill Cemetery and Kelly Mountain, where legendary frontiersman Yellowstone Kelly is buried.

Pictograph Caves State Park (*Lockwood exit. 406-252-4654*) Although archaeologists have unearthed 4,500-year-old artifacts, prehistoric peoples may have lived in these three caves 10,000 years ago. Interpretive trails lead to the caves, where you can take a self-guided tour. Picnic area. *Mid-Apr.–mid-Oct.; adm. fee.*

Barrel racing at a rodeo, Billings, Mont.

Crow Agency **Little Bighorn Battlefield Natl. Monument** (*Exit onto US 212, follow signs. 406-638-2621*) Here, during two days in June 1876, Northern Plains Indians killed more than 260 Americans, including Lt. Col. George Armstrong Custer—an event known as Custer's Last Stand. The Visitor Center provides historical context for a tour of the battlefield and cemetery. *June-Sept.; adm. fee.*

Sheridan, WYOMING (*Visitor Center at 5th St. exit. 307-672-2485*) Part of Indian territory until 1868, Sheridan quickly grew as a farming and coal-mining center dressed in quintessential ranch style. **King's Saddlery** (*184 N. Main St. 307-672-2702. Mon.-Sat.*)—a family-run tack shop, rope maker, and saddler—even smells like the Old West; the museum downstairs is a veritable Louvre of regional gear and memorabilia. Buffalo Bill Cody's favorite haunt, the gabled 1892 **Sheridan Inn** (*5th St. and Broadway. 307-674-5440. Adm. fee for tours*), also hosted Will Rogers, Calamity Jane, Ernest Hemingway, and a few U. S. Presidents; be sure to look at

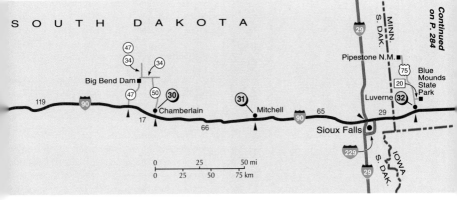

Continued on P. 284

SOUTH DAKOTA

Big Bend Dam

Chamberlain

Mitchell

Sioux Falls

Pipestone N.M.

Blue Mounds State Park

Luverne

MINN. / S. DAK.

IOWA / S. DAK.

0   25   50 mi
0   25   50   75 km

the saloon's magnificent English bar. The **Trail End State Historic Site** (*400 Clarendon Ave. 307-674-4589. Apr.-Dec.*) preserves the 1913 Flemish mansion of "Cowboy Senator" John Benjamin Kendrick.

(20) Big Horn **Bradford Brinton Memorial: A Museum and Historic Ranch** (*Sheridan/Coffeen St. exit, 12 miles S on US 87 to 239 Brinton Rd. 307-672-3173*) Of late 1900s vintage, the beautifully situated Quarter Circle A Ranch was one of the finest in the Big Horn area. Tours cover the sprawling 20-room house and outbuildings. The museum displays Brinton's premier collection of Western art and Native American artifacts. *Mid-May–Labor Day; adm. fee.*

Lt. Col. George A. Custer's grave, Little Bighorn Battlefield National Monument, Crow Agency, Mont.

(21) Fort Phil Kearny State Historic Site (*US 87 exit, follow signs to 528 Wagon Box Rd. 307-684-7629*) Built in 1866, abandoned in 1868, and burned by the Cheyenne, this was the largest—and most turbulent—of three stockade forts along the Bozeman Trail. Signs interpret the eerily empty site, overlooking endless hills and rangeland. Visitor Center and two battle sites. *Daily mid-May–Sept., Wed.-Sun. Apr.–mid-May and Sept.-Nov.; adm. fee.*

Buffalo See I-25, page 76.

(22) Sundance Sioux performed their summer Sun Dance just south of town. Its name was profaned by outlaw Harry Longabaugh, also known as the Sundance Kid, who was jailed here for horse theft.

Devil's Tower Natl. Monument, about 25 miles north on US 14, then 6 miles north on Wyo. 24 to Wyo. 110, follow signs

Original court furnishings and his court records are on view in the **Crook County Museum and Art Gallery** (*309 Cleveland St. 307-283-3666. Closed Sun. June-Aug., closed weekends Apr.-May and Sept.-Dec., closed completely Jan.-March*).

(23) Spearfish, SOUTH DAKOTA Plains Indians speared fish in the local creek, hence the name. The **Black Hills Passion Play** (*St. Joe St. 605-642-2646. Performances June-Aug.; reservations required; fee*), a summer institution in Spearfish since 1939, is staged at an outdoor amphitheater. Art and artifacts honor pioneers, cowboys, and Native Americans at the **High Plains Heritage Center and Museum** (*825 Heritage Dr. 605-642-9378. Adm. fee*), while trout steal the show at the **D.C. Booth Historic Fish Hatchery** (*423 Hatchery Circle. 605-642-7730. Mid-May–mid-Sept.; adm. fee for tours*).

(24) Lead (*4 miles W of Deadwood on US 14A*) Pronounced "leed," meaning "lode," this mile-high company town exists because of the **Homestake Mine** (*101 W. Main St. 605-584-3110. Guided surface tours daily June-Aug., Mon.-Fri. May and Sept.;*

adm. fee). In use since 1876, it's purportedly the world's longest operated gold mine—and one of the most prolific. At the **Black Hills
Mining Museum** *(323 W. Main St. 605-584-1605. Mid-May–Sept.;
adm. fee),* you can tour a simulated mine and pan for gold.

Deadwood *(12 miles W on US 14A or 7 miles S on US 85.
Chamber of Commerce, 460 Main St. 605-578-1876)* Gold fever turned
Deadwood into a boomtown. With some 80 casinos lin-
ing its preserved streets, Deadwood is still booming.
Wild Bill Hickok, gunned down at the **Old Style Saloon
No. 10** *(657 Historic Main St.),* is buried next to Calami-
ty Jane in **Mount Moriah Cemetery** *(Boot Hill. Adm. fee
May-Oct.).* Other attractions: the **Ghosts of Deadwood
Gulch Wax Museum** *(Old Town Hall. 605-578-3583.
May-Sept.; adm. fee)* and the history-rich **Adams Muse-
um** *(54 Sherman St. 605-578-1714. Closed Mon. Oct.-Apr.).*

Rally and Races, Sturgis, South Dakota

Sturgis Normally staid Sturgis cuts loose the first
full week in August, when 100,000 bikers roar in for the
Rally and Races—and the **National Motorcycle Muse-
um & Hall of Fame** *(2438 Junction Ave. 605-347-4875. Adm. fee).*
To the north rises Mato Paha, sacred peak of the Plains tribes and
centerpiece of **Bear Butte State Park** *(7 miles NE of town on S. Dak.
34 and 79. 605-347-5240. Visitor Center open May–mid-Sept.; adm. fee).*

281

Rapid City *(Convention & Visitors Bureau,
444 Mt. Rushmore Rd. 605-343-1744 or 800-487-3223)*
Failed gold diggers founded this wholesale center at
the foot of the Black Hills and named it after Rapid
Creek. For a look back at the past, visit the **Minnilusa
Historical Society's Pioneer Museum** *(515 West
Blvd. in Halley Park. 605-394-6099. Closed Mon. and
Jan.)* and, in the same building, the **Sioux Indian Mu-
seum and Crafts Center** *(605-348-0557. Closed Mon.
Oct.-May).* The South Dakota School of Mines & Tech-
nology's **Museum of Geology** *(501 E. St. Joseph St. 605-
394-2467)* is brimming with local fossils and minerals.

IF TIME PERMITS . . .

The Black Hills This splendid wilderness of rocky, pine-clad slopes and rolling grasslands,
whose gateway is Rapid City**,** lies largely within Black
Hills National Forest. In **Keystone** *(18 miles S on US
16),* exhibits at the **Rushmore-Borglum Story** *(Main
and Roy Sts. 605-666-4448. Mid-April–mid-Oct.; adm.
fee)* commemorate the sculptor of **Mount Rushmore
National Memorial** *(1 mile S of Keystone on US 16A, 2
miles W on S. Dak. 244. 605-574-2523).* The **Black Hills
Central Railroad** *(Board in Keystone on US 16A or in
Hill City on US 16/385. 605-574-2222. Mid-May–mid-*

Inspecting a crack in George Washington's head,
Mount Rushmore NM, near Keystone, S.Dak.

October; fare charge) traverses the scenic 10-mile route between Keystone and Hill City. Mount Rushmore's rival, **Crazy Horse Memorial** (*9 miles S of Hill City on US 16/385. 605-673-4681. Adm. fee)*, features a mountain monument in the making, the studio-home of sculptor Korczak Ziolkowski, and a Native American museum.

Near **Custer** (*14 miles S of Hill City on US 16)*, you'll find the **National Museum of Woodcarving** (*2 miles W on US 16. 605-673-4404. May–mid-Oct.; adm. fee)*, with "talking" characters created by Disneyland's original animator, and **Jewel Cave National Monument** (*15 miles W on US 16. 605-673-2288. Adm. fee May-Sept.)*, roughly 80 miles of colorful limestone caverns connected by narrow passages. To the east of Custer lie two classic Black Hills beauties: 73,000-acre **Custer State Park** (*5 miles E on US 16A. 605-255-4515. Adm. fee)*, where bison still roam a bountiful prairie, and **Wind Cave National Park** (*S of Custer State Park on S. Dak. 87 or US 385. 605-745-4600. Adm. fee for tours)*, site of the world's largest collection of boxworks—calcite fins arranged in a honeycomb pattern.

Longhorn Saloon, Scenic, S. Dak., gateway to South Unit, Badlands National Park

The impossibly varied **Badlands** only look complex. They actually came about by two basic processes: deposition and erosion. Over millions of years, material settled on the bottom of an inland sea, then solidified into layers of sedimentary rock—black shale, yellow and red siltstone, ash-based clay stone. The sea dried up, and the real artistry began 500,000 years ago as water ate away at the rock, exposing ancient soils and serrating the terrain—a work still in progress, ever shaped by wind, rain, and frost.

282

(29) Badlands National Park (*Cactus Flats exit or Wall exit, 3 miles S on S. Dak. 240 Loop Road, follow signs. Visitor Centers at Cedar Pass, for North Unit, and White River, for South Unit. 605-433-5362. Adm. fee)* There is nothing so eerie as the first sight of the Badlands—a landscape of striated spires, knobs, buttes, and canyons floating in the endless grasslands. Roads and trails wind through the park, home to bighorn sheep, bison, prairie dogs, and countless birds and reptiles. A half mile from the park's east entrance, historic **Prairie Homestead** (*605-433-5370. May-Sept.; adm. fee)* preserves a 1909 sod house, outbuildings, and a prairie dog town.

(30) Chamberlain Here, the interstate meets the Missouri River as it cuts across South Dakota, dividing western ranching and mining territory from eastern farmland. Head for the hills on the **Native American Loop,** an exhilarating 54-mile scenic and cultural tour; you can pick up a map at the I-90 Chamberlain Rest Area or the Chamber of Commerce (*115 W. Lawler St. 605-734-6541)*. Highlights include the **Akta Lakota Museum** (*St. Joseph's Indian School, S. Dak. 50. 605-734-3455. Daily May-Sept., Mon.-Fri. Oct.-Apr.)*, dedicated to Sioux culture; the trails at **Roam Free Park** (*1 mile N of Akta Lakota Museum on S. Dak. 50. 605-734-6541. Mem. Day-Labor Day)*; and **Big Bend Dam and Museum** (*In Fort Thompson, 21 miles NW of town on S. Dak. 47. 605-245-2255. Daily tours in summer, by appt. rest of year)*, a 2-mile embankment linking the Crow Creek Sioux and Lower Brule Reservations.

(31) Mitchell This trade hub for grain, corn, and cattle boasts the famous **Corn Palace** (*604 N. Main St. 605-996-7311)*, a Moorish-style monument to the nation's

Corn Palace, Mitchell, South Dakota

breadbasket. Other reasons to stop here: the **Enchanted World Doll Museum** (*615 N. Main St. 605-996-9896. Mid-March–Nov.; adm. fee*), the **Soukup and Thomas International Balloon and Airship Museum** (*700 N. Main St. 605-996-2311. Closed Jan. and Wed.-Thurs. Oct.-Apr.; adm. fee*), and the **Friends of the Middle Border Museum of Pioneer Life** (*1311 S. Duff St. 605-996-2122. May-Sept., by appt. rest of year; adm. fee*). The **Oscar Howe Art Center** (*119 W. 3rd St. 605-996-4111. Closed Sun. Memorial Day-Labor Day, closed Sun.-Mon. rest of year*) displays contemporary Great Plains art, while the **Prehistoric Indian Village Museum and Site** (*N on S. Dak. 37, left on W. 23rd Ave., right on Indian Village Rd. 605-996-5473. May-Oct., by appt. rest of year; adm. fee*) reveals archaeological finds at a thousand-year-old earth-lodge village site.

S i o u x   F a l l s   See I-29, p. 88.

Mayo Medical Center, Rochester, Minn.

L u v e r n e , M I N N E S O T A   A remnant of the once vast tallgrass prairie, along with a small herd of bison, thrives at 1,500-acre **Blue Mounds State Park** (*6 miles N on Minn. 75. 507-283-4892. Adm. fee*), named for the spectacular mile-long quartzite cliffs that turn blue at sunset. Up the road, **Pipestone National Monument** (*18 miles N on Minn. 75, through Pipestone, follow signs. 507-825-5464. Adm. fee*) preserves the site where, for centuries, Plains Indians quarried the sacred red stone used for peace pipes.

A l b e r t   L e a   See I-35, p. 96.

R o c h e s t e r   (*10 miles N on US 63*) Downtown Rochester stands tall in the midst of prime farmland. Dominating the scene are the 43 buildings of the renowned **Mayo Medical Center** (*Tours Mon.-Fri. from Judd Auditorium, 200 1st St. S.W. 507-284-2450*), the largest private medical complex in the world, founded early in this century. Tours of historic **Mayowood,** the 55-room Mayo family mansion, begin at the **Olmsted County History Center Museum** (*Jct. of Rtes. 22 and 25. 507-282-9447. Apr.-Oct. Tues.-Sun., Dec.-March Tues., Sat.-Sun.; reservations required; adm. fee*).

W i n o n a   (*8 miles N on Minn. 43. Convention & Visitors Bureau, 67 Main St. 507-452-2272*) Settled by Yankees, Germans, and Poles, this river town made it rich on lumbering and shipping. Museums to see are the **Julius C. Wilkie Steamboat Museum** (*Main St. at the levee. 507-454-1254. May-Oct.; adm. fee*), housed in a replicated paddle wheeler; the entertaining **Winona Armory Museum** (*160 Johnson St. 507-454-2723. Adm. fee*), one of Minnesota's largest and finest historical museums; and the **Polish Cultural Institute** (*102 Liberty St. 507-454-3431 or 452-5277. May-Oct. Mon.-Fri., weekends by appt.*), displaying the folk arts, artifacts, photographs, and history of the Poles in Winona. **Conway Universal Studios** (*503 Center St. 507-452-9209. Mon.-Fri.*), one of at least four stained-glass producers in town, invites you to watch how it's done.

Those who follow the news from Lake Wobegon, Garrison Keillor's mythical hometown featured on National Public Radio's *A Prairie Home Companion,* know that the blood of *Scandanavians* runs thick in these parts. The land lured the first Scandinavians—mostly farmers, lumberjacks, and miners—after the Civil War. While Swedes settled in towns, Norwegians—more of whom live in Minnesota than in any other state—preferred the countryside, "where all the women are strong." German blood, however, runs even thicker here; about 50 percent of Minnesotans are of German descent.

Devil's Lake State Park, near Baraboo, Wisconsin

(35) Trempealeau, WISCONSIN (8 mi. N on US 53, 3 mi. W on Wis. 35) Spectacular 500-foot bluffs punctuate **Perrot State Park** (Park Rd. 608-534-6409. Adm. fee), where the Trempealeau River meets the Mississippi. Four miles north lies **Trempealeau National Wildlife Refuge** (W. Prairie Rd. to Refuge Rd., follow signs. 608-539-2311), a 5,617-acre wetlands preserve. Spring and fall are the times to see ruffed grouse, thrushes, and other birds.

(36) La Crosse Coulees, bluffs, and valleys lend wild beauty to this Mississippi port city, named for an Indian ball game. The best view in town is from **Grandad Bluff** (2 miles E on Main St.), where you might catch a glimpse of the **La Crosse Queen** riverboat (Riverside Park dock. 608-784-8523. Cruises May-Oct.; fare charge). Historic **Hixon House** (429 N. 7th St. 608-782-1980. Memorial Day-Labor Day, by appt. rest of year; adm. fee) reveals the posh life of a lumber baron.

(37) Coon Valley (15 miles S on Wis. 162, E on US 14/61) In the mid-1800s, Norwegian farmers began settling this rolling countryside, reminiscent of their homeland. Their heritage is preserved at **Norskedalen Nature and Heritage Center** (2 miles NE of town on Rte. PI. 608-452-3424), a 400-acre arboretum with trails, an interpretive center, and a restored Norwegian homestead. Adm. fee.

284

Antique circus wagons, Circus World Museum, Baraboo

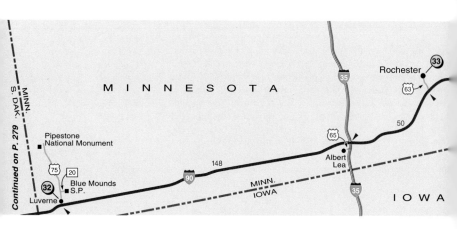

Continued on P. 279

Baraboo *(From the east, take Wis. 33W; from the west, take US 12S)* Baraboo—a corruption of Baribault, the name of a 19th-century French trader—feels a world away. Here, where Ringling Brothers Circus was born, the 50-acre **Circus World Museum** *(426 Water St. 608-356-0800. Adm. fee)* presents big-top performances and exhibits on American circus history. To see 15 species of cranes, including rare whoopers, visit the **International Crane Foundation** *(E-11376 Shady Lane Rd. 608-356-9462. May-Oct.; adm. fee).* The 11,000 acres of **Devil's Lake State Park** *(3.5 miles S on Wis. 123. 608-356-8301. Adm. fee)* contain outstanding glacial features.

Farmers' market, Madison, Wis.

285

Madison *(Convention & Visitors Bureau, 615 E. Washington Ave. 608-255-2537 or 800-373-6376)* Wisconsin's lovely, lively capital embraces four lakes and 150 parks. Its crowning glory is the granite-domed, Roman Renaissance **State Capitol** *(Capitol Sq. 608-266-0382).* The **University of Wisconsin** *(Campus Assistance Center, 420 N. Lake St. 608-263-2400)* offers diverse attractions: the **Elvehjem Museum of Art** *(800 University Ave. 608-263-2246),* the **Geology Museum** *(1215 W. Dayton St. 608-262-2399. Closed Sun.),* the **Arboretum** *(1207 Seminole Hwy. 608-263-7888),* and the **Babcock Hall Dairy Plant and Store** *(1605 Linden Dr. 608-262-3045. Closed Sun.),* where you can watch dairy products in the making, then sample them. Other Mad Town highlights include the **State Historical Museum** *(30 N. Carroll St. 608-264-6555. Closed Mon.),* modern and contemporary works at the **Madison Art Center** *(211 State St. 608-257-0158. Closed Mon.),* and Frank Lloyd Wright's **Unitarian Meeting House** *(900 University Bay Dr. 608-233-9774. Call to arrange tour; adm. fee),* a noteworthy example of his prairie school design.

Rockford, ILLINOIS *(Convention & Visitors Bureau, 211 N. Main St. 815-963-8111 or 800-521-0849)* The **Tinker Swiss Cottage Museum** *(411 Kent St. 815-964-2424. Wed.-Sun.; adm. fee)* shines with Gilded Age opulence, furniture, and art. The

Riverfront Museum Park (*711 N. Main St. 815-962-0105. Daily June-Aug., closed Mon. rest of year*) includes the **Rockford Art Museum** (*815-968-2787. Closed Mon.; adm. fee*) and the **Discovery Center Museum** (*815-963-6769. Closed Mon. Sept.-May; adm. fee*), a science adventure. Next door stands the **Burpee Museum of Natural History** (*813 N. Main St. 815-965-3132. Closed Mon.; adm. fee*).

㊶ Union (*10 miles N on US 20*) On the east side of town, the hands-on **Illinois Railway Museum** (*Olson Rd. 815-923-4391*) houses an 1851 depot, electric trolleys, Pullman and freight cars, and a huge collection of train artifacts. Buffs can ride restored rolling stock. *Daily Memorial Day-Labor Day, weekends May and Sept.–early Oct., Sun. only Apr. and last two weeks of Oct. Train schedules vary; adm. fee.*

㊷ Des Plaines McDonald's Museum (*400 N. Lee St. 708-297-5022*) Four '55 autos parked under the Speedee sign advertising 15-cent burgers hail this monument to American enterprise. Rebuilt on the site where Ray Kroc opened his first restaurant on April 15, 1955, this kitschy museum presents a behind-the-scenes look at the McDonald's gestalt. *Closed Mon. June-Aug., call for hours rest of year.*

㊸ Oak Park (*I-290 to Harlem Ave./Ill. 43N exit. Visitor Center, 158 N. Forest Ave. 708-848-1500*) Less than 5 miles square, this artsy village 10 miles west of Chicago claims more significant architecture per capita than anywhere else in the country. Frank Lloyd Wright developed his prairie school here. The **Historic District** (*Walking tour maps available at Visitor Center*) encompasses 120 prairie-style buildings, 25 by Wright, notably his 1889 **home and studio** (*951 Chicago Ave. 708-848-1976. Adm. fee*) and his 1906 **Unity Temple** (*875 Lake St. 708-383-8873. Adm. fee for tours*). Architect George W. Maher's magnificent **Pleasant Home** (*217 Home Ave. 708-383-2654. Thurs.-Sun.; adm. fee*) holds the local historical society (*708-848-6755. Thurs.-Sun.; adm. fee Fri.-Sun.*). **Ernest Hemingway's Birthplace** (*339 N. Oak Park Ave. Wed. and Sat.-Sun.; adm. fee*) and the **Ernest Hemingway Museum** (*200 N. Oak Park Ave. Wed., Sat.-Sun.; adm. fee*) honor the Oak Park native.

Chicago See I-55, pp. 126-27.

㊹ South Bend, INDIANA (*Convention & Visitors Bureau, 401 E. Colfax. 219-234-0051 or 800-462-5258*) To sports fans, South Bend means only one thing: football. While Notre Dame's Fighting Irish monopolize the city's image, this big-time manufacturing town also spawned the Studebaker brothers, whose legacy lives on at the **Studebaker National Museum** (*525 S. Main St. 219-235-9108. Adm. fee*). Canoers, kayakers, and rafters zip down the **East Race Waterway** (*219-235-9401. June-Aug. Wed., Thurs., Sat.-Sun.; adm. fee*), a man-made whitewater course. The **University of Notre Dame** (*Information at Main Bldg. 219-631-7367*) offers the **Snite Museum of Art** (*Closed Mon. and holidays*), a grotto, and a basilica.

286

Studebaker National Museum, South Bend, Indiana

Elkhart (*Convention & Visitors Bureau, 219 Caravan Dr. 219-262-8161 or 800-262-8161. Ask for information about the 90-mile Heritage Trail that loops through the area.*) At the confluence of the Elkhart and St. Joseph Rivers, this manufacturing center produces, among other things, most of the country's band instruments. The **Midwest Museum of American Art** (*429 S. Main St. 219-293-6660. Closed Mon.; adm. fee*) showcases works by Norman Rockwell, Grandma Moses, and Grant Wood. **Ruthmere** (*302 E. Beardsley Ave. 219-264-0330. Apr.–mid-Dec. Tues.-Sat.; adm. fee*) was the beaux arts mansion of Albert R. Beardsley, an early partner at Miles Laboratories. The **Antique Auto Museum** (*2130 Middlebury St. 219-522-0539. Mon.-Fri. and last weekend of month; adm. fee*) displays S. Ray Miller's prizewinning collection.

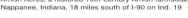

Amish Acres, a restored 19th-century Amish farmstead, Nappanee, Indiana, 18 miles south of I-90 on Ind. 19

Shipshewana (*Middlebury exit, 1 mile S on Ind. 13, 5 miles E on Ind. 120, 3 miles S on Ind. 5*) Named after a local Potawatomi chief and famed for its auction and flea market, this town and surrounding farm region are Amish country. Buggies even get designated parking. Don't miss **Menno-Hof** (*390 S. Van Buren. 219-768-4117*), a multimedia center created by the Mennonite and Amish communities. *Closed Sun. year-round and Mon. Jan.-March; donation requested.*

287

Sauder Farm and Craft Village, OHIO (*Wauseon exit, 1.5 miles S on Ohio 108, 8 miles W on US 20A, 2 miles S on Ohio 66, left on Ohio 2. 419-446-2541*) This living-history compound presents a slice of frontier life with authentic and replicated 19th-century buildings, costumed guides, animals, buggy rides, and artisans. *Mid-Apr.–Oct.; adm. fee.*

Toledo See I-75, p. 189.

Rutherford B. Hayes Presidential Center (*Fremont exit, 3 miles S on Ohio 53, follow signs. 419-332-2081*) Settled as a fur-shipping center on an old Indian trail, Fremont takes pride in Spiegel Grove, the magnificent 25-acre estate of Rutherford B. Hayes, 19th President of the United States. Here you'll find his elegant mansion, a museum, presidential library, and his and his wife's graves. *Adm. fee.*

Milan (*Sandusky-Norwalk exit, 2 miles S on US 250, left on Ohio 113, follow signs*) Linked with Lake Erie by canal in 1839, this New England-style village (pronounced "my-lin") boomed as a grain port, then went bust in 1850. In the bustle of 1847, Thomas Edison was born in a brick house preserved as the **Edison Birthplace** (*9 Edison Dr. 419-499-2135. Closed Mon. and Dec.-Jan., except by appt.; adm. fee*). Across the street, at the **Milan Historical Museum** (*10 Edison Dr. 419-499-2968.*

Corkscrew roller coaster, Cedar Point Amusement Park, Sandusky, Ohio, 11 miles north of I-90 on US 250

Pennsylvania wildflowers

Closed Mon. Apr.-Oct.), a complex of historical buildings houses exceptional glass and doll collections.

50 **V e r m i l i o n** *(11 miles W on Ohio 2 to Ohio 60)* Settled by Connecticut Yankees in the 19th century, this picturesque town—named by the Erie Indians after the local soil color—was once the largest fishing port on the Great Lakes. The **Inland Seas Maritime Museum** *(480 Main St. 216-967-3467)* preserves the lore and history of the lakes through art, artifacts, and an authentic pilothouse. *Adm. fee.*

C l e v e l a n d   See I-77, p. 204.

51 **M e n t o r**   *(Mentor-Kirtland exit, 2 miles N on Ohio 306, right on Mentor Ave. for 2 miles)* In 1880, James Garfield successfully campaigned for President from Lawnfield, his 30-room Victorian home, now the **Garfield National Historic Site** *(8095 Mentor Ave. 216-255-8722. Closed Mon.; adm. fee).* Far from the suburban sprawl, 3,100-acre **Holden Arboretum** *(1 mile S on Ohio 306, 4 miles E on Kirtland-Chardon Rd., left to 9200 Sperry Rd. 216-946-4400. Closed Mon.; adm. fee)* has 7,000 varieties of plants and 20 miles of trails.

E r i e , PENNSYLVANIA   See I-79, p. 212.

52 **C h a u t a u q u a , NEW YORK**   In 1874, a vacation school for Sunday school teachers opened on Lake Chautauqua. From it grew an experimental education movement that flowered as the **Chautauqua Institution** *(Westfield exit, 10 miles SE on N.Y. 394. 716-357-6200 or 800-836-ARTS. Tours late June-Aug.; adm. fee),* now a national forum and center for the arts, education, religion, and recreation. A walk through the village, chockablock with

The idea of digging a canal across the Mohawk River Valley from Lake Erie to the Hudson River was first suggested in 1724. It took a century to become reality. When the **Erie Canal** opened in 1825, linking Buffalo with Albany, it easily moved immigrants and goods westward into the Great Lakes region—thus helping to settle the nation. One of the all-time great engineering feats, the 363-mile-long trench took eight years to hand dig. Laborers also built 83 locks, 18 aqueducts, countless culverts, and wide towpaths for the mules that pulled the barges.

Continued on P. 285

Set impressively on Lake Erie and only a bridge length from Canada, New York's second largest city is one of its best kept secrets (Conv. & Visitors Bureau, 107 Delaware Avenue. 716-852-0511. Mon.-Fri.).

Downtown skyline seen from the Erie Basin Marina

Named for a local creek, Buffalo served as the western terminus of the Erie Canal and grew into a major manufacturing center and rail hub. Its distinguished architecture complements Frederick Law Olmsted's landscapes, notably the *Buffalo and Erie County Botanical Gardens* (2655 S. Park Ave. 716-828-1040). Museum-goers will enjoy the international contemporary art at the renowned *Albright-Knox Art Gallery* (1285 Elmwood Ave. 716-882-8700 or -8701. Closed Mon.; adm. fee), regional works at the *Burchfield Art Center* (1300 Elmwood Ave. 716-878-6011. Closed Mon.), and local history at the *Buffalo and Erie County Historical Society* (25 Nottingham Ct. 716-873-9644. Closed Mon.; adm. fee). Hands-on is the operative word at the

Buffalo Museum of Science (1020 Humboldt Pkwy. 716-896-5200. Closed Mon.; adm. fee). Kids will also take a fancy to the *Buffalo Zoo* (300 Parkside Ave. 716-837-3900. Adm. fee). The *Theodore Roosevelt Inaugural National Historic Site* (641 Delaware Ave. 716-884-0095. Closed Sat. Jan.-March; adm. fee) marks the swearing-in site of the 26th President of the United States.

On the waterfront, World War II Navy ships and military artifacts attract visitors to the *Buffalo and Erie County Naval and Servicemen's Park* (1 Naval Park Cove. 716-847-1773. Daily Apr.-Oct., weekends only in Nov.; adm. fee). Across the canal in North Tonawanda, en route to *Niagara Falls* (20 miles N, off I-190), you'll find the *Herschell Carrousel Factory Museum* (180 Thompson St. 716-693-1885. Daily July-Aug., Wed.-Sun. May-June and Sept.-Nov.; adm. fee). Here you can tour the historic factory, watch carving demonstrations, and ride on a 1916 carousel.

289

Continued on P. 292

Costumed interpreter
Genesee Country Mu
seum, Mumford, N.Y.

Victorian cottages, is a delightful journey into another age. Wine tasting is de rigueur here in the heart of grape-growing country (*Pamphlets available at Chautauqua County Vacationland Assoc., 4 N. Erie St., Mayville. 716-753-4304*).

International Museum of Photography and Film, Rochester, New York

290

54 Mumford Genesee Country Museum (*N.Y. 19 exit, 5 miles S on N.Y. 19 to LeRoy, E on N.Y. 5, left on Flint Hill Rd. 716-538-6822*) Aptly named for New York State's scenic region, from the Iroquois for "pleasant valley," this living-history museum—with 57 buildings, gardens, and costumed guides—re-creates the look and feel of a 19th-century western New York village. Also located here: the **Gallery of Sporting Art** and a **Nature Center.** *Museum and gallery open Mother's Day-third Sun. in Oct.; Nature Center open year-round, except Mon.; adm. fee.*

55 Rochester (*4 miles N on I-390. Visitors Association, 126 Andrews St. 716-546-3070 or 800-677-7282*) Ever linked with Kodak, George Eastman's cultivated hometown honors the man and the medium at the **International Museum of Photography and Film** (*George Eastman House, 900 East Ave. 716-271-3361. Closed Mon.; adm. fee*). The **Susan B. Anthony House** (*17 Madison St. 716-235-6124. Thurs-Sat.; adm. fee*) preserves the memory of Rochester's favorite daughter and her fight for women's rights. Natural and cultural history, along with the Strasenburgh Planetarium, highlight the **Rochester Museum & Science Center** (*657 East Ave. 716-271-1880. Adm. fee*), while the collection at the **Strong Museum** (*1 Manhattan Sq. 716-263-2700. Adm. fee*) documents the industrial revolution and depicts more than 150 years of popular taste through such cultural artifacts as toys, clothing, magazines, and sports equipment. The museum includes a children's hands-on activity center. The **Memorial Art Gallery** (*500 University Ave. 716-473-0350. Closed Mon.; adm. fee*) displays masterworks from ancient times to the present. Be sure to stop at the **Center at High Falls** (*60 Browns Race. 716-325-2030*), overlooking the spectacular gorge and falls.

Women's Rights National Historical Park, Seneca Falls, New York

56 Seneca Falls (*9 miles S on N.Y. 414, left on N.Y. 5/US 20. Visitor Center, 115 Falls St. 315-568-2703*) This mill town was a hotbed of 19th-century activism. Women's rights headed the reform movements, led by Elizabeth Cady Stanton, who organized the first Women's Rights Convention here in 1848. Highlights include the **Women's Rights National Historical Park** (*136 Fall St. 315-568-2991*), **Elizabeth Cady Stanton House** (*32 Washington St.*), and **National Women's Hall of Fame** (*76 Fall St. 315-568-8060. Daily May-Oct., closed Mon.-Tues. Nov.-Apr.*). For a breather, wander the 6,432-acre **Montezuma National Wildlife Refuge** (*5 miles E on N.Y. 5/US 20. 315-568-5987*), or head south to sample Finger Lakes wines along the **Cayuga Wine Trail** (*Information at Visitor Center*).

Syracuse See I-81, p. 239.

Rome *(N on N.Y. 365 or N.Y. 49)* First called Lynchville after its Irish founder, this gritty city straddles the Erie Canal, which links the Great Lakes with the Atlantic Ocean. **Erie Canal Village** *(5789 New London Rd. 315-337-3999. Mid-May–early Oct.; adm. fee)* re-creates an 1840s village with historic buildings, museums, and horse-drawn packet boat rides on the canal. Stop at **Fort Stanwix National Monument** *(112 E. Park St. 315-336-2090. Apr.-Dec.; adm. fee)*, reconstructed on the site of a Revolutionary War fort.

Utica The must-see stop here is the **Munson-Williams-Proctor Institute** *(310 Genesee St. 315-797-0000. Closed Mon.)*, whose acclaimed collection of American art features Thomas Cole's "The Voyage of Life." Next door stands **Fountain Elms** *(Closed Mon.)*, the museum founders' opulent Italianate home. For kids there's the **Children's Museum** *(311 Main St. 315-724-6128. Closed Mon. year-round, closed Tues. Sept.-June; adm. fee)* and the **Utica Zoo** *(Steel Hill Rd., off Memorial Pkwy. 315-738-0472. Adm. fee)*.

Schenectady Cradled in the scenic Mohawk River Valley, this old city began as a Dutch settlement in 1661. Residential **Stockade,** one of several historic districts, preserves the city's architectural heritage with hundreds of 1690s to 1930s buildings lining narrow streets *(Maps at Schenectady Museum & Planetarium; see below)*. Lively exhibits on science, technology, history, and art await at the **Schenectady Museum & Planetarium** *(Nott Terrace Heights. 518-382-7890. Closed Mon., planetarium open weekends only; adm. fee)*.

Albany See I-87, p. 264.

Old Chatham **Shaker Museum and Library** *(From E. Chatham Post Office, 1 mile S on Rte. 13 to Shaker Museum Rd. 518-794-9100)* This 24-gallery museum, housed mainly in a breezy farmhouse, presents a premier collection of simple, elegant Shaker furniture and inventive artifacts gathered from many communities. *May-Oct.; adm. fee.*

Barn at Shaker Museum and Library, Old Chatham, New York

Pittsfield, MASSACHUSETTS *(13 miles N on US 7/20)* Herman Melville fans will delight in **Arrowhead** *(780 Holmes Rd. 413-442-1793. Daily May-Labor Day, closed Tues.-Wed. Labor Day-Oct.; adm. fee)*, where he lived from 1850 to 1863 while writing *Moby Dick*. West of town lies **Hancock Shaker Village** *(5 miles W on US 20. 413-443-0188. Apr.-Nov.; adm. fee)*. Set on 1,200 acres, this 200-year-old town offers 20 restored buildings, including an ingenious round barn, gardens, and craft demonstrations.

Lenox *(Lee-Lenox exit, 4 miles N on US 7/20)* The sound of music fills the Berkshire hills when **Tanglewood** *(Lee-Lenox exit, follow signs to main entrance on West St. 413-637-1940. July to first weekend* in Sept.; adm. fee)—summer home of the Boston Symphony Orchestra—opens its festive season. **Shakespeare & Company** (413-637-3353. Late May-Oct. Tues.-Sun.; adm. fee) stages round-the-clock Shakespeare, plus contemporary theater, dance, and readings, at **The Mount** (Plunkett St. 413-637-1899), the summer estate of novelist Edith Wharton. Across town, the historic **Berkshire Scenic Railway** (1.5 miles E of US 7 at junction of Housatonic St. and Willow Creek Rd. 413-637-2210. Memorial Day-Oct.; fare charge) features a train museum and weekend rides on rolling stock. When sightseeing fatigue sets in, visit the Massachusetts Audubon Society's **Pleasant Valley Wildlife Sanctuary** (472 W. Mountain Rd., follow signs. 413-637-0320. Closed Mon.; adm. fee), where 7 miles of trails thread through 1,150 acres.

Gingerbread House, Tyringham, Massachusetts, 6 miles south of I-90 on Mass. 102

292

63 **Stockbridge** (Lee exit, 3 miles W on Mass. 102) Longtime resident Norman Rockwell drew his classic images of Americana from this early 18th-century town. The **Norman Rockwell Museum** (Mass. 183. 413-298-4100. Adm. fee) houses his studio and the world's largest collection of Rockwell's paintings. The crème de la crème of historic summer "cottages" belonging to Stockbridge society is 122-acre **Chesterwood** (3 miles W of town on Mass. 102, left on Mass. 183, follow signs. 413-298-3579. May-Oct.; adm. fee), the estate of Lincoln Memorial sculptor Daniel Chester French, and **Naumkeag** (Prospect Hill. 413-298-3239. Memorial Day-Labor Day Tues.-Sun., weekends only Labor Day-Columbus Day; adm. fee), designed by Stanford White and noted for its fine landscape architecture.

Springfield See I-91, p. 295.

Old Sturbridge Village See I-84 E, p. 255.

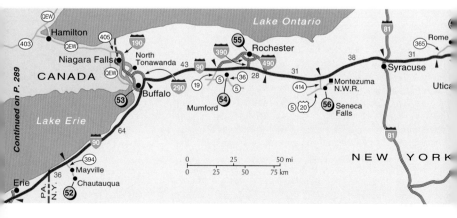

Worcester (*12 miles N on I-290. Visitor Center, 33 Waldo St. 508-753-2920*) New England's second largest city came of age with the industrial revolution. Its legacy of local inventions includes the yellow "smile face" button. The town's story is told at the **Worcester Historical Museum** (*30 Elm St. 508-753-8278. Closed Mon.; adm. fee*). A must-see—the architecturally sublime **Worcester Art Museum** (*55 Salisbury St. 508-799-4406. Closed Mon.; adm. fee*)—showcases 35 galleries of art from ancient to modern times. The **Higgins Armory Museum** (*100 Barber Ave. 508-853-6015. Closed Mon., except July-Aug.; adm. fee*) brings to life the world of knights in shining armor. Another hit with kids: the **New England Science Center** (*222 Harrington Way. 508-791-9211. Adm. fee*), a 60-acre environmental center with an interactive museum, zoo, and more.

Grafton (*Milbury-Worcester exit to Mass. 122, S on Mass. 140, follow signs*) **Willard House and Clock Museum** (*Willard St. 508-839-3500*) Timepieces made by the Willards between 1766 and 1780 tick away at their 1718 farmhouse. *Closed Mon.; adm. fee.*

Lexington and Concord (*8 miles N on I-95 to Mass. 2 or Mass. 2A, follow signs*) See I-93, p. 304.

Brookline (*2 miles S on I-95, 5 miles E on Mass. 9*) On May 29, 1917, the 35th President was born in what is now the **John F. Kennedy National Historic Site** (*83 Beals St. 617-566-7937. Closed Mon.-Tues.; adm. fee*), where the family lived from 1914 to 1921. **Fairsted and the Frederick Law Olmsted National Historic Site** (*99 Warren St. 617-566-1689. Fri.-Sun.*) preserve the enchanting estate of the father of American landscape architecture.

Cambridge See I-93, p. 305.

Boston See I-93, pp. 306-07.

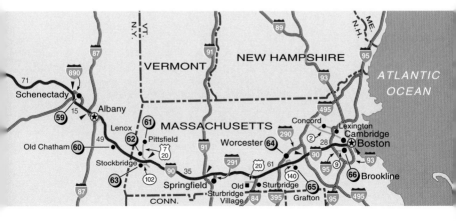

Unless otherwise noted, directions are from interstate, and sites are free and generally open daily. Phone for further information.

(1) Newport, VERMONT The gateway town between Canada and New England sits at the southern end of a lake whose Indian name means "beautiful waters." To see how maple candy is made, stop by **American Maple Products Corp.** *(1 mile N on Bluff Rd. 802-334-6516)* for a 30-minute guided tour. *Closed weekends.*

(2) Danville **Morgan Horse Farm** *(7 miles W on US 2, follow signs. 802-684-2251)* Get to know the state horse at the Lyon family farm. The Lyons have been breeding these handsome animals for 20 years and will be glad to show you the pastures and stables.

Morgan Horse Farm, Danville, Vermont

St. Johnsbury *(2 miles E on US 2)* See I-93, p. 300.

(3) Orford (N.H.) Washington Irving called this town the most beautiful he had ever seen. Its outstanding feature is **Bulfinch Row,** a string of privately owned mansions built between 1773 and 1839 that show the architectural influence of Charles Bulfinch.

(4) Wilder Dam *(Wilder exit, follow signs. Visitor Center 802-295-4873)* This hydroelectric site offers picnicking, fishing, and swimming. A fish ladder at the station was built in 1987 to help Atlantic salmon migrate upstream. *Tours Mem. Day-Labor Day.*

White River Junction See I-89, p. 271.

Quechee Gorge See I-89, p. 270.

(5) Windsor This is where the first Constitution of the "Free and Independent State of Vermont" was adopted in 1777. Elijah West Tavern, the adoption site, has been renamed the **Old Constitution**

House (*Main St. 802-672-3773. Late May–mid-Oct., closed Mon.-Tues.; adm. fee*) and features early Vermont memorabilia. The **American Precision Museum** (*196 Main St. 802-674-5781. Mid-May–Oct.; adm. fee*), dedicated to the history of American industrial technology, shows some of the machinery that made Yankee ingenuity a legend. The **Vermont State Craft Center** (*54 Main St. 802-674-6729. Closed Sun. Jan.-May*), housed in an 1840 Greek Revival structure, displays and sells Vermont crafts. Be sure to drive to Cornish, N.H., on New England's longest **covered bridge**, a 468-foot span built across the Connecticut River in 1866 at a cost of $9,000.

■ **Saint-Gaudens N.H.S. (N.H.)** (*1.5 miles N of the Windsor-Cornish Covered Bridge on N.H. 12A. 603-675-2175*) Sculptor Augustus Saint-Gaudens (1848-1907) came to New Hampshire while working on his "Standing Lincoln," because he was told he'd find "plenty of Lincoln-shaped men" to use as models. He stayed to create this home and studio, with its formal gardens, pools, and fountains. Many of his major works are exhibited here. Chamber music Sundays at 2 p.m. through August. *Mem. Day-Oct.; adm. fee.*

■ **Springfield**   Once northern New England's machine-tool capital, Springfield today combines an old-fashioned workaday ambience with a 1980s spruce-up. The **Eureka Schoolhouse** (*Vt. 11. 802-672-3773. Mid-May–mid-Oct., closed Mon.-Tues.*), of 1790, is the oldest one-room schoolhouse in Vermont. If you show up at the **Hartness House** (*30 Orchard St. 802-885-2115*), an inn, at 6 p.m., you can get a tour of politician-astronomer James Hartness's underground apartment, which houses a collection of telescopes. That stately mansion towering over downtown Springfield is the home of the **Springfield Art and Historical Society** (*9 Elm Hill. 802-885-2415. May–mid-Oct., Tues.-Fri. and Sun. p.m.*), with 19th-century American paintings, artifacts, pewter, pottery, and local crafts.

■ **Charlestown (N.H.)**   Follow Vt. 11 across the Connecticut River toll bridge

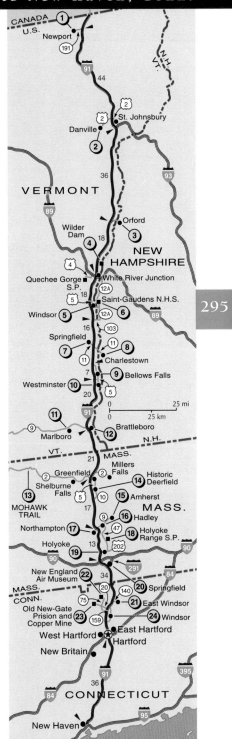

295

to this historic village. Ten downtown structures were built before 1800. The shops offer walking guides. **The Fort at No. 4** (*1 mile N of village on N.H. 11. 603-826-5700*) is a reconstructed outpost recalling life on New England's wild frontier in the 1740s. *Mem. Day-Columbus Day, except Tues. and weekdays Sept. 1-15; adm. fee.*

As you drive south along I-91, take note of the *place names* in Vermont and New Hampshire. When you see them again in Massachusetts and Connecticut, remember that the Connecticut River was once a major migration trail. Throughout the 18th century, colonists from southern New England headed north along the great river for more open space. And they brought along their old town names. Examples are Windsor, Chester, and Hartford in Connecticut and Vermont; and Springfield in Massachusetts and Vermont.

⑨ Bellows Falls   The old mills and railroad-era buildings along the river suggest the town's glory days have passed—but the ruddy brick business district is still very much alive. Climb aboard the **Green Mountain Flyer** (*Depot St. 802-463-3069. Trains run mid-June through foliage season, also over Christmas; adm. fee.*), a diesel-powered vintage train, for a 54-mile round-trip through Vermont's countryside, with its gorges and covered bridges. The train's other terminus is at **Chester**, notable for its tree-lined main street and stone houses. Back in Bellows Falls, New England Power has installed a $6-million **fish ladder** at its Connecticut River station (*Bridge St. 802-463-3226. Late May–mid-Oct.*); exhibits at the Visitor Center will explain it to you. Also worth a stop is the Gothic Revival **Immanuel Episcopal Church** (*Church St.*), with a bell by Paul Revere, and the vintage **Miss Bellows Falls Diner** (*Rockingham St.*).

⑩ Westminster   **MG Car Museum** (*Bellows Falls exit, 2.5 miles S on US 5. 802-722-3708*) "The world's largest private exhibit of a single marque" was assembled by Gerard Goguen, a former trumpet player and race-car driver. On display are 28 classic MGs. *July-Aug. Tues.-Sun., also June weekends; adm. fee.*

⑪ Marlboro Music Festival   (*Brattleboro exit, 8 miles W on Vt. 9 to Marlboro Center; follow signs for Marlboro College. 802-254-2394*) Pianist Rudolf Serkin began this renowned classical music series in 1951; cellist Pablo Casals was its most famous musician-in-residence. *Weekends only from early July to mid-Aug; adm. fee.*

⑫ Brattleboro   Here traditional Vermonters and New Age transplants have come together and made the "Gateway to Vermont" an exciting and vital community. Housed in a restored 1915 railroad depot, the **Brattleboro Museum & Art Center** (*Jct. of Main, Vernon, and Canal Sts. 802-257-0124. Mid-May–Oct. Tues.-Sun.; adm. fee*) rotates exhibits frequently, often showing works of New England artists. The **Creamery Covered Bridge** (*Vt. 9 to Guilford St.*), built in 1879, may be the state's most often photographed bridge. The scenic **Molly Stark Trail** (*Vt. 9*), which extends across southern Vermont to Bennington, has its eastern terminus in Brattleboro.

MG Car Museum, Westminster, Vermont

⑬ The Mohawk Trail, MASSACHSETTS This 63-mile scenic stretch of Mass. 2 from Millers Falls to the New York border follows a former Indian path. Several towns along the trail are near I-91; take the Greenfield exit. In **Greenfield**, drive up Greenfield Mountain to **Poet's Seat Tower** for a superb view of the

Connecticut River Valley. A pocket of 19th-century New England, the town of **Shelburne Falls** *(11 miles W)* has a restored downtown and Victorian architecture. Plants have transformed a former arched trolley bridge over the Deerfield River into a three-season **Bridge of Flowers** *(Bridge St)*, which you can walk across.

On the other side of I-91 in **Millers Falls** *(6 miles E)*, the 750-foot-long, 140-foot-high **French King Bridge**, considered to be one of America's most beautiful, spans the Connecticut River.

Historic Deerfield, Massachusetts

Historic Deerfield *(5 miles N of S. Deerfield on US 5, follow signs. 413-774-5581. Adm. fee)* First settled in 1669, the town's quiet, tree-lined streets belie its colonial history of savage Indian raids. Half the town is a museum, with 14 18th-century buildings open for tours. Period houses display antique furniture; other buildings exhibit textiles, pewter, or ceramics. **Memorial Hall Museum** *(Memorial St. and US 5. 413-774-7476. May-Oct.; adm. fee)*, housed in Deerfield Academy's original 1798 school building, is one of America's oldest museums with what some people believe to be the finest collection of antiquities in New England.

Amherst Chain stores have replaced the hippie shops that once ringed **Amherst Common**, but this quintessential New England town's lovely green is still the site of many a protest; five colleges are located nearby. A tour of the **Emily Dickinson Homestead** *(280 Main St. 413-542-8161. May-Oct. Wed.-Sat.; March-April and Nov.–mid-Dec. Wed. and Sat.; closed mid-Dec. to Feb. Reservations a must; adm. fee)*, now a private residence, includes the bedroom where she wrote most of her poetry. The **Strong House** *(67 Amity St. 413-256-0678. Mid-May–Oct. Wed.-Sat.; adm. fee)* features 18th- to 20th-century rooms as well as an 18th-century garden. The **Pratt Museum of Natural History** at Amherst College *(Mass. 116 and 9. 413-542-2165. Daily during academic year; weekends mid-June–Aug.)* has one of New England's outstanding collections of vertebrate fossils, including mastodon and mammoth skeletons. The **Hitchcock Center for the Environment** *(525 S. Pleasant St. 413-256-6006. Grounds open daily; center closed Sun.-Mon.)* offers 27 acres of gardens, trails, ponds, and a children's nature area.

Hadley Furniture and memorabilia accumulated since 1752 chronicle New England history and daily life at the **Porter-Phelps-Huntington House** *(2 miles N of Mass. 9 on Mass. 47. 413-584-4699. Mid-May–mid-Oct. Sat.-Wed.; adm. fee)*. Formerly a barn on the Porter-Phelps-Huntington estate, the **Farm Museum** *(Jct. Mass. 9 and Mass. 47. 413-584-8279. May–mid-Oct. Tues.-Sun.)* exhibits farm and home implements going back 300 years.

Visitors at the Emily Dickinson Homestead, Amherst, Massachusetts

Northampton Politically outspoken, culturally diverse, and upscale, NoHo boasts

Smith College and a colorful downtown featuring chic shops, restaurants, and art galleries. The **Smith College Museum of Art** *(Elm St. at Bedford Terrace. 413-585-2760. Closed Mon.; limited summer hours)* ranks among the finest art museums in academia, with an outstanding 19th- and early 20th-century collection. Also displayed are objects from a variety of cultures in a wide spectrum of media, ranging from 2500 B.C. to the present. **Historic Northampton** *(46 Bridge St. 413-584-6011. March-Dec. Wed.-Sun.)* houses local artifacts and memorabilia spanning 350 years in three historic buildings.

(18) **Holyoke Range State Park** *(2 miles E on Mass. 9 to Hadley, then 3 miles S on Mass. 47 to Mount Holyoke summit. Visitor Center on Mass. 116 in Amherst. 413-253-2883)* The park comprises nearly 3,000 mostly forested acres and includes Mount Holyoke (part of Skinner State Park), with its historic Summit House. The view from the summit is spectacular. *Adm. fee to Skinner S.P. April-Oct. Fri.-Sun.; summit road closed Dec.-March.*

(19) **Holyoke** One of the nation's first planned industrial cities is showing its age, but its evolution from a quiet farming community to a 19th-century boomtown is fascinating. Learn the story through the multimedia exhibits at the **Holyoke Heritage State Park Visitor Center** *(221 Appleton St. 413-534-1723. Closed Mon.)*. At the park, hop aboard the vintage 1920s railroad for a 5-mile ride through town and the surrounding countryside. *(May-Oct. for train; adm. fee.)* Giant bubble makers, microscopes, handmade paper workshops — there's something for kids of all ages at the **Children's Museum** *(Heritage Park, 44 Dwight St. 413-536-KIDS. Closed Mon.; adm. fee)*. The **Volleyball Hall of Fame**, in the same building as the Children's Museum, traces the evolution of the sport. *Closed Mon.*

(20) **Springfield** This is where James Naismith invented the sport of basketball in 1891, and it's now the home of the **Naismith Memorial Basketball Hall of Fame** *(Springfield Center, 1150 W. Columbus Ave. 413-781-6500. Adm. fee)*. The three-floor structure is packed with exhibits on the game. The **Springfield Armory National Historic Site** *(1 Armory Sq., at Springfield Technical Community College. 413-734-8551. Closed Mon. except summer)* produced military weapons from 1795 to 1968 and displays its outstanding collection. Springfield's four major museums are grouped around the grassy **Quadrangle** *(222 State St. 413-739-3871. Museums closed Mon.-Wed.; one adm. fee for all)*. The **Museum of Fine Arts** features French Impressionist and American paintings and early Chinese ceramics. Highlights at the **Science Museum** are the African and Dinosaur Halls and the Exploration Center for kids. The collection at the **George Walter Vincent Smith Art**

Basketball Hall of Fame, Springfield, Massachusetts

Museum includes Oriental armor, Chinese cloisonné, and Middle Eastern rugs. Period rooms, decorative objects, and domestic artifacts tell area history since l636 in the **Connecticut Valley Historical Museum.** Seven 18th- and early 19th-century buildings were moved from all over New England to the **Storrowtown Village Museum**, on the grounds of the Eastern States Exposition (*US 5 to Mass. 147 W. to 1305 Memorial Ave. in West Springfield. 413-787-0136. Mid-June–Labor Day Mon.-Sat.; adm. fee*).

East Windsor, CONNECTI-CUT At the **Connecticut Trolley Museum** (*1 mile E on Conn. 140. 203-627-6540. Mem. Day-Labor Day, weekends only rest of year; adm. fee*), you can ride on any of three antique trolleys. Whistles blow and brass bells ring as they rattle through the countryside. The **Connecticut Fire Museum** (*Behind trolley museum. 203-623-4732. Memorial Day-Labor Day, weekends only May and Sept.; adm. fee*) exhibits old-time fire trucks.

New England Air Museum, at Bradley International Airport, in Connecticut

New England Air Museum (*2 miles W on Conn. 20, 2 miles N on Conn. 75, follow signs. 203-623-3305*) With more than 75 aircraft, including bombers and jet fighters, this is one of the U. S.'s largest indoor displays of historical planes. *Adm. fee.*

Old New-Gate Prison and Copper Mine (*6 miles W on Conn. 20 to E. Granby, right at Newgate Rd., follow signs. 203-653-3563*) North America's first chartered copper mine (1707) became Connecticut's first prison (1773); the felons worked the copper. You can tour the ruins. *Mid-May–Oct. Wed.-Sun.; adm. fee.*

Windsor Connecticut's first community was begun in 1633 by settlers from Plymouth Colony in Massachusetts. **Ellsworth Homestead** (*2.5 miles toward Windsor on Conn. 159 to 778 Palisado Ave. 203-688-8717. Mid-May–mid-Oct. Tues.-Wed. and Sat.; adm. fee*), an excellent example of 18th-century Connecticut River Valley architecture, was the birthplace of Oliver Ellsworth, a Chief Justice of the U. S. Supreme Court. The 1640 **Fyler House** (*96 Palisado Ave. 203-688-3813. April-Nov. Tues.-Sat., Nov.-March Mon.-Fri.; adm. fee*), home of the Windsor Historical Society, is one of the state's oldest surviving frame dwellings. On the grounds of **Northwest Park** (*145 Lang Rd. off Conn. 75. 203-285-1886*) are a nature center, the **Gordon Taylor Tobacco Cultural Museum** (*March-Nov. Tues.-Thurs., Sat.*), and a sugar-house (*Feb.–mid-March*).

Hartford See I-84 E, p. 254.
West Hartford See I-84 E, p. 254.
East Hartford See I-84 E, p. 255.
New Britain See I-84 E, p. 254.
New Haven See I-95, p. 327.

Along the Connecticut River you'll see fields of *tobacco* and the long barns used for drying the harvested leaves. But isn't tobacco a southern crop? Not necessarily—the climate of the Connecticut Valley is ideal for a variety of *Nicotiana tabacum* used in cigar wrappers, and locally in cigars. (Tobacco was first planted here in 1640 with seeds from Virginia plantations.) In New Haven, a smoke shop near the Yale University campus carries at least a half dozen brands of Connecticut cigars, remnants of a fading New England industry.

Unless otherwise noted, directions are from interstate, and sites are free and generally open daily. Phone for further information.

① St. Johnsbury, VERMONT This old railroad and manufacturing town boasts the eclectic **Fairbanks Museum and Planetarium** (*Main and Prospect Sts. 802-748-2372. Adm. fees*). The handsome Romanesque Revival fortress displays natural science and rural history exhibits, as well as cultural artifacts from around the world. The Children's Nature Corner is open in July and August, and a small planetarium gives shows daily during those months and on weekends the rest of the year. Two blocks away is the **St. Johnsbury Athenaeum and Art Gallery** (*30 Main St. 802-748-8291. Closed Sun.*). The gallery is preserved exactly as it was when dedicated in 1873; most of the paintings are by artists of the Hudson River school and include Albert Bierstadt's enormous "Domes of the Yosemite." Indulge your sweet tooth at the **Maple Grove Farms of Vermont** (*US 2, 167 Portland St. 802-748-5141*), one of the world's oldest and largest maple candy factories. The tour shows candy making and syrup bottling, and a museum has exhibits on maple syrup history. *Closed weekends, museum closed Nov.-March; adm. fee.*

300

Fairbanks Museum and
Planetarium, St. Johnsbury, Vt.

② Frost Place, NEW HAMPSHIRE (*1 mile S on N.H. 116, then follow signs. 603-823-5510*) From 1915 to 1920, Robert Frost lived and wrote in this hilltop farmhouse overlooking Franconia Notch. First editions, photos, and memorabilia are displayed here, and a poet-in-residence gives readings. Save time for the half-mile Poetry-Nature Trail. *Memorial Day-June weekend afternoons; July-Columbus Day afternoons except Tues.; adm. fee.*

③ White Mountain National Forest (*603-528-8721. Info centers in Lincoln and Campton*) For about 30 miles, I-93 cuts through a corner of this 772,108-acre forest. Before it was designated a national forest in 1918, huge logging drives took place here each spring. Now logging is limited, and much of the forest is preserved as wilderness. It includes more than 1,200 miles of hiking trails, 22 campgrounds, and a meals-included hikers' hut system managed by the Appalachian Mountain Club (*hut reservations 603-466-2727*).

Hiking Mount Washington, White Mountain National Forest, New Hampshire

Franconia Notch Parkway
I-93 merges with the parkway for 8 miles to traverse the mountain fastnesses of 6,440-acre **Franconia Notch State Park** (*603-823-5563 or 271-3254*). The first stop is **Echo Lake** (*Closed Labor Day-Memorial Day; adm. fee*). At an elevation of 1,931 feet, it is a lovely—if somewhat cool—spot for swimming, fishing, and boating. You can pick up information about the park just beyond the lake at the **Cannon Mountain**

Old Man of the Mountain, Franconia Notch, N.H.

Aerial Tramway (*Cannon Mt. Ski Area. Late May-Oct., weekends rest of year; adm. fee*). Ride the 80-passenger tram to the 4,200-foot summit. Turn at **Profile Lake**, the "Old Man's Washbowl," to see the **Old Man of the Mountain**—a 200-million-year-old natural rock formation, immortalized in a story by Nathaniel Hawthorne. Farther on is the **Flume** (*Visitor Center 603-745-8391. Late May-Oct.; adm. fee. Combo pass available with Cannon Mt. Aerial Tramway*), an 800-foot-long gorge. Flume Brook cascades between narrow granite walls, crisscrossed by boardwalks, paths, and a covered bridge.

Lost River (*8 miles W on N.H. 112. 603-745-8031*) Walk a half-mile loop across bridges, up ladders, and into caverns, following the river as it courses along a chaotic jumble of glacially-scattered boulders. *Mid-May–mid-Oct.; adm. fee.*

Squam Lake This is the lovely lake made famous by the film *On Golden Pond.* **Golden Pond Tours** of the lake, including Thayer Cottage, Purgatory Cove, and probably a few loons, leave from Squam Boats Dock at the Holderness Bridge (*4.5 miles S of Holderness on US 3. 603-279-4405. Mem. Day-foliage season; adm. fee*). The **Science Center of New**

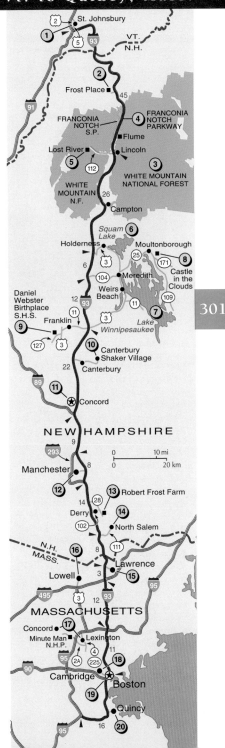

301

Hampshire (*4 miles NE on US 3 to junction with N.H. 113. 603-968-7194*) is a 200-acre outdoor learning center with a three-quarter-mile exhibit trail winding past native wildlife—black bears, otters, white-tailed deer—in natural enclosures. *May-Oct.; adm. fee.*

Moultonborough, on Lake Winnipesaukee, N. H.

302

⑦ **Lake Winnipesaukee** (*7 miles E on N.H. 104 to Meredith*) The boardwalk, water slides, and amusement parks on the state's largest lake are kid heaven. Board one of the restored coaches of the **Winnipesaukee Scenic Railroad** (*603-745-2135 or 279-5253. July–Labor Day, call for additional times; adm. fee*) at Meredith for a two-hour ride, or at Weirs Beach (*Continue down US 3 for 4 miles*) for a one-hour ride along the lakeshore. The **Mount Washington Cruise Line** (*Weirs Beach. 603-366-BOAT. Late May–mid-Oct.; adm. fee*) offers several cruise choices, such as a U. S. mail boat, a 46-foot sloop, and the vintage M.S. *Mount Washington*. **Ellacoya State Beach** (*SE on N.H. 11. 603-293-7821. Adm. fee*) is great for swimming.

⑧ **Castle in the Clouds** (*23 miles E via N.H. 104, 25, 109, and 171. 603-476-2352*) Industrialist Thomas Plant built this mansion, well off the highway but worth the detour, on a 5,200-acre mountain aerie high above Lake Winnipesaukee. The jitney that takes you up the steep, winding drive is an adventure in itself. Horseback riding available. *Mem. Day–mid-Oct.; adm. fee.*

⑨ **Daniel Webster Birthplace S.H.S.** (*9 miles W on US 3/N.H. 11 to junction, then S on US 3 to N.H. 127, follow signs. 603-934-5057 or 271-3254*) The reconstructed frame structure, where the statesman was born in 1782, contains antique furnishings, utensils, and memorabilia. Daniel's father built the two-room cabin to give his family more room than they had ever known. *May-Oct.; adm. fee.*

⑩ **Canterbury Shaker Village** (*Canterbury exit, follow signs E 7 miles. 603-783-9511*) The last Shaker to live in Canterbury died in 1992, but the spirit of the sect lives on in the village they built to be a "heaven on earth." At its peak in 1860, 300 people lived, worked, and worshiped communally here in 100 buildings on 4,000 acres. Today, six buildings are open for tours and eight others to poke around in, and craftsmen keep Shaker workmanship alive. *May-Oct., weekends April and Nov.-Dec.; adm. fee.*

⑪ **Concord** (*Chamber of Commerce, 244 N. Main St. 603-224-2508. Mon.-Fri.*) New Hampshire's capital is compact and easy to tour.

From central New Hampshire to I-495 in northern Massachusetts, I-93 follows much of the course of the **Merrimack River.** Because of its pronounced vertical drop—269 feet in 110 miles—the Merrimack has long been a source of power, first for waterwheel-driven mills and later for hydroelectricity. The great factory cities of Manchester, Nashua, Lowell, and Lawrence grew up along its banks in the mid-1800s, utilizing its energy to weave countless miles of wool and cotton cloth.

Journey through the cosmos at **The Christa McAuliffe Planetarium** (*I-393 to first exit, turn left and follow signs. 603-271-STAR. Closed Mon.; reservations advised; adm. fee*). Computer graphics, videos, a 29-speaker sound system, and 3-D star fields combine on the theater's 40-foot domed screen to create the illusion of flying through space. Head downtown to the **New Hampshire Historical Society** (*30 Park St. 603-225-3381. Donation requested*) to see one of the beautifully restored Concord coaches that helped put the city on the map, as well as 19th-century White Mountain paintings and state-crafted furniture. Pick up a copy of the **Coach and Eagle Trail** self-guided walking tour of 17 historic sites, including the gold-domed **State House** (*107 N. Main St. 603-271-2154. Mon.-Fri.*), the oldest in the nation where the legislature still meets in its original chambers. To learn about New Hampshire's only U. S. President, head up North Main Street to **The Pierce Manse** (*14 Penacook St. 603-225-2068. Mid-June–Labor Day Mon.-Fri.; adm. fee*). Franklin Pierce, the 14th President, and his family lived here from 1842 to 1848, and the house contains many of his furnishings. A few doors up is the far more elaborate 1882 **Kimball-Jenkins Estate** (*266 N. Main St. 603-225-3932. May-late Oct.; adm. fee*), a Victorian Gothic with 11-foot ceilings, hand-carved oak woodwork, Oriental rugs, and formal gardens.

Old gasoline pump

303

Manchester Like its English namesake, Manchester, on the banks of the Merrimack River, once throbbed to the rhythm of power looms. The textile mills are closed now, and rows of empty brick factory buildings have been rehabilitated for small businesses and industries. The largest building complex, the **Amoskeag Mill Yard** (*Commercial St.*), was home to the Amoskeag Manufacturing Co., at one time the world's largest textile manufacturer. **SEE Science Center** (*324 Commercial St. 603-669-0400. Daily in summer, rest of year Thurs. evenings and weekend afternoons; adm. fee*), a science learning center, has made good use of its space in one of the old Amoskeag mills. It offers kids more than 70 hands-on exhibits, including a chance to "walk on the moon." The **Currier Gallery of Art** (*192 Orange St. 603-669-6144. Closed Mon.; adm. fee*) bills itself as "a treasure waiting to be discovered." The collection includes paintings and sculpture from the 13th through the 20th century by European and American masters as varied as Tiepolo, Copley, Matisse, and Picasso. Tours leave the museum for the 1950 **Zimmerman House** (*603-626-4158. Closed Mon.-Wed.; adm. fee*), designed by Frank Lloyd Wright and an example of his low-cost, flat-roofed "Usonian" style.

Robert Frost Farm, Derry, New Hampshire

Robert Frost Farm (*5 miles SE of Derry on N.H. 28. 603-271-3254*) The two-story clapboard house has been restored to look as it did from 1900 to 1911, when the poet lived and farmed here, and the Hyla Brook Nature/Poetry Trail in back is lovely. *Daily in summer, weekends in spring and fall; adm. fee.*

(14) **North Salem** America's Stonehenge (*5 miles E on N.H. 111 to Island Pond and Haverhill Rds., follow signs. 603-893-8300*) Although not nearly as dramatic as its British counterpart, this Stonehenge (formerly called Mystery Hill), a 30-acre complex of erratic stone walls containing large standing stones, is believed by many to have been built some 4,000 years ago by ancient people well-versed in astronomy and stone construction. *Daily mid-April–mid-Nov., last two weekends in Nov., first two weekends in April; adm. fee.*

(15) **Lawrence, MASSACHUSETTS** Lawrence Heritage State Park (*N on I-495 to Marston St. exit, first left onto Canal St., follow signs to Jackson St. 508-794-1655*) There's little green space in this urban park, but a fine Visitor Center chronicles Lawrence's heyday as a textile capital. Exhibits and videos document immigration, factory life, and the Great Lawrence Strike of 1912. Walk the route of the strikers, past the mills along the Merrimack River.

(16) **Lowell** (*10 miles S on I-495 to Lowell Connector, follow signs*) In the 1820s, Boston Brahmin Francis Cabot Lowell returned from a trip to England with the revolutionary idea of creating a city around a complex of textile mills. The stories of Lowell's enterprise, of farm girls-turned-mill workers, of immigrants, and of the eventual eclipse of the local textile industry are documented at **Lowell National Historical Park** (*246 Market St. 508-970-5000. Tours June-Oct.; adm. fee*) through indoor exhibits and a tour of canals and mills. Lowell's other claim to fame is its native son, Beat Generation writer Jack Kerouac. **Jack Kerouac Park** (*Bridge St.*) features a statue and stone markers inscribed with passages from his work.

(17) **Lexington and Concord** To visit the sites of the American Revolution's opening battles, take the I-95 exit and head south for 7 miles to Mass. 4/225 (*Bedford St.*) and follow signs. Here is **Battle Green**, where at dawn on April 19, 1775, some 80 militiamen met 200 redcoats in the first skirmish of the war. Across the street at **Buckman Tavern** (*1 Bedford St. 617-862-1450. Mid-April–Oct.; adm. fee*), costumed guides tell how patriots gathered that morning to await the British. Take Mass. Ave./Mass. 2A ("Battle Road") west toward Concord to **Minute Man National Historical Park** (*Mass. 2A. 617-484-6159 or 508-369-6944. Call for all openings and closings; adm. fee for The Wayside*), a 750-acre strip that extends to Concord's reconstructed **North Bridge**, site of the colonists' first deliberate attack on the British—"the shot heard round the world." At one end of it is Daniel Chester French's statue of **"The Minute Man."** In the park, exhibits, maps, and film-strips re-create the day's events. Also there is **The Wayside**, at various times home to both Nathaniel Hawthorne and Louisa May Alcott. Other worthwhile stops in historic and literary Concord include the **Concord Museum** (*200 Lexington Rd. 508-369-9609. Adm. fee*), which depicts 17th- to 19th-century life in the town; the **Old Manse** (*Monument St., by North Bridge. 508-369-3909. Mid-April*

Massachusetts's literary roots reach back to the dour 18th-century Puritans. In the mid-1800s, an intellectual revolution took place in Concord, fomented by a club of local nonconformists—Ralph Waldo Emerson, Bronson Alcott, and Henry David Thoreau—who together with some high-powered Boston intellectuals called themselves *Transcendentalists.* Their radical new ideas about God and society sparked perhaps the most brilliant period in American literature, known as the American Renaissance.

Costumed "redcoat" at North Bridge reenactment, Concord, Mass.

–Oct. Wed.-Mon.; adm. fee), a Georgian house built in 1770 where both Hawthorne and Ralph Waldo Emerson lived; the **Thoreau Lyceum** (*156 Belknap St. 508-369-5912. Closed Jan., Feb. open weekends only; adm. fee*), with a replica of writer Henry David Thoreau's Walden Pond house out back; and **Sleepy Hollow Cemetery** (*Bedford St. 508-371-6280*), where Thoreau, Emerson, Hawthorne, Daniel Chester French, and the Alcotts lie buried in Authors Ridge.

Cambridge Boston's neighbor across the Charles River is the site of Harvard and MIT, progressive politics, eclectic dining, and a daunting array of bookstores. The social hub of Cambridge is **Harvard Square**, a hodgepodge of cafés, boutiques, and local personalities. At the **Cambridge Discovery** booth (*617-497-1630*) near the entrance to the subway station, you can pick up walking-tour maps of the city. Guided tours of Old Cambridge are also offered in summer by appt. To see the **Longfellow National Historic Site** (*105 Brattle St. 617-876-4491. Closed Mon.-Tues. Reserve for tours; adm. fee*), where George Washington lived during the siege of Boston and poet Henry Wadsworth Longfellow spent 45 years, head out of the square along Brattle Street. Outdoor poetry readings and concerts are held in summer.

Arthur M. Sackler Museum, Cambridge, Mass.

305

Harvard University, Cambridge, Massachusetts

Harvard University, founded in 1636, is the country's oldest institution of higher learning and home to nine museums. For a complete rundown, stop at the **Information Center** (*1348 Mass. Ave. 617-495-1573. Free 45-minute tour of Harvard Yard offered.*). The three art museums (*617-495-9400. One adm. fee for all*)—the **Fogg**, the **Busch-Reisinger**, and the **Arthur M. Sackler**—are near the corner of Quincy Street and Broadway. The **Museums of Cultural and Natural History** (*24 Oxford St. 617-495-3045. One adm. fee for all*) encompass the **Botanical Museum**, with its renowned collection of glass flowers; the **Mineralogical and Geological Museum**; the **Museum of Comparative Zoology**; and the **Peabody Museum of Archaeology and Ethnology**, with its exhibits on American Indians and Central and South American cultures.

Old Burying Ground, near Christ Church, Cambridge

Home of Brahmins, the Red Sox, baked beans, and a half dozen major colleges, Massachusetts's capital is more culturally diverse and rich in history than any other American city its size. Because many of its streets were laid out along winding colonial paths, the best way to explore Boston is on foot. Bring along a good city map and comfortable shoes (Greater Boston Convention & Visitors Bureau, 4th floor, Prudential Tower, 800 Boylston St. 617-536-4100 or 800-888-5515).

U.S.S. *Constitution*

Any visit to Boston should begin with a walking tour along the **Freedom Trail** *(Boston Common Info Booth, or National Park Service Visitor Center, 15 State St. 617-242-5642),* a 3-mile loop incorporating 350 years of history. The trail starts at either **Charlestown Navy Yard** or **Boston Common** and includes stops at the **Paul Revere House** in the North End; **Faneuil Hall** *(Dock Sq.),* the "Cradle of Liberty"; the site of the Boston Massacre at the **Old State House** *(Wash. and State Sts.);* and **King's Chapel** *(58 Tremont St.).* Try to be at **Quincy Market** *(Dock Sq.)* around lunchtime—the domed, granite building

at the center of the city's renewed market district is packed with food stalls.

Boston Common *(Bordered by Tremont, Beacon, and Charles Sts.)* is the oldest public park in the country. Augustus Saint-Gaudens's **Robert Gould Shaw and 54th Regiment Memorial**—to the first free black unit to fight in the Civil War—is at the Beacon St. entrance opposite Charles Bulfinch's magnificent **State House.** Adjacent to the Common in the **Public Garden,** swan boats glide across the lagoon in summer. Walk up Beacon Hill to begin the **Black Heritage Trail** *(46 Joy St. 617-742-5415),* a walking tour of 14 sites highlighting the contribution of blacks to Boston's history. Among the stops: the Abiel Smith School, the first public school for blacks in Boston and the site of the **Museum of Afro American History** *(46 Joy St. 617-742-1854. Mon.-Fri., weekends by appt.).* William Lloyd Garrison began the New England Anti-Slavery Society here in 1832.

Head back down Beacon Hill toward the harbor for the **Boston Tea Party Ship and Museum** *(Congress St. Bridge. 617-338-1773. Closed Dec.-Feb.; adm. fee).*

Faneuil Hall and Quincy Market

The *Beaver II* is a reproduction of one of the ships that tax-protesting Bostonians, masquerading as Indians, boarded in December 1773. Tourists can get into the act by tossing a "bale of tea" overboard. Cross the street to **Museum Wharf** and **The Computer Museum** *(300 Congress St. 617-423-6758. Closed Mon. in winter; adm. fee),* filled with interactive exhibits. Kids are in for a treat next door at the **Children's Museum** *(300 Congress St. 617-426-8855. Closed Mon. Sept.-June; admission fee).* There's a space for toddlers and lots of activities to wear out older kids—including a giant rope "spider's web."

Famous local eatery

Acorn Street, on Beacon Hill

Over on **Central Wharf,** sea turtles, sharks, tropical fish, and eels swim about in a 187,000-gallon cylindrical tank. It's the main exhibit at the **New England Aquarium** *(617-973-5200. Adm. fee).* The best way to get across Boston Harbor to **Charlestown Navy Yard** *(617-242-5601)*—part of Boston National Historical Park—is by water shuttle. Boston Harbor Cruises *(617-227-4320. Adm. fee)* runs one all year. Docked at Pier 1 is the **U.S.S. *Constitution*** *(617-242-5670),* better known as "Old Ironsides." Launched in 1797, it is the oldest commissioned warship afloat. To reach

the **Bunker Hill Monument** *(43 Mon. Sq. 617-242-5641),* follow the Freedom Trail's red path to Breed's Hill.

A water shuttle from **Long Wharf** serves the **John F. Kennedy Library and Museum** in Dorchester *(From I-93 take JFK/U. Mass exit and follow signs. 617-929-4523. Adm. fee),* a stunning structure by architect I. M. Pei. Exhibits chronicle the public and private life of the 35th President.

For a bird's-eye view of Boston and environs, head for Copley Square and take an express elevator to the 60th floor of the city's tallest building, the **John Hancock Tower and Observatory** *(200 Clarendon St. 617-572-6429. Adm. fee).* Next door is H. H. Richardson's **Trinity Church** *(Copley Sq. 617-536-0944),* a Romanesque Revival masterpiece.

Don't miss two outstanding art museums: the **Museum of Fine Arts, Boston** *(465 Huntington Ave. 617-267-9300. Closed Mon.; adm. fee),* one of the world's premier repositories of fine and decorative arts; and the nearby **Isabella Stewart Gardner Museum** *(280 The Fenway. 617-566-1401. Closed Mon.; adm. fee),* a priceless collection in a house modeled after a 15th-century Venetian palazzo.

307

The Common

Quincy The mansion at the **Adams National Historic Site** *(E on Furnace Brook Pkwy. Visitor Center, 1250 Hancock St. 617-773-1177. Mid-April–mid-Nov.; adm. fee)* was home to second U. S. President John Adams and his son, sixth President John Quincy Adams. Their descendants lived here until 1927. The site also includes both Presidents' birthplaces, on Franklin Street.

Unless otherwise noted, directions are from interstate, and sites are free and generally open daily. Phone for further information.

Billings, MONT. See I-90, p. 278.

① **Huntley** **Huntley Project Museum of Irrigated Agriculture** *(Huntley exit; 3 miles E of town on US 312, follow signs. 406-967-2680)* In 1907, the Bureau of Reclamation opened the headgates for this irrigation project, which transformed 29,000 dry Yellowstone River Valley acres into verdant farmland. A memorial to those who homesteaded here, the museum presents more than 5,000 early farm and irrigation artifacts, several historic buildings, and the project's story. *May-Sept.*

Pompeys Pillar, Montana

② **Pompeys Pillar** *(Follow signs. 406-657-6262)* On this 150-foot-high sandstone stump overlooking the Yellowstone River, Capt. William Clark scratched his name on July 25, 1806. Clark named the butte to honor Baptiste, the son of his expedition's Indian guide, Sacajawea. The boy's nickname was Pomp—"chief" in Shoshone. *June-Sept.*

③ **Miles City** Born of a military campaign under Col. Nelson Miles following the Battle of Little Bighorn, Miles City boomed as a stock center and railhead in the 1880s. It's still a roughneck cowtown, known worldwide for its Jaycee Bucking Horse Sale, an annual May blowout. Despite a number of fires, downtown has enough authentic boomtown buildings, saloons, and Stetsons for a Western movie set. Take time to see the **Range Riders Museum** *(West end of Main St. 406-232-4483. Apr.-Oct.; adm. fee)* with all manner of Westerniana; and the unique **Custer County Art Center** *(Water Plant Rd. 406-232-0635. Closed Mon.)* whose award-winning galleries reside in the tanks of the historic waterworks plant.

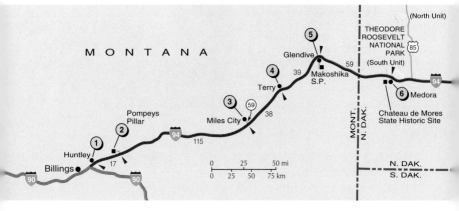

Terry Here on eastern Montana's windblown plains, English photographer Evelyn J. Cameron set up ranch-keeping in 1890. For more than 30 years, she documented the region's life and land. The **Prairie County Museum** (*204 S. Logan St. 406-486-5677*) contains the largest collection of her original prints, along with historical flotsam. Next door, the **Cameron Gallery** displays prints made from glass-plate and nitrate negatives. *Mem. Day–Labor Day.*

Glendive Built by the railroad, ranching, and agriculture, Glendive sits in an oil basin. The main attraction is **Makoshika State Park** (*3 miles S on Snyder Ave. Visitor Center 406-365-8596. Adm. fee*), an 8,123-acre island of fantastic badlands in the Yellowstone River Valley. Rich in fossils, including more than 10 dinosaur species, the park also exposes ancient rock layers. At the **Frontier Gateway Museum** (*1 mile E of town on Belle Prairie Frontage Rd. 406-365-8168. May-Sept.*), you'll find farm machinery to fire engines, historic buildings, and a replicated old downtown street.

Medora, NORTH DAKOTA (*Historic Medora exit*) A lovely oasis ringed by badlands and range, restored Medora is a stylized shadow of its former frontier self. In 1883, aristocratic French entrepreneur Marquis de Mores founded the town, named for his wife. **Chateau de Mores State Historic Site** (*701-623-4355. Open all year; tours mid-May–mid-Sept. and by appt.; adm. fee*) includes his opulent mansion, the ruins of his beef-packing plant, an interpretive center, and a park. De Mores's guests included Theodore Roosevelt, who arrived in 1883 and got hooked on ranching. His inaccessible, 218-acre Elkhorn Ranch is in the wildly beautiful **Theodore Roosevelt National Park** (*Follow signs. Visitor Centers at Medora and Painted Canyon. 701-623-4466. Adm. fee May-Sept.*), the **South Unit** of which is reachable from Medora. A 36-mile loop road wends through the park, past spectacular overlooks of badlands, canyons, and the Little Missouri River. Wildlife includes elk, pronghorns,

Unique among Montana's fauna is the homely ***paddlefish***, a "living fossil" with a prehistoric pedigree. Peculiar to the roily waters of the lower Yellowstone and to China's Yangtze River, this bottomprowler sports a paddle-shaped snout, which can grow to 2 feet. Adults weigh in at 100 pounds average. The only way to land one is to snag it with heavy tackle, then brace for a fight. Long prized for its tasty meat, paddlefish roe now rubs labels with choice caviars.

309

Built in the 1880s

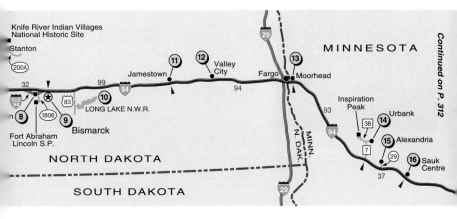

Continued on P. 312

bison, and wild horses. The Medora Visitor Center exhibits Roosevelt memorabilia along with natural history. Also dedicated to the 26th President is the *Medora Musical*, an extravaganza of music, dance, and comedy at the **Burning Hills Amphitheater** *(Follow signs. 701-623-4381. Mid-June to Labor Day; reservations; adm. fee).*

Cowboy gear belonging to Theodore Roosevelt (upper) and bison (lower), in Theodore Roosevelt National Park, North Dakota

310

If Time Permits...

(7) **Knife River Indian Vill. N.H.S.** *(38 miles N via N. Dak. 31, N. Dak. 200A, and Rte. 37 through Stanton. Visitor Center 701-745-3309)* Worth a detour, this is the crème de la crème—for presentation and scale—of earth-lodge village sites found throughout the Upper Missouri River Valley. Self-guided trails access the remains—lodge depressions, storage pits, fortification ditches—of three villages, occupied for centuries by ancestors of the Mandan, Hidatsa, and Arikara tribes.

(8) **Mandan** **Fort Abraham Lincoln State Park** *(4 miles S of town on N. Dak. 1806, follow signs. 701-663-9571)* This 977-acre park sprawls on the banks where the Missouri River meets the Heart. A plaque commemorates Lewis and Clark's 1804 riverside campsite near On-A-Slant Mandan Village. Occupied by the Indians from about 1650 to 1750, the site now exhibits five replicated earth lodges. On the bluff where Fort McKeen Infantry Post, later Fort Lincoln, stood are reconstructed blockhouses and a cemetery. Below is **Lt. Col. George A. Custer's home** *(701-258-0203. May-early Oct.; adm. fee),* **Cavalry Square,** and a Visitor Center.

(9) **Bismarck** *(Convention & Visitors Bureau, 523 N. Fourth St. 701-222-4308. State Capitol exit)* Bismarck became the state capital when North Dakota joined the Union in 1889. A major rail town, it was named to flatter Germany's "Iron Chancellor"—a public relations move to woo German investors. The landmark in this horizontal landscape is the 19-story **State Capitol** *(600 East Blvd. 701-224-2480. Tours Mon.-Fri., plus wknds. Mem. Day-Labor Day),* the "skyscraper of the prairie." Next to the capitol, the **North Dakota Heritage Center** *(701-224-2666)* features a museum dedicated to state heritage and history. Down by the park-lined river is the launch for the **Lewis & Clark Riverboat** *(Port of Bismarck, North River Rd. 701-255-4233. Mem. Day-Labor Day; adm. fee),* which offers assorted cruises, including runs to Fort Lincoln.

State Capitol, Bismarck, N. Dak.

(10) **Long Lake National Wildlife Refuge** *(Sterling exit, 11 miles S on N. Dak. 83, 2 miles E at refuge sign. 701-387-4397)* On the central flyway, this wild and windy refuge centers around a shallow 18-mile-long lake. A wetland management area, more than half of its 22,310 acres are lake bottom, with marsh,

prairie, and cultivated uplands. Sandhill cranes descend in the thousands in autumn.

Jamestown   Home of author Louis L'Amour, the city has as its trademark a 3-story, 60-ton concrete bison overlooking the valley at **Frontier Village** (*17th St. S.W. 701-252-6307. May-Sept.*), a reconstructed prairie town. The unique attraction here is the **National Buffalo Museum** (*Off Louis L'Amour Lane. 701-252-8648. Adm. fee*), which traces the animal from prehistory to the present.

Valley City   Dairy farms and grain fields are the backbone of this Sheyenne River Valley community. Severe drought prompted the building of **Baldhill Dam** (*12 miles NW of town, follow signs. 701-845-2970*), which created 27-mile-long Lake Ashtabula—"fish river." Surrounded by rolling country, its southern shoreline sports eight recreation areas. En route, **Valley City National Fish Hatchery** (*2 miles NW of town at 11515 River Rd., follow signs. 701-845-3464. Weekdays*) offers a fish pond for human small fry, exhibits, tours, and trails in a beautiful setting.

Sunflowers protecting wheat from wind, N. Dak.

Fargo   See I-29, p. 86.

Moorhead, MINNESOTA   Fargo's twin on the east bank of the Red River is an agricultural hub. Highlights include the **Plains Art Museum** (*521 Main Ave. 218-236-7383. Closed Mon.*), with a melange of American, Indian, and African art, and special regional exhibits. Centerpiece of the multicultural **Heritage Hjemkomst Interpretive Center** (*202 First Ave. N. 218-233-5604. Adm. fee*) is a 76-foot replicated Viking vessel that sailed to Norway in 1982. Downstairs, the **Clay County Museum** presents town histories.

Urbank   **Inspiration Peak** (*Brandon exit, N on Rte. 7 for 13.5 miles, left on Rte. 38 for 1.7 miles, then right on Inspiration Peak Rd.*) "There is to be seen," wrote novelist Sinclair Lewis of Minnesota's second highest point (1,785 feet), "a glorious 20-mile circle of some 50 lakes scattered among fields and pastures, like sequins fallen on an old Paisley shawl." A short climb to the top of the knoll will revive the most highway-lagged spirit, especially in fall.

Alexandria   (*3 miles N on Minn. 29*) In 1898, Olaf Ohman found on his nearby farm a large, flat stone covered with strange marks—a Runic inscription, as it turned out, seemingly left by Viking visitors in 1362. Debate still rages over its authenticity, but Alexandrians believe. They call their town the "birthplace of America." Judge for yourself at the **Runestone Museum** (*206 Broadway. 612-763-3160*), which displays the 202-pound stone plus Norse history—and "Big Ole," a 28-foot Viking statue. Out back, **Fort Alexandria** contains replicated 1862 structures. *Adm. fee.*

16 **Sauk Centre** In 1920, novelist Sinclair Lewis published *Main Street*, an exposé of small-town America that helped win him the Nobel Prize. If Lewis won wide critical acclaim, the folks back home were just plain critical. Since then, the town has capitalized on its famous son. Businesses, from drugstore to café, realty to movie theater, flaunt the "Main Street" name. Literary buffs will enjoy the **Sinclair Lewis Boyhood Home** (*810 Sinclair Lewis Ave. 612-352-5201. Memorial Day-Labor Day; adm. fee*) and the **Sinclair Lewis Interpretive Center** (*Jct. with US 71. 612-352-5201. Mon.-Fri., plus weekends Memorial Day-Sept.*).

Sinclair Lewis Boyhood Home,
Sauk Center, Minnesota

17 **St. Cloud** (*6 miles NE on Minn. 23. Chamber of Commerce, 30 S. 6th Ave. 612-251-2940*) An educational center with two universities and a college, this Mississippi River town was named after Napoleon Bonaparte's home in France. It is famed for the premium granite quarried here, a half million pounds of which were used to restore the Statue of Liberty. **Stearns County Heritage Center** (*235 33rd Ave. S. 612-253-8424. Closed Mon., except June-Aug.; adm. fee*) contains a replica of a granite quarry and culture and history exhibits. Among the city's parks is **Riverside Park** (*1515 Riverside Dr. S.E.*), with the dazzling **Munsinger Gardens.**

18 **Elk River** (*5 miles N on Minn. 101*) **Oliver H. Kelley Farm** (*Kelley Farm Rd. 2.5 mi. SE of town off US 10. 612-441-6896*) In 1867, progressive labor organizer Oliver Kelley founded the Grange to help farmers shift from subsistence to market farming. Today, his 189-acre tract is a working Victorian farmstead, where costumed guides plow with oxen and horses, churn butter, and cook molasses. Also here are Kelley's plantation-style home, gardens, and a history center. *May-Oct.; Nov.-April weekends interpretive center only; adm. fee.*

Minneapolis-St. Paul See I-35, pp. 94-95.

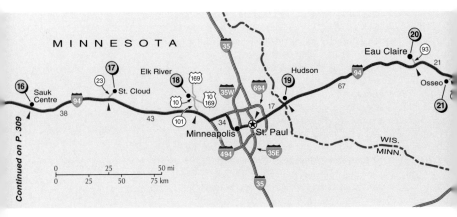

Continued on P. 309

Hudson, WISCONSIN Sitting pretty along the St. Croix River, Hudson evokes the timeless quality of an American small town. The arts are alive and well at **Phipps Center for the Arts** (*109 Locust St. 715-386-2305. Galleries open Mon.-Sat.*), the valley's showcase for art, theater, and music. Claiming a corner of the historic district is the 1855 **Octagon House** (*1004 Third St. 715-386-2654. May-Oct. and Christmastime, closed Mon.; adm. fee*), with fine period pieces, plus a carriage museum and garden house. **Birkmose Park** (*Coulee Rd.*) offers an overlook plus Indian mounds.

Devil's Lake, on Wisconsin's Ice Age Trail, near Baraboo, see p. 284

Eau Claire (*Visitor Center, junction Wis. 53 and Golf Rd. 715-839-2919*) Noting that the muddy Chippewa ran clear where it joined the river here, French explorers dubbed the spot "clear water." In 1857, Eau Claire boomed as a lumber town, boasting 11 mills at its peak, but the industry went bust before 1900. **Paul Bunyan Logging Camp** (*Carson Park Dr. 715-835-6200 or 839-2919. Mid-April–Sept., closed Mon.; adm. fee*) re-creates an 1890s camp, with artifacts and an interpretive center. Next door, **Chippewa Valley Museum** (*715-834-7871. Closed Mon.; adm. fee*) tells the valley's story, from prehistory to the present, with special exhibits and a working turn-of-the-century ice-cream parlor. On the grounds are a historic log cabin (*May-Sept.*) and a one-room schoolhouse. Among worthwhile sights at the **University of Wisconsin-Eau Claire** (*Information for university activities 715-836-4833; tours 836-5415*) are the **Foster Art Gallery, James Newman Clark Bird Museum,** and **L. E. Phillips Planetarium.**

Osseo **Northland Fishing Museum** (*1 block off US 10 at 1012 Gunderson Rd. 715-597-2551*) Aficionados of things fishy will appreciate this unique collector's gallery, with rare 19th-century rods,

313

Continued on P. 316

reels, and lures; antique outboard motors; and vintage boats and decoys. Also contains a wildlife art gallery. *Adm. fee.*

☞ Chances are your Thanksgiving cranberry sauce originated in central Wisconsin's wetlands, one of the country's largest **cranberry-producing regions**. Named after the sandhill crane ("cran"), whose head the berry resembles, cranberries are Wisconsin's number one fruit crop. So mired is this region in the berry business, it even produces all the necessary machines, tools, fertilizers, and chemicals. And Ocean Spray, mother of the cranberry juice cocktail, operates the world's largest cranberry receiving station just off I-94 and I-90 in Tomah.

314

㉒ **W a r r e n s   Cranberry Expo Ltd.** (*6 miles E of town on Rte. E, follow signs. 608-378-4878*) Billed as the "Cranberry Capital of Wisconsin," this beautiful area has the state's largest concentration of bogs. At harvest time, great fragrant flats of ripe berries punctuate green fields. In the heart of it all sits this unique family-run museum, where a fascinating tour details the berry's history and industry. Afterward, be sure to sample the cranberry ice cream and other treats. *Apr.-Oct., other times by appt.; adm. fee.*

B a r a b o o (*7 miles S on US 12*) See I-90, p. 284.

M a d i s o n See I-90, p. 285.

㉓ **L a k e   M i l l s   Aztalan State Park** (*S to town, then 3 miles E on Rte. B and S on Rte. Q. 414-648-8774 or 608-873-9695. Apr.-Nov.*) One of Wisconsin's most important archaeological sites, Aztalan was the seat of a large, stockaded village and distinctive, complex society, which flourished from A.D. 900 to 1200. What remain on this 172-acre preserve are grassy mounds and reconstructed stockade sections, linked by an interpretive path. The **Aztalan Museum** (*Jct. Rtes. Q and B. 414-648-5116. Mid-May–Sept.; adm. fee*) features ancient and pioneer artifacts and historic buildings.

㉔ **W a t e r t o w n** (*9 miles N on Wis. 26*) It was water power that brought New Englanders here in the 1830s to harness the Rock River's rapids for industry. Among the wave of German immigrants who followed, Margarethe Schurz established the country's first kindergarten, which now shares the grounds of the 1854 **Octagon House** (*919 Charles St. 414-261-2796*). Showpiece of the 57-room manse—one of the largest pre-Civil War single-family homes in the Midwest—is the exquisite three-story, cantilevered stairway. *May-Oct.; adm. fee.*

Octagon House, Watertown, Wisconsin

㉕ **A s h i p p u n   Honey Acres** (*12 miles N via Wis. 67 through town; museum is 2 miles N of town. 414-474-4411*) In the bee business since 1852, the Diehnelt family has added to its rural plant here a **Honey of a Museum**. This sweet-scented museum features a film, a "bee tree," entertaining displays on every facet of honeymaking, and samples. Short nature trail out back. *Mon.-Fri., also wknds. mid-May–Oct.*

㉖ **E a g l e   Old World Wisconsin** (*12 miles S on Wis. 67, continue past town 1 mile 414-594-2116*) Hidden in the highlands of Kettle Moraine State Forest, this unique 576-acre museum has stalled time in the 19th century, when European immigrants began settling the heartland. Interpreters do chores in period dress and attitude, enlivening some 60 restored and furnished buildings from around the state, and 10 distinct ethnic farmsteads. Farm animals and seasonal activities. *May-Oct., and winter for sleigh rides; adm. fee.*

Algonquian Indians called this bluff above Lake Michigan Millocki—"gathering place by the waters." In the 1800s, European immigrants gathered here; their diverse folkways and cuisines now spice the city (Conv. & Visitors Bureau, 510 W. Kilbourn Ave. in MECCA complex. 414-273-7222 or 800-231-0903).

The Germans established the city's most famous industry: beer. Headquartered here are two of America's largest breweries, *Miller* (4251 W. State St. 414-931-BEER. Tours Tues.-Sat.) and *Pabst* (901 W. Juneau Ave. 414-223-3709. Tours Mon.-Fri., plus Sat. June-Aug.). The opulent *Pabst Mansion* (2000 W. Wisconsin Ave. 414-931-0808. Adm. fee), built for brew baron Capt. Frederick Pabst, contains 37 art-filled rooms. Other landmark houses with galleries include the *Charles Allis Art Museum* (1801 N. Prospect Ave. 414-278-8295. Wed.-Sun.; adm. fee) and the *Villa Terrace Decorative Arts Museum* (2220 N. Terrace Ave. 414-271-3656. Wed.-Sun.; adm. fee). The dramatic *War Memorial Center* (750 N. Lincoln Memorial Dr. 414-273-5533), graced by the nation's largest outdoor mosaic, houses the world-class *Milwaukee Art Museum* (414-224-3220. Closed Mon.; adm. fee), whose galleries display a range of fine and decorative arts and sweeping lake views. Still more art awaits at Marquette University's *Haggerty Museum of Art* (13th and Clybourn. 414-288-1669) and the 15th-century French *St. Joan of Arc Chapel* (601 N. 14th St. on central mall. 414-288-6873). Spit and polish have turned the old warehouse district into the *Historic Third Ward* (Broadway and St. Paul, by the river), a bohemian quarter, with galleries, cafés, and theaters springing up behind the 19th-century brick. For natural history, the *Milwaukee Public Museum* (800 W. Wells St. 414-278-2702. Adm. fee) ranks among the best, with a superlative rain forest, as well as Indian and dinosaur exhibits. Botanical fans will relish *Mitchell Park Horticultural Conservatory (The Domes)* (524 S. Layton Blvd. 414-649-9800. Admission fee). Other outdoor diversions include the *Boerner Botanical Gardens* in *Whitnall Park* (5879 S. 92nd St. in Hales Corners. 414-425-1130).

Pabst's original copper kettles

315

Racine *(10 miles E on Wis. 20. Conv. & Visitors Bureau, 345 Main St. 414-634-3293)* World headquarters of Johnson Wax, this lakeshore city is a mecca for Frank Lloyd Wright fans. **Wingspread** *(33 E. Four Mile Rd. 414-639-3211. Grounds only open to the public),* the architect's stunning last and largest "prairie house," occupies 30 acres on Wind Point, near the historic **Lighthouse**. Designed as the home of H. F. Johnson, it is now a conference facility. Another Wright design is the **SC Johnson Wax Administration Building** *(1525 Howe St. 414-631-2154. Tours Tues.-Fri., plus summer weekends; reservations),* famed for its "bird-cage" elevators. The spaceship-like **Golden Rondelle Theater**, vestige of the Johnson Wax Pavilion at the 1964-65 New York World's Fair, offers free film programs. *Tues.-Fri.; reservations through admin. building.*

National Bicycle Championship, Kenosha, Wis., 7 miles east of I-94 via Wis. 50

Folks in duneland tell the story of a beautiful hermit, known as 🖙 ***"Diana of the Dunes,"*** who cavorted on Lake Michigan's shore in the early 1900s. The legend grew from the tragic true story of a plain, independent-minded woman named Alice Mable Gray, who graduated Phi Beta Kappa from the University of Chicago. Secreted in the dunes, Alice wished simply to study nature and to write. But her scandalous nude bathing drew the press in 1916, destroying her privacy. Bad luck followed. She died of a mysterious illness in 1925 and was buried in an unmarked grave in Gary.

316

㉙ **Glencoe, ILLINOIS   Chicago Botanic Garden** (*US 41 to 1000 Lake Cook Rd. 708-835-5440*) On these 300 beautifully landscaped acres, more than 20 gardens are enhanced by lagoons, islands, woodlands, and prairie. Themes include aquatic, bulb, English, Japanese, fruit and vegetable, plus greenhouses and a nature trail. Narrated tram tours offered year-round. *Parking fee.*

㉚ **Wilmette**   A fun kid-stop in this affluent lakeshore suburb is **Kohl Children's Museum** (*165 Green Bay Rd. 708-256-6056. Closed Mon. except July-Aug.; adm. fee*), an imaginative hands-on world of art, science, and culture. More peaceful is the **Baha'i House of Worship** (*100 Linden Ave. at Sheridan Rd. 708-256-4400*), a remarkable nine-sided structure that is North America's only Baha'i temple.

㉛ **Evanston**   This lively city at Chicago's northern frontier boasts five institutions of higher learning, the most prestigious being **Northwestern University** (*Sheridan Rd. 708-491-5000*). **Evanston Art Center** (*2603 Sheridan Rd. 708-475-5300. Adm. fee*), in a 1926 Tudor-style mansion overlooking the lake, showcases contemporary work by midwestern artists. Next door is historic **Grosse Point Lighthouse** (*2601 Sheridan Rd. 708-328-6961. Tours June-Sept. wknds.; adm. fee*), now a maritime museum and nature center.

Chicago   See I-55, pp. 126-27.

㉜ **Indiana Dunes, INDIANA** (*Follow signs for Indiana Dunes Rec. Areas*) Hills of sand, formed after the last glacier receded, run nearly the length of Lake Michigan's southern shore. Indiana's portion, pristine save for the looming steel plants, sports two parks. **Indiana Dunes State Park** (*2 miles N on Ind. 49. 219-926-1952. Adm. fee*) has the largest tract of virgin duneland, plus trails, and a 1920s pavilion. Notable for its diverse plant and bird life, 15,000-acre **Indiana Dunes National Lakeshore** (*From Ind. 49,*

3 miles E on US 12. Main Visitor Center on Kemil Rd. 219-926-7561) also features Mount Baldy, a huge "walking" dune; a historic homestead; trails; and events.

▶ **Warren Dunes State Park, MICHIGAN** (Red Arrow Hwy., exit at Bridgman, follow signs. 616-426-4013) Michigan's southernmost preserve of beach, woods, and duneland, wilder and prettier than Indiana's, reaches 240 feet above the lake. Along with the usual recreation, hang gliders flock here, especially in spring and fall, for lofty Tower Hill, smooth winds, and a sandy cushion. *Adm. fee.*

Indiana Dunes State Park, Indiana

Kalamazoo *(Convention & Visitors Bureau, 128 N. Kalamazoo Mall. 616-381-4003)* A highlight here is the **Kalamazoo Institute of Arts** *(314 S. Park St. 616-349-7775. Closed Mon.)*, showcasing contemporary work of varied media. Exhibits on history and culture and a planetarium feature at the **Kalamazoo Public Museum** *(315 S. Rose St. 616-345-7092)*. North of town, **Kalamazoo Nature Center** *(7000 N. Westnedge Ave. 616-381-1574. Adm. fee)*—the state's largest—contains on its 1,000 acres an interpretive center, an arboretum, a family farm, a pioneer homestead, and nature trails. **Kalamazoo Aviation History Museum** *(Portage Rd. exit past airport entrance to 3101 E. Milham Rd., take left. 616-382-6555. Adm. fee)*, the "Air Zoo," memorializes World War II aviation with displays of fighter planes, including a Curtiss P-40 Warhawk and Grumman Cats. Exhibits also include memorabilia, the **Guadalcanal Campaign Veteran's Museum**, and a simulated flight on a Corsair fighter. If you prefer cars, the exceptional **Gilmore-CCCA Museum** *(16 miles NE of Kalamazoo; off Mich. 43 in Hickory Corners.*

Thanks to a marriage of temperate climate and sandy soil, the rolling country along Lake Michigan's southeastern shore abounds in fruit farms, vineyards—and vintners. Among the nation's leading wine producers, the *Michigan wine region* offers diverting tours and tastings. Ask for a guide at the Travel Info. Center just off I-94 in Benton Harbor (616-925-6301). Or call the Michigan Grape & Wine Industry Council at 517-373-1058.

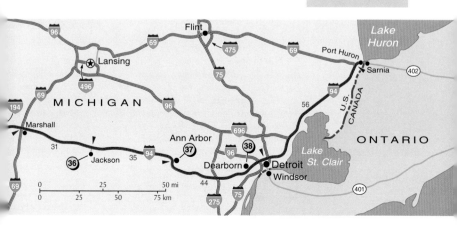

6865 Hickory Rd. 616-671-5089. Mid-May to mid-Oct.; adm. fee) just about has it all—literally, from antiques and classics to steamers and muscle cars, plus a few surprises. All are housed in five meticulous old barns on a 90-acre farm.

(35) Battle Creek *(Visitor & Convention Bureau, 34 W. Jackson. 616-962-2240)* The Kellogg brothers' accidental invention of flaked cereal in 1894 sealed Battle Creek's fate as breakfast city, home to Kellogg, Post, and Ralston Purina. The city made its mark earlier as a major Underground Railroad station—and longtime home of freedom crusader Sojourner Truth, who is buried in **Oak Hill Cemetery** *(255 South Ave. 616-964-7321)*, along with the cereal barons. Set amidst the pastoral landscape at historic **Leila Arboretum** *(928 W. Michigan Ave. at 20th St. 616-969-0270)* is **Kingman Museum of Natural History** *(616-965-5117. Closed Mon. except during July-Aug.; adm. fee)*, a hands-on journey from Ice Age to outer space. Nearby, contemporary Michigan artists show at the **Art Center of Battle Creek** *(265 E. Emmett St. 616-962-9511. Closed Mon. and Aug.).* The star attraction is **Binder Park Zoo** *(7400 Division Dr. Take Beadle Lake Rd. 3 miles S. 616-979-1351. Mid-Apr.–mid-Oct.; adm. fee).* No bars hold in this park, where you walk through the woods on boardwalks, paths, and trails past animals in natural habitats; there's also a children's zoo.

Honolulu House, built in 1860 and open to the public weekends, Marshall, Michigan

318

(36) Jackson In the 1930s, a local industrialist gave the city a 450-acre park with a splashy centerpiece: The Cascades, a series of 16 falls with 6 fountains—supposedly the continent's largest man-made waterfall—illuminated by 1,230 colored lights, is located in **Cascades Park** *(1992 Warren Ave. 517-788-4320. Falls illuminated Mem. Day-Labor Day; adm. fee).*

Vintage automobiles, Henry Ford Museum, Dearborn, Mi

Ella Sharp Park contains the **Ella Sharp Museum** *(3225 4th St. 517-787-2320. Closed Mon.; adm. fee)*, a complex of historic buildings and art, science, and history exhibits. Adjacent is the **Peter F. Hurst Planetarium** *(517-783-2911. Adm. fee)*, with Sunday shows. If astronautics appeal, so will the award-winning **Michigan Space Center** *(Jackson Comm. College campus, 2111 Emmons Rd. 517-787-4425. Closed Mon. except May-Labor Day; call for Dec.-May sched.; adm. fee).* This memorial to space probes displays everything from the Apollo 9 command capsule to astronaut underwear to a moon rock.

(37) Ann Arbor *(Convention & Visitors Bureau, 211 E. Huron. 313-995-7281)* Dominating the scene here is the **University of**

Michigan *(Information 313-764-1817)*, which accounts for the trendy, college-town atmosphere and the plethora of culture. Campus offerings include **Kelsey Museum of Archaeology** *(434 S. State St. 313-764-9304)*; the **Museum of Art** *(525 S. State St. 313-764-0395. Closed Mon.)*; **Exhibit Museum** of natural history *(1109 Geddes Ave. 313-764-0478)*; **Stearn's Musical Collection** *(School of Music. 313-763-4389. Wed.-Sun.)*, with more than 2,000 instruments; **Matthaei Botanical Gardens** *(1800 N. Dixboro Rd. 313-998-7060. Adm. fee)*; and **Nichols Arboretum** *(1827 Geddes Rd. 313-998-7175)*. A special attraction here for kids is the **Ann Arbor Hands-On Museum** *(219 E. Huron. 313-995-5439. Closed Mon.; adm. fee)*, a four-floor world devoted to more than 200 participatory exhibits.

University of Michigan football game, Ann Arbor

Dearborn   With the founding in 1903 of native son Henry Ford's empire, this city—headquarters of the Ford Motor Company—became an indelible mark on the map. Ford's second greatest contribution was **Henry Ford Museum and Greenfield Village** *(20900 Oakwood Blvd., follow signs. 313-271-1620. Adm. fee)*, a massive indoor-outdoor complex celebrating American ingenuity and achievement. The 12-acre museum displays innovations in numerous fields, including transportation, communication, industry, and domestic life. You can see many of the objects in context at the 81-

319

Early Cape Cod windmill and Connecticut saltbox, Greenfield Village, Dearborn, Mich.

acre village, which contains more than 80 original houses and other buildings associated with such luminaries as Abraham Lincoln, Daniel Webster, Thomas Edison, and the Wright brothers. Minutes away is the magnificent, 56-room **Henry Ford Estate-Fair Lane** *(Evergreen and US 12. 313-593-5590. Info centers at Greenfield Village and Fair Lane. Tours daily April-Dec., Sun.-Fri. Jan.-March; fee for tours)* on the University of Michigan-Dearborn campus. The powerhouse, a joint creation of Ford and Edison that made the estate self-sufficient, is also open for tours.

Detroit   See I-75, p. 188.
Port Huron   See I-69, p. 156.

CANADA

Unless otherwise noted, directions are from interstate, and sites are free and generally open daily. Phone for further information.

(1) Patten, MAINE The **Lumberman's Museum** *(Me. 159 for 10 miles, follow signs. 207-528-2650)* traces the history of Maine's logging industry through replica camp buildings, tools, equipment, and dioramas. *Daily July-Labor Day; closed Mon. Mem. Day-June; open weekends Labor Day-Columbus Day; adm. fee.*

(2) Orono The anthropology collection at the **Hudson Museum** *(E on US 2A, follow signs for Univ. of Maine/Maine Center for the Arts. 207-581-1901)* includes works by Native Americans, Pacific islanders, Africans, Asians, and Mesoamericans. *Closed Mon.*

(3) Bangor The former "lumber capital of the world" is a lovely old city of wide, tree-lined streets and handsome 19th-century mansions. The 31-foot **Paul Bunyan Statue** at Bass Park on Main Street is a reminder that the mythical lumberjack is claimed as a Bangor native. The **Bangor Historical Society** is headquartered in the 1834 Greek Revival **Thomas A. Hill House** *(159 Union St. 207-942-5766)*. Tour guides do an excellent job of using furnishings and paintings to recount the city's history. The society has brochures for a town **Walking Tour** and offers guided tours Tues.-Fri. for a fee.

(4) Augusta The state capital, which straddles the Kennebec River, was first settled as a trading post in the 1600s. Today it is a small, bustling city with a small-town personality. The domed **State House** *(207-287-2301. Closed weekends)* in the Capitol Complex was designed by the great Charles Bulfinch; it's topped by a statue of Minerva, Roman goddess of wisdom. The complex's **Maine State Museum** *(Maine State Cultural Bldg. 207-287-2301. Adm. fee except Sun.)* is among New England's best. Displays trace 12,000 years of human history in Maine with emphasis on the state's natural environment and social and industrial history. **Blaine House** *(State and Capitol Sts. 207-287-2301. Tours Tues.-Thurs.)* has been the governor's mansion since 1919. Across the Kennebec River is **Old Fort Western** *(16 Cony St. 207-626-2385. Mid-June–Labor Day; weekends Sept.–mid-Oct.*

 Near the northern end of I-95 is the great wilderness preserve of Maine's *Baxter State Park,* one of the nation's most remarkable examples of private philanthropy. As governor of Maine in the early 1920s, Percival Baxter promoted the idea of public acquisition of Mount Katahdin and its surroundings. The legislature balked at the expense, so Baxter spent the next several decades buying more than 200,000 acres on his own, and presented them to the state as a park to be kept forever wild. From the north, take Me. 159 from Patten and follow signs or, from the south, take Me. 157. 207-723-5140.

White birches, Baxter State Park, Maine

se calf, Baxter State
, Maine

adm. fee), New England's oldest surviving wooden fort. Guides here help bring to life an 18th-century military community.

(5) **Brunswick** *(3 miles E on US 1)* On the Bowdoin College campus, the **Bowdoin College Museum of Art** *(207-725-3275. Closed Mon.)* displays works by Winslow Homer, Mary Cassatt, Gilbert Stuart, and others. Next door, the **Peary-MacMillan Arctic Museum** *(207-725-3416. Closed Mon.)* exhibits mementos of North Pole expeditions by the two Bowdoin alumni. In town are three historical museums: the **Pejepscot Museum** *(159 Park Row. 207-729-6606. Mon.-Sat. in summer, weekdays rest of year),* which explores local history; the 17-room **Skolfield-Whittier House** *(161 Park Row. Summer Mon.-Sat.; adm. fee),* which was virtually sealed from 1925 until 1982, leaving its furnishings and decorations intact; and the **Joshua L. Chamberlain Museum** *(226 Main St. Summer Tues.-Sat.; adm. fee),* honoring the Battle of Gettysburg hero and Maine governor.

Portland *(I-295)* Henry Wadsworth Longfellow called his birthplace a "beautiful town seated by the sea." Portland is now Maine's largest city, but his description still holds. Begin a tour of this compact, walkable seaport with a stroll around **Old Port Exchange.** Stop at the **Convention and Visitor's Bureau** *(305 Commercial St. 207-772-4994)* to pick up a map and then head down the street to the sightseeing- and fishing-boat wharfs. Uphill is the **Portland Museum of Art** *(7 Congress St. 207-775-6148. Closed Mon. year round and Tues. off-season; adm. fee except Thurs. eve.),* with a fine collection of 18th-, 19th-, and 20th-century art from the U. S. and Europe. Next door is the **Children's Museum of Maine** *(142 Free St. 207-828-1234. Adm. fee).* The conical **Portland Observatory** *(138*

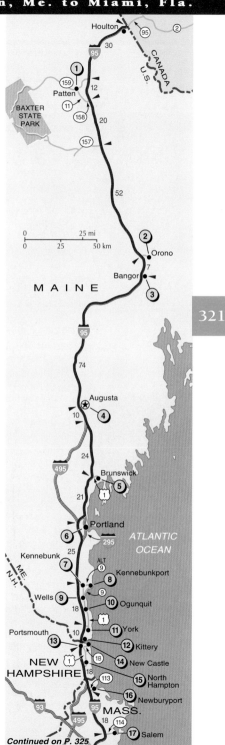

321

Continued on P. 325

Congress St. 207-774-5561. July-Aug. Wed.-Sun., June Fri.-Sun.; adm. fee), built in 1807, is one of the last surviving 19th-century signal towers on the Atlantic coast. The view from the top is worth the climb. Longfellow grew up in the **Wadsworth-Longfellow House** (485-489 Congress St. 207-879-0427. June-late Oct. Tues.-Sat.; adm. fee), built by his grandfather in 1785 and filled with family furniture.

Captain Lord Mansion, Kennebunkport, Maine

(7) Kennebunk (3 miles S on Me. 35) The main attraction of this lovely old inland town is the **Brick Store Museum** (117 Main St. 207-985-4802), which occupies an 1825 brick store and three restored 19th-century buildings. The collections include nautical paintings, ship models, textiles, and 19th-century furniture. Closed Sun.-Mon. year-round and Sat. mid-Dec.–mid-April; adm. fee.

(8) Kennebunkport (4 miles E of Kennebunk on Me. 9A) With New England charm, centuries of history, beautiful beaches, and scenic drives, Kennebunkport is Maine in miniature. Take a drive along **Ocean Avenue,** looking out for **Spouting Rock** and **Blowing Hole Cave**, a sea cave that can be explored at low tide, and at high tide spouts spray up to 30 feet. Former President Bush's summer house is on **Walker's Point**. For a glimpse, take the walk along **Parsons' Way** that begins at Colony Beach and goes north. (If you have time, follow signs to **Cape Porpoise**, a commercial fishing harbor.)

Source of Maine delicacy, Portland

(9) Wells Just off the road between Wells and Kennebunkport are two coastal reserves. At the **Rachel Carson National Wildlife Refuge** (Me. 9. 207-646-9226), a 1-mile, self-guided trail explains the salt marsh ecosystem. **Wells Natl. Estuarine Research Reserve** (N of Wells on US 1, right on Laudholm Farm Rd. 207-646-1555. Adm. fee in summer) at **Laudholm Farm** preserves 1,600 acres of field, forest, wetland, and beach, and offers some 7 miles of trails and special tours. The **Wells Auto Museum** (US 1. 207-646-9064. Mid-June–Sept., weekends Mem. Day–mid-Oct.; adm. fee) exhibits more than 70 antique cars. Kids will love the vintage arcade games.

(10) Ogunquit (5 miles S of Wells on US 1) It's smaller than Kennebunkport, but just as popular with tourists. Walk this delightful town or take the **Trolley** (Summer only; fee). Follow signs from town center to **Perkins Cove** and the **Marginal Way**. The cove, with its picturesque pedestrian drawbridge, is a good place to begin the mile-long, oceanfront walk that runs between village and cove. The **Ogunquit Museum of American Art** (1.4 miles S of Ogunquit Sq. on Shore Rd. 207-646-4909. July–mid-Sept.) overlooks Perkins Cove.

(11) York One of the state's most historic communities, founded in the early 1600s, is preserved as a living museum by the **Old York**

Historical Society (*207-363-4974. Mid-June–Sept. Tues.-Sun.; adm. fee*). The six buildings that make up Old York include the **Old Gaol Museum**, used as a jail from 1719 to 1860, and the **Old School House**, built in 1745. Head to York Harbor for a stroll along **Fisherman's Walk**, beginning at **Hancock Warehouse** and continuing across **Wiggly Bridge** and through the front yard of the **Sayward-Wheeler House** (*79 Barrell Lane. 603-436-3205. June–mid-Oct. Wed.-Sun.; adm. fee*), a 1718 house built by Jonathan Sayward and kept in the family for over 250 years. For beaches, head north on US 1A for 3 miles to York Beach and 2-mile **Long Sands Beach**.

Nubble Head Light, York, Maine

Kittery   Settled in 1623, Kittery is the state's southernmost and oldest town. The first U. S. naval vessel was built here during the Revolutionary War; in 1800, Kittery became the site of the first naval shipyard in America; and in 1917 the U. S. launched its first submarine, the L8, here. The shipbuilding story is told at the **Kittery Historical and Naval Museum** (*Rogers Rd. extended off the circle. 207-439-3080. Weekdays June-Oct.; adm. fee*). The public beach is at **Fort Foster Park** (*Pocahontas Rd. 207-439-3800. Fort open June-Aug.; weekends only May, Sept.; adm. fee to fort*) on Gerrish Island.

Portsmouth, NEW HAMPSHIRE The state's second-oldest city was originally settled in 1630 as Strawbery Banke; for most of the 17th and 18th centuries it was a major shipbuilding center. Today its nautical roots are apparent in the seafarers' houses. The best place to start a tour is at **Strawbery Banke** (*Marcy St., opp. Prescott Park. 603-433-1100. May-Oct.; adm. fee*), a 10-acre collection of buildings dating from 1695 to 1945. Exhibits include eight furnished houses of different periods, historic gardens, and working craft shops. If the kids are restless, walk up Marcy Street to **The Children's Museum of Portsmouth** (*280 Marcy St. 603-436-3853. Closed Mon. during school year; adm. fee*), packed with hands-on exhibits. Virtually every downtown street has historic buildings. Stop at the **Greater Portsmouth Chamber of Commerce** (*500 Market St. 603-436-1118*) for information (ask about cruises to the **Isles of Shoals**). The **Wentworth-Gardner House** (*50 Mechanic St. 603-436-4406. Mid-June–mid-Oct. Tues.-Sun.*), built in 1760, is one of America's finest examples of Georgian architecture. The **John Paul Jones House** (*43 Middle St. 603-436-8420. Mid-May–mid-Oct. weekdays, plus Sun. p.m. July-Oct.; adm. fee*) was once the naval hero's quarters.

New Castle (*1 mile E of Portsmouth on N.H. 1B*) This weathered, 18th-century island community, reminiscent of Nantucket, is the site of **Fort Constitution** (*Follow signs. 603-436-1552*). First fortified in 1632, it played an important role in the region's defense. It offers a superb view of **Portsmouth Light**.

It's only about an hour's drive from the Boston suburbs to Providence, Rhode Island, along I-95, but in the 17th century the trip from the old Puritan capital to the **"Providence Plantations"** was momentous in American intellectual history. Roger Williams, a renegade Puritan divine, believed in the separation of church and state and in the rights of the Indians. In 1635, he was banished from Massachusetts and the next year founded the Rhode Island settlement as an early bastion of American religious freedom.

⑮ **N o r t h   H a m p t o n** Seaside **Fuller Gardens** (*5 miles E on N.H. 51 to N.H. 1A, N to 10 Willow Ave. 603-964-5414*), once part of an estate, feature 2 acres of formal gardens. *May–mid-Oct.; adm. fee.*

⑯ **N e w b u r y p o r t , MASSACHUSETTS** Today, the early 1800s brick-and-stone **Market Square** and the rest of downtown are handsomely restored and given over to chic restaurants and boutiques. The town claims one of the country's largest collections of federal houses. Most were built by wealthy merchants and sea captains along **High Street**. Learn about Newburyport's history at the **Cushing House** (*98 High St. 508-462-2681. May-Oct.; adm. fee*), an 1808 mansion that now holds the historical society collection. Walk down toward the water to the **Custom House Maritime Museum** (*25 Water St. 508-462-8681. April-late Dec.*), which chronicles the birth of the U. S. Coast Guard here and the city's 300-plus years of maritime history. The **Parker River National Wildlife Refuge** (*Follow signs from Water or High Sts. 508-465-5753. Adm. fee*), on a barrier island, is a mecca for birders and beachcombers.

⑰ **S a l e m** (*5 miles E on Mass. 114*) This city is famous both for the witch trials of 1692 and for its fabulous late 18th- to early 19th-century maritime trade. Two museums are devoted to the witch story. Many of the accused were interrogated at the **Witch House** (*310 Essex St. 508-744-0180. Mid-March–Nov.; adm. fee*), home of magistrate Jonathan Corwin. The **Salem Witch Museum** (*Wash. Sq. 508-744-1692. Adm. fee*) uses full-scale stage settings and special lighting to evoke the hysteria. Native son Nathaniel Hawthorne often visited a 1668 house, now the **House of the Seven Gables** (*54 Turner St. 508-744-0991. Adm. fee*), and later used it as his inspiration. The Greek Revival **Custom House** was immortalized by Hawthorne in *The Scarlet Letter*. Today that house and nearby **Derby Wharf** are part of the **Salem Maritime Natl. Historic Site** (*Derby St. 508-744-4323*). The **Peabody Essex Museum** (*E. India Sq. 508-745-9500. Adm. fee*), founded in 1799 to preserve the curiosities and art brought home by sea captains, includes 30 galleries and 7 houses.

Halloween in Salem, Massachusetts

⑱ **S a u g u s** **Saugus Iron Works Historic Site** (*4 miles S on US 1 to Main St. or Walnut St., follow signs to 244 Central St. 617-233-0050*) re-creates the first successful ironworks in the New World, which were built here in the 17th century and flourished for 30 years.

L e x i n g t o n   a n d   C o n c o r d , C a m - b r i d g e , B o s t o n See I-93, pp. 304-07.

B r o o k l i n e (*6 mi. E on Mass. 9*) See I-90, p. 293.

Pawtucket, RHODE ISLAND
Pawtucket is *the* mill town where the U. S. industrial revolution began. The **Slater Mill Historic Site** (*Roosevelt Ave. 401-725-8638. Closed Mon. in summer and weekdays spring, fall; also mid-Dec.–Feb.; adm. fee*) shows how Samuel Slater applied British technology to textile manufacturing. See working 19th-century spinning and weaving machines in an 1810 mill, and a 1700s house where pre-industrial textile crafts are explained. The **Children's Museum of Rhode Island** (*58 Walcott St. 401-726-2591. Closed Mon. and 2 weeks after Labor Day; adm. fee*) approaches history and science with hands-on exhibits.

Providence Rhode Island's capital is part colonial period piece, part busy modern metropolis. Get oriented at the **Roger Williams National Memorial** (*N. Main and Smith Sts. 401-521-7266. Closed weekends except summer*), a park and Visitor Center commemorating the spot where Rhode Island founder Roger Williams settled in 1636.

For a taste of Providence's heyday as a colonial seaport, walk along **Benefit Street**, stopping at the beautifully steepled 1775 **First Baptist Church** (*Thomas and Benefit Sts.*), home of the oldest Baptist congregation in the U. S. Benefit Street itself is a veritable outdoor museum of Georgian and federal architecture, all of it handsomely restored. The street is home of the 1836 Greek Revival **Providence Atheneum** (*251 Benefit Street. 401-421-6970. Closed Sun., also Sat. in summer*). A few blocks away is the **Rhode Island School of Design Museum of Art** (*224 Benefit St. 401-456-6500. Closed Mon., also Sun. in summer; adm. fee.*), a teaching museum with wide-ranging collections. Farther uphill, on the campus of **Brown University,** the **John Hay Library** (*Prospect and College Sts. 401-863-2146. Closed weekends*) contains the remarkable Anne S. K. Brown Collection of toy soldiers in ancient Egyptian to modern uniforms. The **John Brown House** (*52 Power St. 401-331-8575. Closed Mon. and weekdays in Jan.-Feb.; adm. fee*), a magnificent 1786 Georgian mansion, belonged to the wealthiest of the merchant-prince Brown brothers. Rhode Island's **State Capitol** (82

Continued on P. 321

325

Continued on P. 333

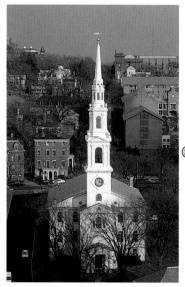

First Baptist Church, Providence, Rhode Island

326

Smith St. 401-277-2357. Closed weekends; call for guided tour schedule) is a 1891 neoclassical structure designed by McKim, Mead & White; it has the world's second largest self-supported dome (after St. Peter's in Vatican City). The zoo at the 430-acre **Roger Williams Park** *(950 Elmwood Ave. 401-785-3510. Adm. fee)* is worth the short drive from downtown; its rain forest and African savanna are especially good.

㉑ Westerly *(6 miles S on R.I. 3)* Near Rhode Island's southwestern point, this town boasts the lovely 18-acre **Wilcox Park** *(71 1/2 High St. 401-348-8362. Guided tours by appt.)*, with an arboretum and garden for the blind. Five miles south via R.I. 1A is **Watch Hill**, a Victorian-era resort with chowder and ice-cream stands, grand (if fading) old hotels, and the 1860s **Flying Horse Carousel** *(Foot of Bay St. Mid-June–Labor Day; adm. fee)*, one of the oldest in the U. S.

㉒ Mystic, CONNECTICUT Most visitors head directly for **Mystic Seaport** *(75 Greenmanville Ave. 203-572-0711. Adm. fee)*, a 17-acre living museum of New England seafaring and harborside life. Along with restored houses, shops, boat-building exhibits, and chandleries is a collection of sailing ships, including America's last wooden whaler. A short drive from the seaport is **Mystic Marinelife Aquarium** *(55 Coogan Blvd. 203-536-3323)*, with 6,000 marine specimens. Dolphin and whale shows.

㉓ Groton The **U.S.S. Nautilus Memorial** *(1.5 miles N on Conn. 12, follow signs. 203-449-3174. Closed Tues.)* includes the U.S.S. Nautilus, America's first nuclear submarine launched in 1954, and a fascinating museum on the history of submarine technology.

㉔ New London Located at the broad mouth of the Thames River, New London has always figured prominently in maritime affairs. The city is the home of the **United States Coast Guard Academy** and the **U. S. Coast Guard Museum** *(15 Mohegan Ave. 203-444-8511. Closed weekends Nov.- April)*, whose collections chronicle the growth of the service since 1790. Artifacts include early lighthouse and lifesaving equipment. On a residential street along the riverfront is **Monte Cristo Cottage** *(325 Pequot Ave. 203-443-5378. April-Dec. weekdays p.m.; adm. fee)*, the boyhood home of playwright Eugene O'Neill, which served as the setting of *Long Day's Journey into Night*. It's filled with turn-of-the-century furnishings and O'Neill memorabilia. The **Lyman Allyn Art Museum** *(625 Williams St. 203-443-2545. Closed Mon.; adm. fee)* has a strong collection of early New England furniture and silver, toys, and dolls, as well as sculpture, paintings, and folk art from around the world.

Mending a net, Mystic Seaport, Connecticut

Essex *(3 miles N on Conn. 9)* Here, near the mouth of New England's longest river, the **Connecticut River Museum** *(Follow Main St. to river. 203-767-8269. Closed Mon.; adm. fee)* tells the story of human interaction with the river, from Indian times to today. Includes paintings, artifacts, and actual sailing craft.

Guilford The **Henry Whitfield State Museum** *(1 mile S on Conn. 77, follow signs. 203-453-2457),* located in a 1639 stone house, the region's oldest, features a great hall and 17th-century furniture. *Closed Mon.-Tues. and mid-Dec.–mid-Jan.; adm. fee.*

New Haven Founded in 1638, New Haven was one of America's first settlements laid out on a grid, which is still visible in the network of streets around the downtown **Green**. It's best known as the home of **Yale University**, founded in 1701 and established here in 1716. To take in the Yale campus, with its splendid array of colonial and early 20th-century Gothic Revival buildings, stop at the **Visitor Information Office** *(Phelps Gate, 344 College St. 203-432-2300)* and pick up a self-guiding brochure, or register for a tour. Among campus highlights are two art museums: the **Yale University Art Gallery** *(1111 Chapel St. 203-432-0600. Closed Mon.),* strong in early American furniture and decorative arts and in contemporary American fine art; and the **Yale Center for British Art** *(1080 Chapel St. 203-432-2800. Closed Mon.),* a striking Louis Kahn building with nearly 500 years of paintings, sculpture, and rare books from the British Isles. Bibliophiles will enjoy the **Beinecke Rare Book and Manuscript Library** *(121 Wall St. 203-432-2977. Closed Sun.),* which displays a Gutenberg Bible. The **Peabody Museum of Natural History** *(170 Whitney Ave. 203-432-5050. Adm. fee)* includes dinosaur fossils and North American habitat dioramas.

Yale University, New Haven, Connecticut

Bridgeport One of Bridgeport's founding fathers was the man who invented American show business. Learn all about P. T. Barnum (1810-1891) at the **Barnum Museum** *(820 Main St. 203-331-1104. Closed Mon.; adm. fee),* bequeathed by the great showman to the city. **The Discovery Museum** *(4450 Park Ave. 203-372-3521. Closed Mon. except July-Aug.; adm. fee)* offers an interactive journey through science, technology, and the visual arts.

Norwalk The **Maritime Center** *(Norwalk exit, follow signs to 10 N. Water St. 203-852-0700)* explores the ecosystems of Long Island Sound, featuring over 125 live species ranging from starfish to seals to sharks. Explore an authentic wooden oyster sloop, and view special presentations on a six-story IMAX screen. *Adm. fee.*

Bluff Point State Park, with views of three states, 3 miles east of Groton, Conn., on US 1

New Rochelle, NEW YORK **Thomas Paine Cottage** *(20 Sicard Ave. 914-632-5376)* was the home of the

Everyone's mind's eye holds the picture of an idealized New York, a montage of George Gershwin and John Cheever, Fifth Avenue fashion and Greenwich Village poets, skyscrapers and Central Park. The great city is also a hundred other places at once, not all of them pretty but each arresting, unique, and unquestionably New York (Convention & Visitors Bureau, 2 Columbus Circle. 212-397-8222).

Start a tour at Manhattan's southern tip, where the Dutch founded their little town of New Amsterdam nearly 400 years ago. The **Statue of Liberty** (212-363-3200) has been the symbol of New York and of America's promise for over 100 years. Now handsomely restored, the statue still offers a "climb to the crown" along a narrow interior staircase. Nearby, **Ellis Island** and its **Immigration Museum** (212-363-3200) represent an even more ambitious restoration effort. The island's main building, where 12 million immigrants arrived and were processed from 1892 to 1954, now tells their fascinating story. Both the statue and the island are accessible only by **Ferry** (212-269-5755.

Snow leopards, Bronx Zoo

Fee for ferry; none for adm.) from Manhattan's Battery Park or from Liberty State Park in Jersey City. The **Museum of the American Indian,** scheduled to relocate in fall 1994 to the 1907 **Custom House** at the foot of Bowling Green *(The Battery. 212-283-2420. Call for new schedule and fees),* comprises one of the world's largest collections of artifacts relating to natives of the Western Hemisphere. Very little remains of colonial New

Manhattan skyline

York, although **Fraunces Tavern** *(54 Pearl St. 212-425-1778. Closed Sun.; admission fee)* has fortunately survived. The restored 1719 tavern, site of Washington's 1783 farewell address to his officers, now holds a museum. Several blocks away is the **South Street Seaport Museum** *(South St. 212-SEA-PORT. Adm. fee. Visitor Center, 12 Fulton St. 212-669-9400),* which includes a restored stretch of early 19th-century waterfront with docked ships, as well as a modern "festival marketplace."

Christmastime on the subway

Head to midtown for an ascent to the top of New York's most famous address, the **Empire State Building** *(Fifth Ave. and 34th St. 212-736-3100).* The graceful 1931 limestone masterpiece has observatories on the 86th and 102nd floors. On the premises is a **Guinness World of Records** *(212-947-2335. Adm. fee)*—a sure hit with kids. For over

Marathon runners on Verrazano Narrows Bridge, N.Y. Harbor

60 years the **Museum of Modern Art** *(11 W. 53rd St. 212-708-9480. Closed Wed.; adm. fee)* has been New York's favorite repository of 20th-century painting, sculpture, photography, and design.

Take a tour of **Carnegie Hall** *(57th St. and 7th Ave. 212-247-7800. Tours weekdays except Wed.; adm. fee),* New York's most beloved venue for musical performances since 1891. But for sheer numbers of performances and stages, the place to go is **Lincoln Center for the Performing Arts** *(Broadway at 65th St. 212-875-5000. Tour info 212-875-5351).* Try to save the better part of a day for the **American Museum of Natural History** *(Central Park W. at W. 79th St. 212-769-5100. Adm. fee),* a superb collection of virtually everything known about human beings and their world, with the giant-screen Naturemax Theater and the Hayden Planetarium. The **Children's Museum of Manhattan** *(212 W. 83rd St. 212-721-1234. Closed Tues.; adm. fee)*

has five stories of hands-on amusement.

Across Manhattan on the East River are the sleek buildings of the **United Nations Headquarters** *(First Ave. and 46th St. 212-963-7713. Guided tours only; adm. fee);* and north on Central Park, a grand parade of art museums beginning with the **Frick Collection** *(Fifth Ave. at E. 70th St. 212-288-0700. Closed Mon.; admission fee),* steel magnate Henry Clay Frick's 1914 Louis XVI mansion filled with works by European masters. The **Metropolitan Museum of Art** *(Fifth Ave. at E. 82nd St. 212-535-7710. Closed Mon.; adm. fee),* with over two

Statue of Liberty

million works, vies only with the Louvre for the title of world's greatest art museum. Farther up Fifth, the **Solomon R. Guggenheim Museum** *(1071 Fifth Ave. at E. 88th St. 212-423-3500. Closed Thurs.; adm. fee),* Frank Lloyd Wright's striking spiral modern art temple, has been restored.

Harlem is the capital of African America, and one of the best ways to sample its variety is to take a tour with **Harlem Spirituals, Inc.** *(1697 Broadway. 212-757-0425. Tour fee).* Tours include such spots as the Apollo Theater and the Cotton Club.

ne Robbins' *Broadway*

revolutionary pamphleteer and author of *Common Sense* in the very early 1800s; the house contains Paine artifacts, including a Franklin stove given to the writer by Franklin himself. *Spring-fall Fri.-Sun.; donation requested.*

From Fort Lee to Perth Amboy, I-95 seems to corroborate all the *New Jersey clichés* about congested cities and stinking oil refineries. Perhaps the clichés stick because this stretch of interstate—which overlaps with the New Jersey Turnpike—is all many visitors ever see of the Garden State. But north Jersey has considerable dairy country, and the south contains not only the vast scrub forest called the Pine Barrens, but also the truck farms where the famous Jersey tomatoes come from.

330

32 Jersey City, NEW JERSEY Liberty Science Center *(Liberty State Park exit from N.J. Tpk./I-95 and follow signs. 201-200-1000. Adm. fee)* Brand-new and chock-full of interactive exhibits combining education and fun, the center covers everything from diet and health to aerodynamics to virtual reality. Don't miss the 100-foot "touch tunnel" or shows on the world's largest OMNI-MAX screen. Liberty State Park also has picnic areas and ferries to the Statue of Liberty, Ellis Island, and Battery Park in Manhattan.

33 West Orange Edison National Historic Site *(Exit onto I-280 W, take Northfield Ave. exit, turn right, follow signs to Main St. and Lakeside Ave. 201-736-5050)* Thomas Edison virtually invented the process of inventing in these laboratories, where he worked for nearly 50 years. Along the way he came up with the phonograph, the incandescent lamp, and over 1,000 other patented inventions. Several blocks away is **Glenmont**, his 23-room mansion. *Labs open daily for tours; Glenmont closed Mon.-Tues.; adm. fee.*

34 Newark Don't overlook New Jersey's largest city—two of its museums are first-rate and located downtown. The collections of the **New Jersey Historical Society** *(230 Broadway. 201-483-3939. Closed Sun.-Mon.; adm. fee for special exhibits)* start with the Garden State's 1664 colonial charter and cover about everything that's happened here since; a "New Jersey History Education Center" is of special interest to kids. The **Newark Museum** *(49 Wash. St. 201-596-6550. Closed Mon.-Tues.)* takes a broad view of the world, from American painting and folk art to a fine Tibetan collection. The museum incorporates the 1885 Renaissance Revival home of John Ballantine, a wealthy brewer.

35 Trenton *(On US 1)* New Jersey's capital is a reminder of why the state has been called the "Cockpit of the Revolution." This is where George Washington crossed the Delaware River on Christmas night in 1776 and defeated a brigade of Britain's Hessian troops in a quick and decisive battle. The revolutionary era comes to life at the **Old Barracks Museum** *(Barrack St. 609-396-1776. Closed Mon.; adm. fee)*, used to billet American troops and as a military hospital. Today, "soldiers" in costume enliven the premises. Around the corner is New Jersey's **State House** *(W. State St. 609-292-4661. Closed weekends, except by appt.; tours by reservation)*, built in 1792. The collection at the nearby **New Jersey State Museum** *(205 W. State St. 609-292-6308. Closed Mon.; adm. fee for planetarium)* ranges from dinosaur fossils to Indian artifacts. There is also a planetarium.

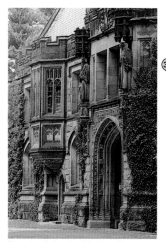

Princeton University, Princeton, New Jersey, 11 miles from N.J. Turnpike/I-95 via N.J. 33 and N.J. 571

William Penn's "City of Brotherly Love" was the second largest city in the British Empire at the time of the American Revolution. The spirit of Benjamin Franklin still presides in old Philadelphia, but later generations have created a cosmopolitan downtown with spirited ethnic neighborhoods. The transportation authority, SEPTA (215-580-7600), offers a Day-Pass good for unlimited riding on all city transit vehicles.

Independence Hall

Philadelphia's *Waterfront and Historic Park* area is called "America's most historic square mile" for good reason—*Independence National Historical Park* (Visitor Center, 3rd & Chestnut Sts. 215-597-8974), within its boundaries, incorporates key sites associated with the founding of the United States. With its central location, the park is also the best place to start a city tour. The park includes the *Liberty Bell Pavilion; Independence Hall,* where the Declaration of Independence was adopted and the Constitution drafted; *Declaration House,*

Aspen Farms, a community garden in W. Philadelphia

where Thomas Jefferson framed the Declaration; *Franklin Court;* and *Christ Church.*

The area is also home to a trove of museums. Among them are the *Afro-American Historical and Cultural*

Museum (701 Arch Street. 215-574-0380. Closed Mon.; adm. fee), which serves as a focal point for black intellectual and cultural activities; and the *National Museum of American Jewish History* (55 N. 5th St. Independence Mall East. 215-923-3811. Closed Sat.; adm. fee), devoted to the role of Jews in America. Other places of interest include: the *Betsy Ross House* (239 Arch St. 215-627-5343. Closed Mon.), where Ross lived when, legend says, she made the first American flag. The *United States Mint* (5th & Arch Sts. 215-597-7350. Weekdays), the largest in the world, offers self-guided tours. *Elfreth's Alley* (2nd St. bet. Arch & Race Sts. 215-574-0560) has 30 houses, most of them private, dating from 1728 to 1836.

Take a stroll through *Fairmount Park,* a 8,700-acre landscaped park. Leading to it, on the Benjamin Franklin Parkway, are several of the city's best museums. The *Franklin Institute Science Museum* (20th St. and the parkway. 215-448-1200. Adm. fee) was the pioneer hands-on science museum. The *Pennsylvania Academy of the Fine Arts* (118 N. Broad St. 215-972-7600. Closed Mon.; adm. fee), founded in 1805, is the nation's oldest art school and museum. The *Philadelphia Museum of Art* (26th St. and the parkway. 215-763-8100. Closed Mon.; adm. fee), one of America's top museums, holds paintings, sculpture, decorative arts, and furniture. And the *Rodin Museum* (22nd St. and the parkway. 215-763-8100. Closed Mon.) has the finest collection of Rodin sculptures and drawings outside Paris.

The famous hoagie

331

37 **Kennett Square** **Longwood Gardens** (*10 miles NW on Del. 52/Pa. 52, 5 miles W on US 1. 610-388-6741. Adm. fee*) was the country home of Pierre S. du Pont and a manicured fantasy of formal gardens and natural woodlands. Nearby is the **Mushroom Museum at Phillips Place** (*US 1. 610-388-6082. Adm. fee*), the country's only such museum.

Longwood Gardens, Kennett Square, Pennsylvania

332

38 **Wilmington, DELAWARE** (*Visitor info at Delaware House Rest Area on I-95. 302-737-4059*) Founded by Swedish settlers in 1638, Wilmington grew with the harnessing of waterpower along the Brandywine River. In 1802, French émigré E. I. du Pont de Nemours established a gunpowder mill on the river; since then, the histories of the city and the Du Pont firm have been entwined. Downtown are the **Holy Trinity Old Swedes Church** and **Hendrickson House Museum** (*606 Church St. 302-652-5629. Mon., Wed., Fri., Sat. p.m.*). The church is one of the country's oldest, built in 1698, and the 1690 farmhouse next door serves as a library and museum of Swedish life in Delaware. This was the site of Fort Christina, the first European settlement in the Delaware Valley. The **Delaware Art Museum** (*2301 Kentmere Pkwy. 302-571-9590. Closed Mon.; adm. fee*) displays works by such American painters as Homer, Eakins, and Hopper. Built in the late 1700s, the federal **Old Town Hall** (*512 Market St. 302-655-7161*) now houses the state historical society collection. The restored jail cells in the basement will fascinate the kids.

Winterthur Museum, Wilmington, Delaware

To the northwest, within 10 miles of downtown, are: **Winterthur Museum, Gardens and Library** (*Del. 52. 302-888-4600. Museum closed Mon.; library closed weekends; adm. fee*), one of America's finest country estates. Built for Henry F. du Pont in 1839, the mansion has 175 period rooms with American 17th- to 19th-century decorative arts and furnishings. Exhibits at the nearby **Delaware Museum of Natural History** (*Del. 52. 302-658-9111. Adm. fee*) include the familiar, the exotic, and the extinct. The **Hagley Museum** (*Del. 141. 302-658-2400. Limited winter hours; adm. fee*) incorporates the original E. I. du Pont family mills, estate, and gardens, built in 1803. Exhibits depict 19th-century home and work life. **Nemours Mansion and Gardens** (*Rockland Rd. 302-651-6912. May-Nov., closed Mon.; adm. fee*) was the estate of Alfred I. du Pont. The modified Louis XVI château is filled with antiques and art.

39 **New Castle** (*5 miles S on Del. 9*) The heritage of this quaint

Maryland state flag

town, founded in 1651, has been well preserved. A walking-tour map for the **Heritage Trail** is available at the **Old Court House** (*Delaware St. 302-652-4088 or 800-758-1550. Tues.-Sun.*).

Havre de Grace, MARYLAND (*3 miles E on Md. 155*) **Concord Point Lighthouse** (*Concord and Lafayette Sts. 410-939-3303. May-Oct. weekends p.m.*), built in 1827, is among the oldest in use in the U. S. The **Havre de Grace Decoy Museum** (*Giles and Market Sts. 410-939-3739. Adm. fee*) traces the role of decoys in hunting on the Chesapeake Bay. Weekend carving demonstrations.

Aberdeen Proving Ground (*3 miles E on Md. 22, follow signs. 410-278-3602*) The **U. S. Army Ordnance Museum** exhibits weapons from the Revolution to the present, including tanks, missiles, artillery, and a 20-foot-high "general purpose bomb."

Baltimore See I-70, p. 179.

Greenbelt NASA/Goddard Visitor Center and Museum (*5 miles E on Md. 193, left on Soil Conservation Rd. 301-286-8981*) The story of space research is told here at NASA's command center.

Chesapeake Bay, in Maryland

Continued on P. 325

333

Continued on P. 337

After George Washington chose 100 square miles of partly mosquito-infested swamp for a Federal City in 1791, Pierre L'Enfant drew up

head east to the **Lincoln Memorial** *(W. Potomac Park and 23rd St. N.W. 202-426-6841)*, with its Daniel Chester French statue of the seated Lincoln; and the nearby **Vietnam Veterans Memorial** *(Constitution Ave.)*. Walk along the Potomac

U. S. Capitol

334

plans for a grid of streets cut across by boulevards and adorned with fountains and statuary. The swamp was filled in, and today L'Enfant's plan still works: Washington is easy to maneuver, once you understand the street pattern. The city has an excellent subway system—**Metro-rail** *(202-637-7000)*. And many of the most visited sites are within walking distance of one another.

The **International Visitors Information Center** *(1630 Crescent Pl. N.W. 202-939-5538. Closed weekends)* offers multilingual information and assistance. Near the White House, there's also a **Tourist Information Center** *(1455 Pennsylvania Ave. N.W. 202-789-7000)*. To avoid doubling back, you might want to plan your sightseeing tour from west to east, beginning at the vibrant **John F. Kennedy Center for the Performing Arts** *(Rock Creek Parkway and N.H. Ave. N.W. 202-416-8340. Free tours mid-day)*. From there,

River, past the Japanese cherry trees, to the neoclassical rotunda of the **Jefferson Memorial** on the south side of the Tidal Basin. The **Washington Monument** *(Constitution Ave. at 15th St. N.W. 202-426-6839)*, a gleaming, 555-foot obelisk with an elevator to the top, is nearby, as is the **U. S. Holocaust Memorial Museum** *(100 Raoul Wallenberg Pl. S.W. 202-488-0400. Tickets required)*, the city's newest museum and America's only national memorial to the Holocaust. Walk north to the **White House** *(1600 Pennsylvania Ave. Tours enter at East Gate. 202-456-7041. Open for tours all year Tues.-Sat.; mid-March to mid-Sept. free tickets required)*, official residence of every President except Washington. Five of the 132 rooms, including the state dining room, are open to the public.

The **Mall** begins at 14th St. A 145-acre park of lawns, a reflecting pool, and tree-lined walkways, it extends to the U. S. Capitol. Along the

Washington National Cathedral

way is the **Smithsonian Institution** *(202-357-2700),* the world's largest museum and research complex. Nine of the Smithsonian museums are here. The **Castle** *(1000 Jefferson Dr. S.W.)* was the first of the museums, and today it houses the Information Center. Among the museums on the Mall are the **National Museum of American History,** the **National Museum of African Art,** the **National Air and Space Museum,** the **Hirshhorn Museum and Sculpture Garden,** and the **National Museum of Natural History.** The immense **National Gallery of Art** *(Constitution Ave. and 7th St. N.W. 202-842-6188)* is also on the Mall. It has one of the world's greatest collections of Old Masters and superb moderns, as well as the single surviving set of portraits by Gilbert Stuart of the first five U. S. Presidents. The Declaration of Independence, the Constitution, and the Bill of Rights are preserved at the **National Archives** *(Constitution Ave. at 8th St. N.W. 202-501-5000).* Before you head to Capitol Hill, make a short detour to the restored, red-brick **Ford's Theatre** and **Lincoln Museum** *(511 10th St. N.W. 202-426-6924),* where President Lincoln was shot on April 14, 1865. The pistol Booth used and Lincoln's theater clothes are among the items in the museum.

Lincoln Memorial

nal Air and Space Museum

Pierre L'Enfant chose Capitol Hill as the site for the nation's **Capitol** *(202-225-6827),* an 83-foot hill now set in a 131-acre park. The original building was burned by the British during the War of 1812. Charles Bulfinch and other architects contributed to the building you see today. Free tours are given daily from the Rotunda area. The **Supreme Court** *(1st St. and Md. Ave. N.E. 202-479-3211. Closed weekends)* is in session from Oct. through June. Next door is the vast **Library of Congress** *(1st and E. Capitol Sts. 202-707-5458. Tours weekdays),* repository of millions of books, photographs, recordings, genealogical research materials, and presidential papers.

Of interest beyond the Mall: the **Frederick Douglass National Historic Site** *(1411 W St. S.E. 202-426-5961),* which preserves the 1850s house and possessions of the black orator, educator, and human rights activist; the **Washington National Cathedral** *(Mass. and Wisc. Aves. N.W. 202-537-6200),* a magnificent Gothic cathedral completed in 1990 after 83 years of work; and the **National Zoological Park** *(3001 Conn. Ave. N.W. 202-673-4717),* with nearly 3,000 animals representing 500 different species.

The **Chesapeake and Ohio Canal National Historical Park** *(301-739-4200),* which parallels the Potomac River for 185 miles from Washington's Georgetown section to Cumberland, Maryland, attracts hikers, bicyclists, and canoeists. You can ride **canal boats** *(202-472-4376 or 301-299-2026. April-Oct.; adm. fee)* staffed by costumed mule skinners. One leaves from Georgetown, another from Great Falls, Maryland.

335

Great Falls of the Potomac River, on the Md.-Va. border

44 **Arlington, VIRGINIA** A guided tour of the **Pentagon** (*From Wash., 1 mile off I-395 on Geo. Wash. Mem. Pkwy., follow signs. 703-695-1776. Closed weekends*) resembles a military briefing: efficient, respectful, and a bit mystifying. On a nearby hill off the George Wash. Mem. Parkway is columned **Arlington House** (*Arlington Cemetery 703-557-0613*), home of Robert E. Lee. The U. S. seized the estate in the Civil War and made the grounds a military graveyard. The 612-acre **Arlington Natl. Cemetery** (*703-692-0931*) is now the resting place for thousands of American veterans. Many visitors come to see John F. Kennedy's grave and the Tomb of the Unknowns.

45 **Alexandria** (*From I-95/495, N on US 1, follow signs*) When the future nation's capital was still a swamp, Alexandria was among the busiest 18th-century Atlantic ports. Founded by Scottish merchants in 1749, its cobblestoned glory days are well-preserved in Old Town. Begin a walking tour at the 1724 **William Ramsay House** (*221 King St. 703-838-4200*), one of the city's oldest buildings, which also serves as the Visitor Center. Nearby stands imposing, castle-like **Carlyle House** (*121 N. Fairfax St. 703-549-2997. Closed Mon.; adm. fee*), built in 1753, which served as a British headquarters in the French and Indian War. Across Market Square, **Gadsby's Tavern Museum** (*134 N. Royal St. 703-838-4242. Closed Mon.; adm. fee*) is restored to its late 1700s appearance, when it was known as America's finest inn. Follow King Street down to the Potomac River, where a World War I munitions plant has been turned into the **Torpedo Factory Arts Center** (*105 N. Union St. 703-838-4565*). African-American culture is spotlighted at the **Alexandria Black History Resource Center** (*638 N. Alfred St. 703-838-4356. Closed Sun.-Mon.*) with archives and photographs.

46 **Lorton** When Washington and Jefferson needed advice, they came to **Gunston Hall** (*4 miles E on Gunston Rd., follow signs. 703-550-9220*), the 1755 home of George Mason, their mentor and the father of the Bill of Rights. He shunned the political spotlight and seldom left his 5,000-acre estate and large family. *Adm. fee.*

47 **Falmouth** On a Rappahannock River bluff sits **Chatham** (*US 17 through town, follow signs to 120 Chatham Lane 703-373-4461*), an 18th-century mansion that became Union headquarters during the Battle of Fredericksburg and also served as a hospital, where Walt Whitman nursed the wounded.

Arlington National Cemetery, Virginia

48 **Fredericksburg** (*3 miles E on Va. 3*) Founded as a tobacco port in the early 18th century, this picturesque town played key roles in both the American Revolution and the Civil War. A walking tour is the best way to take in the 40-block **Historic District** (*Visitor Center, 706 Caroline St. 703-373-1776*), with more than 350 original 18th- and 19th-century buildings. A stroll down Caroline Street in the heart of Old Town should include stops at the **Hugh Mercer Apothecary Shop** (*1020 Caroline St. 703-373-3362.*

Mount Vernon, Virginia, George Washington's house, 8 miles south of I-95/495 on Geo. Wash. Mem. Pkwy.

Adm. fee) and the **Rising Sun Tavern** *(1304 Caroline St. 703-371-1494. Adm. fee),* the quaint 1760 home of Washington's brother, Charles, which later became a drinking place for such notables as the Marquis de Lafayette. A few blocks away is the colonial mansion **Kenmore** *(1201 Wash. Ave. 703-373-3381. Adm. fee),* home of Washington's only sister, Betty, and her husband, Fielding Lewis, who made guns during the Revolution. The **Slave Auction Block,** at the corner of William and Charles Streets, is a reminder of the once flourishing trade. The **James Monroe Museum** *(908 Charles St. 703-899-4559. Adm. fee)* has mementos of the fifth President, who started his law practice here.

Fredericksburg & Spotsylvania N.M.P. Between 1862 and 1864, four major battles took place in or near Fredericksburg. At Marye's Heights, Confederates repulsed Union attacks on Dec. 13, 1862, with heavy casualties. The **Fredericksburg Battlefield** *(Visitor Center, 1013 Lafayette Blvd. 703-373-6122)* has a restored wall above Sunken Road where Southern infantry stood their ground. Surrounded now by farmland and suburbs, **Chancellorsville Battlefield** *(10 miles W on Va. 3, follow signs. Visitor Center 703-786-2880)*

Chancellorsville cemetery, Virginia

Continued on P. 333

Thornburg
Scotchtown 50
Ashland
Richmond
Williamsburg
Petersburg
51
VIRGINIA
Halifax 52
Rocky Mount 53
54 Bailey
Kenly 55
Raleigh
NORTH CAROLINA
Fayetteville 56
0 25 50 mi
0 25 50 75 km

337

N.C.
S.C.
Darlington
57 Florence
58
59 Woods Bay S.P.
Santee N.W.R. 60
SOUTH CAROLINA
Lake Marion
61
Charleston
62
Sheldon
63
Pinckney Island N.W.R.
Savannah
64 Fort McAllister S.H.P.
65
GEORGIA 66
Darien

Continued on P. 343

Monument to George
Washington, Virginia
State Capitol, Richmond

was the scene of Gen. Robert E. Lee's greatest—and most costly—victory in 1863, when 61,000 Rebels defeated 134,000 Federals. Later, Confederate Lt. Gen. Stonewall Jackson was mistakenly shot by his own men and soon died. The Visitor Center also serves the battlefields of the Wilderness and of Spotsylvania Court House, which can be explored on driving tours. The first encounter between Lee and Lt. Gen. U. S. Grant took place in the tangled **Wilderness** *(W on Va. 3, left on Va. 20, follow signs)*, where the armies fought to a draw on May 2, 1864. A week later, the troops met again on fields near **Spotsylvania Court House** *(Follow signs S on Rte. 613)*, an intersection that controlled the shortest route to Richmond.

50 Scotchtown *(11 miles W on Va. 54, follow signs. 804-227-3500)* One of the oldest remaining plantation houses in Virginia, Scotchtown was the home of Patrick Henry during the Revolution. In this rustic frame house, built about 1719, the lawyer and orator composed his stirring "Liberty or Death" speech. *April-Oct.; adm. fee.*

51 Richmond *(Convention & Visitors Bureau, 550 E. Marshall St. 804-782-2777)* Perched on the James River, this hilly city, graced by monument-lined streets and crowned with a modern skyline, epitomizes the Old and New South. In the 1770s, it was a center of dissent against British rule. In 1861, it became the capital of the Confederacy. From the Civil War ashes, Richmond has risen as a major commercial center, but it still moves to old traditions. In the heart of downtown, just blocks from I-95, the **Virginia State Capitol** *(9th and E. Grace Sts. 804-786-4344)* towers over the financial district. Designed by Thomas Jefferson in 1785, the building houses the General Assembly. It once served as the Confederate capitol, to which President Jefferson Davis walked from his wartime executive mansion, now restored as the **Museum** and **White House of the Confederacy** *(1201 E. Clay St. 804-649-1861. Adm. fee)*. The city's black heritage can be found in nearby Jackson Ward, a neighborhood of Italianate houses with ironwork. In 1903, business leader Maggie Walker was the first American woman to found a bank. Her 25-room Victorian house is preserved at the **Maggie Walker Natl. Historic Site** *(110 1/2 E. Leigh St. 804-780-1380. Closed Mon.-Tues.)*. The tap-dancing shoes of native entertainer Bill "Bojangles" Robinson are on display at the **Black History Museum and Cultural Center** *(00 Clay St. 804-780-9093. Closed Sun.-Mon., Wed.; adm. fee)*.

Across town to the northwest, the **Virginia Museum of Fine Arts** *(2800 Grove Ave. 804-367-0844. Closed Mon.; adm. fee)* has a collection of Fabergé eggs among its masterworks. Culture buffs should also visit the **Edgar Allan Poe Museum** *(1914 E. Main St. 804-648-5523. Adm. fee)*, housed in restored Shockoe Bottom, a district to the southeast of downtown that was torched during the Civil War. The writer was well-known in antebellum Richmond.

Continuing south, the Visitor Center on the hilltop site of the **Chimborazo Hospital,** which treated more than 76,000 Confederates, is the starting point for a driving tour of **Richmond Natl-**

al Battlefield Park (*3215 E. Broad St. 804-226-1981*), where Union and Confederate armies fought for control of the Confederate capital. Pick up brochures for a self-guided tour.

Petersburg   See I-85, p. 256.

Halifax, NORTH CAROLINA   Settled in the early 1700s, this river port spurred on the American Revolution by officially urging independence in the "Halifax Resolves." Today's small county seat includes **Historic Halifax** (*5 miles E on N.C. 903, follow signs. 919-583-7191. Closed Mon. Nov.-March*), with restored plantation houses, an antebellum jail, and two 1700s taverns.

Rocky Mount (*4 miles E on US 64*) A 40-year-old throwback to the pre-Nintendo age, the **Rocky Mount Children's Museum** (*1610 Gay St. 919-972-1168*) still thrills today's kids with an array of hands-on exhibits, from a mini-zoo to an ElectriCycle.

Bailey   The **Country Doctor Museum** (*8 miles W on US 264, follow signs. 919-235-4165. Closed Fri.-Sat.; adm. fee*) has a 100-year-old pharmacy and an amazing collection of medical tools, including painful-looking forceps, lancets, and other instruments.

Kenly   The **Tobacco Farm Life Museum** (*1.5 miles N on US 301. 919-284-3431. Adm. fee*) pays tribute to the crop that sustains the area's economy. Exhibits relate the history of the weed, and a sign says, "Thank you for smoking."

Fayetteville (*Visitors Bureau, 515 Ramsey St. 910-483-5311*) Founded by Scotsmen and renamed in 1783 for the Marquis de Lafayette, this railroad town is still dominated by its antebellum **Market House** (*Green St.*), a bell-tower public building where slaves were sold. The **Museum of the Cape Fear** (*801 Arsenal Ave. 910-486-1330. Closed Mon.*) has interpretive exhibits on local history. The **Historic District**'s Victorian buildings abut the city's tenderloin strip, which attracts recruits from nearby Fort Bragg. The large military base is home to the **82nd Airborne Division War Mem. Museum** (*10 miles W on N.C. 24 to Ardennes St. 910-432-5307. Closed Mon.*), with 3,000 artifacts of the famous fighting unit.

Florence, SOUTH CAROLINA (*4 miles E on I-20 Spur, follow signs*) A planned 19th-century railroad town, Florence became known in the pre-interstate era as the midpoint rest stop for New York-Miami travelers on old US 1. A popular attraction of that highway is the **Air and Missile Museum** (*2204 E. Palmetto St. 803-665-5118. Adm. fee*). Its building sits in a graveyard of Cold War relics, including a 95-foot-long Titan ballistic missile, once aimed at the Kremlin. Portraits of antebellum aristocrats hang at the **Florence Museum of Art, Science & History** (*558 Spruce St. 803-662-3351. Closed Mon.*), which also shows works by African-

339

Whether on wood or in bright neon, roadside signs of pigs dot the landscape from Virginia to Georgia, but especially in the Carolinas. These surreal pigs prance, dance, and gleefully cook their own on signs that are beacons to barbecue lovers. Called simply "Q" by locals, this *Carolina-style barbecue* brings together Southerners—rich and poor, black and white—like no other cuisine. Each joint claims its "Q" to be the best in town, if not the world. Served with slaw and hush-puppies, pork barbecue is a delicacy not to be missed. Just look for the dancing pigs.

American artist William Johnson. The building is in **Henry Timrod Park,** named for the Confederacy's poet laureate.

Santee National Wildlife Refuge, South Carolina

58 Darlington A true Dixie shrine, the **Stock Car Hall of Fame/Joe Weatherly Museum** (*8 miles N on US 52, follow signs. 803-393-2103. Adm. fee*) is located at the **Darlington Raceway,** home of the Southern 500 auto race. All the race cars you ever heard of are parked here.

59 Woods Bay State Park (*12 miles via US 378 and US 301, follow signs. 803-659-4445*) Here, visitors can take a boardwalk out into the watery, 1,541-acre forest. For the adventurous, a canoe trail winds through the bayoulike bay, home to alligators and other wildlife. *Thurs.-Tues.*

340

60 Santee Natl. Wildlife Refuge (*Visitor Center, 0.5 mile N on US 301. 803-478-2217*) Anglers fish at Lake Marion in this 15,000-acre refuge, and Canada geese and ducks winter here.

61 Charleston
If Time Permits...

Founded by English colonists in 1670, Charleston (52 miles SE on I-26) soon became the South's largest, most cultivated city. Its Atlantic harbor, at the confluence of the Cooper and Ashley Rivers, provided an international port for the fertile Low Country's planter aristocracy. In the 19th century, Charleston weathered fires, hurricanes, and a bad earthquake. But it was the Civil War that did the most damage, destroying the old plantation economy. By the 1920s, the city had revived enough to inspire a Jazz

Age dance craze, the Charleston. In that era, efforts began to preserve the city's *Historic District,* now fragrant with flowers and fresh paint. Walking is the best way to take it in. Or ride a sightseeing trolley or carriage; they depart from the *Visitor Center* (375 Meeting St. 803-853-8000), located in an antebellum railroad depot. Across the street, the *Charleston Museum* (360 Meeting St. 803-722-2996. Adm. fee), with a Confederate submarine moored at its entrance, encompasses the stern, neoclassical 1803 *Joseph Manigault House* (350 Meeting St. 803-723-2926. Adm. fee). Costumed guides greet visitors at *Market Hall* (Market St.), a Doric building where Rebel soldiers enlisted. Palmettos brush the balconies of the ornate mansions overlooking Charleston Harbor; there, a park marks the April 1861 day when Confederate troops bombarded and captured Fort Sumter, launching the Civil War. Boats embark from City Marina or Patriots Point (803-722-1691. Fare charge) for the *Fort Sumter Natl. Mon.* (803-883-3123), with a museum in the restored fort.

Antebellum houses on the harbor

Sheldon "You are leaving the U. S." warns the sign at the entrance of **Oyotunji African Village** *(5 miles N on US 17, left on Safari Rd., follow signs. 803-846-8900. Guided tours; adm. fee),* a traditional Nigerian community plunked down in the remote countryside. Two decades ago, King Oseijeman Adefunmi and his followers left mainstream America to live in this fenced-in retreat based on Yoruba religious beliefs.

Pinckney Island N.W.R. *(20 miles S on US 278, follow signs. Info 912-652-4415)* Spring and summer bring a spectacular sight to this 4,053-acre refuge, as flocks of white ibis roost on a pond near the entrance. Hiking trails loop around the island.

Savannah, GEORGIA *(10 miles E on I-16)* Designed by Georgia founder James Oglethorpe in the mid-18th century, this lovely port city sits on a bluff at the mouth of the Savannah River. It has shady public squares and storybook Southern buildings. The **Historic Landmark District,** one of the country's largest, encompasses 2.2 square miles of antebellum and Victorian splendor. The district is best seen on a walking tour at a slow, Southern pace. Pick up a brochure at the **Visitor Center** *(301 M. L. King Blvd. 912-944-0460),* which shares a restored 1860s railroad terminal with the **Savannah History Museum** *(912-238-1779. Adm. fee),* a multimedia overview of the town's colorful past. Among the many lavish, pre-Civil War residences are the 1819 **Owens-Thomas House** *(124 Abercorn St. 912-233-9743. Closed Jan.; adm. fee),* the city's foremost example of Regency architecture. A marble bust of the first Girl Scout adorns the parlor of the 1821 **Wayne-Gordon House** *(142 Bull St. 912-233-4501. Closed Wed., also Sun. in Dec.-Jan.; adm. fee),* birthplace of Juliette Gordon Low, Girl Scouts of America founder. The **Negro Heritage Trail Tour** *(502 E. Harris St. 912-234-8000. Adm. fee)* provides a black perspective, starting at the Savannah River where slaves first entered the port in 1749. **Riverfront Plaza,** 9 blocks of cotton warehouses along the wharves, have been turned into shops and taverns. There too is **Factors' Walk,** iron stairways above alleys where slaves loaded goods. Ship models fill the **Ships of the Sea Maritime Museum** *(503 E. River St. 912-232-1511. Adm. fee).*

Historic Landmark District, Savannah, Georgia

Fort McAllister State Historic Park *(10 miles E on Ga. 144, follow signs. 912-727-2339. Closed Mon.; adm. fee)* Confederate earthworks here withstood heavy bombardment by Union vessels on the great Ogeechee River. Explore them on a self-guided tour. The large park has a museum and hiking trails.

Darien *(1 mile E on Ga. 251, 1 mile S on US 17)* Here is an authentically replicated cypress blockhouse of **Fort King George** *(1 mile E on Ga. 25 Spur, follow signs. 912-437-4770. Closed Mon.;*

Scuttling ghost crab

There are few images of the South more enduring than a live oak draped with *Spanish moss.* Responsive to the slightest breeze, the soft, silver-gray strands lend a romantic—some would say mournful—mood to any site, be it a ruined plantation house or a tidy suburban lawn. Neither Spanish nor moss, it is an epiphytic tropical plant that gets its nutrients from moisture in humid air. Unlike parasitic vines, Spanish moss uses trees only as a mechanical support, the spacious, thick limbs of the live oak being a favorite. Sadly, Spanish moss is now in serious retreat in many parts of its native Southeast, probably a victim of air pollution.

adm. fee), the southernmost outpost of the early 1700s British Empire in North America. Though the fort successfully held off the French and Spanish, most of the soldiers stationed here succumbed to disease in the damp climate. A trail into former rice fields, now marsh, at **Hofwyl-Broadfield Plantation State Historic Site** (*S on US 17. 912-264-9263. Closed Mon.; adm. fee*) evokes the days when slaves did their backbreaking labor, an endless cycle of irrigating, planting, and harvesting. The simple 1850 house is typical in the Low Country. A museum details 19th-century rice culture.

67 **B r u n s w i c k** (*5 miles SE on US 341*) Now known mostly as the gateway to Georgia's Golden Isles, this port town was a major shipbuilding center during World War II. A replica of the Liberty Ships made here sits outside the **Welcome Center** (*4 Glynn Ave. 912-265-0620*). These days the city docks along Bay Street are filled with shrimping boats. A driving tour of the historic downtown shows off the Victorian neighborhoods. Locals often take lunch breaks at **Overlook Park** (*On US 17*) for a view of the miles of marshes that stretch hazily toward the barrier islands and the Atlantic. Across scenic causeways, the islands are worth a visit. Pick up brochures for self-guided tours at the Welcome Center. On St. Simons Island, you can see the excavations of **Fort Frederica National Monument** (*N. Frederica Rd. 912-638-3639. Adm. fee*), Georgia's first military post built in 1736. At the turn of the century, Northern industrialists owned **Jekyll Island** (*S on US 17, follow signs. 912-635-2119. Adm. fee for tours*). Now open to the public, their lavish cottages make up the Historic District on Riverview Drive.

68 **C r o o k e d   R i v e r   S t a t e   P a r k** (*8 miles E on Ga. 40. N on Ga. 40 Spur, follow signs. 912-882-5256*) Fallen trees lie on the shores of the aptly-named park, victims of the erosion that has cut dramatic 25-foot cliffs on the banks. Nature trail and camping. *Parking fee.*

69 **A m e l i a   I s l a n d , FLORIDA** (*14 miles E on Fla. A1A*) The Sunshine State's northernmost beach here was bypassed in the early 1900s as tourists flocked to south Florida. The Victorian railroad town Fernandina Beach, which boomed in the late 1800s, is preserved in the **Historic District** along Centre Street. Housed in a Depression-era jail, the **Amelia Island Museum of History** (*233 S. 3rd St. 904-261-7378. Closed Sun.; tour fee*) displays the eight flags that have flown here in the past 400 years. At the island's northern tip, rangers dressed as Union soldiers greet visitors at **Fort Clinch State Park** (*2601 Atlantic Ave. 904-277-7274. Adm. fee*). Abandoned by Confederates, the fort was used by Union forces in the Civil War. Hiking trails and fishing.

J a c k s o n v i l l e See I-10, p. 49.

70 **S t .   A u g u s t i n e** (*8 miles E on Fla. 16. Visitor Center, 10 Castillo Dr. 904-825-1000*) With stone ramparts and narrow streets,

"Du Bignon," historic house, Jekyll Island, Georgia

Former Alcazar Hotel, St. Augustine, Florida

the oldest permanent European city in what is now the U. S., bears the stamp of its Spanish fathers. A half century before its founding in 1565, Ponce de León had come ashore nearby to claim Florida for Spain. An exhibit marks the spot of his landing at **Fountain of Youth Archaeological Park** (*155 Magnolia Ave. 904-829-3168. Adm. fee*) with a navigator's planetarium and a statue. Visitors can also drink from the spring believed to be the legendary fountain. Nearby, a 208-foot cross commemorates the Catholic Mass said in 1565 on the grounds of the **Mission of Nombre de Dios** (*San Marcos and Mission Aves. 904-824-2809*). There is a moat at the 1695 **Castillo de San Marcos Natl. Monument** (*1 Castillo Dr. 904-829-6506. Adm. fee*), a massive, star-shaped fortress that sits near the old city's gates. The restored, 18th-century **Spanish Quarter** (*St. George St. 904-825-6830. Adm. fee*) has costumed guides. From the 1880s, the former Alcazar Hotel now houses city hall and **Lightner Museum** (*75 King St. 904-824-2874. Adm. fee*), with art and Gilded Age relics. **Zorayda Castle** (*83 King St. 904-824-3097. Adm. fee*), a one-tenth-scale copy of a wing of Spain's Alhambra, was used as a casino in the 1920s.

Fort Matanzas Natl. Mon. (*6 miles E on Fla. 206 and S on Fla. A1A. 904-471-0116*) The name of this fort at Matanzas Inlet, meaning "slaughters" in Spanish, recalls the 1565 Spanish massacre of a garrison of French Huguenots. A ferry takes you to the fort, protector of 18th-century St. Augustine.

Continued on P. 337

GEORGIA

66 Darien
St. Simons Island
67 Brunswick
Jekyll Island
CUMBERLAND ISLAND NATIONAL SEASHORE
68 Crooked River S.P.
Fernandina Beach
69 Amelia Island
Jacksonville

St. Augustine
70
71 Fort Matanzas National Monument

Ormond Beach
72 Daytona Beach
New Smyrna Beach
73
CANAVERAL NATIONAL SEASHORE
Titusville
74
Merritt Island N.W.R.

343

John F. Kennedy Space Center
Cape Canaveral

FLORIDA

ATLANTIC OCEAN

75 Stuart
76

0   25   50 mi
0 25 50 75 km

Palm Beach
76

77 Fort Lauderdale
78
Miami Miami Beach
Coral Gables
EVERGLADES NATIONAL PARK
Homestead

Florida conch shell

(72) **Daytona Beach** Cars now obey strict speed limits cruising the hard-sand beaches, where early 1900s daredevils broke speed records. Fans pay homage to today's star drivers at the Gallery of Legends at the **World Center of Racing Visitors Center at Daytona International Speedway** *(1801 W. Intl. Speedway. 904-254-2700).* Cuban general Fulgencio Batista was an avid vacationer at Daytona, and he bequeathed his collection of colorful Cuban art to the city. It is on display at the **Daytona Museum of Arts and Sciences** *(1040 Museum Blvd. 904-255-0285. Closed Mon.; adm. fee).* Just north at Ormond Beach, the **Birthplace of Speed Museum** *(160 East Granada Blvd. 904-672-5657. Closed Sun.-Mon.; adm. fee)* exhibits the fiery machines that pioneer racers drove along the surf. Nearby is **The Casements** *(25 Riverside Dr. 904-676-3216. Closed Sun.),* J. D. Rockefeller's restored winter residence, where he died in 1937.

344

(73) **New Smyrna Beach** *(4 miles E on Fla. 44)* Twisted live oaks poke through the ruins of the **New Smyrna Sugar Mill S. H. S.** *(600 Old Mission Rd. Follow signs. Closed Mon.),* burned by Indians during the Seminole Uprising of 1835. A hiking trail winds into dense woods. Centuries ago, Spanish sailors named the 35-foot-high, 1.5-acre **Turtle Mound** *(Fla. A1A)* that dominates the coastal landscape. The ancient hill of oyster and clam shells and animal bones, one of many that once dotted the area, holds Indian secrets. A boardwalk provides a magnificent view of the 25-mile-long **Canaveral National Seashore** *(904-427-1670).*

(74) **Titusville** *(2 miles E on Fla. 406)* Part of the longest stretch of undeveloped Florida coastline, the 225-square mile **Merritt Island National Wildlife Refuge** *(Fla. 402, follow signs. 407-861-0667)* gives safe haven to more endangered species than any other U. S. refuge. It shares the island with the **John F. Kennedy Space Center** on Cape Canaveral. **Spaceport USA** *(Fla. 405, follow signs. Visitor Center 407-452-2121. Adm. fee for bus tours and IMAX theaters only)* has exhibits on space exploration and security-laden tours of nearby launch pads.

Daytona Beach, Florida

(75) **Stuart** A 19th-century refuge for shipwrecked sailors, **Gilbert's Bar House of Refuge** *(13 miles, NE on Fla. 76 to 301 MacArthur Blvd. 407-225-1875)* now holds a small aquarium and museum of nautical history. *Closed Mon.; fee.*

(76) **Palm Beach** *(3 miles E on Fla. 704)* Florida's first major promoter, railroad tycoon Henry Flagler blanketed the Golden Coast with luxurious hotels. The **Henry M. Flagler Museum** *(1 Whitehall Way. 407-655-2833)* is in his 30-room mansion, built in 1901 for his wife with no expenses spared. *Closed Mon.; adm. fee.*

Fort Lauderdale   This resort city was once a winter training haven for Olympic swimmers. You too can do a few laps at the **Intl. Swimming Hall of Fame** (*1 Hall of Fame Dr. 305-462-6536. Adm. fee*), a wave-shaped water sports temple. Exhibits honor aquatics legends from Weissmuller to Louganis. Technology and ecology meet at the **Museum of Discovery and Science** (*401 S.W. 2nd St. 305-467-6637. Adm. fee*), a futuristic educational playground.

⑦⑧ Miami

A late 19th-century boomtown, Miami really started growing in 1896, when developer Henry Flagler brought his railroad line here. Luxury hotels soon followed, turning the outpost into a glitzy Jazz Age resort. Another hotel building binge occurred after World War II, mostly along 7-mile Miami Beach (Convention and Visitors Bureau, 701 Brickell Ave. 305-539-3000).

Biscayne Bay and downtown

Downtown, the *Historical Museum of Southern Florida* (101 W. Flagler St. 305-375-1492. Adm. fee), part of the Metro-Dade Cultural Center, tells the story of the region starting 10,000 years ago. There too is the *Center for Fine Arts* (305-375-1700. Closed Mon.; adm. fee), with major touring exhibitions. Nearby, *Little Havana* (8th St.— "Calle Ocho") forms the heart of the Cuban community. Corner cafés and cigar stores give it a lively ambience. In North Miami, the *American Police Hall of Fame and Museum* (3801 Biscayne Blvd. 305-573-0070. Adm. fee) is a must-see for crime and punishment fans. Don't miss the gas chamber and the collection of homemade prison weapons.

On Biscayne Bay, *Vizcaya* (3251 S. Miami Ave. 305-579-2708. Adm. fee), is a 10-acre Italian villa with 34 opulent rooms and formal gardens; and the 1891 *Barnacle State Historical Site* (3485 Main Hwy. 305-448-9445. Tours. Closed Tues.-Wed.; adm. fee) was the abode of a homesteader and sea captain.

Across the bay, on Miami Beach, the pastel buildings of the exuberant South Beach *Art Deco Historic District* (Welcome Center, 1244 Ocean Dr. 305-672-2014) gleam with neon at night. For contrast, see the solemn Oriental bronzes and religious art in the *Bass Museum* (2121 Park Ave. 305-673-7530. Closed Mon.; admission fee).

Historic District, South Beach

Adjoining Miami to the south is one of America's loveliest suburbs, the historic, planned community of *Coral Gables.* Pick up a brochure for a tour at the *Chamber of Commerce* (50 Aragon Ave. 305-446-1657). There too are the 83-acre *Fairchild Tropical Gardens* (10901 Old Cutler Road. 305-667-1651. Tours; adm. fee).

Abbreviations for terms appearing below: t-top; b-bottom; l-left; r-right; c-center; NGP-National Geographic Photographer; NGS-National Geographic Staff.

Ken C. Abbott: 78b.
Sam Abell, NGP: 331bl, 337b.
Stewart Aitchison: 6-7, 30t, 30b, 55b, 56b.
William Albert Allard: 44, 133.
ALLSTOCK: 18t (Rich Iwasaki), 18b (Kevin Morris), 20-21 (Vince Streano), 32t (David Muench), 59b (Riley Caton), 69b (Wendell Metzen), 72b (Masa Uemura), 82b (Tom Bean), 83t (Randy Wells), 162 (Karl Weatherly), 164bl & 167 (Tom Dietrich), 198 (Chuck Pefley), 220b (D.C. Lowe), 223b (W.J. Scott), 264 (R. Krubner), 272t (Jim Corwin), 273cl (Nick Gunderson), 274t (John Marshall), 312 (Chuck Pefley), 335bl (Dale E. Boyer).
Amon Carter Museum: 62c.
James L. Amos: 156b, 319t.
Gordon Anderson: 107t.
PETER ARNOLD, INC.: 35 (John Cancalosi), 108t (Alex S. MacLean), 238b & 270 (Clyde H. Smith), 280b (Galen Rowell), 328cl (Dianne Blell).
Craig Aurness: 163c, 229t.
Jose Azel: 25b.
Joseph H. Bailey: 36t, 36c, 127cr, 140b, 200, 228t.
Bill Ballenger: 255b, 322t, 331t.
Des and Jen Bartlett: 87.
Tom Bean: 313.
    Annie Griffiths Belt: 86, 311.
    Nathan Benn: 34, 340b.
    James P. Blair: 116, 119t, 130c.
    William C. Blizzard: 215t.
    Ira Block: 68t.
    Steve Bly: 250t, 250b.
    Matt Bradley: 124.
    Jim Brandenburg: 282t.
Sisse Brimberg: 334b.
Stephen R. Brown: 332b.
Robert W. Busby, Jr.: 259b, 260t.
California Museum of Photography: 59c.
WOODFIN CAMP & ASSOCIATES: 148b (William Strode), 169b (Sepp Seitz), 172 (Sandy Felsenthal), 182b (Michael L. Abramson), 236 & 277 (Mike Yamashita), 337t (Catherine Karnow).
Gary S. Chapman: 202b.
Walter Choroszewski: 214t, 330, 339
Robert C. Clark: 259t.
Vicki Clark-Gourley: 99b, 100, 123t.
Carr Clifton: 242t.
Jodi Cobb, NGP: 26t, 27l, 117t, 328cr, 329bl.
BRUCE COLEMAN, INC.: 12t (Steve Solum), 25t (Willy Spiller), 31b (James Blank), 36b & 43c (John Elk III), 68b (M. Freeman), 94bl & 95t (Steve Solum), 95b (John Elk III), 105br (Melinda Berge), 122 (Wendell Metzen), 127t (D.P. Hershkowitz), 130t (John Elk III), 130b (C.C. Lockwood), 143t (Eric Carle), 152 (Lee Forster), 154b (Wendell Metzen), 164tr (John Elk III), 164br (David Falconer), 166b (Dave Johnson), 174 (Robert E. Pelham), 179cl (Norman Owentomatin), 193t (S.L. Craig, Jr.), 199t (John Elk III), 203b (James H. Carmich), 216t (John Elk III), 218t (Lee Foster), 256 (Steve Solum), 310b (Gary Withey), 344b & 345t (Wendell Metzen).
COMSTOCK: 16c & t (Michael S. Thompson), 43t (Franklin Viola), 63c (Adam Tanner), 179t (Thomas Wear), 204b, 268t & 271 (Gary J. Benson), 272b, 306t, 309 (Phyllis Greenberg).
Richard Alexander Cooke III: Cover-bl, 241b, 246, 246-7.
Bill Curtsinger: 244t.
Bob Daemmrich Photo, Inc.: 41, 42b.
Bruce Dale: 1, 113b, 157, 211t.
Eddie Dean: 196t, 338.
Thomas Defeo: 107b.
Jack Dermid: 341b.
John Dominis: 273b.
William T. Douthitt, NGS: 235.
Dick Durrance II: 148t, 163b.
Rick Edwards: 15.
Sandy Felsenthal: 300b, 301, 324.

FIRST LIGHT ASSOCIATED PHOTOGRAPHERS: 17 (Warren Morgan), 206 (Michael Philip Manheim).
C. Bruce Forster: 16b.
DAVID R. FRAZIER PHOTOLIBRARY: 27r, 46tr, 47, 249 (David Falconer), 251.
FRICK ART & HISTORICAL CENTER: 212t, 212b.
FROZEN IMAGES, INC.: 29c (Larry Brownstein), 94t (Chuck Pefley), 126t (Richard Hamilton Smith), 147 (Everett C. Johnson), 283 (Peter Beck).
Steven Fuller: 278.
Gordon Gahan: 62b, 83b, 102.
Kenneth Garrett: 335br.
Lowell Georgia: 242b, 267bl, 333b.
Todd A. Gipstein: 132t, 132b, 303t.
Lynn Goldsmith: 284b.
Philip Gould: 46c, 46b.
Jay Gourley: 61, 64 and 65 (all), 69t, 74 & 75 all, 101t, 101b.
Farrell Grehan: 227t, 322b.
David Alan Harvey: 62t, 142b.
GRANT HEILMAN PHOTOGRAPHY, INC.: 113t (Runk & Schoenberger), 178 & 208 (Larry Lefever).
David Hiser: 90.
Tom Horan: 163t, 166t, 171, 173, 177, 218b.
Paul Horsted: 281b.
George H.H. Huey: 161.
THE IMAGE BANK: 4-5 (Don Sparks), 10 (Harald Sund), 20t (Andy Caulfield), 29t (Chuck Place), 29b (Grant Faint), 40b (DC Productions), 51 (Patti McConville), 58 (Hank deLespinasse) 231t (Michael Melford), 71 (Anne Rippy), 82c (Mark Romanelli), 96t (Kay Chernush), 111b (Patti McConville), 120b (Michael Quackenbush), 121t (Joe Devenney), 138 (Peter Beney), 145t (Joe Devenney), 150 (Gary S. Chapman), 186 (David W. Hamilton), 188t (John Lewis Stage), 188br (Andy Caulfield), 199b (Patti McConville), 201t (David W. Hamilton), 220t (David Fortney), 222b (Hank deLespinasse), 240t (George Loehr), 248 Hank deLespinasse), 267br (Michael Melford), 307b & 326t & 327t (Steve Dunwell), 344t (James H. Carmichael, Jr.).
Kerrick James: 20b, 21, 22t, 22b, 37, 38t, 216c, 217bl
David P. Johnson, NGS: 210t
Alison Kahn: 7.
Karen Kasmauski: 143b, 144t, 144b.
Steven C. Kaufman: 310t.
Karen Keeney: 135t.
Emory Kristof, NGP: 43b.
Lake George Steamboat Company: 262b.
Robert M. Lightfoot III: 318-319.
Bates Littlehales: 42t, 93, 225b.
Breton Littlehales: 117b.
C.C. Lockwood: 45t, 45b, 66, 201b.
Luray Caverns, Virginia: 243.
Bill Luster: 137t, 192.
Joyce B. Marshall: 238t.
MASTERFILE: 51t (Derek Caron), 111t (Hans Blohm), 273t (Edward M. Gifford), 343t (Bill Brooks).
Stuart McCall/NORTH LIGHT: 11, 12b.
George F. Mobley: 84, 112b.
Yva Momatiuk and John Eastcott: 54, 288.
Gail Mooney: 31t, 304.
Michael Mauney: 315t.
Allan C. Morgan: 39.
David Muench: 40t.
Dean A. Nadalin: 88t, 88b, 89t, 96b.
Tom Nebbia: 341t.
North Carolina Division of Travel and Tourism: 258t.
Michael O'Brien: 103, 104t, 104b.
PHOTOGRAPHERS ASPEN: 217tl (Phil Schermeister), 280t (Nicholas DeVore).
PHOTO RESEARCHERS: 240b (Blair Seitz), 336 (Art Stein).
PICTURESQUE: 28 (T.J. Florian), 119b & 121b (Murray & Associates, Inc), 140t (John Henley), 155t & 155b (Will & Deni McIntyre), 203t (Keith Longiotti).
Michael Pflegar: 315b.
Kevin Poch: 76.
Louie Psihoyos: 55t, 85t.
Jake Rajs: all Cover pictures except bl and br, 105t, 109t, 265t, 267t, 281t, 282b,

310c, 328b, 335t, 340t.
Steve Raymer, NGS: 14, 127b.
John Reddy: 50, 52t, 52b.
Deborah J. Reed: 299.
Lee Romero: 279.
Joel Sartore: 228b.
Kay Scheller: 253, 254.
Phil Schermeister: 320, 321.
Wendy Shattil/Bob Rozinski: 79t, 79c.
Richard Hamilton Smith: 94br, 285.
Ron Snow: 139l, 139tr, 141t, 141b, 176, 207t.
Joseph Sohm/CHROMOSOHM: 38b, 48, 49, 70, 72c, 73, 82t, 89b, 98, 112t, 115, 118l, 120t, 125b, 135b, 145b, 146, 154t, 156t, 158, 168, 169c, 170, 179cr, 181t, 181b, 190t, 191, 207b, 210c, 211b, 223t, 229b, 230b, 233, 237t, 237b, 241c, 252, 260b, 266-267, 274b, 290b, 291-292 (all), 294-297 (all), 298t, 300t, 305 (all), 327b, 328-329, 331br, 333t, 334t, 345b.
TOM STACK & ASSOCIATES: 108b (Tom Algire).
James L. Stanfield, NGP: 169t, 255t.
STOCK BOSTON: 63b (David Woo), 78t (John Elk III), 81 (Eric Neurath), 114 (John Elk III), 123b (Martin Rogers), 136 (William Johnson), 179b (Jim Pickerell), 196b (John Elk III), 202t (Robert E. Schwenzel), 217tr (James Blank), 268b (Bill Gallery), 318 (Robert Eckert).
TONY STONE IMAGES: 26-27 (Ken Biggs), 63t (Charles Thatcher), 80 (Bob Thomason), 97 (James Blank), 99t (Donovan Reese), 118t (Don Smetzer), 125t (James P. Rowan), 127cl (Robert Frerck), 128 (Terry Farmer), 131 (James P. Rowan), 134 (Doris DeWitt), 143c (James P. Rowan), 175 (Michael Ma Po Shum), 182t (Tom Dietrich), 183 (Cathlyn Melloan), 193b (Diane Graham-Henry), 217br (Vince Streano), 226 (James Blank), 227b (Raymond G. Barnes), 230t (Doris DeWitt), 231b (Willard Clay), 232 (Robert Frerck), 261 (Ric Howard), 262tr (Larry Ulrich), 286 & 287t (Cathlyn Melloan), 289 (James Blank), 308 & 314 (Raymond G. Barnes), 317 (Peter Pearson), 326b (Fred M. Dole), 329cr (Jon Ortner), 332t (William Clark), 342 (Arthur Tilley).
William Strode: 149.
James A. Sugar: 287t.
SUPERSTOCK: 9, 13, 105bl, 109b, 110, 137b, 265b, 290tl, 290b, 290tr, 298t, 302, 303b (Alan D. Briere), 306b (Bernard G. Silberstein), 323.
Tennessee Tourist Development: cover-br, 247.
THIRD COAST: 92 (Ken Dequaine), 126b (Peter J. Schultz), 142t (Ken Dequaine), 184t MacDonald Photography), 184b (Ken Dequaine), 216b (Paul R. Meyer), 244b (Ken Dequaine), 257 (Steve Solum) 260c & 284t & 319b (Ken Dequaine).
Thomas County Historical Society: 165.
Tim Thompson: 221t, 222t.
Tomasz Tomaszewski: 276.
TRANSPARENCIES, INC.: 208-209 (Kelly Culpepper), 209 (Tim O'Dell), 210b (J.G. Faircloth), 258b (Kelly Culpepper)
Gary T. Truman: 139br, 215b.
USAF Museum: 190b.
Salvatore Vasapolli: 53t, 53b.
Alice Verbeek: 187.
Randall A. Wagner: 77.
Fred Ward: 164tl, 204t.
Tony Wassell: 225t.
John Wee: 214b.
WEST LIGHT: 24 (Craig Aurness), 26b (Nik Wheeler), 30c (Bill Ross), 32b (Walter Hodges), 46tl (Jim Cornfield), 59t (Craig Aurness), 72t (W. Cody), 79b (Jim Richardson), 153t & b (Bill Ross), 188bl (W. Cody), 194 (Annie Griffiths Belt), 221b (Jim Richardson), 262tl (Charles Campbell), 276t & b (Patrick W. Stoll), 307t (Larry Lee), 307c (Allen Birnbach).
Douglas M. Wilson: 273cr.
Wycheck Photography: 241t.
Gary R. Zahm: 85b.

Index

352

Library of Congress CIP data

Crossing America : National Geographic's guide to the interstates / prepared
  by the Book Division, National Geographic Society, Washington, D. C.
      p.   cm.
    Includes index.
    ISBN 0-87044-985-0. — ISBN 0-87044-984-2 (pbk.)
    1. United States—Guidebooks.   2. Automobile travel—United States—
Guidebooks.   I. National Geographic Society (U.S.). Book Division.
E158.C85   1994
917.304'929—dc20   94-16464
                                                                         CIP

Composition for this book by the National Geographic Society Book Division. Printed and
bound by R. R. Donnelley & Sons, Willard, Ohio. Color separations by Graphic Art Service
Inc., Nashville, Tennessee. Paper by Consolidated/Alling & Cory, Willow Grove, Pa. Cover
printed by Inland Press, Menomonee Falls, Wisconsin.